Best Practices for Online Procurement Auctions

Diane H. Parente
The Pennsylvania State University – The Behrand College,
Black School of Business, USA

Information Science REFERENCE

INFORMATION SCIENCE REFERENCE

Hershey · New York

Acquisitions Editor:	Kristin Klinger
Development Editor:	Kristin Roth
Senior Managing Editor:	Jennifer Neidig
Managing Editor:	Sara Reed
Copy Editor:	Killian Piraro
Typesetter:	Carole Coulson
Cover Design:	Lisa Tosheff
Printed at:	Yurchak Printing Inc.

Published in the United States of America by
Information Science Reference (an imprint of IGI Global)
701 E. Chocolate Avenue, Suite 200
Hershey PA 17033
Tel: 717-533-8845
Fax: 717-533-8661
E-mail: cust@igi-global.com
Web site: http://www.igi-global.com .

and in the United Kingdom by
Information Science Reference (an imprint of IGI Global)
3 Henrietta Street
Covent Garden
London WC2E 8LU
Tel: 44 20 7240 0856
Fax: 44 20 7379 0609
Web site: http://www.eurospanonline.com

Library of Congress Cataloging-in-Publication Data

Best practices for online procurement auctions / Diane H. Parente, editor.

     p. cm.

  Summary: "With the advent of internet communication technologies, the online auction environment has blossomed to support a bustling enterprise. Up until this time, the functional inner workings of these online exchange mechanisms have only been described using anecdotal accounts. this book offers a systematic approach to auction examination that will become invaluable to both practitioners and researchers alike"--Provided by publisher.

  Includes bibliographical references and index.

  ISBN 978-1-59904-636-5 (hardcover) -- ISBN 978-1-59904-638-9 (ebook)

  1. Internet auctions. I. Parente, Diane H.

  HF5478.B47 2008

  658.7'2--dc22

                              2007024465

British Cataloguing in Publication Data
A Cataloguing in Publication record for this book is available from the British Library.

All work contributed to this book set is original material. The views expressed in this book are those of the authors, but not necessarily of the publisher.

Table of Contents

Section IV
Online Reverse Auction Success

Section V
A Review of the Literature

Detailed Table of Contents

Section I
Online Reverse Auctions Today

In this chapter, the online reverse auction is introduced through a series of points and counterpoints on the use of the tool. Tom Gattiker, Boise State, and M. L. (Bob) Emiliani, Central Connecticut State, identify and debate eleven points in the use of online reverse auctions.

Section II
Input Side of Online Reverse Auctions

Section II.a
Buyers, Suppliers, and the Dyad

Competition between supply chains has resulted in firms carefully examining the relationships that they have, or are contemplating having, with other links in their chain. While the main focus of this book is on a specific type of relationship, that of the reverse auction, other forms of buyer-supplier relationships exist. In order to better understand the implications of the reverse-auction relationship, managers should also analyze the alternatives and the environment of relationships in which reverse auctions operate. The focus of this chapter is on an alternative buyer-supplier relationship, that of the supplier consortia. Within the six dimensions of the framework proposed by Parente, et al. (2004), this chapter examines this little-studied collaborative group and proposes a spectrum to begin to understand some aspects of buyer-supplier relationships. The chapter includes a theoretical classification framework for supplier consortia. It then compares and contrasts supplier consortia to the reverse auction, concluding with a prescriptive decision process that can help managers better analyze the most appropriate form of buyer-supplier relationship for their firm and their supply chain.

Chapter III

This chapter views online reverse auctions from the purchasing agent's perspective. In this study, purchasing agents with a high level of buying experience perceived that online reverse auctions have a negative impact on the trust and cooperation in supplier relationships. Purchasing agents did not see a negative impact of online reverse auctions on long-term viability of suppliers. The chapter discusses the evolution of the buyer-supplier relationship, emphasizing the critical success factors in supplier selection. Further, it discusses the role of the online reverse auction in the buyer-supplier relationship. By understanding the lens through which purchasing agents view online reverse auctions, managers can do a better job of managing the procurement function through improved training programs for purchasing agents that incorporate the appropriateness of online reverse auctions vs. other sourcing strategies. In addition, they will be able to better manage online reverse auctions, minimizing any negative impact of the auction on existing supplier relationships.

Chapter IV

Once a company implements an internet reverse auction platform, buyers often have considerable discretion as to whether or not to utilize it. This paper discusses many reasons for nonadoption of Internet reverse auctions. The focus is on factors that impact the fit between the Internet reverse auction technology and the characteristics of the particular purchasing task that the buyer must carry out (i.e., characteristics of the material or service to be purchased in the market that it is to be purchased from). Data (qualitative comments) were collected from buyers within one firm. The comments detail the reasons that buyers have not used reverse auctions for particular commodities. Of the nine factors identified in the literature review, four were actually cited by buyers. These are: specifiability, level of competition for the buyer's business, importance of non-price factors, and dollar volume.

Chapter V

This chapter describes the economic effects caused by the use of electronic reverse auctions along the procurement process. It argues that an analysis of these economic effects requires the consideration of the whole transaction process. The approaches of the new institutional economics provide a theoretical foundation for the analysis. The second part of the chapter deals with the single steps of an auction-inte-

grated procurement process. Through this holistic view of the procurement process the authors emphasize the additional benefits and the danger caused by auctions. A better awareness of the procurement process enables better decisions concerning the choice of benefits that are worth pursuing.

This chapter discusses the challenges involved with developing trust and commitment in online procurement auctions. Online procurement auctions, otherwise known as e-auctions, are becoming increasingly more popular for conducting business-to-business transactions. However, many studies suggest that the success rate for e-auctions is down considerably. This may be due, in large part, to the absence of trust between the buyer and seller in this virtual arena. This chapter summarizes the current literature on trust and collaboration in the e-auction supply chain and discusses the processes in place that may contribute to the lack of trust between parties. Viewpoints of the buyer and seller are presented. Common issues are identified and the challenges associated with creating trust and fairness in the e-auction environment are revealed. Proactive strategies must be in place in order for stakeholders to maintain trust in this environment and to gain benefits from this virtual supply chain process. Future areas of study in this area are critical to its success.

The massive wave of enthusiasm for B2B (business-to-business) e-commerce generated with the "dot-com" boom led many to believe that a fundamental transformation of how firms bought and sold products was just around the corner. The new "wired" world of commerce would lead to real-time, Internet-driven trading, with significant implications for—amongst other things—the nature of buyer-supplier relationships, pricing, and the management of industrial capacity. Despite the excitement, such a transformation has largely failed to materialize, and whilst there has been a limited uptake of B2B innovations (for example, the use of online reverse auctions), the fundamental character of B2B trade has remained mostly unchanged. Drawing on a multi-stranded empirical study, this chapter seeks to explain the divergence between the expected and realized degrees of innovation.

Section II.b
The Product

This chapter provides insights into bundling practices for online reverse auctions by exploring approaches and reporting experiences of 252 companies in the U.S. manufacturing industry. Within the context of Parente et al.'s (2004) conceptual framework for the analysis of online auctions, aspects of the "Product Characteristics" component were explored. Bundling issues investigated include content, goals, structure, and performance. Following the theme of the book, differences and similarities in bundling behavior and outcomes between small and large enterprises are emphasized, highlighting the impact of firm size and the resulting strategies explored. While large corporations are usually on the forefront of information technology adoption and use, the potential is significant for smaller firms as well. As such, this chapter provides managerial insights, useful especially to smaller companies, for successfully employing bundles in reverse auctions.

This chapter highlights the promise and importance of reverse multi-attribute auctions (RMAA). It outlines the major benefits of RMAAs over other traditional auction mechanisms, such as reverse single attribute auctions, and then presents a structured and critical assessment of the current state of RMAA research. The intention of this chapter is not only to review both experimental and theoretical studies that have been conducted on RMAAs, but also to provide a starting point and specific recommendations for future research directions on RMAAs.

Section III
The Auction Process

The Winner's Curse is a common phenomenon mostly in auctions, even though it has applications in a diverse range of fields. We define the idea of a Winner's Curse and specify the types of auctions in which this could be prevalent. We look at the data provided by a major multinational corporation on online procurement auctions conducted by them. We specify the relationship that the prevalence of the Winner's Curse would have on the success of such procurement auctions. Using this theoretical background, we analyze the given data and show that in some cases, the presence of the Winner's Curse and the subsequent need for bidders to show caution in the presence of the Winner's Curse could lead to lower auction success for the firm. We specify the particular cases where this is true. This leads to managerial implications for firms wishing to conduct procurement auctions online, and we spell them out. We also provide some examples of how firms might try and lower the negative effects of the Winner's Curse. Finally, we provide some future research ideas that may be pursued and some additional readings for the curious reader.

With the advent of the Internet, traditional auction forms have evolved to fit into a plethora of business niches, either integrating into traditional approaches or simply creating new opportunities. This chapter examines two novel uses for auctions in a business context, namely sponsored search auctions and prediction markets. Understanding the potential auction benefits and limitations can hopefully provide practitioners with a more informed and successful approach when employing these auction-based tools in their business.

This chapter considers reverse auctions in the context of the supply chain and the type of end user product being produced. It contends that in order to successfully utilize a reverse without alienating their suppliers, buyers need to classify their product as innovative or standardized. An innovative product is one that is undergoing rapid changes in functionality or specifications. A standardized or functional product is one that has stabilized its specifications and functionality. It also argues that the buyer must consider whether their supply chain is responsive or efficient. A responsive supply chain is one that rapidly adapts to changes in product characteristics without placing undue financial burdens on any members of the supply chain. An efficient supply chain is one that has reduced costs to their minimum but has a reduced flexibility when compared with a responsive supply chain. It is hoped that an understanding of this relationship will allow purchasers to better evaluate their use of reverse auctions as a purchasing tool in the context of buyer supplier relations.

Today a high volume of goods and services is being traded using online auction systems. The growth in size and complexity of architectures to support online auctions requires the use of distributed and cooperative software techniques. In this context, the agent software development paradigm seems appropriate for their modeling, development, and implementation. This paper proposes an agent-oriented patterns analysis of the best practices for online auction. The patterns are intended to help both IT managers and software engineers during the requirement specification of an online auction system while integrating benefits of agent software engineering.

In this chapter we present a generic electronic market platform that is designed to run different kinds
of auctions and exchanges. Researchers can use the platform to implement different electronic market
mechanisms, simulate the market behavior of their interests, and experiment with it. A generic OR/XOR
bidding language that can express different OR/XOR combinations is implemented for Web interfaces.
Different auctions, including combinatorial auctions, multiple-round reverse auctions, and multiple
homogeneous good auctions, have been built and run successfully on the platform.

Section IV
Online Reverse Auction Success

This chapter studies the effect of bidder conduct on auction success by examining a business to business
(B2B) online procurement auction market. In particular, it investigates whether collaborative bidding is
more likely when suppliers compete with each other on multiple auctions and/or over a longer period
of time. Multiple regression analysis confirms that in online reverse auctions, winning bids are higher
or auction success is lower when the same set of suppliers bid against each other regularly. In a supply
chain framework, existence of such collaborative bidder behavior would reduce the cost savings for the
buyer. It is therefore important for the practitioners to be alert to such activities and introduce measures
that curtail the resulting costly outcomes.

During the e-business boom of the 1990s, reverse auctions became a new business tool for purchasing
and procurement that promised increased reductions in supplier costs. The benefits of reverse auctions
have been substantiated, but not without debate. One of the debates is the ethical considerations inherent
to these new business processes. Our study investigates whether reverse auctions violate corporate or
professional standards of conduct. This chapter examines some of the professional standards and codes
of ethics available, including the Institute of Supply Chain Management (ISM) and a selected number
of organizations including Dell and GE. Further, the chapter presents a framework that can help an
organization determine whether reverse auctions, and the way they run them, are ethical.

The case describes the initial implementation and evaluation of an e-procurement system, using reverse auctions, for a large manufacturer of brown coal in the Slovak Republic. One of the biggest problems when making decisions on e-business investments is unclear return on investment (ROI) and uncertainty about what method should be used for measuring the results. An outline of the reverse auction process is provided, followed by the presentation of a number of metrics that evaluate the current performance of the system vs. intended future performance matrix. Specifically, it focuses on the ROI and other performance indicators that have been adjusted according to e-commerce specifics, particularly to procurement with dynamic pricing transactions. The case results prove that the investment into the e-commerce solution is highly effective in reducing input costs.

The reverse auction tool has evolved to take advantage of Internet technology and has been identified by many large organizations as a tool to achieve substantial procurement savings. As companies adopt this technology it is important for them to understand the implications of this type of procurement. This chapter revisits a reverse auction event and discusses the impacts the reverse auction format had upon all participants involved in the auction. In late 2001, a small Australian supplier of transport and logistics services was asked to participate in a reverse auction for services they had provided for 5 years to a multinational organisation. They were not successful in retaining their contract position and this chapter looks at the reverse auction and its business impacts 2 years after the initial auction. The case study is viewed through the eyes of the winning supplier, losing supplier, auction vendor, and buyer. The main outcomes show that the reverse auction struggles to adapt to fluid business conditions and is limited if it is used as only a price-fixing mechanism. It did not engender cooperative supply chains or win-win situations between the auction players.

**Section V
A Review of the Literature**

Online reverse auctions are a relatively new phenomenon in business, although the practice of traditional auctions is centuries old. The online aspect of auctions is an example of a disruptive technology and its impact on the business world. The use of the Internet has changed the face of competition in supply and also changed the way buyers and suppliers interact. This chapter is a topological classification of the current literature on e-procurement auctions, with the intent of organizing current and future research in online procurement auctions. Over 200 articles have been abstracted and reviewed. The authors develop three classification frames: content, theory, and methodology. Nineteen content areas are populated, including significant reference to the impact of auctions on the supply chain. In summary, this chapter seeks to increase the topic clarity of current research. The quality of each individual reverse auction paper is not evaluated. However, the classification should stimulate academics to pursue current and new avenues of reverse auction research.

xiv

Preface

My first introduction to the online reverse auction was at an organization's professional development event. The two speakers were from a very large firm engaged in a private auction site. The speakers related the procurement of safety glasses—originally $300,000 in purchased safety glasses. The buying firm invited 24 suppliers—eight suppliers did not respond at all; eight suppliers signed in to the online auction at the designated time, but only submitted one bid; and the remaining eight signed in and bid multiple times until there was a "winner" of the auction. The speakers related that the firm saved 15% from the prior price. My mind went into overdrive. If this savings was 15%, what about the next set of bids on safety glasses? Who was the winner? Who was losing the profit on the transaction? How low could they go? Would this work on other products? Would small firms go out of business?

Auctions have long been a staple of business practices. Selling and buying goods has intrigued participants for many years. Auctions have been studied from many perspectives, particularly by economists in light of such traditional principles as game theory and auction theory.

TRADITIONAL AUCTIONS

The original idea of an auction is that one can procure goods and services through the use of a bidding mechanism. Traditional auctions are based on long-standing theoretical foundations and tested empirical work. Engelbrecht-Wiggans (1980) presented classifications for various types of auctions and bidding models based on the assumptions used in the models.

Others studying traditional auctions have attempted to link auction theory to everyday transactions. Rothkopf and Harstad (1994) presented an essay in *Management Science* that attempts to model the competitive bidding process. Since this work was done on a traditional auction, a fundamental issue of the advancement of knowledge in auctions is revealed: the lack of a large sample size. Gathering information on competitive bidding is difficult in the traditional auction arena.

Other issues have also been studied in traditional auction research. These include proposing a methodology for profit-maximized bidding (Swider & Weber, 2007), identifying the winner's curse (Neeman & Orosel, 1999; Parlour, Prasnikar, & Rajan, Shaffer, 1998), and behavior in the bidding process under a variety of scenarios (Linzert, Nautz, & Breitung, 2006; Neugebauer & Selten, 2006; Peters & Bodkin, 2007).

Traditional auctions, as stated previously, have some limitations. They are constrained by time, place, number of bidders, number of bids, and the bidding experience. The advent of the Internet has, frankly, given researchers an opportunity to study auction theory with much larger data sets. The Internet, as a disruptive technology (Christiansen, 1997), has opened the door to not only a significantly different way to do research but also a different way to do business.

ONLINE PROCUREMENT AUCTIONS

Auctions have long been a popular method for allocation and procurement of products and services. With the advent of the Internet and the proliferation of Web users, auctions are moving online. Online auctions have become popular in business because they reduce transaction costs, enable a larger number and variety of bidders, and, of course, reduce costs along the supply chain. However, as noted earlier, there is a cost that someone pays for the use of the auctions. There is the potential for a significant impact on profitability of both the buyers and the sellers in the online procurement auction environment (Klein, 1997; Van Heck, 1998).

Growth in online auctions reinforces the need for understanding the factors important in auctions and the caveats that both researchers and practitioners need to know in order to effectively study and use the auction tool. Although the basis for understanding traditional auctions are well known (see for example Engelbrecht-Wiggans, 1980), research is still somewhat limited in online auctions (Van Heck, 1998).

It is with this in mind that *Best Practices in Online Procurement Auctions* was initiated.

ORGANIZATION OF THE BOOK

Best Practices is organized in five sections and nineteen chapters. The organization follows the conceptual framework of Parente, Venkataraman, Fizel, and Millet (2004) by using systems theory to frame the study of auctions. In the model, the input, process, and output of auctions are examined. While each chapter will be discussed in the section that follows, a high-level overview is given in the remainder of this section.

The input side of the model is specifically focused on the participants in the auction and the product characteristics. As such, this section has two subsections—one dealing with the buyers' concerns, the suppliers' issues, and the buyer-supplier dyad; and one consisting of two papers addressing product characteristics.

The process portion of the model, and the organization of the book, deals with how the auction is conducted, specific issues related to technology, auction theory (i.e., winner's curse), and issues surrounding the auction in a business.

The output side of the model attends to performance metrics and success of auctions. This includes addressing issues of collusion and ethics.

Finally, the chapters are book-ended with an introductory chapter that is a debate on online procurement auctions and an ending chapter that is an extensive literature review that results in a typology of online reverse auctions.

THE CHAPTERS

The first section of the book, Online Reverse Auctions Today, addresses the ongoing controversy of the online procurement auction. Chapter I, **Point Counterpoint: The Online Reverse Auction Controversy**, frames the remainder of the volume.

Online reverse auctions have been extensively used in business since the early 1990s. However, there is reason to believe, on one hand, that the reverse auction is gaining in popularity. Buyers are able to increase their supplier pool and obtain lower prices. However, this is not necessarily the case. Some would argue that the reverse auction has outlived its usefulness and is merely a cost-cutting, nonstrategic, and actually detrimental way of doing business.

In this chapter, Thomas F. Gattiker of Boise State and M. L. Emiliani of Central Connecticut State square off in an eleven-point debate on the usefulness of online procurement auctions.

The next section deals with the **Input Side of Online Reverse Auctions**. Clearly, this is a popular area of research, as six chapters are devoted to the buyers, suppliers, and the buyer-supplier dyad, while another two chapters focus on the product part of the auction equation.

In Chapter II, Peter B. Southard discusses **Reverse Auctions and Supplier Consortia.** The notion of a supplier consortium is introduced. The supplier consortium is an alternative buyer-supplier relationship and is examined within the dimensions of the Parente et al. framework (Parente et al., 2004). The chapter addresses various consortia and the potential impact on the reverse auction. Southard concludes with a prescriptive decision process to help managers better analyze the most appropriate form of buyer-supplier relationship for their firm and their supply chain.

Chapter III, by Peggy D. Lee, is an empirical study that views the reverse auction from the perspective of the purchasing agent. **The Purchasing Agent's View of Online Reverse Auctions** surveys purchasing agents in multiple businesses on their use and satisfaction with online reverse auctions. Lee found that purchasing agents with a high level of buying experience will perceive that online reverse auctions have a negative impact on the trust and cooperation in supplier relationships. Purchasing agents did not see a negative impact of online reverse auctions on long-term viability of suppliers. By understanding the lens through which purchasing agents view online reverse auctions, managers can do a better job in sourcing strategies and the decision to use online reverse auctions.

Internet Reverse Auctions: Listening to the Voices of Non-adopters is written by Thomas F. Gattiker. He targets non-adopters of auctions and challenges us to understand the reason for the lack of use of the online reverse auction in a specific business. The focus is on factors that impact the fit between the Internet reverse auction technology and the characteristics of the particular purchasing task that the buyer must carry out (i.e., characteristics of the material or service to be purchased in the market that it is to be purchased from). Gattiker presents an empirical study with links to the literature and advice for practitioners.

Chapter V, **Economic Effects of Electronic Reverse Auctions: A Procurement Perspective**, describes the economic effects caused by the use of electronic reverse auctions along the procurement process. The authors, Ulli Arnold and Martin Schnabel, argue that the economic effects must be viewed from a holistic perspective. The whole transaction process must be considered. The approach of the new institutional economics provides a theoretical foundation for the analysis. The second part of the chapter deals with the single steps of an auction-integrated procurement process. Through this holistic view of the procurement process, the authors emphasize the additional benefits and the danger caused by auctions. The development of better procurement process awareness enables better decisions concerning the choice of benefits which are worth to be pursued.

Janet M. Duck moves the reader into some of the more organizational issues of auctions, in **Developing Trust-Based Relationships in Online Procurement Auctions.** Chapter VI revolves around the challenges involved with developing trust and commitment in online procurement auctions. While many studies suggest that the success rate for e-auctions is down, Duck proposes that absence of trust between the buyer and seller in this virtual arena is a critical issue in online reverse auctions. Viewpoints of the buyer and seller are presented. Common issues are identified and the challenges associated with creating trust and fairness in the e-auction environment are revealed. Duck suggests proactive strategies in order for stakeholders to maintain trust in this environment and to gain benefits from this virtual supply chain process.

Chapter VII is a reprint of a previously published article by Steve New, **Innovation and B2B E-Commerce: Explaining What Did Not Happen.** I have added the Implications for Practitioners for consistency throughout the volume. This chapter deals with the massive wave of enthusiasm for B2B e-commerce. The issue of Internet-driven trading is paramount in this work. The author talks about the "wired" world of commerce that leads to real-time, Internet-driven trading and the significant implications for the nature of buyer-supplier relationships, pricing, and the management of industrial capacity. Drawing on a multistranded empirical study, this chapter seeks to explain the divergence between the expected and realized degrees of innovation in Internet-driven trading.

The next subsection of the volume relates to issues concerning the product in the online reverse auction equation. Chapter VIII, **Bundling for Online Reverse Auctions: Approaches and Experiences**, was written by Tobias Schoenherr and Vincent A. Mabert. The authors provide insight into bundling practices for online reverse auctions by exploring approaches and reporting experiences of 252 companies in the U.S. manufacturing industry. Within the context of Parente et al.'s (2004) conceptual framework for the analysis of online auctions, aspects of the "Product Characteristics" component were explored. Bundling issues investigated include content, goals, structure, and performance.

Differences and similarities in bundling behavior and outcomes between small and large enterprises are emphasized, highlighting the impact of firm size and the resulting strategies explored. As such, this chapter provides managerial insights, especially useful to smaller companies, for successfully employing bundles in reverse auctions.

Chapter IX, **Multi-Attribute Auctions: Research Challenges and Opportunities,** is by Kholekile L. Gwebu and Jing Wang. This chapter highlights the promise and importance of reverse multi-attribute auctions (RMAA). It outlines the major benefits of RMAAs over other traditional auction mechanisms, such as reverse single attribute auctions, and then presents a structured and critical assessment of the current state of RMAA research.

Section III deals with the auction process itself. How do auctions run? What are the issues? **Competition and the Winner's Curse in B2B Reverse Auctions**, is an empirical study using data from industry. Indranil K. Ghosh, John L. Fizel, Ido Millet, and Diane H. Parente, authors of Chapter X, use the data provided by a major multinational corporation on online procurement auctions. They specify the relationship that the prevalence of the Winner's Curse would have on the success of such procurement auctions. They show that the presence of the Winner's Curse and the subsequent need for bidders to show caution in the presence of the Winner's Curse could lead to lower auction success for the firm. They identify specific cases in which this phenomenon holds true. Further, they identify implications for firms wishing to conduct procurement auctions online.

Novel Business-Oriented Auctions, by Tracy Mullen, introduces the reader to the concept of "agents" in the auction process. Chapter XI demonstrates that with the advent of the Internet, traditional auction forms have evolved to fit into a plethora of business niches, either integrating into traditional approaches or simply creating new opportunities. This chapter examines two novel uses for auctions in a business context, namely sponsored search auctions and prediction markets. Understanding the potential auction benefits and limitations can hopefully provide practitioners with a more informed and successful approach when employing these auction-based tools in their businesses.

Chapter XII, by Eric C. Jackson, deals with the reverse auction in the context of the supply chain. **Implications for Reverse Auctions from a Supply Chain Management Perspective** considers reverse auctions in the context of the supply chain and the type of end-user product being produced. Jackson contends that in order to successfully utilize a reverse auction without alienating their suppliers, buyers need to classify their product as innovative or standardized. He also argues that the buyer must consider whether its supply chain is responsive or efficient. Firms with an understanding of this relationship will allow buyers to better evaluate their use of reverse auctions as a purchasing tool in the context of buyer supplier relations.

Chapter XIII is another reprint for *Best Practices:* **Multi-Agent Patterns for Deploying Online Auctions**, by Ivan Jureta, Manuel Kolp, and Stéphane Faulkner. In this chapter, they discuss the high volume of goods and services that is being traded using online auction systems. They also note the growth in size and complexity of architectures to support online auctions. They also discuss the agent software development paradigm and its appropriateness for modeling, development, and implementation. This article proposes an agent-oriented pattern analysis of best practices for online auctions. The patterns are intended to help both IT managers and software engineers during the requirement specification of an online auction system while integrating benefits of agent software engineering. I have written the section on Implications for Practitioners for this chapter.

Haiying Qiao, Hui Jie, and Dong-Qing Yao produced a previously published paper that appeared to be a good fit for Chapter XIV. **An Internet Trading Platform for Testing Auction and Exchange Mechanisms** discusses a generic electronic market platform that is designed to run different kinds of auctions and exchanges. This is particularly important to practitioners. Knowledge of the existence of such tools in academia can present wonderful options for practitioners. Different auctions, including combinatorial auctions, multiple-round reverse auctions, and multiple homogeneous good auctions, have been built and run successfully on the platform.

Section IV, Online Reverse Auction Success, focuses on the performance or results of the auction. Sbrana Gupta, Indranil Ghosh, and Ido Millet wrote **An Empirical Study of Collusion Potential Metrics and their Impact on Online Reverse Auction Success.** In Chapter XIII, they study the effect of bidder conduct on auction success by examining a business to business (B2B) online procurement auction market. In particular, they investigate whether collaborative bidding is more likely when suppliers compete with each other on multiple auctions and/or over a longer period of time. The analysis confirms that in online reverse auctions, winning bids are higher or auction success is lower when the same set of suppliers bid against each other regularly. In a supply chain framework, existence of such collaborative bidder behavior would reduce the cost savings for the buyer. It is therefore important for the practitioners to be alert to such activities and introduce measures that curtail the resulting costly outcomes.

Auction success, as an issue, has its share of caveats. Joseph R. Muscatello and Susan Emens present a discussion of the popular topic of ethics. Chapter XVI is entitled **Do Reverse Auctions Violate Professional Standards and Codes of Conduct?** Muscatello and Emens discuss the debate as to the ethical considerations inherent in the new business processes of online reverse auctions. The chapter examines some of the professional standards/codes of ethics available including the Institute of Supply

Chain Management (ISM) and a selected number of organizations, including Dell and GE. Further, the chapter presents a framework that can help an organization determine whether reverse auctions, and the way they are run, are ethical.

Chapter XVII is a reprint of a previously published work by Radoslav Delina and Anton Lavrin. **Reverse Auction Impact on a Mining Company** is a case study that describes the initial implementation and evaluation of an e-procurement system, using reverse auctions, for a large manufacturer of brown coal in the Slovak Republic. They address one of the biggest problems when making decisions on e-business investments. The issue is one of defining return on investment (ROI) and uncertainty about what method should be used for measuring the results. They provide a wonderful outline of the reverse auction process and present metrics to evaluate the current performance of the system versus intended future performance matrix. The case results proved that the investment into the e-commerce solution is highly effective in reducing input costs. The editor has provided a section for Implications for Managers, consistent with other chapters in the body of the volume.

Chapter XVIII, **A Reverse Auction Case Study: The Final Chapter**, is a reprint of a previously published article by Andrew Stein, Paul Hawking, and David C. Wyld. The authors present a review of a reverse auction event and discuss the impact that the reverse auction format had on all participants involved in the auction. The previous supplier was not successful in retaining its contract position. This chapter looks at the reverse auction and its business impacts two years after the initial auction. The case study is viewed through the eyes of the winning supplier, losing supplier, auction vendor, and buyer. This is a good assessment for anyone looking to get into—or out of—the reverse auction procurement strategy. The main outcomes show that the reverse auction struggles to adapt to fluid business conditions and is limited if it is used as only a price fixing mechanism.

Finally, in the last section, the single chapter deals with the review of the literature. In Chapter XIX, Barbara Sherman and Joseph R. Muscatello did an extensive literature review that results in **Reverse Auctions: A Topology and Synopsis of Current Research Efforts.** This chapter is a topological classification of the current literature on e-procurement auctions with the intent of organizing current and future research in online procurement auctions. Over 200 articles have been abstracted and reviewed. The authors develop three classification frames: content, theory, and methodology. Nineteen content areas are populated, including significant reference to the impact of auctions on the supply chain.

In summary, this chapter seeks to increase the topic clarity of current research. The quality of each individual reverse auction paper is not evaluated. However, the classification should stimulate academics to pursue current and new avenues of reverse auction research.

THE CONTRIBUTION

Best Practices in Online Procurement Auctions is unique in that it attempts to transfer academic research to the practitioner. At the end of Chapters II-XVII, a section entitled Implications for Practitioners briefly summarizes the substance of the paper, findings, recommendations for practitioners, and the limitations of the study or theoretical proposal. It is my intent to provide practitioners with a window to the rich world of academia and an easy tool with which to use the research in practice.

REFERENCES

Christiansen, C. (1997). *The Innovator's Dilemma.* New York: Harvard Business School Press.

Engelbrecht-Wiggans, R. (1980). Auctions and bidding models: A survey. *Management Science, 26*(2), 119-142.

Klein, S. (1997). Introduction to electronic auctions. *Electronic Markets, 7,* 3-6.

Linzert, T., Nautz, D., & Breitung, J. (2006). Bidder behavior in central bank repo auctions: Evidence from the Bundesbank. *Journal of International Financial Markets, Institutions and Money, 16*(3), 215-230.

Neeman, Z., & Orosel, G. O. (1999). Herding and the sinner's curse in markets with sequential bids. *Journal of Economic Theory, 85*(1), 91-121.

Neugebauer, T., & Selten, R. (2006). Individual behavior of first-price auctions: The importance of information feedback in computerized experimental markets. *Games and Economic Behavior, 54*(1), 183-204.

Parente, D. H., Venkataraman, R. R., Fizel, J. L., & Millet, I. (2004). A conceptual framework for analyzing online auctions. *Supply Chain Management: An International Journal, 9*(4), 287-294.

Parlour, C. A., Prasnikar, V., & Rajan, U. Compensating for the winner's curse: Experimental evidence. *Games and Economic Behavior.*

Peters, C., & Bodkin, C. D. (2007). An exploratory investigation of problematic online auction behaviors: Experiences of eBay users. *Journal of Retailing and Consumer Services, 14*(1), 1-16.

Rothkopf, M. H., & Harstad, R. M. (1994). Modeling competitive bidding: A critical essay. *Management Science, 40*(3), 364-384.

Shaffer, S. (1998). The winner's curse in banking. *Journal of Financial Intermediation, 7*(4), 359-392.

Swider, D. J., & Weber, C. (2007). Bidding under price uncertainty in multi-unit pay-as-bid procurement auctions for power systems reserve. *European Journal of Operational Research, 181*(3), 1297-1308.

Van Heck, E. (1998). How should CIOs deal with Web-based auctions? *Communications of the ACM, 41,* 99-100.

Acknowledgment

I would like to acknowledge the help of all involved in the collaboration and review process of the book. I could not have done it without all of you.

Most of the authors of chapters included in this book also served as referees for articles written by other authors. Thanks go to all who provided constructive feedback and reviews.

I would like to thank Cheryl Southard for serving as copy editor. She did yeoman's work on this volume. I would also like to thank Eric Jackson, Peter Southard, and Ido Millet for taking on extra reviews with short, short turnaround. I would also like to thank Joe Muscatello for contributions to the book and for being a "go to" colleague when I really needed it.

I would like to thank John Fizel for sharing his wisdom in the editing of this book. I didn't always listen to his advice, but in hindsight, I wish I had.

I would especially like to thank my colleague, friend, and collaborator, Tom Gattiker from Boise State. Tom has been supportive in every aspect of getting this book done.

Special thanks go to all the staff at IGI Global, especially Ross Miller and Kristin Roth. Ross began the project with me and Kristin has really helped to bring it to fruition. Her advice and counsel has been critical in getting the project done.

In closing, I want to thank all of the authors for their insights and excellent contributions. They were very responsive in doing all of the little "extras" necessary for publication and making this a book for both academics and practitioners.

Finally, I want to thank my husband, John. He really helped me to complete the project on time, in spite of the many other things "on the table" for us. He helped me to get through my eleventh hour panic without making me feel guilty for letting other things slip.

Diane H. Parente, PhD
Hershey, PA, USA
November 2007

List of Reviewers

Ulli Arnold, University of Stuttgart, Germany

Craig Carter, University of Nevada – Reno, USA

Janet Duck, The Pennsylvania State University – Great Valley, USA

John Fizel, The Pennsylvania State University – Erie, USA

Thomas F. Gattiker, Boise State University, USA

Indranil Ghosh, Winston-Salem State University, USA

Sbrana Gupta, St. Thomas University, USA

Eric C. Jackson, The Pennsylvania State University – Erie, USA

Heinzpeter Kärner, University of Stuttgart, Germany

Peggy D. Lee, The Pennsylvania State University – Great Valley, USA

Vincent A. Mabert, Indiana University, USA

Ido Millet, The Pennsylvania State University – Erie, USA

Tracy Mullen, The Pennsylvania State University , USA

Joseph Muscatello, Kent State University, USA

Martin Schnabel, University of Stuttgart, Germany

Tobias Schoenherr, Eastern Michigan University, USA

Loay Sewali, Indiana State University, USA

Peter Southard, The Pennsylvania State University – Erie, USA

Jing Wang, University of New Hampshire, USA

Section I
Online Reverse Auctions Today

Chapter I
Point Counterpoint:
The Online Reverse Auction Controversy

Thomas F. Gattiker
Boise State University, USA

M. L. Emiliani
Central Connecticut State University, USA

ABSTRACT

In this chapter, the online reverse auction is introduced through a series of points and counterpoints on the use of the tool. Tom Gattiker, Boise State, and M. L. (Bob) Emiliani, Central Connecticut State, identify and debate eleven points in the use of online reverse auctions.

INTRODUCTION

Reverse auctions used in industrial business-to-business procurement have continued to be a controversial practice since their introduction in 1995. The controversy extends to buying organizations, suppliers, the business press, industry trade associations, and to the academics who study them.

Regardless of their merit, reverse auctions are likely to be with us for some time. As a result, buyers and sellers who participate in reverse auctions should thoroughly understand the benefits, shortcomings, risks, and costs of using or not using Internet-enabled reverse auction technology.

In this chapter, we offer a debate on the subject of Internet-enabled reverse auctions. Thomas F. Gattiker, Boise State University, develops a series of points in favor of the use of reverse auctions as a procurement tool, while M. L. Emiliani, Central Connecticut State University, develops the counter arguments.

This eleven issue point-counterpoint chapter is intended to provide readers with a brief outline of the key issues surrounding reverse auctions.

POINT-COUNTERPOINT

In the following pages, there are eleven points that Gattiker and Emiliani debate on reverse auctions. While Emiliani, who provided the counterpoints, is a strong opponent in his research on auctions, Gattiker, who provided the points, is neither a proponent nor an opponent of the reverse auction tool. Both authors make convincing arguments on the advantages and disadvantages of auctions.

Point #1: Reverse auctions yield significant purchase price savings.

For example, 65% of auctions studied by Wagner and Schwab (2004) resulted in purchase price savings of over 5 percent. Greater savings have been reported by others. The total cost savings are likely to be less than the purchase price savings due to contract leakage, non-conformances, and other post-award problems (Emiliani & Stec, 2002, 2004). However, even when we take these factors into account, savings still remain in many instances.

Counterpoint: Buyers should not assume reverse auctions will deliver savings in every case, either on a unit price or total cost basis.

While there is much emphasis on total cost, the primary measure of reverse auction success is unit price savings using the purchase price variance (PPV) or similar metric. This metric is known to be defective and leads to higher total costs (Emiliani, Stec, & Grasso, 2005). Reverse auction savings can range from negative value, which costs the buyer money; to neutral, where no savings are

achieved; to a positive average gross savings of 10-20%, but where net savings are typically half or less (Emiliani & Stec, 2002).

Point #2: Reverse auctions decrease the time and resources needed to conduct the sourcing process.

For example, Smeltzer and Carr (2003) report that companies achieve a 25-35% reduction in time required to go from RFQ distribution to choosing a supplier. Time savings are accompanied by similar decreases in administrative costs. Since much of the work (supplier pre-qualification, RFQ preparation, development of award strategy, and so on) is reusable, time and administrative cost savings for subsequent auctions may be greater than for first auctions. In fact, subsequent auctions may take only one tenth of the time required for the first auction (Carter, Beal, Carter, Hendrick, Kaufman, & Petersen, 2004).

Counterpoint: The use of reverse auctions does not guarantee a decrease in the time and resources needed to source goods and services (Emiliani & Stec, 2004, 2005).

The bulk of the time savings is in price negotiation, though additional pre- or post-auction activities may take place, thus offsetting the expected time savings. The time it takes to source via reverse auctions will also depend upon the use or non-use of decision-support tools. Likewise, administrative costs may or may not decrease. The purchase of reverse auction software and related services will offset some or all administrative savings. Subsequent auctions may not take a fraction of the time required for the first auction if sellers determine it is not in their interest to participate in reverse auctions.

Point #3: Reverse auctions also allow companies to more efficiently manage purchasing human resources.

This is because auctions reportedly enable the average buyer to achieve price savings that are as good as those achieved by the company's best negotiator (Kaufmann & Carter, 2004; Gattiker, 2005). This increases the fungibility of human capital within the supply chain function.

Counterpoint: Reverse auctions typically constitute an average of about 5% of total corporate spend for goods and services (CAPS, 2006).

Thus, reverse auctions offer minimal opportunity to more efficiently manage purchasing human resources on a broad basis. Additionally, purchasing personnel using reverse auctions are ostensibly negotiating total cost, while normal day-to-day purchasing activities typically focus on negotiating unit price and delivery. Thus, a comparison between the two activities may not be valid.

Point #4: Reverse auctions drive improvements to underlying purchasing processes of many companies.

Using electronic auctions requires a sourcing process that is more formalized than the practices commonly encountered at many companies. In many organizations, transitioning to auctions has revealed that procurement processes were not as disciplined as management would like to have believed. For example, at Shell Chemical, management believed that reverse auctions would be an incremental extension of existing competitive bidding processes. However, initial attempts at implementing auctions revealed a lack of solid supplier selection procedures in many areas of the company. In this case, implementing auctions provided the catalyst for improving many areas of the sourcing process. Many of the improved practices were then imbedded in templates. As one manager reported, "It's [using reverse auctions is] a way that the average buyer can raise his game to really perform like an exceptional buyer" (Gattiker, 2005).

Counterpoint: Reverse auctions represent a form of power-based bargaining whose success relies on zero-sum outcomes—that is, the buyer

benefits at the sellers' expense—and coercion (Giampietro & Emiliani, 2007).

This invalidates any characterization of reverse auctions as an improvement in purchasing process. Electronic reverse auctions are not required as a means to initiate more formalized sourcing processes. The managers of companies whose sourcing processes are ad hoc or less formalized suffer from a lack of process focus. To remedy this, managers can adopt alternate manual or electronic supplier selection and sourcing templates for strategic and non-strategic goods and services. Organizations that apply these processes consistently, and with discipline typically realize lower total costs than those achieved using reverse auctions. These outcomes are the result of the existence of many more opportunities for bilateral learning, joint cost management, and interfirm capability building (Bounds, 1996; Dyer & Nobeoka, 2000; Liker & Choi, 2004). In contrast, reverse auctions are very narrow in scope and less collaborative, thus offering fewer opportunities.

Point #5: The buyer firm benefits from the "internal transparency" that reverse auctions insert into the purchasing process.

This is especially beneficial to purchasing managers and executives. These managers value an archival record of how the final price was reached. One such person has been quoted as saying, "Now I can literally look into the negotiation room and see what was going on—I need to base my judgments far less on what I am told by my buyers than on what I can't really see in the system" (Kaufmann & Carter, 2004, p. 21).

Counterpoint: Buyers should not assume there is always transparency in reverse auctions.

This purported benefit assumes that supplier prices and related data are accurate. Reverse auctions have long been plagued by data integrity issues, for both the buyer's data as well as the seller's data (Emiliani & Stec, 2002), in addition to the market-maker's data. Prices input by suppliers may not have been precisely calculated. In many cases, the seller inputs rough price estimates they hope to achieve if they win the work.

Point #6: The overall reverse auction process can expand the supply base.

Because the distribution of RFQ's becomes highly automated, buyers can invite additional suppliers to participate with very small increases in marginal cost. Assuming these suppliers can be prequalified, this can be a significant benefit. Some reverse auction services even provide for the translation of RFQ's into other languages, which facilitates international sourcing. Translating specifications runs the risk of distorting them, but apparently some organizations have found this practice to be effective (Kaufmann & Carter, 2004).

Counterpoint: Expansion of the supply base may or may not be beneficial to the buyer's interests.

A smaller supply base is generally more manageable from the standpoint of transactions and maintenance. Reverse auctions often require the addition of many new suppliers before incumbent suppliers can be eliminated. In many cases, the work will be split between an incumbent and a new supplier based upon the distribution of winning bids among the various lots of work. Thus, the buyers may experience growth in their supply base, which is the opposite of what most senior managers wish to achieve.

Point #7: Sellers benefit from the increased efficiency of the reverse auction process.

While suppliers view auctions less favorably than buyers (Beall et al., 2003), suppliers have realized considerable benefits. Sellers report that reduced cycle time pays off for them in several ways. First, the time required for negotiation and other aspects of the process reduces suppliers' administrative costs. A second result of decreased cycle time is increased cash flow due to the reduction in the

time from submitting price proposals to the time that revenue is actually generated from the sale (Carter et al., 2004).

Counterpoint: The benefits of reverse auctions to suppliers have been consistently overstated or misrepresented by market makers and by buyers (Emiliani & Stec, 2004, 2005).

Fundamentally, power-based bargaining rooted in zero-sum outcomes does not create a basis for suppliers to benefit from in any meaningful way. Sellers who report benefits tend to be very much in the minority, typically one supplier here and another there. Reduction in supplier's administrative costs is largely unproven. Supplier cash flow is usually negatively impacted if they win work from reverse auctions. This is because buyers use reverse auctions as a means to establish new terms and conditions that are more favorable to buyer's interests and less favorable to seller's interests (Emiliani & Stec, 2001). For example, payment terms are often extended from 30 days to 60 or 90 days, and suppliers may be required to carry finished goods inventories.

Point #8: Sellers benefit from market information they gain from participating in reverse auctions.

In the past, sellers have often had to rely on buyers' accounts of competitive conditions and the like. Due to the transparency of the process, reverse auctions (under most formats) provide a good understanding of the "true market" (Kaufmann and Carter, 2004). In addition to benefiting sellers, buyers benefit (assuming they do not want to mislead sellers) because rather than buyers having to convince sellers, sellers can "see for themselves."

Counterpoint: Sellers may or may not gain useful insight into the prices offered by other entities.

This benefit can only exist if all suppliers' selling prices are accurately determined and if the buyer's RFQ requirements are also accurate. In other words, data integrity issues can lead to a "false market" if seller's prices or lead-times are defective, and buyer's requirements are incorrect or will soon change in ways that are unfavorable to supplier's interests (Emiliani & Stec, 2002). False markets are easily created when sellers who are not qualified to do the work are invited to bid, if bidders participating in the auction do not actually have available capacity, or if sellers' lead-times are incorrect.

Point #9: Transparency inherent in reverse auctions also benefits suppliers in the post-bidding stages of the procurement process.

A good auction process includes well-articulated award criteria. Additionally, a good bidding process creates more internal transparency (within the buying organization) into how the competing suppliers compare on the award criteria. Due to this, suppliers report that auctions create greater impartiality in the way buyers award business (Carter et al., 2004).

Counterpoint: Buyers and sellers should view with caution the often-stated benefit of transparency in reverse auctions.

This benefit must be qualified by the potentially negative impact originating from problems in the integrity of buyer or seller data. If buyers used standard sourcing process in a disciplined way, suppliers would also likely report greater impartiality in the way buyers award business. This, like many other purported benefits, is not the exclusive domain of reverse auctions.

Point #10: Like any tool, the results achieved from deploying reverse auctions depend partially on the conditions under which they are used.

Researchers have investigated numerous factors. A preponderance of the research (e.g., Kaufmann & Carter, 2004; Wagner & Schwab, 2004) suggests that reverse auctions are appropriate when

competition for the buyer's business is high (e.g., a sufficient amount of available capacity among potential suppliers), when purchase volumes are high, and when the characteristics of the material or service being purchased can be fully specified in advance (i.e., in an RFQ). These material and service characteristics include physical descriptions, quality, certifications such as ISO 14000, transportation requirements, expected services, and so on (Smeltzer & Carr, 2003).

Counterpoint: The goods and services to which reverse auctions can be successfully applied is limited to about 5% of total corporate spending.

The amount of corporate spending that meets requirements—competition, available capacity, existence of new suppliers, high purchase volumes, and so forth—is typically 50-70%. The low amount of corporate spending subject to reverse auctions indicates that they suffer from structural deficiencies that are not easily overcome. These include use of the PPV metric as the measure of success, zero-sum basis of operation, coercion (Giampetro & Emiliani, 2007), and perpetually destructive short-term management thinking (Emiliani, 2006). Further, a tool that promotes destructive power-based bargaining whose success relies on coercion and zero-sum outcomes is certain to be of very limited use.

Point #11: A logical extension of the previous point is that many of the ill-effects that have been observed are due to using reverse auctions under the wrong conditions.

Purchasers have numerous tools at their disposal. There are very few tools that are exclusively "good" or "bad." Rather, most tools will produce undesirable results when they are applied in the wrong circumstances. As mentioned under the previous point, reverse auctions are likely to produce poor results when applied when volumes, competition, or specifiability is low. Unfortunately, it is not unusual for individuals to apply tools in situations to which they are ill-suited, especially when those tools are in vogue. Therefore, it is probable that many of the poor results reported with reverse auctions occurred when they were misapplied.

Counterpoint: Reverse auctions are nothing more than a shortcut for achieving price concessions from suppliers, with little or no regard to suppliers' costs.

As such, it is not surprising that both buyers and sellers commonly experience undesirable outcomes. Shortcuts are often nothing more than a method to cheat—that is, to avoid having to do the necessary hard work. In this case, reverse auctions help buyers avoid having to do the hard work and establish intraorganizational discipline for creating non-zero sum outcomes with their key suppliers (Bounds, 1996; Dyer & Nobeoka, 2000; Liker & Choi, 2004).

CONCLUSION

There are many opinions regarding reverse auctions. Therefore, it is useful to look beyond opinion to the research on the topic, much of which the debaters have cited above. Even in the research there are differing findings. Like any tool, the results achieved from deploying reverse auctions depend partially on the conditions under which they are used. Researchers have investigated numerous factors. A preponderance of the research (e.g., Kaufmann & Carter, 2004; Wagner & Schwab, 2004) suggests that reverse auctions are appropriate when competition for the buyer's business is high (e.g., a sufficient amount of available capacity among potential suppliers), when purchase volumes are high, and when the characteristics of the material or service being purchased can be fully specified in advance (i.e., in an RFQ). These material and service characteristics include physical descriptions, quality, certifications such as ISO 14000,

transportation requirements, expected services, and so on (Smeltzer & Carr, 2003). Other research (e.g., Emiliani & Stec, 2004, 2005) suggests that even under these "ideal" conditions, the costs of reverse auctions outweigh the benefits.

It is incumbent on the buyer and the seller to understand the many issues. Each aspect of the reverse auction adds another layer of complexity to the issue of whether to use the tool or not, and further, whether it will add long-term value to the business or not. Buyers, in particular, need to be wary of being oversold on the tool. At the most, reverse auctions should be one component in a portfolio of sourcing tools and strategies that reside in the buyer's toolchest.

ACKNOWLEDGMENT

The students in Tom Gattiker's MBA supply-chain management class at Boise State University participated in the creation of this essay (Barbara Acker; Benjamin Goode; Carrie Sandirk; Clint Adams; Eric Hackett; Jared Heward; Kasthuri Munirajah; Robin Evans; Ryan Carlson; Sara Anderson)

REFERENCES

Beall, S., Carter, C., Carter, P., Germer, T., Hendrick, T., Jap, S., et al. (2003). *The role of reverse auctions in strategic sourcing* (CAPS Research Report). Tempe, Arizona: Institute of Supply Management.

Bounds, G. (1996). Toyota supplier development. In G. Bounds (Ed.), *Cases in quality* (pp. 3-25). Chicago: R. D. Irwin.

CAPS (2006). *CAPS research: Report of cross-industry standard benchmarks.* Retrieved May 22, 2006, from http://www.capsresearch.org/publications/pdfs-protected/CrossInd052006.pdf

Carter, C., Beal, S., Carter, P., Hendrick, T., Kaufman, L., & Petersen, K. (2004). Reverse auctions-grounded theory from the buyer and supplier perspective. *Transportation Research Part E, 40*(3), 229-254.

Dyer, J., & Nobeoka, K. (2000). Creating and managing a high-performance knowledge sharing network: The Toyota case. *Strategic Management Journal, 21,* 345-367.

Emiliani, M. (2006). Executive decision-making traps and B2B online reverse auctions. *Supply Chain Management: An International Journal, 11*(1), 6-9.

Emiliani, M., & Stec, D. (2001). Online reverse auction purchasing contracts. *Supply Chain Management: An International Journal, 6*(3), 101-105.

Emiliani, M., & Stec, D. (2002). Realizing savings from on-line reverse auctions. *Supply Chain Management: An International Journal, 7*(1), 12-23.

Emiliani, M., & Stec, D. (2004). Aerospace parts suppliers' reaction to online reverse auctions. *Supply Chain Management: An International Journal, 9*(2), 139-153.

Emiliani, M., & Stec, D. (2005). Wood pallet suppliers' reaction to online reverse auctions. *Supply Chain Management: An International Journal, 10*(4), 278-287.

Emiliani, M., Stec, D., & Grasso, L. (2005). Unintended responses to a traditional purchasing performance metric. *Supply Chain Management: An International Journal, 10*(3), 150-156.

Gattiker, T. (2005). Individual user adoption and diffusion of internet reverse auctions at Shell Chemical. *Practix: Best Practices in Purchasing and Supply Chain Management, 8*(4), 1-6.

Giampietro, C., & Emiliani, M. (2007). Coercion and reverse auctions. *Supply Chain Management: An International Journal, 12*(2), 75-84.

Kaufmann, L., & Carter, C. (2004). Deciding on the mode of negotiation: To auction or not to auction electronically. *Journal of Supply Chain Management, 40*(2), 15-26.

Liker, J., & Choi, T. (2004). Building deep supplier relationships. *Harvard Business Review, 82*(12), 104-113.

Smeltzer, L. R., & Carr, A. S. (2003). Electronic reverse auctions: Promises, risks and conditions for success. *Industrial Marketing Management, 32*(6), 481-488.

Tassabehji, R., Taylor, W., Beach, R., & Wood, A. (2006). Reverse e-auctions and supplier-buyer relationships: An exploratory study. *International Journal of Operations and Production Management, 26*(2), 166-184.

Wagner, S. M., & Schwab, A. P. (2004). Setting the stage for successful electronic reverse auctions. *Journal of Purchasing and Supply Management, 10*(1), 11-26.

Section II
Input Side of
Online Reverse Auctions

Section II.a
Buyers, Suppliers, and the Dyad

Chapter II
Reverse Auctions and Supplier Consortia

Peter B. Southard
The Pennsylvania State University, USA

ABSTRACT

Competition between supply chains has resulted in firms carefully examining the relationships that they have, or are contemplating having, with other links in their chain. While the main focus of this book is on a specific type of relationship, that of the reverse auction, other forms of buyer-supplier relationships exist. In order to better understand the implications of the reverse-auction relationship, managers should also analyze the alternatives and the environment of relationships in which reverse auctions operate. The focus of this chapter is on an alternative buyer-supplier relationship, that of the supplier consortia. Within the six dimensions of the framework proposed by Parente, Venkataraman, Fizel, and Millet (2004), this chapter examines this little-studied collaborative group and proposes a spectrum to begin to understand some aspects of buyer-supplier relationships. The chapter includes a theoretical classification framework for supplier consortia. It then compares and contrasts supplier consortia to the reverse auction concluding with a prescriptive decision process that can help managers better analyze the most appropriate form of buyer-supplier relationship for their firm and their supply chain.

INTRODUCTION

Recently, Parente et al. (2004) proposed a conceptual framework for analyzing certain types of business-to-business transactions classified as reverse auctions. In their framework, they identified six dimensions on which to perform this analysis, namely supplier characteristics, the dyad or relationship characteristics, buyer characteristics, product characteristics, the auction process and the auction outcome. In order to better analyze and understand these transactions, a manager needs to also understand the environment in which reverse auctions exist. To do this, it is useful to analyze other comparable or competitive types of buyer-supplier relationships. This chapter facilitates that analysis by examining one type of entity, **supplier consortia**, which could impact several dimensions, including supplier characteristics, dyad or relationship characteristics, and outcomes. The information gleaned from such analysis can be useful to the managers of both supplier and buyer organizations.

Most research in buyer-supplier relationships has been focused on the downstream side of the supply chain, that of the buyer's perspective. Even more specifically, it has been focused on the buyer's interaction with, or selection of, a single supplier. Studies have been conducted on buyers banding together to accomplish various objectives, the most common one being to achieve economies of scale in their purchases in order to lower their overall costs of purchasing. Research on buyers' consortia has been documented from the characteristics of the buyers that are doing it (Huber, Sweeney, & Smyth, 2004) as well as their rationale (Tella & Virolainen, 2005). Other ways of reducing purchasing costs have also been studied. In particular, and in reference to this edited series, much has been written on the use and benefits to buyers of reverse auctions to reduce the costs of purchases. On the other hand, nearly as much information has been provided on the disadvantages to buyers (and, accordingly, to the end customer) of these same reverse auctions.

Little attention has been paid to the perspective and activities of the upstream, or supplier, side of the supply chain equation. In many cases, however, this link, or set of supply chain links, not only possesses considerable market power, but in some cases has learned (or is learning) how to exercise it. In other cases, smaller, less powerful suppliers have been banding together to form consortia to gain both visibility and market power. The intent is that such an association would allow them to survive and prosper. These situations depend on basic objectives of both the buyer and supplier; those of reducing costs and/or building

relationships. Companies in the role of suppliers need to understand not only the implications of a reverse auction relationship with a buyer but also what other relationship alternatives exist and their implications. One objective of this chapter is to provide that perspective and information.

This chapter specifically looks at various supplier consortia from the perspective of what their role is in the technology-enabled marketplace, the relationship they have to reverse auctions, the new paradigm of buyer-supplier relationships with which they compete and, finally, the managerial actions the managers of both suppliers and buyers can or should take to rationalize or improve their relationships with their respective supply chain links. This discussion is preceded by a brief definition of terms and a review of frameworks for classifying supplier consortia. The basis of some of the material presented here, including the supplier consortia framework, comes from an article by Southard and Parente (2007).

SCOPE

One of the primary reasons for the rise in use of e-marketplaces has been both the evolution of Internet technology and the increase in competition that it has generated. This competition either exists currently between suppliers or, in more fragmented industries and markets, is created by buyers through the use of technology. The e-marketplace environment, therefore, is primarily of interest to the supplier that operates in a medium- to highly competitive environment. There are those situations in which the market consists of one, or just a few, suppliers, as in the case of a monopoly or an oligopoly. Suppliers in this market have little need for e-marketplaces, or consortia, as the buyers are well aware of the actual suppliers. Most relationships in this market are of a strategic nature since the products are usually highly technical or specialized. This article, therefore, does not directly address that type of market.

MOTIVATIONS

As mentioned, the business-to-business (B2B) marketplace has often been characterized as being highly fragmented, meaning there has been little coordination or organization. In many cases, suppliers are often, relatively speaking, much smaller in size than their purchasers. This fragmentation has been one reason why there has been an explosion in the number and size of electronic marketplaces. Several different approaches have tried to provide a logical set of criteria for the motivation behind the formation of these marketplaces. One of the more comprehensive was provided by Standing, Love, Stockdale, and Gengatharen (2006), who based their framework on M. E. Porter's Five Competitive Forces Model (1980). They proposed that organizations form electronic marketplaces for one or more of four reasons: economic (lower costs and/or increased revenue), relational (to establish a particular relationship for social, political or other specific purpose), service (providing improved service to the customer), or community benefits (e.g., general economic development). While the relational, service, and community motives have specific goals, as their titles imply, all three eventually summarize to the basic proposition of lowering transaction costs or increasing revenues for the supplier members, both of which are also economic motives. The question then arises, is this economic motive the same reason for the formation of e-marketplaces involving supplier consortia and, if so, how do these unique associations of supply chain links relate to e-marketplaces? A second, and equally important, question is what motives do buyers then have to establish relationships with these associations through e-marketplaces? Before either question may be answered, some basic definitions and classification schema need to be clarified to establish an appropriate foundation for discussion.

DEFINITIONS AND CLASSIFICATIONS

The Oxford Modern English Dictionary (*The Oxford Modern English Dictionary*, 1996) defines a consortium (plural: consortia) as "an association, esp. of several business companies" and comes directly from the Latin for partnership. Since no definition was found in business literature, for the purposes of this article the first step is to define the term supplier consortium as it pertains to e-marketplaces and to distinguish supplier consortia from a purchasing, or buyer's, consortium as well as from reverse auctions. A simple definition of a supplier consortium, therefore, is a partnership of cooperating sellers that have formed, or joined, an association or relationship for the common purpose of promoting and selling the product(s) they produce to the potential buyers of their products. Notice that this, in general, differs from reverse auctions in that there is voluntary cooperation and communication among the members of the group. Having provided a basic definition, the next step is to place these consortia into a classification scheme.

In classifying supplier consortia, it is useful to examine a generic structural framework such as the one proposed by Standing et al. (2006), which they developed to classify electronic marketplaces (both buyer and supplier). They placed these marketplaces into one of four categories: an intermediary, a hierarchy, a consortium (not the same term as defined above), or a large group ownership.

Intermediary, or public, e-markets serve as third party players to bring buyers and sellers together, receiving compensation for that service primarily (or usually) from the buyer. An example of this is eBay, a company that provides an electronic market for sellers to advertise, auction, and sell their products to buyers. Sellers pay eBay based on the starting or reserve price, called the insertion fee, as well as a percentage of the final sales price. These fees can change based on the type of auction conducted. Other service fees can also apply. In a primarily commercial setting, FreeMarkets was a first-mover in this area. It operated as an intermediary and consultant for the buying organization, bringing together suppliers to bid through an online reverse auction scenario. Other types of intermediaries are also possible. In a report to the European Commission, Sairamesh, Stanbridge, Ausio, Keser, and Karabulut (2005), proposed a business model whereby a consortium of sellers form a trusted independent third party (TTP), which manages the contracts between the consortium and the buyer. In this arrangement, the intermediary is a branch or subsidiary of the consortia.

Hierarchy, or private e-marketplaces, are owned and administered by a single party, normally the seller, such as in the reverse auction markets administered by General Electric Corporation. Other examples are electronic marketplaces created by the United States government for use in selecting their suppliers.

The third category is the large group ownership, also known as community or cooperative marketplaces, where many organizations share ownership of the marketplace. An example of this is the group PASourcing.com. This particular consortium consists of a nonprofit initiative developed by suppliers and supported by two state industry groups, the Northwest Pennsylvania Regional Planning and Development Center and the Northwest Pennsylvania Industrial Resource Center. It serves as an economic development and marketing tool that allows small manufacturers access to an electronic marketplace.

In the last group, which the previous study termed a consortium, the marketplace is jointly owned by a small number of large companies. Buyer's consortia such as Covisint in the automobile industry, GoCargo.com in the shipping industry, and Quadrem in the mining industry, all began life as a small group of large organizations forming alliances to increase their buyer and supply chain power.

A second, slightly different, classification schema for e-markets was proposed by Le, Rao, and Truong (2004). It categorized e-markets into three segments based on their transaction governance, which was defined as how the members controlled the flow of information, resources, and products based on the member's power within the market. These three categories were 3PXs (third party exchanges), ISMs (industry-sponsored marketplace), and private e-markets.

3PXs were defined in a similar fashion to the intermediary classification above. They provide a supposedly neutral go-between in a many-to-many marketplace such as the company FreeMarkets provided. The ISM functions as its name implies and, similar to the large group or cooperative ownership in the prior framework, consists of many buyers or sellers from the same industry associating together.

The private e-market is equivalent to the hierarchy marketplace from the previous framework. While the first framework was based on ownership structure, the second was based on power or control within the structure. It appears there is a relationship between ownership structure and power/control since both of these studies proposed similar descriptions of groupings.

The organizational structure of the consortium varies as well. One structural type is a series of joint ventures between suppliers and clients, such as the kyoryokukai created by Japanese automaker suppliers. A second structure is a special purpose organization created when suppliers create a consortium to service a particular project, such as governmental projects. A third is the consortium consisting of a prime contractor who then engages several subcontractors to form a consortium. Many construction and consulting projects are designed in this format.

These frameworks, developed primarily for electronic marketplaces, appear to provide a very adequate description of consortia as well, since the examples used fall into the categories already established. With various classifications of consortia identified, the next step is to examine what role or function consortia play in the supply chain. This information can be used to define a subsequent framework for making managerial decisions regarding association with consortia on the part of sellers and buyers.

ROLE AND FUNCTION OF THE SUPPLIER CONSORTIA

Supplier consortia, and reverse auctions to a certain degree, serve in the role of an intermediary in the industries in which they operate. Many people believed that the growth of Internet technology would eventually mean that market **intermediaries** would no longer be required since companies would have complete access to all of the information needed to eliminate information asymmetry, or problems with discovery, within the supply chain. Unfortunately, it appears that the opposite has happened. Internet technology has enabled more suppliers than ever to enter the market place, further fragmenting it and increasing the need for a coordinating link. As reverse auctions serve to gather suppliers together to aggregate or mitigate transaction and other relationship costs to battle this fragmentation, so do consortia provide a similar function as well as serving as an intermediary.

From an information perspective, Internet technology has led to a virtual information overload, or even gridlock, where gathering information is more costly and time consuming than ever. In this more complex marketplace arena, intermediaries still provide at least as much value as ever, although as electronic intermediaries their role may still be changing. This is the opinion of Anderson and Anderson (2002), who emphasized that the need for intermediaries in the electronic market will have to adapt to the Internet form of electronic business or else face extinction.

Many supplier consortia have recognized this need for change due to the changes in technology

and either developed within, or transformed to, the electronic form necessary to compete for that middle spot, or intermediary, in the buyer-supplier relationship. Electronic marketplaces, which include both reverse auctions and the electronic forms of supplier consortia, have provided the opportunity for, among other things, smaller suppliers to gain access to larger markets without incurring many of the associated marketing costs. These lowered costs provide a definite economic benefit if they can be passed along. Buyers often base their purchasing decisions on price, so these cost savings provide the supplier members of such a marketplace a competitive advantage. These are some of the motivating factors behind the formation of supplier consortia. Like reverse auctions, supplier consortia provide a market or pool of suppliers that will attract buyers seeking inputs that place these consortia in a similar role to that of the reverse auction. These similarities, along with distinct differences, lead to further questions about the relationship between reverse auctions and supplier consortia.

THE EVOLUTION OF BUYER-SUPPLIER RELATIONS AND A RELATIONSHIP SPECTRUM

In the days of Frederick Taylor and Henry Ford, around the turn of the century, if an organization was not completely vertically integrated, as many such as Ford were, the general relationship between a buyer and a supplier was an adversarial one. In the postwar and Cold War eras of the 1950s and 1960s, there was a movement toward horizontal integration that increased the need for more and different suppliers, yet the relationships still tended to be more competitive than cooperative. Then the movement toward quality management and lean production systems of the 1970s and 1980s led to a reversal in thought, as companies were urged by industry leaders and academics alike to form long-term strategic partnerships with suppliers. These new strategic relationships were supported and enabled by trust, cooperation, and the sharing of information among the partners. At the heart of this relationship were the benefits in product and process design resulting from the collaboration between buyer and seller that resulted in cost reductions and quality improvements for both. An economic downturn in the 1990s, however, forced many companies to look for new ways to cut costs. At the same time, tremendous advances in technology were making Internet business, or e-business, not only possible but also cost-effective. Enter the reverse auction and a rethinking of the drive toward totally strategic relationships.

The development of electronic reverse auction marketplaces altered the buyer-supplier relationship models, particularly with regards to the strategic selection of, and relationship with, suppliers. For the last couple of decades, business schools, and management experts have touted the formation of strategic relationships with an organization's suppliers. As competition increased exponentially, driven by new advances in technology and Internet adoption, top management felt forced to seek ways to use that same technology to improve their bottom line and hence shareholder equity. Reverse auctions provided that short-term reduced cost, but usually at the expense of supplier collaboration and cooperation. Thus emerged a polarized spectrum of buyer-supplier relationship models where strategic partnerships anchored one end and reverse auctions the other. Unlike the frameworks provided earlier that described the structure of the consortium, this continuum allows managers to classify a consortia based on how it interacts with a buyer and the role it plays

in the supply chain, directly relating it to the relationship created by reverse auctions.

Note that this continuum describes the relationship between the buyer and the supplier and not necessarily the role of the product being sourced or the sourcing decision itself. Companies can and do use reverse auctions to source strategic inputs.

Firms such as General Electric chose managerial objectives that pulled them toward developing relationships on the auction end of the spectrum. Those firms following the lean, responsive supply chain model, such as Toyota and Dell, still seek managerial objectives that foster longer term, single-supplier relationships more toward the strategic end. In this latter environment, even commodity suppliers are encouraged to participate in more strategic relationships with their supply chain partners. In these relationships, pioneered by the Japanese automobile industry, inputs are provided by sole suppliers who have long-term agreements. This is done with the belief that these long-term commitments encourage the supplier to reinvest profits to create further efficiencies in both the product and process, which benefits both themselves and their customer.

This polarized spectrum gives rise to the question of where on the line does the supplier consortium reside. It also raised the question as to whether the membership in a consortium and the participation in a reverse auction are mutually exclusive relationships.

The simple answer as to whether they are mutually exclusive decisions is no, since each sourcing decision is independent and based on the idiosyncratic sourcing needs of the buyer. The relationship between the two organizations hinges on the fact that the visibility presented

Figure 1. Buyer/supplier relationship models

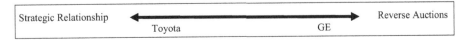

Strategic Relationship   ←——————————————————→   Reverse Auctions
                 Toyota   GE

by the consortium may actually enable the seller to gain access to the markets and relationships offered by reverse auctions. Such an initial contact or introduction of supplier to buyer may, in fact, lead to other, longer term relations between the two. It may also lead the buyer to additional prospects presented by the seller's other partners in the consortium. In this manner, one seller's short-term auction relationship may actually lead to long-term strategic relations with the consortium itself.

The answer to the question as to where on the spectrum the consortium resides depends greatly on what value the consortium brings to the supply chain. It also depends on the specific kind of buyer the consortium is targeting.

HOW DO CONSORTIA COMPETE OR WHAT VALUE PROPOSITION DO THEY CREATE IN THESE RELATIONS?

The value proposition provided by a consortium consists of two parts. The first is the possible value proposition to each supplier to become a member of the consortium. The second stream is what value consortium brings to the supply chain or, put another way, why a buyer would consider a consortium a better value than a reverse auction with which to form a relationship.

The first stream, the value to the supplier, can flow from two possible objectives, as proposed by Jost, Dawson, and Shaw (2005). They studied supplier consortia that formed in Great Britain as a prerequisite for serving the public sector entities. This is not unlike the situation in which a supplier must participate in a reverse auction in order to be considered by a buyer. Their study suggested two reasons for joining a consortium, self-interest and efficiency. In self-interest, a supplier joins a consortium because it sees the

partnership as the means to a particular end it is seeking, such as legitimacy. As the study noted, this reason may not necessarily be intended to occur at the expense of other suppliers, nor even need to be profitable in and of itself. Self-interest motives may also refer to the idea of improving organizational effectiveness, whereby the partners provide synergies or compliments in terms of expertise, skill sets, technology, and resources. This motivation is more unique to supplier consortia, as it provides less motivation for participating in a reverse auction. The second reason, however, pertains to both.

Efficiency, the study's second motive, was gained through economies of scale, the sharing or transfer of risk, increased visibility through access to new markets, and collaboration on product and process developments. Note the similar motives to that of the reverse auction, particularly the increased visibility that the new market structure provides and the economies of scale that reduces the transaction costs to all parties.

The second part of the value proposition is the value that the consortium brings to the supply chain. No entity can survive in business without offering value to the supply chain in which it resides. The value created by a consortium can fall into one or more of several categories. The first is the value created by its role as an intermediary as discussed earlier. The value offered by such an intermediary can fall into one of three subcategories as described by Anderson and Anderson (2002). They noted that e-commerce intermediaries add value through matching (providing information about themselves and their products to match the needs of the buyer), through requisitioning (providing for economies of scale, scope, time, and location), and through providing problem-solving capabilities to the buyer (such as qualifying sellers for quality, preserving the anonymity of the buyer, or customization of the product to the buyer). Both intermediaries in the reverse auction industry (e.g., Free Markets) and intermediary types in the supplier consortia market (e.g., WeddingChannel.com) exist primarily to provide those value-added services.

As an intermediary, then, a supplier consortium must determine what value it intends to provide to its supply chain. Some consortia may not have a choice, as they are required to maintain membership in order to even qualify as a supplier to certain organizations such as governmental agencies or branches. For those in voluntary situations, however, there is a choice as to which of those values it can and will provide. Buyers, too, have differing needs for the value that consortia can provide.

In the study of British supplier consortia (Jost, Dawson, & Shaw, 2005), three reasons were cited for the government seeking a relationship with a consortium rather than with a single arms-length affiliation such as that formed through a reverse auction. The first was that the size of the project meant that a wide range of skills and products were needed that exceeded the capability of any one supplier. The second reason was that no one supplier was willing to dedicate all of its resources to a single project. This was due to both the inherent risk to and prior commitments made by the supplier. The third reason was related to the second, and that was risk. A consortium is much better, as is a financial portfolio, to spread and share risk, effectively creating a hedging effect for the suppliers.

The conclusion is, then, that the consortium must offer some kind of benefit to the buyer in order to attract it to do business, and that it must take the form of some kind of financial gain to the buyer. That conclusion infers that the buyer and the consortium must form some kind of relationship and that the consortium brings some value to that relationship.

VALUE AND THE SPECTRUM: WHERE DO CONSORTIA AND REVERSE AUCTION INTERMEDIARIES LIE?

In general, it is questionable how much value an intermediary provides on either of the two extreme ends of the relationship spectrum described in Figure 1. On the strategic end, the highly specialized nature of the product or component normally dictates the need for a strategic alliance since there are usually only one or two vendors for the product in the first place (e.g., PC microprocessor chips) and the buyer is very interested in obtaining long-term commitments toward the manufacture and improvement of that input. As mentioned in the earlier section on scope, this is similar to a monopoly or oligopoly where competition and information asymmetry are reduced such that intermediaries are unneeded.

At the other end of the spectrum, where the product is a true commodity, there are so many suppliers available and there is so little difference between products that no intermediary is necessary or cost effective since information asymmetry and price discovery are not problems (e.g., corn or soybeans). These arguments (at both ends of the spectrum) hold true for all kinds of intermediaries—not only for supplier consortia, but also for reverse auctions.

Away from the poles of the spectrum are those situations in which the inputs are coming from more fragmented industries. In those situations, an intermediary of some kind is almost essential to provide buyers with needed information on what products and suppliers are available and to assist in setting, meeting, and maintaining quality standards. Prior to the rise of technology, this intermediary role was often performed by salespersons (e.g., manufacturers' representatives, or "reps"). The mid-1990s saw the reduction in sales forces and the introduction of electronic third-party intermediaries, such as FreeMarkets.

com (acquired later by Ariba), that pioneered the concept of reverse auctions. Around that same time, electronic buyer and supplier consortia began to form, such as Covisint (a buyers' consortium made up of several major automobile manufacturers).

How far out from the center of the spectrum an intermediary may be and still provide value to the supply chain is dependant in large part on what portion of that value is in the problem-solving capabilities that were discussed earlier. To some buying organizations, that answer is zero, regardless of the type of input or of the intermediary's position. Such is the case with one large multinational company whose management objective specifies that its goal is to purchase all inputs through a private reverse auctions site.

Two types of market intermediaries have been presented in this chapter: reverse auctions and supplier consortia. Both have been identified as providing similar value attributes to the supply chains in which they operate. For managers to decide which to use, they must better understand the relationship between the two.

RELATIONSHIP OF SUPPLIER CONSORTIA TO REVERSE AUCTIONS

One way to begin to evaluate the relationship between supplier consortia and reverse auctions is to classify supplier consortia based on a two-dimensional matrix with the number of different products they supply on one axis and the number of different markets they supply on the other. This is illustrated in Figure 2.

In Quadrant 1, suppliers provide a single product (or product family) to a single market or industry. An example of this is the Residential Multiple Listing Service that provides real estate products to the general consumer. In this situation, the buyer is able to view the sellers' offerings and select the lowest cost that meets their needs. Quadrant 2 offers a single product or family to several markets or industries, such as the combination Multiple Listing Services that services both the individual consumer and corporate customers. In Quadrant 3, the consortium acts as sort of a "supermarket" that gathers different kinds of suppliers together to serve various markets. MusiciansFriend.com represents many kinds of suppliers providing musical instruments, sound and light electronics,

Figure 2. Supplier consortia classification

Markets / Products	Single Product	Different Products
Single Market	1. SS Residential MLS	4. SD PASourcing.com Single relationship or consortia
Multiple Markets	2. MS Residential & Commercial MLS	3. MD MusiciansFriend.com eBay

and other products of interest to a wide range of commercial customers such as churches, schools, and professional sound providers, as well as the general consumer. One example of consortium in Quadrant 4 is National CAPITOL Solution, a supplier consortium made up of information technology and accounting firms, developed for and by the Ministry of Defense of Great Britain. PASourcing.com, discussed earlier, also fits this category in the commercial plastics industry.

Consortia whose members target a single product (Quadrants 1 & 2) are likely to be more competitive, since all participants are marketing the same product, and therefore tend to fit on the line toward the reverse auction end of the spectrum. Consortia whose members offer different products to different markets have a tendency to operate as an exponential outgrowth of the single-single model (Quadrant 1) and also tend to fit down toward the reverse auction end of the spectrum. Another scenario is where there are multiple competitors offering the same or similar products through a single source.

Consortia can also offer one-stop shopping in noncompetitive situations. Both Quadrant 3 and 4, the multiple product side of the matrix, offer this capability to the buyer. In these, the buyer can view multiple products from a single source.

In Quadrant 4, however, where the participants are offering multiple products to a single market, the consortium moves more toward the strategic end. In this quadrant, the suppliers offer both visibility and a kind of one-stop shopping to their buyer clients for all of its industry needs. This type of consortium not only gives buyers the ability, but also encourages them, to form cooperative relationships with more than one member of that consortium. These relationships may be quite temporary, as in the case of a reverse auction, but most likely they create longer-term relationships, mimicking that of a strategic partnership. In some cases, the relationship forms with the consortium as a whole, which now serves as a supplier itself.

Consortia, therefore, can have similarities to both ends of the spectrum. If the consortium lies toward the auction end, it may actually serve as a substitute or a proxy for a reverse auction. Both structures represent a group of suppliers gathered for similar purposes. Remember that the definition of consortium at the beginning, however, included voluntary cooperation and communication among the members. This type of consortium offers the opportunity for buyers to compare sellers side-by-side in terms of characteristics, capabilities, and even price and cost structure. It allows the buyer to select a supplier from the consortium based on lowest overall total cost. In this situation, consortia may actually have an advantage over electronic auctions because of the latter's drawbacks.

In addition to the implied adversarial relationship that a reverse auction creates, there are other negative issues as well. Emiliani and Stec (2001, 2002a, 2002b) consistently argue that reverse auctions encourage business practices that are detrimental to both buyer and seller in the long run. Sairamesh, et al. (2005) also noted that, based on selected business criteria, the model representing reverse auctions tended to incur higher costs, including transaction monitoring costs, and less flexibility when compared to developing or creating relationships with independent third parties that aggregated the sellers. It may be possible, therefore, that supplier consortia are able to offer the benefits of lower transaction and per-item cost associated with an auction without these drawbacks.

Understanding the relationships between the two and the relative characteristics of each, managers need to establish a logical approach for making decisions on what supply chain links to include and why.

MANAGERIAL ACTIONS OR PRESCRIPTIONS

The path of managerial actions to be taken depends on whether an organization is approaching decision making from the perspective of the buyer or the seller. From the perspective of the continuum view, the issue is where on the line between strategic and reverse auctions does that party view itself in terms of where its buyer-supplier relationship lies or where the firm wants it to lie.

The decisions that need to be made by the supplier can be illustrated in the form of a process flow diagram as presented in Figure 3. Note that the lower part of this chart is based on the framework developed by Standing et al. (2006) and discussed at the beginning of this chapter. The initial decision involves evaluating the basic characteristics of the product to determine the particular buyer-supplier relationship that best supports that particular product or product line. An in-depth discussion of this kind of product/

market analysis can be found in Simchi-Levi, Kaminsky, and Simchi-Levi (2000, Chapter 7) and in Chopra and Meindl (2007, Chapter 14). Note that this implicitly assumes that there can be more than one type of relationship between the same supplier and buyer. It also means that supplier-consortia relationships and reverse auction relationships can not only coexist, but can actually compliment one another.

As mentioned in the introduction, firms in markets where they are the sole supplier, or one of a handful of members, are usually involved in strategic relations already. Those in more competitive and fragmented industries are forced to make harder choices as to what kind of buyer-supplier relationship is best suited to achieve the strategic goals of the supplier's organization. The supplier must determine the type of relationship sought by the buyer and whether that is the type of relationship beneficial to the supplier based on those goals. Many suppliers have entered into reverse auction relationships without fully analyzing its true and

Figure 3. Supplier decision process

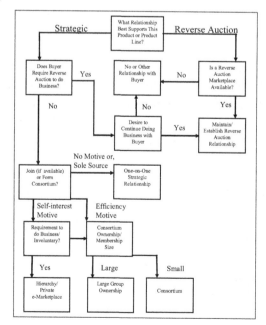

total costs of production, particularly since overhead costs are often allocated on an average basis (Sparks & Wagner, 2003). This leads to smaller margins than projected or even negative margins, which can cause problems with the long-term viability of the supplier. On the other hand, reverse auctions do present certain profit and marketing opportunities to those organizations that are able to calculate total costs and successfully cover them in the bidding process.

If the seller determines that there is sufficient motivation to move toward the more strategic end of the relationship spectrum, either through the value proposition presented by such an entity or by other motives, the seller will move away from the reverse auction relationship and down the left side of the diagram. At the next fork, however, the supplier's decision is dictated by the buyer. If the buyer requires a reverse auction relationship in order to do business, the supplier's only choices are to either enter that type of relationship or to forgo any relationship at all. That decision is determined by the supplier's market needs.

If there is no requirement for a reverse auction relationship, the supplier then needs to evaluate its motives or needs for either joining or forming a consortium. Since at this point the manager has already decided that reverse auctions are not the appropriate market structure for them, the decision now is which type of consortium should the supplying company join or possibly take the lead in forming. That decision hinges on the perceived value proposition offered by consortia discussed earlier and whether there is sufficient motivation. If there is sufficient motivation, the supplier can decide whether that motivation is primarily for self-interest or for efficiency reasons. In some cases, the self-interest motivation is created by the fact that membership in the consortium is a requirement of doing business with the buyer. In this case, there is little choice and the normal resulting consortium is a private one established and managed by the buyer, often a governmental unit.

If it is not a requirement, then the last decision is based on the size and number of participants desired in the association as discussed by Standing et al. (2006).

The reverse auction side of the chart is, for purposes of this chapter, relatively simple. Once the decision has been made that the reverse auction relationship is the most appropriate, the only other diversion point is whether such a market is available. If it is not, another type of relationship is necessary, or none at all.

The buyer organization must also determine what type of sourcing model fits the strategic goals of its organization. Chopra and Meindl (2007) discussed some alternatives to consider in the supplier selection process that fit well into this discussion. The first decision is likely to be whether the buyer desires sole sourcing or whether it wants to look at multiple suppliers. Once this decision is made, the buyer has at least three methods of selecting its choice or choices. The first is direct negotiations. Here, the buyer believes it has sufficient knowledge of the market, and price structure of that market, to approach a single supplier and agree to a contract. This method inherently assumes less competition and therefore would tend to be the method used to develop a more strategic relationship. Businesses seeking more competition in their supplier relationships will choose different methods that involve multiple suppliers, usually directly contending with one another. The major method to accomplish that is some type of an auction. To place reverse auctions and supplier consortia in context, a brief review of auction types may be helpful.

An auction can take place with each competitor's bids either transparent to the other suppliers or opaque to the other bidders. Opaque bidding is the traditional sealed-bid selection process with either the lowest bidder winning at the lowest price (first-price) or the lowest bidder winning at the second-lowest price (second-price or Vickrey auction). Transparent bid auctions include the subject of this book, the reverse, or English, auction.

It also includes the Dutch auction in which the auction begins low and then the price is gradually raised until a supplier accepts the bid. One major advantage of the transparent auction methods is that both parties avoid the negative connotations left by the winner's curse, where the seller determines that it could have won the auction without sacrificing as much in price as it did.

Each of these competitive bidding methods has its advantages and disadvantages, which are well documented in other literature. For purposes of this discussion, suffice it to say that the key to auctions, for both buyers and sellers, is to thoroughly understand one's own cost structure. The buyer's objective is to obtain its resources at the lowest cost, yet auctions stress the focus on only one dimension of that cost, price per item.

Supplier consortia seem to offer buyers a middle-of-the-road approach to supplier selection and relationship building that blends aspects of strategic selection and maintains the essence or flavor of competition. Since the consortium consists of more than one supplier, the basic element of competition remains. Even in those consortium where the participants are from different industries (Quadrant 2—multiple market, single product, and Quadrant 3—multiple market, different products), there is almost always a common theme that binds suppliers together and provides the knowledge that a buyer can approach another member, if not for direct services, at least for a referral to competition. Cost structure information on each member may not be directly available, but simply being a member of the consortium identifies the member and allows buyers to compare it to others.

A buyer can then use the classification schema described in Figure 2 to evaluate possible consortia, determining where within the framework a particular group would lie. The consortium's placement in the diagram will give the buyer a general direction as to what kind of relationship it is likely to encounter or establish with the consortium or the members therein. The closer to Quadrant 1 a consortium lies, the more competi-

tive the resulting relationship is likely to be. The closer to Quadrant 3, the more strategic it is likely to be. The buyer then has the choice as to where on the buyer-supplier spectrum it wishes to reside based on its corporate goals and objects, and can select the appropriate supplier and structure.

Consortia can also fit the buyer's strategy when it offers one-stop shopping for noncompetitive sellers (also Quadrant 3). The possible disadvantage to this scenario, however, is that the buyer generally only has a single choice for each category or market from which to purchase.

With the consortium selected, the buyer then establishes a particular supplier within the organization, or with the consortium as a whole. For Quadrants 1 and 2, the buyer may, even at this point, wish to use an auction method of selection within the consortium, employing the consortium as a kind of identification and screening tool to prequalify its auction participants. It may allow the consortium's third party entity, if present, willing, and able, to do the same. The buy may also move directly to one-on-one negotiations with selected members, particularly in Quadrants 3 and 4.

The final buyer methodology exists when the buyer has exercised its market power to force the creation of the consortium in the first place as in the case of governmental agencies or another large buyer, as is the case in many reverse auction situations. In these events, the buyer has usually formed the consortium for one of two reasons alluded to earlier. Either the buyer has the market power to bring Quadrant 1 type suppliers together for competitive reasons, similar to a reverse auction, or it needs the Quadrant 3 suppliers to cooperate and coordinate for efficiency and effectiveness due to the size of the project (e.g., Jost, Dawson, & Shaw, 2005).

Supply chain management is a very contemporary and very critical topic in the field of business operations. Much has been written regarding the actions and strategies for buyers, yet the term "supply chain" implies multiple links. Supplier consortia have existed since businesses have, and yet little attention has been focused on them. This discussion has attempted to place these associations and partnerships into the context of buyer-supplier relations and compare them to another popular relationship, that of reverse auctions. Supplier consortia offer another method of establishing relationships both between suppliers themselves and also between suppliers and sellers. This link in the chain has the capability to offer its other links many advantages that combine some of the positive qualities of strategic alliances and the competitive savings of the auction relations. This discussion has sought to identify those advantages through providing a possible classification of consortia, an investigation into their possible value propositions, their relation to reverse auctions, and finally, a prescriptive methodology for managers to walk through those alternative decisions. Hopefully, this will assist in providing information to make the best decision on the relationship between an organization and its supply chain partners, the kind of cooperative relationship that creates its own kind of "consortium."

FUTURE RESEARCH DIRECTIONS

One area of future research in this area needs to consist of refining and validating the classification framework and the decision-making flowchart. This will require empirical study to validate the framework and the impacts proposed. Research should begin with focused interviews of selected participants of, and buyers from, consortia inhabiting each of the four quadrants to refine the characteristics, axis, and implications. Once this is completed, a survey of consortia members and administrators would be conducted, as well as a survey of buyers who purchase from consortia members or the consortia themselves.

Even in the consortia area, most studies have been relatively short term in nature. While reverse auctions are by their very nature, short-term rela-

tionships, it is possible for long-term relationships to develop with consortia. To date, there have been no studies on the long-term effects on the supply chain of such a relationship. If such a relationship can be identified, a longitudinal study could be very useful.

In addition to this research, there may be other alternative forms of relationships that can exist either in competition with or in conjunction with reverse auctions. These other forms, and the impacts on reverse auctions, need to be identified and studied.

REFERENCES

Anderson, P., & Anderson, E. (2002). The new e-commerce intermediaries. *MIT Sloan Management Review, 43*(4), 53-62.

Chopra, S., & Meindl, P. (2007). *Supply chain management: Strategy, planning, operation* (3rd ed.). Upper Saddle River, NJ: Prentice Hall.

Emiliani, M. L., & Stec, D. J. (2001). Online reverse auction purchasing contracts. *Supply Chain Management, 6*(3/4), 101-105.

Emiliani, M. L., & Stec, D. J. (2002a). Realizing savings from online reverse auctions. *Supply Chain Management, 7*(1), 12-23.

Emiliani, M. L., & Stec, D. J. (2002b). Squaring online reverse auctions with the Caux Round Table principles for business. *Supply Chain Management, 7*(2), 92-100.

Huber, B., Sweeney, E., & Smyth, A. (2004). Purchasing consortia and electronic markets: A procurement direction in integrated supply chain management. *Electronic Markets, 14*(4), 284-294.

Jost, G., Dawson, M., & Shaw, D. (2005). Private sector consortia working for a public sector client—factors that build successful relationships:

Lessons from the UK. *European Management Journal, 23*(3), 336-350.

Le, T. T., Rao, S. S., & Truong, D. (2004). Industry-sponsored marketplaces: A platform for supply chain integration or a vehicle for market aggregation? *Electronic Markets, 14*(4), 295-307.

The Oxford Modern English Dictionary. (1996). (2nd ed.) . New York: Oxford University Press.

Parente, D. H., Venkataraman, R., Fizel, J., & Millet, I. (2004). A conceptual research framework for analyzing online auctions in a B2B environment. *Supply Chain Management, 9*(3/4), 287-294.

Porter, M. E. (1980). *Competitive strategy: Techniques for analysing industries and competitors.* New York: Macmillan, Free Press.

Sairamesh, J., Stanbridge, P., Ausio, J., Keser, C., & Karabulut, Y. (2005). *Business models for virtual organization management and interoperability*: Deliverable document 01945 prepared for TrustCom. and the European Commission, 1-20.

Simchi-Levi, D., Kaminsky, P., & Simchi-Levi, E. (2000). *Designing and managing the supply chain: Concepts, strategies, and case studies* (1st ed.). Boston: Irwin McGraw-Hill.

Southard, P. B., & Parente, D. H. (2007). Supplier consortia: A classification framework. *In process*, 1-16.

Sparks, L., & Wagner, B. (2003). Retail exchanges: A research agenda. *Supply Chain Management, 8*(1), 17-25.

Standing, C., Love, P. E. D., Stockdale, R., & Gengatharen, D. (2006). Examining the relationship between electronic marketplace strategy and structure. *IEEE Transactions on Engineering Management, 53*(2), 297-311.

Tella, E., & Virolainen, V.-M. (2005). Motives behind purchasing consortia. *International Journal of Production Economics, 93-94*, 161-168.

ADDITIONAL READING

Akacum, A., & Dale, B. G. (1995). Supplier partnering: Case study experiences. *International Journal of Purchasing and Materials Management, 31*(1), 37-44.

Chopra, S., & Meindl, P. (2007). *Supply chain management: Strategy, planning, operation* (3rd ed.). Upper Saddle River, NJ: Prentice Hall.

Davila, A., Gupta, M., & Palmer, R. (2003). Moving procurement systems to the Internet: The adoption and use of e-procurement technology models. *European Management Journal, 21*(1), 11-23.

Dyer, J. H., & Hatch, N. W. (2004). Using supplier networks to learn faster. *MIT Sloan Management Review, 45*(3), 57-63.

Hines, P., & Rich, N. (1997). Supply-chain management and time-based competition: The role of the suppler association. *International Journal of Physical Distribution & Logistics Management, 27*(3/4), 210-221.

Hines, P., & Rich, N. (1998). Outsourcing competitive advantage: The use of supplier associations. *International Journal of Physical Distribution & Logistics Management, 28*(7), 524-536.

Hines, P., Rich, N., & Easin, A. (1999). Value stream mapping: a distribution strategy application. *Benchmarking, 6*(1), 60-71.

Izushi, H. (1999). Can a development agency foster co-operation among local firms? The case of the welsh development agency's supplier association programme. *Regional Studies, 33*(8), 739-750.

Min, H., & Galle, W. P. (2003). E-purchasing: Profiles of adopters and nonadopters. *Industrial Marketing Management, 32*, 227-233.

Simchi-Levi, D., Kaminsky, P., & Simchi-Levi, E. (2000). *Designing and managing the supply chain: Concepts, strategies, and case studies* (1st ed.). Boston: Irwin McGraw-Hill.

Stuart, I., Deckert, P., McCutcheon, D., & Kunst, R. (1998). Case study: A leveraged learning network. *Sloan Management Review, 39*(4), 81-93.

Yen, B. P.-C., & Ng, E. O. S. (2003). The impact of electronic commerce on procurement. *Journal of Organizational Computing and Electronic Commerce, 13*(3 & 4), 167-189.

IMPLICATIONS FOR PRACTITIONERS

Title: Reverse Auctions and Supplier Consortia

Short Description

Competition between supply chains has resulted in firms carefully examining the relationships that they have, or are contemplating having, with other links in their chain. While the main focus of this book is on a specific type of relationship, that of the reverse auction, other forms of buyer-supplier relationships exist. In order to better understand the implications of the reverse-auction relationship, managers should also analyze the alternatives and the environment of relationships in which reverse auctions operate. The focus of this chapter is on an alternative buyer-supplier relationship, that of the supplier consortia.

Within the six dimensions of the framework proposed by Parente, et al. (2004), this chapter examines this little-studied collaborative group and proposes a spectrum to begin to understand some aspects of buyer-supplier relationships. The chapter includes a theoretical classification framework for supplier consortia. It then compares and contrasts supplier consortia to the reverse auction concluding with a prescriptive decision process that can help managers better analyze the most appropriate form of buyer-supplier relationship for their firm and their supply chain.

Findings

- Buyer-supplier relationships tend to lie along a spectrum with reverse auctions on one end and strategic relationships on the other.
- Supplier consortia, like reverse auctions, can be classified based on supplier characteristics, the relationship characteristics, buyer characteristics, and product or industry characteristics.
- Supplier consortia, depending on classification, can fit on several places on the spectrum, including that of the reverse auction, providing many of the same benefits of a reverse auction without some of the disadvantages.
- A decision flowchart was developed to help managers begin to analyze factors for the most appropriate form of buyer-supplier relationship.

RECOMMENDATIONS

- Organizations need to carefully examine and analyze the relationship that they currently have with their supply chain links.
- Managers of both buying and supplying firms need to understand all the alternatives that they have available for such relationships.
- Managers should understand the characteristics of alternative relationship structures.
- Managers should make use of logical approaches to decision making such as the flowchart provided in this chapter.

LIMITATIONS

This is a theoretical framework and decision process. Though conceptually based on past literature, it needs to be tested and validated by empirical research.

Chapter III
The Purchasing Agent's View of Online Reverse Auctions

Peggy D. Lee
The Pennsylvania State University – Great Valley, USA

ABSTRACT

This chapter views online reverse auctions from the purchasing agent's perspective. I found that purchasing agents with a high level of buying experience will perceive that online reverse auctions have a negative impact on the trust and cooperation in supplier relationships. Purchasing agents did not see a negative impact of online reverse auctions on long term viability of suppliers. The chapter discusses the evolution of the buyer-supplier relationship, emphasizing the critical success factors in supplier selection. Further, it discusses the role of the online reverse auction in the buyer-supplier relationship. By understanding the lens through which purchasing agents view online reverse auctions, managers can do a better job of managing the procurement function through improved training programs for purchasing agents that incorporate the appropriateness of online reverse auctions vs. other sourcing strategies. In addition, they will be able to better manage online reverse auctions, minimizing any negative impact of the auction on existing supplier relationships.

INTRODUCTION

Auctions have been used to buy and sell goods and services throughout the centuries (Smeltzer & Carr, 2003). However, technological innovation, improvements in communications, and the Internet have made online auctions more popular in business-to-business purchasing as well as in consumer sales. The online reverse auction (ORA) is one of the latest tools to improve purchasing costs by giving buyers access to a broader range of suppliers and allowing suppliers to bid on items that they might not have had the chance to bid on in the past. Online reverse auctions have saved buyers and sellers millions of dollars in the last decade and estimates are that this can only continue. Academics and practitioners alike have extolled the benefits of online reverse auctions, primarily in the form of reductions in the costs to procure goods and services as well as to bid.

The research in this area has focused on the decision to implement an ORA (Parente, Venkataraman, Fizel, & Millet, 2004; Stein, Hawking, & Wyld, 2003) how to structure an ORA (Nair, 2005); how to determine the suppliers to invite to bid (Talluri & Ragatz, 2004) and the impact of the auction on the suppliers (Gattiker, Huang, & Schwarz, 2007; Jap, 2007). The success of ORAs usually is measured by how much purchasers' and sellers' costs are reduced, estimated to be about 10% (Griffiths, 2003). Few researchers have studied the purchasing agent's perceptions on the success of the auction, despite the fact that an online reverse auction is one of the many methods that purchasing agents use to procure goods for their companies (Emiliani & Stec, 2001). Consequently, the purpose of this chapter is to view online auctions from the purchasing agent's perspective. The next two sections discuss the evolution of the buyer-supplier relationships, emphasizing the success factors in supplier selection; and ORAs in the buyer-supplier relationships. The second section ends with the hypotheses derived from prior research in supplier relationship and online reverse auctions. The last sections describe the study methodology, followed by survey results, a discussion of my findings, limitations of the study and thoughts on the direction of future research.

SUPPLIER RELATIONSHIPS: EVOLUTION AND SUCCESS FACTORS

Strategic sourcing involves creating a plan to discover, evaluate, select, develop, and manage a viable supply base (Burt, Dobler, & Starling, 2003; Kumar, Bragg, & Creinin, 2003). This systematic approach to sourcing positively affects a firm's performance (Chen, Paulraj, & Lado, 2004; Paulraj & Chen, 2005). Of the activities involved in strategic sourcing, supplier management is perhaps one of the most important tasks of the purchasing agent since the cost of externally procured goods can account for nearly 50% of total costs (Degraeve & Roodhooft, 1999). The buyer-supplier relationship is a crucial component in strategic sourcing (Leenders & Fearon, 1997). Buyer-supplier relationships are characterized by a high level of communication and information sharing between the partners, often including their cost structures and production plans (Burt et al., 2003). Thus, researchers have identified trust, quality, delivery reliability, economic performance of the supplier and the supplier's financial stability as important decision factors in selecting a supplier (Choi, 1996; Ellram, 1990; Kannan & Tan, 2002; Kumar et al., 2003; Min, 1994).

The buyer-supplier relationship is a dyadic relationship formed for the purpose of purchasing goods and/or services and it has evolved over the years from an adversarial one to one characterized by partnerships, strategic alliances, and collaborative relationships (Burt et al., 2003; Hoyt & Huq, 2000). In the early years of the purchasing profession, supplier management meant that the purchasing agent's job was to negotiate the best price, quality and delivery terms with his or her vendors and suppliers, once the decision was made to buy vs. make a component used in the manufacturing process. Grounded in transaction cost theory (Williamson, 1979), procurement activities were basically arms' length transactions with no relational content and were governed by a contractual arrangement. Burt, Dobler, and Starling (2003) refer to this as reactive purchasing, where the buyer-seller relationship is transactional rather than being collaborative. They describe transactional relationships as having "an absence of concern by both parties about the other party's well being" (p. 81). Each transaction is an independent deal. Costs, production schedules, and demand forecasts are not shared. Transactional relationships are arm's-length transactions where if one party "wins", the other "loses". The role of the purchasing agent was to manage (i.e., reduce) risk and transaction costs (Hoyt & Huq, 2000). Trust was artificially maintained by the threat of losing the business and power resided with the buyer (Burt et al., 2003).

In the late 1990s, suppliers recognized that there were advantages in partnering with their customers. Salespersons were encouraged to development relationships with their key customers. At the same time, purchasing managers recognized that partnerships and strategic alliances with a few, carefully selected suppliers was preferable to many independent transactions with many suppliers (Hoyt & Huq, 2000). Although price was still an important criterion used to select a supplier, purchasing managers began to realize that the lowest priced supplier may be the most costly, considering costs related to unreliable delivery, inadequate product quality, and poor communication. Reducing the number of suppliers meant that the purchasing firm had to have a higher level of trust in the supplier, especially when the supplier was the sole source of the good or service (Burt et al., 2003).

When the buyer-supplier relationship is founded on strategic initiatives of benefit to both parties, an alliance usually results (Burt et al., 2003). Alliances and cooperative buyer-supplier relationships are characterized by trust, collaboration, and cooperation. Partners often share a common vision (Buono, 1997); communicate frequently (Cooper, Ellram, Gardner, & Hanks, 1997); use electronic media (Scott & Westbrook, 1991) and have access to shared business systems (Bowersox & Closs, 1996). All of these actions require a high degree of trust between the buyer and the seller (Claro, Claro, & Hagelaar, 2006; Doney & Cannon, 1997; Smeltzer & Carr, 2003). In short, the non-quantifiable supplier selection criteria (such as supplier's strategic commitment to the buyer and suppliers' willingness and ability to share information) have a greater impact on

buyer's business performance than quantifiable variables (Kannan & Tan, 2002).

ONLINE REVERSE AUCTIONS AND THE BUYER-SUPPLIER RELATIONSHIP

In an online reverse auction the supplier is selected based on its self-expressed ability to meet the requirements described in the auction documentation. The purchasing manager might not even be familiar with the supplier prior to the auction. This means that often the sole basis for selecting a supplier in an online reverse auction is price. In fact, online reverse auctions have been found to work best in situations where the requirements are defined precisely and do not require interaction between the buyer and seller except for the bid (Jap, 2002; Smeltzer & Carr, 2003). Since the two firms may not have had a previous business relationship, trust, information sharing, and/or cooperation, have not been established. The presence of a buyer-supplier relationship (partnership, strategic alliance, etc.) is not needed in order for an ORA to be successful, However, researchers have found that it increases the likelihood of establishing a buyer-supplier relationship in the long term (Hohner, Rich, Ng, & Reid, 2003). Therefore, the non-quantifiable variables (e.g., trust, information sharing, and collaboration, cooperation) are not likely to be critical success factors in an auction. In fact, researchers have found that online reverse auctions work best in situations where the product to be purchased is a commodity and the requirements are very well defined (Parente et al., 2004).

Hohner, et al. (2003) reported on collaboration in a Web-based auction between Mars Inc. and IBM that reflect the complex bid structures of a strategic sourcing situation. They found that the auction must be a win-win for the buyer and the suppliers in order for relationships to be sustained over the long term. Trust significantly affects the level of commitment of the parties, which in turn promotes the formation (and the ability to sustain) a long term relationship. Long term relationships were found to be helpful in achieving a buyer's operational performance (Hsieh, 2004). Johnston (2004) found that the supplier's trust in the buyer was strongly linked to cooperative behaviors such as shared planning and flexibility in coordinating activities. (Prahinski & Benton, 2004) found that when there is collaboration and communication, the supplier perceives a positive influence on the relationship. The purchasing agent manages the process of collaboration and is responsible for communicating with suppliers.

Online reverse auctions are used extensively as part of a firm's sourcing strategy (Smeltzer & Carr, 2003). This research focuses on the purchasing agent's perception of the impact of the online reverse auction on the firm's relationship with its suppliers in terms of trust and cooperation. The purchasing agent's attitude towards the online reverse auction can affect the success of the auction. When the auction has not been handled properly, the experience can be negative for all involved (Jap, 2000, 2007; Kwak, 2001).

Jap (2000) warns that not all online reverse auctions are positive experiences. While they save money for the buyers, online reverse auctions can undermine the buyer's relationship with its suppliers. A long term relationship with a valued supplier can be ruined when the customer initiates an online reverse auction. The supplier sees this as a betrayal and the loss of many years of cultivating the customer relationship (Tassabehji, Taylor, Beach, & Wood, 2006). Opportunism can also be seen as a byproduct of online reverse auctions (Jap, 2000). Suppliers suspect that the buyer is taking advantage of the auction to gain cost advantages or to switch suppliers without notifying the current supplier (Jap, 2007). This involves matters of trust since a collaborative transactional relationship requires more trust than an arm's length relationship. If the supplier suspects that the buyer is engaging in opportunistic

behavior by initiating the online reverse auction, the relationship between the two parties is likely to be irreparably damaged (Jap, 2007). Some suppliers might elect not to bid even if they are invited to participate in the auction.

Pressey and Tzokas (2004) provided support for the assertion that more experienced purchasing agents may not value ORAs very highly. They found that long term relationships diminish over time unless they have relational content. Pressey and Tzokas (2004) further assert that high relational content positively affects firm performance. Increased use of ORAs can lead to a lower level of relational content in the buyer-seller relationship. Therefore, experienced purchasing agents (i.e., those who have been in long term relationships with suppliers) would see ORAs as having a negative impact on the level of trust and cooperation with suppliers.

Millet, Parente, Fizel, and Venkataraman (2004) posited that the more experienced a firm is in participating in online auctions, the more successful that firm is likely to be. This argument can be extended to the purchasing agent in the buying firm; namely that the more experienced purchasing agents will be well versed in strategic sourcing methods that make positive contributions to his or her firm's performance. Therefore, experienced purchasing agents are more likely to use multiple supplier selection strategies, including ORAs, making them more conversant about the positive and negative traits of online reverse auctions.

Consequently, I hypothesize the following:

H1: There is a significant difference between experienced and inexperienced buyers in the perceived impact of online reverse auctions on the trust in the buyer-seller relationship.

H1a: Experienced buyers will perceive a negative impact on trust.

H2: There is a significant difference between experienced and inexperienced buyers

Table 1. Descriptive statistics

	Mean	Std Deviation	N
Buying Experience (Buy_exp)	6.51 years		144
Trust in relationship with suppliers (Sup_Trst)	4.03	7.0021	144
Cooperation in relationships with suppliers (Sup_CoOp)	4.16	1.563	144
Long term viability of suppliers (Sup_viab)	4.07	1.331	144
Ability to gain cost leadership (Cost)	5.47	1.509	144

in the perceived impact of online reverse auctions on cooperation in the buyer-seller relationship.

H2a: Experienced buyers will perceive that online reverse auctions will negatively impact cooperation in the buyer-seller relationship.

H3: There is a significant difference between experienced and inexperienced buyers in the perceived impact of online reverse auctions on the long term viability of suppliers.

H3a: Experienced buyers will perceive that online reverse auctions will negatively impact long term viability of the suppliers.

METHODOLOGY

A survey was administered to purchasing agents of a major multinational corporation, which has been the buying firm in millions of online reverse auction transactions. The purchasing agents represent many industries, including manufacturing, financial services, aerospace technologies, health care, and transportation. The respondents were a diverse group, representing a wide range of products purchased, size of purchasing responsibility, geographical areas, and cultures. Given this high level of diversity in respondents, they represent a broad range of environments within which the procurement decisions are made. The respondents were asked:

"What is the impact of online reverse auctions on:

1. Trust in relationship with suppliers
2. Cooperation in relationship with suppliers
3. Long term viability of suppliers
4. Ability of your business area to gain leadership in cost.

A 7-point Likert scale was used, with 1 indicating very negative and 7 indicating very positive. They were also asked how long (in years) they had been a buyer and how long they had been working their current product buying category. The means and standard deviations for the answers to these questions are presented in Table 1.

We can see from Table 1 that, as a group, the purchasing agents believe that the impact of ORAs on the level of trust within the supplier relationship (mean = 4.03), cooperation within the supplier relationships (mean = 4.16) and on the long term viability of suppliers (mean = 4.07) is somewhat positive. As would be expected, the purchasing agents rated the impact of ORAs on cost (mean = 5.47) higher than the other three variables.

RESULTS

The initial analysis involved determining whether a correlation exists between a purchasing agent's years of experience as a buyer and his or her

Table 2. Correlation Matrix—Buyer experience, supplier trust

		SUPPLIER TRUST	**BUYER EXPERIENCE**
SUPPLIER TRUST	Pearson Correlation	1	-.223(**)
	Sig. (2-tailed)	.	.007
	N	144	144
BUYER EXPERIENCE	Pearson Correlation	-.223(**)	1
	Sig. (2-tailed)	.007	.
	N	144	144

** Correlation is significant at the 0.01 level (2-tailed)

Table 3. Correlation Matrix—Buyer experience, supplier viability and cooperation

Buyer Experience	Pearson Correlation	1	-.130	-.202(*)
	Sig. (2-tailed)		.119	.015
	N	144	144	144
Supplier Viability	Pearson Correlation	-.130	1	.425(**)
	Sig. (2-tailed)	.119		.000
	N	144	144	144
Supplier Cooperation	Pearson Correlation	-.202(*)	.425(**)	1
	Sig. (2-tailed)	.015	.000	
	N	144	144	144

* Correlation is significant at the 0.05 level (2-tailed).

** Correlation is significant at the 0.01 level (2-tailed).

perception of the impact of ORA on trust in the supplier relationship. The Pearson correlation was significant at the 0.01 level (see Table 2). This confirmed my belief that there is a negative relationship between trust in a relationship and years of experience. The longer a purchasing agent has been a buyer, the less likely that he or she will believe that ORAs will have a positive impact on trust within the relationship with suppliers. This finding is supported by other researchers who warn that initiating an online reverse auction has the potential to damage a long term relationship with the supplier (Jap, 2000, 2007; Kwak, 2001).

Next, I looked to see whether there was a relationship between the purchasing agents' years of buying experience and the impact of ORAs on cooperation in the supplier relationships and long term supplier viability. The Pearson Correlation coefficients are included in Table 3.

Again, as the purchasing agents' experience increases, his or her perception of the impact of the online reverse auction on cooperation becomes negative, as indicated by the negative correlation coefficient. This result is significant at the .05 level. The correlation between long term supplier viability and buyer experience is not significant.

Table 4. Group statistics

	Buyer Experience terciles	**N**	**Mean**	**Std. Deviation**	**Std. Error Mean**
SUPPLIER TRUST	1.00 (low experience)	53	4.17	1.638	.225
	3.00 (high experience)	50	3.56	1.752	.248
SUPPLIER COOPERATION	1.00 (low experience)	53	4.36	1.360	.187
	3.00 (high experience)	50	3.74	1.688	.239
SUPPLIER VIABILITY	1.00 (low experience)	53	4.09	1.290	.177
	3.00 (high experience)	50	3.84	1.462	.207

There is a slight relationship between these variables, in a negative direction, meaning that as the buying experience increases, the purchasing agents' perceptions of the impact of online reverse auctions on trust, cooperation and supplier's long term viability decreases. We found these results to be significant at the 0.05 and 0.01 levels for trust and cooperation, respectively. The rationale for this may be that as a buyer gains experience in strategic sourcing, online reverse auctions become just one more method used in the firm's sourcing strategy. Therefore the impact of this sourcing method alone is perceived to be less.

In order to determine whether there was a significant difference between purchasing agents with low and high experience levels, Richins and Dawson's methodology (1992) was followed to create three groups for buyer experience based on the buyers' self-report of years of experience as a buyer. Three groups seemed appropriate, given the frequency distribution across years of experience. To create a clear separation between groups following the Richins and Dawson methodology (1992), we chose Group 1 (N=53) to represent buyers with a low experience level (mean experience level of 1.5 years) and Group 3 (N=50) to represent buyers with a high experience level (mean experience level of 12.58 years). In this manner, the original sample was reduced from 144 to 103 through eliminating the medium experience level group (n = 41). The high and low

groups were then compared using *t* tests to assess significant differences between the two groups regarding the impact of online reverse auctions on trust in the supplier relationship; cooperation in the supplier relationship; and the long term viability of suppliers. The means and standard deviations for trust, cooperation and long term viability of suppliers for the two groups are included in Table 4.

The average values for high experience buyers on all variables tend toward the impact being negative, which supports the hypotheses. Thus, the high experience buyers tend to believe that ORAs have a negative impact on trust, cooperation and long term viability of their suppliers.

The independent samples t-test was conducted to determine if there was a significant difference between the groups on these three variables. The results are in Table 5.

These results are decidedly mixed. The difference between the high experience and low experience purchasing agents on supplier trust and supplier cooperation is significant at the 0.10 and 0.05 levels, respectively. This might be because all of the purchasing agents work for the same company. Even though they are a very diverse group, representing a broad range of industries, geographical locations and cultures, the fact that the firm has been the buying company in millions of online reverse auction transactions may mean that there would be less difference between newer

Table 5. Independent samples test results

		t	df	Sig. (2-tailed)	Mean Difference	Std. Error Difference
Supplier Trust	Equal variances assumed	1.826	101	.071	.610	.334
Supplier Viability	Equal variances assumed	.938	101	.351	.254	.271
Supplier Cooperation	Equal variances assumed	2.053	101	.043	.618	.301

purchasing agents and those with more experience. It is interesting to note that the difference between the two groups on supplier cooperation is the most significant. This is perhaps because the high experience buyers have worked on building supplier relationships longer than the low experience buyers, so see the ORA as a threat to those relationships. All of our hypotheses were supported except H3a: Experienced buyers will perceive that online reverse auctions will negatively impact long term viability of the suppliers.

DISCUSSION

The purpose of this study was to extend the research in online reverse auctions to include the purchasing agents' perceptions of online reverse auctions. In particular, I wanted to determine their perceptions of how ORAs impact trust and cooperation with suppliers and suppliers' long term viability. The more experienced buyers view ORAs as having a negative impact on trust and cooperation with suppliers, but not supplier long term viability. A possible explanation could be that the high-experience purchasing agents were trained to develop supplier relationships and alliances which were built on trust and cooperation with their suppliers. These purchasing agents might see ORAs as going back to the past when the relationships between buyers and sellers were transactional, sometimes adversarial, and based on a contractual arm's length relationship. National purchasing associations (for example, the Institute for Supply Management and APICS)

have worked to promote the purchasing function such that it is now recognized as a competitive weapon and value adding function within organizations. Purchasing agents are no longer order takers, but develop long term partnerships with their suppliers. Relationships take time to build. The high experience purchasing agents might see the online auction as a threat to strategic sourcing and alliance building. The high experience purchasing agents may also view ORAs as just one more tool in the strategic sourcing tool box, and will only use ORAs when they deem them to be appropriate. Therefore, they would not rate one specific sourcing methodology as being a greater contributor to firm performance than another.

On the other hand, the low experience buyers might view ORAs as a "quick fix" to reducing costs. Since they have less experience as buyers they may not have had a chance to build relationships with suppliers. Reducing spend, while improving quality, can be a way for a low experience purchasing agent to make a positive impact on the firm's performance, especially in the short term. Purchasing agents with low experience may see more opportunity to gain cost advantages from auctions than the purchasing agents with higher experience levels.

Executives and supply managers should not take these results to mean that high experience purchasing agents are against online reverse auctions. The findings lead us to conclude that we should use ORAs when appropriate and structure them such that the potentially negative impact of an ORA on the buyer-supplier relationship is first understood; and then minimized. The implementation of ORAs can send mixed messages to the purchasing agents. On the one hand, they are to develop long-term relationships with suppliers, focusing on trust, delivery, flexibility, and product quality as well as cost (i.e., relational purchasing transactions). On the other hand, an online reverse auction can be implemented in a fairly short time frame and the purchasing agent may never interact with the winner of the bid. These two types of procurement activities are likely to require different skills sets. If a firm intends to use both sourcing methods on a routine basis, then the training received by purchasing agents should include the structure of ORAs, when they are appropriate, how to select suppliers for inclusion and the management of incumbent suppliers in the auction.

From a supplier relationship perspective, incumbent suppliers should be notified of the impending ORA, preferably by the purchasing agent. This communication, if not done correctly, could cause a rift in the relationship with a valuable supplier; especially if it is a Tier 1 supplier. Thus, it should probably be handled at the executive level. Although all of the hypotheses except H3a were supported, these results are not definitive since I have simply shown that there is a difference between the perceptions of purchasing agents with low experience levels as buyers and those with high experience levels as buyers. The next step would be to determine why this difference exists using more sophisticated statistical methods. In addition, further study of ORAs in different firms and industries would be instructive.

LIMITATIONS AND FUTURE RESEARCH

As with any research effort, this study has limitations. Although the respondents come from a very broad range of industries, product categories, geographical areas and cultures, they are all from one multinational organization. Consequently, there

are not enough individuals from each industry, product category, geographical area, etc. to be able to generalize about each category. Future research should explore, at more depth, whether these findings would differ by industry, value of products and services purchased, corporate culture, type of products and services purchased, culture, and/or geography. A further limitation is how trust, cooperation and long term viability of the suppliers are defined. It is likely that the perceptions and definitions of these terms vary among the respondents. Future work should use validated scales for trust and cooperation and multiple questions to determine long term supplier viability.

The purpose of this chapter was to take the purchasing agent's perspective and look at online reverse auctions in the context of supplier selection and strategic sourcing. We found, as hypothesized, that high experience purchasing agents view online reverse auctions as having a negative impact on trust and cooperation in supplier relationships; but they do not view ORAs as having a negative impact on the long term viability of suppliers. Although I have only scratched the surface in exploring the perceptions of purchasing agents about online reverse auctions, these findings have implications for managing and structuring online reverse auctions as well as long term buyer-supplier relationships. The training received by purchasing agents and managers must address the potential conflicting goals of online reverse auctions and building a long term relationship with suppliers. The training should also address when online reverse auctions are (and are not) appropriate, how to address incumbent suppliers' concerns, and how to structure an auction such that opportunism is not the unintended result.

FUTURE RESEARCH DIRECTIONS

Given the lack of previous work in the buyer-supplier relationships and strategic sourcing areas that take the purchasing agents point of view, future research in this area is only limited by the researcher's imagination and resources. Future research should explore whether these findings would differ by industry, value of products and services purchased, corporate culture, type of products and services purchased, demographic culture and/or geography. The concepts of trust and cooperation need further definition and refinement. Therefore, additional research should use established scales on trust and cooperation to explicitly measure trust and cooperation rather than relying on the respondent's definition of trust and cooperation. Multiple and more specific questions designed to measure the long term supplier viability construct should also be conducted. The definition of each of these variables is open to interpretation by the respondent. Further studies should remove this potential for bias in the study. An additional contribution to this body of work would be to study buyer-supplier dyads who have participated in an online auction and a traditional procurement process. Looking at dyads over a period of time (i.e., longitudinal study analyses) would shed light on the issue of supplier long term viability. Ethnographic studies, case studies of successful and unsuccessful auctions, and other research methodologies would also provide a rich area for further research efforts. Finally, an effort geared toward looking at the link between purchasing agent perceptions, online reverse auctions and firm performance (of both the buying and supplying firm) would significantly contribute to the discourse in this area.

REFERENCES

Bowersox, D. J., & Closs, D. J. (1996). *Logistical management*. New York: McGraw-Hill.

Buono, A. F. (1997). Enhancing strategic partnerships: Intervening in network organizations. *Journal of Organizational Change, 10*(3), 251-266.

Burt, D. N., Dobler, D. W., & Starling, S. L. (2003). *World class supply management - the key to supply chain management* (7th ed.). New York: McGraw-Hill Higher Education.

Chen, I. J., Paulraj, A., & Lado, A. A. (2004). Strategic purchasing, supply management, and firm performance. *Journal of Operations Management, 22*(5), 505-523.

Choi, T. Y. (1996). An exploration of supplier selection practices across the supply chain *Journal of Operations Management, 14*(4), 333-343.

Claro, D. P., Claro, P. B. d. O., & Hagelaar, G. (2006). Coordinating collaborative joint efforts with suppliers: The effects of trust, transaction specific investment and information network in the Dutch flower industry. *Supply Chain Management, 11*(3), 216-224.

Cooper, M. C., Ellram, L., Gardner, J. T., & Hanks, A. M. (1997). Meshing multiple alliances. *Journal of Business Logistics, 18*(1), 67-89.

Degraeve, Z., & Roodhooft, F. (1999). Effectively selecting suppliers using total cost of ownership. *Journal of Supply Chain Management, 35*(1), 5-10.

Doney, P. M., & Cannon, J. P. (1997). An Examination of the nature of trust in buyer-seller relationships. *Journal of Marketing, 61*(2), 35-51.

Ellram, L. (1990). The supplier selection decision in strategic partnerships. *Journal of Purchasing & Materials Management, 26*(4), 8-14.

Emiliani, M. L., & Stec, D. J. (2001). Online reverse auction purchasing contracts. *Supply Chain Management, 6*(3/4), 101-105.

Gattiker, T. F., Huang, X., & Schwarz, J. L. (2007). Negotiation, email, and Internet reverse auctions: How sourcing mechanisms deployed by buyers affect suppliers' trust. *Journal of Operations Management, 25*(1), 184-202.

Griffiths, A. (2003). Trusting an auction. *Supply Chain Management, 8*(3/4), 190-194.

Hohner, G., Rich, J., Ng, E., & Reid, G. (2003). Combinatorial and quantity-discount procurement auctions benefit Mars, Incorporated and its suppliers. *Interfaces, 33*(1), 23-35.

Hoyt, J., & Huq, F. (2000). From arms-length to collaborative relationships in the supply chain: An evolutionary process. *International Journal of Physical Distribution & Logistics Management, 30*(9), 750-764.

Hsieh, L.-F. (2004). The buyer-supplier long-term partnership effects upon the buyer's operational performance in the Taiwan center-satellite factory system. *International Journal of Technology Management, 28*(2), 243.

Jap, S. D. (2000). Going, going, gone. *Harvard Business Review, 78*(6), 30-38.

Jap, S. D. (2002). Online reverse auctions: Issues, themes, and prospects for the future. *Academy of Marketing Science Review, 30*(4), 506-525.

Jap, S. D. (2007). The Impact of online reverse auction design on buyer-supplier relationships. *Journal of Marketing, 71*(1), 146-159.

Johnston, D. A., McCutcheon, D. M., Stuart, F. I., & Kerwood, H. (2004). Effects of supplier trust on performance of cooperative supplier relationships. *Journal of Operations Management, 22*(1), 23-38.

Kannan, V. R., & Tan, K. C. (2002). Supplier selection and assessment: Their impact on business performance. *Journal of Supply Chain Management, 38*(4), 11-21.

Kumar, S., Bragg, R., & Creinin, D. (2003). Managing supplier relationships. *Quality Progress, 36*(9), 24-30.

Kwak, M. (2001). Searching for search costs. *MIT Sloan Management Review, 42*(3), 8-9.

Leenders, M. R., & Fearon, H. E. (1997). *Purchasing and Supply Management* (11th ed.). Chicago: Richard D. Irwin.

Millet, I., Parente, D. H., Fizel, J. L., & Venkataraman, R. R. (2004). Metrics for managing online procurement auctions. *Interfaces, 34*(3), 171-179.

Min, H. (1994). International supplier selection: A multi-attribute utility approach *International Journal of Physical Distribution & Logistics Management, 24*(5), 24-33.

Nair, A. (2005). Emerging Internet-enabled auction mechanisms in supply chain. *Supply Chain Management, 10*(3/4), 162.

Parente, D. H., Venkataraman, R. R., Fizel, J. L., & Millet, I. (2004). A conceptual research framework for analyzing online auctions in a B2B environment. *Supply Chain Management, 9*(3/4), 287-294.

Paulraj, A., & Chen, I. J. (2005). Strategic supply management and dyadic quality performance: A path analytical model. *Journal of Supply Chain Management, 41*(3), 4-18.

Prahinski, C., & Benton, W. C. (2004). Supplier evaluations: communication strategies to improve supplier performance. *Journal of Operations Management, 22*(1), 39-62.

Pressey, A., & Tzokas, N. (2004). Lighting up the "dark side" of international export/import relationships: Evidence from UK reporters. *Management Decision, 42*(5/6), 694-708.

Richins, M. L., & Dawson, S. (1992). A consumer values orientation for materialism and its measurement: scale development and validation. *Journal of Consumer Research, 19*, 303-316.

Scott, C., & Westbrook, R. (1991). New Strategic Tools for Supply Chain Management. *International Journal of Physical Distribution and Logistics Management, 21*(1), 23-33.

Smeltzer, L. R., & Carr, A. S. (2003). Electronic reverse auctions: Promises, risks and conditions for success. *Industrial Marketing Management, 32*(6), 481-488.

Stein, A., Hawking, P., & Wyld, D. C. (2003). The 20% solution?: A case study on the efficacy of reverse auctions. *Management Research News, 26*(5), 1-20.

Talluri, S., & Ragatz, G. L. (2004). Multi-attribute reverse auctions in B2Bexchanges: A framework for design and implementation. *Journal of Supply Chain Management, 40*(1), 52-61.

Tassabehji, R., Taylor, W., Beach, R., & Wood, A. (2006). Reverse e-auctions and supplier-buyer relationships: an exploratory study. *International Journal of Operations & Production Management, 26*(2), 166-184.

Williamson, O. E. (1979). Transaction-cost economics: The governance of contractual relations. *Journal of Law and Economics, 22*, 3-61.

ADDITIONAL READINGS

Bartholomew, D. (2004, Sep). Procurement's new role. *Industry Week, 253,* 62.

Bowersox, D. J., Stank, T. P., & Daugherty, P. J. (1999). Lean launch: Managing product introduction risk through respone-based logistics. *Journal of Product Innovation Management, 16*(6), 557-568.

Carr, S. M. (2003). Note on online auctions with costly bid evaluation. *Management Science, 49*(11), 1521.

Carter, P. L., Carter, J. R., Monczka, R. M., & Swan, A. J. (2000). The future of purchasing and supply: A ten-year forecast. *The Journal of Supply Chain Management, 36*(1), 14-26.

Dash, J. (2000). Reverse auction cuts training cost. *Computerworld, 34,* 24.

Deeter-Schmetz, D. R., Bizzari, A., Graham, R., & Howdyshell, C. (2001). Business-to-business online purchasing: Suppliers' impact on buyers' adoption and usage intent. *The Journal of Supply Chain Management, 37*(1), 4-10.

Dowlatshahi, S. (2000). Designer-buyer-supplier interface: Theory versus practice. *International Journal of Production Economics; Amsterdam, 63*(2), 111-130.

Dwyer, F. R., Schurr, P. H., & Oh, S. (1987). Developing buyer-seller relationships. *Journal of Marketing, 51*, 11-27.

Emiliani, M. L. (2004). Sourcing in the global aerospace supply chain using online reverse auctions. *Industrial Marketing Management, 33*(1), 65.

Emiliani, M. L. (2005). Regulating B2B online reverse auctions through voluntary codes of conduct. *Industrial Marketing Management, 34*(5), 526.

Emiliani, M. L. (2006). Executive decision-making traps and B2B online reverse auctions. *Supply Chain Management, 11*(1), 6.

Emiliani, M. L., & Stec, D. J. (2001). Realizing savings from online reverse auctions. *Supply Chain Management, in press.*

Ford, D. I. (1980). The development of buyer-seller relatins in industrial markets. *European Journal of Marketing, 14*(5-6), 339-353.

Handfield, R. B., Krause, D. R., Scannell, T. V., & Monczka, R. M. (2000). Avoid the pitfalls in supplier development. *Sloan Management Review, 41*(2), 37-49.

Jap, S. D., & Ganesan, S. (2000). Control mechanisms and the relationship life cycle: Implications for safeguarding specific investments and developing commitment. *Journal of Marketing Research, XXXVII*, 227-245.

Johnson, P. F., & Klassen, R. D. (2005). E-Procurement. *MIT Sloan Management Review, 46*(2), 7.

Karras, C. L. (1995). Reverse auction tactic. *Purchasing, 118,* 21.

Klein, S. (1997). Introduction to electronic auctions. *Electronic Markets, 7,* 3-6.

Kwak, M. (2002). Potential pitfalls of e-auctions. *MIT Sloan Management Review, 43*(2), 18.

Pinker, E. J., Seidmann, A., & Vakrat, Y. (2003). Managing online auctions: Current business and research issues. *Management Science, 49*(11), 1457.

Richardson, J., & Roumasset, J. (1995). Sole sourcing, competitive sourcing, parallel sourcing: Mechanisms for supplier performance. *Managerial and Decision Economics (1986-1998), 16*(1), 71.

Ruiz-Torres, A. J., & Mahmoodi, F. (2007). The optimal number of suppliers considering the costs of individual supplier failures. *Omega, 35*(1), 104.

Schrader, R. W., Schrader, J. T., & Eller, E. P. (2004). Strategic implications of reverse auctions. *Journal of Business to Business Marketing, 11*(1,2), 61.

IMPLICATIONS FOR MANAGERS

Title: The Purchasing Agent's View of Online Reverse Auctions

Description of Manuscript

A survey was administered to purchasing agents of a multinational corporation, which has been the buying firm in millions of online reverse auction transactions. The purchasing agents represent many industries, including manufacturing, financial services, aerospace technologies, health care, and transportation. The respondents were a very diverse group, representing a wide range of environments within which procurement decisions are made. They were asked about the impact of online reverse auctions on trust and cooperation in relationships with suppliers and the long term viability of suppliers.

Findings

- The longer a purchasing agent has been a buyer, the less likely that he or she will believe that ORAs will have a positive impact on trust and cooperation with suppliers.
- There is a significant difference between the perceptions of purchasing agents with low buying experience and those with high buying experience with respect to trust in the buyer-supplier relationship.
- There is a significant difference between the perceptions of purchasing agents with low buying experience and those with high buying experience with respect to cooperation in the buyer-supplier relationship.
- There was no significant difference between the perceptions of purchasing agents with low buying experience and those with high buying experience with respect to long term viability of their suppliers.
- Experienced buyers perceive that ORAs have a negative impact on trust and cooperation with suppliers.
- Experienced buyers do not perceive that ORAs have a negative impact on the long term viability of suppliers.

RECOMMENDATIONS

These findings should be used by practitioners in the following manner:

- To develop appropriate training programs for purchasing agents which stress that there should be a mix of sourcing strategies and supplier selection methods.
- The training should include the critical factors for a successful online reverse auction, how it should be implemented, and more importantly, how incumbent supplier relationships should be handled.
- Managers should recognize that the decision to use ORAs will require a different purchasing skill set than other supplier selection and strategic sourcing initiatives, which stress relationship building.

- Managers should also recognize that the cooperation (or lack of cooperation) of a purchasing agent in the ORA might be because of their perception that it will have a negative impact on his or her relationships with suppliers.

LIMITATIONS

Although these results are indicative of the need for further research in this area, managers should be cautioned that this is one study with 144 purchasing agents' perceptions. Before wholesale changes are made in purchasing organizations, managers are urged to discuss these issues with the purchasing agents in their companies to determine the proper role for ORAs in the supplier selection and strategic sourcing processes.

Chapter IV
Internet Reverse Auctions:
Listening to the Voices of Non–Adopters

Thomas F. Gattiker
Boise State University, USA

ABSTRACT

Once a company implements an Internet reverse auction platform, buyers often have considerable discretion as to whether or not to utilize it. This chapter discusses many reasons for non-adoption of Internet reverse auctions. The focus is on factors that impact the fit between the Internet reverse auction technology and the characteristics of the particular purchasing task that the buyer must carry out (i.e., characteristics of the material or service to be purchased in the market that it is to be purchased from). Data (qualitative comments) were collected from buyers within one firm. The comments detail the reasons that buyers have not used reverse auctions for particular commodities. Of the 9 factors identified in the literature review, 4 were actually cited by buyers. These are: specifiability, level of competition for the buyer's business, importance of non-price factors, and dollar volume.

INTRODUCTION

An important question for companies is what characteristics make an item a good candidate for reverse auctioning. When items that are not appropriate are auctioned, the results are typically undesirable. For example, sellers deliver materials or services that do not meet buyer's needs because the buyer and the seller did not develop an adequate mutual understanding of the product and service requirements. Or an insufficient amount

of competition is generated and the low bid turns out to be higher than existing contract price.

The academic literature has a lot to say on this topic. Scholarly articles on Internet reverse auctions have identified a number of conditions when auctions are a good and bad fit to the purchasing task. Much of the focus has been on characteristics of the material to be purchased and the market from which it is sourced.

The objectives of this chapter are to review the existing literature on reverse auction fit and then to validate and extend this body of knowledge using an approach that is somewhat different from approaches used in other studies. The findings of this and other studies are interpreted for buyers and managers who desire a deeper understanding of (1) factors that contribute to and inhibit reverse auction fit-to-task and (2) of how to increase the utilization and effectiveness of auctions when they are appropriate.

BACKGROUND

When organizations adopt a new technology, they have an interest in their employees using it. In order to understand what makes employees use and not use a technology, it is useful to listen to the voices of non adopters.

The level of fit between the information system and the task at hand increases both information systems utilization and IS benefits. The fit of reverse auction to a particular sourcing decision is influenced by characteristics of the commodity (item) being sourced, the supply base for that commodity and the buying firm (Mabert & Skeels, 2002).

The following factors may influence the fit of reverse auction to the purchasing task:

Importance of non-price factors (as compared to part price): Reverse auctions may fit best with items for which price is the most important attribute in the vendor selection decision. Jap (2002) finds that when price is the dominant factor in the supplier selection decision then reverse auctions are more likely to be successful than when other factors (such as quality, delivery, design assistance and other types of support) are as important as price. Similarly Kaufmann and Carter (2004, p. 20) state that buyers using eRA's should be willing to pursue a "satisficing (Simon, 1955) or 'ticket to the game' strategy" on factors that, unlike price, cannot be easily quantified. Other reverse auction

papers (e.g., Smeltzer & Carr, 2003) echo this finding, as do the widely accepted prescriptions for when to adopt and avoid competitive bidding (e.g., Burt, Dobler, & Starling, 2003; Leenders, Fearon, Flynn, & Johnson, 2002; Monczka, Trent, & Handfield, 2005).

Specifiability: Specifiablilty refers to the buyer's ability to provide a clear specification in advance of bidding. Low specifiablilty exists when the buyer cannot fully enumerate the material or service characteristics in advance. Often in these cases, the buyer and seller may work together to determine the final design after supplier selection. Or sellers submit design proposals (or other types of proposals) along with or prior to their bids or pricing proposals. In this latter case, the buyer may only allow potential suppliers with adequate design proposals to participate in the competitive bidding or reverse auction. The lower the specifiability, the more difficult it becomes to make "apples to apples" comparisons among competing bids. Thus the reverse auction literature holds that the lower the specifiability, the lower the fit of Internet reverse auctions to the purchasing task (Beall et al., 2003; Jap, 2002; Mabert & Schoenherr, 2001; Mabert & Skeels, 2002; Parente, Venkataraman, Fizel, & Millet, 2004; Smeltzer & Carr, 2003).

Standardization: Standardized materials are made to meet the requirements of many buying firms. By contrast non-standard commodities are designed to the unique requirements of a particular buyer. These items are "made to order," "made to print" or "engineered to order." Researchers (Jap, 2002; Parente et al., 2004) have suggested that the more standardized the item, the greater the fit of reverse auction to the sourcing task . A survey by Emiliani and Stec (2004) of suppliers of make-to-print parts in the aerospace industry found a great deal of dissatisfaction with reverse auction. (However, a later survey on standardized items was not positive either).

Standardization is similar to specifiability, but the two concepts should not be confused. For example, an automobile seat is a complex, non-standard item (i.e. a supplier makes a particular seat only for one customer); however, it is one that a buyer can specify fully without the seller's input. On the other hand, a fuel cell to be used in a hybrid vehicle is an item that an OEM (for example an auto manufacturer) likely does not have the expertise to specify fully without a great deal of input from the supplier. In this example, the seat is specifiable and the fuel cell is not. Of course, both are non-standard.

Level of competition for the buyer's business: In general, a substantial amount of competition in the supply base is necessary for any form of competitive bidding to be successful. Without an adequate number of suppliers who actively want a buyer's business, the market is unlikely to yield the "right" price (Burt, Norquist, & Anklesaria, 1990). By this same token, the amount of competition for a buyer's business increases the appropriateness of a reverse auction. A large number of potential suppliers increases competition and thus the likelihood of a successful auction. Auctions are unlikely to be successful when the competitive situation in the particular market gives sellers more power than buyers (Emiliani & Stec, 2000; Parente et al., 2004). Some buyers have attempted to have an auction only to find that sellers will not participate (Mabert & Schoenherr, 2001). Researchers have offered estimates from two to five sellers as the minimum number needed. In addition to the number of potential suppliers, another determinant of competition is the amount of unused capacity in the supply base. Even if there are a handful of viable suppliers, low current capacity utilization among these suppliers may generate substantial competition and thus make reverse auctions a good choice (Beall et al., 2003; Emiliani & Stec, 2000; Jap, 2002; Mabert & Skeels, 2002; Parente et al., 2004; Smeltzer & Carr, 2003).

A related concept is *channel power*. Channel power is an organization's ability to get suppliers and/or customers to do what it wants (Bucklin, 1973). A buyer's channel power depends on the number of suppliers, the number of similarly situated buyers, recent increases in the number of competing buyers or suppliers, the amount of a supplier's business accounted for by the buyer and switching costs (Dickson, 1994). When buyers lack channel power, suppliers have the ability to withhold participation in a reverse auction—i.e. by refusing to participate or by not bidding aggressively. In other words, it is difficult for buyers to insist that suppliers participate, and thus it might not be feasible to attract a sufficient number of good suppliers into the auction (Emiliani & Stec, 2000; Parente et al., 2004). Several studies (Beall et al., 2003; Mabert & Skeels, 2002; Parente et al., 2004) have identified switching costs in particular as a barrier to reverse auction success.

Stakeholder preferences: Purchasing's internal customers (e.g. manufacturing) may have an overwhelming preference for the incumbent supplier. This may make it politically difficult to switch business to another bidder or it may result in contract leakage if the business is switched. For example, GE has curtailed using reverse auctions to contract for employee lodging because of the difficulty of convincing employees to actually use the contracted providers (Boehmer, 2005).

Dollar volume: Is a function of the dollar volume unit cost and unit volume and (for lots consisting of multiple items) the number of different items in the lot. Reverse auctions require a lot of up front work in order to ensure that specifications and volumes are clear and accurate, to do due diligence on suppliers and so on. A significant dollar volume is necessary to justify this investment of time and company resources. Furthermore, all else equal, a greater dollar volume will generate more interest from the supplier community. Generally the greater the dollar value of the contract up for bid, the more appropriate reverse auction will be (Beall et al., 2003; Mabert & Skeels, 2002; Smeltzer & Carr, 2003) Other lot characteristics such as the homogeneity of the items in the lot may affect the ability of the buyer to attract suppliers and they may affect auction results (Schoenherr & Mabert, 2005).

Strategic nature of item: A strategic item has great importance to product performance or customer acceptance. Following Krajlic's (1983) classification system Beal et al (2003) state that reverse auctions are appropriate for leverage, commodity and bottleneck items, but not strategic items. Other researchers have also suggested this (Jap, 2002; Parente et al., 2004). This may be for a number of reasons. For example, the technical complexity of the commodity may be quite high, specifiability may be low or the supply market may be highly complex, for example there may be only a few viable suppliers. Finally purchasers may believe that other forms of price discovery, such as negotiation, are more conducive to the highly cooperative relationships that buyers often desire for strategic materials and services.

Price elasticity: Price elasticity must exist. In other words, there must be some likelihood that suppliers will reduce their prices in response to increasing competition (Mabert & Skeels, 2002). Suppliers may reduce costs (perhaps in response to price pressures applied by auction participation) or reduce their margins. With respect to the latter case, suppliers' ability to reduce their margins and still remain viable are limited (Margins are not infinite and thus cannot be infinitely reduced). Thus buyers often see declines in price elasticity (and hence price reductions) if they repeatedly auction the same part or service.

METHODOLOGY

The majority of articles that have studied reverse auction fit have been based on a case study approach, with a smaller number of surveys (e.g. Hartley, Duplaga, & Lane, 2005; Wagner & Schwab, 2004) and even several lab experiments (Carter & Stevens, forthcoming; Gattiker, Huang, & Schwarz, 2007). Typically with this approach, researchers gather information about a company's reverse auction experience by interviewing one or a few key informants. This a well-accepted approach that has generated many of (perhaps most of) the supply chain field's key insights into reverse auctions. This notwithstanding, most fields of inquiry benefit from multiple approaches to the same problem. A "triangulation approach" allows us to corroborate existing findings and produce new insights. Therefore this chapter takes a different approach to gathering data on auction fit and auction utilization. First, this study focuses on auction non-adopters. Second, rather than utilizing a few key informants to understand the behavior of an organization, this study is more fine grained. The unit of analysis is the individual buyer's decision to adopt reverse auctions for a particular material for which he or she is responsible. The hope is that by examining buyers' explanations of why they would not use reverse auction in a particular situation, we can better understand the variables that affect auction utilization and auction fit to a variety of purchasing tasks.

To collect data, we constructed a survey aimed at individual rank-and-orfile purchasing professionals (i.e. buyers). The suitability of reverse auctions depends heavily on the characteristics of materials being purchased and the markets from which they are sourced. This can be seen from the literature review in the previous section. Therefore the survey collected data from the buyer on a commodity-by-commodity basis,

Table 1. Reasons given by buyers for not using reverse auctions for a particular commodity for which they have responsibility (ranked by frequency)

Reason	Frequency of mention
Specifiability	13
Insufficient competition (number of suppliers)	8
General concerns about effectiveness *	4
Difficulty of using tool (ease of use)	3
Insufficient volume	3
Commodity/part complexity	2
Insufficient time to conduct process	2
Importance of non-price factors	1
Total	36

rather than about their reverse auction utilization in general. (A *commodity* is a group of materials sharing similar characteristics, for example memory or surface-mount printed circuit boards in the electronics industry).

Data Collection

Data were collected from the North American division of a global OEM, which is one of the top fifty companies in the world in terms of revenue. The company employs approximately 90 North American direct material buyers, who collectively spend over $25 billion annually. At the time the data were collected the company was one of the world's top users of Internet reverse auctions in terms of the volume of business sourced via this channel.

At the time the data were collected, company policy was that unless there was an overriding reason *not* to adopt eRA's for a particular commodity (e.g. insufficient number of potential suppliers), buyers were expected to utilize eRA's. However, in reality there is little review of individual buyers' adoption decisions or "enforcement." There were no explicit performance incentives for eRA

usage, and the overall incentive pay structure is the same across all buyers. Thus individual buyers exercised their own discretion regarding whether or not to adopt eRA's in a particular situation.

ANALYSIS AND RESULTS

Data were collected in 2003 using a survey which was sent to all direct material buyers in the company. The response rate was approximately sixty percent. An input to the survey was a company database detailing which buyers were responsible for which commodities. This enabled the survey program to ask buyers for information with respect to specific commodities for which they had responsibility. For each commodity for which buyers had not used reverse auction, the survey program asked buyers why they had not used the tool. Respondents were provided with space to type in an open-ended response. Thirty-four usable responses were received and were then categorized. Categories corresponded to the determinants of auction fit in the literature review above. New categories were created for content that did not correspond to the *a priori* categories.

In a few cases, multiple reasons were provided. Each one of these was categorized separately. Table 1 lists the results.

DISCUSSION AND RECOMMENDATIONS

This section discusses the results and dissects the data in more detail. Analyzing the data in this way points out some actionable knowledge for managers.

Of the 9 factors identified in the literature review, 4 were mentioned at least once. These are:

- Specifiability
- Level of competition for the buyer's business
- Importance of non-price factors
- Dollar volume

The results here validate the findings of other studies that these four factors influence the fit of reverse auctions to the purchasing task and that these characteristics affect whether reverse auctions are actually adopted for a particular task.

Turning to the factors individually, a lack of specifiability was cited as the reason for non-adoption for approximately one-third of the commodities. It was cited much more frequently than any other factor. This validates the assertions of Beal et al (2003) and Kaufmann and Carter (2004) that specifiability is a paramount determinant of auction suitability. Or as one interviewee told Beal et al. (2003, p. 51), "If you can spec it you can bid it." The majority of the specifiability-related comments indicated that supplier selection occurs before all design work is completed, usually because the supplier will participate in the design process or because design proposals will be part of the information solicited from suppliers as part of the supplier selection process. However, specifiability manifested itself in several other ways. Two comments noted that it was difficult

for suppliers to understand the specs and that they could be interpreted multiple ways. One way to overcome this issue is to conduct supplier conferences prior to the bid event. One of these comments noted that the specification format was unusual and it suggested that as buyers became more familiar with the format over time, there would be a better common understanding of requirements and reverse auctioning would be more feasible. A lesson here for managers is that the decision to auction or not auction should not be static. As factors change over time, auctions may become more suitable to the situation. Another comment noted the difficulty in predicting costs in advance due to the nature of the manufacturing process. In this type of situation, negotiation would be preferable because it allows the parties to discuss how various contingencies will be handled. One comment stated that selection is done by testing suppliers' samples followed by competitive quoting and that reverse auctions are not feasible because they would require bypassing the test phase. This indicates poor understanding of the reverse auction process. Many companies have had success with testing or otherwise evaluating material from potential suppliers followed by allowing those suppliers whose materials pass the test to participate in the auction.

The amount of competition for the buyer's business also plays a key role in buyers' decisions not to adopt reverse auctions. This factor accounts for over twenty percent of the comments. The findings here validate assertions from existing case study research and from a data mining-based study (Millet, Parente, Fizel, & Venkataraman, 2004) that an adequate number of suppliers is important in making auctions work. When other factors favoring reverse auctions (e.g. specifiability) are in place, but buyers are constrained by a small supply base, it is worth considering using one of the established methods for testing the assumption that there are only a few viable suppliers. These include revisiting specifications to determine whether specifications are too restrictive or written to favor one supplier, as well as using third party research services to investigate new potential sources of supply. In some cases, a limited number of suppliers are qualified by engineering during a new product's design phase. However, other viable suppliers may exist or develop with time. Therefore, as with the specifiability criterion, companies may wish to periodically revisit the decision not to reverse auction a part because conditions may change.

The importance of non-price factors and dollar volume of the business that can be put up for bid were not cited as reasons for non-adoption as frequently as specifiability and competition in the supply base. Nevertheless, their being mentioned here adds to the evidence from other studies that they are important determinants of auction fit. Companies wishing to attack the dollar volume factor may want to consider their approaches to bundling. Readers interested in current research on this topic should consult (Schoenherr & Mabert, 2006).

The data contained two other reasons for non-adoption:

- Difficulty in using tool
- Insufficient time to conduct process

While these factors were mentioned by the buyers, they were not among the factors identified in the literature review. Researchers may gain from including these factors in future studies.

Turning to each of the factors individually, difficulty (or its opposite *ease of use*) surfaces regularly in the management information systems literature as a determinant of adoption of various information systems (Davis, Bagozzi, & Warshaw, 1989; Davis, 1989; Venkatesh & Davis, 2000; Venkatesh, Morris, Davis, & Davis, 2003). Managers interested in facilitating reverse auction adoption should address employee perceptions of difficulty of use. Training and assistance from power users are two ways to accomplish this. Successfully using reverse auctions requires that

buyers apply a highly disciplined overall sourcing process (e.g. a sound supplier qualification process, clear specifications, and a well-articulated award strategy). It is possible that comments about ease of use belie reluctance to embrace these practices, which some buyers perceive as an excessive amount of work. Therefore it is important for managers to be on guard that ease of use concerns really reflect problems with the technology and not a reluctance to engage in a rigorous sourcing process.

The general purchasing literature recognizes that successfully executing any competitive bidding process requires substantial time for thoroughly defining requirements, consolidating volumes, qualifying suppliers and so on (Burt et al., 2003). Reverse auctions are no different. While auctions may save time on the "back end" by reducing days spent negotiating to an hour of bidding, the up front-time is usually longer. However, as similar materials are auctioned repeatedly, it is possible to develop templates that can cut down the up-front time. A resource within the company, such as an on-line auction coordinator, can serve as a clearinghouse for this kind of material and can thus avoid "reinventing the wheel" within the organization. Auction providers may also be able to provide templates that cut down on up front time. Nevertheless, companies should not under-estimate the time required. Especially when purchasing is at the end of a longer process, such as a new product development effort, activities that occur earlier must not be allowed to consume the time needed to execute the sourcing process.

Notably, five factors from the literature review received no mention in the data:

- Standardization
- Channel power
- Stakeholder preferences
- Strategic nature of item
- Price elasticity

This by no means asserts that these factors are unimportant. However, this study is unable to validate their importance. The factors may be less important in the context in this study than in other contexts. Alternatively, the factors may be quite important in this context, but they were not ones that the buyers were able to articulate. Additionally there is some overlap between the non-mentioned factors and factors that were mentioned. For example, when there are few suppliers (which was mentioned) buyers' channel power (which was not mentioned) is relatively low.

The findings here may be instructive with respect to standardization, which received no mention among the buyers in this study. Some research has suggested that reverse auctions are appropriate for made-to-stock materials, but should be avoided for made-to-order or made-to-print parts. Most of the direct material purchases of the company in this study are non-standard and yet reverse auctions have been used successfully for many of these. The results here seem to support the view that it is specifiability, not standardization that makes the difference.

The strategic nature of an item may be a good reason not to auction an item. However, recent research suggests that buyers have difficulty operationalizing this concept (Terpend and Krause, under review), which may be why it did not receive mention by the buyers in this study. On the other hand, assuming it is going to be sourced in the first place, rather than made in-house, there may be no reason not to use an auction for a strategic item, assuming the specifiability and competition criteria are met.

Comments in the *general concerns about effectiveness* category essentially state the buyer did not think reverse auctions would provide good results for the commodity with respect to the results already being achieved, but they did not list a specific reason or rationale. A representative comment is, "A reverse auction might result in higher than world class pricing." One notable element in several of the comments was that other

novel approaches were being used to source the commodity—in particular an initiative to consolidate and leverage requirements on a global basis. Several buyers indicated that they believed that these approaches were more effective for the particular part than a reverse auction would be. In the academic community, we often think of buyers as having a choice between reverse auctions, sealed bidding and negotiation processes. In other words if a company does not use a reverse auction, they will use one of the latter two tools. As these buyer comments suggest, this oversimplifies the situation. In many organizations, reverse auctions are one choice that occurs in a milieu of tools and approaches available to the buyer.

FUTURE TRENDS

As reverse auctions become an established tool in many organizations, the decision whether to use an RA will become more structured. Past practice and past results may be more influential than commodity and market characteristics. However it is critical for companies to review the choice of price discovery mechanism for each commodity periodically because conditions change. It is important to have a system for regularly reviewing commodity strategies, and the suitability of reverse auctions should be part of this review.

CONCLUSION

By listening to the voices on non-adopters, this chapter took a "deep look" within one company into the issues of auction fit-to-task and rationales for adoption and non-adoption that are actually used by buyers. In addition to shedding light on the validity of existing research on auction fit, this chapter provided a window into the thinking processes employed by approximately thirty professional buyers in one of the world's largest organizations. It is hoped that this provides insights that are usable by managers seeking to understand employee behavior with respect to auctions and who have an interest in seeing that auctions are used under the conditions when they are likely to produce good results. Future trends, gaps in the existing research literature and potential research directions were also identified.

FUTURE RESEARCH DIRECTIONS

Trade press accounts suggest that many organizations' explicit criteria for when to employ reverse auctions boil down to only a few factors, especially competition among suppliers, specifiability, and volume. Taking this into account, one might expect to see greater reverse auction usage than we see presently. This raises the question, why aren't reverse auctions used more frequently when there are a sufficient number of suppliers (typically 3 or more), clear specifications and adequate volumes? Richer models are probably needed to identify other factors that play a role—factors that are limited to characteristics of commodities and markets. Models of information technology usage decision, such as the task-technology fit model (Goodhue & Thompson, 1995; Goodhue, 1995) suggest that individual person-level characteristics make a difference as do habit and various beliefs and social norms (in the company, the industry, and so on). The impact of these factors on auction utilization is important to understand.

An additional direction for future inquiry is the auction decision process. The research community has produced a great deal of information on commodity and market characteristics that influence the alignment of auctions with particular purchases. However, we need to document and understand the process that organizations actually go through when deciding what sourcing mechanisms to use in a particular situation. For example, who makes the decision? Who provides input? What is the level of process formality and centralization? When and how often does the

process occur? What is the relationship between these process-oriented factors and success?

REFERENCES

Beall, S., Carter, C., Carter, P., Germer, T., Hendrick, T., Jap, S. et al. (2003). *The role of reverse auctions in strategic sourcing (CAPS Research Report)*. Tempe, Arizona: Institute of Supply Management.

Boehmer, J. (2005). GE curtails hotel auctions. *Business Travel News, 22*(8), 6.

Bucklin, L. (1973). A theory of channel control. *Journal of Marketing, 37*, 39-47.

Burt, D., Dobler, D., & Starling, S. (2003). *World class supply management*. Boston: McGraw-Hill-Irwin.

Burt, R., Norquist, W., & Anklesaria, J. (1990). *Zero base pricing: Achieving world class competitiveness through reduced all-in-cost*. Chicago: Probus Publishing.

Carter, C., & Stevens, C. (Forthcoming). Electronic reverse auction configuration and its impact on buyer price and supplier perceptions of opportunism: A laboratory experiment. *Journal of Operations Management*.

Davis, F., Bagozzi, R. P., & Warshaw, P. R. (1989). User acceptance of computer technology: A comparison of two theoretical models. *Management Science, 35*(8), 982-1003.

Davis, F. D. (1989). Perceived usefulness, perceived ease of use, and user acceptance of information technology. *MIS Quarterly, 13*(3), 319-340.

Dickson, P. (1994). *Marketing management* (2nd ed.). Fort Worth: Dryden Press/Harcourt-Brace.

Emiliani, M., & Stec, D. (2000). Business to business online auctions: Key issues for purchasing process improvement. *Supply Chain Management, 5*(4), 176-186.

Emiliani, M., & Stec, D. (2004). Aerospace parts suppliers' reaction to online reverse auctions. *Supply Chain Management, 9*(2), 139-153.

Gattiker, T., Huang, X., & Schwarz, J. (2007). Negotiation, email, and Internet reverse auctions: How sourcing mechanisms deployed by buyers affect suppliers' trust. *Journal of Operations Management, 25*(1), 184-202.

Goodhue, D., & Thompson, R. (1995). Task-technology fit and individual performance. *MIS Quarterly, 19*(2), 213-236.

Goodhue, D. L. (1995). Understanding user evaluations of information systems. *Management Science, 41*(12), 1827-1844.

Hartley, J. L., Duplaga, E. A., & Lane, M. D. (2005). Reverse e-auctions: Exploring reasons for use and buyer's satisfaction. *International Journal of Integrated Supply Management, 1*(4), 410-420.

Jap, S. (2002). Online reverse auctions: Issues, themes and prospects for the future. *Marketing Science Institute—Journal of the Academy of Marketing Science—Special Issue on Marketing to and Serving Customers through the Internet, 30*(4), 506-525.

Kaufmann, L., & Carter, C. (2004). Deciding on the mode of negotiation: To auction or not to auction electronically. *Journal of Supply Chain Management, 40*(2), 15-26.

Leenders, M., Fearon, H., Flynn, A., & Johnson, P. (2002). *Purchasing and supply management* (12 ed.). Boston: McGraw-Hill Irwin.

Mabert, V. A., & Schoenherr, T. (2001). Evolution of on-line auctions in b2b procurement. *Praxtix, 5*(1), 15-19.

Mabert, V. A., & Skeels, J. (2002). Internet reverse auctions: Valuable tool in experienced hands. *Business Horizons*, 70-76.

Millet, I., Parente, D., Fizel, J. L., & Venkataraman, R. R. (2004). Metrics for managing online procurement auctions. *Interfaces., 34*(3), 171-180.

Monczka, R., Trent, R., & Handfield, R. (2005). *Purchasing and supply chain management* (3rd ed.). Cincinnati: Southwestern.

Parente, D. H., Venkataraman, R. R., Fizel, J. F., & Millet, I. (2004). A conceptual research framework for analyzing online auctions in a b2b environment. *Supply Chain Management: An International Journal.*

Schoenherr, T., & Mabert, V. A. (2006). Bundling for b2b procurement: Current state and best practices. *International Journal of Integrated Supply Management, 2*(3), 189-213.

Simon, H. (1955). A behavioral model of rational choice. *Quarterly Journal of Economics, 69*(1), 99-118.

Smeltzer, L. R., & Carr, A. S. (2003). Electronic reverse auctions: Promises, risks and conditions for success. *Industrial Marketing Management, 32*(6), 481-488.

Terpend, R. and Krause, D. R., under review. Thinking Outside the Box: A Typology of Commodity Sourcing Strategies. *Journal of Operations Management.*

Venkatesh, V., & Davis, F. (2000). A theoretical extension of the technology acceptance model: Four longitudinal field studies. *Management Science, 46*(2), 186-204.

Venkatesh, V., Morris, M. G., Davis, G. B., & Davis, F. D. (2003). User acceptance of information technology: Toward a unified view. *MIS Quarterly, 27*(3), 425-478.

Wagner, S. M., & Schwab, A. P. (2004). Setting the stage for successful electronic reverse auctions. *Journal of Purchasing and Supply Management, 10*(1), 11-26.

ADDITIONAL READING

Anonymous (2002). E-auction participants strive for fair, ethical events. *Purchasing.* http://www.manufacturing.net/pur/index.asp?layout=article&articleId=CA263504&stt=001&text=reverse+auction

Anonymous (2002). Motorola's success with e-sourcing inspires 2000 $billion e-auction goal. *Supplier Selection and Management Report (IOMA), 6*(1), 13-15.

Anonymous (2002). Motorola's Success With e-sourcing inspires 2002 $billion e-auction goal. *Supplier Selection & Management Report, 2*(6), 1-4.

Anonymous (2002). Owens Corning builds major savings from reverse auctions. *Supplier Selection & Management Report, 2*(1), 13-15.

Atkinson, W. (2003). New buying tools present different ethical challenges. *Purchasing,* 27-29.

Battalio, R., Kogut, C., & Meyer, D. (1990). The effect of varying number of bidders in first price private value auctions: an application of a dual market bidding technique. In Green, J. (Ed) *Advances in Behavioral Economics.* Norwood, NJ: Ablex Publishing.

Carter, C., Beal, S., Carter, P., Hendrick, T., Kaufman, L., & Petersen, K. (2004). Reverse auctions-grounded theory from the buyer and supplier perspective. *Transportation Research Part E, 40*(3), 229-254.

Carter, C., & Stevens, C. (Forthcoming). Electronic reverse auction configuration and its impact on buyer price and supplier perceptions of opportunism: A laboratory experiment. *Journal of Operations Management.*

Cohn, L. (2000). The hottest net bet yet. *Business Week, 17,* 36-37.

Cox, J., Smich, V., & Walker, J. (1988). Theory and individual behavior of first price auctions. *Journal of Risk and Uncertainty, 1*(1), 61-99.

Dyer, D., Kagel, J., & Levine, D. (1989). Resolving uncertainty about the number of bidders in independent priviate-value auctions: An experimental analysis. *Rand Journal of Economics, 20*(2), 268-279.

Emiliani, M., & Stec, D. (2001). Online reverse auction purchasing contracts. *Supply Chain Management, 6*(3), 101-105.

Emiliani, M., & Stec, D. (2002). Realizing savings from on-line reverse auctions. *Supply Chain Management, 7*(1), 12-23.

Emiliani, M., & Stec, D. (2002). Squaring online revere auctions with the caux round table principles for business. *Supply Chain Management, 7*(2), 92-100.

Gattiker, T. (2005). Individual user adoption and diffusion of Internet reverse auctions at Shell Chemical. *Practix: Best Practices in Purchasing and Supply Chain Management, 8*(4), 1-6.

Gattiker, T., Huang, X., & Schroeder, R. (2007). The Relationship between TQM orientation and electronic commerce adoption among manufacturers: Does a plant's quality management orientation affect its use of electronic procurement tools? *Proceedings of the 18th Annual North American Research/Teaching Symposium on Purchasing and Supply Chain Management,* Tempe, Arizona.

Gattiker, T., Huang, X. and Schwarz, J. (2005). *Why do sellers dislike Internet reverse auctions? Some experimental results.* Proceedings of the 16th Annual North American Research/Teaching Symposium on Purchasing and Supply Chain Management, Tempe, Arizona.

Handfield, R., & Straight, S. (2003). What sourcing channel is right for you. *Supply Chain Management Review 2003, (Jul/Aug),* 62-68.

Hartley, J. L., Lane, M. D., & Hong, Y. (2004). An exploration of the adoption of e-auctions in supply management. *IEEE Transactions on Engineering Management, 51*(2), 153-161.

Hur, D., Hartley, J. L., & Mabert, V. A. (2005). *Implementing reverse e-auctions: an organizational learning perspective.* 36th Annual Meeting of the Decision Sciences Institute, San Francisco, CA, USA.

Jap, S. (2003). An exploratory study of the introduction of online reverse auctions. *Journal of Marketing Research, 67*(3), 96-107.

Johnson, P., & Klassen, R. (2005). E-Procurement. *MIT Sloan Management Review, 46*(2), 7-10.

Metty, T., Harlan, R., Quentin, S., Moore, T., Morris, T., Sorensen, R., Schneur, A., Raskina, O., Schneur, R., Kanner, J., Potts, K., & Robbins, J. (2005). Reinventing the supplier negotiation process at Motorola. *Interfaces, 35*(1), 7-23.

Olson, J., & Boyer, K. (2002). Factors influencing the utilization of Internet purchasing in small organizations. *Journal of Operations Management, 21*, 225-245.

Pearcy, D., Giunipero, L., & Dandeo, L. (2002). *The Impact of Purchase Type on the Reverse Auction Process: A Conceptual Model.* The 13th Annual North American Research and Teaching Symposium on Purchasing and Supply Chain Management, Dallas.

Rosenberg, M., & van Wassenhove, L. N. (2001). *Do I hear 5 million euros? The story of a reverse auction: Econia.com and Scotts* (case study, 601-029-1). Fountainebleau, France: INSEAD-CEDEP.

Smeltzer, L., & Carr, A. (2002). Reverse auctions in industrial marketing and buying. *Business Horizons, 45*(2), 47-52.

Smeltzer, L. R., & Carr, A. S. (2003). Electronic reverse auctions: Promises, risks and conditions for success. *Industrial Marketing Management, 32*(6), 481-488.

Stein, A., Hawking, P., & Wyld, D. C. (2003). The 20% solution? a case study on the efficacy of reverse auctions. *Management Research News, 26*(5), 1-20.

Talluri, S., & Ragatz, G. (2004). Multi-attribute reverse auctions in B2B exchanges: A framework for design and implementation. *Journal of Supply Chain Management, 40*(1), 52-60.

Tulder, R. V., & Mol, M. (2002). Reverse Auctions or Auctions Reversed: First Experiments by Philips. *European Management Journal, 20(5)*, 447-457.

IMPLICATIONS FOR PRACTITIONERS

Title: Internet Reverse Auctions: Listening to the Voices of Non-Adopters

Description

Once a company implements an Internet reverse auction platform, buyers within the company often have considerable discretion as to whether or not to use it. This chapter discusses reasons for buyer non-adoption of Internet reverse auctions. Using a survey with open ended responses, data were collected and analyzed from buyers on why they had opted not to adopt reverse auctions. Surveys were collected from the North American division of a global OEM. The findings were as follows:

Findings

Most cited reasons for not using reverse auctions:

- Specifiability if the item/material being purchased
- Insufficient competition among suppliers
- Importance of non-price factors in the supplier selection decision
- Dollar volume of the business being put out to bid
- Difficulty in using tool
- Insufficient time to conduct the auction process

RECOMMENDATIONS

- When deciding whether or not to use an Internet reverse auction, managers should make sure that the item that is up for bid is specifiable. In order to make sure that suppliers understand the specs, conferences or other activities should be conducted prior to the bid.
- The amount of competition between suppliers plays a key role in the decision. When buyers are constrained by a small supply base, it is worth considering using one of the established methods.
- Managers interested in facilitating reverse auction adoption should address employee perceptions of difficulty of use. Training and assistance from power users are two ways to accomplish this.
- While auctions may save time on the "back end" by reducing days spent negotiating to an hour of bidding, the up-front time is usually longer. However, as similar materials are auctioned repeatedly, it is possible to develop templates that can cut down the up-front time. A resource within the company, such as an on-line auction coordinator, can serve as a clearinghouse for this kind of material and can thus avoid "reinventing the wheel" within the organization.
- Results from the surveys suggest that specifiability, not standardization makes the difference in the decision to use eRAs. Most of the direct material purchases of the company in this study are non-standard and yet reverse auctions have been used successfully for many of these.

- The decision to auction or not auction should not be static. As factors change over time, auctions may become more suitable to the situation.

CAVEATS

- The study was conducted in the United States. The findings may not generalize to other cultures.

Chapter V
Economic Effects of Electronic Reverse Auctions:
A Procurement Process Perspective

Ulli Arnold
University of Stuttgart, Germany

Martin Schnabel
University of Stuttgart, Germany

ABSTRACT

This chapter describes the economic effects caused by the use of electronic reverse auctions along the procurement process. It argues that an analysis of these economic effects requires the consideration of the whole transaction process. The approaches of the new institutional economics provide a theoretical foundation for the analysis. The second part of the chapter deals with the single steps of an auction-integrated procurement process. Through this holistic view of the procurement process the authors emphasize the additional benefits and the danger caused by auctions. A better awareness of the procurement process enables better decisions concerning the choice of benefits which are worth pursuing.

INTRODUCTION

The efficiency and effectiveness of traditional procurement processes can be improved by using electronic sourcing tools. New concepts and software solutions can support the procurement process in different phases of the market transaction. The electronic reverse auction (eRA) is one of these new tools which can be used in the negotiation phase. It seems to be a common idea that eRA influences the item price. Both practitioners and academia concentrate on analyzing the real price savings and they look at eRA only because of this benefit (see also Emiliani, 2004, p. 66). However, there are other economically relevant effects of using eRA: there are impacts on transaction costs, cycle time of transaction and eventually item quality (see also Carter et al., 2004). In order to obtain a better understanding of the complex economic effects, it is necessary to extend the focus of analysis from a single transaction view to a dynamic process (Arnold et al., 2005). This chapter concentrates on the economic effects stimulated by an eRA-integrated procurement process.

To explain the different economic effects, a substantial theoretical basis is necessary. We begin the chapter by discussing the theoretical basis for auction. We follow with the differences between forward and reverse (procurement) auctions. These differences explain the necessity of considering the whole transaction process in our analysis. Then, we take a closer look at the different approaches of the new institutional economics. Transaction cost theory, in the next section, refers to a transaction as the basic unit of analysis. Transaction cost theory explains that electronic applications are an enabler for using reverse auctions in procurement processes. It is through this theoretical foundation that the origin of savings and the process-related effects can be demonstrated. Adding information economics theory to our analysis illustrates that an eRA is more than an information seeking tool, while agency theory allows us to analyze the resulting shifts in information asymmetry. The fact that some of these shifts take place outside the negotiation phase emphasizes the necessity of analyzing the whole eRA-integrated procurement process in detail. It is there that we look at the different procurement phases in detail to identify the economic effects described previously. As we evaluate and explain the various economic theories, we follow the perspective of a buying company.

THEORETICAL APPROACHES EXPLAINING ECONOMIC EFFECTS OF ELECTRONIC REVERSE AUCTIONS

Modern IT-tools and infrastructure have created a "new" business world. The idea of a "perfect market model" became - maybe for the first time ever—realistic and revitalized neoclassical economic theory. There the price is the dominant instrument to coordinate supply and demand. Auction theory and new institutional economics are influenced by neoclassical theory but go beyond this.

Auction Theory

"An auction is a market institution with an explicit set of rules determining resource allocation and prices on the basis of bids from the market participants" (McAfee & McMillan, 1987, p. 701). Market institutions are mechanisms which compensate market failures. An auction helps to allocate resources more efficiently than other allocation mechanisms such as fixed price or bilateral negotiations. The auction theory investigates the characteristics of this allocation mechanism such as auction rules, auction types, but also the context in which the auction takes place. The standard setting therefore is a monopoly - a situation where one seller sells a product to a group of potential buyers (forward auction). Correspondingly the standard case for procurement auctions (reverse auction) is a monopsony—a situation with one buyer and a group of sellers. Experts of experimental oriented economics literature analyzed forward auctions, consisting of many buyers and one seller, and some of them suggested transferring the results to reverse auctions (e.g. Kräkel, 1992). However, there are important differences between forward and reverse auctions.

Jap (2002) subdivides these differences between the forward auction and reverse auctions in:

- **Differences in degree:** The general premises of forward auctions are that the configuration of the transaction is fixed and the price is the only remaining criteria of the auction object. This also matters for some reverse auctions. However, the selection of suppliers requires the consideration of non-price attributes, such as quality, delivery performance and cycle time.

- **Differences in kind:** Contrary to forward auctions, reverse auctions do not always determine a winner. They determine just one of the parameters—the price—which is not necessarily the last step of the negotiation before setting the contract. Reverse auctions are often just a supplier pre-selection tool which is followed by traditional face-to-face negotiations with the selected supplier(s). Another important difference is the bidding on multiple item lots. Depending on the auction rules, the bids of different lots are interdependent. The challenge for suppliers is to allocate their fixed capacity across different lots.

In addition to these differences the fact that buyers conduct reverse auctions electronically creates other effects. The bidding event no longer depends on geographical constraints. The buyers identify and invite qualified suppliers worldwide, who participate in the eRA without additional time consuming efforts. The identity of the participating suppliers remains typically anonymous, which allows the buyer additional options to regulate the visibility among suppliers. In manual reverse auctions the buyer regulates the amount of information provided to the bidder through the choice of the auction type (English,

Dutch, etc.). In addition, the electronic application normally contains features to vary the visibility of competitors' information for the bidder, e.g. showing the suppliers just their relative rank yield instead of providing price visibility.

Because of these differences eRAs, "appear to be a fundamentally different phenomenon" (Jap, 2002, p. 510). Applying an appropriate auction design—the main concern of the auction theory—is a very important step of the procurement process. However, the auction has to be designed in the context of the situation-specific procurement process. Although the eRA is just a tool which supports the negotiation, it has to be integrated thoroughly into the strategic sourcing process (Emiliani, 2000; Smeltzer & Ruzicka, 2000; Meier et al., 2002; Beall et al., 2003; Kaufmann, 2003; Kaufmann & Carter, 2004).

New Institutional Economics

Referring to neoclassical economic theory, which considers the price mechanism as the best instrument for coordination in a market economy, Coase (1937) asked "why is there any organization?" When describing the "costs for using the price mechanism" (transaction costs), he developed the theory of the firm and set the basis for different new institutional approaches. The perfect market conditions of the neoclassical theory were extended by dealing with the origins of imperfections:

- **Bounded rationality** refers to incomplete information and restrictions in human information and decision processing. Rationality therefore can never be complete.

- **Opportunism** means that individuals attempt to maximize their own benefit (self-interest seeking assumption; Williamson, 1990). Because of asymmetrical distribution of information one individual market party can acquire extra benefits which burden the other party.

Figure 1. Coordination mechanisms supported by electronic infrastructure

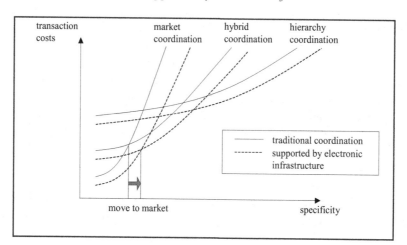

Transaction Cost Theory

The basic unit of analysis is the transaction defined as a transfer of property rights between two parties. The argumentation of the transaction cost theory follows the principle of cost efficiency. Williamson (1990) distinguished between two types of costs: transaction (or coordination) costs and production costs. The transaction costs exist because of information asymmetry, bounded rationality and opportunism. Such costs arise in every stage of the transaction from activities which include: evaluating suppliers, negotiation, control function etc. (Picot, 1991). The basic idea of the transaction cost theory is the reduction of these costs by selecting the appropriate organization for the transaction (transaction design). This design consists of institutions and their supporting infrastructure, e.g. information and communication technology. The organization of transactions follows two steps: first the selection of an appropriate coordination mechanism and secondly the creation of a transaction design within that mechanism (Picot et al., 1997).

There are three major coordination mechanisms for economic activities:

- **Markets** coordinate transactions by the price mechanism. Price is a direct incentive for all transaction partners. If a supplier can not meet customers' requirements, he will no longer be able to participate in economic exchanges.
- **Hierarchies** are based on the centralization of property rights by management. Administrative control mechanisms within a company facilitate the orientation on only one goal (e.g. the production of automobiles).
- There are many governance structures which are neither clear markets nor clear hierarchies. Examples are long-term contracts or strategic alliances between independent companies. All these in-between governance structures combine hierarchical and market elements. Therefore they are called **hybrids** (Williamson, 1991).

To select an appropriate coordination mechanism, we need deeper insights into the transaction's characteristics. According to Williamson (1990) *specificity* is the most important attribute of a transaction. The specificity of a transaction comprises every characteristic which "makes a

Figure 2. The transaction process

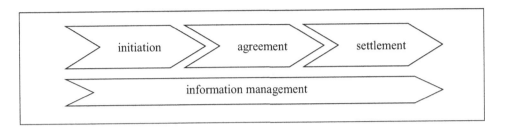

difference" to the buyer. The specificity results from the required know-how and physical assets (object specificity), the logistics requirements (site specificity) and the investments, which the supplier has to make for this transaction (dedicated asset specificity). In other publications Williamson (1989) also added the brand name capital as a further type of specificity. Malone et al. (1987) adds time specificity, which means that the value of an asset depends on its arrival to the user within a defined period of time. Much information has to be exchanged before, during and after the exchange of goods and services with high specificity. Normally the effects are extremely high market transaction costs. It is not possible to realize large scale effects because only a few customers exist (or perhaps only one). Objects with low specificity can be coordinated by market mechanisms. Low specificity means that there is almost no information transacted between the partners and possibly only information regarding price is exchanged. Market partners are able to bundle demand and to exploit economies of scale (see Figure 1).

The negotiation process is a market element. Thus it is part of the coordination effort in governance structures with market elements. These elements are usually external but also may be internal markets. The existence of an external market means spot transactions or possibly, long-term relationships with suppliers. Having an internal market refers to a higher degree of hierarchical

steering: by forming independent profit centers instead of hierarchical departments, market elements become relevant within a company (Krüger & Homp, 1997). Sometimes this structure is referred to as intra-company transfer.

After choosing markets as a suitable coordination mechanism, the transaction - a process consisting of different tasks - has to be designed. The transaction process can be subdivided into major phases: *initiation*, *agreement* and *settlement*. The *information management* takes place along the whole process so that it represents a support function and has a cross-sectional character (Figure 2). Each of these phases is organized by institutions. Picot et al. (1997) distinguishes between:

- **Transparency institutions** determine the visibility of other market members' activities.
- **Access institutions** require a certain data format for an order.
- **Price discovery institutions** define the negotiation design, e.g. whether an eRA will be integrated in the negotiation phase.
- **Settlement institutions** lay down the rules for settlement activities, e.g. the payment.

These institutions become more efficient and effective with the proper supporting infrastructure. The new possibilities of the information technology focus specifically on the problems of

Table 1. Net savings conducting an eRA

	historic price of traditional buying
-	last bid (new price) of the chosen supplier
=	realized price reduction
+	savings due to the eRA-procedure
-	costs due to the eRA-procedure
-	switching costs (due to the change of supplier)
=	net savings

coordination. Malone et al. (1987) describe that the coordination of markets as well as hierarchies will become more efficient by using information technology. The effects can be described as:

- **Electronic communication effect** referring to the higher data processing capabilities of the information and communication technology.
- **Electronic brokerage effect** which means the substitution of brokers by information and communication technology, which allows a buyer a quicker and inexpensive screening, comparison and selection of potential suppliers.
- **Electronic integration effect** which stands for the use of information and communication technology in order to integrate tasks through data processing without disruption, e.g. linking the suppliers and buyers inventory systems so that the supplier can ship the goods just in time.

Markets benefit from the electronic communication effect and the electronic brokerage effect. Virtualization of markets has caused a shift from more traditional face-to-face negotiation towards the auction paradigm lowering transaction costs through high reaction speed for all market partners and high market transparency. Even though a reverse auction is the better allocation mechanism for certain goods and services, this complex process can only be performed if carried out

electronically (Gampfer, 2003). The transaction costs for a manual (non-electronic) reverse auction are usually higher than the improved market efficiency (i.e. lower market prices) created by the auction mechanism. The electronic infrastructure - i.e. the use of the electronic application for reverse auctions in combination with other electronic tools, such as electronic requests for information, requests for proposal and requests for quote - reduces the transaction costs, so that it pays to use the auction mechanism (see Figure 1). It allows buyers to invite more suppliers to the bidding event —from all around the world, facilitating global sourcing—and requires fewer resources to organize them. If suitable items are identified a remaining question must be answered: What is the appropriate amount to be invested to implement an eRA-integrated transaction process? Compared to a traditional transaction —e.g. without the integration of an auction—the eRA-integrated process can save additional transaction costs. However, buyers sometimes put up with increased transaction costs—e.g. more up-front efforts and additional face-to-face negotiations (Carter & Petersen, 2005)—if the expected market price reductions are higher. To handle this trade-off we need deeper insights into the cost and value components incurred while conducting eRAs.

There are different terms used to describe the savings that result from eRAs. In general the (maximal achievable) savings will be calculated as the difference between the historic price of

Figure 3. Information problems in procurement transactions (Backhaus et al., 1994)

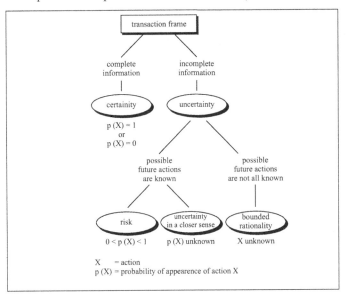

the traditional buying and the lowest bid of the conducted eRA. Considering the fact that there are some changes in the procurement process the overall savings will be calculated as shown in Table 1 (see also Emiliani & Stec, 2002).

The table contains both the improved market efficiency (i.e. lower market prices) created by the auction mechanism and the changes in transaction costs (arising due to the eRA-procedure). The transaction cost drivers along the procurement process related to the eRA-procedure are personnel time (i.e. internal administrative costs) and the costs for the third-party provider (i.e. external administrative costs and the fee for the software solution). The costs of switching suppliers includes transaction costs, which arise regardless of whether the procurement process is eRA-integrated or traditional. However, the probability of changing suppliers is higher when using an eRA.

Critics of transaction cost theory emphasize that cost orientation neglects the corresponding results or output respectively. Therefore Zajac and Olsen (1993) suggested a shift from transaction cost to transaction value. We discuss different value impacts along the eRA-integrated procurement process later.

Information Economics Theory

A fundamental characteristic of transactions, or rather sourcing decisions, is *uncertainty*. As complex contracts can never cover all possibilities of future developments, management has to deal with information deficits and their consequences. Backhaus et al. (1994) differentiate between three types of uncertainty caused by incomplete information (Figure 3):

- **Risk:** The buyer knows all possible actions of the supplier and future developments and has an expectation about the probability of appearance $[0 < p(x) < 1]$.
- **Uncertainty in a closer sense:** In contrast to risk the buyer has no expectation about the probability of the anticipated events $[p(x) = \text{unknown}]$.
- **Bounded rationality:** Both future disturbance variables and their probabilities are unknown $[X = \text{unknown}]$.

There are two perspectives of information situations which have to be differentiated along the transaction process:

Figure 4. The Information economics triangle (Weiber & Adler, 1995)

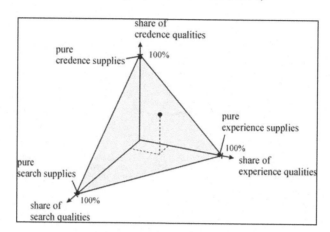

- • **Ex-ante information deficits** exist in the transaction phases before awarding the contract to the supplier. These information deficits could be partly eliminated by information-seeking activities. However, information is not free; the transaction costs generally increase.
- • **Ex-post information deficits** are part of the information situation in the settlement phase, when the supplier could react in an opportunistic way. The buyer has to think about agreements—sanctions and incentives - before awarding the contract to reduce these ex-post information risks.

Nelson (1970) and Darby, Karni (1973) differentiated three information-based exchange situations (Darby & Karni call them "qualities"): "Search qualities which are known before purchase, experience qualities which are known only after purchase, and credence qualities which are expensive to judge even after purchase" (Darby & Karni, 1973, p. 69). Complex procurement situations are often a combination of these different qualities. For analyzing the information problems each transaction should be positioned within the information economics triangle (see Figure 4).

The procurement function reduces uncertainty by information seeking mainly through the use of modern information technology systems (Arnold & Essig, 2001). The eRA is basically an ex-ante information discovery tool. It allows buyers to make a real-time bidding comparison of significantly more alternative suppliers. That way they eliminate the so-called "noise" of traditional negotiations as the participants bid at the same time and on the same basis. However, to create this same basis - i.e. to make all bids comparable - the process requires additional up-front preparation efforts consisting mainly of information discovery, e.g. through analyzing the supplier base and improving specifications. (see section "The Auction-Integrated Procurement Process"). Additional information discovery is necessary to avoid ex-post information problems caused by the use of eRA. There are new challenges such as phantom bidding (Kaufmann, 2003). From the buyers' perspective this means that a supplier places his bid although he is not able to deliver in accordance to the specification. From the suppliers' perspective phantom bidding means that the buyer himself places bids in order to drive down the price. The understanding of new uncertainty problems coming from the use of eRAs is one of the prerequisites for an appropriate procurement process design. As a result, we will discuss the information seeking requirement aligned with the eRA-integrated procurement process (see section "Economic Effects along the Auction-Integrated Procurement Process").

Agency Theory

Due to the assumption of bounded rationality the agency theory analyzes the relationship between transaction partners in situations with asymmetrical information. A principal employs an agent in order to use his superior problem-solving capabilities and provides compensation for his effort. Information defects are the reason for numerous activities which offer the possibility to the better informed party (agent) to act for it's benefit. Considering the theoretical assumption of opportunism, the other party (principal) runs the risk of being cheated. Agency theory analyzes the increasing opportunistic scopes of action which create further costs which further reduce the efficiency of the transaction. These are the so-called agency costs which are defined as the difference between the coordination costs with complete information and the coordination cost of the situation with incomplete information. There are three opportunistic scopes of action (Spremann, 1990):

- **Hidden characteristics** describe the ex-ante uncertainty of the principal, while evaluating the qualification of the agent, before awarding the contract. This could lead to adverse selection. This problem can be prevented either by suppliers signaling with credible characteristics (e.g. certificates) or by self-selection devices used by the buyer.
- **Hidden intention** occurs after a contract is signed. It means that the principal has made a specific investment in the relationship and the agent behaves in a manner that destroys this specific investment. The principal can counteract this problem through control activities.
- **Hidden action** stands for the inability of the principal to observe the actions of the agent. This problem can be reduced by aligning the interests of the two parties through incentive schemes.

A reverse auction helps to choose the right supplier(s). It has a self-selection effect on the suppliers, because the buyer will select the supplier who has the lowest production costs. Moreover, the auction reveals private cost information reducing the information asymmetry (Kräkel, 1992). However, there is the danger of selecting the supplier whose calculation is based on the most positive assumptions about future developments - a phantom bid mentioned before. To evaluate the bids, the buyer should consider non-price variables of the supplier's performance (such as quality, delivery performance, etc.), e.g. the signaling characteristics.

In general, the buyer is the principal and the supplier the agent. However, using eRAs the information asymmetry has to be analyzed in more detail. As described above, the supplier knows more about the auction object (e.g. production costs) but on the other hand the buyer knows more about his supplier selection process. For instance, the buyer decides about the degree of transparency of the selection rules for the suppliers regulating the information asymmetry concerning the competitiveness of the bids (hidden information). The buyer might use the eRA as a negotiation ploy (hidden intention), i.e. prior to the eRA he has no intention of switching suppliers and is just using the bids as a comparison standard to strengthen his power position in subsequent negotiations (Smeltzer & Carr, 2003). Phantom bids are another important concern for suppliers (hidden action). In many cases the buyer has to reduce these uncertainty factors if he wants the supplier to participate in the eRA. This can be done by explaining the tool and the procure-

Figure 5. The auction-integrated procurement process

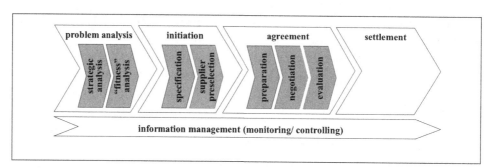

ment process, promising fairness, efficiency and transparency, following this promise and giving feedback to the participants. Some firms developed voluntary codes of conduct or other forms of guidance for eRA participants (Emiliani, 2005) trying to create and improve their auction reputation (Kaufmann, 2003).

Other principal-agent relations become relevant while introducing eRAs as a sourcing tool: the relation between the purchasing manager (user of eRAs) and his superior (e.g. the head of purchasing department). The use of eRAs leads to an increased procurement process transparency which comes from the higher degree of process determination. If the employee feels threatened by eRAs, sabotage could occur. The purchasing manager has to realize that eRAs do not replace him but give him space to concentrate on his strategic tasks: instead of exercising buying options he will spend his time valuing and creating those options. Resistance might also come up from any internal department other than purchasing. Communicating with and educating employees is important to overcome these resistance barriers (Beall et al., 2003).

ECONOMIC EFFECTS ALONG THE AUCTION-INTEGRATED PROCUREMENT PROCESS

In this section we illustrate the procurement process. We will analyze the changes caused by use of eRAs in each step. Afterwards we discuss the economic effects presented in the previous section in the context of the auction-integrated procurement process.

The Auction-Integrated Procurement Process

As presented in the section "Transaction Cost Theory", the transaction process consists of four different phases: initiation, agreement, settlement and information management (Figure 2). Describing the strategic procurement process we must regard *problem analysis* as an additional phase. Within this phase a comprehensive strategic analysis takes place concerning the internal and external conditions, the potentials and the demand, resulting in the development of sourcing strategies. Figure 5 illustrates the relevant process steps. The end of each of these steps can be seen as a key milestone which has to be achieved along the process.

Problem analysis

Generally the strategic analysis does not differ from traditional methods. However, with respect to electronic procurement in general, and to eRAs in particular, the companies "struggle with assessing the suitability of the different solutions for their specific commodities, supplier relations and portfolio of purchasing requirements" (De Boer et al., 2002, p. 25). eRAs are one alternative to be used in conjunction with other tools within the procurement process, if the conditions are favorable. These conditions have to be inspected. We call this step a "fitness" analysis. Kaufmann and Carter (2004) describe them as a set of requirements related to the auction object, the market and the involved parties.

Generally buyers associate eRAs with the procurement of items characterized by low specificity (standard goods and services). However, in practice this tool is used also for complex and strategic goods and services. High specificity is not necessarily a reason to exclude eRAs. The most important characteristic of the auction object is its speciability, i.e. the buyer is able to translate the demand into unambiguous specifications, making the purchase goods and services homogeneous and thus the bids comparable. However, some aspects of specificity are important in this context. Site specificity might reduce the number of potential suppliers. The suppliers would be reluctant to commit any dedicated assets—e.g. tooling, employee training, etc.—if the renewal of the contracts takes place using eRAs. Suppliers will protect their brand equity and will not allow a dissociation of the product from its brand through an eRA.

The competition among the participating suppliers is the main market-related requirement for a successful eRA. This competition depends on factors such as the number of qualified bidders and the attractiveness of the auction object (e.g. order volume) for the bidders. A careful analysis of the potential bidders prevents an overestimation of the competition intensity among suppliers or collusion in certain markets. It considers dependence on the supplier as one aspect in assessing the competitive environment. For example, if a supplier provides other products to the buyer, the confrontation with an eRA might destroy suppliers' trust, signaling the buyer's general intention to switch sources. If the supplier provides other products, an eRA could disturb the cooperation in these fields thus increasing transaction costs. If the supplier is also a customer, an eRA may have a negative direct effect on the firm's revenues.

All parties involved must trust the new procurement process (i.e. the reduction of bidders' uncertainty regarding the selection process and the lack of internal acceptance described in the "Agency Theory" section). When introducing eRAs, the employees within the purchasing function must be qualified so that they are skilled to use this new tool. However, cross-functional teamwork already needs to be in place prior to this. Buyers often have to overcome the resistance in other departments.

The process phase of "problem analysis" is always necessary regardless of whether eRAs will be used. However, there is an interesting effect coming from eRAs. As Smeltzer and Carr (2003, p. 486) noticed "the greatest advantage of reverse auctions was that it forced the organization to implement strategic sourcing." The requirement of such a process leads firms to carefully complete the tasks in the process. As a result, it creates an improvement of the data basis, pooling and even standardization efforts. Thus eRAs contribute strongly to change management of strategic sourcing.

Specification

Similar effects come about in this process step, the buying company being forced to write more precise specifications for the goods and services through the use of eRAs. Interactions with the supplier will happen less frequently and with fewer difficulties—the so-called "ping pong" resulting from incomplete specifications will stop. Leaving space in specifications means giving the supplier an opportunity to make a (unnecessary) difference, i.e. to add spurious object specificity.

The eRAs may cause the firm to review existing specifications. ERAs are an important argument for standardization efforts—leading to a decrease in specificity.

Proper specifications avoid redundancy and adjustments in later phases. Lack of clarity or later changes lead to post-eRA negotiations, interrupted or failed eRA, and thus an increase in administrative costs on both sides. Unclear specifications increase the uncertainty for the bidders. Suppliers will be reluctant to respond to a solicitation facing unclear conditions.

Suppliers' Pre-Selection

The eRA process requires the buyers to evaluate other capable suppliers which they otherwise might not consider under traditional conditions. On one hand the up-to-date market information about potential suppliers increases the competitive tension for an eRA. On the other hand the change to newly identified suppliers with better performance has the positive impact of improving the supply base quality and can even lead to a supply base reduction.

The use of well-written (e)RFx (request for information, request for proposal and request for quote) is a major step in developing clear specifications and in qualifying potential suppliers. Issuing specifications needed by the suppliers to provide quotations is information of interest to competing companies. A large number of invited suppliers means these specifications will be widely disseminated. The trade-off between the necessity of giving a precise specification to the invited supplier and the problem of making information available to the competitors can be met with proper specifications based only on cost drivers. Another possibility is to hide the buyer's identity and shift the whole interaction with the suppliers to a third-party provider.

Preparation

The decision to use an eRA to source items must be made at the beginning of this process step. The development of an adequate auction design and thus corresponding know-how is crucial to the eRAs' success. Most of the firms have a corporate standard, nevertheless all of them vary the auction design and adjust it to the specific situation. For instance, the auction design has to consider the experience of the potential bidders. If they are not experienced with eRAs, they might perceive a Dutch auction more unfair than an English auction reacting with boycott and/or collusion. The adjustment possibilities also depend on the software solution used.

On the basis of the evaluated (e)RFx, the buying company can develop different bid options and/or define and weight non-price variables (such as quality, delivery performance, etc.) in order to consider further specificity aspects of the different suppliers during the eRA event. This consideration is usually done by automatically adjusting each supplier's bid price up or down based on the pre-eRA analysis.

The buyer has to explain these developed bid options to the bidders, but also the auction rules, procurement process, the software application and the codes of conduct. This instruction (training, briefing) is an important task in order to reduce bidders' uncertainty described in the section "Agency Theory".

Negotiation

All the previous decisions have influences on this process step. Simultaneous bidding considerably increases the competition and the number of negotiation rounds.

In many cases *post-eRA negotiations* follow the bidding event for different reasons. On one hand the post-eRA negotiations can be planned as an additional process step for the final supplier selection. Additional price reductions are

Figure 6. Cost savings conducting an eRA

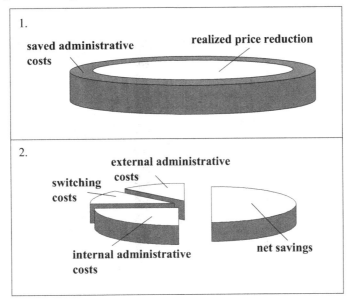

the most frequent motives. Sometimes it is made conditional on the course of the eRA event whether a post-eRA negotiation takes place, e.g. attaining to the target price. Another motive is a more detailed consideration of non-price variables. On the other hand, a post-eRA negotiation may not be planned, but necessary, due to changes in the specification. These changes may result from poor specifications (e.g. if the lot sizes were not achieved) or as an accepted risk of the buyer (e.g. goods in the development phase).

At this process step the buyer also has to pay attention to possible time lags between completion of the bid event and awarding the business. If the lags become extensive, circumstances on the supplier's side may change and alter their decisions. For instance, the supplier might not be able to honor his bids due to a change of capacity, so that the buyer has to re-evaluate the eRA data or award the business to an incumbent supplier (Emiliani, 2000).

Evaluation

Usually the firms document their eRA success in various measures, e.g. price reduction, number of (identified, invited and participating) suppliers, ratio of utilization, etc. In contrast to the traditional way, this documentation happens automatically. Feedback conversations with the participants is additional work compared to the traditional procurement process. However, it is important for building up auction reputation. Switching suppliers results in additional work created by qualification and auditing.

The evaluation creates a lot of findings for the buying firm (experience qualities). The results of eRAs improves the firm's database concerning market prices and suppliers' cost structures. The price level created by the eRA will become the new benchmark of future negotiations. The learning effects from each step will positively impact future eRAs, e.g. suppliers' acceptance of the tool and

Figure 7. Information qualities along the eRA-integrated procurement process

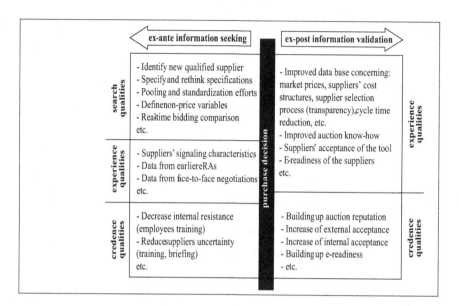

auction design. An added value for the manager is additional process transparency. This allows better control and adjustment of the procurement process. The buyer might draw conclusions about the e-readiness of the suppliers, i.e. about their capability to perform business transactions by using modern information and communication technologies (see also Arnold & Kärner, 2003).

Finally, eRAs help to build up the firm's e-readiness. Every successfully conducted eRA represents powerful experience which helps the buyer overcome internal resistance to this tool on every level of the company. The tool can be seen as a catalyst for other e-procurement systems. ERAs are often considered as an entry tool for e-procurement, because they can be used in a stand-alone mode independently of other sourcing systems. They allow quick low-cost and low-risk testing and provide a first feeling for internet based applications (Schwab, 2003).

Discussion and Managerial Implications

Besides price reductions the eRA-integrated procurement process can save additional transaction costs (see Case 1 in Figure 6), especially in the form of personnel time (i.e. internal administrative costs). These time savings arise mainly during the negotiation phase - the most time consuming phase in the traditional procurement process. However, additional internal administrative costs before and after the eRA event, the costs for the third-party provider (i.e. external administrative costs and the fee for the software solution) and the cost of switching suppliers might neutralize a part of these savings (see Case 2 in Figure 6).

There is a third economic effect besides price reductions and changes in transaction costs. The additional efforts along the different phases increase the quality and stability of the procurement process. The information economics theory

Figure 8. Personnel vs. cycle time reduction

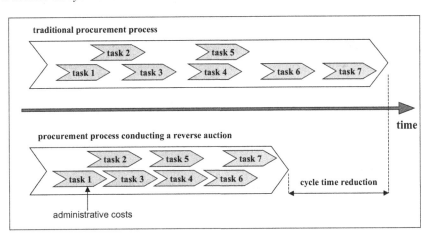

describes performance qualities—in our case the performance quality of the eRA-integrated procurement process. The additional efforts illustrated in the previous section are mainly ex-ante information seeking activities in order to meet the conditions for the successful use of the tool and to avoid post-eRA information problems. The ex-post information valuation activities increase the experience and credence qualities for later eRA-integrated as well as traditional procurement processes. Figure 7 summarizes the different qualities along the eRA-integrated procurement process.

Not all of these activities are eRA-specific. Pooling and standardization efforts and identification of new qualified suppliers are part of every proper (traditional) strategic sourcing process. However, in practice, the buyer often neglects some of these tasks for different reasons, e.g. time restrictions. The integration of an eRA in the procurement process forces the buyer to consider all these tasks in detail. Thus the eRA is a welcome *change management* instrument for strategic sourcing.

Only a part of the quality components affect the auction result and become visible in lower purchase prices, changed transaction costs and

costs for switching suppliers. For instance, when talking about time savings we have to differentiate two perspectives (see Figure 8). Time savings in the sense of less manpower means reduced transaction costs. Through certain decisions some tasks may become unnecessary or some tasks can be executed within less time, so that less manpower is needed. However, economies of time in a sense of cycle time reduction indicate that the time lags between the execution of the different tasks became shorter. The procurement process is completed earlier, although the transaction costs may remain equal or go up. The short cut procurement process may bring about time advantages on the production and the sales side, which is a positive contribution to the company's value (e.g., improved cash flow). An increase in value may also be interpreted as a decrease in transaction costs. Note that the decrease does not concern the present but the following transactions (subsequent).

CONCLUSION

Economic effects from eRAs are usually not only what practitioners are expecting, namely pure price savings, i.e. the difference between the historic price of traditional buying and the lowest bid of the auction. Buyers often ignore the additional resources which are necessary to prepare and conduct an eRA (transaction costs). They also overlook the additional value effects coming from eRAs. The dynamic process view reveals additional potentials. ERAs bring about considerable changes - although not fundamental ones - of the procurement process with a lot of design options. Thus they generate many different effects on the transaction and beyond, showing the importance of a strongly developed procurement process awareness when conducting eRAs.

FUTURE RESEARCH DIRECTIONS

Many buying organizations have become experienced in using eRAs. This allows in-depth research into the relationship between eRA-experience and influencing factors. More research is needed to examine how process awareness changes during the time period of the tool integration into the procurement processes. This time period begins at the first use of eRAs and continues until its routine use as a standard tool. Furthermore, the eRA-experience allows research into the way the companies handle subsequent auctions for identical or similar goods and services. Do the buyers' goals (i.e. pursued economic effects) and eRA-associated strategies change over time?

Most of the eRA-related research is limited to the perspective of the supply management function in the buying organization, perhaps because the buyers accepted the tool first. Future research might include the perspectives of other functional areas such as engineering and manufacturing in the buying organization. How do the buyers use their knowledge to support their own sales department when their company participates in an eRA as a supplier?

It seems that the suppliers accepted the confrontation with eRAs. But does this shift of information asymmetry in favor of the buyer

stimulate reactions on the suppliers' side? Do eRAs stimulate sellers to cooperate ex-ante in order to decrease competition forces and price pressure?

Another important issue is the international dimension of negotiations. Culture plays a crucial role in international negotiations. The depersonalization of the "unpleasant" price negotiation by the eRA might remove some of the cultural factors. However, many other parameters might be affected by cultural issues, e.g. the overall acceptance of the tool or the applicability of eRA-related strategies within different cultural contexts. Until now this field remained completely untouched by researchers.

REFERENCES

Arnold, U., & Essig, M. (2001). Electronic procurement in supply chain management: An information economics-based analysis of electronic markets, their facilities and their limits. *Journal of Supply Chain Management, 37*(4), 43-49.

Arnold, U., & Kärner, H. (2003). eReadiness deutscher Lieferanten - Empirische Erhebung zum aktuellen Stand und den zukünftigen Entwicklungen. *quiBiq.de, DeSK Deutscher eSupplier Katalog*, (pp. 7-35). Stuttgart, Germany.

Arnold, U., Kärner, H., & Schnabel, M. (2005). Target oriented use of strategic sourcing tools: A critical analysis creating process awareness for electronic reverse auctions. *Journal of Purchasing and Supply Management, 11*(2-3), 116-128.

Backhaus, K., Aufderheide, D., & Späth, G. M. (1994). *Marketing für Systemtechnologien: Entwicklung eines theoretisch-ökonomisch begründeten Geschäftstypenansatzes*. Stuttgart.

Beall, S., Carter, C., Carter, P.L., Germer, T., Hendrick, T., Jap, S., Kaufmann, L., Maciejewski, D., Monczka, R., & Petersen, K. (2003). The role of reverse auctions in strategic sourcing. *CAPS Research*, Tempe (Arizona).

Carter, C.R., Kaufmann, L., Beall, S., Carter, P.L., Hendrick, T.E., & Petersen, K.J. (2004). Reverse auctions—grounded theory from the buyer and supplier perspective. *Transportation Research: Part E 40*, pp. 229-254.

Carter, P., & Petersen, H.J. (2005). Impact of technology on purchasing and supply. In: Essig, M. (Ed.), *Perspektiven des Supply Management*, (pp. 251-290), Berlin.

Coase, R. H. (1937). The Nature of the firm. *Economica, 4*, 386-405.

Darby, M. R., & Karni, E. (1973). Free Competition and the Optimal Amount of Fraud. *Journal of Law and Economics, 16*(4), 67-88.

De Boer, L., Harink, J., & Heijboer, G. (2002). A conceptual model for assessing the impact of electronic procurement. *European Journal of Purchasing & Supply Management, 8*(1), 25-33.

Emiliani, M.L. (2000). Business-to-business online auctions: key issues for purchasing process improvement. *Supply Chain Management: An International Journal, 5*(4), 176-186.

Emiliani, M.L. (2004). Sourcing in the global aerospace supply chain using online reverse auctions. *Industrial Marketing Management, 33*(1), 65-72.

Emiliani, M.L. (2005). Regulating b2b online reverse auctions through voluntary codes of conduct. *Industrial Marketing Management, 34*(5), 526-534.

Emiliani, M.L., & Stec, D.J. (2002). Realizing savings from online reverse auctions. *Supply Chain Management: An International Journal, 7*(1), 12-23.

Gampfer, R. (2003). *Auktionen und Auktionsplattformen zwischen Unternehmen im Internet*, Aachen.

Jap, S.D. (2002). Online reverse auctions: issues, themes, and prospects for the future. *Journal of the Academy of Marketing Science, 30*(4), 506-525.

Kaufmann, L., & Carter, C.R. (2004). Deciding on the mode of negotiation: To auction or not to auction electronically. *The Journal of Supply Chain Management, 40*(2), 15-26.

Kaufmann, L. (2003). Elektronische Verhandlungen—Erste empirische Befunde zu Auktionen im Einkauf. In: Weber J. & Deepen, J. (Eds.), *Erfolg durch Logistik—Erkenntnisse aktueller Forschung,* (pp. 197-216), Bern.

Kräkel, M. (1992). *Auktionstheorie und interne Organisation*, Berlin.

Krüger, W., & Homp, C. (1997). *Kernkompetenz-management: Steigerung von Flexibilität und Schlagkraft im Wettbewerb.* Wiesbaden: Gabler.

Malone, T.W., Yates, J., & Benjamin, R.I. (1987). Electronic markets and electronic hierarchies. *Communication of the Association for Computing Machinery, 30*(6), 1987, 484-497.

McAfee, R.P., & McMillan, J. (1987). Auction and bidding. *Journal of Economic Literature, 25*(2), 669-738.

Meier, R.L., Williams, M.R., & Singley, R.B. (2002). The strategic role of reverse auctions in the quotation and selection process. *PRACTIX, Best Practices in Purchasing & Supply Chain Management, 5*(3), 13-17.

Nelson, P. (1970). Information and consumer behavior. *Journal of Political Economy, 78*(2), 311-329.

Picot, A. (1991). Ein neuer Ansatz zur Gestaltung der Leistungstiefe. *Zeitschrift für betriebswirtschaftliche Forschung, 43*(4), 336-357.

Picot, A., Bortenlänger, C., & Röhrl, H. (1997). Organization of electronic markets: Contributions from the new institutional economics. *Information Society, 13*(1), 107-123.

Schwab, A.P. (2003). *Elektronische Verhandlungen in der Beschaffung.* St. Gallen.

Smeltzer, L.R., & Carr, A.S. (2003). Electronic reverse auctions: Promises, risks and conditions for success. *Industrial Marketing Management, 32*(6), 481-488.

Smeltzer, L., & Ruzicka, M. (2000). Electronic reverse auctions: Integrating the tool with the strategic-sourcing process. *PRACTIX, Best Practices in Purchasing & Supply Chain Management, 3*(4), 1-6.

Spremann, K. (1990). Asymmetrische Information. *Zeitschrift für Betriebswirtschaft, 60*(5/6), 561-586.

Weiber, R., & Adler, J. (1995). Informationsökonomisch begründete Typologisierung von Kaufprozessen. *Zeitschrift für betriebswirtschaftliche Forschung, 47*(1), 43-65.

Williamson, O. E. (1989). Transaction cost economics. In: Schmalensee, R. & Willig, R.D. (Eds.), *Handbook of Industrial Organization:Vol. 1*, (pp. 135-182). Amsterdam.

Williamson, O. E. (1990). *Die ökonomischen Institutionen des Kapitalismus: Unternehmen, Märkte, Kooperationen.* Tübingen, Germany.

Williamson, O. E. (1991). Comparative economic Oorganization: Vergleichende ökonomische organisationstheorie: Die Analyse diskreter Strukturalternativen. In: Ordelheide, D., Rudolph, B. & Büsselmann, E. (Eds.), *Betriebswirtschaftslehre und ökonomische Theorie* (pp. 13-49). Stuttgart, Germany.

Zajac, E. J., & Olsen, C. P. (1993). From transaction cost to transaction value analysis: Implications for the study of interorganizational strategies. *Journal of Management Studies, 30*(1), 131-145.

ADDITIONAL READINGS

Arnold, U., & Meyle, R. (2006). Elektronische Beschaffungslösungen. In: Arnold, U./ Kasulke, G. (Eds.), *Praxishandbuch innovative Beschaffung* (pp. 487-511). Weinheim, Germany.

Buchwalter, J. (2001). *Elektronische Ausschreibungen in der Beschaffung: Referenzprozessmodell und prototypische Realisierung*, Lohmar & Köln.

Daly, S.P. & Nath, P. (2005). Reverse auctions for relationship marketers. *Industrial Marketing Management, 34*(2), 157-166.

Daly, S.P., & Nath, P. (2005). Reverse auctions and buyer-seller relationships: a rejoinder to Emiliani and Stec's commentary. *Industrial Marketing Management, 34*(2), 173-176.

Emiliani, M.L., & Stec, D.J. (2001). Online reverse auction purchasing contracts. *Supply Chain Management: An International Journal, 6*(3), 101-105.

Emiliani, M.L., & Stec, D.J. (2002). Squaring online reverse auctions with the caux round table principles for business. *Supply Chain Management: An International Journal, 7*(2), 92-100.

Emiliani, M.L., & Stec, D.J. (2004). Aerospace parts suppliers' reaction to online reverse auctions. *Supply Chain Management: An International Journal, 9*(2), 139-153.

Emiliani, M.L., & Stec, D.J. (2005). Commentary on "Reverse auctions for relationship marketers" by Daly and Nath. *Industrial Marketing Management, 34*(2), 167-172.

Emiliani, M.L., & Stec, D.J. (2005). Wood pallet suppliers' reaction to online reverse auctions. *Supply Chain Management: An International Journal, 10*(4), 278-288.

Essig, M. (2006). Electronic procurement—Konzeption und Anwendung. In J. Zentes (Ed.), *Handbuch Handel: Strategien, Perspektiven, internationaler Wettbewerb* (pp. 737-758). Wiesbaden, Germany.

Essig, M., & Kaerner, H. (2001). Buyer-driven electronic marketplaces: Developing business models for an integrated e-procurement strategy. *PRACTIX, Best Practices in Purchasing & Supply Chain Management, 5*(1), 1-9.

Eyholzer, K., Kuhlmann, W., & Münger, T. (2002). Wirtschaftlichkeitsaspekte eines partnerschaftlichen Lieferantenmanagements. In: *Handbuch der maschinellen Datenverarbeitung: Praxis der Wirtschaftsinformatik, 39*(228), 7-15.

Germer, T. (2006). *Beschaffungsauktionen: Theoretische Grundlagen und empirische Befunde aus Europa und den USA*. Unpublished doctoral dissertation, WHU—Otto Beisheim School of Management, Vallendar (Germany).

Griffiths, A. (2003). Trusting an auction. *Supply Chain Management: An International Journal, 8*(3), 190-194.

Jap, S.D. (2003). An exploratory study of the introduction of online reverse auctions. *Journal of Marketing, 67*(3), 96-107.

Jap, S.D. (2007) The Impact of online reverse auction design on buyer-supplier relationships. *Journal of Marketing, 71*(1), 146-159.

Jap, S.D., & Mohr, J.J. (2002). Leveraging internet technologies in B2B relationships. *California Management Review, 44*(4), 24-38.

Kaufmann, L., Carter, C.R., & Germer, T. (2004). Purchasing auctions—A synthesis of current research. *Proceedings of The 15th Annual North American Research Symposium on Purchasing and Supply Management* (pp. 119-139), Tempe, AZ.

Mabert, V.A., & Schoenherr, T. (2001). Evolution of online auctions in B2B e-procurement, in: *PRACTIX, Best Practices in Purchasing & Supply Chain Management, 5*(1), 15-19.

Smart, A., & Harrison, A. (2002). Reverse auctions as a support mechanism in flexible supply chains. *International Journal of Logistics: Research and Applications, 5*(3), 275-284.

Smart, A., & Harrison, A. (2003). Online reverse auctions and their role in buyer-supplier relationships. *Journal of Purchasing & Supply Management, 9*(5/6), 257-268.

Smeltzer, L.R., & Carr, A. (2002). Reverse auctions in industrial marketing and buying. *Business Horizons, 45*(2), 47-52.

Wildemann, H. (2003). Schnelle und transparente Preisfindung durch Online-Auktionen im Einkauf. In: Boutellier, R., Wagner, M.S. & Wehrli, H.P. (Eds.), *Handbuch Beschaffung: Strategien—Methoden—Umsetzung* (pp. 217-244). München & Wien.

IMPLICATIONS FOR PRACTITIONERS

Title: Economic Effects of Electronic Reverse Auctions: A Procurement Process Perspective

Description

This chapter provides the theoretical background of the economic effects stimulated by the use of eRAs based on a literature review. This is followed by a synoptical analysis of all involved procurement process steps with their potentials and design options.

Findings

In practice the use of eRAs is associated with several problems. The discussion of this topic has become more common recently. This shows that eRAs have became a part of the ordinary business in buying organizations. Nevertheless, practitioners often allocate their resources in an inefficient way. Procurement auctions are often an information technology topic - but not always. The core of the eRA and all related mechanisms - e.g. electronic requests for information, requests for proposal and requests for quote - is not its IT-implementation but the question, when, how, and where this mechanism should be used. The best (game theoretically optimized) auction design or the best software doesn't matter, if the user does not accept the tool or if the specification is unclear.

The eRA supports the negotiation targeting the price. However, the use of eRA initiates many other economic effects. Most of them emerge in the procurement process steps, before or after the negotiation, but also in later transactions. Some of these effects do not concern the buying department but other functions within the company. Therefore, the buyers are not aware of all these effects. Thus they do not consider these effects for their decisions during the preparation and realization of an eRA-integrated procurement process. The procurement process design, and thereby the resource allocation, is based on inappropriate goals.

RECOMMENDATIONS

- A strong procurement process awareness enables the buyer to identify, counteract or support crucial factors at the right time.
- Such activities might increase the costs in the respective process step, however, they enable relatively higher savings in other process steps and avoid negative impacts on following transactions.
- The practitioner must change its short-term view focusing on the price reduction in single transactions to a wider and long-term oriented perspective including all economic effects which occur during the time period beginning from the first use of eRAs until its routine use as a standard tool.

LIMITATIONS

This model should be empirically tested.

Chapter VI
Developing Trust–Based Relationships in Online Procurement Auctions

Janet M. Duck
The Pennsylvania State University – Great Valley, USA

ABSTRACT

This chapter discusses the challenges involved with developing trust and commitment in online procurement auctions. Online procurement auctions, otherwise known as e-auctions, are becoming increasingly more popular for conducting business-to-business transactions. However, many studies suggest that the success rate for e-auctions is down considerably. This may be due, in large part, to the absence of trust between the buyer/seller in this virtual arena. This chapter summarizes the current literature on trust and collaboration in the e-auction supply chain and discusses the processes in place that may contribute to the lack of trust between parties. Viewpoints of the buyer and seller are presented. Common issues are identified and the challenges associated with creating trust and fairness in the e-auction environment are revealed. Proactive strategies must be in place in order for stakeholders to maintain trust in this environment and to gain benefits from this virtual supply chain process. Future areas of study in this area are critical to its success.

INTRODUCTION

As you have read in previous chapters, online reverse auctions, also known as *downward price auctions* or *e-auctions*, is a forum wherein several suppliers compete online for contracts offered by a customer. Supplier bids are posted in real-time, and successive bids decrease until "a theoretically rational market price is reached" (Smeltzer & Carr, 2002, p. 49). Due to the process efficiencies and immediate financial savings for companies, this type of supply chain management is expected to experience continued growth in the upcoming decade. Johnson and Klassen (2005) state that e-procurement, including sourcing, e-coordination, and e-communities, (Jap, 2002) is critical to building and maintaining competitiveness for manufacturing and service firms. Potential benefits of online reverse auctions include reducing direct costs, clearly establishing market prices and shortening cycle times. Virtually every major industry has begun to use these types of auctions on a regular basis (Smith, 2002). Some of the leading providers of online reverse auction services include Caterpillar, Emerson Electric, Frigidaire, General Motors, PepsiCo, and Proctor & Gamble (Emiliani & Stec, 2001). Although it is in the initial stages of its lifecycle, it is evident that the reverse e-auction has been accepted in most major industrial sectors.

Although some claim that e-auctions are here to stay, (Jap, 2002) others are more skeptical about their long-term viability (van Tulder & Mol, 2002). Some criticism has been offered (Emiliani & Stec, 2002; Skjott-Larsen, Kotzab, & Grieger, 2003) about the capability of these virtual environments to sustain good supply chain management relationships founded on shared trust and collaboration. It has been argued that open-bid auctions, such as e-auctions, are unethical to collaborative relationship development strategy (Emiliani & Stec, 2002). The dilemma occurs because open bid pricing reveals pricing information to the competition. This interaction is known to drive the focus of bids solely on pricing, which negates the importance of other critical contract issues, such as customer service and quality. Building a supply chain system based on this premise will eventually lead to distrust and suspicion between parties. This contemporary marketplace requires buyers and sellers to conduct vital business transactions having had little or no prior interaction. Both economists and sociologists agree that trust is a critical enabling factor in relations where there is uncertainty, interdependence, and fear of opportunism (Gefen, Karahanna, & Straub, 2003;

Mayer, Davis, & Schooman, 1995; Williamson, 1985). So, although the increase in online reverse auctions is evident, what is not clear is the sustainability of the virtual supply chain relationships in the virtual environment. The ability to create and maintain trust and collaboration will likely be more difficult between all stakeholders. Empirical evidence has been emerging from specific industries (Emiliani & Stec, 2004) on this issue; however, more research is needed to properly assess the impact that e-auctions have on the supplier-buyer relationship (Smart & Harrison, 2003; Stein, Hawking, & Wyld, 2003).

Throughout this chapter we will explore the current literature pertaining to trust and collaboration within the e-auction format and discuss how the online procurement auction affects the contemporary supply chain. We will also discuss proposed strategies that will help to create trustworthy supply chain relationships within e-auction formats. This chapter will include: (1) a clear definition of the e-auction setting, (2) understanding trust and ethics in e-auctions, (3) a thorough literature review of the most recent studies conducted relating to trust and commitment from both the buyer and the seller perspective, (4) a discussion on the possible causes of the changes in supply chain relationships, (5) a strategic approach to cultivating trust and commitment in virtual supply chain management so as to benefit all stakeholders, and (6) implications for the future.

WHAT DOES *TRUST* MEAN IN E-AUCTIONS?

To begin, we must first understand the meaning of trust and its applicability in reverse e-auction formats. Trust is "a firm's belief that another company will perform actions that will result in positive outcomes for the firm as well as not take unexpected actions that result in negative outcomes," (Anderson & Narus, 1990, p. 45).

Trust is a crucial element in many such transactional, buyer-seller relationships, especially those containing an element of risk, as in interacting with an e-vendor (Reicheld & Schefter, 2000). It is an essential requirement for successful supply chain management to have effective supply chain planning that is based on shared information and trust among partners (Kwon & Suh, 2004). A lack of trust among supply chain partners often results in inefficient and ineffective performance. A recent study (Kwon & Suh, 2004) indicates that a firm's trust in its supply chain partner is greatly associated with both sides' specific asset investments (positively) and behavioral uncertainty (negatively). In a reverse e-auction, all parties assume a high level of risk that leads to a more uncertain and vulnerable setting. The seller and buyer must have a good sense that each party will not behave opportunistically by taking advantage of the situation (Kwon & Suh, 2004). So what does it mean to be untrustworthy in an e-auction environment? Untrustworthy behaviors in an e-auction setting may include:

- Establishing unfair pricing
- Offering inaccurate information
- Manipulating contracts in favor of a particular seller
- Modifying or amending contracts without prior agreement,
- Violating confidentiality agreements, and
- Intentionally providing bias for or against a particular seller

Based on the obvious risks associated with e-auction settings, organizations must be open to finding new ways to build trustworthy relationships.

CAN WE LEARN TO TRUST IN AN ONLINE ENVIRONMENT?

A number of academic studies have identified trust as a key partnership characteristic that fosters collaborative behaviors (Morgan & Hunt, 1994; Wilson, 1995). However, the literature to date shows limited research on the topic of trust and the proactive measures necessary to learn trustworthy behaviors in the online auction setting. The most recent literature by Emiliani and Stec (2004) is not optimistic. The authors write about the uncertain environment that exists within reverse e-auction environments and the increased risks that serve to damage the relationship between the buyer-seller. Their study of 23 leading suppliers and users of online reverse auctions resulted in the following findings that either directly or indirectly relates to trust and commitment between partners in online reverse auctions (Emiliani & Stec, 2004, p.150-151):

- Over 70% of incumbent suppliers responding to the survey actively seeking opportunities to charge their customer higher prices as a direct result of their participation in online reverse auctions when the opportunity to do so arises.
- The incumbent suppliers surveyed view online reverse auctions as a divisive purchasing tool that damages relationships with long-time customers.
- The incumbent suppliers surveyed realized few benefits, if any, from participating in online reverse auctions.
- Most incumbent suppliers drop out of the bidding process after one or two years.
- A few suppliers responded to online reverse auctions with efforts to improve productivity by adopting lean production practices.

An interesting component of this study, involving aerospace parts suppliers, addresses the issue of ethical business practices, including trustworthiness, as it relates to reverse e-auctions. Participants were asked if they felt that online reverse auctions represented ethical business practices that represented a trustworthy environment. Most suppliers (21 of 23) judged this new purchasing tool as an *unethical* business practice due to the inability of the environment to present a "level" playing field. Although this finding is not conclusive, it does present a clear challenge for the future of reverse e-auctions.

It should be noted that participants of the study did recognize published reports in both academic journals and business press suggesting that similar results would be found among incumbent suppliers from other industries, and that the findings from this study can be broadly applicable. However, it is possible that more successful outcomes may exist between specific pairs of buyers and incumbent sellers from certain commodities such as bulk materials or nontechnical services that can be very easily specified (Emiliani & Stec, 2004). However, the resounding message from this study states that online procurement auctions exist in a somewhat unethical arena. The following literature review broadens our view on this topic and presents perspectives of the buyer and seller.

LITERATURE REVIEW

To clarify, an *auction* is defined as a market institution with an explicit set of rules determining resource allocation and prices on the basis of bids from market participants (Jap, 2002). So, do these *rules* clearly define the level of trust and commitment required for successful reverse e-auctions? What happens to the supply chain when trust and commitment do not exist? Is there a psychological contract established that clearly defines the degree of trust expected between parties? In most cases, the answer to these questions is *no* (Emiliani & Stec, 2004; Presutti, 2003; Stein et al., 2003 and Emiliani & Stec, 2002). The information below outlines the findings of current research pertaining to the importance of trust and commitment in online procurement auctions.

The Buyer's Perspective

On the surface, online reverse auctions appear rather straightforward. However, after close review, it is evident that the relationships within the e-auction setting are dynamic and somewhat complex. Let us first consider the buyer's perspective. As noted by Griffiths (2003), the buyer is charged with facilitating three critical relationships. Each relationship requires an earnest level of trust and commitment.

- The first relationship that the buyer has is with its *company*. In this role, the buyer is responsible for managing the price contract of products as well as quality and customer service.
- The second relationship is with the *company and the existing suppliers*. In this role, the buyer strives to maintain or reduce pricing while preserving a commitment to quality and cost issues.
- Lastly, the buyer is responsible for building relationships with *new suppliers* to ensure that the company does not place undue reliance on a core group of suppliers.

The critical tight rope that buyers face is that each party is focused on its own objectives and goals during the life of the e-auction (Tassabehji, Taylor, Beach, & Wood, 2006). It is the role of the buyer to establish and maintain trust with all parties without sacrificing trust or representing information or processes unethically. For example, a buyer has an obligation to his employer to follow defined organizational goals regarding price, quality, and delivery. The buyer also has an obligation to manage the relationship with suppliers, keeping in mind fair pricing and quality. This effort can be a daunting task for some buyers operating in a virtual supply chain (Griffiths, 2003). Lack of trust in these relationships can lead to a failed transaction and could cost the company millions of dollars. For example, in initiating a reverse e-auction, a buyer can be perceived as having a lack of trust in his supplier's prices (Emiliani & Stec, 2002). Loss of supplier commitment can reduce the likelihood that suppliers will invest further in the company (Goldsby & Eckert, 2003). The buyer must carefully facilitate each relationship in order for successful auctions to take place in a trustworthy environment.

The Supplier's Perspective

Reverse e-auctions can be positive in that they can act as a "wake-up call" to suppliers (Jap, 2002), requiring them to consider things such as real cost reduction, waste elimination and stronger supply chain management with their customers (Presutti & Zuffoletti, 2002; Sashi & O'Leary, 2004). On the flip side, reverse e-auctions have been criticized for being corrosive (Presutti, 2003) and undermining supply chain relationships. Some arguments (Grieger, 2003; Skjott-Larsen et al., 2003) propose that reverse e-auctions send inconsistent messages to suppliers about collaboration by falsely advertising a "win-win" partnership, and dismissing previous supplier-buyer relationships by treating all bidders equally and at arm's length. These propositions lead some to think of e-auctions as unethical business transactions that severely damage the supply-change link between parties (Emiliani & Stec, 2004; Presutti, 2003; Stein et al., 2003 and Emiliani & Stec, 2002).

Emiliani and Stec (2001) go further by stating that e-auctions only serve as a short-term, quick-fix solution to critical underlying problems within the organization. Beliefs, such as these, surrounding reverse e-auctions are of critical importance because of the implications that they have on the future of e-auctions. Companies who have invested time and money in reverse e-auctions, and who plan on using this business strategy in the future, must carefully consider how well they develop and maintain trust with their e-auction environments, both from a buyer and seller per-

spective. The competitive strategies that result from virtual reverse e-auctions can discourage suppliers from sharing product innovations and can eventually diminish loyalty, such that the supplier will be less likely to help the buyer in a future crisis or in cost reduction (Emiliani & Stec, 2001; Presutti, 2003). The ramifications of lost trust and commitment in these environments can be detrimental to buyers and suppliers engaged in e-actions.

Researchers (Jap, 2002; Wathne & Heide, 2000) have identified several tactics used in the e-auction environment that may result in a direct loss of trust and commitment. For example, the nature and format of reverse e-auctions can leave suppliers feeling vulnerable and exploited (Jap, 2002). For example, suppliers sometimes feel that there are *unqualified* bidders participating in the auction who are unfairly undercutting their chances of winning the bid (Wathne & Heide, 2000). This perception leads suppliers to think that buyers are unethical, in that they are using less capable suppliers to push the contract price below a reasonable level (Kisiel, 2002). Additionally, suppliers frequently suspect that buyers enter a supplier in *phantom bids* in order to manipulate price reduction (Kwak, 2002). Unfortunately, perceptions of this type of buyer behavior exist, and although they are largely unsubstantiated, there is some evidence that this type of behavior increases after initial participation in e-auctions (Jap, 2003).

Suppliers also find the e-auction format very stressful due to the time constraints and the *down-bidding* feature of the e-auction setting (Smeltzer & Carr, 2002). You may have also experienced the same type of *auction stress* when bidding in an online format, such as eBay. Due to the intensity of the environment, suppliers have been known to bid lower than their minimum cost figure (Smeltzer & Carr, 2002). Consequently, the company loses money on the contact and potentially causes permanent supplier damage to the business—a phenomenon sometimes referred to as the "winners curse" (Kern, Willcocks, & Heck, 2002). Additional frustration and loss of trust from a supplier perspective can occur when, as often happens, the buyer does not select the *lowest bidder*, as may be implied by the process of *down bidding*. Keep in mind that the e-auction buyers understandably reserve the right to select the supplier that they determine to offer the *best package* (Bulow & Klemperer, 1996). The buyer's decision could be based on factors other than product price, such as proximity, customer service, and sustainability of the supplier. So, although the selection process may be well intended from a buyer's perspective, the nature of reverse e-auctions can cause some suppliers to feel insecure, vulnerable, and exploited. This feeling of distrust may prevent suppliers from participating in future e-auction transactions.

Another key source of supplier suspicion and distrust is the likelihood of buyers to engage in further negotiation with the selected supplier after conclusion of the auction (Jap, 2002). Some studies show that buyers have been known to adjust the terms and conditions of the contract *after* the bidding period has ended and a supplier has been selected (Emiliani & Stec, 2001, p. 104). For example, by:

- Purchasing fewer items than originally specified while benefiting from the lower agreed unit cost, based on higher volume
- Extending payment periods to improve the buyer's own cash flow and
- Requiring the supplier to carry extra stock to meet its lead-time requirements.

Attempts by the buyer to modify the contract terms and conditions to meet the special needs or requests of a particular seller can negatively impact the relationships within reverse e-auctions (Tassabehji et al., 2006). While it should be noted that the buyer does have the option to establish new terms and conditions based on the change in business practice, the intent to modify the contract

terms so as to favor one seller is unfair and may result in a loss of trust and fairness in the process. These unfair *adjustments* in the contract serve as another source of distrust that exists within the e-auction supply chain. This type of modification to contracts can substantially affect the supplier's production costs and profit margins and can be detrimental to the organization (Tassabehji et al., 2006).

Given the observations to date, it is apparent why suppliers are often unhappy and skeptical with the reverse e-auction format, having been coerced into price reductions, in an environment that has been known to breed feelings of distrust and uncertainty (Emiliani & Stec, 2004; Presutti, 2003; Stein et al., 2003; Emiliani & Stec, 2002).

However, there is hope for the future of e-auctions if the appropriate strategies are implemented. There are ways in which suppliers may retaliate in the future due to damage in the buyer-supplier relationship and the erosion of trust (Tassabehji et al., 2006). For example, many suppliers indicate a reluctance to share cost-saving technological developments with their customers. Another pro-action is to participate in developing collaborative buyer-seller relationships where it is understood that price is the principal criterion. This strategy must be clearly understood by all parties at the onset of the auction. Other studies suggest that suppliers are beginning to retaliate against reverse e-auctions by not selling products *under value*, in terms of price, rather than getting caught up in the bidding war and offering products at *bargain prices*. In these instances, suppliers must be pro-active in gaining back the trust that is sometimes lost in transaction during e-auctions.

CREATING TRUST IN VIRTUAL SUPPLY CHAIN MANAGEMENT

In order to move forward with e-auctions in a positive perspective, it is important to uncover the specific sources of distrust and determine exactly

Figure 1. Embedding trust in reverse e-auction transaction processes (Pavlou, 2002a, p. 220)

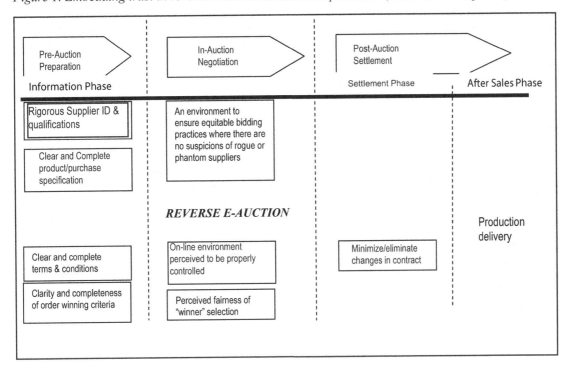

when, in the auction process, these opportunities exist. Consider the e-auction process progressing in three phases—pre-auction, in-auction, and post-auction. Experienced suppliers in the e-auction format have speculated on the source of skepticism, and have also offered solutions to overcome the breakdown that occurs in these phases. Recent research (Tassabehji et al., 2006) shows that dishonest buyer behavior, present throughout all phases of the e-auction, serves as a core cause of uncertainty between parties.

For example, at the pre-auction stage, studies (Tassabehji et al., 2006) have uncovered that suppliers have serious concerns about the credibility of the prequalification process and the lack of systematic vendor rating. During in-auction, suppliers feel suspicious that unqualified buyers and phantom buyers were participating in the process with intentions of falsely driving down bids. For example, one study showed that in the supplier survey, where respondents were the lowest bidder, most did not win the contract, where they did win the contract without the lowest bid; they were the incumbent supplier on 70% of the occasions. A similar incident of questionable buyer behavior deals with lack of clarity and completeness of product specification; this leaves suppliers uninformed about the critical details of the contract. Given this vulnerability among players, suppliers often become apprehensive and doubtful of the e-auction environment and the buyers fairness (Tassabehji et al., 2006).

Post-auction buyer behavior continues to create uncertainty and distrust on the part of the suppliers. In some cases, as noted earlier, buyers have been known to amend or modify the initial product contract, even after the auction has ended, in order to satisfy business strategies for their own organization. This behavior not only displays outright dishonesty but displays direct conflict with the open environment practiced in traditional supply chain systems. Buyer behavior continues to erode the integrity of the reverse e-auction format and creates apprehension on the part of all stakeholders to participate in future e-auctions.

HOW CAN E-AUCTIONS BECOME TRUSTWORTHY?

In order for e-auctions to experience continued growth and success in the future, actions must be taken on the part of the buyer and seller to ensure a credible, trustworthy relationship. The diagram below (Figure 1) responds to sources of distrust, as noted above, and provides suggestions on how to create and integrate trust-building mechanisms within the e-auctions phases (Pavlou, 2002a).

To improve the trustworthiness of the e-auction environment, buyer behavior must continually provide suppliers with a clear sense of purpose and completeness in regards to specifications and product contract. Several strategies are provided in Figure 1 that help to increase the level of trust in the virtual supply chain environment. First, originating contracts should be thoroughly examined and discussed in detail *prior* to the auction so that the chances of amending or modifying final contracts *after* the auction finalized, are minimized. Originating contracts should be honored by buyers without rights to modify or amend the agreed-upon specifications. Wagner and Schwab (2004) found that the most important precondition leading to a successful reverse auction was investing time in the preparation stage to understand clearly the competitive situation in the supply market before conducting the auction. By taking the time to examine this information, an open and honest environment based on trust can be the foundation of the e-auction relationship.

Second, buyers should exercise a more rigorous supplier qualification process (Heide & John, 1990) and endeavor to convince all suppliers of their robustness (Pavlou, 2002b). Buyers that implement a reliable qualifying process will assure an even playing field for the supplier base. Third, qualifications and winning criteria should be clearly stated with complete details. Lastly, to address the concern of opportunistic buyer behavior and false bidding, suppliers could be permitted to have representatives observe the buyer's personnel during the auction, or auction facilitators could devise additional assurance procedures to allay supplier's fears that the auction is not properly controlled (Hsiao, 2003). Steps such as these must be implemented in order to change the current perception of dishonesty and discontent within e-auctions.

CONCLUSION

The usual method of evaluating a reverse e-auction is to consider the cost savings, the time commitment, and the efficiency of the system. However, when evaluating the effectiveness of online reverse auctions it is imperative that we review the buyer-supplier behaviors in relation to the perceived level of trust and commitment between parties. The staggering growth and interest in reverse e-auctions challenges us to uncover the sources of distrust and uncertainty and respond to them proactively. Finding ways to develop and maintain trustworthy relationships within online reverse auction environments is vital to its continued success. As stated by Kwon and Suh (2004), it is an essential requirement for successful supply chain management to have effective supply chain planning that is based on shared information and trust among partners.

Supporting research (Deise, Nowikow, King, & Wright, 2000) believes that using the Internet as a medium for business can create a positive outcome that is founded on trust and commitment between supply chain partners. If reverse online auction e-procurement is to enhance enterprise competitiveness, then value must be delivered to ease industry pain points, with trust being enhanced between suppliers and buyer (Emiliani & Stec 2002; Jap, 2000). Jonsson and Zineldin (2003, p. 226) state that "in many situations it is not enough to know that the other is trustworthy, but also that the other will actively support the commitment." This proactive effort is essential to successful buyer-seller relationships. Commitments can only be built on trustworthy actions, not on empty promises.

Trust and commitment must be built over time as two parties share a variety of experiences that help each other's ability to predict behaviors of the individuals (Doney & Cannon, 1997). Such would be the case with online reverse auctions when buyers and sellers maintain the commitments and obligations that surround contract terms and conditions. Consequently, trust is more than just a list of promises and commitments; it is a proactive move toward long-term commitment. Thus, each single relationship will have a specific history in terms of how the parties have treated each other and the degree of trust and commitment that has been built up over time. In fact, the supplier and the dealer may at times have to pass "tests" set by the other in order to establish credibility and gain the trust of the other (Hakansson, 1982). Jonsson and Zineldin (2003, p. 236) conclude that "a major determinant of future business opportunity is the extent to which dealers are satisfied with and trust the supplier."

Regardless of the challenges that exist within the e-auction environment, it is likely that many companies will continue to test the waters for the sake of potential sales growth opportunities and simply because the auctions change the nature of competition. However, management must resist the temptation for quick results and focus instead on maintaining a trustworthy environment based on open exchange of information and fairness (Emiliani, 2000). Companies participating in online procurement auctions must have a proactive strategy in place that fosters a level playing field and encourages trust between parties. The following information will identify additional proactive measures that help to establish and maintain trust in a virtual supply chain management system.

FUTURE RESEARCH DIRECTION

It is obvious that future success of online procurement auctions depends on the ability for seller and buyers to establish and nurture trust and commitment within the virtual supply chain management system. A number of academic studies have identified trust as a key partnership characteristic that fosters collaborative behaviors (Morgan & Hunt, 1994; Wilson, 1995). Collaborative buyer-supplier relationships, based on trust, are necessary as the move to a more electronically based supply chain system is at the forefront. The idea of trust is eloquently stated by Spekman (1988): For supply-chain partnerships to become truly collaborative in nature, trust is not only a desired characteristic, but a necessary one.

REFERENCES

Anderson, J. C., & Narus, J. A. (1990). A model of distributor-firm and manufacture-firm working partnership. *Journal of Marketing, 54*(January), 42-58.

Bulow, J., & Klemperer, P. (1996). Auctions versus negotiations. *The American Economic Review, 86*(1), 180-194.

Diese, M., Nowikow, C., King, P., & Wright, A. (2000). *Executive's guide to e-business from tactics to strategy.* New York: Price, Waterhouse Coopers, John Wiley & Sons, Inc.

Doney, P. M., & Cannon, J. P. (1997). An examination of the nature of trust in buyer-seller relationships. *Journal of Marketing, 61*(2), 35-52.

Emiliani, M. L. (2000). Business-to-business online auctions: Key issues for purchasing process improvement. *Supply Chain Management, 5*(4), 176-186.

Emiliani, M. L., & Stec, D. J. (2001). Online reverse auction purchasing contracts. *Supply Chain Management, 6*(3-4), 101-105.

Emiliani, M. L., & Stec, D. J. (2002). Squaring online reverse auctions with the Caux round table principles for business. *Supply Chain Management, 7*(2), 92-100.

Emiliani, M. L., & Stec, D. J. (2004). Aerospace parts suppliers' reactions to online reverse auctions. *Supply Chain Management: An International Journal, 9*(2), 139-153.

Gefen, D., Karahanna, E., & Straub, D. W. (2003). Trust and TAM in online shopping: An integrated model. *MIS Quarterly, 27*(1), 51-90.

Grieger, M. (2003). Electronic marketplaces: A literature review and a call for supply chain management research. *European Journal of Operational Research, 144*(2), 280-294.

Griffiths, A. (2003). Trusting an auction. *Supply Chain Management, 8*(2/3), 190-194.

Goldsby, T. J., & Eckert, J. A. (2003). Electronic transportation marketplaces: A transaction cost perspective. *Industrial Marketing Management, 32*(3), 187-198.

Hakansson, N. H. (1982). Changes in the financial market: Welfare and price effects and the basic theorems of value conservation. *The Journal of Finance, 37*(4), 977-1005.

Heide, J. B., & John, G. (1990). Alliances in industrial purchasing: The determinants of joint action in buyer-supplier relationships. *Journal of Marketing Research, 37*(1), 24-36.

Hsiao, R. L. (2003). Technology fears: Distrust and cultural persistence in electronic marketplace adoption. *Journal of Strategic Information Systems, 12*(3), 169-199.

Jap, S. D. (2000). Going, going, gone. *Harvard Business Review, 778*(6), 30.

Jap, S. D. (2002). Online reverse auctions: Issues, themes and prospects for the future. *Journal of the Academy of Marketing Science, 30*(4), 506-525.

Jap, S. D. (2003). An exploratory study of the introduction of online reverse auctions. *Journal of Marketing, 67*(3), 96-107.

Johnson, P. F., & Klassen, R. D. (2005). E-procurement. *MIT Sloan Management Review, 46*(2), 7.

Jonsson, P., & Zineldin, M. (2003). Achieving high satisfaction in supplier-dealer working relationships. *Supply Chain Management, 8*(3-4), 224-241.

Kern, T., Willcocks, L. P., & Heck, E. V. (2002). The winner's curse in IT outsourcing: Strategies for avoiding relational trauma. *California Management Review, 44*(2), 47-69.

Kisiel, R. (2002). Supplier group seeks conduct code for auctions. *Automotive News, 67,* 16F.

Kwak, M. (2002). Potential pitfalls of e-auctions. *MIT Sloan Management Review, 43*(2), 18.

Kwon, I., & Suh, T. (2004). Trust, commitment and relationships in supply-chain management: A path analysis. *Supply Chain Management, 10*(1), 26-34.

Mayer, R. C., Davis, J. H., & Schooman, F. D. (1995). An integration model of organizational trust. *Academy of Management, The Academy of Management Review, 20*(3), 709-735.

Morgan, R. M., & Hunt, S. D. (1994). The commitment-trust theory of relationship marketing. *Journal of Marketing, 58*(3), 20-38.

Pavlou, P. A. (2002a). Institution-based trust in interorganizational exchange relationships: The role of online B2B marketplaces on trust formation. *Journal of Strategic Information Systems, 11*(3/4), 215-243.

Pavlou, P. A. (2002b). Trustworthiness as a source of competitive advantage in online auction markets. *Best Paper Proceedings, Academy of Management, Denver, CO*, 9-14.

Presutti, W. D. (2003). Supply management and e-procurement: Creating value added in the supply chain. *Industrial Marketing Management, 32*(3), 219-226.

Presutti, W. D., & Zuffoletti, J. (2002). The buyer-seller relationship and the impact of reverse auctions. In G. Antionette, L. C. Giunipero, and C. Sawchuk (Eds.), *E-purchasing Plus* Goshen, NY: JGC Enterprises.

Reicheld, F. F., & Schefter, P. (2000). E-loyalty: Your secret weapon on the Web. *Harvard Business Review, 78*(4), 105-113.

Sashi, C. M., & O'Leary, B. (2002). The role of Internet auctions in the expansion of B2B markets. *Industrial Marketing Management, 31*(2), 103-110.

Skjott-Larsen, T., Kotzab, H., & Grieger, M. (2003). Electronic marketplaces and supply chain relationships. *Industrial Marketing Management, 32*(3), 199-210.

Smart, A., & Harrison, A. (2003). Online reverse auctions and their role in buyer-supplier relationships. *Journal of Purchasing & Supply Management, 9*(5-6), 257-268.

Smeltzer, L. R., & Carr, A. (2002). Reverse auctions in industrial marketing and buying. *Business Horizons, 45*(2), 47-52.

Smith, N. (2002). Dynamic pricing effects on strategic sourcing and supplier relations. *Leaders for Manufacturing Thesis.* Massachusetts Institute of Technology.

Spekman, R. F. (1988). Strategic supplier selection: Understanding long-term buyers' relationship. *Business Horizon, July-August,* 75-81.

Stein, A., Hawking, P., & Wyld, D. C. (2003). The 20 percent solution: A case study on the efficacy of reverse auctions. *Management Research News, 26*(5), 1-20.

Tassabehji, R., Taylor, W. A., Beach, R., & Wood A. (2006). Reverse e-auctions and supplier-buyer relationships: An exploratory study. *International Journal of Operations & Production Management, 26*(1/2), 166.

van Tulder, R. J. M., & Mol, M. (2002). Reverse auctions or auctions reversed: First experiments by Philips. *European Management Journal, 20*(5), 447-56.

Wagner, S., & Schwab, A. (2004). Setting the stage for successful electronic reverse auctions. *Journal of Purchasing & Supply Management, 10*(1), 11-27.

Wathne, K. H., & Heide, J. B. (2000). Relationship governance in supply chain network. *Journal of Marketing, 68*(1), 73-89.

Williamson, O. E., (1985). *The economic institutions of capitalism.* New York: Free Press.

Wilson, D. T. (1995). An integrated model of buyer-seller relationships. *Journal of the Academy of Marketing Science, 23*(4), 335-345

ADDITIONAL READING

Anderson, E., & Weitz, B. (1992). The use of pledges to build and sustain commitment in distribution channels. *Journal of Marketing Research, 29,* 18-24.

Ball, J. (2001, January 22). New Chrysler boss plans to cut jobs, squeeze suppliers in overhaul mission. [Electronic version].*The Wall Street Journal Online.*

Bapna, R., Goes, P., & Gupta, A. (2001). Comparative analysis of multi-item online auctions; Evidence from the laboratory. *Decision Support Systems, 32*(2), 135-53.

Barber, B. (1983). *The logic and limits of trust.* New Brunswick, NJ: Rutgers University Press.

Bowersox, D. J., Closs, D. J., & Stank, T. P. (2000). Ten mega-trends that will revolutionize supply chain logistics. *Journal of Business Logistics, 21*(2), 1-16.

Bulow, J., & Klemperer, P. (1996). Auctions vs. negotiations. *The American Economic Review, 86*(1), 180-94.

Drew, S. (2003). Strategic uses of e-commerce by SMEs in the east of England. *European Management Journal, 21*(1), 79-88.

Emiliani, M. L. (2000b). The false promise of "what get measured gets managed." *Management Decision, 38*(9), 612-15.

Gao, T., Sirgy, M. J., & Bird, M. M. (2005). Reducing buyer decision-making uncertainty in organizational purchasing: Can supplier trust, commitment and dependence help. *Journal of Business Research, 58,* 397-405.

Gounaris, S. P. (2005). Trust and commitment influences on customer retention: Insights from business-to-business services.*Journal of Business Research, 58,* 126-140.

Handfield, R. B., Krause, D. R., Scannell, T. V., & Monczka, R. M. (2000). Avoid the pitfalls in supplier development.*Sloan Management Review, 41*(2), 37-49.

Jap, S. D. (2001). *The impact of online, reverse auctions on buyer-supplier relationships.* Retrieved from http://gbspapers.library.emory.edu/archive/00000033/01/GBS-MKT-2001-001.pdf

Jap, S. D., & Mohr, J. J. (2002). Leveraging Internet technologies in B2B relationships. *California Management Review, 44*(4), 24-40.

Johnston, D. A., McCutcheon, D. M., Stuart, F. E., & Kerwood, H. (2004). Effects of supplier trust on performance of cooperative supplier relationships. *Journal of Operations Management, 22*(1), 23-38.

Judge, P. (2001). How I saved $100 million on the Web. *Fast Company, 43,* 174-181.

McCraken, J. (2001, November 21). Ford at bottom of supplier's ranking [Electronic version]. *Detroit Free Press.*

Mohr, J., & Spekman, R. (1994). Characteristics of partnership success: Partnership attributes, communication, behavior and conflict resolution techniques. *Strategic Management Journal, 15*(2), 135-152.

OESA (2003, March). *Guidelines for the conduct of reverse auctions.* Original Equipment Suppliers Association. Retrieved from www.oesa.org/publications/conduct.pdf

Pavlou, P. A. (2002). Trustworthiness as a source of competitive advantage in online auction markets. *Best Paper Proceedings, Academy of Management* (pp. 9-14), Denver, CO.

Presutti, W. D. (2003). Supply management and e-procurement: Creating value added in the supply chain. *Industrial Marketing Management, 32*(3), 219-226.

Richards, B. (2000). Dear supplier: This is going to hurt you more than it hurts me... *Ecompany Now, 1*(1), 136-142.

Stanley, L. L., & Wisner, J. D. (2001). Service quality along the supply chain: Implications for purchasing. *Journal of Operations Management, 19*(3), 287-306.

Tully, S. (2000). The B2B tool that really is changing the world. *Fortune, 20,* 132-45.

Womak, J., & Jones, D. (1996). *Lean thinking.* New York: Simon & Schuster.

Womak, J., Jones, D., & Roos, D. (1990). *The machine that changed the world.* Rawson Associates, New York, NY, 39-68.

IMPLICATIONS FOR PRACTITIONERS

Title: Developing Trust-Based Relationships in Online Procurement Auctions

Description

Online procurement auctions, otherwise known as e-auctions, are becoming increasingly more popular for conducting business-to-business transactions. However, many studies suggest that the success rate for e-auctions is down considerably. This may be due, in large part, to the absence of trust between the buyer/seller in this virtual arena. Viewpoints of the buyer and seller with respect to trust between the parties are presented. Common issues are identified and the challenges associated with creating trust and fairness in the e-auction environment are revealed. Proactive strategies must be in place in order for stakeholders to maintain trust in this environment and to gain benefits from the virtual supply chain process.

Findings

While progress has been made in the e-auction environment, the participant needs to be aware of specific contractual and process-oriented details to help establish trust and commitment between stakeholders. It is imperative to outline the specific measures that help to ensure an even "playing field" among players. Buyers and sellers must be proactive in developing and maintaining trustworthy virtual supply chain management system. In order for online procurement auctions to survive it is imperative that the process create value for all participants.

RECOMMENDATIONS

10 Guidelines for Implementing Trust-Based Relationships in E-Auctions

The following list provides practitioners with a strategic approach to creating trustworthy relationships in online procurement auctions and also offers direction for future research areas in this field. If you are new to the e-auction environment, the following guidelines will help you to build trustworthy relationships within the e-auction environment based on honest and open communication.

1. Establish clear, well-designed terms and conditions of the buyer's contract. Provide all relevant and critical information in the contract at the onset of the process. Contracts should be designed with *trust-building* mechanisms in mind.
2. Buyers must treat each seller the same. Be aware of unintentional bias towards a particular company or individual seller. Once written, the contract should not be modified to meet the "specifications" of a specific seller.
3. Be sure that open bid auctions are implemented with the right intention and are not intended to survey market prices.
4. It is unethical for the buyer to participate in "shilling" the bids, or posing as a seller, only to inflate the bids.
5. Strive for collaborative relationships based on trust.

6.   Keep in mind that successful buyers must juggle three relationships:

     1. They need to manage the relationship they have with their own company
     2. They need to manage the relationship between their company and existing suppliers, and
     3. They need to foster relationships with new suppliers (Griffiths, 2003)

7.   Keep at the forefront the goals and objectives of all parties involved.
8.   Invite suppliers who are true potential suppliers. If there is something that will cause the supplier to be automatically disregarded, you have allowed them to be misrepresented.
9.   Conduct an assessment. Reverse auctions are not appropriate for every sourcing process. Conducting an assessment will eliminate the potential risks involved with damaging supplier chain relationships.
10. Placing sole focus on "lowest price" can ultimately deteriorate the buyer/seller relationship. Define all relevant factors, aside from price, that are critical decision factors in seller selection. Keep all factors in mind during the selection process.

CAVEATS OR LIMITATIONS

Lack of research in this area may be a limitation at this point. More efforts need to be focused on identifying the specific value for each participant and the proactive strategy to create these benefits in an open environment. By expanding this knowledge base we can ensure trust and collaboration among parties.

Chapter VII
Innovation and B2B E–Commerce:
Explaining What Did Not Happen

Steve New
Univeristy of Oxford, UK

ABSTRACT

The massive wave of enthusiasm for B2B (business-to-business) e-commerce generated with the "dot-com" boom led many to believe that a fundamental transformation of how firms bought and sold products was just around the corner. The new "wired" world of commerce would lead to real-time, Internet-driven trading, with significant implications for—amongst other things—the nature of buyer-supplier relationships, pricing, and the management of industrial capacity. Despite the excitement, such a transformation has largely failed to materialise, and whilst there has been a limited uptake of B2B innovations (for example, the use of online reverse auctions), the fundamental character of B2B trade has remained mostly unchanged. Drawing on a multi-stranded empirical study, this chapter seeks to explain the divergence between the expected and realised degrees of innovation.

INTRODUCTION

The extraordinary rise and fall of the late 1990s **technology bubble** was not the first speculative boom of its kind—and presumably will not be the last. As with the successive 19th century booms relating to the railways, the frenzy was accompanied by an astonishing explosion of rhetoric, folklore, and intellectual and mana-gerial fashion—crudely, "hype." This led to a significant flurry of innovation, particularly in the founding of large numbers of **Internet-based intermediaries** ("hubs" or "exchanges" Bakos, 1991, 1998; Bloch & Catfolis, 2001; Barratt & Rosdahl, 2002; Le, Rao, & Truong, 2004). Investors and organisations poured vast sums into these ventures and, for the most part, lost their money. Consultants and investment banks made shrill claims that **interorganisational trade** would be transformed, but the predicted revolution failed to materialise.

I address two central questions in this chapter. The first is the simple question: Why did the revolution not happen? The second is: What substantive ideas for business practice can be salvaged from the wreckage? This is an important task; to adapt George Santayana's famous quip, those who do not understand the past are condemned to repeat it.

One feature of published work in this field is that there has been relatively little solid empirical material; on the other hand, there has been a great deal of generalised comment and unsupported speculation regarding the causes and consequences of the bursting of the **B2B bubble**. Day, Fein, and Ruppersberger (2003) present an analysis that emphasises the similarities with other "shakeouts" associated with disruptive technologies.

This chapter reports the results of a multistranded investigation into the extent to which organisations are prepared to make use of the Internet in buying and selling, and into the patterns of life and death of **B2B exchanges**. Unlike much of the literature in this area, which has largely focused on leading companies or the few successful hubs, this chapter concentrates more on the opportunities and obstacles that face "ordinary" organisations, and the innovations which failed. The logic behind this is that there is often much to be learnt about the process of innovation from the mundane and the typical. The purpose of this study was not to recount the organisational success stories of leading firms—others have done that before, and the *potential* benefits of B2B e-commerce are well documented (e.g., Sculley & Woods, 1999; Timmers, 2000; DeMaio, 2001; Raisch, 2001). For this study, the challenge was to understand the reality of organisations' experiences, and to gauge the key issues and obstacles that they face.

BACKGROUND: THE B2B PHENOMENON

A simple starting point to the complex origins of the **B2B e-commerce** phenomenon lies in the well-established technologies of **electronic data interchange (EDI)**. At the beginning of the 1990s, for many industries, the direct system-to-system transfer of data over proprietary networks following industry standard protocols had become a routine element of doing business. The technology allowed significant savings from both increasing the speed and accuracy of data transmission, and in some cases was progressing to more advanced uses whereby buyers and suppliers could not only manage routine transactions but also "see" into each others' systems, facilitating such operational innovations as *collaborative planning forecasting and replenishment*, and *vendor managed inventory*. In addition, electronic linkages also were developing for the easier sharing of technical and design data, encouraging inter-firm collaboration in technical design. The downside of these **"inter-organisational information systems"** were the considerable "hook up" costs incurred by the parties involved, a fact which limited the adoption of the technologies by smaller suppliers, often faced with meeting the costs of linking their own systems with the non-matching requirements of several customers. In parallel, in the academic literature, there was a limited debate as to the long-term effects of these technologies on firms' switching costs, and good arguments could made for expecting both a reduction and increases in market "stickiness," and the consequential shift to purer "markets" or growing "hierarchies," respectively (Malone, Yates, & Benjamin, 1987; Bakos, 1991). The debate was rather theoretical, and was rather neglected outside of a handful of learned journals.

The arrival of the Internet, and its adoption by businesses as a serious tool for business, however, radically changed the character of the debate. Three key features of the Internet and two innovations transformed the horizons of possibility. The Internet was ubiquitous, cheap, and—being built around the idea of a standard and simple set of technical protocols—relatively easy for firms to adopt. The two innovations—the *search engine* and the *online auction*—opened up a range of new possibilities for online B2B trading. Over time, two basic connected perceptions emerged regarding the potential for a new approach.

The first of the perceptions was that the Internet could radically transform procurement and sales processes, collapsing the costs and timescales of trading. Prospective buyers could seek out prospective suppliers very rapidly, and suppliers could present vast quantities of searchable information on their products and capabilities. Furthermore, buyers could use Internet mechanisms to identify the cheapest supplier in real time using multilateral reverse auctions. Correspondingly, suppliers could be more responsive in their pricing. The scope for these new approaches to yield substantive benefits was widely acknowledged.

The second perspective, however, took these new potentials as heralding something far more significant than some dollars shaved off administrative transaction costs. As Bill Gates (1995) stated, the Internet will "carry us into a new world of low-friction, low-overhead capitalism, in which market information will be plentiful and transaction costs low." This vision of the future initially fuelled enthusiasm for online **business-to-consumer (B2C)** retailing, but after a while many observers realised that the B2B market was of a vastly larger scale. B2B e-commerce was held to signify a "fundamental change in the way capitalism works" (Prigg, 2000; Tapscott et al., 2000). A report by AT Kearney (2001) suggested the emergence of "differentiated value networks" that would "redefine entire industries and value chains," and that that e-markets "can dramatically affect the power balance in today's value chain." Partly driven by an almost ideological faith in the nature of "markets," this position assumed that supply markets for corporate purchasers would

be transformed: The features which stopped industrial markets behaving like the theoretical, equilibrium-finding markets of the neoclassical model (small numbers, constrained flows of information, high switching costs, high barriers to entry) could be removed by the new technology, reaping substantial efficiency gains. For these gains to be realised, however, new market institutions would be needed to act as "hubs" between buyers and sellers, and these—even if charging just a tiny fraction of the throughput—stood to reap phenomenal economic rewards. These hubs were to be the "killer application of the B2B Internet revolution" (Sculley & Woods, 1999). As a result, an Internet "land grab" emerged as entrepreneurs and existing market participants sought to establish themselves in the controlling positions in their chosen market or industry.

As time has passed, many of these new intermediaries have fallen by the wayside—and their fate is examined later in the chapter. However, it is important to note that there is far more to B2B e-commerce than online exchanges and marketplaces, and some organisations have achieved significant advantage through the use of e-procurement and the use of so-called "private exchanges." However, many organisations have struggled to develop their e-procurement or e-marketing activities, and it is interesting to explore why this might be so.

METHODOLOGY

The investigation described here used multiple research methods. First, an e-mail questionnaire was sent to over 4,000 firms who supply the major UK utilities, generating 240 usable replies that provided information on these companies as both buyers and sellers. Second, follow-up telephone interviews with a dozen of these firms helped provide greater insight into their experiences. Third, this was complemented by nine case studies (involving site visits, multi-informant interviews, and documentary analysis) involving a range of both public and private sector organisations. Fourth, the work used a database of 663 e-marketplaces and B2B hubs constructed by Meakin (2002). This large database represents a significant slice of the population, although there is no way of definitively establishing what percentage it represents. Grubb (2000) estimated 1,400 B2B exchanges had been launched; Levaux (2001) "estimated a thousand or so." Caspar (2000) cited an Andersen Consulting study that claimed there were 7,500 by late 2000. Day et al. (2003) claim a peak of 1,520. (For reasons discussed next, all these figures must be taken with considerable caution).

The sample for the e-mail survey was firms in the **Utilities Vendor Database** of the Achilles Group—a B2B company whose activities concentrate on public and regulated procurement (see www.achilles.com). The pool of companies represented a broad range of firms supplying the UK utilities sector. Our approach was to initially use a very brief questionnaire and to use the immediacy of e-mail feedback to refine the structure and examine the effect on response rates by adapting the number and sequence of questions asked. The survey was administered in the autumn of 2001, and we e-mailed just over 4,000 organisations, reaping over 240 usable replies (we asked firms about either their purchasing or selling, or both). However, due to our adaptive design, we did not collect data on all questions from every respondent. Participants were entered into a drawing to win a £50 gift voucher.

The mechanism of the questionnaire was to send a plain text e-mail, for which the answers could be simply overtyped on the reply and returned. We did this to avoid using e-mail attachments (which might be blocked by firms' firewalls), and to avoid the need for respondents to access a Web page (we knew that for at least some of the smaller firms involved, whose access to the Internet was by standard telephone line, this requirement would be a disincentive). We also offered each participant access to the

findings of the report, and a brief benchmarking report comparing their response with other (anonymous) firms. Due to the exploratory nature of the research, we have not employed formal scaling or rigorous hypothesis testing in the interpretation of the data; the full analysis is still in progress. Here, we present an overview of the descriptive data, which in this case we believe is more instructive than looking for intricate correlations of scores. As we were dealing with non-anonymous returned questionnaires, we were able to additionally incorporate further public domain information about the organisations into our analysis, including financial information and (subject to data protection constraints) data from the original database. The median turnover of the respondents was £11m, with the median number of employees being 124.

The qualitative aspects of the research entailed a series of visits to nine organisations with a view to finding out which issues and aspects of B2B e-commerce at the top of their agendas; we sought (within the time and budget available) as wide a selection of organisations as possible (large, small, public, and private sector), and sought to let managers and staff in these organisations largely steer the direction of the discussions. This rather unstructured approach meant that we did not (nor did we expect) to collect commensurate or matching data from these organisations; however, it helped us engage with some of the underlying issues regarding B2B and e-procurement, which we suspect would have been rather lost if we had framed the meetings too strictly in our own terms. We believe this trade-off to be particularly important given managers' propensity to discuss aspiration in these areas as if it were current fact, and the way in which interviewees' responses may sometimes encapsulate that which they have read in professional magazines rather than the actual experience of their organisations. However, the serious downside to this approach is that much of the material generated is not directly relevant to issues at hand, and of course generalisations are even more problematic than with survey data.

Methodological trade-offs also were needed in the analysis of the B2B hubs. Much of the writing on these initiatives has assumed that relatively few of them would survive, for example, Levaux (2001) estimated that only 200 would still be around by 2003. Drawing from the prior database, this phase of the research worked through 302 e-marketplaces with a highly structured search process which entailed examining the Web site (where available) and using two search engines (*Factiva*™ and *Lexis-Nexis*™) to collate news and PR-agency coverage (typically from trade journals). There are obvious problems with these secondary sources not being wholly accurate or reliable; on the other hand, for some of the initiatives we examined, these reports are the only accessible information left. Where necessary and possible, e-mail messages were sent to the exchange to gain further information.

This highly structured process allowed the systematic analysis of data regarding each of the initiatives and also allowed a rational decision to abandon the search for information on a particular exchange and move on to the next one. This Taylorist approach to data gathering proved particularly effective, as experimentation showed that without a programmed cut-off point, a great deal of time could be spent searching fruitlessly for exchanges which were the equivalent of "vapourware"—initiatives which were announced in the press but subsequently disappeared without trace.

A key aspect of the data collection process was the classification of the B2B initiative according to a set of dimensions (such as type of exchange, industry, etc.). These included whether the site was alive, dead, or had a continued existence via merger with or acquisition by another initiative. Sites that appeared to be dormant were contacted via e-mail, but if the link was broken and the e-mail returned, it was assumed the operation had closed. If the site appeared to be in a state "yet to go live" it was left until the end of the project

and then rechecked—if it was still pending, it was ignored.

During the course of the data collection, it became clear that it was not easy to judge the level of activity or indeed in some cases the seriousness of intent of the initiatives. Many of the marketplaces described what they did in principle, but displayed no evidence that the site or the services provided were genuinely operational. This transpires to be a major problem when investigating organisations that may or not be viable, and which exist in a business context where it is not in the actors' interests to be completely honest about their current degree of success. What was needed was an indication of substantive activity—an "Activity Test." We eventually settled on a simple proxy for being "genuinely alive": whether there was any reported quantitative indication of the transaction volume (in number of transactions or dollar value) or throughput. These were deemed to be "Actives." However, this does not imply that the initiatives were financially viable; an exchange could have throughput but not make any profit. There is clearly a risk of "type one" error in this classification, in the cases where an Active site has simply not gotten around to releasing some indicative numbers, or there is some other strategic reason for obfuscation. There is also a "type two" error for marketplaces that falsely declare activity. However, as there will be a general incentive for initiatives to publicise their vitality in order to attract participants, this seems a reasonable criterion to apply. Büyüközkan (2004) describes another attempt to "score" the activity of e-marketplaces, but, from the experience gained in the current study, it is difficult to see how his approach could be operationalised in practice.

SUDDEN BIRTH AND LINGERING DEATH OF B2B EXCHANGES

Figure 1 illustrates that—given the extensive reportage of the death of B2B—a surprising

Figure 1. Survival of B2B e-marketplaces: Comparison of whole sample with those passing the 'Success Test'

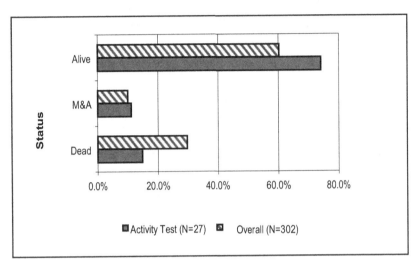

number of initiatives remained "alive," in that there was still a Web presence of some kind. However, out of the 302 studied, we identified only 29 who passed the "Activity Test" of providing quantitative evidence of any substantial kind of any kind of activity.

Interestingly, the small difference between sites passing the Activity Test and those not was not statistically significant (using the chi-squared test at the 0.1 level of significance). So marketplaces able to publish throughput figures seem to be no more likely to be still "alive" than those not. This can be explained by two ideas: The relatively low capital and operating costs for "pure play" Internet-based businesses (and the relative ease of fundraising during the boom years) can mean that sites with meagre levels of real activity may be able to sustain some type of Internet presence for some time as they simply burn off the initial investment. This is a significant point. Day et al.'s (2003) study uses the construct that a marketplace "exists and continues to operate"—our

work points to the fact that these two things are separable concepts.

Second, one way of attracting sufficient buyers and suppliers to participate in an exchange would be to charge minimal fees, or to offer attractive but expensive-to-provide services, thereby making continuing operations unviable.

There are a very wide range of schemes for classifying different types of exchange. Here we adopt that proposed by Ramsdell (2000), which is summarised in Table 1.

The classification of exchanges transpires to be a rather complex matter, as there are many instances of hybrid and unconventional approaches. However, in this study we found that the total sample—where categorisation was possible—was split roughly equally between the categories as shown in Table 2. Figure 2 illustrates the status of these categories; again, there is no statistical significance between the types of exchange.

The lesson that emerges here is that despite the widespread assumption in the prescriptive and

Table 1. B2B marketplace Types (after Ramsdell 2000)

Type	Typical Owners	Type of market	Description
Product	Suppliers or 3rd parties	Fragmented	Horizontal e-marketplace usually formed around a supply market that cuts several industries. E.g. MRO market
Industry	Buyers	Buyer power dominated	Vertical e-marketplace, usually revolving around an industry sector. E.g. Chemical Industry
Function	3rd parties	Non-fragmented	Focuses on services and capabilities rather than products, such as Supply Chain Integration (SCI) or Project Management.

Table 2. Breakdown of marketplaces by category

Type	Percentage
Function	38%
Product	35%
Industry	27%

Figure 2. Status of exchange types

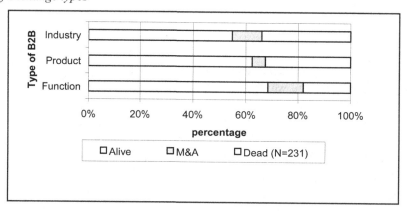

speculating writing at the time, no one particular exchange model turned out to be dominant.

The emergence of B2B needs to be understood in the context of the technology boom of the late 1990s, and Figure 3 plots the date of first announcement against the value of the NASDAQ composite index. This pattern is illustrated in more detail in Figure 4, which illustrates the lifelines of exchanges by category.

The data presented in Figures 3 and 4 points to some interesting speculation. On the one

hand, the close match of announcements to the NASDAQ index is suggestive that much of the enthusiasm for B2B intermediaries was driven as much by the potential of making money from investors in the heat of the technology investment boom as it was by the desire to build genuinely viable businesses. Simply setting up some kind of intermediary B2B organisation is not in itself capital intensive (although making it really deliver value to buyers and suppliers may be). Therefore, it seems unlikely that the decline in the launching

Figure 3. Announcements of marketplaces

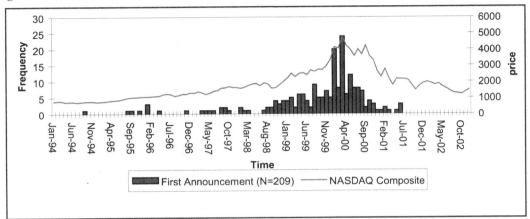

of B2B initiatives is completely explained by the difficulty of raising funds as the boom subsided. If, on the other hand, the motivation for many of the enterprises was simply to get to the investment markets quickly, then the sharp drop off in announcements between April 2000 and February 2001 makes more sense.

Figure 4, however, suggests that the fate of the initiatives cannot be explained by looking at the launch date. A very cynical view might expect that those launched at or just before the frenzy might be the least likely to survive, being the most driven by fashion and being subject to the least rigorous degree of scrutiny. However, if this is the case, it is not clear from the data. Furthermore, it does not seem that the early initiatives were more or less likely to fail than the later starters. A key point in the consideration of this data is that many of the initiatives may well be alive, and yet not very active, and not generating very much or any revenue. As nearly all the initiatives are small private businesses, it is generally very difficult to get convincing or informative data on their financial and operating performance. The fact, however, that so few pass the "Activity Test" is perhaps indicative that the task of bringing buyers and suppliers together is far more complex than many initially thought. To explain why this might

be, it is sensible to begin by reviewing the impact of e-commerce to "ordinary" companies—and this brings the discussion to the survey and case studies.

EXPERIENCES OF B2B E-COMMERCE: INITIAL OBSERVATIONS

Before we turn to the substantive data gathered by the survey and the cases, it is worth noting some incidental aspects of the research that we found interesting. First, an immediate feature of the survey was the large number of e-mails (roughly 10%) that were returned as undeliverable—even though we had used contact e-mails provided by the firms themselves to a database to which they paid a fee. Following up these cases revealed several potential problems: Many firms had changed the format of their e-mail addresses; individuals had left the organisation; and a surprising number were addresses based on non-company e-mail systems (for example, Hotmail™ or Freeserve™), and the addresses were no longer active. For reasons we discuss next, we think this is a significant finding. A second and surprising observation was that eight of the

Figure 4. Birth and death of e-marketplaces (n = 193)

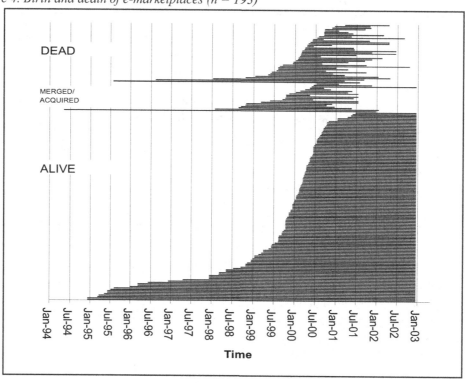

responses were returned by conventional post rather than by e-mail.

For reasons of available space, we concentrate here on just three aspects of the substantive research findings: the impacts of e-commerce on buying, selling, and the character of the buyer-seller relationship.

Buying: Commodification and Specification

We suspected that much of the hype surrounding B2B e-commerce was based on a naïve view of corporate procurement. For example, many of the B2B enthusiasts over-emphasise the extent to which corporate purchasing is about buying commodities or highly standardised products for

which price is the only salient variable. We sought data from supplier organisations about the nature of their sales on two dimensions: First, the degree to which their output was commoditised—in the sense that the goods or services provided were standard "off-the-shelf" items, or bespoke for a particular customer's needs. Second, we asked about the extent to which buyers play a role in the specification of their own requirements: In some cases, buyers spell out exactly what they want; in others, the seller specifies the solution according to an assessment of the buyer's needs; in many cases, the exchange requires a process of dialogue between the buyer and seller. Much of what has been written about B2B e-commerce has assumed a particular model of inter-company trade, emphasising standardized products specified by the

Figure 5. Purchasers' use of the Internet

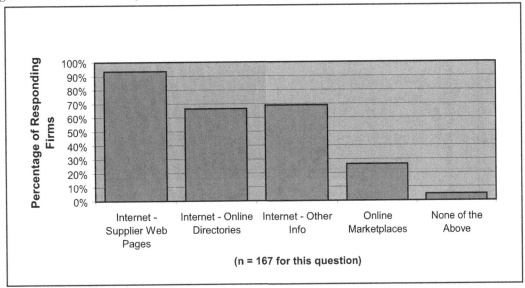

customers (e.g., from an online catalogue). From the supplying firms who responded to the e-mail questionnaire in this study, this amounted to less than 19% of sales. This is a significant finding, as it indicates that (if the result were indicative of the general case) more than 80% of B2B trade is not amenable to the impersonal, price-oriented, online catalogue mechanisms which have been one of the key archetypal images of B2B. Firms also differ from each other by supplying different combinations of goods, services, and works. The firms in the e-mail survey provided a good mix here, with 60% providing goods alone or in some combination with works and services, and the remainder selling some combination of works and services. Of the firms that sold goods, three quarters sell them as part of a more complex package involving more intangible elements. Again, much of the discussion about B2B has thought only in terms of simple "products," but the reality is far more complex.

Buying: Use of the Internet

We asked organisations about the use of the Internet in the purchasing process and found extensive

use, especially in terms of seeking information from suppliers' Web pages (see Figure 5).

Telephone interviews confirmed that respondents interpreted the term "online marketplaces" very broadly—and organisations often view distributors in these terms. Also, it seems that a crucial role of suppliers' Web pages is simply providing further contact data—postal addresses and telephone numbers. The "other info" response includes using standard search engines to find, for example, press coverage on a supplier. This mundane but valuable facility transpired to main current impact of the Internet on the procurement function, and is a significant observation only in as much as that it falls considerably short from the idea of a "closely-coupled supply chain" or a "virtual community." In our case studies, we noted that the opportunity for "finding new suppliers" did not seem to excite much enthusiasm amongst the organisations; the Internet could make getting information slightly faster, but was not perceived by the case participants as being fundamentally different from using the Yellow Pages. This is an apparently mundane but significant finding; much of the early excitement about the role of the Internet

Figure 6. Purchasing organisation and methods

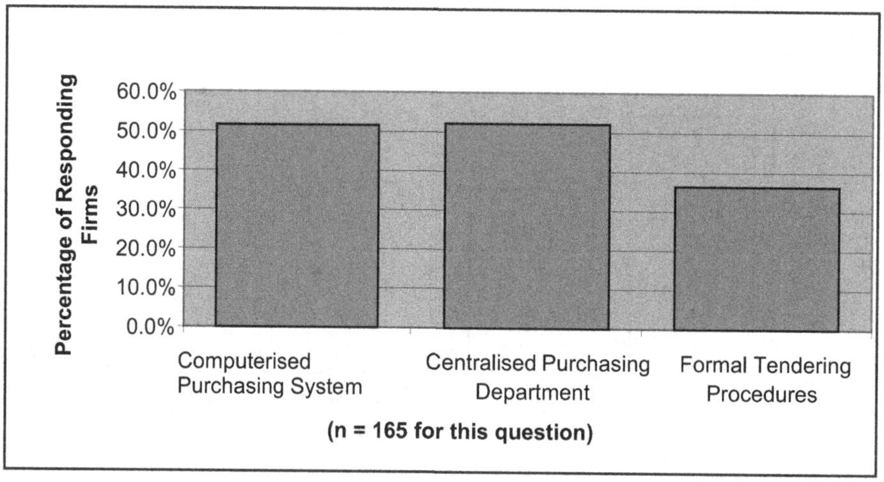

was based around a notion that it would reduce search costs (see Bakos, 1991). This appears not to be much of an issue—or, if it is, there is only marginal advantage in a marketplace system over a simple Google™ search.

Buying: Inter-Organisational Systems

Although the B2B hype emphasises the electronic linking of organisations' procurement systems to their suppliers' systems, we found that only half of the supplying firms had computerised purchasing systems, with the same proportion having centralised purchasing systems (see Figure 6).

These findings are interesting in that it suggests that for smaller organisations at least, the idea of inter-linked systems along the supply chain is likely to remain something of a fantasy without considerable innovation in both information technology and business practice amongst many firms. This is not to say that this cannot or will not happen; however, were these findings to be representative, it would appear that there is a major task of supplier development ahead for those firms which wish to cascade integrated supply chain practices.

Buying: Purchasing Measurement and Control

Much of the enthusiasm for **e-procurement** has focused on the enormous scope for reducing the costs of purchasing bureaucracy and transactions processing. Rather than go through an internal purchasing department, "users" can order what they need from their desktop, with automatic budget controls keeping spending within predefined limits: Many B2B enthusiasts have predicted the demise of purchasing departments as a result.

While not denying the great potential for these types of savings, this study points to some important qualifications. This is because there is more to purchasing than transaction processing. First, effective procurement requires higher-level, strategic management in regard to external issues—such as supplier development, collaboration on business processes, and supply policy. In other words, there is much more to good purchasing than simply finding the lowest price. Second, there are more complex internal issues than simple budgetary controls—a prime function of procurement systems is the control of fraud, and, in the public sector in particular, organisations' procurement systems are constrained by a complex regulatory framework. So while e-procurement can yield significant savings on elements of the procurement process, it does not do away with the need for specialist procurement staff with real purchasing expertise.

These considerations of organisation and structure lead to the questions of measurement. The participants in our study all struggled with quantifying both the performance of purchasing and in determining reliable costs for the purchasing process itself. This issue has two important consequences for the adoption of e-procurement and B2B.

First, without effective metrics of how well a purchasing process is performing, the appeal of using Internet-based innovation to reduce costs is rather blunted. Indeed, for managers in some of the organisations in this study, the key motivation was to ensure compliance with a system of bureaucratic controls rather than a hunger to reduce expenditure. This seems a particular issue if an organisation's culture rewards risk aversion; we found organisations where purchasing managers' principal goals seemed to be to stop things going wrong and to maintain a steady equilibrium. In such organisations, mechanisms of measurement and reward work against dynamic innovation in procurement systems.

Second, in other types of organisations, the measurement of purchasing works to give a misleading focus on short-term savings. In some organisations, the dazzle of dramatic savings in headline prices achieved by B2B innovation (for example, online reverse auctions) has mesmerized firms into forgetting that the important cost is the total cost of acquisition and ownership. The phenomenon of suppliers "lowballing" to win a contract, then working hard to claw back their margin by, for example, raising post-contract complexities, is well known and understood by procurement professionals. Equally, costs associated with delivery, quality, warranties, and post-sale support can easily dominate the initial purchase price. It appears, however, that in some organisations it has become politically convenient to brush aside these concerns and focus on impressive sounding reductions in headline prices. In such cases, there is a clear risk that such an approach may backfire in the longer term.

Selling: Communication and Customer Relationships

B2B has often been presented as though it is all about purchasing. But is essential to understand the other side of the coin—how it affects selling organisations. We asked suppliers about various aspects of their relationships with customers (see Figure 7).

Although only roughly one-third used electronic links such as EDI, the use of e-mail was very widespread. E-mail is clearly a dominant aspect of firms' use of the Internet, but it is useful at this point in the discussion to consider the earlier finding regarding the poor quality of e-mail addresses. It seems fair to say that although the firms in our study are largely reliant on electronic communications, there are many examples where the process of managing these communications is rather amateurish, and, specifically, where the organisational infrastructure for managing these systems are underdeveloped. (It is worth noting that in the author's own institution, there are cases of administrators continuing to use e-mail addresses to send and receive messages from accounts labeled after long-departed colleagues; published "contact" e-mail addresses are often personalised; and there are few managerial systems for systematically managing the "filing" of e-mails). Electronic communication—for all its benefits—brings with it a need for an administrative infrastructure, and associated investment and training.

Selling: Use of Web Sites

The use of Internet pages for selling firms varied considerably, with many firms using the

Figure 7. Customer relationships

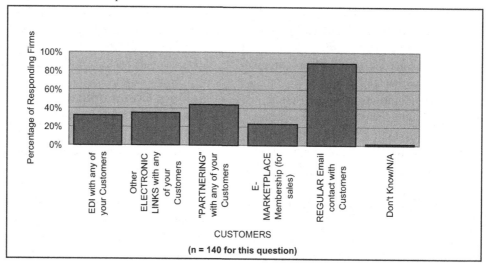

opportunity for both information and handling queries. Far fewer organisations used the Web sites for transactional purposes—and for many the mechanism for handling orders was merely the provision of an e-mail address for the sales department (see Figure 8).

The study highlighted the various roles that the Internet might play in the sales and marketing strategies of supplying firms. Much of the B2B literature presents a very passive role for suppliers—their role reduced to supplying commoditised goods and participating in price-driven auctions, or merely providing the fulfilment of orders placed through online catalogues. In contrast, we found that organisations have various proactive approaches to using the Internet. Our case studies included a small manufacturer of specialist architectural electrical equipment, who made considerable use of the Internet as a marketing intelligence tool—a member of the marketing team systematically trawled the Web for news relating to suitable building projects in key overseas markets. For this firm, the crucial marketing activity was working with the "specifiers" rather than the immediate customers, and to avoid any type of marketing which presented their

products as commodities, or easily comparable to competitors' products. In this case, the use of online catalogues was not at all a priority, as this would be entirely out of step with its relationship marketing philosophy.

Impact on Buyer-Seller Relationships

A key question for B2B e-commerce is its effect on the power balance in supply relationships. Figures 9 and 10 indicate some interesting contradictions in participants' perspectives. ("High" and "Low Impact" here refer to participants' expectation of the impact of the Internet on customer relationships in the next five years. "Don't Knows" and "Not Applicables" are not included on these graphs).

An interesting contrast here is that a large group of respondents expect their suppliers' prices to decline while the prices they charge to customers remain unaffected. This imbalance is also reflected in the way in which firms viewed the likely shifts in power (see Figures 11 and 12).

One interpretation of these data is that there is perhaps an unwarranted degree of optimism—and

Figure 8. Use of websites for selling

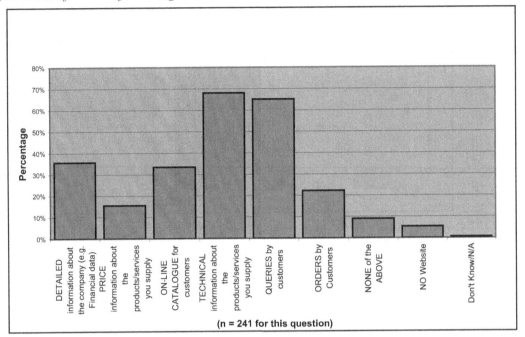

maybe even complacency—in the responding firms. This intriguing and contradictory finding echoes previous findings regarding firms' views regarding the power consequences of supply chain integration and partnership relationships (see Burnes & New, 1996; New, 1998).

CONCLUSION

This chapter has presented some of the data from a multi-method study into the reality of B2B e-commerce. Its general conclusions are to point toward a picture which is considerably at variance to the extraordinary hyperbole generated by the business media, consultants and some academics about the potential impact of B2B.

A key element of this picture is that much of the theorising about the potential impact of B2B has started from an inaccurate and deeply misleading image of a) what organisational buying and selling is like, and b) the degree of sophistication

of much of the supply base. Here, we found firms who were a considerable distance from "supply chain cybermastery" (Berger & Gattorna, 2001) and appeared not to be "surging forward on the crest of the Internet wave" (Friedman & Blanshay, 2001, p. 2) and for whom the reality of B2B relationships are more complex and richly textured than the rather Spartan and highly depersonalised images of the electronic marketplace.

The boom and bust in B2B e-commerce could be accounted for by a number of explanatory stories. Day et al. (2003) focus on the idea of a competitive opportunity attracting many players, many of whom die in the rush. The fact that so many of the e-marketplaces have failed simply reflects brutality of the "land grab." Good ideas attract much interest, and there is not enough gold to go around. An analogy could be that the innovations at the turn of the 20th century that initially encouraged the founding of hundreds of car companies—but only a few can become Ford and GM.

Figure 9. Predicted effects on price changes to customers

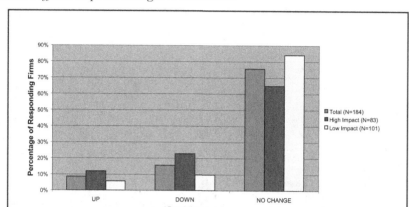

Figure 10. Predicted effect on prices paid to suppliers

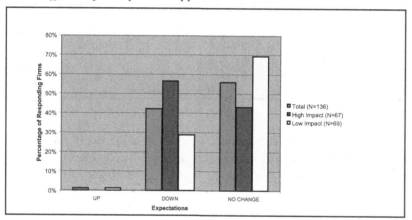

Figure 11. Predicted effect on power position relative to customers

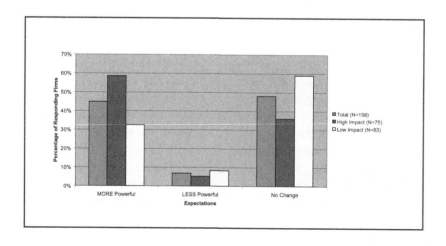

Figure 12. Predicted effect on power position relative to suppliers

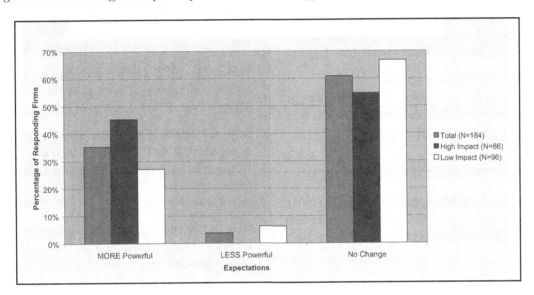

The story that emerges from the research described here is different. It suggests that the B2B hype was based on a fundamental misreading of the nature of inter-organisational buying and selling, and the rush was for fool's gold. Many of the presumptions of the B2B model were not true, and, in consequence, innovators lost a great deal of money. From this wreckage, one might salvage a reminder of the idea that innovators have a duty to understand in detail the nature of the markets into which they wish to enter.

These observations are clearly contingent on the degree to which the data gathered here is representative of other populations. However, the use of the triangulated approach in the broader research project has indicated to us that this line of inquiry is worth continuing.

ACKNOWLEDGMENT

The author would like to acknowledge the significant contributions of Tony Meakin, Ruth Southworth, and Mark Siddall, to this work, and to Achilles Group Ltd for financial assistance.

Earlier versions of this work were presented at the EurOMA conference, Lake Como, in June 2003.

REFERENCES

AT Kearney (2001). *Creating differentiated value networks: How companies can get real value out of e-markets*. Chicago: AT Kearney.

Bakos, J.Y. (1991). A strategic analysis of electronic marketplaces. *MIS Quarterly, 15*(1), 295-310.

Bakos, J.Y. (1998). The emerging role of electronic marketplaces on the Internet. *Communications of the ACM, 41*(8), 35-42.

Barratt, M.A., & Rosdahl, K. (2002). Exploring business-to-business marketsites. *European Journal of Purchasing and Supply Management, 8*(2), 111-122.

Bloch, N., & Catfolis, T. (2001). B2B e-marketplaces: How to succeed. *Business Strategy Review, 12*(3), 20-28.

Berger, A.J., & Gattorna, J.L. (2001). *Supply chain cybermastery*. Aldershot: Gower.

Burnes, B., & New, S. (1996). *Strategic advantage and supply chain collaboration*. London: AT Kearney.

Büyüközkan, G. (2004). A success index to evaluate e-marketplaces. *Production Planning and Control, 15*(7), 761-774.

Casper, C. (2000). B2B exchanges: All buzz, not bite? *Food Logistics, 34*, (September 15), 14.

Day, G.S., Fein, A.J., & Ruppersberger, G. (2003). Shakeouts in digital markets: Lessons from B2B exchanges. *California Management Review, 45*(2), 131-250.

DeMaio, H.B. (2001). *B2B and beyond: New business models built on trust*. New York: Wiley.

Friedman, M., & Blanshay, M. (2001). *Understanding B2B*. Chicago: Dearborn Trade.

Gates, B. (1995). *The road ahead*. London: Viking.

Grubb, A. (2000). *B2B Darwinism: How e-marketplaces survive (and succeed)*. New York: Deloitte Research.

Le, T.T., Rao, S.S., & Truong, D. (2004). Industry-sponsored marketplaces: A platform for supply chain integration or a vehicle for market aggregation? *Electronic Markets, 14*(4), 295-307.

Levaux, J. (2001). B2B exchanges: Will they survive? *World Trade, 14*(3), 32-35.

Malone, T.W., Yates, J., & Benjamin, R. (1987). Electronic markets and electronic hierarchies. *Communications of the ACM, 30*(6), 484-497.

Meakin, A. (2002). *Options and opportunities in business-to-business e-commerce*. Unpublished MEng dissertation, University of Oxford.

New, S.J. (1998). The implications and reality of partnership. In B. Burnes & B. Dale (Eds.), *Working in partnership: Best practice in customer-supplier relationships* (pp. 9-20). Aldershot: Gower.

New, S.J. (2002). *Understanding the e-marketspace: Making sense of B2B*. Saïd Business School, Oxford.

Prigg, M. (2000, December 3). How sharing can change the way business works. *Sunday Times Special Supplement, B2B: Collaborating with Partners in the Digital Economy*, pp. 2-3.

Raisch, W.R. (2001). *The eMarketplace: Strategies for success in B2B eCommerce*. New York: McGraw-Hill.

Ramsdell, G. (2000). The real business of B2B. *McKinsey Quarterly, 3*, 174-185.

Sculley, A.B., & Woods, W.W.A. (1999). *B2B exchanges: The killer application in the business-to-business Internet revolution*. Hamilton, Bermuda: ISI Books.

Timmers, P. (2000). *Electronic commerce: Strategies and models for business-to-business trading*. Chichester, UK: Wiley.

IMPLICATIONS FOR PRACTITIONERS[1]

Title: Innovation and B2B E-Commerce: Explaining What Did Not Happen

Description

B2B E-commerce was expected to change the way buyers and sellers did business. In the face of the dot.com boom, many believed that this would be a fundamental change in business. Many expected that the internet as a disruptive technology would lead to real-time internet-based trading with implications for changes in the nature of buyer-supplier relationships, pricing, and industrial capacity.

This study was undertaken in order to learn the extent to which organizations are prepared to use the Internet for organizational buying and selling.

Findings

- The changes have failed to materialize and there is a disparity between the potential and the realized impact of B2B business.
- The procurement of commodities and other highly standardized products for which price is the supreme variable is grossly overstated. Less than 19% of the products fell in this category.
- A supplier's website is often used for information gathering as opposed to purchasing.
- There is only marginal value in a marketplace system as opposed to a website that would be found with a Google search.
- Only half of the supplying firms had computerized purchasing systems. The same proportion had centralized purchasing systems. Thus the linking of purchasing and supplying systems only exists in a small number of organizations and small firms are not likely to be engaged in this practice.
- While the e-commerce movement hypes the savings in purchasing costs, there is no chance for early demise of purchasing departments. High level sourcing strategies are needed.
- The use of web sites and internet pages for selling firms is primarily for information provision and handling queries. Fewer organizations used the web for transactional sales.
- The study indicated that the impact on buyer-seller relationships was that suppliers would become more powerful, prices paid to suppliers would go down, and that there would be no change in the price charged to customers would remain the same.

RECOMMENDATIONS

- Firms should enter into the e-commerce world with complete data on the markets into which a firm might enter.
- Interorganizational systems should be used cautiously. They typically have high entry fees that may not be recovered.
- The high entry fees may also limit their use by smaller organizations.

CAVEATS

- The study was conducted via email. Interestingly, although they used a database that was a paid membership, a large number of the surveys came back as undeliverable.

ENDNOTE

[1]   Note that this section was written by D. H. Parente, editor of *Best Practices for Online Procurement Auctions*, in order to be consistent with other chapters and provide value to practitioners reading the volume.

Section II.b
The Product

Chapter VIII
Bundling for Online Reverse Auctions:
Approaches and Experiences

Tobias Schoenherr
Eastern Michigan University, USA

Vincent A. Mabert
Indiana University, USA

ABSTRACT

This chapter provides insights into bundling practices for online reverse auctions by exploring approaches and reporting experiences of 252 companies in the U.S. manufacturing industry. Within the context of Parente, Venkataraman, Fizel, and Millet's (2004) conceptual framework for the analysis of online auctions, aspects of the "Product Characteristics" component were explored. Bundling issues investigated include content, goals, structure, and performance. Following the theme of the book, differences and similarities in bundling behavior and outcomes between small and large enterprises are emphasized, highlighting the impact of firm size and the resulting strategies explored. While large corporations are usually on the forefront of information technology adoption and use, the potential is significant for smaller firms as well. As such, this chapter provides managerial insights, useful especially to smaller companies, for successfully employing bundles in reverse auctions.

INTRODUCTION

An important aspect in online reverse auctions is the design/configuration of the order lot that is put up for bid to potential suppliers (Mabert & Skeels, 2002). The order lot can consist of a single stock-keeping unit (SKU), but is most often comprised of several different products and/or services bundled together in a single request for quotation (RFQ) (Schoenherr & Mabert, 2006).

We define this ***bundling*** activity as the aggregation of two or more products (SKUs) and/or services by an industrial buyer into a bundle that is put up for bid to potential suppliers as part of a single RFQ.

The practice of bundling has received some attention in economics (e.g., Adams & Yellen, 1976) and marketing (e.g., Stremersch & Tellis, 2002), but bundling research for the purchasing function in an enterprise has been sparse. Furthermore, while bundling (that is, lotting, combining, and aggregating) is frequently practiced in offline procurement, its criticality is heightened in online bidding events, especially in online reverse auctions used today, due to their usual short duration and constrained environment (Mabert & Schoenherr, 2001; Beall et al., 2003; Schoenherr & Mabert, 2006). Despite the importance of this task, little systematic discussion or evaluation has taken place concerning this practice. Therefore, the objective of this chapter is to provide insight into bundling approaches and experiences gained during online reverse auctions by enterprises, and following the theme of the book, to identify differences and similarities that exist between small and large enterprises in this regard. Past studies have shown that firm size is a particularly influential factor in explaining adoption, implementation, and use of information systems (e.g., Raymond, 1990; Yap, 1990; Mabert, Soni & Venkataramanan, 2003).

Within the context of Parente et al.'s (2004) conceptual framework for the analysis of online auctions, which is based on systems theory, this chapter provides analyses and results about the "Product Characteristics" component, influencing auction dynamics and, ultimately, auction outcomes. Both products and services are considered in this chapter for outside provisioning, and therefore the term "item" is used instead of "product." As such, "item" denotes one purchasable component of a bundle, whether it is a product or a service (cf., Cavinato & Kauffman, 1999). The narrative below not only explores item characteristics, but also the impact that the *combination* of items auctioned off in a single auction event may have.

Specifically, this chapter provides detailed insight about bundle usage in online reverse auctions, including the predominant types of items chosen, the number of items, the spend included in a bundle, the contract length associated with the bundled items, the preparation time to set up the bundle, and what goals are pursued by having items bundled together. In addition, bundle structure in terms of item difficulty (i.e., the degree of complexity the individual items possess, such as highly-engineered components vs. off-the-shelf commodities) and overall bundle complexity (i.e., the degree of homogeneity vs. heterogeneity of the items in the bundle, or a bundle with similar items vs. one with diverse items) will be discussed. The impact of these characteristics on purchase performance, as measured by percent savings achieved, is also assessed. In line with the theme of this book, differences and similarities are discussed, with implications, especially as they relate to small-and-medium-sized enterprises.

To explore these issues in detail, data were collected with a large-scale survey from purchasing professionals in manufacturing, randomly drawn from the membership database of the Institute for Supply Management (ISM). A total of 252 respondents, having indicated using bundles for online reverse auctions, fully completed the questionnaire.

This chapter proceeds as follows. The subsequent section presents an overview of relevant literature in bundling and online auctions, providing background and stressing the need for research in this area. Next, the methodology is described, followed by a discussion of respondent characteristics. The following section then presents the results, which are split into the four subsections of bundle content, bundle goals, bundle structure, and bundle performance. The next section provides a summary of the research findings and managerial insights, with the last providing conclusions.

BACKGROUND

The concept of bundling was first discussed in the field of economics, most notably by the seminal work of Adams and Yellen (1976). Many econometric models have been devised since then, often dealing with optimal bundling policies in auctions, as well as factors influencing the success of a bundle (e.g., McAffee, McMillan, & Whinston, 1989; Avery & Hendershott, 2000). More recently, the marketing discipline has looked at bundling in terms of creating the best product/service combination for sale to consumers (e.g., Stremersch & Tellis, 2002). Related works cross over into the domain of information technology, dealing with the aggregation of information goods (e.g., Bakos & Brynjolfsson, 2000), and the area of ethics and law, discussing consequences of bundling that may include potentially unfair competition (e.g., Rogers, 2001).

Nevertheless, many of these studies focused on offering bundled items to consumers, rather than to other businesses. In addition, bundles were created by the seller, rather than by the buyer as is the case in reverse auctions. Furthermore, the context was usually the offline world, whereas here we are dealing with online auctions. All of this makes bundling for online reverse auctions a compelling research topic.

Based on bundling definitions in marketing (e.g., Stremersch & Tellis, 2002) and finance (e.g., Mizrachi, 2002), as well as case study insight of the authors, bundling is defined as the aggregation of two or more products (SKUs) and/or services by an industrial buyer into a bundle that is put up for bid to potential suppliers as part of a single RFQ in an online reverse auction (cf., Schoenherr & Mabert, 2006). The bundle can include any combination of items, where the term "item" stands for one purchasable component of the bundle, that is, a product or a service. Usually a single overall price needs to be quoted on the order lot, although an additional per-SKU price breakdown may be required by the purchasing firm.

While bundling is frequently done for offline negotiations, its criticality is heightened in online reverse auctions due to their usual short duration and constrained environment. Mabert and Schoenherr (2001) provide the first published account of the importance of bundle composition, and the potential detrimental impact it can have on auction outcome. In their case study, 20% of the bundles did not receive any competitive bids, with follow-up analysis identifying the bundle composition as one main contributor for this result. Other purchasing research confirms this observation. For example, Emiliani (2004) states poor bundle structure as a factor in the decline of online reverse auction usage by major U.S. aerospace companies. However, if bundling is correctly done, it can lead to significant benefits for the buyer. As such, if supplier competencies and synergies in manufacturing or distribution are taken into consideration, and if the potential bundle spend is large enough, the practice of bundling can lead to increased supplier competition and subsequent purchase performance (Jap, 2002; Smeltzer & Carr, 2003). The appropriate bundling strategy, however, requires careful selection because of the potential interdependence of individual lots auctioned during the same time frame (Jap, 2002). Bundling strategies were also discussed by Beall et al. (2003), who stress the consideration of the suppliers' capabilities and market environment. Schoenherr and Mabert (2006) confirm that obtaining valid and relevant information, as well as subsequent cautious analysis, is key in successfully bundling items together. Their study provides an exploratory overview of the current state of bundling practice, based upon 30 case studies. The article furthermore describes conditions, uses, and contents of bundles, and discusses the benefits and challenges of bundling.

With the exception of Schoenherr and Mabert (2006), no published research article was identified that specifically focused on bundling for online reverse auctions. However, due to the small sample size received in the survey by Schoenherr and

Mabert (2006), no sophisticated statistical tests could be applied with confidence; their study is therefore descriptive and exploratory in nature. This chapter reports results from the follow-up study to Schoenherr and Mabert (2006) involving a large-scale survey. The data are split into two company-size groups to investigate similarities and differences between large and small firms to better understand bundling practice.

METHODOLOGY

The questionnaire for the large-scale survey was developed in a structured and systematic way, based on a series of case studies and past literature. The survey started with questions about general issues related to bundling for online reverse auctions. Afterwards, respondents were asked to think about the most recent reverse auction incident in which bundles were used, and with which they were familiar. The following questions then referred back to this focal bundled purchase. Answers to such specific instances tend to be more accurate, compared to responses to general practices (cf., Choi & Hartely, 1996).

Since reverse auctions are most commonly used in the manufacturing industry (e.g., Beall et al., 2003), the focus was on this sector. The Institute for Supply Management (ISM), a major U.S. association for purchasing professionals, provided addresses of members with standard industrial classification (SIC) codes of 2000 through 3900. The survey was administered online, following closely Dillman's (2000) tailored design method. A detailed description of the methodology can be found in Schoenherr (2005).

A total of 252 complete and useable responses were received, which represents an effective response rate of 4.4%. The response rate is rather small, compared to other surveys using ISM members as respondents, but the requirements for participating in the study were quite stringent, eliminating individuals that did not use reverse auctions and that did not practice bundling. However, starting out with a large sample population (a total of 5,671 solicitation e-mails were sent out) assured us the receipt of a large enough number of responses with which reliable statistical analysis could be performed (252 questionnaires). Nonresponse bias was not considered a serious problem in this study, based on several statistical tests (e.g., Armstrong & Overton, 1977).

RESPONDENT CHARACTERISTICS

Most respondents (29%) belong to miscellaneous manufacturing industries (SIC code 390), followed by manufacturers of electric and electronic equipment (13.9%; SIC code 360), and manufacturers of chemicals and allied products (9.5%; SIC code 280). Besides these main groups, a wide variety of manufacturing industries is represented, which comprised 7.5% or fewer per SIC code.

The respondents came from mostly large companies. This is not surprising, since smaller firms are less likely to use reverse auctions (Hartley, Lane, & Hong, 2004). Table 1 presents information about the firms' total annual revenue profile; unfortunately 72 respondents did not respond to this question, leading to 180 records with size information. To obtain some insight about the impact of company size on bundling behavior in online reverse auctions, and especially the potentially different approach that smaller firms may take, which is the focus of this book, the sample with size information (180 records) was split into two groups. As such, this study labels "small and medium size companies" as firms having an annual revenue of $1 billion or below, and "large companies" as above $1 billion. We are aware that this classification is not consistent with the common cutoff value of $50 or $100 million for SMEs. However, given the characteristics of our respondents, especially their distribution in terms of revenue (cf., Table 1), we feel that the higher cutoff value provides more insightful analysis.

Table 1. Total annual revenue of firms

Total Annual Revenue ($)	Frequency*	Percent	Cum. Percent	Classification for Analysis Purposes
100 million and below	14	7.778	7.778	Small and Medium Sized Enterprises
101 million – 500 million	23	12.778	20.556	
501 million – 1 billion	23	12.778	33.333	
1.1 billion – 3 billion	27	15.000	48.333	Large Enterprises
3.1 billion – 10 billion	45	25.000	73.333	
10.1 billion – 100 billion	43	23.889	97.222	
100.1 billion and above	5	2.778	100.000	
*Missing data for 72 respondents				

Subsequent analysis and discussion will report the overall results, as well as any significant differences between the two size groups. When overall numbers are reported, the sample base consists of the 252 received responses. When results for the size groups are reported, the sample base is 180, as discussed above. Unless otherwise stated, to test for significant differences between the two groups, the independent samples t test is used if the variables are measured on ratio or interval scales, the Mann-Whitney U test is used for variables measured on an ordinal scale, and the Pearson chi-square test is used to assess whether the proportions of answer choices across the two groups are the same (cf., Green & Salkind, 2003).

Purchasing authority at responding firms was organized as a hybrid of both centralization and decentralization for almost half of the respondents (49.2%). A pure centralized structure was present in 38.1% of the cases, and a mere 10.3% were a pure decentralized structure. A visual examination of the two size groups via crosstabs shows that SMEs tend to have a more centralized purchasing structure, whereas larger ones have a predominant hybrid organizational context. However, statistically, SMEs and large corporations do not differ in their purchasing authority structure (Pearson chi-square, χ^2 (2, $N = 177$) =

4.336, $p = 0.114$). Respondents had been employed in purchasing for an average of 14.5 years; an independent samples t test detected no significant differences between the two sized groups in this regard ($t(107)=1.795$, $p=0.075$).

The earliest use of reverse auctions among the sample was in January 1998, with most responding companies conducting their first auction events around April 2002. No statistical difference was detected between small and large companies ($t(101)=-1.425$, $p=0.157$). An average of 230 bidding events had been conducted to date, with over half of the respondents having conducted only 25 bid events. This shows that there are a few "super-users" of reverse auctions, but that the majority of firms have limited experience with this sourcing tool. In addition, large companies had significantly more auction experience, having conducted an average of 228 auctions more than their smaller counterparts (76 vs. 304) ($t(165)=-2.284$, $p=0.024$). This was, however, not reflected in a significant difference in mean savings realized, which averaged 19.3% ($t(121)=-1.470$, $p=0.119$).

The significance of research in bundling for online reverse auctions was substantiated by respondents' answers to three statements, to which they had to indicated their degree of agreement on a seven-point Likert scale ranging from "strongly

Table 2. Significance of bundling for reverse auctions

Statement	Overall		SMEs		Large Firms	
	Mean	Std.Dev.	Mean	Std.Dev.	Mean	Std.Dev.
Bundling is important for reverse auctions	4.857	1.618	4.883	1.606	4.883	1.605
The composition of a bundle determines the competitiveness of the auction	5.262	1.630	5.200	1.624	5.333	1.652
Coming up with the best bundle is difficult	4.199	1.640	3.763	1.418	4.342	1.713

Table 3. Term used for the concept of bundling

Term	Overall*		SMEs		Large Firms	
	Frequency	Percent	Frequency	Percent	Frequency	Percent
Putting together a bid package	110	43.7	33	55.0	49	40.8
Bundling	55	21.8	13	21.7	29	24.2
Putting together a market basket	37	14.7	1	1.7	23	19.2
Lotting	36	14.3	10	16.7	12	10.0
Other	14	5.6	3	5.0	7	5.8
* Cumulative frequencies for "Overall" differ from the sum of the frequencies of "SMEs" and "Large Firms," since not all respondents provided company size information (see Table 1).						

disagree" (value=1) to "strongly agree" (value=7). As such, respondents confirmed that the concept of bundling is important for online reverse auctions, that the composition of a bundle clearly determines the competitiveness of the auction, and that coming up with the best bundle for the auction event poses challenges and requires significant consideration. As can be seen from Table 2, all means are above the scales' midpoints. Mann-Whitney U tests only detected a difference in the answers between large and small companies in regards to the last statement (z=-2.200, $p = 0.028$); large corporations agreed more to this point, with an average higher agreement rating of 0.6 on the seven-point scale (3.763 vs. 4.342).

The importance of bundling was also noted when respondents indicated the percentage of online auctions that consist of bundles. As such, an average of 74% of all auctions were for a bundle of items, rather than an individual product. While

SMEs practice bundling in online reverse auctions to a bigger extent than their larger counterparts (79.281% vs. 71.047%), this difference was not confirmed statistically ($t(116)$=1.748, p=0.084).

The concept of bundling has different labels, but all refer to the same idea of aggregating two or more products (SKUs) and/or services into a single lot, which is then put up for bid as a single RFQ. To assess what label is most frequently used, respondents were asked to indicate with what term they refer to the activity under study. Table 3 presents the answer options given and the response frequencies. The term "putting together a bid package" received the most mention, probably because of the online reverse auction context investigated. Differences in term usage across the two different size groups were significant (Pearson chi-square, χ^2 (4, $N = 180$) = 12.561, $p = 0.014$). While both groups use the terms "putting together a bid package" and "bundling" as their first and

Table 4. Number of SKUs in bundle—answer ranges

Range	Frequency*	Percent
1-5	36	16.000
6-10	31	13.778
11-20	41	18.222
21-50	40	17.778
51-200	45	20.000
201-500	20	8.889
> 500	12	5.333
* Numbers do not add up to the total sample size of 252 due to missing values		

Table 5. Predominant type of items in the bundle

Type	Overall*		SMEs		Large Firms	
	Frequency	Percent	Frequency	Percent	Frequency	Percent
Direct (production) material	127	50.397	40	66.667	55	45.833
MRO / indirect material	71	28.175	12	20.000	34	28.333
Services	27	10.714	3	5.000	18	15.000
Capital equipment	14	5.556	3	5.000	6	5.000
Other	13	5.159	2	3.333	7	5.833
* Cumulative frequencies for "Overall" differ from the sum of the frequencies of "SMEs" and "Large Firms, since not all respondents provided company size information (see Table 1).						

second most frequent choice, SMEs favored as a third alternative "lotting," while larger firms used "putting together a market basket."

For the main part of the survey, respondents were requested to focus on one particular bundle in the most recent online reverse auction event, rather than answering based on their collected experience. The goal was to elicit a wide range of purchases and bundling approaches that are still fresh in the minds of the respondents. The next section provides detailed insight about this focal bundled purchase.

RESULTS

Bundle Content

The focal bundle contained an average of 269 different SKUs on which potential suppliers had to submit bids; however, over half of the respondents' bundles contained less than 50 SKUs (Table 4). No significant differences between the two size groups were recorded ($t(160)=-1.611$, $p=0.109$).

Predominantly direct material was auctioned, followed by indirect or MRO-type items (Table 5).

Table 6. Most frequent examples mentioned

Description	Frequency	Percent
Packaging material	27	10.714
Fasteners	9	3.571
Electronic components	8	3.175
Office supplies	7	2.778
Chemicals	6	2.381
Janitorial supplies	5	1.984
Automotive components	4	1.587
Bearings	4	1.587
Machined parts	3	1.000

Table 7. Spend of the bundle—answer ranges

Range	Frequency*	Percent
$100,000 and below	19	8.482
$100,001 - $250,000	22	9.821
$250,001 - $500,000	23	10.268
$500,001 - $1,000,000	38	16.964
$1,000,001 - $2,000,000	38	16.964
$2,000,001 - $5,000,000	35	15.625
$5,000,001 - $10,000,000	23	10.268
$10,000,001 - $50,000,000	24	10.714
$50,000,001 and above	2	0.893
* Numbers do not add up to the total sample size of 252 due to missing values.		

Smaller firms use auctions proportionally more for direct material than their larger counterparts, but fewer indirect items. Furthermore, services comprise a greater percentage for the larger firms, in contrast to the SMEs. However, a difference test did not detect statistically significant differentiation between the two size groups (Pearson chi-square, χ^2 (4, $N = 180$) = 8.305, $p = 0.081$). In addition to this classification, respondents had to verbally describe the items in the bundle. Table 6 provides a summary of the most frequently mentioned items.

The spend of the bundle ranged from $5,000 to $130 million, and averaged around $5.4 million;

differences between the two size groups were not significant ($t(131)=-1.007, p=0.316$). A breakdown is provided in Table 7. Most of the time it was a repeat buy of the material via online auctions (86.9%), which turned out to be independent of company size (Pearson chi-square, χ^2 (1, $N = 176$) = 0.439, $p = 0.508$). Savings for the focal bundled purchase averaged 16.7% compared to the prior purchase of the bundle for repeat events, which is lower than the percentage saved in general during first-time auction events (19.3%) reported above. The focal bundle described was thus less successful on average, in terms of savings achieved, than the overall experience of the respondents.

While SMEs and large firms did not differ in their answers to the general savings achieved, the percentage provided differed significantly for the particular focal bundled purchase; smaller firms achieved on average 4.7% less savings than bigger companies ($t(158)=-2.617$, $p=0.010$). Savings for the group of SMEs in our study were 13.285%, whereas larger firms reported savings of 18.046% on average for the focal purchase.

For 9.5% of the bid events, the purchase was a one-time buy with immediate fulfillment; company size did not impact this result (Pearson chi-square, χ^2 (1, $N = 174$) = 0.084, $p = 0.773$). In all other instances a multi-month contract was the outcome. The most frequently employed contract period was three years (31.4%), followed by two-year (29.5%) and one-year (26.8%) arrangements. Comparing these three most-frequently mentioned options, the two size groups showed no significant differences (Pearson chi-square, χ^2 (2, $N = 135$) = 3.217, $p = 0.200$). In 5.2% of the cases the duration of the contract was longer than three years.

It took the buyer around six weeks to prepare the bundle and put together the auction event; the two company size groups do not differ in this regard ($t(164)=-1.091$, $p=0.277$).

Bundle Goals

Bundling is done for a reason, with specific objectives targeted when creating the order lot. Just by looking at the significant preparation time of six weeks for a bundle lets one suspect that this effort is not expended without a good rationale behind it. Case study research led to the identification of key motivators why bundling may be practiced. These were presented to survey respondents, who indicated their degree of agreement on a seven-point Likert scale ranging from "strongly disagree" (value=1) to "strongly agree" (value=7). In order to identify common themes, factor analysis (Principal Components, Varimax Rotation with Kaiser Normalization) was performed with the answers. Four one-dimensional

Table 8. Factor analysis results

Goal Statement	Mean	Standard Deviation	Long-Term α=0.731	Efficiency α=0.707	Price α=0.694	Cherry-Picking α=0.796
Securing of supply	4.484	1.436	**0.771**	0.063	0.089	0.082
Having the least possible risk in sourcing the bundle	4.555	1.513	**0.710**	0.158	0.251	0.094
Having a collaborative buyer-supplier relationship	4.577	1.520	**0.698**	0.433	0.055	0.011
Finding new supplier(s)	3.675	1.595	**0.627**	0.091	-0.037	0.192
Supply base consolidation	4.799	1.816	0.058	**0.818**	0.119	0.184
A resulting simpler purchasing environment	4.574	1.536	0.267	**0.818**	0.022	0.101
More efficient purchasing	5.534	1.364	0.315	**0.538**	0.451	0.110
Achieving the best price possible	6.269	0.994	-0.078	0.134	**0.868**	0.077
Making the bidding as competitive as possible	5.947	1.223	0.278	0.039	**0.834**	0.017
Combining attractive and unattractive items in the bundle	4.267	1.744	0.121	0.086	0.019	**0.912**
Avoiding "cherry-picking"	4.882	1.653	0.177	0.213	0.105	**0.846**

factors were identified, explaining 69.3% of the variance. Factor loadings are presented in Table 8, together with means and standard deviations of the goal statements.

The first factor, which we label *Long-Term*, is composed of goal statements related to ensuring the long-term sustainability and securing of supply. Risk is minimized when a collaborative buyer-supplier relationship is a goal. In addition, the long-term orientation is supported by locating alternate sources of supply. Statements loading on the second factor, *Efficiency*, are concerned with making the sourcing environment simpler and more efficient, which can be achieved via supply base consolidation. The third factor, labeled *Price*, represents goals that are aimed for the creation of a competitive environment in which the best possible price can be achieved. The two items loading on the fourth factor, *Cherry-Picking*, are concerned with designing bundles that combine both attractive and unattractive items, to encourage suppliers to also submit competitive bids on the less desirable products and/or services in the bundle.

The validity of the constructs is supported by content validity, unidimensionality, and reliability. Content validity was achieved by developing from and thus grounding the goal statements in case study research. Unidimensionality was accomplished by the exploratory factor analysis above, resulting in four unique factors. Reliability was confirmed by Cronbach alpha, values of which range from 0.694 to 0.796 (Table 8).

Table 9 shows means, standard deviations, and correlations among the constructs. *Price* is the highest rated goal among our respondents, followed by *Efficiency, Cherry-Picking,* and *Long-Term*. The goals are highly correlated with each other ($p < 0.01$), with only *Price* and *Cherry-Picking* showing a moderate correlation ($p < 0.05$).

Due to the significant correlations, multivariate analysis of variance (MANOVA) was selected to examine the impact of firm size on the four different goal orientation constructs, similar to the approach taken by Hartley et al. (2004). The model was not significant (Wilks' Λ: 0.975; $F(4, 166)=1.067, p = 0.374$), indicating that SMEs and

Table 9. Correlation matrix for goal constructs

Construct	Mean	Std. Dev.	Long Term	Efficiency	Price
Long Term	4.322	1.127			
Efficiency	4.966	1.261	0.508**		
Price	6.104	0.977	0.270**	0.335**	
Cherry-Picking	4.571	1.550	0.316**	0.356**	0.150*
** $p < 0.01$; * $p < 0.05$					

Table 10. ANOVA results comparing SMEs and large firms

Construct	Mean		F-statistic	p-value
	SMEs	Large Firms		
Long Term	4.267	4.324	0.095	0.759
Efficiency	4.684	5.077	3.847	0.052
Price	6.025	6.185	1.075	0.301
Cherry-Picking	4.552	4.606	0.049	0.824

large firms do not differ in regard to the goals they are pursuing when bundling for online reverse auctions. Follow-up analysis was conducted with univariate analyses of variance (ANOVAs), using a p-value of 0.0125 (0.05 / 4 dependent variables). Table 10 presents the means for the two groups, as well as the corresponding F-statistics and p-values. While larger firms consistently agree more with the four goals than their smaller counterparts, especially for *Efficiency, Long-Term,* and *Price,* this difference is not statistically significant.

Bundle Structure

The difficulty or complexity of a product and/or service can impact industrial buying in general (Fisher, 1976; Lilien & Wong, 1984) and online reverse auction outcome specifically (Parente et al., 2004). Therefore, it is worth looking at the bundle structure in online auction events. In this exploratory study, bundle structure is examined in terms of individual item specification difficulty (i.e., the degree of complexity the individual items possess, such as highly-engineered components vs. off-the-shelf commodities) and overall bundle composition complexity (i.e., the degree of homogeneity vs. heterogeneity of the items in the bundle, as in a bundle with similar items vs. one with diverse items).

Individual item specification difficulty describes how challenging the individual items in the bundle are to specify for the RFQ. This aspect was included for the following reasons. First, Parente et al. (2004) suggested that the degree of item customization influences the outcome of an online auction. This is especially true in the context of bundling, since individual items with higher specification difficulty can be more difficult to bundle together with other products. And second, Mabert and Skeels (2002) cautioned that unclear or imprecise specifications can lead to an unsatisfactory auction outcome; more complex and difficult items usually possess specifications that are harder to quantify.

Bundle structure can also be described in terms of how the individual items are combined with each other, which is referred to here as overall bundle composition complexity. This aspect describes how complex the overall bundle is, and is considered for the following reasons. First, Mabert and Skeels (2002) and Schoenherr and Mabert (2006) suggested that when the individual items are very different from each other, or a wide variety of capabilities is needed to produce them, the

Table 11. Individual item specification difficulty characteristics

Characteristic	Overall		SMEs		Large Firms	
	Mean	Std.Dev.	Mean	Std.Dev.	Mean	Std.Dev.
Complex	3.857	1.662	3.810	1.605	3.821	1.633
Technical	4.004	1.693	3.898	1.739	4.136	1.627
Easy specifications *(reverse coded)*	3.650	1.624	3.746	1.657	3.638	1.639
Low engineering content *(reverse coded)*	3.704	1.830	3.821	1.759	3.681	1.844
Unique	3.645	1.716	3.672	1.721	3.624	1.721
Custom-designed	3.895	1.966	4.085	1.985	3.812	1.982

Table 12. Overall bundle composition complexity characteristics

Characteristic	Overall		SMEs		Large Firms	
	Mean	Std.Dev.	Mean	Std.Dev.	Mean	Std.Dev.
It was difficult for suppliers to provide all items *(reverse coded)*	2.944	1.713	2.424	1.303	3.195	1.873
The bundle was composed of similar items	2.476	1.521	2.367	1.551	2.496	1.556
Suppliers had the necessary production capabilities to produce the items	2.458	1.467	2.390	1.462	2.429	1.406
The bundle's volume did not place strain on suppliers' capacities	2.474	1.440	2.356	1.323	2.487	1.449
The manufacturing processes for the items were similar	2.585	1.473	2.600	1.597	2.552	1.447
The items in the bundle were from the same product family	2.345	1.527	2.450	1.682	2.297	1.521
The items in the bundle had similar application(s)	2.448	1.505	2.283	1.485	2.429	1.565

bundle is less attractive to suppliers. And second, the diversity or heterogeneity of items combined together in the bundle can also determine how many suppliers are able and willing to bid on the bundle; when the individual items are very different, or a wide variety of capabilities is needed to produce them, the number of available suppliers willing to bid is likely to be lower.

To assess these two aspects, several measurement items were developed based on scales and insights found in Heide and John (1988), Mabert and Skeels (2002), Beall et al. (2003), and Schoenherr and Mabert (2006). Respondents were asked to indicate their degree of agreement with descriptors of the individual items in the bundle, as well as the bundle overall, on a seven-point Likert scale, ranging from "strongly disagree" (value=1) to "strongly agree" (value=7). These measurement item means and standard deviations for the overall sample, the SME sample and the large firm sample are presented in Tables 11 and 12.

Mann-Whitney U tests were conducted to find differences between the two firm-size groups along the above characteristics. The only significant difference was detected in regards to the characteristic "it was difficult for suppliers to provide all items" ($z=-2.390, p=0.017$); large firms

agreed with this characteristic significantly more than their smaller counterparts (2.424 vs. 3.195). All other characteristics were not significantly different across the two groups.

Bundle Performance

A key supplier performance measure, besides reliable delivery and quality, is the cost for the items, or the purchase price (e.g., Millet, Parente, Fizel, & Venkatraman, 2004). The proliferation of online reverse auctions was primarily aided by the often significant purchase price savings that could be obtained. These savings can be directly influenced by the bundle characteristics (Mabert and Schoenherr, 2001). Our survey respondents confirm this by indicating high agreement on the statement that the bundle determines the competitiveness of the auction (Table 2). Therefore, the percent saved compared to the most recent purchase of the bundled products represents a measure of bundle performance.

To investigate what influences bundle performance, a stepwise regression analysis on percent savings achieved in the focal auction event was conducted. Independent variables included the number of SKUs in the bundle, the predominant item type, the spend, the contract length, the preparation time for the bundle, purchase authority structure, all goal statements, all individual item specification difficulty statements, all overall bundle composition complexity statements, as well as the firm size group variable. These variables were allowed to enter the model when the probability level of their F value was less than 0.05; variables were removed once this value exceeded 0.10. The final model includes the firm size group variable ($\beta = 0.255$; $p = 0.005$), the contract length ($\beta = 0.234$; $p = 0.010$), and the number of SKUs ($\beta = -0.254$; $p = 0.006$). Altogether this model is able to explain 13.236% of the variance in the percent savings achieved. As such, in order to achieve higher savings, purchasing professionals should extend the contract length and minimize the number of different items included in the bundle. In addition, the regression results show that larger firms are usually more successful in obtaining higher savings.

SUMMARY AND MANAGERIAL INSIGHTS

The above analysis highlighted some of the main differences between large firms and SMEs on a variety of aspects related to bundles in B2B online reverse auctions. This section summarizes these issues, as well as discusses managerial insights that can be gained. First, general observations:

- No statistically significant difference was found between the first use of auctions by large firms versus SMEs. While larger firms had conducted more auction events to date than their smaller counterparts, similar savings were achieved on average for the two size groups. This indicates that smaller firms have sufficient experience and are capable of achieving similar savings on average, when compared to larger corporations. This should serve to encourage SMEs, who have

not used reverse auctions for their purchasing activities, to consider this tool. Please note that this observation refers to the average experience of firms since their first use of the online tool, and not to the most recent auction event experience, which is discussed in later paragraphs. As will be seen, firm size *does* impact savings when considering the most recent auction event.

- Larger firms, when compared to their smaller counterparts, confirmed to a greater degree that coming up with the best bundle for the auction event poses challenges and requires significant consideration. Larger companies may find bundling more challenging since they may have to satisfy more internal and external stakeholders, their purchasing situations may be more complex, or because bundle information may be more difficult to gather from many constituents in the large enterprise.

- An average of 74% of all auctions conducted by the respondents were for a bundle, rather than a single product or service. When split by size, smaller firms used bundles to a greater extent (79.3% of all auction events) than the larger companies (71.1% of all auction events). A reason for this can be that smaller companies need to combine more spend in a bundle to receive more competitive prices, whereas larger firms already have the necessary clout by their mere name and reputation, or are simply able to achieve a considerable spend with a significant volume for just a single item. This confirms case study findings by Schoenherr and Mabert (2006) who found that increased leverage is a primary motivator for bundling. It must be noted though that, while a visual comparison indicated such distinction, the difference test in this study was not statistically significant. More focused future research on online auction use by SMEs needs to bring light into this area.

The following bullet points summarize the insight gained by the analysis of the answers given to the focal bundled purchases (a bundle is the most recent online reverse auction) the respondents were asked to think about.

- Regression analysis detected a significant relationship between the number of SKUs included and the percent saved, with bundles containing fewer items achieving higher savings. This represents a tradeoff between higher efficiencies gained by bundling several items together and the resulting potential for purchase price savings; efficiencies achieved by bundling more items together may outweigh a possible loss in savings.

- Direct material was most often sourced in the auction, followed by indirect material and services; statistical differences between the size groups were significant. Smaller firms put up for bid more direct material, but less indirect material and service requests, compared to their larger counterparts. Smaller firms are usually not able to bundle as much indirect material together as their larger competitors, due to their smaller scale of operations. Most often, direct materials represent the biggest spend areas for smaller companies, making this material group a feasible candidate to bundle together for a more competitive environment. As Schoenherr and Mabert (2006) noted, an insignificant purchase spend can be a factor impeding the use of online auctions. Therefore, smaller firms source indirect materials and services, for which similar arguments can be made, via traditional sourcing methods, rather than via online auctions, since the spend would not be large enough for a reverse auction. SMEs should thus focus on material that can be easily bundled together for a large spend, which will be direct material in most cases. Follow-up analysis with the spend included in the bundle expressed as a percentage of total revenue confirmed this conclusion.

- In contrast to the average savings reported in online auctions, savings for the particular focal bundled purchase differed with firm size, with larger firms being able to obtain almost five percentage points more than smaller enterprises. This may result from bigger companies usually possessing larger clout and bargaining power, increasing the willingness of suppliers to make greater concessions. Case study insight by the authors confirms this reasoning, indicating that new suppliers are willing to reduce the price even more for reputable large companies to "get a foot in the door" for more future business. Future research should investigate the stated observation of firm size on the one hand impacting savings in the focal bundled reverse auction event, but on the other hand *not* influencing average savings over the usage time horizon.

- Preparation time for the bundle (six weeks on average) and contract length (most frequently three years) did not differ across large and small firms. Larger available resources for bigger firms apparently do not add to the speed with which a bundle can be prepared; the same careful planning needs to be undertaken. Similarly, smaller firms are not disadvantaged when it comes to the average contract length for the bundled items.

- A variety of bundling goals were identified by respondents, with price-related aspects receiving the highest agreement. Other goal statements were grouped into the themes *Cherry-Picking, Efficiency*, and *Long-Term* orientation/risk minimization. Bigger firms consistently agree more with the four goals than smaller companies, especially for *Efficiency*. Although not statistically different, this observation suggests that larger firms tend to have more goal orientation than their smaller counterparts, and pursue their goals more specifically.

- Firm size did not impact individual item specification difficulty and overall bundle composition complexity, except for the characteristic "it was difficult for suppliers to provide all items," which received higher agreement from larger companies (again, a further reason why bigger firms find bundling more challenging). Overall, the characteristics of the individual items included in the bundle, as well as the way they are combined with each other, does not differ across large and small firms. A visual comparison of the means also did not lead to any pattern, letting one conclude that, in general, the bundle structure created by small and large firms does not differ in terms of these two characteristic themes.

- Bundle performance, as measured by savings achieved in the auction event, is influenced by firm size, contract length, and number of SKUs. It is not impacted by the predominant item type, the spend, the preparation time for the bundle, purchase authority structure, the goal statements, the individual item specification difficulty statements, and the overall bundle composition complexity statements. While these latter aspects are important, greater emphasis should be placed on the former. The longer the contract length and the smaller the number of SKUs included in the bundle, the more savings can be achieved. These two aspects should therefore be carefully assessed and determined. It was again confirmed that firm size impacts the percent savings, with larger corporations achieving higher savings, as discussed above.

CONCLUSION

This chapter provided insights into bundling practices for online reverse auctions by exploring approaches and reporting experiences of 252 companies in the U.S. manufacturing industry. Within the context of Parente et al.'s (2004) conceptual framework for the analysis of online auctions, aspects of the "Product Characteristics" component were investigated. Following the theme of this book, differences and similarities between small and large enterprises were emphasized. The chapter presented detailed analyses of bundle usage for online reverse auctions, including the predominant types of items chosen, the number of items and the spend included in a bundle, the contract length associated with the bundled items, the preparation time to set up the bundle, and what goals are pursued by having items bundled together. Furthermore, bundle structure in terms of item difficulty and overall bundle complexity were conferred, and their impact on purchase performance was assessed. Differences between small and large firms were highlighted and discussed.

As with all research, this study has limitations. It was noted that the entire sample was comprised of primarily larger firms. The skewed distribution suggests that mostly larger corporations have adopted online reverse auctions so far, or at least at the time of the survey, which was conducted during fall 2004. This pattern of B2B online auction users is consistent with Beall et al.'s (2003) findings. However, in order to provide some insight for smaller firms (at least relative to our sample), and derive insights for true SMEs, two logical groups were formed. The revenue cutoff point for inclusion in the group of smaller and medium-sized firms was much higher than in other studies, and higher than many commonly-accepted cutoff points, such as $100 million or less (Beall et al., 2003). However, if the $100 million cut point was used, only 7.8% of the respondents would fall in this category, making a group-wise comparison unreliable. Future studies should therefore look at true SMEs, especially as their use of the online reverse auction tool increases, and investigate how they are approaching the bundling decision. The results reported here provide a starting point for further exploration.

FUTURE RESEARCH DIRECTIONS

Exciting opportunities for future research exist. First, as noted above, the sample in this study consisted of primarily large companies. A more focused investigation into how SMEs are using bundles, and adopting and implementing reverse auctions is therefore needed. This effort should start with detailed case studies to identify common themes. It can then be followed up with a large-scale survey targeted specifically at SMEs that have implemented reverse auctions. Since the present study was conducted, many more SMEs have adopted this new bidding tool, and obtaining a large SME sample should therefore be attainable.

Second, advanced bundling practices are emerging. For example, Mars implemented combinatorial and quantity discount auctions (Hohner et al., 2003), and Proctor & Gamble used an approach called expressive competition (Sandholm et al., 2006). Part of these new methods is the possibility for suppliers to create their own preferred bundles, taking into consideration their capacities and capabilities. The resulting bundles should thus be more competitive than the buyer-generated lots that were the norm in the past and also the focus of this study. Advanced algorithms can then determine, among the potentially numerous different bundles submitted by suppliers, which proposed item combination is the most beneficial for the buyer. In addition, new methodologies allow for the incorporation of non-price aspects, such as quality, delivery and service performance of the supplier. This fact should make reverse auctions a viable tool for many more buyers, especially for those that have been reluctant to use the reverse bidding approach since it focused only on price.

And third, research is needed concerning the implementation of reverse auction results. While the savings achieved in bidding events can be quite high compared to offline procurement, it needs to be examined whether these saving can also be realized over the long run, and what hap-pens upon implementation of the contract. For example, a supplier could offer low pricing in a reverse auction to get the business of the buyer, and then later on, once the buyer is committed to the relationship, increase its prices. Similarly, suppliers could charge additional fees for services that may have been included for free in the past, or the quality could suffer. This can especially be the case when suppliers were forced to bid on bundled items that did not really match their competencies (in all-or-nothing bids). They possibly overcommitted themselves or fell victim to the "winner's curse." All these could be potential retaliatory actions by the supplier in response to having been "forced" to such a low price. Therefore, future research should investigate the satisfaction of the buyer with reverse auction results over the long-run. It will also be insightful to explore whether buyers then decide to conduct second-round auctions with the same items, once the current contract expires, or whether they went back to traditional sourcing.

REFERENCES

Adams, W. J., & Yellen, J. L. (1976). Commodity bundling and the burden of monopoly. *The Quarterly Journal of Economics, 90*(3), 475-498.

Armstrong, J. S., & Overton, T. S. (1977). Estimating nonresponse bias in mail surveys. *Journal of Marketing Research, 14*(3), 396-402.

Avery, C., & Hendershott, T. (2000). Bundling and optimal auctions of multiple products. *Review of Economic Studies, 67*(3), 483-497.

Bakos, Y., & Brynjolfsson, E. (2000). Bundling and competition on the Internet. *Marketing Science, 19*(1), 63-82.

Beall, S., Carter, C., Carter, P. L., Germer, T., Hendrick, T., Jap, S., et al. (2003). *The role of reverse auctions in strategic sourcing* (Focus Study). Tempe, Arizona: CAPS Research.

Cavinato, J. L., & Kauffman, R. G. (Eds.). (1999). *The purchasing handbook* (6th ed.). New York: McGraw-Hill.

Choi, T. Y., & Hartley, J. L. (1996). An exploration of supplier selection practices across the supply chain. *Journal of Operations Management, 14*(4), 333-343.

Dillman, D. A. (2000). *Mail and Internet surveys: The tailored design method* (2nd ed.). New York: Wiley & Sons.

Emiliani, M. L. (2004). Sourcing in the global aerospace supply chain using online reverse auctions. *Industrial Marketing Management, 33*(1), 65-72.

Fisher, L. (1976). *Industrial marketing: An analytical approach to planning and execution.* London: Business Books Limited.

Green, S. B., & Salkind, N. J. (2003). *Using SPSS for Windows and Macintosh.* Upper Saddle River, NJ: Prentice Hall.

Hartley, J. L., Lane, M. D., & Hong, Y. (2004). An exploration of the adoption of e-auctions in supply management. *IEEE Transactions on Engineering Management, 51*(2), 153-161.

Heide, J. B., & John, G. (1998). The role of dependence balancing in safeguarding transaction-specific assets in conventional channels. *Journal of Marketing, 52*(1), 20-35.

Hohner, G., Rich, J., Ng, E., Reid, G., Davenport, A. J., Kalagnanam, J. R., et al. (2003). Combinatorial and quantity-discount procurement auctions benefit Mars, Incorporated and its suppliers. *Interfaces, 33*(1), 23-35.

Jap, S. D. (2002). Online reverse auctions: Issues, themes, and prospects for the future. *Journal of the Academy of Marketing Science, 30*(4), 506-525.

Lilien, G., & Wong, M. A. (1984). An exploratory investigation of the structure of the buying center

in the metalworking industry. *Journal of Marketing Research, 21*(1), 1-11.

Mabert, V. A., & Schoenherr, T. (2001). An online RFQ system: A case study. *PRACTIX—Best Practices in Purchasing/Supply Chain, 4*(2), 1-6.

Mabert, V. A., & Skeels, J. A. (2002). Internet reverse auctions: Valuable tool in experienced hands. *Business Horizons, 45*(4), 70-76.

Mabert, V. A., Soni, A. K., & Venkataramanan, M. A. (2003). The impact of organization size on enterprise resource planning (ERP) implementations in the US manufacturing sector. *Omega, 31*(3), 235-246.

McAfee, R. P., McMillan, J., & Whinston, M. D. (1989). Multiproduct monopoly, commodity bundling, and correlation of values. *The Quarterly Journal of Economics, 104*(2), 371-383.

Millet, I., Parente, D. H., Fizel, J. L., & Venkatraman, R. R. (2004). Metrics for managing online procurement auctions. *Interfaces, 34*(3), 171-179.

Mizrachi, J. (2002). Focusing on "bundling" and "IRS" (no, not that IRS) in real estate transactions. *The Real Estate Finance Journal, 17*(3), 13-17.

Parente, D. H., Venkataraman, R., Fizel J., & Millet, I. (2004). A conceptual research framework for analyzing online auctions in a B2B environment. *Supply Chain Management: An International Journal, 9*(4), 287-294.

Raymond L. (1990). Organization context and information systems success: A contingency approach. *Journal of Management Information Systems, 6*(4), 5-20.

Rogers, D. L. (2001). The future of software bundling after United States v. Microsoft. *Intellectual Property and Technology Law Journal, 13*(12), 1-11.

Sandholm, T., Levine, D., Concordia, M., Martyn, P., Hughes, R., Jacobs, J., et al. (2006). Changing the game in strategic sourcing at Procter & Gamble: Expressive competition enabled by optimization. *Interfaces, 36*(1), 55-68.

Schoenherr, T. (2005). *An exploratory study of bundling in B2B online procurement auctions.* Doctoral dissertation, Indiana University, Indiana.

Schoenherr, T., & Mabert, V. A. (2006). Bundling for B2B procurement: Current state and best practices. *International Journal of Integrated Supply Management, 2*(3), 189-213.

Smeltzer, L. R., & Carr, A.S. (2003). Electronic reverse auctions: Promises, risks, and conditions for success. *Industrial Marketing Management, 32*(6), 481-488.

Stremersch, S., & Tellis, G. J. (2002). Strategic bundling of products and prices: A new synthesis for marketing. *Journal of Marketing, 66*(1), 55-72.

Yap C. S. (1990). Distinguishing characteristics of organizations using computers. *Information and Management, 18*(2), 97-107.

ADDITIONAL READING

Bendoly, E., & Schoenherr, T. (2005). ERP system- and implementation-benefits: Implications for B2B e-procurement. *International Journal of Operations and Production Management, 25*(4), 304-319.

Carter, C. R., Kaufmann, L., Beall, S., Carter, P. L., Hendrick, T. E., & Petersen, K. J. (2004). Reverse auctions grounded theory from the buyer and supplier perspective. *Transportation Research Part E, 40*(3), 229-254.

Daly, S. P., & Nath, P. (2005). Reverse auctions for relationship marketers. *Industrial Marketing Management, 34*(2), 157-166.

Hartley, J. L., Duplaga, E. A., & Lane, M. D. (2005). Reverse e-auctions: Exploring reasons for use and buyer's satisfaction. *International Journal of Integrated Supply Management, 1*(4), 410-420.

Hartley, J. L., Lane, M. D., & Duplaga, E. A. (2006). Exploring the barriers to the adoption of e-auctions for sourcing. *International Journal of Operations and Production Management, 26*(2), 202-221.

Hur, D., Hartley, J. L., & Mabert, V. A. (2006). Implementing reverse e-auctions: A learning process. *Business Horizons, 49*(1), 21-29.

Hur, D., Mabert, V. A., & Hartley, J. L. (2007). Getting the most out of reverse e-auction investment. *Omega, 35*(4), 403-416.

Jap, S. D. (2000). Going, going, gone. *Harvard Business Review, 78*(6), 30.

Jap, S. D. (2003). An exploratory study of the introduction of online reverse auctions. *Journal of Marketing, 67*(3), 96-107.

Jap, S. D. (2007). The impact of online reverse auction design on buyer-supplier relationships. *Journal of Marketing, 71*(1), 146-159.

Kaufmann, L., & Carter, C. R. (2004). Deciding on the mode of negotiation: To auction or not to auction electronically. *Journal of Supply Chain Management, 40*(2), 15-26

Kinney, S. (2000). RIP fixed pricing: The Internet is on its way to "marketizing" everything. *Business Economics, 35*(20), 39-44.

Mabert, V. A., & Schoenherr, T. (2001). Evolution of online auctions in B2B e-procurement. *PRACTIX—Best Practices in Purchasing/Supply Chain, 5*(1), 15-19.

Min, H., & Galle, W. P. (2003). E-purchasing: Profiles of adopters and nonadopters. *Industrial Marketing Management, 32*(3), 227-233.

Pearcy, D. H., & Giunipero, L. C. (2006) The impact of electronic reverse auctions on purchase price reduction and governance structure: An empirical investigation. *International Journal of Services Technology and Management, 7*(3), 215-236.

Pearcy, D. H., Giunipero, L. C., & Wilson, A. (2007). A model of relational governance in reverse auctions. *Journal of Supply Chain Management, 43*(1), 4-15.

Sahay, B. S., Mohan, R., & Sachan, A. (2006). E-procurement: Systems and implementation. *International Journal of Services Technology and Management, 7*(5/6), 490-511.

Schoenherr, T. (2004). Deciding on the appropriateness of B2B reverse auction technology: An AHP approach combined with integer programming. *Journal of International Technology and Information Management, 13*(1/2), 21-32.

Schoenherr, T. (2007). *Diffusion of online reverse auctions for B2B procurement.* Working paper, Eastern Michigan University.

Schoenherr, T., & Mabert, V. A. (2003). A conceptual study of developments in B2B reverse online auctions: The changing role of the online auction provider/intermediary. In A. Chikan (Ed.), *Advances in Purchasing and Supply Chain Management, 4.* IFPSM Publications.

Schoenherr, T., & Mabert, V. A. (2007). Online reverse auctions: Common myths versus evolving reality. *Business Horizons, 50*(5), 373-384.

Schoenherr, T., & Mabert, V. A. (2007). *The current state of B2B online reverse auctions.* Working paper, Eastern Michigan University.

Schoenherr, T., & Mabert, V. A. (2007). The effect of buyer-imposed bidding requirements and bundle structure on purchase performance. *The Journal of Supply Chain Management: A Global Review of Purchasing and Supply, 43*(3), 27-39.

Schoenherr, T., & Mabert, V. A. (in press). The use of bundling in B2B online reverse auctions. *Journal of Operations Management.*

Schrader, R. W., Schrader, J. T., & Eller, E. P. (2004). Strategic implications of reverse auctions. *Journal of Business to Business Marketing, 11*(1/2), 61-82.

Smart, A., & Harrison, A. (2003). Online reverse auctions and their role in buyer-supplier relationships. *Journal of Purchasing and Supply Management, 9*(5/6), 257–268.

Smeltzer, L. R., & Carr, A. (2002). Reverse auctions in industrial marketing and buying. *Business Horizons, 45*(2), 47-52.

Talluri, S., & Ragatz, G. L. (2004). Multi-attribute reverse auctions in B2B exchanges: A framework for design and implementation. *Journal of Supply Chain Management, 40*(1), 52-60.

Tassabehji, R., Taylor, W. A., Beach, R., & Wood, A. (2006). Reverse e-auctions and supplier-buyer relationships: An exploratory study. *International Journal of Operations and Production Management, 16*(2), 166-184.

Van Tulder, R., & Mol, M. (2002). Reverse auctions or auctions reversed: First experiments by Philips. *European Management Journal, 20*(5), 447-456.

Wagner, S. M., & Schwab, A. P. (2004). Setting the stage for successful reverse auctions. *Journal of Purchasing and Supply Management, 10*(1), 11-26.

IMPLICATIONS FOR PRACTITIONERS

Title: Bundling for Online Reverse Auctions: Approaches and Experiences

Short Description

This chapter provides insights into bundling practices for online reverse auctions by exploring approaches and reporting experiences of 252 companies in the U.S. manufacturing industry. Within the context of Parente et al.'s (2004) conceptual framework for the analysis of online auctions, aspects of the "Product Characteristics" component were explored. Bundling issues investigated include content, goals, structure, and performance.

Following the theme of the book, differences and similarities in bundling behavior and outcomes between small and large enterprises are emphasized, highlighting the impact of firm size and the resulting strategies explored. While large corporations are usually on the forefront of information technology adoption and use, the potential is significant for smaller firms as well. As such, this chapter provides managerial insights, useful especially to smaller companies, for successfully employing bundles in reverse auctions.

Findings

- No statistically significant difference was found between the first use of auctions, as well as average savings over time, by large firms versus SMEs. However, in the most recent auction event, larger firms were able to achieve higher savings than smaller firms.
- The majority of reverse auctions is conducted for bundles, rather than single items. Smaller firms used bundles to a greater extent.
- Larger firms found bundling more challenging than their smaller counterparts.
- An increase in the number of SKUs in the bundle led to a decrease in savings.
- Direct material was most often sourced in the auction, followed by indirect material and services.
- Bundle preparation time averaged six weeks, and most negotiated contracts were over three years.
- Goals pursued with bundling included best price, avoidance of cherry-picking, increased efficiency, and risk minimization via long-term relationships.
- Overall, the characteristics of the individual items included in the bundle, as well as the way they are combined with each other, did not differ across large and small firms.
- Bundle performance, as measured by savings achieved in the auction event, was influenced by firm size, contract length, and number of SKUs.

RECOMMENDATIONS

- Smaller firms should feel confident using reverse auctions, since average savings over time can be comparable to savings experienced by their larger counterparts. However, when looking at the most recent auction event, larger corporations achieved an average savings of 5% more than smaller firms. Nevertheless, savings of 13.3% for the smaller companies were still significant.

- Smaller companies should take greater advantage of bundling in order to increase the spend of the order lot, especially since results indicate that small firms are more easily able to create bundles.
- Efficiencies achieved by bundling more items together may outweigh a possible loss in savings. Before bundling, purchase goals must be assessed and the order lot should be constructed accordingly. As such, savings achieved may not always be the most important performance measure assessing the purchase.
- SMEs should focus on material that can be easily bundled together for a large spend, which will be direct material in most cases.
- When bundling for purchase price savings, emphasis should be placed on a long contract length and a smaller number of SKUs included in the bundle, since these two aspects significantly influence the percent of savings achieved.

LIMITATIONS

The sample was comprised primarily of larger firms, suggesting that mostly large corporations had adopted online reverse auctions at the time of the survey, which was conducted during fall 2004. However, in order to provide some insight for smaller firms (at least relative to our sample), and derive insights for true SMEs, two logical groups were formed. The revenue cutoff point for inclusion in the group of smaller and medium-sized firms was much higher than in other studies, and higher than many commonly-accepted cutoff points, such as $100 million or less (Beall et al., 2003). However, if the $100 million cut point was used, only 7.8% of the respondents would fall in this category, making a group-wise comparison unreliable. Future studies should therefore look at true SMEs, especially as their use of the online reverse auction tool increases, and investigate how they are approaching the bundling decision.

Chapter IX
Multi–Attribute Auctions:
Research Challenges and Opportunities

Kholekile L. Gwebu
University of New Hampshire, USA

Jing Wang
University of New Hampshire, USA

ABSTRACT

This chapter highlights the promise and importance of reverse multi-attribute auctions (RMAA). It outlines the major benefits of RMAAs over other traditional auction mechanisms, such as reverse single attribute auctions, and then presents a structured and critical assessment of the current state of RMAA research. The intention of this chapter is not only to review both experimental and theoretical studies that have been conducted on RMAAs, but also to provide a starting point and specific recommendations for future research directions on RMAAs.

BACKGROUND

In recent years online reverse auctions have grown in prominence and in use. Both the academic community and practitioners have taken an active interest in their research and development due to the numerous benefits they offer over traditional auction mechanisms. For instance, one of the most important benefits is that they are able to automate negotiations between buyers and sellers, resulting in time and money savings. The bid-taker and bid-ders need not converge in a single physical location to negotiate. Rather, this can be done remotely via the Internet at any time of day. However, despite these important benefits one major limitation of many contemporary online reverse auctions is that they only automate negotiation on a single attribute—price. Thus, they are inflexible since they do not to allow bidders and bid-takers to negotiate on other aspects of a deal. Yet in many cases especially in the business-to-business (B2B) arena, buyers often wish to negotiate with sellers on several aspects of a deal such as warranty, delivery time, payment terms, and so on.

Online reverse multi-attribute auctions (RMAA) are a potential solution to this problem. They allow bid-takers and bidders to negotiate on multiple aspects of a deal rather than just on price alone. A bid-taker determines the attributes of an item she wants bidders to submit bids on. For instance, to purchase a truck using a RMAA, after specifying minimum required features of the truck, the bid-taker invites bidders to submit bids on various attributes such as price, warranty, and lead time. To automate the submission and evaluation of bids, the bid-taker can employ an online RMAA. The RMAA has an interface conducive for bid submission on the pre-specified attributes and a set of algorithms based on Multi-attribute Utility Theory (MAUT) for bid evaluation. Each combination of price, warranty, and lead time submitted by bidders gives the bid-taker a certain level of utility, with higher levels of utility being preferred to lower ones. After several rounds of

bidding, the contract to supply the truck is awarded to the bidder who is able to submit a combination of attribute values which generates the highest level of utility for the bid-taker.

CHAPTER OBJECTIVES

Although there has been recent research activity devoted to analyzing the design and use of RMAAs, the academic literature in this area is relatively scarce compared to that found in other branches of auction literature (Bichler, 2000; Branco, 1996, 1997; Che, 1993; Laffont & Tirole, 1991; Pinker, Seidmann, & Vakrat, 2003; Teich, Wallenius, Wallenius, & Koppius, 2004). Therefore, this chapter analyzes the current state of research on multi-attribute online auctions and develops a broad research agenda for issues such as the solicitation of bid-taker preferences, bidders' perception of auction fairness, and the influence of information architecture on auction

Figure 1. RMAA components

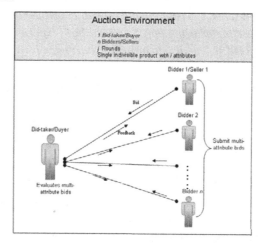

Auction platform /environment: The platform may either be a manual one (e.g., sealed bid auction) or one that is electronic and automated. The current chapter focuses on electronic automated mechanisms.
Bid-taker: A bid-taker solicits, evaluates multi-attribute bids, and decides the auction rules, procedures, and feedback to be used during bidding.
Bidders: Bidders submit competitive multi-attribute bids. Unlike bids in single attribute auctions where bids are single values, bids in multi-attribute auctions are vectors.

performance. It is important to note from the onset that it is not our aim to present an exhaustive review of the literature on online auctions in general and RMAAs in particular, nor is it our intention to suggest detailed solutions to any particular problems identified in the RMAA area. Rather, we seek to map out through a structured, critical evaluation of the current state of research the major open issues about RMAAs that we believe could be addressed by the research community to help practitioners make more informed decisions about their design and use. By doing so, we hope to develop a broad research agenda for the open issues and spur valuable research activity in this area. Before examining extant work on RMAAs we begin with a description of its components.

COMPONENTS OF A RMAA

A RMAA generally consists of three major components: bidders who are the sellers of the item, a bid-taker who is the buyer of the item, and the auction platform/environment that is the electronic mechanism that connects the bidders and the bid-takers. Among other things the platform manages the auction protocols and procedures, such as the number of auction rounds, the attributes

bidders can bid on, the number of bids permitted per time period, communication between auction participants, bid evaluation, and bid feedback, and so forth.

This chapter considers the opportunities and challenges that confront RMAA research. Most of the key issues relating to RMAAs can be understood by looking at the sequence of events in the RMAA process. This sequencing includes the bid submission, bid evaluation, feedback, and winner determination (see Figure 2). Mirroring this sequence are relevant research questions such as: What is the optimal number of attributes bidders can handle when submitting their bids? What information elements should a bid taker reveal to bidders? The RMAA process (Figure 2) serves as our framework for the identification, classification, and discussion of important open research issues relating to RMAAs. For the sake of brevity, issues falling outside this framework are not considered in this study. Moreover, issues falling outside this framework tend to be similar if not identical to those found in single attribute auction research, and considering them here would not add considerable value to extant auction literature.

Figure 2. Research framework

	Bid Submission	**Bid Evaluation**	**Feedback**	**Winner Determination**
Reverse Single Attribute Auction (RSAA)	Bidders submit *price bid*	The bid-taker compares *prices* submitted. Prefers *lower* prices to higher ones	Bidders can be shown: • All prices submitted by bidders • Rankings based on price • Directions for improvement	The bid-taker awards contract to the bidder with the *lowest price* bid
Reverse Multi-Attribute Auction (RMAA)	Bidders submit bid with *values for n-attributes*	The bid-taker compares *utility* given by each bid. Prefers *higher* utility to lower utility	Bidders can be shown: • All values submitted by bidders for each attribute • Rankings based on utility scores • The bid-takers' scoring function • Directions for improvement on some or all the attributes	The bid-taker awards contract to the bidder who provided the *highest level of utility*

BID SUBMISSION

In the majority of RSAA, bidders simply submit price-only bids to a bid-taker. Their goal is to offer the bid-taker an acceptable price that is lower than those of other competing bidders. Throughout the duration of the auction, bidders continuously lower their prices in response to changing market conditions in order to enable themselves to win the auction and profit from the subsequent transaction. RMAAs differ from RSAAs in that the bidders submit bids on several attributes simultaneously. Thus the bidding process involves a more complex multi-criteria bidding process. Take for instance the example provided earlier in this chapter, where bidders are competing to supply a bid-taker with a truck. Rather than simply offering the bid-taker a certain price for a particular make and model of truck, the bidders also concurrently offer a warranty (e.g., 1 year, 2 years,... n years) and a delivery date of the vehicle, that is, lead-time (1 day, 2 days,...n days). Therefore, the bid will be a vector composed of three values for each of the attributes (price, warranty and lead-time). During the course of the auction, bidders try to improve on values for each of the attributes in response to changing market conditions.

The main research issue that arises due to this complex bidding process revolves around the following question:

How will the number of attributes affect the quality of bids submitted by bidders?

The Number of Attributes and the Quality of Bids Submitted

The majority of studies conducted to date have considered differences in utility obtained by bid-takers when either one or three attributes are involved. For instance, Bichler (2000) conducts an experiment where he constructs an electronic brokerage service application, and over the counter (OTC) financial derivatives were auctioned. The study found that single-attribute auctions yield statistically significant lower utility scores for the bid-taker than do multi-attribute auctions. Bichler and Segev (2001) suggest that this could be because bidders in multi-attribute auctions had more possibilities to improve their bids for the bid-taker, and in some cases they could do so without increasing their own costs. The study indicates no statistically significant difference between the two formats in terms of efficiency and no evidence of the revenue equivalence theorem for the multi-attribute auction setting.

Recently, Chen-Ritzo, Harrison, Kwasnica, and Thomas (2005) conducted a similar study to the one by Bichler (2000). They compare the performance of single attribute auctions to multi-attribute auctions. Their study differs in that it makes use of a feedback mechanism which does not fully reveal the utility function of the bid-taker. Rather bidders were only given information on how they could improve on different attributes (direction of improvement and magnitude of improvement) of an existing bid. They also seek to determine whether or not bidder experience affects the performance of multi-attribute auctions.

As with Bichler's (2000) study, Chen-Ritzo et al. (2005) found that multi-attribute auctions tend to result in significantly higher utility levels for a bid-taker than single attribute auctions. Interestingly, they also found that multi-attribute auctions do not degrade bidders' profits. On the contrary, in some cases bidders' profits actually increased. Finally, they found that the bid-takers' utility and bidders' profits rarely change significantly from the inexperienced to the experienced bidders; however, the auctions appeared to perform more consistently when the bidders were experienced.

There have also been a few simulation studies that do not make use of human subjects to determine the difference between RSAAs and RMAAs. For instance, Bichler and Klimich (2000) conduct a simulation study to assess whether or not higher levels of utility can be achieved in multi-attribute auctions compared to single attribute auctions.

They use a process-based discrete event simulation package to model a multi-attribute auction of a generic product with price and nine other non-price attributes. They find that when attribute weights are uniformly distributed, the higher the number of negotiable attributes, the higher utility scores achieved in a multi-attribute auction compared to a single attribute auction. If attribute weights are not uniformly distributed and emphasis is placed only on a single attribute, then there is no difference in terms of utility score between multi-attribute or singe attribute auctions. The problem with this particular simulation study as acknowledged by the authors is that it is very sensitive to alterations made to the initial underlying assumptions such as the distribution of the individual attribute values or the cost parameters (Bichler, 2000; Bichler & Klimesch, 2000; Bichler & Segev, 2001).

Based on the general simulation model discussed above, Bichler (2001) creates another simulation study to simulate over the counter (OTC) market derivatives. In this study, three negotiable attributes are considered, namely strike price, option maturity, and option price. Again, he seeks to determine whether or not multi-attribute auctions produce higher utility scores than single-attribute auctions. He finds similar results to the previous study, that is, there was a positive correlation between the number of negotiable attributes and utility scores. However, compared to the previous study, the utility scores were lower in this study when the attribute weights were uniformly distributed. He concludes that the special nature of the attributes used in this study had a significant impact on the results. The results of these two simulation studies indicate one important implication. When bid-takers define a scoring function they should ensure that they have included all the relevant attributes.

Despite the significant and important contributions made by the above studies, the issue of the effect of having a large number of attributes has not been fully explored. Future research may wish to consider the following questions:

1. Will the quality of bids deteriorate or improve as more attributes are considered? Past experimental work only considers two or three attributes. The effect on bid quality of four or more attributes in this competitive multi-criteria decision making environment needs to be considered.

2. What is the optimal number of attributes bidders can handle? From a bidder's cognitive perspective, is there a point beyond which bidders will fail to submit quality bids?

3. Are decision support tools necessary for aiding bidders during the bidding process? If yes, what types of decision support tools should be provided? Such tools should be simple and intuitive to use and require little or no training, and should not give any of the competing bidders an unfair competitive environment.

4. What is the optimal amount of time bidders should be given to submit bids?

Some clues to answer these questions may be found in the multi-criteria decision-making literature. However, the competitive nature of RMAA mechanisms distinguishes them from other multi-criteria decision-making environments, and therefore necessitates specific research into these questions for RMAAs. Moreover, work addressing such questions is necessary, as it would allow designers of RMAAs to develop better quality auctions.

BID EVALUATION

In an RSAA a bid-taker evaluates bids by simply comparing the prices bidders submit, with lower prices being preferred to higher ones. In an RMAA a bid-taker needs to use some form of scoring rule that takes into consideration the relative importance of each attribute when determining how much utility each bid gives to a bidder. For instance, Bichler (2001) makes use of the following scoring rule in some of his experiments:

$$S(B_i) = \sum_{i=1}^{n} w_i S(x_i)$$

and

$$\sum_{i=1}^{n} w_i = 1, w_i > 0$$

and

$$S(x_i) = \frac{x_i - x_{worst}}{x_{best} - x_{worst}}$$

where,

$S(B_i)$ is the utility score for Bid i

w_i - weight/importance of attribute i

$S(x_i)$ - function used to assess individual utility score for attribute i

x_i = values submitted for attribute i

x_{worst} - worst possible value for attribute i

x_{best} - best possible value for attribute i

Other researchers studying RMAAs appear to employ variations of this scoring rule when conducting experimental research. However, use of various scoring functions gives rise to issues which have not been adequately addressed in the current literature namely:

1. What form should a scoring function take?
2. How can one elicit the bid-taker utility function in order to specify a scoring rule?

Scoring Function Form

Beil and Wein (2003) consider an inverse optimization-based auction mechanism for electronic multi-attribute auction, which attempts to maximize the utility of the bid-taker. In their model, the bid-taker is assumed to know the parametric form of the suppliers' cost function but has no

information on the parameter values. The paper demonstrates an inverse optimization approach on how a bid-taker can continuously adjust his scoring function over multiple rounds and learn bidders' cost functions. Armed with this information, the bid-taker can then maximize his utility during the final round of the auction. However, the authors acknowledge that an auction, which employs a scoring function that is continuously being adjusted in order to learn the bidders' cost function, may be practically infeasible.

The majority of scoring rules used in RMAA research are linear additive functions that assume preferential independence of attributes. In the truck example provided earlier, warranty is assumed to be preferentially independent from delivery time if preferences for specific outcomes of warranty do not depend on the value for delivery time (Bichler & Kalagnanam, 2005). However, if an additional attribute such as quantity (i.e., bidders can offer more than one truck) were included, the preferential independence assumption may fail to hold true because the price and quantity may not be preferentially independent. Such a scenario is feasible and often occurs in many practical settings. The work by Bichler (2001) provides insights into potential solutions to such problems. However, more work on alternative scoring functions appropriate for RMAAs where preferential independence cannot be assumed still needs to be conducted.

Eliciting the Bid-Taker's Utility Function

Eliciting the exact preferences of a bid-taker has proved to be difficult, mainly because bid-takers may not know all the attributes they wish bidders to negotiate on or they may not be capable of providing exact weights to be assigned to the attributes in their scoring function. Several approaches have been devised to address this issue. For instance, Teich et al. (2004) propose a technique they call "pricing out," where attributes are eliminated by expressing them in monetary terms. However, this technique may not be feasible in situations in which bid-takers cannot express attributes in monetary terms. Other approaches include the use of fuzzy decision analysis techniques (Bichler & Kalagnanam, 2005; Ribeiro, 1996). Much of the research on how to elicit a bid-taker's utility function has turned to literature on utility theory and decision analysis techniques (Bichler, 2001). Bichler (2000), Bichler and Kalagnanam (2005) and Beam, Segev, Bichler, and Krishnan, (1999) indicate that a multitude of techniques such as the analytical hierarchy process (AHP), the simple multi-attribute ranking technique (SMART), conjoint analysis, and MAUT can be employed to elicit the bid-taker's utility function in order to develop a scoring function for use in RMAA bid evaluation. Although the above-listed utility theory and decision analysis techniques have been used extensively in numerous settings to elicit decision makers' preference functions (Beam et al., 1999; Bichler, 2000; Bichler, 2001) they often assume that attributes are preferentially independent (Bichler & Kalagnanam, 2005). However, the utility derived by a bid-taker from various attributes in an auction may not necessarily be the sum of the attributes, but may be related in some way to the proportions in which those attributes are combined. If mutual independence of preferences cannot be established, it may be necessary to use more complex models for combining scores across criteria (Bichler, 2001). This may be an issue which future research probes deeper into.

FEEDBACK

The importance of information and its effect on auction performance have recently come under the spotlight in the RMAA literature. It is generally agreed that information may play an important role in influencing auction performance. However, literature on this issue is still in its infancy. This section seeks to examine the work that has been

done and then map out important research opportunities and challenges in this area. However, because this area remains largely unexplored in the context of RMAAs, we first turn our attention to single attribute auction studies for insights, since that literature is relatively more mature. Thereafter, we focus on multi-attribute auction studies and identify some of the shortcomings of previous studies.

Information Revelation in Single-Attribute Auctions

Among some of the most important findings on the effects of information on single attribute auction performance are papers by Milgrom and Weber (1982), Mares and Harstad (2003), Campbell and Levin (2000) and Dasgupta and Maskin (2000). Perhaps the most influential paper on this topic is by Milgrom and Weber (1982), who suggest that a bid-taker can employ one of several information disclosure policies on the item under auction, namely:

1. **A full revelation policy:** All information known by the bid-taker about the item is disclosed to all the bidders.
2. **A censoring policy:** Only information favorable to the bid-taker is revealed to all bidders.
3. **A concealment policy:** No information is reported to any bidder.
4. **A summarizing policy:** Only rough summary statistics are revealed to all bidders.
5. **A randomizing policy:** Information with "noise" is revealed to all the bidders.

They find that in situations in which a bid-taker must commit to a revelation policy, full revelation is the best for English or a sealed-bid second-price or a sealed-bid first price auction because it maximizes bid-taker revenue.

Mares and Harstad (2003) analyzed discriminatory information revelation policies in two bidder auctions and their impact on bid-taker revenue. They evaluate situations in which bid-takers chose to reveal important information they have about the item being auctioned to a bidder who is at an information disadvantage, while concealing the information from a bidder who is at an information advantage. They argue that private revelation, in situations in which bidders are already asymmetric in the precision of their private information, yields higher revenue than public revelation. Private information in such cases has the effect of reducing asymmetry and creating a more competitive environment.

Campbell and Levin (2000) consider auctions with heterogeneously informed bidders. In particular, they investigate auctions in which one bidder (an "insider") has superior information to other bidders about the value of the item under auction. They develop a two-bidder model for a pure common-value first-price auction to assess the impact of information revelation on the bid-taker revenue. No difference in revenue was observed between environments where bidders were initially heterogeneously or homogenously informed. However, like Milgrom and Weber (1982), Campbell and Levin (2000) find that in environments where bidders have heterogeneous information, public revelation of information yielded higher revenue for bid-takers.

Mikoucheva and Sonin (2004) examine the impact of information revelation on auction efficiency. The question they tackle is "does more information lead to increased auction efficiency?" Dasgupta and Maskin (2000) in a seminal article prove that if information signals are multi-dimensional, full efficiency is impossible to attain in single attribute auctions. This is because in single attribute auctions, bidders must convert multi-dimensional information signals into a single dimensional bid and this complex conversion inherently contributes to auction inefficiency. Thus, the efficiency achieved in single attribute auctions is constrained by the multi-dimensional nature of the bids and is often referred to as "con-

strained efficiency." Mikoucheva and Sonin (2004) demonstrate that disclosing additional information leads to increased constrained efficiency (measured by expected additional value of the item to the winning bidder). However, this result is not generalizable to the second-price sealed-bid case. In such auctions, additional information may actually lead to auction inefficiency.

The above discussion of extant literature on information revelation and single attribute auctions brings to light three important points. First, although interesting, the above findings may not be directly applicable to the multi-attribute auction setting due to the complexity of multi-attribute auctions. Several authors have indicated that the impact of information on multi-attribute auctions may differ from that found in single attribute auctions due to the complex nature of the bidding process in such auctions (Bichler, 2001; Koppius & Van Heck, 2002).

Second, most studies have been analytical in nature with game theoretical approaches dominating. Although such studies are important because they provide interesting insights into auction performance under various conditions, their findings are constrained by the assumptions made.

Third, the majority of papers only consider the effects of the bid-taker disclosing information about the item under auction to bidders and not the effects of disclosing information about other auction elements such as the number of bidders and bid-rankings. An exception to this is a recent paper by Millet, Parente, Fizel, and Venkatarman (2004) that reveals that such elements may affect the outcome of single attribute reverse auctions. They found that if bidders are only given rank information and there are a large number of bidders competing in the auction, the auction may perform poorly, because lower ranked bidders may not be motivated to participate. However, telling bidders how far their bid is from the leading bid in addition to their ranking may motivate them to submit better bids.

Information Revelation in Multi-Attribute Auctions

The significance of information and its relationship to auction performance has recently emerged as an important issue in the multi-attribute auction literature. Small changes in an information architecture (the manner in which information is disclosed to auction participants) may potentially affect the overall performance of an auction, that is, the winning bidder and the overall utility of the bid-taker (Koppius, 2002; Strecker and Seifert, 2003; Chen-Ritzo et al., 2005). Therefore, it is imperative that the information architecture be designed and implemented with careful consideration. The questions related to this issue, which researchers currently are attempting to tackle, primarily revolve around the following basic questions:

1. What information elements should a bid taker reveal to bidders?
2. When should information be revealed?
3. To whom should information be revealed?

The bid-taker typically controls the information architecture in multi-attribute auctions, and can determine which information elements bidders may or may not receive before bidding commences and what feedback they receive during the bidding process. Typical information elements under the bid-taker's control include the bid-taker's utility function/scoring rule, the number of competing bidders, identity of competing bidders, the bid elements submitted, and the bid rankings. The bid-taker can choose to reveal all, some, or none of these information elements.

The information presented is essential as it may guide bidders in their bidding process. If bidders are unaware of the utility function or scoring rule they may assign incorrect weights to attributes, which could ultimately result in lower utility scores for the bid-taker. However, bid-takers may not always be in a position to reveal

their utility scores or scoring rules to bid-takers. In some cases, bid-takers fear that bidders may exploit this information and shift the gains from trade to themselves (Strecker and Seifert, 2003). In other cases, such information may be sensitive and bid-takers may have security concerns over releasing it (Chen-Ritzo et al., 2005). Still in other cases bid-taker may not know the details of the function with certainty (Bichler, 2001).

Strecker and Seifert (2003) conducted an interesting study to determine whether or not revealing a bid-taker's preferences affects bid-taker utility scores and whether or not bidders would take advantage of this information and shift the gains of trade to themselves. Their findings do not indicate significantly higher utility scores for the bid-taker, nor do they indicate significantly higher profits for bidders when preference information is provided. However, the sample size used in their study was small. Future studies may wish to revisit this issue and make use of large sample sizes.

Future research may also wish to investigate other alternatives to explicitly revealing utility functions or scoring rules. Chen-Ritzo et al.'s (2005) study provides a good alternative in which the utility function is concealed and only marginal values that indicate how bidders can improve on previously placed bids are revealed. Future research may want to compare Chen-Ritzo et al.'s (2005) scheme to other non-explicit utility function/scoring rule revelation schemes.

Information such as the number of competing bidders, bidder identities, bid elements submitted by other bidders, and bid rankings provides a sense of competition in the auction. Arguably this type of information may spur bidders to submit their best possible bid in order to outperform their competitors. The choice of when to reveal such information and to whom it should be revealed may vary. However, this issue has not yet been tackled in detail in RMAA literature and needs to be addressed. Future research may wish to consider the following questions:

- Will RMAA performance differ considerably if a bid-taker chooses not to reveal the number of competing bidders, or the bidder identities, or the bid elements submitted by other bidders, or the bid rankings compared to when such information is revealed?
- Does the timing of the release of such information matter? Will there be a difference in utility scores if the bid-taker releases ranking information during the final round (assuming a hard-stopping rule is adopted) of bidding vs. if it is released continually throughout the auction?
- Who should the bid-taker reveal these information elements to? A bid-taker can for example make use of an information revelation policy that discriminates based on ranking. For example, bidders who are near or at the bottom third of the rankings after bids are evaluated may not be informed about their ranking as this may discourage them from further participation. Instead the bid-taker may privately inform them to make various improvements on their previous bid in order to remain competitive. Existing technology can easily facilitate such disclosure and can ensure that it is discrete. This approach differs considerably from conventional information revelation schemes where various types of details are indiscriminately revealed to all bidders. Research looking into how private or discriminatory revelation schemes affect the overall auction outcomes as compared to public ones is important but lacking.

In summary, there are numerous information revelation schemes a bid-taker can use when conducting RMAAs, however some schemes may be impractical for certain bid-takers. The question then becomes what are the next best alternatives. Future research needs to provide answers to such questions by investigating and clearly outlining the pros and cons of various information revelation schemes in RMAAs.

WINNER DETERMINATION

The final component in our framework considers winner determination. In RSAAs winner determination is straightforward. The bid-taker simply compares all the price bids submitted and selects the lowest price bid. With RMAAs, since the bid is a vector of values that gives the bid-taker differing levels of utility, the bid-taker uses a scoring function to determine which bid gives the highest level of utility. However, since bid-takers may not always be in a position to reveal their utility function or other auction information, the issue of fairness may arise.

Fairness

One of the most crucial elements for the long-term success of any market mechanism is that all participants who utilize it perceive it as being fair. Beil and Wein (2003) highlight that in a multi-attribute auction setting, if a mechanism is not transparent and auction participants do not perceive equity, they may be reluctant to use it. They indicate that "the rules of an auction must strike a delicate balance between the perception of fairness and the mitigation of strategic behavior" (Beil & Wein, 2003, p.1545). Pekec and Rothkopf (2003) note that fairness is a vital goal of auctions despite the difficulty to define it. Pinker et al.(2003) rightfully state that:

A market built on the premise that one side, the buyer, reaps the entire economic surplus will not attract many suppliers in the long run. There must be gains to both parties to get participation in the market and sufficient liquidity. (pp. 1477-1478)

The issue of fairness in multi-attribute auctions emerges when bidders attempt to determine how the scoring function relates to the winning bid. If bidders feel that there is discrimination in terms of winner determination, they are unlikely to return in the future. The more transparent a mechanism, the higher the likelihood that bidders will perceive it as being fair since they can easily determine why the winning bid was better than their own. If they have no access to this information, they may be suspicious, sense discrimination from the bid-taker, and may be unsatisfied with the winner determination process. They may feel that their final bid was the best one out of all the submitted bids. However, for some other reason (e.g., bid-taker has a special relationship with the winning bidder) the bid-taker discriminated against them, and therefore they will not be inclined to participate in future auctions.

Although fairness is difficult to assess due to its subjective nature, a good proxy may be auction efficiency. An efficient auction is one in which the bidder with the highest valuation wins the auction (Teich et al., 2004). One can assess efficiency of a multi-attribute auction mechanism by looking at a set of auctions, then determining how many times the bidder with the lowest cost structure won an auction (Koppius, 2002). If in the majority of cases the winning bidder was the one with the lowest cost structure, then the auction mechanism may be deemed efficient, and if not it is inefficient. If a multi-attribute auction mechanism is found to be inefficient, it may also be perceived by bidders as being unfair.

Factors that influence bidders' perceptions of fairness in multi-attribute auctions need to be explicitly identified and studied. Currently, both empirical and theoretical work in this area is lacking. As stated above, for a mechanism to enjoy long-term success it is essential that bidders perceive the auction mechanism as being fair. Research in this area would help the design and implementation of more successful RMAAs.

CONCLUSION

RMAAs are new types of auction mechanisms that have been enabled by contemporary technology. They offer several advantages over con-

ventional single attribute auction mechanisms, which may lead to their rapid adoption especially in the B2B arena. There are however a number of issues surrounding their design that are yet to be addressed. The purpose of this chapter was to provide a detailed outline of these issues and propose directions for future research, thus laying a clear foundation for research on these types of mechanisms. In brief, the paper synthesized the current state of research on RMAA and developed a broad research agenda for issues relating to bid submission, bid evaluation, feedback, and winner determination. Our intention is to motivate research in this area, so as to improve existing RMAA mechanisms and stimulate their adoption and use by practitioners.

FUTURE RESEARCH DIRECTIONS

Online reverse multi-attribute auctions are relatively novel market mechanisms which differ significantly from online reverse single attribute auctions in several important ways including bid submission, bid evaluation, feedback, and winner determination. These differences are not yet fully explored in extant literature. Therefore there exist numerous research opportunities that can allow researchers to enhance the design of online reverse multi-attribute auctions.

Bidding in online reverse multi-attribute auctions tends to be a more complex process than in reverse single attribute auctions. Future research needs to explore issues surrounding bidder support in such complex decision making environments. Specifically, researchers and auction designers need to understand how additional attributes influence the quality of bids submitted and whether there is a point beyond which bidders will fail to submit quality bids in these competitive multi-criteria decision-making environments. Such research will aid in the design of appropriate decision support systems for reverse multi-attribute auctions.

Another important difference between reverse multi-attribute auctions and reverse single attribute auctions is in bid evaluation. Reverse multi-attribute auctions make use of scoring functions that are used to determine the amount of utility a particular bid gives to a bid-taker. More research is required to determine the form scoring functions should take in various situations. Moreover, work which investigates how to elicit a bid-taker's utility function in order to specify an appropriate scoring function is necessary.

Another major issue that requires further investigation is information disclosure: what information elements should be provided to bidders as feedback to enhance bidding and auction performance. There are various types and combinations of information elements that may or may not be revealed to bidders, such as ranking information, the number or identity of competing bidders, the bids submitted by competitors, and so forth. There are numerous information revelation schemes a bid-taker can use when conducting reverse multi-attribute auctions, however some schemes may be impractical for certain bid-takers. The question then becomes what are the next best alternatives. Future research needs to provide answers to such questions by investigating and clearly outlining the pros and cons of various information revelation schemes in reverse multi-attribute auctions.

Finally, when winners are determined it is important that bidders perceive the process as being fair; otherwise they may choose not to participate in future auctions. Factors that influence bidders' perceptions of fairness in multi-attribute auctions need to be explicitly identified and studied. Currently, both empirical and theoretical work in this area is lacking. For an auction mechanism to enjoy long-term success it is essential that bidders perceive the auction mechanism as being fair. Research in this area would help in the design and implementation of more successful reverse multi-attribute auctions.

REFERENCES

Beam, C., Segev, A., Bichler, M., & Krishnan, R. (1999). On negotiations and deal making in electronic markets. *Information Systems Frontiers, 1*(3), 241-258.

Beil, D. R., & Wein, L. M. (2003). An inverse-optimization-based auction mechanism to support a multi-attribute RFQ process, *Management Science, 49*(11), 1529-1545.

Bichler, M. (2000). An experimental analysis of multi-attribute auctions. *Decision Support Systems, 29*(3), 249-268.

Bichler, M. (2001). *The future of e-Markets: Multi-dimensional market mechanisms.* Cambridge: Cambridge University Press.

Bichler, M., & Kalagnanam, J. (2005). Configurable offers and winner determination in multi-attribute auctions. *European Journal of Operational Research, 160*(2), 380-394.

Bichler, M., & Klimesch, R. (2000). Simulation multivariater auktionen—eine analyse des otc-handels mit finanzderivaten. *Wirtschaftsinformatik, 42*(3), 244-252.

Bichler, M., & Segev, A. (2001). Methodologies for the design of negotiation protocols on e-markets. *Computer Networks, 37*(2), 137-152.

Branco, F. (1996). Common value auctions with independent types. *Economic Design, 2*(3), 283-309.

Branco, F. (1997). The design of multidimensional auctions. *RAND Journal of Economics, 28*(1), 63-81.

Campbell, C. M., & Levin, D. (2000). Can the seller benefit from an insider in common-value auctions? *Journal of Economic Theory, 91*(1), 106-120.

Che, Y. K. (1993). Design competition through multidimensional auctions. *RAND Journal of Economics, 24*(4), 668-680.

Chen-Ritzo, C., Harrison, T. P., Kwasnica, A. M., & Thomas, D. J. (2005). Better, faster, cheaper: An experimental analysis of a multi-attribute reverse auction mechanism with restricted information feedback. *Management Science, 51*(12), 1753-1762.

Dasgupta, S., & Maskin, E. (2000). Efficient auctions. *The Quarterly Journal of Economics, 65*(2), 341-388.

Klemperer, P., (1999). Auction theory: A guide to the literature. *Journal of Economic Surveys, 13*(3), 227-286.

Koppius, O. R. (2002). *Information architecture and electronic market performance.* Unpublished Doctoral Dissertation, Erasmus University, Rotterdam, The Netherlands.

Koppius, O. R., & Van Heck, E. (2002). The role of product quality information, market state information and transaction costs in electronic auctions. *Academy of Management Proceedings, TIM,* I1-16.

Laffont, J., & Tirole, J. (1991). Auction design and favoritism. *International Journal of Industrial Organization, 9*(1), 9-42.

Mares, V., & Harstad, R. M. (2003). Private information revelation in common-value auctions. *Journal of Economic Theory, 109*(2), 264-282.

Mikoucheva, A., & Sonin, K. (2004). Information revelation and efficiency in auctions. *Economics Letters, 83*(3), 277-284.

Milgrom, P., & Weber, R. (1982). A theory of auctions and competitive bidding. *Econometrica, 50*(5), 1089-1122.

Millet, I., Parente, D., Fizel, R., & Venkatarman, R. (2004). Metrics for managing online procurement auctions. *Interfaces, 34*(3), 171-179.

Pekec, A., & Rothkopf, M. H. (2003). Combinatorial auction design. *Management Science, 49*(11), 1485-1503.

Pinker, E. J., Seidmann, A., & Vakrat, Y. (2003). Managing online auctions: Current business and research issues. *Management Science, 49*(11), 1457-1484.

Ribeiro, R. A. (1996). Fuzzy multiple attribute decision making: A review and new preference elicitation techniques. *Fuzzy Sets and Systems, 78*(2), 155-181.

Strecker, S., & Seifert, S. (2003). *Preference revelation in multi-attribute bidding procedures: An experimental analysis.* Paper presented at the 14th International Workshop on Database and Expert Systems Applications (DEXA'03).

Teich, J., Wallenius, H., Wallenius, J., & Koppius, O. (2004). Emerging multiple issue e-auctions. *European Journal of Operational Research, 159*(1), 1-16.

ADDITIONAL READINGS

Chao, H. P., & Wilson, R. (2002). Multi-dimensional procurement auctions for power reserves: Robust incentive-compatible scoring and settlement rules. *Journal of Regulatory Economics, 22*(2), 161-183.

Che, Y. K. (1993). Design competition through multidimensional auctions. *RAND Journal of Economics 24*(4), 668-680.

Cripps, M., & Ireland, N. (1994). The design of auctions and tenders with quality thresholds: The asymmetric case. *Economic Journal 104*(423), 316-326.

Dasgupta, S., & Spulber, D. (1990). Managing procurement auctions. *Information Economics and Policy, 4*(1), 5-29.

Dyer, D., Kagel, J. H., & Levin, D. (1989). A comparison of naive and experienced bidders in common value offer auctions: A laboratory analysis. *Economic Journal, 99*(394), 108.

Hansen, R. G. (1988). Auctions with endogenous quantity, *RAND Journal of Economics, 19*(1), 44-58.

Jehiel, P., Moldovanu, B., & Stacchetti, E. (1999). Multidimensional mechanism design for auctions with externalities. *Journal of Economic Theory, 85*(2), 258-293.

Johns, C. L., & Zaichkowsky, J. L. (2003). Bidding behavior at the auction. *Psychology and Marketing, 20*(4), 2003, 303-322.

Klemperer, P. (1999). Auction theory: A guide to the literature. *Journal of Economic Surveys, 13*(3), 227-286.

Koh, W. T. H., Mariano, R. S., & Yiu, K. T. (2007). Open vs. sealed-bid auctions: Testing for revenue equivalence under Singapore's vehicle quota system. *Applied Economics, 39*(1), 125-134.

Koppius, O. R., & van Heck, E. (2003). Information architecture and electronic market performance in multidimensional auctions. *ERIM PhD Research Series in Management,* No. 13, Erasmus University of Rotterdam, The Netherlands.

Kwak, M. (2002). Potential pitfalls of e-auctions. *MIT Sloan Management Review, 43*(2), 18.

Milgrom, P. (2000). An economist's vision of the B-to-B marketplace., Perfect.Com. Executive White Paper available at http://www.stanford.edu/~milgrom/publishedarticles/An Economist's Vision.pdf

Rothkopf, M. H., Harstad, R. M., & Fu, Y. (2003). Is subsidizing inefficient bidders actually costly? *Management Science, 49*(11), 71-84.

Strecker, S., & Seifert, S. (2004). *Electronic sourcing with multi-attribute auctions.* Paper presented at the 37th Annual Hawaii International Conference on System Sciences, HICSS 2004, Big Island, Hawaii, USA.

Teich, J., & Wallenius, H. (1999). Multiple-issue auction and market algorithms for the World Wide Web. *Decision Support Systems, 26*(1), 49-66.

Thiel, S. (1988). Multidimensional auctions. *Economics Letters, 28*(1), 37-40.

Vickrey, W. (1961). Counterspeculation, auctions, and competitive sealed tenders. *Journal of Finance, 16*(1), 8-37.

Walley, M., Fortin, J. C., David R. (2005). Behavioral outcomes from online auctions: Reserve price, reserve disclosure, and initial bidding influences in the decision process. *Journal of Business Research, 58*(10), 1409-1418.

Wilcox, R. T. (2000). Experts and amateurs: The role of experience in Internet auctions. *Marketing Letters, 11*(4), 363-374.

IMPLICATIONS FOR PRACTITIONERS

Title: Multi-attribute Auctions: Research Challenges and Opportunities

Description

The primary purpose of this chapter is to assess the current state of research on reverse multi-attribute auctions (RMAA). As an emerging auction mechanism, RMAAs have the potential to offer tremendous benefits over traditional reverse single attribute auctions (RSAA). For instance, rather than only offering bidders the ability to submit bids on price alone, RMAAs allow the bidders to bid on several dimensions of an item simultaneously. They also provide bid-takers with the ability to automatically evaluate complex multidimensional bids. Traditional time consuming and labor intensive processes in procurement such as the Request for Quotation (RFQ) process can be automated using RMAAs, thereby resulting in time and money savings for firms. Due to the aforementioned potential benefits of RMAAs, issues surrounding how to design, architect, and deploy effective, efficient, and fair RMAAs have become essential for both practitioners and academicians. Therefore, the goal of this work is to identify important research issues that still need to be explored in order for RMAAs to be successfully designed and eventually incorporated into firms' procurement processes. We achieve this goal by conducting a structured and critical assessment of the current state of research on RMAAs and based on this assessment, we develop a broad research agenda for issues that are important but yet to be addressed in order to help firms make informed decision on the design and use of RMAAs.

IMPORTANCE OF THE WORK

This work is of great importance for practitioners for the following reasons:

- It highlights the promise and importance of RMAAs, novel auction mechanisms that overcome some of the limitations of RSAAs and the RFQ process.
- By reviewing the literature, it provides a comprehensive set of references on both experimental and theoretical studies that have been conducted on RMAAs.
- It highlights some of the current limitations of RMAA research and RMAA mechanisms in general.
- It serves as an indispensable link between past and future work on RMAA and provides a starting point and specific recommendations and strategies for future research directions.

The following is a summary of some of the important research issues that remain unsolved in the RMMA literature.

- **Bid submission:** The bid submission process in RSAAs is fairly straight forward: Bidders simply submit a price bid that they believe will allow them to win the auction and profit from the subsequent transaction. In RMAAs the bidding process is more complex and bidders have to structure a vector of bids based on the number of attributes the bid-taker wishes to receive bids on. Given the cognitive demands of RMAA mechanisms, a major issue becomes what is the maximum number of attributes bidders can handle?

- **Bid evaluation:** In RSAAs the bid-taker compares the prices submitted by bidders when evaluating bids, whereas in RMAAs the bid-taker compares vectors. Price comparison is straight forward, however when comparing vectors, the scoring function used may raise some issues. In the book chapter, we explore the limitations of current bid evaluation techniques.
- **Bid feedback:** The issue of what information should be given to bidders is important, as it may influence the outcome of the auction regardless of whether one is dealing with an RSAA or an RMAA. Should bidders be told their ranking and the rankings of other competing bidders after bid submission? Should they be told who they are competing with? Should they be told the details of what other bidders have submitted? Information may provide guidance for bidders during auctions. RMAAs are complex and highly competitive bidding environments, and bidders need as much guidance as possible to allow them to structure and submit competitive bids. However, bid-takers may not always be in a position to reveal certain information elements such as the identities of other competing bidders and rankings. Will this affect auction performance? If so what are the consequences of not revealing various information elements?
- **Winner determination:** It is imperative that bidders perceive the auction mechanism as fair in determining winners. Failure to do so may result in a decrease in the number of auction participants. What are some of the factors that influence bidders' perceptions on fairness in RMAAs? How can bid-takers ensure that bidders perceive winner determination as being fair?

With the information presented in this chapter, practitioners can make more informed decisions about whether or not RMAA mechanisms in their current state can benefit their organizations. They may also be able to determine what areas in the research and development of RMAAs to direct their efforts to in order for the benefits of RMAAs to be fully realized in their organizations.

LIMITATIONS

This is not an empirical piece. Rather, it is a review article. We do not conduct any experiments or test any hypotheses. The empirical findings and recommendations presented in the chapter are primarily based on work conducted by previous research.

Section III
The Auction Process

Chapter X
Competition and the Winner's Curse in B2B Reverse Auctions

Indranil K. Ghosh
Winston-Salem State University, USA

John L. Fizel
The Pennsylvania State University – Erie, USA

Ido Millet
The Pennsylvania State University – Erie, USA

Diane H. Parente
The Pennsylvania State University – Erie, USA

ABSTRACT

This chapter studies the negative effects of the Winner's Curse, a phenomenon found commonly in auctions. We define the idea of a Winner's Curse an specify the types of auctions in which this could be prevalent. We look at the data provided by a major multinational corporation on online procurement auctions conducted by them. We specify the effect that this Winner's Curse would have on the success of procurement auctions. Using this theoretical background, we analyze the given data and show that in some cases, the presence of the Winner's Curse and the subsequent need for bidders to show caution in the presence of the Winner's Curse could lead to lower auction success for the firm. We specify the particular cases where this is true. This leads to managerial implications for firms wishing to conduct procurement auctions online, and we spell them out. We also provide some examples of how firms might try and lower the negative effects of the Winner's Curse. Finally we provide some future research ideas that may be pursued and some additional readings for the curious reader.

INTRODUCTION

Auctions have been widely used as an important purchasing tool in industrial, governmental, and personal consumption environments dating back to 500 B.C. (Milgrom & Weber, 1982). Before the Internet and online revolution, auctions would be conducted mainly through the RFQ (request for quotes) route in governmental and industrial contexts, and through auction houses in the context of personal consumption products. However, with the advent of the Internet for commercial use in approximately 1993, the breadth of online auction activity has increased tremendously. According to Lucking-Reiley (2000), the earliest Internet auction based on Internet news groups appeared in 1993. The first Internet auction Web sites, OnSale and eBay, appeared in 1995. Right now, there are many thousands of Web sites that are dedicated to online auctions. The variety of goods being auctioned online includes books, stamps, coins, computers, cars, airline tickets, hotel rooms, machine tools, handyman services, and many others. In this chapter, we will look at several procurement auctions conducted online by a reputed multinational firm, and analyze the existence of an interesting characteristic of auctions called the Winner's Curse in these auctions. The rest of this chapter is organized as follows: In Section 2, we provide a brief introduction of various auction types and mechanisms. In Section 3 we provide a theoretical background to the idea of the Winner's Curse, explain the presence of the Winner's Curse under private and common value auctions, and give an example of an auction where the Winner's Curse could affect the outcome. In Section 4 we review the literature. In Section 5 we briefly describe the dataset that we use for our models. In Section 6 we discuss the various models that we use and look at all our results. Section 7 provides some managerial implications that we believe would be useful to practitioners. We conclude our chapter with some ideas of further research.

CLASSIFICATION OF AUCTION TYPES AND AUCTION MECHANISMS

In general, there are four basic types of auction mechanisms. An English auction is an ascending bid auction, in which individual bids are generally transparent. The winner is the highest bid that is also equal to the price paid. An example would be the bidding for goods on eBay. A first-price sealed-bid auction is a secret auction with individuals making a single bid that is sealed. The winner is the highest bidder, with the price also being the highest bid. An example would be the Chicago Wine Company auctions. A second-price sealed-bid auction, also called a Vickrey auction, is similar to a first-price auction in that it is a single secret bid. However, the winning bidder is the one with the highest bid, but the winner pays a price equal to the second highest bid. In a Dutch auction, the seller lowers the price from a starting price. The winner is the first bidder to pay the current price.

In general, auctions can be classified as a C2C or a consumer to consumer auction, B2C or a business to consumer auction, a C2B or a consumer to business auction, and a B2B or a business to business auction, depending on the types of agents involved in the transactions. For online auctions, we can classify auction types by characterizing them as forward or reverse auctions, a forward auction being one with one seller and many buyers, while a reverse auction is one with many sellers and one buyer.

In this chapter, we look at the process of online auctions, or what is sometimes called as Web-based dynamic pricing mechanisms. The most popular category of online auctions is business to consumer (B2C) forward auctions. However in recent times business to business (B2B) forward and reverse auctions have become a significant model for businesses to auction their products and services to each other. Typically, when a business wants to sell its product through an auction to different buyers they use a forward auction, while if they are looking to buy products and services from their suppliers they are looking to operate a reverse auction. Within the realm of supply management, electronic (or online) reverse auctions, or eRAs, have become a widespread and extremely popular topic for research and practical application. Parente, Venkatraman, Fizel, and Millet (2001) provide a research framework for analysis of auction data. In this chapter we look at a product characteristic (private and common value) that will affect the auction process (by means of the Winner's Curse) and hence will affect the auction outcome (in this case the success of the auction). In the next section we will discuss the characteristics of the products that are bought and sold in these auctions and will introduce the concept of the Winner's Curse.

THE WINNER'S CURSE

A Brief Theoretical Background

It is a well-known economic fact that under the ideal conditions of perfect competition, an increase in the demand for a product increases equilibrium prices. In this regard, the Walrasian analysis of markets, which can be thought of as an auction in which an auctioneer (or the online mechanism) raises prices until the supply equals the demand. If the number of bidders increase in the limit to an infinitely large number, then the auction process would equal the competitive market setting i.e. in a perfect setting, any increase in the number of bidders in an ascending price auction would lead to more aggressive bidding and hence a higher final equilibrium price. In the case of a descending price or reverse auction, as is common among firms conducting procurement of intermediate goods or raw materials over the Internet, a larger number of bidders under ideal conditions would lead to a lower buying price for the firm conducting the auction. By perfect conditions, assuming an ascending price auction, we mean a situation in which a buyer has some estimate of the value of the product, and this estimate is independent of any other consumers' estimate of the product. In this sort of perfectly competitive or Adam Smith world, each individual buyer would be willing to

pay up to their individual valuation of the product—that is, pay their reservation price—thus choosing consumption points maximizing their utility. This analysis would be relevant for a private value model of auctions, which would be analogous to the assumptions of perfect conditions described above.

However, not all markets or products give rise to private value auctions. Consider the case where different consumers or buyers have differentiated information about the value of a product; however all buyers would have identical valuations of the product if they all had the same complete information about the value (i.e., the ex post value of the product is the same for all individuals). These are common value auctions. Oil fields and oil drilling rights are cited as the best example of a common value product. Most products have both a common and private value component. For example, a valuable art object being auctioned has a common value element which is the expected value of the painting, while each individual may have individual private values about the painting. The problem with such auctions involving a common value element is the presence of what is called the Winner's Curse.

The Winner's Curse Under Common and Private Value Auctions

In the presence of the Winner's Curse, a rational bidder would internalize the curse by bidding less aggressively. Going back to our initial premise of increasing competition or the number of bidders, if we consider a low price or "reverse" procurement auction, there can be two distinct counteracting effects on equilibrium bidding behavior: An increase in the number of bidders leads to more aggressive bidding and consequently lower winning prices, while the same increase in bidders can lead to a more severe Winner's Curse. Thus, taking this into account, rational bidders will bid less aggressively and it is entirely possible that this Winner's Curse effect may overwhelm the low price effect of more bidders, and as a result could lead to higher equilibrium prices in a reverse auction. The impact of this Winner's Curse effect can be different depending on the auction format. In a sealed-bid first- or second-price auction, individuals bid at the same time and have no idea about the bids of their competitors. Thus, the conditions are ripe for the Winner's Curse to exist. In the case of ascending (or descending) auctions the argument suggesting the existence of a Winner's Curse is a little bit more complicated. In both these auction formats bidders have at least partial information about competitors who drop out of the bidding process at particular bid values. Individuals can thus reformulate the values that they place on the product being bought or sold. However, because of imperfect information, there is no guarantee that the bids at which competitors drop out of the auction are the true values placed on the product by these competitors. In fact, bidders may drop out of the auction at values more or less than the true values of the product. If a bidder sees a large number of other competitors still in the auction they may revise their valuations, assuming that their competitors have better information about the product. Or, keeping in mind the assertion that a larger number of bidders may force everyone to bid more aggressively and thus exacerbate the Winner's Curse, they may revise their valuations in the opposite direction. Thus, in the presence of such imperfect information a bidder does not have the necessary tools to eradicate the Winner's Curse.

An Example of the Winner's Curse

To make the understanding of the concept of the Winner's Curse a little simpler, we provide an example of the consequences of the Winner's Curse described above. In this example of a second-price or Vickrey auction, we look at the case of bidding to win the rights of an oil lease. Company X is preparing to bid for an oil lease. To get an idea of the value of the tract that they are going to bid for, the company hires a geologist. According to the geologist the value of the lease is $5000. However, we are talking here of imperfect information: that is, until the oil is dug up, no one can be exactly sure of the value of the lease. Thus, the value given by the geologist is an estimate and may be incorrect. Let us assume that the true value of the lease is $4000, and this fact is unknown to anyone—Company X, the geologist employed by Company X, or any other company bidding for the lease or any geologist employed by them. The maximum that Company X would bid, given the information they got from their geologists estimate, is thus $5000. If we assume that X is the highest bidder and the next highest bidder stops at $4499, then Company X would win the bid for the lease at $4500. However, since the true value of the lease is $4000, they have overbid and will lose $500 on the transaction, which is the Winner's Curse. If the companies bidding for the lease had perfect information about the value of the lease, we would not have this problem. But, given that they have imperfect information about the value, it is not unreasonable to assume that some of them will have estimated values below the correct value while some will have estimated values above the actual value. The winner of the auction is going to be the person with the highest estimated value (since they have the highest bid), and thus we could easily expect the winner to pay more than the true value for the lease. The only way to reduce the Winner's Curse is for the bidders to be more cautious about their bids—that is, Company X should find an estimate of the variation of the geologist's estimate and the true value, and place its bids taking this variation into account. Let us assume in the previous example that there are three companies bidding, and each gets an estimate that is within $1000 dollars of the true value, $4000. Since we conjectured that the estimates could be equally dispersed around the true value, it is evident that the highest estimate is going to be somewhere between $4000 and $5000, giving an expected high estimate of

$4500. Similarly, the middle expected estimate should be $4000 and the lowest expected estimate should be $3500. If Company X takes the Winner's Curse effect seriously they should not bid higher than $4500, the second bidder should not bid higher than $4000, and thus we should expect that Company X will win the bid paying (approximately) $4000, the true value of the bid. This is how bidders who are aware of the Winner's Curse should bid. Thus, in an ascending price (or forward auction) awareness of the Winner's Curse would lead to a reduction in the prices paid. In a reverse auction, conversely, if bidders are aware of the Winner's Curse, it would lead to an increase in the prices paid. In the presence of more competition (more bidders) it is not clear which effect would prevail—the presence of more competitors should lead to a lower price being offered by the suppliers, but on the other hand, being aware of the Winner's Curse could cause the suppliers to bid more cautiously and thus offer higher prices. If the competition effect is larger than the Winner's Curse effect, the net result of having more bidders would be a lowering of the price. If however the Winner's Curse effect dominates, the net result of having more bidders would be an increase in the price.

LITERATURE REVIEW

In this section we provide a brief description of the literature with reference to the Winner's Curse. This "Winner's Curse" was first commented on by three petroleum engineers Capen, Clapp, and Campbell (1971) who suggested that oil companies had suffered unexpectedly low rates of return on outer continental shelf (OCS) lease sales year after year in the 1960s and the 1970s. They argued that such low rates of return resulted from the fact that winners ignored the informational consequences of winning and naively based their bids on the unconditional expected value of the item. However, having

a winning bid against rivals following similar bidding strategies implies that the unconditional expected value of the item (which is true on average) is nevertheless an overestimate of the value of the item conditional upon the event of winning. More simply put, you only win the auction when your estimate happens to be the highest (or one of the highest) and this adverse selection effect ensures that below normal or even negative profits are produced. Examples of such Winner's Curse have been claimed in the oil industry (Capen, Clapp, & Campbell, 1971; Lorenz & Dougherty, 1983), in auctions for book publication rights (Dessauer, 1981), in major league baseball free agency (Cassing & Douglas, 1980; Blecherman & Camerer, 1998), in corporate takeover battles (Roll, 1986), in real estate auctions (Ashenfelter & Genesore, 1992), timber auctions (Athey & Levin, 2004), and procurement auctions in the state of New Jersey (Hong & Shum, 2002). Such Winner's Curse phenomena are however not necessarily restricted to auctions with pure common values or partial common value elements. We could also see the Winner's Curse effect under private value auctions with independent valuations. This has been effectively argued in Compte (2002), and Crawford and Irriberi (2005).

We also provide at the end of the chapter a list of further readings that can provide valuable insight into the problems surrounding the Winner's Curse. The interested reader is referred to this section for further literature.

DATA

The data set used in this analysis consists of online reverse auctions conducted by a large multinational firm between the years 2000 and 2002 to procure a variety of products ranging from nuts and bolts to IT services. The data set comprises of first-price auctions where the lowest bidder wins the contract at its bid price. For each item auctioned, the purchasing agent of the firm specified the auction formats, identified the potential suppliers, and invited them to place bids in the auctions. The firm employed different auction designs that offered different degrees of information to the suppliers. The participating suppliers at all points in time were aware of the bidding terms, time remaining in the auction, and their own bidding history, but had only partial or no information about the bidding history of their competitors. At one end of this spectrum were auctions where the bidders only knew whether their own bid was accepted. These auctions are equivalent to traditional sealed-bid or blind auctions. However, we only have 109 observations for this type of auction. The other auction formats provided the bidders with varied levels of transparency about the bids tendered. The degree of information available to the competitors ranged from knowing only their ranks in the auction to knowing all three of the following: their own current rank, the lowest bid submitted in that auction, whether they lead the auction or not, and a combination of their rank and the lowest bid. We have a total of 6,875 observations. To protect the confidentiality of the data, the dependent variable P depicting the auction success is computed by multiplying the percentage deflation in bid price by a secret positive constant.[1]

THE MODEL: METHODOLOGY AND RESULTS

As described above, if we follow the arguments acknowledging the existence of the Winner's Curse not only in common value auctions, but also in private value auctions, we do not need to worry whether our products are pure common value products, pure private value products, or a combination of the two. Our hypothesis is that in the presence of the Winner's Curse, with the bidders being aware of its presence, the auctioneer would face the problem of having overcautious bidders. In fact, contrary to competitive market economic theory, the more competition there is, the more cautious the bidders will become, and if it so happens that the Winner's Curse effect dominates the competition effect, in our case of reverse auctions, we would have an increase in the final price if we increase the number of bidders or suppliers. To capture this particular hypothesis, we define the dependant variable as success, which is formally defined as:

SUCCESS = (last price - minimum bid)/last price

That is, we look at a quantitative measure of the success of the auction. The minimum bid is set by the firm that is the buyer, thus the measure SUCCESS looks at proportionally how much the price has dropped below the required minimum bid. Initially we look at a total of 6,875 observations, the observations being the auctions conducted by the large multinational firm whose dataset we use, to procure a variety of products from its suppliers ranging from nuts and bolts to paper to IT services. In our first model, we only have one independent variable N. We take a look at results for two broad variants of the auction: rank known, auctions where the bidders are aware of their bid ranks, and rank unknown, where bidders are unaware of their bid ranks. There are a total of 6,171 observations for known ranks, this includes 1,911 observations where just the rank is known and 4,260 observations for which both the rank and the low bid are known. For the broad case of rank unknown, there are 704 observations, of which 364 observations are where only the low bid is revealed, and 231 observations are where the only information is whether the participant is leading in the bidding or not. We will also present results using all these control variables of auction characteristics, such as rank, rank and low bid, low bid, and lead/not lead. In our second model we will add a couple of new explanatory variables into our model, experience and presence of overtime (see Table 1).

Table 1. First model (rank known)

	Coefficient	Standard Error	t-statistic	p-value
Intercept	0.28	0.006	44.6	2.3E-298
N	-0.0025	0.0002	-9.01	4.48E-19

R-squared =0.04

Table 2.

	Coefficient	Standard Error	t-statistic	p-value
Intercept	0.2802	0.0062	44.63	1.4E-298
N	-0.002531	0.0002	-9.01	4.59E-19

R-squared =0.04

Table 3.

	Coefficient	Standard Error	t-statistic	p-value
Intercept	0.2482	0.0048	51.16	0
N	0.0010	0.0005	1.871	0.06

R-squared =0.0008

First Model (Rank Known)

We are essentially interested in the significance of the slope coefficient and the sign of the slope coefficient which is N. As we can see from Table 1, both the intercept and the slope term are significant. As for the sign on N, it is negative, which implies that there is an inverse relationship between the SUCCESS variable and N—the higher the number of competitors in our auction, the lower (value) will be the success parameter or the higher will be the last price. This does indicate the presence of a Winner's Curse effect that is larger than the competition effect for our data set. Let us now look at the two sub categories under this category of Rank Known. The two sub categories would be *Rank* and *Rank and Low Bid*. Under *Rank* the only information given to the bidders are the ranks of their bids. Under *Rank and Low Bid* the bidder knows not only their own rank but

the lowest bid in the auction as well. This latter category would give the bidders a little bit more information about the auction and their position in the auction. For the subcategory *Rank* we have the following results (see Table 2).

In this subcategory we see that the Winner's Curse does force the bidders to be cautious, and thus an increase in the number of bidders leads to lower auction success. Both the intercept and the slope in the regression are significant.

The following are the results for the next sub category, which is *Rank and Low Bid* (see Table 3).

In this case, the slope variable in the regression has a positive value and is significant at the 94% confidence level. This suggests that the additional information to the bidders may be either getting rid of the Winner's Curse problem or is making the effect of the Winner's Curse on auction success statistically independent.

First Model (Rank Unknown)

Now, we present the results for the situations where the bidders do not know the rank of their bids. This could have two sub categories in our data: *Low Bid* and *Lead/Not Lead* (see Table 4).

In this case, the sign on the variable N is positive, indicating that the competition effect is larger than the Winner's Curse effect. The coefficient is significant only at the 93% confidence interval or lower. We could intuitively conjecture that the case of known rank has a Winner's Curse effect larger than the competition effect, while the case of unknown rank has a lower Winner's Curse effect because if the bidders know their ranks they automatically tend to become more cautious (especially the bidders that are likely to be successful) to avoid the Winner's Curse. In the case of unknown rank the bidders are unaware of their standing relative to the other bidders and thus do not tend to become more cautious. The

other observation about the results here is that the R-squared term is very low. This would suggest the introduction of new explanatory variables, which is presented in our second model. Let us now look at the two subcategories under Rank Unknown: *Low Bid* and *Lead/Not Lead*.

The following are the results for *Low Bid* (see Table 5)

In this case the slope variable of the regression, the number of bidders becomes insignificant. Thus the Winner's Curse effect on auction success becomes statistically insignificant.

Given below are the results for *Lead/Not Lead* (see Table 6).

In this case the slope variable is positive and significant at the 95% confidence level, meaning that the Winner's Curse effect is overshadowed by the competition effect and the Winner's Curse ceases to cause any loss of auction success. Again, as noted under the broad category Rank Unknown above, what seems to be happening here

Table 4. First model (rank unknown)

	Coefficient	Standard Error	t-statistic	p-value
Intercept	0.2505	0.0044	56.30	0
N	0.0009	0.0005	1.751	0.07

R-squared =0.0006

Table 5.

	Coefficient	Standard Error	t-statistic	p-value
Intercept	0.3076	0.0177	17.31	2.47E-49
N	0.0011	0.0033	0.346	0.729

R-squared =0.0003

Table 6.

	Coefficient	Standard Error	t-statistic	p-value
Intercept	0.2834	0.0361	7.85	1.58E-13
N	0.0152	0.0080	1.8995	0.05

R-squared =0.015

is that if the bidders are unaware of their specific rank they seem to do better in competitive bidding. Also comparing the results with the broad category Rank Known, if the bidders are given more information than just the Ranks, they seem to be more comfortable bidding competitively and not being cautious because of the Winner's Curse effect. Thus it seems to be important from a practitioner's standpoint that the bidders be given information more than just their ranks or be given information other than their ranks.

Second Model (Rank Known)

In this model we add several more independent variables to the model to give us a richer interpretation of the data set. In many instances with

our firm, which is borne out by the large number of both theoretical and practical literature on the subject, there is at least one overtime period in the auctions. According to the theory, an auction with a fixed and prespecified ending time will tend to have a flurry of behavior at the end that will not be beneficial to the interests of the firm conducting the auction, nor to the interests of the suppliers participating. In the case of reverse auctions, the firm will tend to see sudden drops in prices by some suppliers, leading to frustration among the others that in the long run may hurt the buyer due to lessened participation. From the point of view of the suppliers, they may be suspicious that there is a dummy supplier that is really an agent of the buyer indulging in shill bidding in the end to promote a price war. Usually the overtime rules

Table 7. Second model (rank known)

	Coefficient	Standard Error	t-statistic	p-value
Intercept	0.208	.005	35.44	1.2E-250
N	-0.00143	.0002	-6.1	8.64E-10
Overtime	.049	.005	7.67	1.92E-14
Experience	.0033	.0003	12.55	1.02E-35

R-squared = 0.044

Table 8.

	Coefficient	Standard Error	t-statistic	p-value
Intercept	0.2427	.009	24.94	4.5E-119
N	-0.0020	.0002	-7.3	3.97E-13
Overtime	.0089	.009	0.909	0.36
Experience	.0028	.0003	7.22	7.04E-13

R-squared =0.06

Table 9.

	Coefficient	Standard Error	t-statistic	p-value
Intercept	0.1809	.0075	23.95	4.4E-119
N	0.0003	.0005	0.566	0.57
Overtime	0.06	.0077	7.86	4.77E-15
Experience	.004	.0003	10.73	1.49E-26

R-squared =0.04

are set such that if there is a specified amount of activity in the last few moments of the auction, the auction automatically goes to overtime. Thus, there is no incentive for one firm or the other to try and win the auction at the last minute.

The other variable that we introduce is experience. Often buyers will only invite those suppliers that have sufficient experience both in participation in such auctions and in supply chain relationships with the buyer. Again under this broad category, we have two subcategories: *Rank* and *Rank and Low Bid.* The first result table looks at the broad category of Rank Known and after that we present the results for the two subcategories. We thus have the following results (see Table 7).

As we can see from the above table, all the independent variables are significant, which suggests the importance of all of them. Coefficients of overtime and experience both have positive signs, which are what we would expect from our hypothesis, while N has a negative value, which implies that the Winner's Curse effect dominates the competition effect, as we had in our first model with known rank.

Let us now look at the specific model with the additional control variable of the bidders knowing just their rank. The following are the results (see Table 8).

We can see from these results that our discussions in the first model are also borne out by the addition of the two new variables: Information

about the ranks of the bidders does have an adverse effect on auction success.

We next present results for the subcategory *Rank and Low Bid* (see Table 9).

Again, what we see here is that the additional information about the low bids makes the Winner's Curse effect on auction success statistically insignificant.

Second Model (Rank Unknown)

In this case, like in our first model, the bidders do not have any idea about what the ranks of the bidders are. However, in this case the coefficient of N is negative, implying that if we include our variables of experience and overtime situations, the Winner's Curse effect will dominate the competition effect even though the effect is marginally smaller than the case where all the ranks of the bidders were known. We note that just like in the first model with unknown ranks of bidders, the coefficient of N is insignificant. Both these results suggest that if we are looking at a situation where the bidders do not know their ranks, the number of bidders has an insignificant effect on the price deflation variable—neither the Winner's Curse effect nor the competition effect have any consequence on the final price. All other coefficients are significant and have the expected signs (see Table 10).

As we see above, comparing the situation in model one where the ranks were unknown with the results above the R-squared term has increased

Table 10. Second model (rank unknown)

	Coefficient	Standard Error	t-statistic	p-value
Intercept	0.2196	0.0153	14.35	3.89E-41
N	-0.00236	0.0030	-0.7631	0.445621
Overtime	0.0832	0.0160	5.186	2.82E-07
Experience	0.0014	0.0008	1.759	0.078903

R-squared = 0.043

quite a bit—however, the coefficient of N is still insignificant. It does seem that the lack of information about ranks of bidders leads to an insignificant relationship between the number of bidders and the price deflation or success of the auction. If we split up the category into sub categories, the coefficient of N is still insignificant, and we need not show the results here again. Thus, looking at all our results we could come to the conclusion that information about just the ranks of the bidders forces the bidders to be cautious about their bids, and this affects the auction success.

CONCLUSION

We conclude by reiterating the basic premise of this chapter, that online reverse auctions could lead to a Winner's Curse problem, for both common value and private value auctions. Thus bidders in such reverse auctions would be cautious about their bids to avoid overbidding, and they would tend to be more cautious the higher the number of bidders, thus giving rise to the problems described here associated with trying to avoid the Winner's Curse.

FUTURE RESEARCH DIRECTIONS

One idea worth exploring in the future would be to look at blind or sealed-bid auctions and compare them with results from an open auction to see if we have a worsening of the Winner's Curse. Typically, sealed-bid auctions provide less information to the bidders about competitors' bids. Thus, bidders may be a lot more concerned about their bids since they have no means of knowing how their bids stack up against their fellow bidders. Hence, they would tend to be cautious about their bids and may exacerbate the Winner's Curse problem. A second idea would be to look at the data for auction values, and see if higher auction values would exacerbate the Winner's Curse or not, the idea being that firms would be more eager to win higher valued auctions and would thus bid more aggressively. We could also explicitly try to see whether experience can help mitigate the problem, in the sense that more experienced firms would tend to understand the Winner's Curse better. Intelligent firms would thus be able to perceive the potential of a Winner's Curse in this situation without being more cautious about their bidding. The intuition here is that if all the firms are experienced and are aware of the Winner's Curse, they would all tend to have confidence that no one was overbidding. Thus, everyone could have perfect information or close to perfect information about the products being auctioned and we would see less chance of diminished auction success. Another idea worth exploring would be to find data for bundled goods and see if the Winner's Curse is less prevalent. Theoretically, since bundling would "tie up" a few products together, bidders would be bidding for all these products as a group rather than individually, thus we should expect the Winner's Curse for a group of products to be less than the combined Winner's Curse for individual products. Such new research may probably find a place in a follow up to the current chapter.

REFERENCES

Ashenfelter, O., & Genesore, D. (1992). Testing for price anomalies in real estate auctions. *American Economic Review: Papers and Proceedings, 82,* 501-505.

Athey, S., & Levin, J. (2001). Information and competition in U.S. forest service timber auctions. *Journal of Political Economy, 109*(2), 375-417.

Blecherman, B., & Camerer, C. (1998). *Is there a winner's curse in the market for baseball players?* mimeograph, Brooklyn Polytechnic University, Brooklyn.

Capen, E., Clapp, R., & Campbell, W. (1971). Competitive bidding in high-risk situations. *Journal of Petroleum Technology, 23*(6), 641-653.

Cassing, J., & Douglas, R. (1980). Implication of the auctions mechanism in baseball's free agency draft. *Southern Economic Journal, 46,* 110-120.

Compte, O. (2002). *The winner's curse with independent private values*, Mimeograph CERAS-ENPC.

Crawford, V., & Irriberi, N. (2005). *Level-k auctions: Can a non-equilibrium model of strategic thinking explain the winner's curse and overbidding in private value auctions?* Working Paper.

Davies, G. (2002). Entering the second generation of online reverse auctions. *Inside Supply Management, 5*(6), 54.

Dessauer, J. (1981). *Book Publishing*. New York: Bowker.

Gupta, S., Ghosh, I., & Millet, I. (2008). An empirical study of collusion potential metrics and their impact on online reverse auction success In D. Parente (Ed.), *Best Practices in Online Procurement Auctions*. Hershey, PA: IGI Global Publishing.

Hong, H., & Shum, M. (2002). Increasing competition and the winner's curse: Evidence from procurement. *Review of Economic Studies, 69*(4), 871-898.

Kagel, J., & Levin, D. (1986). The winner's curse and public information in common value auctions. *American Economic Review, 76,* 894-920.

Lorenz, J., & Dougherty, E. (1983). *Bonus bidding and bottom lines: Federal off-shore oil and gas*. SPE 12024, 58th Annual Fall Technical Conference.

Lucking-Reiley, D. (2000). Auctions on the Internet: What's being auctioned, and how? *Journal of Industrial Economics, 48*(3), 227-252.

Milgrom, P., & Weber, R. (1982). A theory of auctions and competitive bidding. *Econometrica, 50*(5), 1089-1122.

Parente, D., Venkatraman, R., Fizel, J., & Millet, I. (2001). A conceptual research framework for analyzing online auctions in a b2b environment. *Supply Chain Management: An International Journal, 9*(4), 287-294.

Pinker, E., Seidmann, A., & Vakrat, Y. (2003). Managing online auctions: Current business and research issues. *Management Science, 49*(11), 1457-1484.

Roll, R. (1986). The hubris hypothesis of corporate takeovers. *Journal of Business, 59,* 197-216.

ADDITIONAL READINGS

Astbro, T., & Bernhardt, I. (2005). The winner's curse of human capital. *Small Business Economics, 1,* 63-78.

Ausubel, L., & Cramton, P. (2004). Auctioning many divisible goods. *Journal of the European Economic Association, 2*(2-3), 480-493.

Bajari, P., & Hortacsu, A. (2003). The winner's curse, reserve prices, and endogenous entry: Empirical insights from eBay auctions. *RAND Journal of Economics, 34*(2), 329-355.

Bajari, P., & Hortacsu, A. (2004). Economic insights from Internet auctions. *Journal of Economic Literature, 42*(2), 457-486.

Banerjee, P., & Chakraborty, A. (2004). *Auctions with ceilings*. Unpublished manuscript, Rutgers University at Newark.

Biais, B., & Faugeron-Crouzet, A. (2002). IPO auctions: English, Dutch, French, and Internet. *Journal of Financial Intermediation, 11*(1), 9-36.

Bulow, J., & Klemperer, P. (2002). Prices and the winner's curse. *RAND Journal of Economics, 33*(1), 1-21.

Cable, J., Henley, A., & Holland, K. (2002). Pot of gold or winner's curse? An event study of the auctions of 3G mobile telephone licenses in the UK. *Fiscal Studies, 23*(4), 447-462.

Chakraborty, I. (2002) Bundling and the reduction of the winner's curse. *Journal of Economics and Management Strategy, 11*(4), 663-684.

Chakraborty, A., & Yilmaz, B. (2003). Multi-stage financing and the winner's curse. *Economics Bulletin, 4*(32), 1-8.

Eschker, E., Perez, S., & Siegler, M. (2004). The NBA and the influx of international basketball players. *Applied Economics, 36*(10), 1009-1020.

Eso, P., & White, L. (2004). Precautionary bidding in auctions. *Econometrica, 72*(1), 77-92.

Eyster, E., & Rabin, M. (2005). Cursed equilibrium. *Econometrica, 73*(5), 1623-1672.

Goeree, J., & Offerman, T. (2002). Efficiency in auctions with private and common values: An experimental study. *American Economic Review, 92*(3), 625-643.

Goeree, J., & Offerman, T. (2003). Winner's curse without overbidding. *European Economic Review, 47*(4), 625-644.

Goeree, J., Offerman, T., & Schram, A. (2006). Using first-price auctions to sell heterogeneous licenses. *International Journal of Industrial Organization, 24*(3), 555-581.

Gordy, M. (1999). Hedging winner's curse with multiple bids: Evidence from the Portuguese treasury bill auction. *Review of Economics and Statistics, 81*(3), 448-465.

Hauser, J., & Toubia, O. (2005). The impact of utility balance and endogeneity in conjoint analysis. *Marketing Science, 24*(3), 498-507.

Kagel, J. (2003). Common value auctions and the winner's curse: Lessons from the economics laboratory. *The economics of risk* (pp. 65-101). Kalamazoo, MI: W. E. Upjohn Institute for Employment Research.

Kagel, J., & Levin, D. (2002). *Common value auctions and the winner's curse.* Princeton, NJ: Princeton University Press.

Keloharju, M., Nyborg, K., & Rydqvist, K. (2005). Strategic behavior and underpricing in uniform price auctions: Evidence from Finnish treasury auctions. *Journal of Finance, 60*(4), 1865-1902.

Leite, T. (2005). Returns to sentiment investors in IPOs. *Economics Letters, 89*(2), 222-226.

Levin, J., Athey, S., & Seira, E. (2004). *Comparing open and sealed bid auctions: Theory and evidence from timber auctions.* (Working Paper No. 2004.142). Italy: Fondazione Eni Enrico Mattei

Lind, B., & Plott, C. (2001). The winner's curse: Experiments with buyers and with sellers. *Collected papers on the experimental foundations of economics and political science: Vol. 2. Market institutions and price discovery*, (pp. 332-43), Economists of the Twentieth Century series. Cheltenham, UK and Northampton, MA: Elgar.

Mandell, S. (2005). The choice of multiple or single auctions in emissions trading. *Climate Policy, 5*(1), 97-107.

Ockenfels, A., Reiley, D., & Sadrieh, A. (2006). *Online auctions.* National Bureau of Economic Research, Inc, NBER Working Papers: 12785.

Parlour, C., & Rajan, U. (2005). Rationing in IPOs. *Review of Finance, 9*(1), 33-63.

Pinkse, J., & Tan, G. (2005). The affiliation effect in first-price auctions. *Econometrica, 73*(10), 263-277.

Povel, P., & Singh, R. (2006). Takeover contests with asymmetric bidders. *Review of Financial Studies, 19*(4), 1399-1431.

Selten, R., Abbink, K., & Cox, R. (2005). Learning direction theory and the winner's curse. *Experimental Economics, 8*(1), 5-20.

Wang, J., & Zender, J. (2002). Auctioning divisible goods. *Economic Theory, 19*(4), 673-705.

Welch, I. (1991). An empirical examination of models of contract choice in initial public offerings. *Journal of Financial and Quantitative Analysis, 26*(4), 497-518.

ENDNOTE

[1]   Parts of the description of the data are taken from our companion paper "An Empirical Study of Collusion Potential Metrics and their Impact on Online Reverse Auction Success," by Gupta, Ghosh, and Millet (2007).

IMPLICATIONS FOR MANAGERS

Title: Competition and the Winner's Curse in B2B Reverse Auctions

Description

In this chapter we have analyzed the data for a major multinational company that uses online reverse auctions for its procurement purposes. In most auctions, we have the potential problem of a Winner's Curse described in the chapter. Should the Winner's Curse exist in an online reverse auction, suppliers would engage in bidding that would result in prices below competitive levels and thus great savings for the procurement agent. However, the possibility of a Winner's Curse may make suppliers more hesitant to participate in the auction and potentially reduce the number of bidders and/or result in cautious bidding. The result is a trade-off for buyers: give information to reduce likelihood of Winner's Curse to promote more supplier participants and competitive buying or give less information, possibly reduce number of bidders and hope for the uninformed participants to result in Winner's Curse. If Curse not the result, the reduction in number of bidders may actually result in prices higher than would result with informed suppliers. Using the company auction data we have, the Winner's Curse is less likely in auctions where information of the ranking of bids is available to the bidders. In most other cases where the bidders have less or more information than the ranks of their bids, they do not tend to be that cautious and consequently the auctioning firm can be expected to have competitive price savings.

Findings

- The Winner's Curse is prevalent in all types of auctions.
- As a result of the Winner's Curse, bidders may choose to be cautious about their participation in the auction and, if participating, their bids, both responses which may diminish the potential price savings and success for the auctioneer.
- In our data set, we find that the more information given to the bidders about ranks of bids tends to lower the auction success.
- If the auctioneer gives more information to the bidders than just bidding ranks, as in Ranks and Low Bid, or less information, as in Low Bid or Lead/Not Lead, the bidders tend to be less cautious about their bidding.
- Practitioners of procurement auctions need to analyze their data and see when the Winner's Curse is most likely to occur and then be aware of the potential negative impact on their auction success.
- Practitioners may need to provide either more information than just Bidding Ranks or less information in order to have insignificant effects of the Winner's Curse. However, as a caveat, it is not necessary that all auctions will provide the same results. Hence, we emphasize the need to properly analyze data from each individual auction data in order to follow the best firm strategy for success.
- An example of how to analyze auction data is provided in this chapter.
- Below we provide some interesting ideas about getting rid of the negative impacts of the Winner's Curse.

RECOMMENDATIONS

An interesting example of the Winner's Curse in reverse auctions is found in construction contracts. Construction contracts are true reverse auctions in the sense that a given number of companies will bid against each other for the right to a construction project. After bidding for a project has closed, the winner is announced and the contractor who won the job will look for subcontractors and materials. In these types of reverse auctions, the Winner's Curse thus comes from bidding too low. However in general construction contracts are able to avoid the Winner's Curse in general. This has been done using some innovative ideas. Besides the obvious idea that more experienced bidders are more easily able to avoid the Winner's Curse, construction contracts have laws in many states where they can withdraw their bids because of arithmetic errors. The interpretation of these arithmetic errors is quite liberal, and hence if a contractor feels that they have bid too low on a project they can withdraw from the project citing the above-mentioned arithmetic errors. Another way to escape the Winner's Curse is to renegotiate the contracts with the subcontractors. The subcontractors know that if they do not renegotiate with the contractor, the latter will withdraw the bid for the project citing arithmetic errors and the subcontractor will be out of a project. Also the contractor can overcharge for change orders which are inevitable in the construction business. The idea here is that being aware of and escaping the Winner's Curse in reverse auctions means charging a price higher than what would have been charged through the bidding process if the bidders were unaware of the curse.

LIMITATIONS

The limitation of this study is that it uses construction contracts.

Chapter XI
Novel Business–Oriented Auctions

Tracy Mullen
The Pennsylvania State University, USA

ABSTRACT

With the advent of the Internet, traditional auction forms have evolved to fit into a plethora of business niches, either integrating into traditional approaches or simply creating new opportunities. This chapter examines two novel uses for auctions in a business context, namely sponsored search auctions and prediction markets. Understanding the potential auction benefits and limitations can hopefully provide practitioners with a more informed and successful approach when employing these auction-based tools in their business.

SPONSORED SEARCH AUCTIONS

Introduction

Search engines are big business on the Internet. The two main players, Google and Yahoo!, made $6 billion and $5 billion in 2005, respectively. This bonanza mainly comes from *sponsored search*, where search engines charge advertisers to display their ads when users search for particular terms. Instead of large banner ads directed to everyone, sponsored search allows advertisers to target their audience. Real estate agents can display their ads

only to users searching on the term "real estate." In Figure 1, Google's unpaid (or native or organic) search results are in the middle of the screen, while its advertising network's paid results (or sponsored links) are on the right-hand side.

To advertise via sponsored search, advertisers first identify potential search terms of interest and then bid on the *cost per click* (CPC) that they are willing to pay to the search engine if a user clicks on their advertisement. Each time a user searches, an auction occurs based on what advertisement keywords match the search terms. The auction ranks advertisements based on bid

Figure 1. Search for "buy real estate" on Google

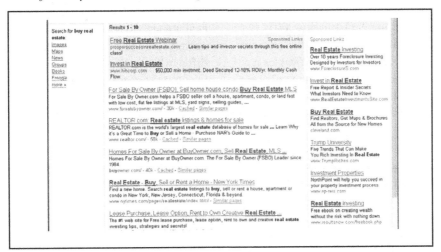

amount, desired geographic location, and other criteria, then displays the advertisements according to their ranking in the paid results slots (e.g., Google Adwords, Yahoo! Search Marketing). Alternatively, Google's AdSense serves ads when users visit Web sites enrolled in their program. Instead of matching using a user's search query, they match advertisement keywords according to the Web site's content.

Search engines make money from advertisers, who can choose to take their business to any one of several search engine companies. For a search engine to attract advertisers, they must attract or be able to target the users an advertiser desires, and to attract users, they must have good unpaid search results. So Yahoo! Search Marketing's main competitor in the sponsored search business is not Google Adwords, but Google's unpaid search results, and vice versa (Balcan, Chen, Devanur, & Kumar, 2006).

Behind the scenes in sponsored search, huge numbers of transient auctions are occurring, one for every time a user enters a query (Jansen, 2006). Instead of the standard one-shot one-item auction, sponsored search auctions are continuous real-time multi-item auctions. Instead of two main participants, there are three: the search engine,

the advertiser, and the user. Academic research is just starting to evaluate auction mechanism tradeoffs in terms of properties such as maximizing revenue, consumer welfare, price stability, and robustness to fraud. In this chapter, we describe some current research results in this area and their implications for practitioners.

Auction Mechanism Background

Google and Yahoo! are currently the major players in the sponsored search business, with several smaller players such as AskJeeves and LookSmart, and the more recent addition of the Microsoft adCenter. We focus here on the Yahoo! and Google contributors to the present day sponsored search auction format. GoTo.com (renamed Overture in 2001, and acquired by Yahoo! in 2003) originated the sponsored search auction in 1998, while Google's first sponsored search auction followed in 2002 (Fain & Pedersen, 2005). The original GoTo.com auction used a first-price payment mechanism. The bidder with highest bid received the top advertising slot and was charged a price equal to the bid amount. The second highest bidder was assigned to the second highest slot, paying its bid amount, and so forth. This payment mechanism led to strategic bidding-war cycles that consumed advertiser time and diminished search engine profits (Edelman & Ostrovsky, 2005). For example, suppose advertiser X values the keyword "real estate" at $2, while advertiser Y values it at $1. If X starts the bidding by bidding the lowest possible price, say $0.10, then Y bids $0.11 to win the first ad slot. Advertiser X responds by bidding $0.12, and so forth. Once X bids $1, then Y will not bid $1.01 since Y only values the keyword at $1. To acquire the second ad slot, Y simply has to bid $0.10. But now X only needs to bid $0.11 to win the first slot, and so the cycle starts over.

Google AdWords added two significant twists to the auction mechanism. First, inspired by auction theory, they changed from a first-price payment mechanism to a more robust second-price one. In a second-price auction, the highest bidder wins but only pays the second highest bid price (plus some small delta). For example, suppose the bids are $10, $9, $8 for a single item, then the $10 bidder wins but only pays $9. Under certain conditions (e.g., sealed-bid, one-shot), a second-price auction is *incentive compatible*, meaning that the optimal strategy for bidders is to bid their true valuation (Vickrey, 1961). This eliminates time-consuming strategic game play and ensures that the item is sold to the bidder who values it the most. The Vickrey-Clark-Groves (VCG) auction is a multi-item extension to the single-item second price auction that retains the incentive compatibility property by charging each bidder the opportunity cost imposed upon the other bidders by being there (Krishna, 2002). Google's multi-item second price auction is known as generalized second price (GSP) auction, and is a straightforward extension of the single-item second price auction, where the kth highest bidder pays the $(k + 1)^{st}$ highest price plus some delta. Consider our previous example where advertiser X pays up to $2 for the keyword "real estate," and advertiser Y will pay $1. In a sealed-bid environment, where only the auctioneer knows the value of all bids, if X bids $2, and Y bids $1, then X pays

$1 + $0.1 (the minimum delta) while X pays the minimum bid amount of $0.10. If only one slot is available to advertisers, then the GSP and VCG auctions are equivalent. However, their properties differ when multiple slots are offered. Namely, the GSP is not incentive compatible, but is easier to understand than the VCG, and can reduce the bidding war cycles of the first-price mechanism. Also, while VCG maximizes consumer welfare, it may not maximize revenue or hold up well in the face of collusive and anti-social behavior by bidders (Ausubel & Milgrom, 2005; Brandt & Weiss, 2001).

The second main twist Google added to the original first-price auction mechanism is ranking its ads not by bid price alone, but by computing a quality score derived from the bid amount, the ad's click-through rate, keyword relevancy along with landing-page and site quality. The *click-through-rate* (CTR) measures the rate that Web searchers click through to the advertiser's Web site when shown the ad. Google's other quality-based criteria serve to penalize sites that use deceptive practices or have exceptionally poor Web sites, and is assessed through both human and automated methods. In this way, Google can protect the user's search experience, and also increase their profits, since users are more likely to click on relevant ads and thereby generate Google revenue. These two auction mechanism changes have helped make Google's auction more stable and more profitable. Google's second-price auction debuted in February 2002, and Overture (rebranded to Yahoo! Search Marketing in 2005) updated to a second-price auction in May 2002. However, Yahoo! has only recently decided to add a Quality Index (Yahoo!) to their ranking as of early 2007.

Sponsored search auctions demonstrate how markets can evolve to forms more suitable to their commercial environment. Researchers have also begun to formally describe both current properties of sponsored search auctions and consider potentially desirable modifications. However, it is difficult to formalize the full-fledged sponsored search auction environment where there are a multitude of continuously repeated auctions. In game theory, the Folk Theorem states that any feasible and individually rational outcome of a repeated game can be sustained as an equilibrium. In other words, almost any reasonable outcome can be shown to happen across infinitely repeated games. Some researchers have simplified the problem by considering the auction mechanism for a one auction, one keyword setting. Under these conditions, the GSP auction has been shown theoretically to have a local equilibrium where advertisers find a bid amount such that they neither want to raise their bid to move up to the next highest slot, nor lower it to move to the next lower slot. This equilibrium concept was discovered independently as a *locally envy-free equilibrium* (Edelman, Ostrovsky, & Schwarz, 2005) or equivalently a *symmetric Nash equilibrium* (Varian, 2006).

Researchers have also stepped back to look at the entire competitive landscape by considering the problem facing an advertiser with multiple advertising campaigns, each consisting of multiple keywords. Optimizing bidding strategy for a single auction, may not be the best strategy across all auctions of interest (Balcan, Chen, Devanur, & Kumar, 2006). Most have focused on using the budget to evaluate the overall return on investment (ROI). One proposed bidding heuristic is that advertisers equalize their ROI across all keywords (Borgs et al., 2007). Others have incorporated minimum ROI into their bidding strategies, or applied budget constraints to single auctions (Abrams, 2006; Borgs et al., 2007; Lahaie, 2006; Szymanski & Lee, 2006).

Budget can also serve as a proxy for risk management (e.g., against click fraud or unexpected user query surges). Auction payment mechanisms can also effect how risk is shared between the search engine and the advertiser. Pay-per-action (PPA) pricing allows advertisers to specify what action (e.g., selling a product, sales lead, etc.) a user would have to take on their Web site before

they would have to pay. PPA advertising can help mitigate the risks of fraudulent clicks since the advertiser pays only if a customer takes a further action. Both pay-per-click and pay-per-action allow the search engine to bear more of the market variation risk than pay-per-impression. For example, if an ad gets shown more often at 5 a.m., but users are less likely to buy then, an advertiser will not incur any budgetary loss. Another possibility is extending the auction mechanism to include futures—florists who want to lock up advertisements on and shortly before Valentine's Day might buy a keyword future for the word "flowers" (Balcan, Chen, Devanur, & Kumar, 2006). Finally, different auction mechanisms can also serve to apportion risk differently across search engine and advertiser (Liu, Chen, & Whinston, 2006).

Click Fraud

Click fraud occurs when an advertiser's ad is clicked with the sole intent of generating a charge to the advertiser. It can be done automatically by computer scripts or directly by humans, and can occur for a variety of reasons, including a competitors desire to minimize the impact of an ad campaign, simple vandalism, or a desire by a publisher to increase their income (Jansen, 2006). To see this, consider Google's Adwords and AdSense programs. In the Adwords program, Google displays advertiser's ads on their search engine as a response to user queries. Clicking on an advertisement costs the advertiser and runs down their ad budget. In the AdSense program, Google serves ads to a Web site whenever a user visits that Web site. Clicking on an advertisement costs the advertiser, but also provides revenue to the Web site owner. Google and Yahoo! search for suspicious patterns of clicking, and automatically do not charge advertisers for any clicks deemed to be an instance of click fraud. However, the process of assessing click fraud is complex and not provided to the public. Since the advertising networks benefit from the increased traffic, albeit unintentionally, both advertisers and Web site owners have concerns that fraudulent clicks be classified correctly.

The class action lawsuit, the Lane's Gifts vs. Google, charged Google with not doing enough to detect click fraud. As part of the settlement, Dr. Alexander Tuzhilin from NYU was commissioned to do an independent study of Google's handling of click fraud (Tuzhilin, 2006). He was given access to Google's engineers and inside documents. His main finding was that Google's efforts to detect and combat click fraud seem to be "reasonable," with Google efforts becoming more effective by 2005. However, given the lack of full conversion data, there was way to give hard scientific evidence as to exactly how well the measures were working. Indeed, for some clicks, especially human ones, it may be impossible to determine whether it was click fraud simply from the data. Given this, Tuzhilin lends support to the notion that using CPA pricing may be necessary to reduce or eliminate click fraud. He also confirmed that AdSense is more prone to fraud than AdWords. Other involve designing click fraud resistant algorithms (Goodman, 2005; Immorlica, Jain, Mahdian, & Talwar, 2005).

Recommendations

Identify Business Objectives

Online advertising is here to stay. In 2005, Proctor & Gamble was the nation's biggest advertiser, spending $33.5 million of its $4.6 billion ad budget on online ads. Similarly, the second-biggest advertiser, General Motors, spent 2.5% of its total ad budget of $4.35 billion online (Story, 2006). However, these large established companies tend to be more interested in furthering their brand recognition online, and concentrating on banner ads and other display advertisements rather than search ads. Clearly before starting a sponsored-search advertising campaign, a company must identify

their business objectives and see if sponsored search is a good match. Some standard business objectives include selling products online, gathering contact information, generating traffic on your Web site, or providing information to drive visitors to local physical business locations. While most sponsored search pricing is based on CPC, it may be more straightforward for a business to evaluate its objective using different metrics. Cost-per-mille (CPM) measures the number of times (in thousands) that users have seen the ad, or the user impressions. It is most valuable when brand recognition is the goal, and comes directly from offline advertising. Cost-per-action (CPA) measures how many of the clicks on an advertisement result in a sale or some other valuable "action." This is known as the *conversion rate*. For example, if the objective is to generate customer leads, then the action being measured might be how many users fill out a form with their name and e-mail address for further contact. Pricing based on CPM and CPA may be offered directly by the search engine, or advertisers can buy advertisements using CPC pricing and then use the CTR, CPM, or CPA rates supplied by the search engine data to evaluate how well their ad campaign outcome aligns with their business goals.

Devote Time to Discovering the Best Keywords

Discovering the right keywords for a sponsored search ad campaign can make a big difference in the CTR and conversion rate. For example, consider the keywords "real estate" vs. "buy real estate." Users who clicked on ads for "buy real estate" were much more likely to generate actions that led to sale leads, at least in 2003 (Ellam et al., 2003). While there might be fewer searches for "buy real estate" vs. "real estate," users who include the keyword "buy" in their search had a higher conversion rate and thus were more valuable. Advertisers bidding on "real estate" would need to bid higher to rank highly in a "buy real estate" auction. However, by bidding higher, they then show up as highly ranked when more casual users searched for "real estate" and end up paying a higher price for users with a lower conversion rate. To help address this issue, a common bidding strategy for advertisers was to estimate their conversion rate for the different keyword phrases, and then set their bid to maximize return on investment (ROI). So the lesson learned here is that these keyword markets are highly interrelated, and it may take some exploration to discover the market with the best ROI for a given business objective or product.

Similarly, although advertisers do not pay when an ad is shown and users do not click on it, bidding for a large number of general keywords is not an effective strategy, as your advertisement and site may not have a high relevance for a general keyword, and your CTR will probably be low. Recall that in quality-based bidding, both of those factors can negatively impact the final advertisement ranking, requiring the advertiser to increase their bid price to keep the same final ranking.

Finding the right set of "golden-nugget" keywords requires knowing the market and demographics for a given business or product. In additional, competitors' Web sites may help give insight into useful keywords. Determining the right set of keywords can also be used to upgrade a business' Web site, thereby improving both its bidding quality score as well as its unpaid search placement results. Google (Google) and Yahoo! (Yahoo!) provide advice on keyword selection, guidelines for increasing the quality score of an ad or site, along with tools that can help track hits for individual keywords. For example, when advertising for a particular product, Google recommends sending the user directly to that product's Web page rather than to the site's home page (Google). Negative keywords can also be used to further target the audience. If you are a chocolate company specializing in truffles, you may want to exclude searches on "mushroom truffles" (i.e., "-mushroom").

Estimator tools that can be used without signing up for an advertising campaign include Google's Adword Keyword (Google) and Traffic Estimator tools (Google). The Adword Keyword tool helps select keywords by displaying alternate potential keyword phrases, their cost and ad position estimates for a given bid, potential negative keywords, and other related information. The Traffic Estimator tool provides estimates of ad position, clicks per day, and budget per day for multiple keywords. Figure 2 shows the Traffic Estimator output for the "buy real estate" and "real estate" keyword phrases given a $1 maximum CPC, a $20 daily budget, for the United States. The keyword phrase "buy real estate" receives fewer clicks than "real estate" for the above parameters, but to determine the better ROI, we would need to know the conversion rate.

Monitor for Click Fraud

Some recommendations from a short, 10-day experiment by the Marketing Experiments Blog and Clicks2Customers for reducing click fraud include (Click Fraud, 2005):

1. Monitor for variations in clicks and conversions in ad campaign performance.
2. Be conservative using ads placed on third-party Web sites (e.g., Google's AdSense). Click fraud from search engines tends to be quite low, not so for third-party Web sites.
3. Only display ads in the geographic areas where products and services are sold.
4. Review server logs, including repeated IP addresses or IP ranges. If click fraud occurs mainly during certain times of day, then pause ad campaigns for those hours. Consider applications like KeywordMax, Urchin, Clicktracks, or companies like ClickDefense to track click fraud levels if the campaign size warrants it.

Figure 2. Google's Adwords Traffic Estimator tool for "buy real estate" and "real estate"

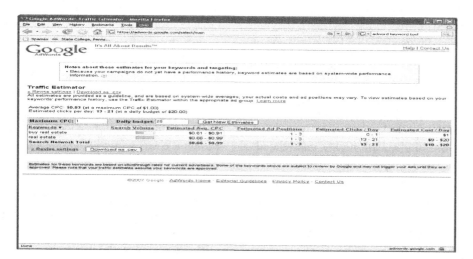

5. Do not simply bid to be number one, measure your results and try to maximize your ROI.
6. High traffic, expensive keywords tend to attract more fraud, try to find alternatives.

Consider Companies that Setup, Monitor, and Track Ad Campaigns

Depending on the size of an ad campaign and the in-house support available for creation and ongoing tracking of campaign success, a business may want to outsource their marketing effort. The Buyer's Guide to Paid Search Ad (PPC) Agencies 2007 profiles 65 firms. Two major players include iProspect (www.iprospect.com) and Clicks2Customers (www.clicks2customers.com), and each provides substantial details on their respective Web sites about their services.

PREDICTION MARKETS AS DECISION SUPPORT TOOLS

Introduction

Increasingly competitive market pressures, driven by globalization and enabled by information technology, have spawned new products and innovations at a rapid pace. Accurately assessing future demand for a new product, given nonexistent or limited historical data, is challenging. Some companies are experimenting with a potential new addition to traditional forecasting tools called prediction markets. A *prediction market* is a financial market created for the sole purpose of producing forecasts, or predictions. Conventional wisdom holds that futures market prices can accurately forecast the likelihood of future events, in part as participants generally have a clear incentive to be honest and "put their money where their mouth is." This insight has been backed up by more quantitative studies, including Roll's 1984 demonstration that the price of orange-juice futures is a better predictor of Florida weather than the National Weather Service (Roll, 1984). Companies such as Hewlett Packard, Google, and Lily are exploring the use of prediction markets as decision support tools to forecast sales, new product demand, or product release dates (King, 2006; Kiviat, 2004). By harnessing the distributed knowledge of their employees and other stakeholders, they hope to use market-driven consensus to arrive at an accurate forecast for questions that may not be easily addressed using other methodologies. Exactly when and where prediction markets can best be used as a decision support tool is still an open question.

Existing Markets

Early prediction markets were set up to forecast events of interest to the general public. The Iowa electronic markets (www.biz.uiowa.edu/iem/) is a limited real-money online futures market founded in 1988 that focuses on predictions of economic and political events, such as who will win presidential elections. Figure 3 shows the **IEM daily midnight closing prices** for the 2004 US Presidential Winner Takes All Market. Analysis of their trading data shows that prices in these markets generally predict the election outcomes better than polls (Berg, Forsythe, Nelson, & Rietz, 2001). The Hollywood Stock Exchange (www.hsx.com) is a play-money exchange that predicts how new films will perform at box office and trading data is sold to entertainment companies. Other examples include Yahoo! Tech Buzz (buzz.research.yahoo.com), Tradesports (www.tradesports.com) and NewsFutures (us.newsfutures.com).

Hewlett-Packard was one of the first to use internal prediction markets for enterprise forecasting, setting up markets to forecast computer workstation sales from 1996-1999 (Chen & Plott,

2002). The traders were mostly product and finance managers, and their market forecasts came closer than official forecasts six out of eight times. As the discipline matures, more companies such as Eli Lilly, Intel, and Microsoft are starting to use prediction markets for internal consumption (Kiviat, 2004). Google reports having run 143 markets so far, on questions from product launch dates to new office openings (Cowgill, 2005). Eli Lilly has experimented with drug development markets to predict the most successful drugs (Kiviat, 2004). Prediction markets have also been used as a means to provide early information on the expected benefits of a given aid project (Hahn & Tetlock, 2005) and to predict influenza outbreaks (Polgreen, Nelson, & Neumann, 2006). Third parties, such as NewsFutures and ConsensusPoint, currently provide commercial market platforms and support to companies wanting to run prediction markets.

Given ethical and legal constraints against real-money gambling, play-money markets are often used for internal markets, which begs the question of whether market accuracy results still apply. Several studies have shown that results are just as accurate (Feng, Bhargava, & Pennock, in press) and that the prices of securities in these play money markets gave as accurate or more accurate predictions than expert opinions (Chen, Chu, Mullen, & Pennock, 2005; Feng, Bhargava, & Pennock, in press; Pennock, Lawrence, Nielsen, & Giles, 2001). The key is to attract a knowledgeable and motivated pool of traders, and money is not the only means of doing that (Servan-Schreiber, Wolfers, Pennock, & Galebach, 2004). Play-money markets typically offer participants small prizes along with public acknowledgement of their trading skills.

Simple Enterprise Market Example

Setting up a prediction market to capture this distributed knowledge requires first determining the appropriate market securities. A *security* pays

Figure 3. Kerry versus Bush aggregate probabilities from IEM

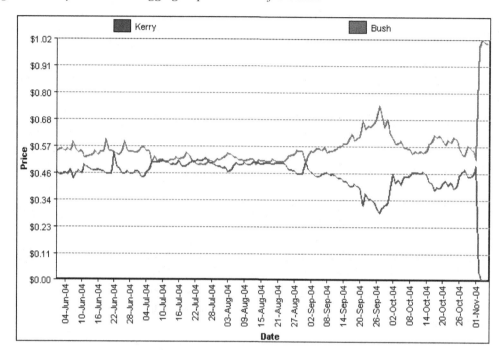

some amount of money (real or play) contingent on future event(s). Consider the security "one dollar if sunny tomorrow." A trader who purchases this security at 30 cents gets a profit of 70 cents if it is sunny tomorrow, or else loses 30 cents if not. In the Iowa electronic markets model, traders initially purchase "unit portfolios." For each dollar a trader receives a basket of related securities. For example, in the 2008 presidential election they might receive three contracts: "one dollar if Republican candidate wins," "one dollar if Democratic candidate wins," and "one dollar if another 3rd party wins."

Moving to the enterprise domain, Figure 3 shows how different stakeholders' might think about an internal product release deadline. An example of a market security here might be "one dollar if product meets March deadline," where "meets the deadline" would be specified with measurable criteria such as "implemented at least 90% of the features in the final require-

ments document." However, there is more relevant information here to discover than just whether the product will meet the deadline. We might also want to know if the project will finish early (when has that ever happened?) or late. If it will finish late, then how late will it finish. To cover the entire space of possibilities, these securities can be sold in *bundles* or *baskets*: "one dollar if meet March deadline," "one dollar if meet April deadline," "one dollar if not done until May or after." Each security would trade in a separate market, and following the IEM approach each user would initially receive a bundle containing one of each security. A user who thought that the product would meet the April deadline with 100% probability would keep the "one dollar if meet April deadline" security and sell the other securities to achieve the greatest expected profit. A user who thought that the April deadline had a 75% probability of being met would keep the "one dollar if meet April deadline" security as

Figure 4. Harnessing distributed stakeholders' explicit and tacit knowledge

long as the price in the April market was 75 cents or below and sell otherwise, and similarly for the other markets.

Theory

Theoretical and empirical research by economists shows that under certain conditions, markets aggregate less-than-perfect, diverse information across many individual traders, so that security prices summarize all the relevant information across traders into a *rational expectations equilibrium*, which is the assumption underlying the strong form of the *efficient markets hypothesis* in finance (Chen, Mullen, & Chu, 2004, 2006; Feigenbaum, Fortnow, Pennock, & Sami, 2003; Grossman, 1981; Jackwerth & Rubinstein, 1996; Plott & Sunder, 1988). Prediction markets are virtual security markets to aggregate information from a diverse set of traders. Depending on the context, prediction markets are also called information markets, forecasting markets, decision markets, or game markets. The process of creating a prediction market starts with identifying a random variable of interest X (e.g., product meets deadline?), then turning it into a financial instrument where the payoff is the realized value of variable (e.g., "Pays one dollar if task completed by May 31st"). If the security price incorporates all available information from market traders, it can be viewed as a consensus prediction about the value of the security reflecting not only individual trader beliefs, but also the effects of

traders updating their beliefs in reaction to the market price and feeding this update back into the market. So ideally, at time t, price(t) $\Box E_t[X]$. (Feng, Bhargava, & Pennock, in press). Recent preliminary theoretical work shows that a general interpretation of prediction market prices depends the joint distribution of trader's beliefs, budgets, and risk preferences (Szymanski & Lee, 2006; Wolfers & Zitzewitz, 2005).

Compared with statistical forecasting methods, prediction markets can incorporate real-time information, which may not be contained in historical data. Conversely, price movements can be mined to indicate when new information has arrived into the system (Feng, Bhargava, & Pennock, in press). Compared with eliciting expert opinions, prediction markets are less constrained by space and time—they eliminate the effort of identifying experts and soliciting their participation, and they do not need to deal explicitly with conflicting opinions (French, 1985; Genest & Zidek, 1986). Most importantly, prediction markets make real-time predictions that take advantage of dispersed information, both explicit and tacit, which can sometimes be hard to capture using other forecasting methods. The market reaches its equilibrium only when all participants believe that the market price represents their predictions (otherwise they would trade).

Laboratory experiments have provided simplified environments for understanding how prediction market accuracy can be affected by a variety of factors such as market structure, aggregate uncertainty (i.e., even if traders pool their information freely, the outcome remains uncertain), and trader heterogeneity. In the case of market structure, negative effects can occur when the composition of available securities makes it difficult or too complex for traders to aggregate their information in the market (O'Brien & Srivastava, 1991; Plott & Sunder, 1988). Also, not surprisingly, outcomes with more aggregate uncertainty lead to less efficient information aggregation (Lundholm, 1991). However, the more heterogeneous the trader profiles, the more efficient the information aggregation (Forsythe & Lundholm, 1990). Sunder (1995) extensively summarized experimental work on information aggregation, concluding that identifying and understanding which factors facilitate or prevent information aggregation in these markets remains a key research issue.

Recommendations

Given the plethora of choices of market and asset design, we describe some of the strategic prediction market requirements that should drive subsequent tactical decisions. The first is to carefully select the events that the prediction market is to forecast. The second is to make the prediction markets simple and easy to use. The third is ensuring management buy-in and recruiting a diverse set of participants.

Carefully Select What to Forecast and Provide Participants with Proper Incentives

Determining the right data to collect to make a good forecast, and gathering it, can comprise a large portion of the forecasting effort. Prediction markets are no exception. The markets themselves require overhead to run and administer, while the participants must invest time to trade. The knowledge should be valuable enough to justify this time and effort. Hewlett Packard has modified

their sales forecast markets to use a market-based method, rather than a prediction market per se, in part because a forecast accuracy increase of a few percentage points was not worth the effort of running markets continuously (Chen, Fine, & Humberman, 2004; King, 2006).

Markets must also attract a reasonable number of participants with an interest in or knowledge of the forecasted events. At the simplest level, the more traders, the more market liquidity results in a more accurate market. In real-money markets, profit is a straightforward motivator. For play-money markets, while some will play for fun, most participants have to be provided with incentives to participate. The top few traders can be rewarded with prizes or their winnings can be converted to lottery tickets where the best traders have the best chance of winning lottery prizes (e.g., iPods, laptops, etc.). Another incentive is recognizing the top players through announcements or a "Top Five Traders" list.

Once the decision about what is worth forecasting is determined, then the appropriate market security must be designed. Our earlier example described a standard security of the form "one dollar if sunny tomorrow," but there are several variations. One possibility is that if the early forecasting of events is critical, market creators can design a security with the appropriate weighted measures of performance, call *scoring rules*, that encourage early predictions (e.g., "one dollar if meet February deadline and predicted by Dec 31st, otherwise $.90").

Another example is conditional securities, which can be used for forecasts that involve assessing policy choices, such as whether to use development package X vs. Y (Berg & Rietz, 2003; Hanson, 1999). Thus given two conditional market securities: (1) "If using development package X, can meet product deadline," and (2) "If using development package Y, can meet product deadline," the relative value of the two asset prices reveals something about the confidence traders have in using development package X vs. Y. This can in turn be folded back into the enterprise decision-making process. Of course, given that the results of these conditional markets may affect future decisions, such contacts will need to be set up to avoid self-defeating properties, so that they predict the outcome *given* the choices.

Simplify User Interfaces and Interactions

This requirement impacts both the user interface design and the market setup (e.g., markets should be easy to navigate, understand, and bid in). To keep the number of markets to a reasonable level, potential forecasting events should be prioritized. For example, not all deadlines should have prediction markets associated with them, only those with critical risk factors that can benefit from real-time monitoring.

Possible choices for prediction market mechanisms include continuous double auctions (CDAs), essentially stock market auctions, or pari-mutual markets similar to those used in horse betting. CDAs are used in exchanges such as Iowa Electronic Market, Hollywood Stock Exchange, Tradesports, NewsFutures, while dynamic pari-mutuel markets can be seen at Yahoo! Tech Buzz. In a CDA, buyers and sellers continually place offers, and as soon as a buy offer is at least as great as a sell offer, a transaction occurs. A few exchanges use a market maker, or "virtual specialist," who will always be willing to buy or sell, but it may lose money (although for fake money markets, this is not an issue). The Yahoo Tech Buzz pari-mutuel auction also provides a market maker mechanism that ensures immediate trading, and does not lose money, but the interface interactions may not be as intuitive as the CDA. Some CDAs require traders to buy long or sell short to express their probabilities (i.e., if you don't believe the product will meet the deadline, you don't buy anything, you sell it short). However, unsophisticated and novice traders seem to feel uncomfortable with these concepts.

Get Buy-In from Management and Ensure a Diverse Set of Participants

In addition to aggregating information, internal prediction markets allow workers to anonymously telegraph concerns to upper management. Thus it may be easier for workers to trade honestly and anonymously in the market (and get rewarded by the market for correct predictions) than to tell their manager directly that sales may go down next quarter, or that critical deadlines may not be met. However, for the same reason, it can be difficult to get support from upper management to implement such markets. They may not want other employees to know that deadlines may not be met, fearing that it may impact morale. As cited by *Business Week* online (2006): "The risk of creating markets is that it's not fudgible, and if you ask the question, then you better want to know the answer," says Robin Hanson, a professor in the department of economics at George Mason University (King, 2006). Clearly this is an area where market designers need to be very sensitive to management concerns. There are also concerns regarding whether market results would create a disclosure dilemma. As Google's Cowgill puts it, "Prediction markets could make everyone in the company an insider from the SEC [Securities Exchange Commission] perspective, if you don't manage it well" (King, 2006). Thus companies generally steer away from forecasting revenue or other financial indicators.

Diversity of knowledge and skills across participants is also important since prediction markets aggregate information best when they combine the forecasts of a heterogeneous set of traders (Forsythe & Lundholm, 1990). Market designers should actively seek to recruit developers, project managers, financial and sales people, and other types of stakeholders. No one person, indeed, no one department can independently track the emerging factors involved in forecasting complex events.

FUTURE RESEARCH DIRECTIONS

In both sponsored search auctions and prediction markets, market design requires the consideration complex tradeoffs to work effectively. In the case of sponsored search auctions, the mechanisms have evolved from simple first-price auctions to GSP auctions to GSP plus quality-based bidding. Driven by commercial pressures, the only constant in this arena is likely to be rapid innovation and change for the near future. A variety of pricing mechanisms, appropriate for different business objectives and for reducing click fraud, are either being offered or planned. More sophisticated bidding software agents could assist advertisers in achieving their campaign objectives by implementing and monitoring more complex bidding strategies. Yahoo! is exploring how to target mobile devices with sponsored search, especially within a given geographic region (Yahoo!, 2006). However, there are numerous potential personalization and privacy issues involved in this extension (Yuan & Zhang, 2003; Minch 2004).

Business prediction markets are starting to move from internal ones to industry-specific ones. For example, StorageMarkets (www.storagemarkets.com) focuses on using prediction markets to gather competitive intelligence about the IT Storage industry. However, as prediction markets get more widely used, the there is a danger that the financial payoffs involved in market outcomes may outweigh the market gains themselves (Rhode & Strumpf, 2007). While market methods have shown initial promise as enterprise forecasting tools, they are not a panacea, and come with their own set of pros and cons. Instead of viewing them as a stand-alone tool, they should be viewed as an integral part of the whole decision support system (Berg & Rietz, 2003). Further research and experience is needed to help determine when the market outperforms more traditional forecasting methods, and where it can be used synergistically with other decision support tools.

REFERENCES

Abrams, Z. (2006). *Revenue maximization when bidders have budgets.* Paper presented at the seventeenth annual ACM-SIAM Symposium on Discrete Algorithms, Miami, FL.

Ausubel, L. M., & Milgrom, P. (2005). The lovely but lonely Vickrey auction. In P. Crampton, R. Steinberg, & Y. Shoham (Eds.), *Combinatorial auctions* (pp. 17-40). Cambridge, MA: MIT Press.

Balcan, M.-F., Chen, J., Devanur, N., & Kumar, A. (2006). Transcript of Panel discussion: Models for Sponsored Search: What are the right questions? [Electronic Version]. *Second Workshop on Sponsored Search Auctions* Retrieved April 5, 2007. from http://research.microsoft.com/~hartline/papers/panel-SSA-06.pdf

Berg, J. E., Forsythe, R., Nelson, F. D., & Rietz, T. A. (2001). Results from a dozen years of election futures markets research. Forthcoming in C. A. Plott & V. Smith (Eds.), *Handbook of Experimental Economic Results.*

Berg, J. E., & Rietz, T. A. (2003). Prediction markets as decision support systems. *Information Systems Frontiers, 5*(1), 79-93.

Borgs, C., Chayes, J., Etesami, O., Immorlica, N., Jain, K., & Mahdian, M. (2007, May). *Dynamics of bid optimization in online advertisement auctions.* Paper presented at the 16th International World Wide Web Conference (WWW2007), Banff, Alberta, Canada.

Brandt, F., & Weiss, G. (2001). Antisocial agents and Vickrey auctions. In J. J. C. Meyer & M. Tambe (Eds.), *Intelligent Agents, 8*(2333), 335-347. Springer-Verlag.

Chen, K. Y., Fine, L., & Humberman, B. A. (2004). Eliminating public knowledge biases in information-aggregation mechanisms. *Management Science, 50*(7), 983-994.

Chen, K. Y., & Plott, C. (2002). *Information aggregation mechanisms: concept, design, and implementation for a sales forecasting problem.* Unpublished manuscript, California Institute of Technology.

Chen, Y., Mullen, T., & Chu, C. H. (2004, June). *Theoretical investigation of prediction markets with aggregate uncertainty.* Paper presented at the 7th International Conference on Electronic Commerce Research (ICECR-7), Dallas, TX.

Chen, Y., Mullen, T., & Chu, C. H. (2006). An in-depth analysis of information markets with aggregate uncertainty. *Electronic Commerce Research, 6,* 201-220.

Chen, Y., Chu, C. H., Mullen, T., & Pennock, D. M. (2005, June). *Information Markets vs. Opinion Pools: An Empirical Comparison.* Paper presented at the ACM Conference on Electronic Commerce (EC-05), Vancouver, British Columbia, Canada.

Click Fraud (2005). [Electronic Version]. *Marketing Experiments Journal.* Retrieved April 5, 2007, from www.marketingexperiments.com/internet-online-advertising/click-fraud.html

Cowgill, B. (2005). *Putting crowd wisdom to work.* Retrieved April 5, 2007, from http://googleblog.blogspot.com/2005/09/putting-crowd-wisdom-to-work.html

Edelman, B., & Ostrovsky, M. (2007). Strategic bidder behavior in sponsored search auctions. *Decision Support Systems, 43*(1), 192-198.

Edelman, B., Ostrovsky, M., & Schwarz, M. (2007). Internet advertising and the generalized second price auction: Selling billions of dollars worth of keywords. *American Economic Review, 97*(1), 242-259.

Feigenbaum, J., Fortnow, L., Pennock, D. M., & Sami, R. (2003, June). *Computation in a distributed information market.* Paper presented at the 4th Annual ACM Conference on Electronic Commerce (EC'03), San Diego, CA.

Feng, J., Bhargava, H. K., & Pennock, D. M. (2007). Implementing sponsored search in Web search engines: Computational evaluation of alternative mechanisms. *Informs Journal on Computing, 19*(1), 137-148.

Forsythe, R., & Lundholm, F. (1990). Information aggregation in an experimental market. *Econometrica, 58,* 309-347.

French, S. (1985). Group consensus probability distributions: A critical survey. *Bayesian Statistics, 2,* 183-202.

Genest, C., & Zidek, J. V. (1986). Combining probability distributions: A critique and an annotated bibliography. *Statistical Science, 1*(1), 114-148.

Goodman, J. (2005). *Pay-per-percentage of impressions: An advertising method that is highly robust to fraud.* Paper presented at the Workshop on Sponsored Search Auctions.

Google. Adwords Help Center. Retrieved April 5, 2007, from https://adwords.google.com/support/

Google. Keyword Tool. Retrieved April 5, 2007, from https://adwords.google.com/select/KeywordToolExternal

Google. Tips for success. Retrieved April 5, 2007, from https://adwords.google.com/select/tips.html

Google. Traffic Estimator. Retrieved April 5, 2007, from https://adwords.google.com/select/TrafficEstimatorSandbox

Grossman, S. J. (1981). An introduction to the theory of rational expectations under asymmetric information. *Review of Economic Studies, 48*(4), 541-559.

Hahn, R. W., & Tetlock, P. C. (2005). Making development work. *Policy Review, 132,* [Electronic version]. Stanford, CA: Hoover Institution.

Hanson, R. D. (1999). Decision markets. *IEEE Intelligent Systems, 14*(3), 16-19.

Immorlica, N., Jain, K., Mahdian, M., & Talwar, K. (2005). *Click fraud resistant methods for Learning click-through rates.* Paper presented at the Workshop on Internet and Network Economics (WINE), (pp. 34-45).

Jackwerth, J. C., & Rubinstein, M. (1996). Recovering probability distribution from options prices. *Journal of Finance, 51*(5), 1611-1631.

Jansen, B. (2006). Paid search. *IEEE Computer, 39*(7), 88-90.

King, R. (2006). Workers, place your bets [Electronic Version]. *Business Week online.* Retrieved April 5, 2007 from www.businessweek.com/technology/content/aug2006/tc20060803_012437.htm

Kiviat, B. (2004). The end of management? *Time, July 6.*

Krishna,V. (2002). *Auction theory*: Academic Press.

Lahaie, S. (2006). *An analysis of alternative slot auction designs for sponsored search.* Paper presented at the Seventh ACM Conference on Electronic Commerce, Ann Arbor, MI.

Liu, D., Chen, J., & Whinston, A. B. (2006). *Weighted unit-price auctions.* Paper presented at the Second Workshop on Sponsored Search Auctions, Ann Arbor, MI.

Lundholm, R. (1991). What affects the efficiency of the market? Some answers from the laboratory. *The Accounting Review, 66,* 486-515.

O'Brien, J., & Srivastava, S. (1991). Dynamic stock markets with multiple assets: An experimental analysis. *Journal of Finance, 46,* 1811-1838.

Pennock, D. M., Lawrence, S., Nielsen, F. A., & Giles, C. L. (2001). *Extracting collective probabilistic forecasts from Web games.* Paper presented

at the 7th ACM SIGKDD International Conference on Knowledge Discovery and Data Mining, San Francisco, CA.

Plott, C., & Sunder, S. (1988). Rational expectations and the aggregation of diverse information in laboratory security markets. *Econometrica, 56,* 1085-1118.

Polgreen, P. M., Nelson, F. D., & Neumann, G. R. (2006). Using prediction markets to forecast trends in infectious diseases. *Microbe, 1*(10), 459-465.

Rhode, P. W., & Strumpf, K. S. (2007). *Manipulating political stock markets: A field experiment and a century of observational data.* University of Arizona.

Roll, R. (1984). Orange juice and weather. *American Economic Review, 74,* 861-880.

Servan-Schreiber, E., Wolfers, J., Pennock, D. M., & Galebach, B. (2004). Prediction markets: Does money matter? *Electronic Markets, 14*(3), 243-251.

Story, L. (2006, October 30). Marketers demanding better count of the clicks. *New York Times.*

Sunder, S. (1995). Experimental asset markets. In J. H. K. a. A. E. Roth (Ed.), *The handbook of experimental economics* (pp. 445-500). Princeton, NJ: Princeton University Press.

Szymanski, B. K., & Lee, J. S. (2006, June). *Impact of ROI on bidding and revenue in sponsored search advertisement auctions.* Paper presented at the Second Workshop on Sponsored Search Auctions, Ann Arbor, MI.

Tuzhilin, A. (2006). *The Lane's Gifts v. Google Report.* Retrieved Oct 16, 2007 from http://google-blog.blogspot.com/pdf/Tuzhilin_Report.pdf

Varian, H. R. (2006). *Position auctions.* (Technical Working Paper). Berkeley, CA: Univeristy of California. Forthcoming in *International Journal of Industrial Organization.*

Vickrey, W. (1961). Counterspeculation, auctions, and competitive sealed tenders. *Journal of Finance, 16*, 8-27.

Wolfers, J., & Zitzewitz, E. (2005). *Interpreting prediction market prices as probabilities.* Wharton School, University of Pennsylvania.

Yahoo! (2007). *Search marketing overview: Quality index.* Retrieved April 5, 2007, from http://help.yahoo.com/1/us/yahoo/ysm/sps/start/overview_qualityindex.html

Yahoo! Search Marketing: Sponsored Search. Retrieved April 5, 2007, from http://searchmarketing.yahoo.com/srch/index.php

Yahoo! (2006, August 16, 2006). *Yahoo! and go2 Sign Mobile Search Advertising Distribution Agreement; Yahoo! Advertisers to Reach Consumers Through go2's Mobile Local Content Channels.* Retrieved April 5, 2007, from http://yhoo.client.shareholder.com/press/ReleaseDetail.cfm?ReleaseID=207538

ADDITIONAL READING

Asdemir, K. (2006). *Bidding patterns in search engine auctions.* Paper presented at the Second Workshop on Sponsored Search Auctions, Ann Arbor, MI.

Camerer, C. (1998). Can asset markets be manipulated? A field experiment with racetrack betting. *Journal of Political Economy, 106,* 457-82.

Even-Dar, E., Kearns, M., & Wortman, J. (2007) *Sponsored search with contexts.* Paper presented at the Third Workshop on Sponsored Search Auctions, Banff, Canada.

Giles, J. (2005). Wisdom of the crowd: Decision makers, wrestling with thorny choices, are tapping into the collective foresight of ordinary people. *Nature, 438,* 281.

Hansen, J., Schmidt, C., & Strobel, M. (2004). Manipulation in political stock markets: Preconditions and evidence. *Applied Economics Letters, 11,* 459-463.

Hanson, R. (1999). Decision markets. *IEEE Intelligent Systems, 14,* 16-19.

Hanson, R., Oprea, R., & Porter, D. (2006). Information aggregation and manipulation in an experimental market. *Journal of Economic Behavior and Organization, 60*(4), 449-459.

Kitts, B., Laxminar, P., LeBlanc, B. J., & Meech R. (2005). *A formal analysis of search auctions including predictions on click fraud and bidding tactics.* Paper presented at the Second Workshop on Sponsored Search Auctions.

Kitts, B. & LeBlanc, B. J. (2004). *A trading agent and simulator for keyword auctions.* Paper presented at the Third International Joint Conference on Autonomous Agents and Multiagent Systems (AAMAS 2004), New York.

Malone, T. W. (2004). *The future of work.* Harvard Business School Press.

Mehta, A., Saberi, A., Vazirani, U., & Vazirani V. (2005) *AdWords and Generalized online matching.* Paper presented at Proceedings of the 46th Annual IEEE Symposium on Foundations of Computer Science (FOCS).

Milgrom, P. (2004). *Putting auction theory to work.* Cambridge, UK: Cambridge University Press.

Oliven, K., & Rietz, T. (2004). Suckers are born but markets are made: Individual rationality, arbitrage, and market efficiency on an electronic futures market. *Management Science. 50,* 336-351.

Pennock, D., Lawrence, S., Giles, C. L., & Nielsen, F. A. (2001). The real power of artificial markets. *Science, 291,* 987-988.

Pennock, D. (2004). *A dynamic pari-mutual market for hedging, wagering, and information aggregation.* Paper presented at the 5th ACM conference on Electronic commerce, New York.

Rhode, P. W. & Strumpf K. (2004). Historical presidential betting markets. *Journal of Economic Perspectives, 18*(2), 127-142.

Surowiecki, J. (2004). *The wisdom of crowds.* New York: Random House.

Wolfers, J., & Zitzewitz, E. (2004). Prediction markets. *Journal of Economic Perspective, 18,* 107-126.

Zhang, X.M., & Feng, J. (2005) *Price cycles in online advertising auctions.* Paper presented at the 26th International Conference on Information Systems (ICIS), Las Vegas, NV.

Zhou, Y., & Lukose, R. (2006) *Vindictive bidding in keyword auctions.* Paper presented at the Second Workshop on Sponsored Search Auctions,

IMPLICATIONS FOR PRACTITIONERS (POST-MANUSCRIPT)

Title: Novel Business-Oriented Auctions

Short Description of the Manuscript

With the advent of the Internet, traditional auction forms have evolved to fit into a plethora business niches, either integrating into traditional approaches or simply creating new opportunities. This chapter examines two novel uses for auctions in a business context, namely sponsored search auctions and prediction markets. Understanding the potential auction benefits and limitations can hopefully provide practitioners with a more informed and successful approach when employing these auction-based tools in their business.

Findings

- Sponsored search is big business, making Google and Yahoo! $6 and $5 billion dollars, respectively in 2005.
- Sponsored search allows advertisers to target their audience and only pay when users click on their advertisement.
- Sponsored search auctions have evolved from standard first-price auctions into variations of second-price auctions that are more suitable to their commercial environment.
- Click fraud is a major concern in sponsored search.
- Academic research is just starting to evaluate sponsored search auction mechanism tradeoffs in terms of properties such as maximizing revenue, consumer welfare, price stability, and robustness to fraud.
- A prediction market is a futures market where prices forecast the likelihood of future events, in part since participants generally have a clear incentive to be honest and "put their money where their mouth is."
- Companies such as Hewlett-Packard, Eli Lilly, Intel, Microsoft, and Google have used prediction markets internally for enterprise forecasting.
- Prediction markets make real-time predictions that take advantage of dispersed information, both explicit and tacit, which can sometimes be hard to capture using other forecasting methods.
- Prediction markets they should be viewed as an integral part of the whole decision support system rather than a stand-alone tool.

Recommendations or how the practitioners should put the findings to use and how they should interpret them:

- To use sponsored search auctions to best effect (1) identify business objectives, (2) devote time to discovering the best keywords, (3) monitor for click fraud, and (4) consider using companies that setup, monitor and track ad campaigns.
- To use prediction markets to best effect (1) carefully select what to forecast and provide participants with proper incentives, (2) keep user interfaces and interactions simple, and (3) get buy-in from management and ensure a diverse set of participants.

Caveats or limitations of using the results in practice:

Both sponsored search auctions and prediction markets are relatively new and practitioners should expect a certain amount of learning about how best to use them in their specific business environment. In the case of prediction markets, while they offer an alternative and potentially powerful forecasting methodology, it may not be appropriate to all business environments.

Chapter XII
Implications for Reverse Auctions from a Supply Chain Management Perspective

Eric C. Jackson
The Pennsylvania State University – Erie, USA

ABSTRACT

This chapter considers reverse auctions in the context of the supply chain and the type of end user product being produced. It contends that in order to successfully utilize a reverse auction without alienating their suppliers, buyers need to classify their product as innovative or standardized. An innovative product is one that is undergoing rapid changes in functionality or specifications. A standardized or functional product is one that has stabilized its specifications and functionality. It also argues that the buyer must consider whether their supply chain is responsive or efficient. A responsive supply chain is one that rapidly adapts to changes in product characteristics without placing undue financial burdens on any members of the supply chain. An efficient supply chain is one that has reduced costs to a minimum but has a reduced flexibility when compared with a responsive supply chain. It is hoped that an understanding of this relationship will allow purchasers to better evaluate their use of reverse auctions as a purchasing tool in the context of buyer supplier relations.

INTRODUCTION

Undoubtedly you have surmised from the other chapters in this book that reverse auctions or e-auctions have become a major factor in the procurement of goods and services in business today, and possibly could impact purchasing to an even greater extent in the future. In the recent past the use of reverse auctions has been predicted to increase steadily. In 2000 it was reported that while less than 20% of buyers utilized e-auctions, approximately 47% of the non-users planned to make use of reverse auctions in the future (Porter, 2000). However, despite this optimistic projection for their adoption, reverse auctions have not developed into the panacea of purchasing predicted seven years ago (Hur, Mabert, & Hartley, 2007). As with any new tool questions have arisen as to the value and the effective use of reverse auctions.

The benefits for buyers in reverse auctions include lower prices, reduced transaction costs, a reduction in information asymmetries, potential identification of new suppliers, and shortened cycle times in gaining price quotations. At the same time, sellers may gain access to new markets, information on competitors, and faster responses to bids. While the benefits, particularly lower prices, tend to favor the buyer in a reverse auction, the disadvantages in a similar manner tend to be absorbed by the supplier.

One significant drawback to the buyer is that they are exposed to potentially unqualified suppliers, especially if they simply accept the lowest bid as the winner. This circumstance is avoided because most buyers add a caveat to their bid document reserving the right not to accept the lowest bid as the auction winner. This actually exacerbates some of the drawbacks to reverse auctions for suppliers. Many of these drawbacks center on expectations a supplier has when his is involved in a supply chain relationship.

Suppliers feel that while participating in a supply chain relationship they provide more value than simply the lowest price. For example, the supplier may be expected to keep a buyer informed of design or engineering advances so that the buyer can incorporate these changes into his product line. So when a buyer sends a contract to be bid on in a reverse auction, where price is the principal selection criteria, the supplier feels that it negates any value-added services he provides. A supplier in an effective relationship is expected to leverage all of his capabilities for the benefit of the buyer as well as the entire supply chain. As such, a buyer that opens contracts

to any participant, regardless of capabilities or a willingness to contribute to the relationship in order to gain lower prices, is viewed as having violated the trust and commitment supposedly endemic in the relationship. The structure of the auction itself might alleviate this destruction of trust in the supply chain.

The structure of an e-auction provides some potential mechanisms to maintain trust between the buyer and the seller, while allowing the buyer to check the marketplace for competitive pricing. What the structure of the auction cannot address is whether or not the auction is a viable tool within the type of supply chain, whether that supply chain is efficient or responsive. If the auction is taking place in a reasonable position in the supply chain given the type of the supply chain, or if the auction is in alignment with the product requirements the supply chain was designed to provide.

It is the intent of this chapter to examine reverse auctions in the context of the supply chain. Consideration will be given to the particular type of supply chain in use by the buyer and supplier engaged in the reverse auction, and to whether the auction is disruptive to that type of supply chain. The chapter will consider whether the disruptive tendencies perceived by suppliers and attributed to reverse auctions are a result of using the tool in an inappropriate position along the chain. Lastly, the chapter will consider whether the detrimental impact of reverse auctions should be attributed to the more general problem of a mismatch between the type of supply chain and the product(s) being delivered by the supply chain itself.

REVERSE AUCTIONS LITERATURE REVIEW

The advantages to buyers utilizing reverse auctions have been well documented. Price reductions naturally head the list of the advantages gleaned by firms utilizing reverse auctions. In 2000 it was reported that Quaker Oats saved over $8 million in the prior three years because of their participation in reverse auctions (Brunelli, 2000). In addition to a price reduction, purchasers may be able to use information from auctions as a source of price discovery in general (Chen-Ritzo, Harrison, Kwasnica, & Thomas, 2005). As a mechanism for market coordination auctions have been identified as a means of reducing transaction costs for buyers (Garcia-Dastugue & Lambert, 2003). E-auctions have also been noted as a tool that may be used to identify world-class suppliers (Hartley, Lane, & Hong, 2004).

Suppliers have also been able to glean benefits from reverse auctions. Suppliers are able to gain new markets by participating in reverse auctions (Smeltzer & Carr, 2003). They may be able to gain insight into competitors pricing (Hartley, Lane, & Hong, 2004; Plouffe, Vandenbosch, & Hulland, 2001). This information may be used by suppliers to reexamine their practices forcing them to identify waste or to initiate lean programs which would in turn make it possible for them to lower their prices (Jap, 2002) and remain competitive. Both suppliers and buyers stand to gain from faster cycle times present when a reverse auction is used (Hartley et al., 2004; Plouffe et al., 2001).

Despite the advantages, disadvantages have also been espoused for reverse auctions. The focus that reverse auctions place on price tend to deemphasize other important factors such as quality and service (Hartley et al., 2004), which could leave the buyer without critical resources associated with other suppliers. Reverse auctions have been identified as undermining supply chain relationships by applying unfair pressure on supplier profits (Drew, 2003), by dismissing past relationships (Grieger, 2003), by undermining the supplier's sense of cooperation and collaboration (Skjott-Larsen, Kotzab, & Grieger, 2003), and by creating the perception that buyers use reverse auctions as a short-term solution to complex problems (Emiliani & Stec, 2001). Since relationship building has been identified as a critical factor for

value creation in supply chains (Jayaram, Kannan, & Tan, 2004) the potential negative impact reverse auctions might have on supply chain relationships would be significant.

A substantial body of work has developed to address the question of how a buyer might use a reverse auction as a procurement tool and not damage the trust that is an essential element in the buyer-supplier relationship. It has been noted that the design and implementation of the reverse auction is a critical element in preventing damage to the buyer-seller relationship (Jap, 2007). In a study of 274 buyers randomly selected from Amazon's auction Web site, Pavlou and Gefen (2004) examined what institutional mechanisms might enhance a perception of trust on the part of buyers and concluded that those mechanisms should include legally binding mechanisms and institutional mechanisms. Beyond legal means, researchers have also considered relationships or trust between buyers and sellers relative to reverse auctions.

Tassabehji, Taylor, Beach, and Wood (2006) studied several suppliers involved in reverse auctions and examined the characteristics that damaged trust. They found that suppliers were greatly concerned that unqualified or "rogue" bidders were included in the auctions for the sole purpose of driving prices down. There was also concern among suppliers that specifications for the products in the auction were vague and that buyers frequently changed the specifications during the bidding process. Suppliers expressed concerns that bids were awarded without a complete explanation of why the bid winner was selected. Specifically, suppliers were concerned that bids were not awarded to the lowest bidder despite the indication that the lowest bid was the selection criteria. Furthermore, in many cases when the contract was awarded, the lowest bidder also happened to be the incumbent supplier before the auction took place. This resulted in the perception that the only reason the auction took place was to force prices down in an existing relationship. Suppliers also expressed concerns that having been awarded the contract they were then subject to further negotiations with the buyer when amendments were made to the bid contract. Finally, Tassabehji et al. (2006) conclude that buyers could alleviate many of these concerns by incorporating trust-building mechanisms into the transaction process of the auction, as proposed by Pavlou (2002).

While examining the mechanics of trust retention during a reverse auction, this stream of research has overlooked some critical factors that moderate trust in a buyer-seller relationship during a reverse auction. In particular, the type of the supply chain, the basic fit of the supply chain with its end product or products, and the level of collaboration within the supply chain all need to be taken into consideration when assessing the desirability or viability of reverse auctions.

SUPPLY CHAIN IMPLICATIONS

A supply chain as defined by Mabert and Venkataramanan (1998, p. 538) is "...the network of facilities and activities that performs the functions of product development, procurement of material from vendors, the movement of materials between facilities, the manufacturing of products, the distribution of finished goods to customers, and after-market support for sustainment." While it is not the intent of this chapter to provide an in-depth analysis of supply chains, it is necessary to establish some basis for considering reverse auctions within the context of supply chains.

In their most basic form supply chains may be considered either efficient or responsive (Fisher, 1997). An efficient supply chain is one that is competing in an environment where products are primarily functional in nature. Products falling into this category tend to be standardized with few or no variants available in any given category. The order qualifying criteria for standardized

products are well established and understood by all members of the supply chain. Inventory is aggressively controlled in an efficient supply chain and high manufacturing utilization rates are typical, as are short lead times and relatively low contribution margins.

Fisher (1997) uses the Campbell Soup Company as a good example of a firm that utilizes an efficient supply chain. Most of their products have been established for many years with well-established consumer demand. Their ingredients are commodity items and suppliers know the demand and specifications well in advance of orders. It is interesting to note at this point that many of these characteristics also apply to Quaker Oats, which saved several millions of dollars via reverse auctions (Brunelli, 2000).

In contrast to the functional product produced with an efficient supply chain, the innovative product is produced with a responsive supply chain. An innovative product is one that is subject to great demand variation and is also present in great variety, that is, there are several variants in each category (Fisher, 1997). Firms in a responsive supply chain must be adaptable in terms of their manufacturing ability so that the variation in design may be accommodated. They also must have larger inventories so that they can quickly respond to changes in demand. This is essential since innovative products tend to have a higher contribution margin relative to functional goods and the loss of sales has a greater impact per unit (Fisher, 1997). A good example of an innovative product produced in a responsive supply chain would be computers in the time before they became standardized enough to allow them to be produced by mass customization. Computers in the 1960s and 1970s were made to order. This required flexibility so that each unit could meet potentially different specifications. Demand was unpredictable, so suppliers were required to inventory finished goods so that lead times would be reasonable. Fisher (1997) explains how a change in the market changed the requirements for the supply chain, which resulted in a mismatch between IBM's computers and the supply chain it had designed to manufacture them. This type of mismatch between product and supply chain is detrimental to all firms participating in the supply chain and may be magnified when reverse auctions are utilized.

If we consider the two types of products, functional and innovative, and pair them with the two types of supply chains, we get four possible combinations with two of those combinations being mismatches and two being matches. The two appropriate matches are a responsive supply chain producing an innovative product and an efficient supply chain producing a functional product. If a reverse auction is used in a responsive supply chain that is producing an innovative product, the reverse auction could be viewed as disruptive to the supply chain in the eyes of the supplier. Suppliers in a responsive supply chain are expected to be able to adjust rapidly to changes in demand and have the ability to modify product components for changes in design as needed. This type of responsiveness requires that suppliers have inventories available or have excess production capacity to meet that demand. Changes in design require suppliers to have flexible production capacity and possibly the ability to make design changes internally so that delays are not encountered in subcontracting modifications. This ability adds value to the buyer because it enables him to be agile in the market. At the same time it increases costs to the supplier and ultimately to the buyer. A reverse auction that emphasizes price as the principal criteria signals the supplier that flexible manufacturing or the ability to respond rapidly to demand changes has little or no value to the buyer. Suppliers have one of two options: they may elect to absorb the added cost which reduces their profits at the margin, or they may eliminate value-added functions so that they can provide their products at the market clearing price established by the auction. If they elect the latter position the result is seen in two ways. First, their ability to respond to changes in

demand or design will be reduced. Second, they will begin to apply pressure to their suppliers to reduce cost, which leads to an innovative product being produced by an efficient supply chain, a mismatch.

The second product supply chain dyad that matches is when a functional product is produced by an efficient supply chain. In this case all firms have accurate demand information and product design is frozen. A reverse auction in this environment is not disruptive since all members of the supply chain are already aggressively reducing waste so that they may obtain the lowest possible cost. A buyer who initiates an auction in this setting is not expecting suppliers to be agile in their ability to make design changes or to be able to respond quickly to sudden fluctuations in demand. As such, price is the principal order winner and any suppler that is not already at the rational market clearing price should not be surprised that the buyer is attempting to reduce his costs, nor should it disturb him. Having examined the impact of reverse auctions in supply chains that match their needs in terms of the final product, an examination of reverse auctions in supply chains that do not match their needs is in order.

As in the cases where the supply chain matched effectively with the needs of the final product, there are two possible combinations when the target product and the supply chain do not match. First is a product that needs a responsive or agile supply chain but is being produced in an efficient supply chain, and second is a product that best fits into an efficient supply but is being produced in a responsive supply chain. In the latter case a reverse auction would actually be beneficial to the system as a whole.

Since the suppliers do not need the ability to respond to changes in design or to fluctuations in demand, maintaining this ability is actually a waste of resources. A reverse auction seeking a market clearing price would force the suppliers to reexamine how they are doing business and aggressively reduce the waste. In this case, the reverse auction would serve as the "wake-up-call" noted by Jap (2000) and actually benefit both the supplier and the buyer in that it lowers prices for the buyer and forces the supplier to become more competitive in the long run. The application of reverse auctions to the mismatch case of a product that needs a responsive supply chain but is being produced in an efficient one has a less positive result. If the product that a supply chain has been developed to produce requires flexible production in order to meet changes in demand or design, but the supply chain is not capable to adjust to these changes, a reverse auction could actually compound the problems. Rapid or frequent changes in design result in stocks of unsold goods that must be sold at high discounts as modifications in the product are introduced (Fisher, 1997). If a buyer uses a reverse auction to induce a low price in an attempt to defray these costs the auction might be viewed by the supplier as an attempt to force the supplier to absorb the risk associated with the innovations in the product line instead of sharing the risk across the supply chain. This would effectively poison the relationship between the buyer and the supplier. In this case, the suppliers see a buyer that needs flexibility in design and demand, but clearly signals that the principal order winner is price, so much so that the buyer is willing to abandon relationships in favor of a low price. This situation effectively is the "quick-fix" solution sought by buyers to create temporary shareholder values discussed by Emiliani and

Stec (2001). A summary of these matches between product and supply chain type and the impact a reverse auctions has on the relationships is provided in Figure 1.

SUPPLY CHAIN RELATIONSHIPS

While it is not the intent of this section to address the extensive body of literature on supply chain relationships, it is valuable to touch on the importance of relationships in supply chains since these relationships frequently impact the success or failure of the supply chain in general. Many researchers (Bowersox, 1990; Fisher, 1997; Lee, Padmanabhan, & Whang, 1997) have noted the importance of collaboration between supply chain partners to enhance the competitive performance of all the members of the supply chain, and therefore the supply chain itself, when in competition with other supply chains. Collaborative planning, forecasting, and replenishment (CPFR) has been identified as having been successfully applied by GM, Hewlett-Packard, and Proctor and Gamble, among others (Barratt & Oliveira, 2001). Specifically Hewlett-Packard has developed a set of tools that allows for improved communications, collaboration, and understanding between members of their supply chain (Billington, Callioni, Crane, Ruark, & et al., 2004). Barratt and Oliveira (2001) note that an enabler of successful CPFR is the development of a trust-based relationship, which

Figure 1. Reverse auctions relationship impact by product and supply chain types

	Actual Supply Chain	
Supply Chain as Needed by Product	**Responsive Supply Chain**	**Efficient Supply Chain**
Responsive Supply Chain	RA Disruptive	RA Disruptive
Efficient Supply Chain	RA Beneficial	RA Neutral

they note only occurs with time. Simatupang and Sridharan (2005) developed an index that may be used to measure collaboration based on three dimensions—information sharing, decision synchronization, and incentive alignment. All of these depend on having a viable relationship between the members that allows these behaviors to be optimized. In other words, supply chain members must be trustworthy partners in a relationship.

Barney and Hansen (1994) discuss three types of trustworthiness and whether or not each can be used to create a competitive advantage. These are a weak form, a semistrong form, and strong form. A weak form of trust exists because there is little or no opportunity for opportunism on the part of either party. Trust in this case is based on a lack of opportunity and not on any characteristics of the parties or any relationship between them. A semistrong form of trust develops because of governance mechanisms such as contracts. While stronger than the weak form because of the legal aspects, the parties still have no relationship beyond the contract and realize that contracts may be violated or negated at any given time. A strong form of trust develops when vulnerabilities exist but no governance mechanisms dictate behavior, but rather that the parties are in and of themselves trustworthy. Barney and Hansen (1994) note that the weak form of trustworthiness can be a competitive advantage only because of the legal governance incorporated in the relationship. This explains why, when a supplier wins an auction with little or no up-front conditions but is then faced with the buyer negotiating to specify additional conditions, a detrimental impact on the relationship results. The trust in the relationship has been shifted to a weak form. It has also been shown that trust and commitment must be in place before supply chain partners may initiate value creation.

Jayaram, Kannan, and Tan (2004) examined over 500 firms who were members of the Institute for Supply Management (ISM) and the American Production and Inventory Control Society (APICS) in an effort to establish the mechanisms that lead to value creation in supply chains. They found that two factors are essential precursors to the creation of stainable high levels of value creation: their ability to control structural mechanisms and their relationship building abilities. Thus relationships are essential to high-performing supply chains. Actions that have a negative impact on the supply chain relationship have negative impact on the performance of the supply chain. As a result it is imperative that a buyer consider the context of their reverse auction within their supply chain before choosing to engage in reverse auctions.

CONCLUSION

Trust and relationship building are essential factors in the creation of value for a supply chain. As the competition between supply chains begins to become more paramount, more and more attention must be paid by all members of the supply chain to its competitive position. When considering the advantages of using reverse auctions as a procurement tool, purchasing agents need to give consideration to the impact that an auction might have on the supply chain as a whole.

In the same manner that firms need to build a supply chain to match their products, they need to examine if a reverse auction hinders, aids, or has a neutral effect on the supply chain as a whole. If a mismatch exists, as it would in the case of an innovative product with an efficient supply chain, the use of a reverse auction is likely to exaggerate the problem and create disruptions in the relationships. In the case of a responsive supply chain being used to produce innovative products, a reverse auction is also likely to be disruptive since it sends incorrect signals to suppliers, specifically that price is more important than agility. In cases where the supply chain is correctly matched with a product that needs to be produced by an efficient supply chain, reverse auctions may be neutral in their impact or actually be beneficial in that suppliers may be forced to reduce waste in order to compete.

From a practitioner's perspective the implications of determining the type of supply chain and product before implementing a reverse auction as a purchasing tool are significant in two ways. The first is the importance of matching products with their supply chain in general. If the product is improperly aligned with the supply chain, costs in general will not be optimized and the implementation of a reverse auction will potentially exacerbate the problem by alienating suppliers. Forcing price cuts while continuing to emphasis supplier flexibility places undue risk and costs on suppliers. In turn this eventually forces the supplier to exit from the relationship completely or to be driven out of business. Buyers then must absorb the cost of finding new suppliers. The second important point for practitioners is that in the right situation the use of reverse auctions may not be detrimental to supply chain relationships. Efficient supply chains producing functional or standardized goods should already have eliminated any wasteful practices. Reverse auctions in this case are cost-neutral to the supplier since no other suppliers are more efficient in producing the goods or services in question. If not, the supplier is motivated to reexamine their process to eliminate waste and reduce their price, a process that should be ongoing in any case.

FUTURE RESEARCH DIRECTIONS

Empirical studies or case studies testing these relationships would be of great benefit. In particular an examination of how the supply chain relationships are affected by reverse auctions in each of the four possible scenarios is needed. Examining each combination of product type and supply chain type—functional-efficient, functional-responsive, innovative-efficient, and innovative-responsive—as moderators it would

be possible to determine if reverse auctions have the detrimental impact on relationships that some have indicated.

REFERENCES

Barney, J. B., & Hansen, M. H. (1994). Trustworthiness as a source of competitive advantage. *Strategic Management Journal, 15*, 175.

Barratt, M., & Oliveira, A. (2001). Exploring the experiences of collaborative planning initiatives. *International Journal of Physical Distribution & Logistics Management, 31*(4), 266.

Billington, C., Callioni, G., Crane, B., Ruark, J., D., & et al. (2004). Accelerating the profitability of Hewlett-Packard's supply chains. *Interfaces, 34*(1), 59.

Bowersox, D. J. (1990). The strategic benefits of logistics alliances. *Harvard Business Review, 68*(4), 36.

Brunelli, M. (2000). Online auctions save millions for Quaker Oats and SmithKline Beecham. *Purchasing, 128*(4), S22.

Chen-Ritzo, C.-H., Harrison, T. P., Kwasnica, A. M., & Thomas, D. J. (2005). Better, faster, cheaper: An experimental analysis of a multiattribute reverse auction mechanism with restricted information feedback. *Management Science, 51*(12), 1753.

Drew, S. (2003). Strategic uses of e-commerce by SMEs in the east of England. *European Management Journal, 21*(1), 79.

Emiliani, M. L., & Stec, D. J. (2001). Online reverse auction purchasing contracts. *Supply Chain Management, 6*(3/4), 101.

Fisher, M. L. (1997). What is the right supply chain for your product? *Harvard Business Review, 75*(2), 105.

Garcia-Dastugue, S. J., & Lambert, D. M. (2003). Internet-enabled coordination in the supply chain. *Industrial Marketing Management, 32*(3), 251.

Grieger, M. (2003). Electronic marketplaces: A literature review and a call for supply chain management research. *European Journal of Operational Research, 144*(2), 280.

Hartley, J. L., Lane, M. D., & Hong, Y. (2004). An exploration of the adoption of e-auctions in supply management. *IEEE Transactions on Engineering Management, 51*(2), 153.

Hur, D., Mabert, V. A., & Hartley, J. L. (2007). Getting the most out of reverse e-auction investment. *Omega, 35*(4), 403.

Jap, S. (2000). Going, going, gone. *Harvard Business Review, 78*(6), 30.

Jap, S. (2002). Online reverse auctions: Issues, themes, and prospects for the future. *Academy of Marketing Science Journal, 30*(4), 506.

Jap, S. (2007). The impact of online reverse auction design on buyer-supplier relationships. *Journal of Marketing, 71*(1), 146.

Jayaram, J., Kannan, V. R., & Tan, K. C. (2004). Influence of initiators on supply chain value creation. *International Journal of Production Research, 42*(20), 4377-4399.

Lee, H. L., Padmanabhan, V., & Whang, S. (1997). The bullwhip effect in supply chains. *Sloan Management Review, 38*(3), 93.

Mabert, V. A., & Venkataramanan, M. A. (1998). Special research focus on supply chain linkages: Challenges for design and management in the 21st century. *Decision Sciences, 29*(3), 537.

Pavlou, P. A., & Gefen, D. (2004). Building effective online marketplaces with institution-based trust. *Information Systems Research, 15*(1), 37.

Pavlou, P. A. (2002). Institution-based trust in interorganizational exchange relationships: The role of online B2B marketplaces on trust formation. *The Journal of Strategic Information Systems, 11*(3-4), 215-243.

Plouffe, C. R., Vandenbosch, M., & Hulland, J. (2001). Intermediating technologies and multi-group adoption: A comparison of consumer and merchant adoption intentions toward a new electronic payment system. *The Journal of Product Innovation Management, 18*(2), 65.

Porter, A. M. (2000). Buyers turn wary eyes on electronic auctions. *Purchasing, 129*(3), 109.

Simatupang, T. M., & Sridharan, R. (2005). The collaboration index: A measure for supply chain collaboration. *International Journal of Physical Distribution & Logistics Management, 35*(1), 44.

Skjott-Larsen, T., Kotzab, H., & Grieger, M. (2003). Electronic marketplaces and supply chain relationships. *Industrial Marketing Management, 32*(3), 199.

Smeltzer, L. R., & Carr, A. S. (2003). Electronic reverse auctions: Promises, risks and conditions for success. *Industrial Marketing Management, 32*(6), 481.

Tassabehji, R., Taylor, W. A., Beach, R., & Wood, A. (2006). Reverse e-auctions and supplier-buyer relationships: An exploratory study. *International Journal of Operations & Production Management, 26*(1/2), 166.

ADDITIONAL READINGS

Altman, B. (2003). Reverse auctions destroy relationships. *Manufacturing Engineering, 130*(6), 112.

Asare, A. K., & Brashear, T. G.. (2006). A framework for the adoption of interfirm technologies in customer driven supply chains. *American

Marketing Association. Conference Proceedings, 17, 324.

Bandyopadhyay, S., Rees, J., & Barron, J. M. (2006). Simulating sellers in online exchanges. *Decision Support Systems, 41*(2), 500.

Biehl, M., Cook, W., & Johnston, D. A. (2006). The efficiency of joint decision making in buyer-supplier relationships. *Annals of Operations Research, 145*(1), 15.

Carter, C. R, & Kaufmann, L. (2007). The impact of electronic reverse auctions on supplier performance: The mediating role of relationship variables. *Journal of Supply Chain Management, 43*(1), 16.

Chang, S.-C., Hsieh, M.-M., & Chen, C.-W. (2007). Reverse auction-based job assignment among foundry fabs. *International Journal of Production Research, 45*(3), 653.

Claro, D. P., Claro, P. B. d. O., & Hagelaar, G. (2006). Coordinating collaborative joint efforts with suppliers: The effects of trust, transaction specific investment and information network in the Dutch flower industry. *Supply Chain Management, 11*(3), 216.

Cuganesan, S. (2006). The role of functional specialists in shaping controls within supply networks. *Accounting, Auditing & Accountability Journal, 19*(4), 465.

Debasis, M., & Dharmaraj, V. (2006). An ascending price procurement auction for multiple items with unit supply. *IIE Transactions, 38*(2), 127.

Engelbrecht-Wiggans, R., & Katok, E. (2006). E-sourcing in procurement: Theory and behavior in reverse auctions with noncompetitive contracts. *Management Science, 52*(4), 581.

Gattiker, T. F., Huang, X., & Schwarz, J. L. (2007). Negotiation, e-mail, and Internet reverse auctions: How sourcing mechanisms deployed by buyers

affect suppliers' trust. *Journal of Operations Management, 25*(1), 184.

Giampetro, C., & Emiliani, M. L. (2007). Coercion and reverse auctions. *Supply Chain Management, 12*(2), 75.

Hazra, J., & Mahadevan, B. (2006). Impact of supply base heterogeneity in electronic markets. *European Journal of Operational Research, 174*(3), 1580.

Hill, R. M., & Omar, M. (2006). Another look at the single-vendor single-buyer integrated production-inventory problem. *International Journal of Production Research, 44*(4), 791.

Jain, K., Nagar, L., & Srivastava, V. (2006). Benefit sharing in inter-organizational coordination. *Supply Chain Management, 11*(5), 400.

Jin, M., & Wu, S. D. (2006). Supplier coalitions in online reverse auctions: Validity requirements and profit distribution scheme. *International Journal of Production Economics, 100*(2), 183.

Kehoe, D. F., Dani, S., Sharifi, H., Burns, N. D., & Backhouse, C. J. (2007). Demand network alignment: Aligning the physical, informational and relationship issues in supply chains. *International Journal of Production Research, 45*(5), 1141.

Lindorff, D. (2006). In this case, talk isn't so cheap. *Treasury and Risk Management, 16*(4), 15.

Malik, M. A. K., & Peter, M. (2006). Innovating for supply chain integration within construction. *Construction Innovation, 6*(3), 143.

Meij, S., & Pau, L. F. (2006). Auctioning bulk mobile messages. *Computational Economics, 27*(2-3), 395.

Melton, H. L. (2006). Antecedents and consequences of social influence strategies in supply chain management. *American Marketing Association. Conference Proceedings, 17*, 263.

Mihiotis, A., Mylonakis, J., & Ntalakas, G. (2007). Value chain analysis: An ECR tool for assessing business competitive advantage. *International Journal of Management Practice, 2*(3), 240.

Morrissey, W. J., & Pittaway, L. (2006). Buyer-supplier relationships in small firms: The use of social factors to manage relationships. *International Small Business Journal, 24*(3), 272.

Pearcy, D., Giunipero, L., & Wilson, A. (2007). A model of relational governance in reverse auctions. *Journal of Supply Chain Management, 43*(1), 4.

Pearcy, D. H, & Giunipero, L. C. (2006). The impact of electronic reverse auctions on purchase price reduction and governance structure: An empirical investigation. *International Journal of Services Technology and Management, 7*(3), 215.

Rabinovich, E., & Knemeyer, A. M. (2006). Logistics service providers in Internet supply chains. *California Management Review, 48*(4), 84.

Rao, B. V., & Smith, B. C. (2006). Decision support in online travel retailing. *Journal of Revenue and Pricing Management, 5*(1), 72.

Rooks, G., Raub, W., & Tazelaar, F. (2006). Ex post problems in buyer-supplier transactions: effects of transaction characteristics, social embeddedness, and contractual governance. *Journal of Management & Governance, 10*(3), 239.

Sahay, B. S., Mohan, R., & Sachan, A. (2006). E-procurement: Systems and implementation. *International Journal of Services Technology and Management, 7*(5/6), 490.

Sampath, K., Saygin, C., Grasman, S. E., & Leu, M. C. (2006). Impact of reputation information sharing in an auction-based job allocation model for small and medium-sized enterprises. *International Journal of Production Research, 44*(9), 1777.

Sandholm, T., Levine, D., Concordia, M., Martyn, P., & et al. (2006). Changing the game in strategic sourcing at Procter & Gamble: Expressive competition enabled by optimization. *Interfaces, 36*(1), 55.

Sheridan, M., Moore, C., & Nobbs, K. (2006). Fast fashion requires fast marketing. *Journal of Fashion Marketing and Management, 10*(3), 301.

Sucky, E. (2006). A bargaining model with asymmetric information for a single supplier-single buyer problem. *European Journal of Operational Research, 171*(2), 516.

Suh-Yueh, C., & Wen-Chang, F. (2006). Exploring the relationships of trust and commitment in supply chain management. *Journal of American Academy of Business, Cambridge, 9*(1), 224.

Suh, T., & Kwon, I. W. G. (2006). Matter over mind: When specific asset investment affects calculative trust in supply chain partnership. *Industrial Marketing Management, 35*(2), 191.

Tassabehji, R., Taylor, W. A., Beach, R., & Wood, A. (2006). Reverse e-auctions and supplier-buyer relationships: An exploratory study. *International Journal of Operations & Production Management, 26*(1/2), 166.

Teich, J. E, Wallenius, H., Wallenius, J., & Zaitsev, A. (2006). A multi-attribute e-auction mechanism for procurement: Theoretical foundations. *European Journal of Operational Research, 175*(1), 90.

Tulder, R. V., & Mol, M. (2002). Reverse auctions or auctions reversed: First experiments by Philips. *European Management Journal, 20*(5), 447.

Wu, Y., & Zhang, D. Z. (2007). Demand fluctuation and chaotic behaviour by interaction between customers and suppliers. *International Journal of Production Economics, 107*(1), 250.

Yang, M.-F. (2006). A two-echelon inventory model with fuzzy annual demand in a supply chain. *Journal of Information & Optimization Sciences, 27*(3), 537.

Zaccone, S. (2004). Supply chain initiatives: The yin and the yang of reverse auctions and trust. *Converting Magazine, 22*(5), 34.

Zhu, K., Zhang, R. Q, & Tsung, F. (2007). Pushing quality improvement along supply chains. *Management Science, 53*(3), 421.

IMPLICATIONS FOR MANAGERS

Title: Implications for Reverse Auctions from a Supply Chain Management Perspective

Short Description

The impact of reverse auctions on supply chain relationships are examined from a conceptual perspective. The type of product and the type of supply chain are discussed as being essential moderators on the effectiveness of reverse auctions and how auctions may affect the relationships between suppliers and users of reverse auctions. If used in an inappropriate setting, reverse auctions may have a detrimental impact on essential supply chain relationships. If used in an appropriate setting they serve as an effective tool to determine the market-clearing price for goods or services, and may also demonstrate to suppliers that improved, more cost-effective processes need to be implemented.

Findings

- When used with functional products in an efficient supply chain, reverse auctions are not disruptive to buyer-supplier relationships and may be beneficial to both the supplier, as a warning that more efficient processes are needed, and to the buyer as a tool to lower prices
- When used with functional products in a responsive supply chain reverse auctions are signals from buyers to suppliers that changes need to be made in the supply chain and that conditions no longer support the need for a responsive supply chain.
- When used with innovative products in a responsive supply chain reverse auctions are detrimental to supply chain relationships because they signal the supplier that the buyer is not interested in the mechanisms that allow the supply chain to be adaptive to changes, and is only interested in a low price.
- When used with innovative products in an efficient supply chain reverse auctions exacerbate a bad situation by further deemphasizing the adaptability chain, instead of increasing its adaptability to meet the changing of the supply needs of the product.

RECOMMENDATIONS

- Practitioners should make sure that their interpretation of the product's needs and the type of supply chain they are using are accurate and that they are in agreement with the suppliers' interpretations.

LIMITATIONS

This theoretical frame will be tested empirically.

Chapter XIII
Multi–Agent Patterns for Deploying Online Auctions

Ivan Jureta
University of Namur, Belgium

Manuel Kolp
University of Louvain, Belgium

Stéphane Faulkner
University of Namur, Belgium

ABSTRACT

Today high volume of goods and services is being traded using online auction systems. The growth in size and complexity of architectures to support online auctions requires the use of distributed and cooperative software techniques. In this context, the agent software development paradigm seems appropriate both for their modelling, development and implementation. This chapter proposes an agent-oriented patterns analysis of best practices for online auction. The patterns are intended to help both IT managers and software engineers during the requirement specification of an online auction system while integrating benefits of agent software engineering.

INTRODUCTION

The emergence and growing popularity of electronic commerce in general and online auctions in particular, has raised the challenge to explore scalable global electronic market information systems, involving both human and automated traders (Rachlevsky-Reich, Ben-Shaul, Tung Chau, Lo & Poggio, 1999).

Online auctions are a particular type of Internet-based electronic markets, i.e. worldwide-open markets in which participants buy and sell goods and services in exchange for money. Most online auctions rely on classical auction economics (Bikhchandani, de Vries, Schummer & Vohra, 2001; Beam & Segev, 1998). In the economics literature, "an auction is an economic mechanism for determining the price of an item. It requires a pre-announced methodology, one or more bidders who want the item, and an item for sale" (Beam & Segev, 1998). The item is usually sold to the highest bidder. An online auction can be defined as an auction which is organized using an information system (IS), and is accessible to auction participants exclusively through a Web site on the Internet.

Recently, online auctions have become a popular way to trade goods and services. During 2002, the leading online marketplace, eBay. com provided a trading platform for 638 million items of all kinds. The value of all goods that were actually traded amounted to nearly $15 billion, which represented, at the time, a third of all online sales in the US. This trend results from specific advantages of online auctions over traditional ones as well as the fact that people are becoming increasingly comfortable with online shopping, which is reflected in strong growth of online sales, on both auction-based and other e-commerce platform types (e.g., fixed-price marketplaces, such as Amazon.com).

Today, with the increasing number of online auctions being organized, there is a need for distributed, large-scale and dynamic IS architectures to support online auction marketplaces (Rachlevsky-Reich, Ben-Shaul, Tung Chau, Lo & Poggio, 1999). From the IS development perspective, multi-agent systems (MASs) are a powerful new software engineering paradigm for designing and developing complex ISs (Yu, 1997). The use of agents as intentional, autonomous, and social entities which act according to their self-interest (Yu, 2001) provides advantages in both the modelling of an online auction system, and in its implementation using an agent-oriented IS.

In this chapter, we propose agent-oriented analysis patterns for deploying online auction information system (OAIS). These patterns are intended to help both IT managers and software engineers during the analysis of OAIS. We develop the social dimension of patterns on the basis of the analysis of leading existing OAIS.

Our motivation stems from the fact that auction mechanisms for exchanging goods and services will become more and more popular with both consumers and companies (see e.g., Resnick & Zeckhauser 2002). Providing agent-oriented patterns for such systems can reduce their development cost and time, while integrating benefits of agent-orientation in software development. Patterns of current best practices in the online auction domain facilitate the development of new auction systems, by clearly showing the functionalities that are particularly valued by auction participants. These should be included in any auction system if it wishes to attract both consumers and corporate users.

The rest of this chapter is organized as follows. Section 2 gives an overview of the core concepts and of their relevance in the context of online auctions. Section 3 describes our analysis method and identifies existing online auction systems on which we base our analysis. Section 4 describes the patterns of a basic OAIS. Section 5 describes best practices in the domain of OAIS. Section 6 concludes the text and discusses the limitations of our approach.

ONLINE AUCTIONS, AGENTS, AND AGENT PATTERNS

Our work revolves around three main concepts: online auctions, agents, and patterns. In the following subsections, we present each one and we discuss reasons why agent-orientation is appropriate for modelling, design, and implementation of OAIS.

Figure 1. Classification of online auction types, according to (Pinker, Seidmann & Vakrat, 2001)

	ONE BUYER	**MANY BUYERS**
ONE SELLER	Bilateral negotiations	Web-based sales auctions
MANY SELLERS	Web-based reverse procurement auctions	Web-based exchanges

Current State of Online Auctions

There is currently multi-billion dollar annual activity in the online auction market with a growing variety of sophisticated trading mechanisms (Pinker, Seidmann & Vakrat, 2001). There are numerous reasons for the popularity of online auction marketplaces (Lucking-Reiley 2000; Re, Braga, & Masiero 2001; Pinker, Seidmann & Vakrat, 2001). We classify them into following categories: *Market efficiency, Accessibility, Managing complexity, Information gathering.*

There have been several studies presenting online auction business models (see e.g., (Beam & Segev, 1998; Lucking-Reiley, 2000)). These studies propose different classification criteria for online auctions, such as the auction mechanism (English, Vickrey, Dutch, etc.), the type of participants (businesses and/or consumers), the number of participants, etc. We retain here the classification proposed by (Pinker, Seidmann & Vakrat, 2001) which is primarily based on the number of participants. This classification is shown in Figure 1.

In bilateral negotiations, the two parties negotiate the sale of an item. Negotiation involves the price of the item, but may also involve its qualitative characteristics.

In Web-based reverse procurement auctions, many sellers compete to win a single buyer (e.g., a government accepts bids for a construction project from several companies).

In Web-based exchanges, many buyers face multiple sellers (e.g., the stock market). In Web-based sales auctions, a single seller offers an item for sale to many bidders (e.g., eBay.com).

In Web-based sales auctions on the Internet, the most common auction mechanism is the "English", "Vickrey", "Dutch", and "first-price sealed bid" auctions. We briefly describe their mechanisms.

English Auction. Each bidder sees the highest current bid, can place a bid and update it many times. The winner of the auction is the highest bidder who pays the price bid, i.e. the final auction bid that this bidder placed. An example is eBay. com. English auctions are by far the most popular auction type and their success lies most probably in the familiarity of English auctions as well as in the entertainment they provide to participants (in the form of bidder competition).

First-Price Sealed Bid Auction. Each bidder makes a single secret bid; the winner is the highest bidder, and the price paid is the highest bid. An example is The Chicago Wine Company (tcwc.com).

Vickrey Auction. Each bidder makes a single secret bid; the winner is the highest bidder. However, the price paid is the amount of the second highest bid. Some online auction systems propose it as an option (e.g., iauction.com).

Dutch Auction. The seller steadily lowers the price of the item over time. The bidders can see the current price and must decide if they wish to purchase at that price or wait until it drops further. The winner is the first bidder to pay the current price (e.g., klik-klok.com).

In the context of the classification proposed in Figure 1, our analysis focuses on *Web-based sales auctions*. The analysis is applicable on any type of auction as far as the participant type is concerned: both the seller and buyers may be either customers and/or businesses. Our analysis is independent of the auction mechanism, as long as it is a mechanism involving a single seller and many buyers.

Benefits of Agent-Orientation

An agent can be defined as an intentional, autonomous, and social entity, which acts according to its self-interest (Yu, 2001). In the IS development perspective, an agent is an autonomous software entity that is responsive to its environment, proactive (in that it exhibits goal-oriented behavior), and social (in that it can interact with other agents to complete goals) (Kauffman &Walden, 2001). Multi-agent systems involve the interaction of multiple agents, both software and human, so that they may achieve common or individual goals through cooperative or competitive behavior.

The use of agent-orientation in the modeling, design, and implementation of OAIS provides at least the following benefits:

- When modeling an OAIS, we can represent (using e.g., the *i** modeling framework (Yu, 1995)) the intentional dimension of agents participating in the auction process, as well as their interdependencies. Consequently, the use of agents as the core modeling concept, makes it possible to understand more profoundly the environment in which the IS will be used. We can then explore alternative IS structures incorporating different functionalities during the requirements engineering phase of the IS development. We can evaluate alternative IS structures in terms of their contribution to user's needs (such as e.g., ease of use, speed, etc.) and to the system's other non-functional requirements (such as e.g., security, reusability, development cost, development time, etc.) in order to select the most adequate IS structure.

- OAIS are large-scale, complex, and distributed systems. The use of MAS as a powerful new software engineering paradigm for designing and developing complex IS has been advocated in e.g., (Faulkner, Kolp & Do, 2004). Social organization-based MAS (see e.g., (Kolp, Giorgini & Mylopoulos, 2003; Faulkner, Kolp & Do, 2004) match the system architecture with its operational environment (Do, Kolp, & Pirotte, 2003). They provide a strong basis for the development of robust and highly customizable software able to cope with the changing environment, while being sufficiently secure to protect personal data and other belongings of system agents. Agent architectures are more flexible, modular and robust than e.g., object-oriented ones. They tend to be open and dynamic as their components can be added, modified or removed at any time (Yu, 1997).

Online Auction Patterns

Patterns are reusable solutions to recurring IS design problems, and provide a vocabulary for communicating these solutions to others (Weiss, 2003). They aid in the reuse of IS analysis and design experience, as each pattern describes a reusable and flexible solution for a specific problem type.

Patterns for OAIS have already been proposed by (Re, Braga & Masiero, 2001) However, these patterns are specified using the UML. Consequently, they do not show agents as intentional, autonomous, and social entities. In addition, the pattern language provided by (Re, Braga & Masiero, 2001) does not integrate best practices that can be identified on currently operating auction IS on the Internet. (Kumar & Feldman, 1998) only provides a global architecture of a basic online auction system in the context of object-oriented software development. GEM (Rachlevsky-Reich, Ben-Shaul, Tung Chau, Lo & Poggio, 1999) provides system architecture for developing large distributed electronic markets but it only addresses the system's basic functionalities required to organize trading among agents. It provides patterns without treating intentional aspects, and uses agents at implementation level.

ANALYSIS METHOD

Our analysis is based on three leading OAIS on the Internet: eBay.com, Amazon.com Auctions, and Yahoo.com Auctions. We examined the Web sites of these systems, and used literature that provides either strategic analysis (see e.g., (Pinker, Seidmann & Vakrat, 2001)), and/or economic analysis (see e.g., (Lucking-Reiley, 2000; Resnick & Zeckhauser, 2002)) of aspects of auctions being conducted on these systems.

We do not provide a comparative analysis of the three. However, it is necessary to note that eBay is by far the leading online auction marketplace, and provides most advanced functionalities that support both the auction process and the exchange of items and valuables that follows the auction. eBay is also the only one for which online auctions constitute its core business, making it particularly sensible to the needs of its users (Amazon is specialized in fixed-price retailing, and Yahoo is an all-purpose Web portal). We have found that both Yahoo.com Auctions and Amazon.com Auctions are late entrants to the online auction market, and that they copy the eBay business model. Consequently, we focus the analysis of the IS structure and the identification of best practices on eBay, while comparing our findings with its two main competitors.

We model the social dimension of each pattern using the *i** modelling framework (Yu, 1995). *i** is an agent-oriented modelling framework used to support the early phase of requirements engineering (Yu, 1997), during which we wish to represent and understand the wider context in which the IS will be used. The framework focuses on dependencies that exist among actors, and provides two types of models to represent them: a strategic dependency (SD) model used for describing processes as networks of strategic dependencies among actors, and the strategic rationale (SR) model used to describe each actor's reasoning in the process, as well as to explore alternative process structures.

Main modelling constructs of the *i** framework are Actors, Roles, Goals, Softgoals, Resources, and Tasks. Both the SD and SR models can represent dependencies among Actors or Roles. A dependency is a relationship in which an Actor or Role A_1 depends on some other Actor or Role A_2, for the provision of a dependum. We call A_1 the depender, and A_2 the dependee in the relationship. Each dependency can be seen as a matching of a want from the depender side to an ability on the dependee side (Liu & Yu, 2004). The following dependency types exist:

- **Goal dependency:** A Goal is a condition or state of affairs in the environment that

Figure 2. Actors and roles in the online auction information system

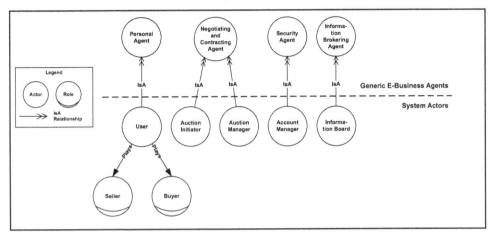

the actors would like to achieve. In a Goal dependency, the depender depends on the dependee to achieve a Goal. The dependee has the freedom to choose the way in which the goal will be achieved.

- **Softgoal dependency:** A Softgoal is similar to a Goal, but differs in that there are no clear-cut criteria for knowing whether the Softgoal has been achieved or not. It is then up to the stake holders to judge whether a particular IS structure sufficiently satisfies the Softgoal. In a Softgoal dependency, the depender depends on the dependee to act in such way as to contribute to the softgoal.
- **Task dependency:** A Task specifies a particular way of doing something. In a Task dependency, the depender specifies the course of action to be taken by the dependee.
- **Resource dependency:** A Resource is a physical or informational entity which may serve some purpose. In a Resource dependency, the depender requires the dependee to provide some Resource.

In *i**, software agents are represented as Actors. Actors can play Roles. A Role is an abstract characterization of the common behavior of an Actor in some specific context (e.g., a consumer, a salesman, a buyer, a seller, etc.).

BASIC AGENT-ORIENTED PATTERNS ANALYSIS

We focus on an online auction process that is appropriate for the cited auction types (English, Vickrey, Dutch, and First-Price Sealed Bid Auction) involving a single seller and multiple buyers. We first provide the social dimension of separate patterns required to run an OAIS. We then integrate these patterns in order to show how they constitute an OAIS that provides basic auction functionality.

Basic Patterns

In our analysis, we identified system actors shown in Figure 2. The figure shows that these actors are specializations of common generic e-business agents from the business agent typology proposed in (Papazoglou, 2001). This is useful since much work has been put into their specification, development and testing of these generic agent types (see e.g., Guttman, Moukas & Maes, 1998; Papazoglou 2001).

Personal Agents work directly with the human user to help support the creation and management of the user's profile. *User Agents* can play the roles of *Buyers* and *Sellers* with regards to sell-

Figure 3. Social dimension of the user authentication pattern

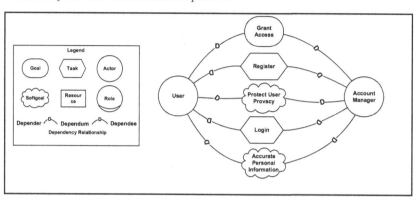

ing and/or buying in auctions. *Negotiating and Contracting Agents* negotiate terms of business transactions, in terms of e.g., transaction rules, payment methods, etc. *Security Agents* manage security aspects of the system such as e.g., user registration, access authorization, etc. *Information Brokering Agents* manage, summarize, and manipulate information. They search for information on behalf of *User Agents*.

We have identified a set of generic features that compose the online auction process. We provide analysis patterns for these features by allocating responsibilities to agents according to their capabilities briefly described above.

The rest of this section presents each of these analysis patterns through the social and dynamic dimensions. The dynamic dimension is represented with classical state-machine diagrams.

User Authentication. In order to use the system, *Users* first need to register on the system, by providing personal data. This data is necessary for identification when they return to participate in auctions. They can then access and use the system by logging on.

Auction Setup. A *User* will set up an auction when he/she wishes to sell an item. In such case, the *User* plays the role of the *Seller* in the auction. The *Seller* must provide a description of

the item using a procedure specified by the *Auction Initiator* (e.g., by filling out a series of Web forms on the auction Web site). Ideally, the *Seller* would *Provide Exact Item Details*, which would contribute to the quality of service of the system, with regards to the *Buyers*. The *Seller* depends on the *Auction Initiator* to provide a procedure for selecting among alternative auction rules (e.g., English Auction, Dutch Auction, etc.), and to specify the schedule of the auction. The *Seller* depends on the *Auction Initiator* to advertise the item that the *Seller* has put on auction, so that the potential *Buyers* can be informed about the auction event.

The Auction Setup pattern is independent of the auction type. However, specific constraints do apply for specific auction types. For example, if the *User* selects the English Auction rules, he must specify the minimum bid increment. The same information is irrelevant for e.g., a Dutch Auction. The specification of such constraints is outside the scope of this text, and should be discussed with specialists of the auction domain.

Auction (Item) Search. A *User* looks for auctioned items by using either a search interface, or by browsing the catalogue which provides a hierarchical organization of items. Search and browsing features are provided by the *Information Board*. The *User* depends on the *Information Board* to maintain an up-to-date database of current auctions.

Figure 4. Dynamic dimension of the user authentication pattern

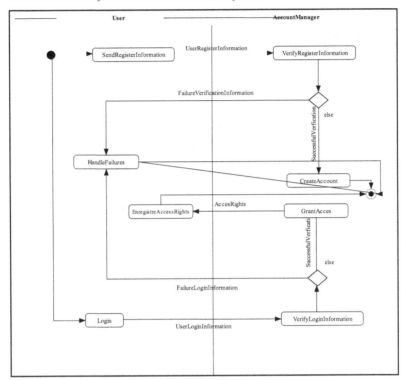

Figure 5. Social dimension of the auction setup pattern

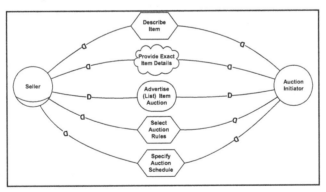

Auction Bidding. *Buyers* can *Place Bids*, and *Retract Bids*. The way in which these tasks are accomplished is defined in the IS (e.g., through a specific web/wap/i-mode interface). *Buyers* depend on the *Auction Manager* to *Verify Bids* that they place, in terms of bid coherence with the auction rules (e.g., Is the minimum bid increment respected?). The *Auction Manager* provides notifications to all *Buyers* participating in the auction whenever a new high bid is placed. The *Auction Manager* depends on the users to *Respect System Policies*, in terms of incorrect behaviour such as "multiple bidding". Finally, both *Buyers* and the *Seller* in the auction depend on the *Auction Manager* to supply the *Winning Bid Notification* so that the *Seller* and the winning *Buyer* can then proceed to the trade settlement. In addition, they both depend on the *Auction Manager* to supply the *New High Bid Notification*.

Figure 6. Dynamic dimension of the auction setup pattern

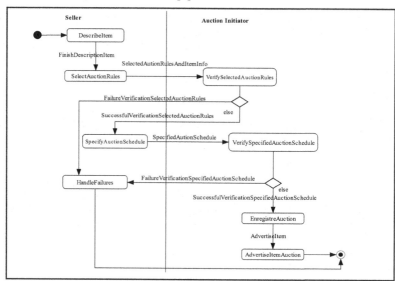

Figure 7. Social dimension of the auction search pattern

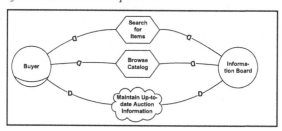

Figure 8. Dynamic dimension of the auction search pattern

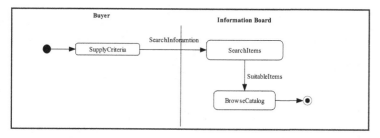

BEST PRACTICES PATTERNS ANALYSIS

Today's OAIS offer additional features to those that automate the traditional auction. In addition to enhancing the user experience, these additional features are essential to the commercial success of an OAIS. We provide patterns for several additional features that we consider being best practices in the domain of online auctions.

We will see that some of the features can be introduced in the system in several ways, requiring comparison and evaluation. To select the most adequate alternative, we represent relevant system qualities (e.g., security, privacy, usability, etc.) as softgoals and use contribution links to show how these softgoals are affected by each alternative, as in the Non-Functional Requirements framework (Chung, Nixon, Yu & Mylopoulos, 2000).

Figure 9. Social dimension of the auction bidding pattern

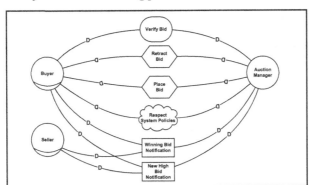

Figure 10. Dynamic dimension of the auction bidding pattern

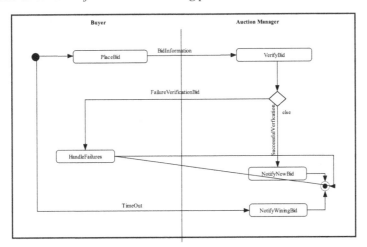

Proxy Bidding. Online auctions can last for several days, making it impossible for human buyers to follow the auction in its integrity, as is the case in traditional ones. Proxy bidding allows buyers to specify their maximum willingness to pay. A procedure is then used to automatically increase their bid until the specified maximum is reached, or the auction is closed (Kurbel & Loutchko, 2001). This enables human buyers to be represented in the auction, without requiring their physical presence in order to interact with their *Buyer* agent. It is important to note that proxy bidding is applicable only when English Auction rules are enforced in the auction.

Proxy bidding can be introduced in the basic OAIS in several ways in terms of responsibility

assignment. Two alternatives are shown in Figure 11. Each alternative is represented as a simple Strategic Rationale model. A series of softgoals have been selected as criteria for alternative comparison—*Privacy, Security, Reliability, Speed,* and *Workload.* These are non-functional requirements (Chung, Nixon, Yu & Mylopoulos, 2000) for the information system and were selected according to issues often raised in e-commerce IS design (e.g., (Mylopoulos, Kolp & Castro, 2001; Weiss 2003)), OAIS design (e.g., (Kumar & Feldman, 1998)), etc.

The first alternative seems more adequate. In this alternative, the responsibility of managing proxy bidding is allocated to the *Buyer* agent.

Figure 11. *Two alternative responsibility assignments expressed in two strategic rationale models of the proxy bidding feature. Positive (favorable) (+) and negative (not favorable) (-) contributions of each alternative structure are shown. They aid in alternative selection*

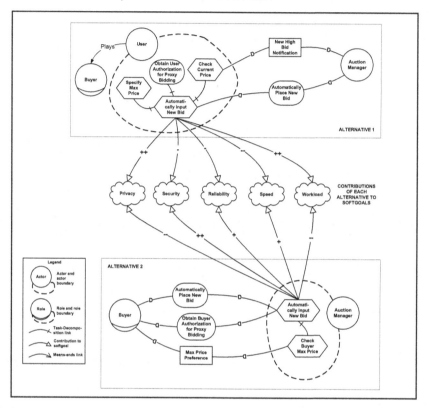

Several reasons support this choice:

- When the *Buyer* manages proxy bidding, price preferences are not communicated to outside agents. Consequently, *Privacy* is higher than in the second alternative which requires the transfer of price preferences to the *Auction Manager*.
- *Workload* of the system is lower, since automatic bidding is distributed among multiple *Buyer* agents participating in the auction. We consider that system *Workload* is much higher when all proxy bidding activity in one auction is centralized at the *Auction Manager*.
- We consider that *Security* of data transfers between the *Buyer* and *Auction Manager* is not of high priority in an English online

auction, since the bid made by the *Buyer* is made publicly available by the *Auction Manager*.

Reliability concerns the probability of error in terms of e.g., a new proxy bid not being taken into account by the *Auction Manager*. This probability is higher when proxy bidding is distributed among multiple *Buyers*. Finally, it is probable that speed of bid input is higher when proxy bidding is centralized, since there are no data transfers between the *Auction Manager* and *Buyer* agents.

Based on this discussion, we select the first alternative on Figure 11. Consequently, proxy bidding is introduced in the IS as a service that a *User* agent playing *Buyer* role can provide to the human user, and requires the human user to specify the maximum price that he/she is willing to pay. In addition, the *Buyer* agent needs to obtain an authorization from the user in order to initiate proxy bidding.

Reputation management. In classical exchanges where buyers and sellers actually meet, trust results from repeated buyer-seller interactions, from the possibility to inspect items before the purchase, etc. In online auctions, sellers and buyers do not meet, and little personal information is publicly available during the auction. In addition, product information is limited to information provided wilfully by the seller. In such a context, a mechanism for managing trust should be provided in order to reduce uncertainty in transactions among auction participants.

According to (Ramchurn, Huynh & Jennings, 2004), "trust is a belief an agent has that the other party will do what it says it will (being honest and reliable) or reciprocate (being reciprocate for the common good of both), given an opportunity to defect to get higher payoffs." Trust can be favoured in an OAIS through a reputation mechanism, which should satisfy specific requirements (Ramchurn, Huynh & Jennings, 2004): it should be costly to change identities in the community; new entrants should not be penalized by initially having a low reputation rating; participants with low ratings should be able to rebuild reputation; it should be costly for participants to fake reputation; participants with high reputation should have more

influence on reputation ratings they attribute to other participants; participants should be able to provide more qualitative evaluations than simply numerical ratings; and finally, participants should be able to keep a memory of reputation ratings and give more importance to the latest ones. Such reputation mechanism can reduce the hesitancy of new buyers and sellers when using the OAIS for the first time, as it implicitly reduces the anonymity and uncertainty among trading partners.

It is difficult to construct a reputation system that satisfies all of these requirements. Seller reputation can be established through feedback of buyers on the behavior of sellers during the trade settlement which follows the closure of the auction (Resnick & Zeckhauser, 2002). As a result of buyer feedback in repetitive sales, a seller receives a rating which is indicative of the trust that the trading community has in him/her.

In order to enable the management of trust in the OAIS, we introduce an additional agent: *Reputation Manager*, which is a specialization of the *Information Brokering Agent* (Papazoglou, 2001). Informally, its responsibility is to collect, organize, and summarize reputation data. The *Reputation Manager* depends on the winning *Buyer* of each auction to provide feedback on the *Seller* after the trade settlement. *Reputation Manager* uses *Qualitative* (textual) and *Quantitative* (numerical) *Feedback on Seller* to establish reputation ratings of *Users* that have played the

Figure 12. Social dimension of the reputation management pattern

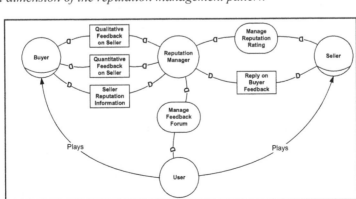

Figure 13. Strategic rationale model of the dispute resolution pattern with focus on negotiation assistant agent rationale

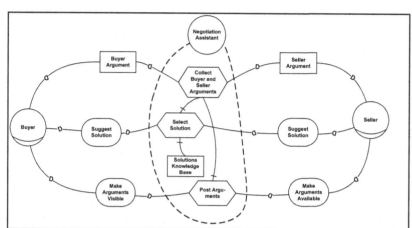

role of *Sellers* in auctions. As information on reputation is valuable to any *User* of the OAIS, any *User* depends on the *Reputation Manager* to *Manage Feedback Forum*, in which the feedback and rating information is contained and organized. Each *Buyer* depends on the *Reputation Manager* to provide summarized *Seller Reputation Information*, so that the *Buyer* can have an indication on the trust he/she can put into the relationship with the *Seller*. The *Seller* can post replies on feedback provided by *Buyers*. Finally, the *Seller* depends on the *Reputation Manager* to *Manage Reputation Rating*.

This pattern satisfies all but one of the requirements specified above: it does not make it costly for participants to change identities. For example, eBay deals with this problem by requiring each seller to provide a valid credit card number. We do not introduce such possibility into the pattern as it is not a standardized solution (eBay applies it only for its US users and none of its competitors applies it anywhere in the world).

Dispute Resolution. The trade settlement that follows the closure of the auction may not be successful for many reasons (e.g., late deliveries, late payment, no payment at all, etc.). It then results in dispute that can require mediation by a third party in order to be resolved. The third party (here, a

Negotiation Assistant) can be either a software agent that manages an automated dispute resolution process, or a human mediator.

The *Negotiation Assistant* collects *Buyer* and *Seller Arguments*, and makes them available to both parties. On the basis of these *Arguments* and its *Solution Knowledge Base*, the agent *Selects Solution*—both the *Buyer* and the *Seller*—depend on the agent to *Suggest Solution* to their dispute.

Payment. Payment can be accomplished by numerous ways in the context of an online auction. They can be either managed (in part) through the OAIS (e.g., credit card based transactions), or outside the scope of the IS (e.g., cash, checks, etc.). The payment choice of auction participants is not repetitive and differs according to the payment cost, convenience, and protection. Consequently, it is important to take these criteria into account when structuring an OAIS.

In the Payment pattern, the *Payment Agent* (specialization of the *Negotiating and Contracting Agent* (Papazoglou, 2001)) mediates the payment interaction between the *Seller* and the *Buyer*. This agent depends on the *Account Manager* for data on *Users*, which is then used in providing *Payment Details* to the *Payment System*. In addition to user identification, *Payment Details* should also contain transaction-related data. The *Pay-*

Figure 14. Social dimension of the payment pattern

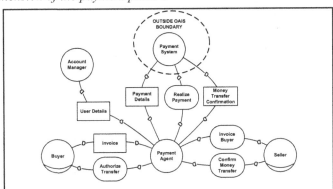

ment Agent depends on the *Payment System* to *Realize Payment* and to provide *Money Transfer Confirmation*, which is used to *Confirm Money Transfer* to the *Seller.* The *Payment System* is outside the boundary of the OAIS. Upon closure of the auction, the *Seller* depends on the *Payment Agent* to *Invoice Buyer.* The *Buyer* depends on the *Payment System* to provide *Invoice* and in return, the *Buyer* is expected to *Authorize Transfer.*

The pattern structure in Figure 14 is adapted to all common credit card based payment systems. Any of these payment systems intervenes in the pattern as the *Payment System*, which is specialized in money transfers.

CONCLUSION

Online auctions have become increasingly popular in e-business transactions. Companies require such systems to be developed on tight budgets and in short time, in order to deploy auctions in managing relationships with their suppliers and clients. Patterns of best practices of online auctions can provide significant aid in the development process of such systems.

This chapter explores such patterns, by analyzing some advanced online auctions functionalities through the lens of the agent paradigm. Compared to the literature, our approach is innovative in

several respects: we consider that multi-agent systems are particularly adapted to modelling and implementing online auction systems; we provided the *i** agent-oriented modelling perspective of each of the patterns we consider and we focused on specifying best practices in current online auction systems.

There are limitations to our work. We have not provided other dimensions than the *i** (social and intentional) ones for the patterns. This is well beyond the scope of this chapter as it requires much more time and space. As future work, the patterns will be modelled using UML-based notations as well as formally specified with the Z language.

REFERENCES

Beam, C. & Segev, A. (1998). Auctions on the Internet: A Field Study. *Working Paper 98-WP-1032, The Fisher Center for Management and Information Technology,* University of California, Berkeley.

Bikhchandani, S., de Vries, S., Schummer, S. & Vohra, R.V. (2001). *Linear Programming and Vickrey Auctions: Mathematics of the Internet: E-auction and Markets.* Springer-Verlag.

Buyya, R., Stockinger, H., Giddy, J. & Abramson, D. (2001). Economic Models for Management of Resources in Peer-to-Peer and Grid Computing. *Proceedings of the international symposium on the convergence of information technologies and communications, ITCom '01*, Denver, USA.

Chung, L.K., Nixon, B.A., Yu, E. & Mylopoulos J. (2000). *Non-Functional Requirements in Software Engineering*. Kluwer Publishing.

Do, T.T., Faulkner, S. & Kolp, M. (2002). The Structure-in-5 as a Multi-Agent Architectural Pattern. *IAG Working Paper 38/02, IAG School of Management*, Université catholique de Louvain.

Do, T.T., Kolp, M. & Pirotte, A. (2003). Social Patterns for Designing Multiagent Systems. *Proceedings of the 15th International Conference on Software Engineering and Knowledge Engineering, SEKE '03*, San Francisco, USA.

Faulkner, S., Kolp, M. & Do, T.T. (2004). The SKwyRL Perspective on Agent-Oriented Design Patterns. *Proceedings of the 6th International Conference on Enterprise Information Systems, ICEIS '04*, Porto, Portugal.

Faulkner, S. (2004). *An Architectural Framework for Describing BDI-Multi-Agent Information Systems*. Unpublished doctoral thesis, University of Louvain, Belgium.

Guttman, R.H., Moukas, A.G. & Maes, P. (1998). Agent-mediated Electronic Commerce: A Survey. *Knowledge Engineering Review, 13*(3), 45-69.

Kauffman, R.J. &Walden, E.A. (2001). Economics and Electronic Commerce: Survey and Research Directions. *International Journal of Electronic Commerce, 5*(4), 5-117.

Kolp, M., Giorgini, P. & Mylopoulos, J. (2003). Organizational Patterns for Early Requirements Analysis. *Proceedings of the 15th International Conference on Advanced Information Systems Engineering, CAiSE '03*, Velden, Austria.

Kumar, M. & Feldman, S.I. (1998). Internet Auctions. *Proceedings of the 3rd USENIX Workshop on Electronic Commerce*, Boston, USA.

Kurbel, K. & Loutchko, I. (2001). A Framework for Multi-agent Electronic Marketplaces: Analysis and Classification of Existing Systems. *Proceedings of International Congress on Information Science Innovations, ISI '0*1, American University in Dubai

Liu, L. & Yu, E. (2004). Designing information systems in social context: a goal and scenario modelling approach. *Information Systems, 29*, 187-203.

Lucking-Reiley D. (2000). Auctions on the Internet: What ís Being Auctioned, and How?. *Journal of Industrial Economics, 48*(3), 227-252.

Mylopoulos J., Kolp M. & Castro J. (2001). UML for Agent-Oriented Software Development: The Tropos Proposal. *Proceedings of the 4th International Conference on the Unified Modeling Language, UML '01*, Toronto, Canada.

Papazoglou M.P. (2001). Agent-Oriented Technology in Support of E-Business. *Communications of the ACM, 44*(4), 71-77.

Pinker, E.J., Seidmann, A. & Vakrat, Y. (2001). The Design of Online Auctions: Business Issues and Current Research. *Working Paper CIS-01-05, W. E. Simon Graduate School of Business Administration*, University of Rochester, Canada.

Rachlevsky-Reich B., Ben-Shaul, I., Tung Chau, N., Lo, A. & Poggio, T. (1999). GEM: A Global Electronic Market System. *Special issue on information systems for electronic commerce, Information Systems, 24*(6), 495-518.

Ramchurn, S.D., Huynh, D. & Jennings N.R. (2004). Trust in Multi-Agent Systems. *The Knowledge Engineering Review, 19*(1), 1-25.

Re R., Braga R.T.V. & Masiero P.C. (2001). A Pattern Language for Online Auctions Management. *Proceedings of the 8th Conference on Pattern Languages of Programs*, PLoP '01, Illinois, USA.

Resnick P. & Zeckhauser R. (2002). Trust Among Strangers in Internet Transactions: Empirical Analysis of eBayís Reputation System. *Advances in Applied Microeconomics, 11,* 77-106.

Schafer, J.B. (2002). *MetaLens: A Framework for Multisource Recommendations.* Unpublished doctoral thesis, Department of Computer Science, University of Northern Iowa, USA.

Weiss M. (2003). Pattern-Driven Design of Agent Systems: Approach and Case Study. *Proceedings of the 15ᵗʰ International Conference on Advanced Information Systems Engineering, CAISE '03,* Velden, Austria.

Yu E. (1995). *Modelling Strategic Relationships for Process Reengineering.* Unpublished doctoral thesis, Dept. of Computer Science, University of Toronto, Canada.

Yu E. (1997). Why Agent-Oriented Requirements Engineering. *Proceedings of 3rd International Workshop on Requirements Engineering: Foundations for Software Quality,* Barcelona, Spain.

Yu E. (2001). Agent-Oriented Modelling: Software Versus the World. *Proceedings of the 2nd International Workshop on Agent-Oriented Software Engineering,* AOSE '01, Montreal, Canada.

ENDNOTE

[1] The issue of trust between buyers and sellers in online auctions is an often treated topic in economics research (see e.g., (Resnick & Zeckhauser, 2002; Pinker, Seidmann & Vakrat, 2001)).

This work was previously published in the International Journal of Intelligent Information Technologies, Vol. 2, Issue 3, edited by V. Sugumaran, pp. 21-39, copyright 2006 by IGI Publishing, formerly known as Idea Group Publishing (an imprint of IGI Global).

IMPLICATIONS FOR PRACTITIONERS[1]

Title: Multi-Agent Patterns for Deploying Online Auctions

Description

A high volume of goods and services is being traded using online auction systems. This growth requires a larger size and complexity in order to support the online auction systems.

This chapter proposes that there be an analysis of the patterns to identify best practices in the development of online auction information systems. These patterns should help both IT managers and software engineers during the requirements specifications phase of developing an online auction system.

Findings

- Several features of online auctions should be developed. These include:
  - Proxy bidding
  - Reputation management
  - Dispute resolution

RECOMMENDATIONS

- Firms that wish to develop their own private auction software should look to intelligent agents for some of the development.
- Pattern analysis is something that should be done periodically in order to identify areas for improvement in the system development.

LIMITATIONS

- The study did not provide dimensions other that the social and intentional ones for the patterns. This is a much larger analytical effort.

ENDNOTE

[1]   Note that this section was written by D. H. Parente, editor of *Best Practices for Online Procurement Auctions*, in order to be consistent with other chapters and provide value to practitioners reading the volume.

Chapter XIV
An Internet Trading Platform for Testing Auction and Exchange Mechanisms

Haiying Qiao
University of Maryland, USA

Hui Jie
Shanghai Jiao Tong University, China

Dong-Qing Yao
Towson University, USA

ABSTRACT

In this chapter we present a generic electronic market platform that is designed to run different kinds of auctions and exchanges. Researchers can use the platform to implement different electronic market mechanisms, simulate the market behavior of their interests, and experiment with it. A generic OR/XOR bidding language that can express different OR/XOR combinations is implemented for Web interfaces. Different auctions including combinatorial auctions, multiple-round reverse auctions and multiple homogeneous good auctions have been built and run successfully on the platform.

INTRODUCTION

The Internet and information technologies (IT) have brought in dramatic changes to the traditional auction marketplace. Many companies are using online channels for buying and selling goods/services, sometimes referred to as e-procurement in the areas of supply chain management. With the widespread online auction practices to meet different requirements of the electronic marketplaces, the success of online auctioneer such as eBay.com also has been attracting more research on online auctions.

One big advantage of auction is that a successful auction can reveal the market values according to the bidders' and auction items' values. Even for the goods whose value can not be easily determined in advance, auctions have a particularly convenient property to find the market values of the goods, i.e., auctions can be adopted to discover the equilibrium price of the supply and demand. Under some simplified assumptions, auction theories can prove that some basic auctions are efficient and have equilibriums. For example, Milgrom and Webber (1982) developed a model of competitive bidding under the assumption that the winning bidder's payoff may depend upon his personal preferences, the preferences of others and the intrinsic qualities of items being sold. However, some of the assumptions may not be held in the real world as pointed out by Banks et al. (2005). More often than not, the winner is determined not only by the price, but also by other attributes such as quality or transportation service (arrival time, dispatch time, weight, volume etc), which make auction more complicated to solve theoretically. Lucking-Reiley's (1999) experiment on the Internet auction shows more extensive research needs to be done for the trading behaviors of Internet auction. Among them, two critical issues are worth addressing here:

1.   For particular goods or types of goods, the market structure and mechanism should be carefully designed to make sure that the real market values are obtained through the auction and the goods are allocated to the bidders efficiently. A bad market design could not only result in inefficiency, winner's curse, reduced revenue, but also legal problems if fairness is not well maintained. Different auction mechanisms may be designed for different auction items. The auction could be a single item auction, multiple homogeneous

items or multiple heterogeneous items auction. Although heterogeneous items auction is a generalization of the other auctions, the inherent difficulty of combinatorial auction has forced researchers to find other alternative ways.

2.   Information revelation mechanism is another important part of an auction design. For example, according to Milgrom and Webber (1982), under some circumstances, the English auction generates higher average prices than the second-price auction since the bidders have more information of the auction.

As we mentioned before, it is hard to predict the bidding behaviors and auction results theoretically due to complexity of the problem. Therefore many researchers turn to experiments or simulations. For example, McCabe et al. (1991) tested traditional Vickrey's and other simultaneous multiple unit versions of the English auction. Banks et al. (2005) ran an experiment on the FCC spectrum auctions.

A challenging problem of these experiments and simulation is that customized auction software has to be developed for each of them. A reusable auction software platform is needed for researchers to quickly design prototype and develop different auction mechanisms to test and experiment different research ideas. So far, some research auction software has been developed on the Internet. For example, FM 96.5 (Rodriguez-Aguilar et al., 1997) is an electronic auction house that is a complete implementation of the trading conventions of the fish market, which allows for a real-time concurrent operation of the complete fish market auction process. The Michigan Internet AuctionBot (Wurman et al., 1998) is a configurable auction server, where classic auctions such as English auction, Dutch auction, Vickery auction and Sealed auction can be implemented by different configurations. eAuctionHouse (Sandholm, 2002) is an auction server based on the eMediator server developed by CMU. Instead of implementing the classic auctions, eAuctionHouse focuses more on combinatorial auctions. It also implements the XOR of OR bidding language and includes CABOB algorithm to solve the winner determination problem. Other researchers focus on how to solve the problems that could happen during the auction processes such as security, privacy, trust, and fraud. Secure auction marketplace (SAM) architecture[1] is a framework to address such issue.

However all the above products limit users to the auction mechanism that they can support. Auction designers cannot define auctions as they want with current auction software. To this end, we developed a reusable software auction framework and platform in an attempt to run different types of auctions and exchanges. The main purpose of the platform is to provide an auction software platform and framework where researchers can quickly develop, deploy, experiment and simulate different auction mechanisms.

The remainder of the chapter is organized as follows: in Section 2, we discuss some considerations, requirements and services of the platform. We discuss the framework design and implementation in Section 3, and introduce bidding language in Section 4. We provide a demo in Section 5. Section 6 concludes the chapter with some future research ideas.

REQUIREMENTS AND SERVICES OF OUR FRAMEWORK

Auction process is a marketing mechanism to discover the market equilibrium. This process sometimes is not efficient if it is done in a single round. For example, FCC uses the simultaneous multi-round auction to sell spectrum license. For multiple-item auction, it is popular to use multi-round in an auction. An auction framework should have built-in multi-round auction support.

It will be challenging for an individual auction software platform to support all different types of auctions. Therefore instead of implementing configurable auction software as Michigan Auctionbot, we generalize and implement the fundamental auction activities and leave some implementation details to specific auctions. In our approach, the framework only abstracts and implements the general activities. We will discuss the detailed implementation in Section 4. In this section, we first list all key features that an auction platform is supposed to support, which are implemented in our platform:

- The platform should support different kinds of auction items. From basketball ticket to air spectrum, all auctions of different kinds of goods should be supported by the platform. Although it is possible to create an auction to sell any items on eBay.com, the item specification is not clearly defined. For example, you cannot search two tickets whose seats are next to each other on eBay.com.

- The platform should support single and multiple auction items. This requirement is important since the obvious benefit of combinatorial auction has attracted more and more researchers. A simple but powerful bidding language that fits the Internet technology should be developed to let bidder place a package bid easily.

- The platform should support multi-round auction. A new round should be triggered in different ways, e.g., triggered by scheduled time, specific event or manual initiation.

- The platform should support different kinds of bid format and flexible bidding language.

- The platform should allow different algorithms to be plugged to clear auction or auction round. It should be able to run multiple algorithms simultaneously to compare the performance among them.

- The platform should support multi-seller and multi-buyer exchanges in the same auction.
- The platform should take into account different kinds/levels of information revelation mechanism. Since an auction is a game, different information revelation mechanisms have significant impacts on the bidder's valuation, strategy, and auction efficiency. Therefore the platform should provide convenient ways for auction designer to deliver different information to bidders. For example, auction can deliver bid information or results at a scheduled time.
- The platform should support bidding both through the Web by bidders and through software agent.
- The platform should build in security. Although the security is not a critical concern in this framework, some access control such as bidders' privileges and seller's access privileges should be defined and implemented.
- The platform should provide data persistence and retrieval mechanism.

Additionally, The platform should also provide necessary services so that the auction designer can focus on specific auction mechanism design instead of dealing with the details of software implementations such as Web publishing, access control, data retrieval, task scheduling etc.

For multiple-item auction, a challenging task is how to place a bid. An auction platform should also provide a simple, expressive and user-friendly bidding language compatible with Web applications and be easy to use. Again, the bidding language should be generic enough so that auction designers have the freedom to design their own bidding structures. In the next section, we propose our composite bidding language specially designed for Web applications.

BIDDING LANGUAGE FOR MULTI-ITEM AUCTIONS

For single item English auction, the bidding language is very simple: a bidder may just specify the price that the bidder wants to pay. For Dutch auction, a bid just needs to specify whether the bidder will take the item at the current price or not, and the auction ends when someone submits such a bid.

However, when an auction includes multiple items, whether the items are identical or non-identical, a bid can be very complicated if the bidder is allowed to bid combinations of items. The exponential number of the possible combinations will make the computation intractable. Nisan (2000) analyzed different kinds of bidding languages. He defined atomic bid that includes a subset of bid items and the associated price. He also formally defined six bidding languages: OR-bids, XOR-bids, OR of XOR bids, XOR of ORs, OR/XOR-formulae and OR*-bids. The first four languages are the special types of OR/XOR-formulae. OR*-bids can represent all other types by using phantom items. Sandholm (2002) implemented two auction languages in the eAuctionHouse: the XOR bidding language and the OR-of-XOR, which is more convenient than traditional OR bidding language.

Although these languages can express a bid, sometime it is not succinct enough due to the simple definition of atomic bid. For example, assume that three items (A, B, C) are totally substitutable and that the bidder wants to bid on any two of them at price of 2. If using XOR language, the bid will be as follows:

(A, B, 2) XOR (A, C, 2) XOR (B, C, 2)

If atomic can be defined with more flexible expression, the bid can be easily expressed as:

((A, B, C), 2, 2)

where the first "2" denotes any two-item set. The second "2" is the price. If the size of the items is large, the benefit is self-explanatory in the sense that it can significantly reduce the size of the expression. Auction designers can interpret the language as they wish because they can normally define such bidding language on their own.

By generalizing the atomic bid, the platform allows richer and more convenient input languages without losing expressive power. Other atomic bid formats may allow bidders to specify a step-wise or continuous curve demand functions.

As a general framework, our platform takes into account this flexibility since the main purpose of the framework is to provide a platform where auction designers can play different auction mechanisms and different algorithms. To implement the OR/XOR-formulae, we introduce the concept of composite bid and expand Nisan's definition of atomic bid as follows:

Atomic bid is specified by auction designer. It could be different kinds of bids such as a package bid, a matrix bid (Day & Raghavan 2003), or step-wise quantity bid, etc.

Composite bid is a collection of atomic bids and composite bids, with the relationship (OR or XOR) between the atomic bids and composite bids. Composite bid can be implemented with a design pattern called Composite pattern (Gamma et al. 1995). Each composite bid has two or more composite bids or atomic bids and the relationship between them. The relationship can be defined as OR, XOR, or any kinds of relationship defined by auction designer.

Figure 1 shows the bid structure of the composite bidding language. From the diagram, we can see that the atomic bid and composite bid can be combined together with different OR/XOR relations. As such it can easily implement OR-bids, XOR-bids, OR of XOR bids, XOR of Ors,

Figure 1. Illustration of a composite bid

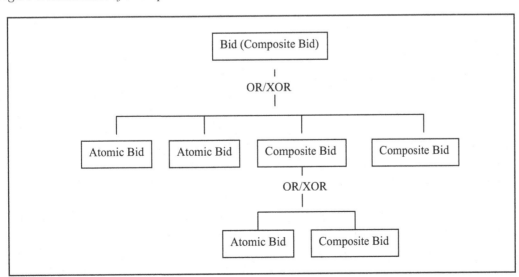

Figure 2. High-level component relationship

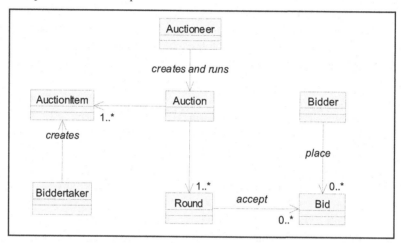

OR/XOR-formulae bids through different combinations of composite bids and atomic bids.

FRAMEWORK DESIGN AND IMPLEMENTATION

Although there are different types of auctions, some relationships between components in an auction are pretty static. Figure 2 shows the high level relationship between the components in an auction.

From Figure 2, it can be seen that an auction system has the following components:

1. **Auction:** The exchange where the auction takes place.
2. **Auctioneer:** Who creates, runs and ends an auction.
3. **Bid-taker:** Who places auction items in an auction.
4. **Bidder:** Who places bid(s) on items in the auction.
5. **Auction round:** An auction may have one or more rounds. An auction round can be a sealed auction or an iterative auction.
6. **Auction item:** An auction may have one or more auction items.
7. **Bid:** Bidders can place one or more bids on the auction.

The implementation guidelines of the platform is to specify and implement these high-level relationships, generic attributes and behaviors of these components, but leave the details of different auction design including user interfaces to auction designers.

All components include two different kinds of attributes: *general attributes* and *specific attributes*. General attributes are those that a component possesses in most cases, whereas specific attributes are attributes that are unique to an individual or specific auction. For example, auction name and start time are general attributes of auction components while the auction rules such as whether there is a reserve price are different for different auctions.

All specific attributes of these components are coded using XML. The auction developer can extend the components to manipulate these specific data. Good Web interfaces or agent interfaces are needed to create these specific attributes easily. We provide many utilities to help creating these specific attributes in XML through WEB interface including a Web publish framework that extends Jakarta Strut framework[2].

By using XML, we can depict any specific attributes of an auction item, auction rules, information revelation mechanism, etc. Auction designer designs the XML schema, understands the meaning of these attributes and processes these data as needed while the platform has no knowledge of these data; however it can run these auctions according to the high-level activities and rules specified by these auctions.

Based on the high level relationships between these components defined in Figure 2, currently we have designed six framework level activities:

1. **Create an auction:** Auctioneer can create an auction in the auction container. He or she can specify the general auction information, specific auction information, and auction rules.

2. **Create a round and specify round information:** The auction creator can specify the auction round information such as the round numbers, round schedules or round proceeding rules, etc.

3. **Add auction items:** Sellers can add one or more items to an auction. Again, they can specify general and specific information of an item.

4. **Place bids:** Bidders can place one or more bids on an auction. The bidding language and bidding interface should be carefully designed by the auction designer. A generic bidding language implementation for combinatorial auctions is described in the previous section.

5. **Information Revelation:** During the process of an auction, the system can deliver different kinds of information about the scheduled time, upon some events or bidders' request.

6. **Clearing:** Clearing may happen at the end of each round or the end of the auction.

Figure 3. Architecture overview

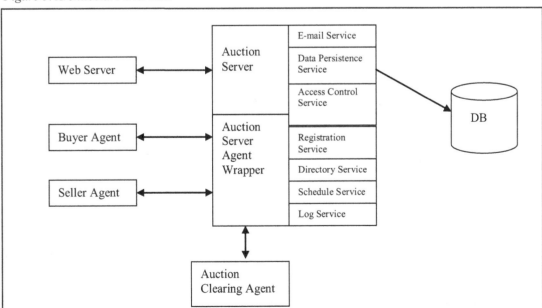

The auction platform architecture is shown in Figure 3. The components of the system are described as follows:

Auction server. Handles most basic activities as describe before. It also provides a client side API so that clients can talk to the server directly. The auction service is implemented as a JAVA Enterprise Java Bean, which is run in JBoss application server. Because the server provides the basic auction service, it is generic enough to support different types of auctions. Some implementation details are left to different agents or components. For example, the clearing details are left to clearing agents. Basically, auction server is responsible for taking information from buyer agent, seller agent and clearing agents. The details of how to process the information are delivered to other components in the systems.

Auction Server Agent Wrapper. The wrapper provides message-based communication between agents. This wrapper wraps up all functions provided by the auction server. Since the auction server is implemented as Enterprise Java Bean, the buyer agent or seller agent can use either the client API to call auction server directly or auction server agent wrapper to communicate with the auction server. In addition, the wrapper also provides communications between the server and other agents or components, especially the event notification. For example, seller can subscribe to price change event and get notified from the auction server through server agent wrapper.

Buyer Agent. This agent could be a real buyer or a virtual buyer that simulates the buyer's behavior. The framework just provides high level of communication and event subscription-notification service for these agents. The implementation of these agents depends on different projects and varies with different agent frameworks such as Cougaar[3], IMPACT[4], etc. Again the framework only provides communication services between these agents and server, but leaves the bidder's logic implementation to specific auction projects.

If the buyer is a real person, the agent is only a software component that represents the buyer to communicate with server to place a bid or get information such as auction status from server.

Seller Agent. This agent could also be a real seller or a virtual seller. Similar to buyer agent, the underlying logic and the implementation of such agents depends on the specific project. The server agent wrapper provides two-way communication between the server and these agents.

Web Server. Provides Web interface for real buyers and sellers to interact with the auction server. To provide more flexible Web publish, we extend Struts Web publishing framework to provide more generic and dynamic Web publishing.

In addition, our framework provides several services that are required to run an auction. These services include authentication and authorization service, persistence service, log service, registration service, and scheduling service, etc.

The framework abstracts the high-level auction activities and service. However, different auctions have different implementations and requirements, so we provide the XML interface for users and implementers to specify specific auction, round and item information, etc. All information is specified and managed by users themselves.

DEMO IMPLEMENTATION

The auction is implemented in Java based on several open source projects such as Struts for Web publishing, JBoss as server container, Xercex for XML parsing, Jakarta Slide for Access control, log4J for logging, Repast for Agent based simulation, Jfreechart for chart generation. One of the reasons why we chose the above tools is that they are all available for free. Since our framework is designed to support different research and classroom projects, by not having to worry about

Figure 4. Create an auction screen

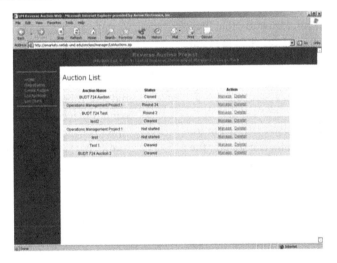

Figure 5. List auction screen

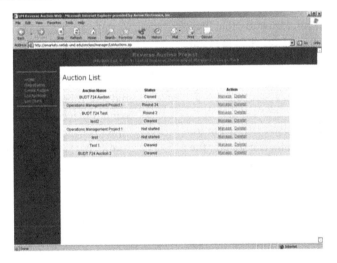

licensing issues, we can focus on implementing and testing different applications quickly. Next we will introduce a demo implementation based on the above auction framework.

The application is a Web-based procurement auction that is used in an operation management course. The application is developed for business students to understand the procurement auction process and make decisions in gaming environment. The class is divided into several groups, each of which has different production capacity, production cost, initial inventory, scheduled sales order and uncertain demand. As such each student group has different costs of the products, production capacity and production plan. In addition, one group has no knowledge of other groups' information (i.e., this is a game with incomplete information). The auctioneer (the instructor) can create an auction first, which may have one item and the required quantity. The auction is multi-round. In each round, the auctioneer specifies the price of the auction item

Figure 6. Manage auction screen

based on bid information of the previous round. Each group places a bid with a quantity that they want to provide. The auction stops when the total bid quantity is less than the required quantity.

The application includes the following functions:

a. **Create an auction:** In the screen (see Figure 4), the auction administrator can specify the basic auction information such as name, round duration, auction item name, quantity, etc.

b. **List Auction:** This screen (see Figure 5) shows a list of auctions where the instructor can select one to manage or delete.

c. **Manage the auction:** This screen (see Figure 6) manages the round, start a new round, clear or close the auction. This is the main screen for auction administrator. The student cannot place a bid until the auctioneer (administrator) starts the auction/create a new round. In addition to the price, the auctioneer can specify some basic rules for the rounds, such as minimum bidding quantity and maximum bidding quantity. The auctioneer also can view current auction status and close the auction so that nobody can place a bid within this auction.

d. **View auction detail image:** The application can also create image of the auction process dynamically.

e. **Place a bid:** In this screen, the bidder can place a bid based on his or her previous bid and other auction rules such as he/she cannot place a bid quantity larger than the previous bid, he/she has to place the bid before the end of the round (the system will alert the bidder 30 seconds before the round ends), the bidder will be notified of new events (a new round is created, the auction is closed or cleared, etc.) if the browser's Java plug-in is enabled. A bid cannot be changed after the current round is closed.

We do release some bid information such as the total bid amount in each round to the groups so that each group knows how close they are to their required quantity. We run this auction in a classroom setting, and all groups are in the same classroom. Some interesting bidding behaviors are observed during the auction, such as collaboration and collusion through body languages or expressive words.

Furthermore, we find that although groups have their own pre-plan bidding strategies, they do change their strategies in the auction since

Figure 7. View auction detail image

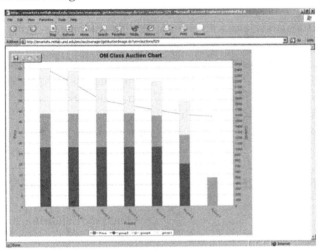

Figure 8. Place a bid screen

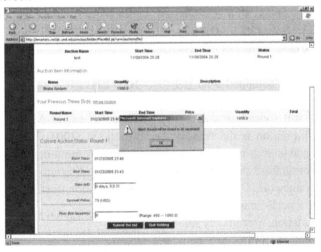

bidding strategies may be adjusted according to other behavior, for example, some make bid mistakes because they thought other groups have the same cost factors as theirs. Winner's curse is also observed, since each group wants to win a bid in a competitive environment.

We also run the same auction twice and try to find whether the bidding behaviors change with the knowledge learned from the first auction. The results show that they do change the bidding behavior due to the learning curve effect.

All the data including bidding quantity and price for each round are finally stored in a Oracle database through data persistence service, which is implemented as enterprise java entity bean. However since the discussion of the auction results is out of the scope of this chapter, we will not discuss more detailed results of this auction demo.

The auction platform is generic and flexible, which can help auction designers quickly design, deploy, modify and test their auction designs. We have implemented several other auctions using the framework, i.e. matrix auction (Day & Raghavan 2003), UM Game ticket auction and an agent based auction simulation, etc. with our composite bidding language. Furthermore we can easily implement other traditional auctions such as English, Dutch and sealed-bid auction. As a research auction platform, our platform can be easily adopted for instructional use, research simulation and experiment.

CONCLUSION AND FUTURE RESEARCH

The purpose of this chapter is to present a software auction platform that can support different kinds of auctions. We introduce a new composite biding language that can express all five bidding languages suggested by Nisan (2000): OR-bids, XOR-bids, OR of XOR bids, XOR of ORs, OR/XOR-formulae. By extending the concept of atomic bid, researchers are equipped with rich choices of the bidding languages.

However there are still some limitations in our framework. One limitation is the tradeoff between performance and generic requirements. To describe the different auctions and bids, XML is widely used in the framework. One drawback of this language is slow performance, which is critical for auction simulation. Fortunately some performance improvement efforts are being conducted for a simulation project based on this framework. Another limitation is that the framework cannot totally eliminate the programming efforts although it has provided several high level services. The auction designer still has to learn the API and JAVA programming. However, the framework has greatly helped the development and deployment of different auction projects. For example, one PhD student can quickly prototype an auction simulation by using the auction framework.

In the future, we will extend the framework to include workflow support, which means auc-

tion designers have the capability to define the workflow for the auction process instead of hard coding the process. Also we feel the need to extend the commercial XML Standards such as ebXML[5], cXML[6] to support auction. Mao et al. (2001) suggest an XML based configurable auction framework, however they focus more on the communication protocol between agents instead of the description of the auction itself.

ACKNOWLEDGMENT

We thank the Editor-in-Chief and two anonymous reviewers for their constructive comments on the drafts of this chapter. The research of the first author is sponsored by NSF Grant (ITR-0205489): "Rapid Response Electronic Markets for Time Sensitive Goods".

REFERENCES

Banks, J., Olson. M., Porter. D., Rassenti, S., & Smith, V. (2005) Theory, experiment and the Federal Communications Commission spectrum auctions. *Journal of Economic Behavior and Organization* (forthcoming).

Day, R., & Raghavan, S. (2003). *CAMBO: Combinatorial Auctions using Matrix Bids with Order.* Working Paper, University of Maryland.

Erich, G., Helm, R., Johnson, R., & Vlissides, J. (1995). *Design Patterns.* Addison-Wesley.

Lucking-Reiley, D. (1999) Using field experiments to test equivalence between auction formats: Magic on the Internet. *American Economic Review, 89*(5), 1063-1080.

Weiliang, M., Sheng, H., & Peng, D. (2001). An XML-based language for coordination protocol description in multi-agent system. In *Proceedings of 14th International Conference on Industrial and Engineering Applications of Artificial Intel-*

ligence and Expert Systems (IEA/AIE2001) (pp. 708-717).

McCabe, K., Rassenti, S., & Smith, V. (1991). Testing Vickrey's and other simultaneous multiple unit versions of the English auction. Isaac, R.M. (Ed.), *Research in Experimental Economics, Vol. 4* (pp. 45-79). JAI Press.

Milgrom, P., & Weber, R. (1982). A theory of auctions and competitive bidding. *Econometrica. 50,* 1485-1527.

Nisan Noam. (2000). Bidding and allocation in combinatorial auctions. In *Proceedings of the 2nd ACM Conference on Electronic Commerce* (pp. 1-12).

Rodriguez-Aguilar J. A., P. Noriega, C. Sierra, & J. Padget (1997). FM96.5: A Java-based electronic auction house. *Proceedings of the Second International Conference on the Practical Application of Intelligent Agents and Multi-Agent Technology (PAAM'97).* 207-224.

Sandholm T. (2002). eMediator: A next generation electronic commerce server. *Computational Intelligence. 18*(4), 656-676.

Wurman P. R., M. P. Wellman, & Walsh W. E. (1998). The Michigan Internet auctionbot: A configurable auction server for human and software agents. In *Proceedings of the Second International Conference on Autonomous Agents (AGENTS)* (pp. 301-308).

ENDNOTES

[1] http://www.ece.cmu.edu/~adrian/projects/SAM/a2.html
[2] http://jakarta.apache.org
[3] http://www.cougaar.org
[4] http://www.cs.umd.edu/projects/impact
[5] http://ebxml.org
[6] http://cxml.org

This work was previously published in the International Journal of Intelligent Information Technologies, Vol 1, Issue 4, edited by V. Sugumaran, pp. 20-35, copyright 2005 by IGI Publishing, formerly known as Idea Group Publishing (an imprint of IGI Global).

IMPLICATIONS FOR PRACTITIONERS[1]

Title: An Internet trading platform for testing auction and exchange mechanisms

Description

In this chapter, the authors discuss a generic electronic market platform. It was designed to run a variety of different auctions and exchanges. The users can simulate market behaviors and identify actions and reactions that can be employed in the real situation.

Findings

- Development of a generic software auction platform and composite bidding language.

RECOMMENDATIONS

- If you are considering development of an auction platform, you might turn to a generic or packaged tool that could be customized for your use.

LIMITATIONS

- The study has its limitations in the tradeoff between performance and generic requirements.
- The framework developed has limitations in the speed of running an auction.

ENDNOTE

[1] Note that this section was written by D. H. Parente, editor of *Best Practices for Online Procurement Auctions*, in order to be consistent with other chapters and provide value to practitioners reading the volume.

Section IV
Online Reverse Auction Success

Chapter XV
An Empirical Study of Collusion Potential Metrics and their Impact on Online Reverse Auction Success

Srabana Gupta
St. Thomas University, USA

Indranil Ghosh
Winston-Salem State University, USA

Ido Millet
The Pennsylvania State University - Erie, USA

ABSTRACT

This chapter studies the effect of bidder conduct on auction success by examining a business to business (B2B) online procurement auction market. In particular, it investigates whether collaborative bidding is more likely when suppliers compete with each other on multiple auctions and/or over a longer period of time. Multiple regression analysis confirms that in online reverse auctions, winning bids are higher or auction success is lower when the same set of suppliers bid against each other regularly. In a supply chain framework, existence of such collaborative bidder behavior would reduce the cost savings for the buyer. It is therefore important for the practitioners to be alert to such activities and introduce measures that curtail the resulting costly outcomes.

INTRODUCTION

Auctions are market mechanisms that have played a crucial role in determining the price of a variety of goods and services for thousands of years. Recent growth in Internet technology has spilled over to auction markets; businesses, consumers, and government organizations are buying and selling goods and services via auctions conducted over the Internet. Popular Internet auction houses such as eBay and Yahoo! sell consumer products using a standard or forward auction format. In a forward auction, there is one seller and multiple buyers with the highest bidder winning the object at the end of the designated time period. In contrast, when businesses and government procure goods and services, they use what are known as reverse auctions. An online reverse auction is defined as an online, real-time dynamic auction between a buyer organization and a group of prequalified suppliers who compete against each other to win the business to supply goods or services that have clearly defined specifications for design, quantity, quality, delivery, and related terms and conditions (Beall, Carter, Carter, Germer, Hendrick, Jap, et al.,2003). Regardless of the format of the auction, the ultimate goal is the same: obtaining the best possible price for the auctioned item, also known as auction success. In a forward auction, auction success refers to the organization securing the highest possible price for the traded article, whereas in a reverse auction, auction success entails the organization procuring an item at the lowest possible price.

Theoretical and empirical literature in traditional auctions have established that auction success depends on a variety of factors, such as type of product, number of bidders, auction format, bidder behavior, and so forth. In an online reverse auction, while the buyer firm can control the auction format, the type of product, and to some extent the number of bidders, they have no control over bidder conduct. One of the crucial concerns pertaining to bidder behavior is the inefficient market outcome arising from the possibility of collusion among the suppliers.

Collusion refers to an agreement among competing firms that lowers the degree of competition and distorts the price in the market to benefit the member firms. In a forward auction market it would amount to a lower winning bid price, and in a procurement or reverse auction market it would result in an artificial high bid price. Any profit-motivated collaborative conduct reduces the efficiency in the market, and is deemed illegal in many countries, including the United States.

In a supply chain framework, existence of collusion would reduce the cost savings for the buyer, or would equivalently depress the auction success. It is therefore important for the practitioners to be alert to such activities and introduce measures that curtail the resulting costly outcomes. Economic literature has documented a variety of exogenous and endogenous factors that can facilitate noncompetitive behaviors among the firms. It has been established that cooperation among rivals is easier to sustain in a long-term relationship than in a one-time encounter. We examine whether collaborative bidding is more likely when bidders compete with each other on multiple auctions and/or over a longer period of time by studying 10,573 business to business (B2B) online procurement auctions carried out by a large multinational firm between 2000 and 2002. We apply two different metrics representing recurring contacts among firms to investigate whether repeated interaction among suppliers has an effect on online reverse auction success. The repeated interaction metrics in our analysis are based on *all* logged-in bidders, instead of those that actually submitted bids. This allows the possibility of no-bid behavior by certain participants as a strategy to collude, adding a new dimension to the existing research in this area. Multiple regression analysis confirms that winning bids are higher in online reverse auctions, or auction success is lower when the same set of suppliers bid against each other regularly.

The rest of the chapter is organized as follows: The next section lays out the conceptual background of our work and offers a brief account of the pertinent literature. It is followed by a discussion of why B2B online reverse auctions are particularly susceptible to possible bidder cartel that lowers the auction success. Next, we specify the empirical model and illustrate the construction of the metrics representing repeated interaction among the firms. A description of the auction market, data, and the summary statistics follow immediately thereafter. The next two segments depict the empirical results and provide a guide to practitioners respectively. Finally, we summarize our findings and suggest directions for future research.

CONCEPTUAL BACKGROUND AND LITERATURE

Collusion has long been recognized as a threat to competition and market efficiency. Collusion can be either explicit or tacit. Explicit collusion exists in a market when firms communicate with each other directly to fix price. The OPEC cartel is a common example of explicit collusion where the participants coordinate their actions *openly*. Explicit collusion can also be present in markets where, due to fear of prosecution, firms collaborate in a *covert* fashion to drive up the price. These secret negotiations do not involve any sort of documentations or records and therefore, are not easily identified. Under tacit collusion, on the other hand, firms do not directly communicate with each other but coordinate their strategies by reacting to their competitors' actions. Uniform pricing, price matching, certain market sharing schemes, advance announcement of price alterations are all examples of tacit collusion. While tacit collusion is not customarily challenged by the authorities, it still is detrimental to competition.

Interestingly, though collusive schemes result in an inflated profit for the suppliers, most of these schemes are vulnerable to breakdown. Without any legally binding contract, sustaining an illegal conspiracy is challenging as the participants in a collusive ring seldom have incentives to adhere to the agreed upon price. By charging a slightly lower price, a firm can capture a larger market share and increase its own profit. Possibility of such defection can be lowered if there is a credible and enforceable mechanism to discipline the defecting member. Given that the firms in a

collusive ring cannot turn to the court to penalize a cheating member, a cartel without a self-enforcing punishment strategy would be difficult to preserve. An effective punishment must cause severe loss to the straying firm in post defection period to discourage it from cheating. Thus, when the suppliers compete with each other repeatedly in different markets or over time, by breaching an agreement in one market or in one period, they jeopardize their future payoffs significantly. Consequently, the probability of maintaining a successful collusion is higher when suppliers compete with each other frequently, either over time or in different markets. For a buying firm that acquires its goods and services through reverse auction, inviting the same suppliers recurrently to participate in the bidding process may create an environment conducive to possible collusive activity and can drive up the bid price.

Theoretical and empirical studies have suggested that likelihood of collusion is a critical issue in auctions. However, most of the research in this area has been conducted in traditional auction markets. This includes studies by Feinstien, Block, and Nold (1985), Bajari and Ye (2003), Froeb, Koyak, and Werden (1993), Gupta (2001, 2002), Mcmillan, J. (1991), and Porter and Zona (1993, 1999). Each of these studies confirms that auction success is negatively affected by cartel activity. Our research is most closely related to that of Feinstien, Block, and Nold (1985) and Gupta (2001, 2002). All three of these analyses have focused on possible existence of collusion and its effect on bid price in a market setting in which bidders have the opportunity to bid together frequently.

Among the research conducted on bidder behavior in Internet auction markets, only two studies so far have explored the issue of collusion. Both reports address the issue of possible bidder collaboration related to late bidding and its effect on auction success in reference to business to consumer (B2C) online auctions. Roth and Ockenfels (2002) examines eBay auctions and concludes that late bidding or sniping facilitates tacit collusion and increases the price in an ascending bid auction. Bapna, Goes, and Gupta (2003) demonstrate that proxy bidding by sniping agents such as e-snipe can encourage collusive bidding and reduce economic efficiency. While the incidence of possible bidder collaboration emerging from recurrent contact and its effect on winning bid price have been examined in the context of traditional first-price sealed bid auctions, to our knowledge no one thus far has investigated the same in a dynamic B2B online auction market. In this study, we partially replicate and extend the previous research done by Gupta (2001) to explore whether repeated interaction among bidders is likely to affect the auction success in a B2B online reverse auction. We follow the basic principles described in Gupta (2001) to generate the metrics for repeated contact among the bidders. However, we go a step further and include all logged-in bidders in our calculation to reflect the fact that a ring member can participate in a conspiracy not only by submitting a fake bid but also by withholding his or her bid.

B2B ONLINE REVERSE AUCTIONS AND POSSIBILITY OF COLLUSION

Auctions can benefit both buyers and suppliers in the supply chain. However, these benefits can be seriously compromised by unscrupulous bidder behavior when the suppliers form a bidding ring and agree on not undercutting each other's bids. B2B online reverse auctions can be susceptible to possible collusion among suppliers due to several reasons. First, participation of bidders in a B2B auction is monitored by the relevant institution to ensure a dependable trading relationship. The buyer firm invites the suppliers to participate in the auctions, and typically the suppliers are subject to some sort of precertification process. This restriction is likely to lower the number of participants in each auction. It is well known that forming and sustaining a collusive scheme is much easier when only a few firms have to coordinate their actions. Second, in a B2B auction, the items traded are standardized with strict quality, quantity, and delivery stipulations. Product homogeneity makes coordination among suppliers easier since the cost of production would not vary much from supplier to supplier, and the suppliers will have to agree on fewer issues while forming a collusive ring. In particular, with similar cost of production, setting a common price would be less complicated, facilitating the likelihood of collusion among the suppliers. Third, in B2B auctions, all suppliers are professionals with considerable amounts of resources. Coordination requires less effort when supplying firms are more or less symmetrical and have similar long-term goals. Additionally, likelihood of coordinated interaction increases when suppliers are better equipped both in terms of knowledge of the market and access to adequate finances. Fourth, the goods and services traded in B2B auctions are usually big-ticket items making conspiracy among suppliers to bid high more enticing as it may result in large potential payoffs. Fifth, in an online auction, competing suppliers observe pricing information almost immediately. Thus, it is easier for the ring members to orchestrate a pricing scheme, monitor participants' responses, and detect cheating. Lastly, in a B2B supply chain setting, the buying agency often holds a trade event where the suppliers meet with the representatives of the buyer in order to learn the details of the products being auctioned. While the goal of these trade events is to improve the sourcing process, it may also have some negative consequences in terms of auction success simply because it provides the suppliers the opportunity to be acquainted with their potential rivals, gather information, and conspire with them.

EMPIRICAL MODEL AND DEFINITION OF METRICS

The dependent variable in our model is the metric for auction success. Existing research in online auctions has mostly used percentage price reduction from the prior purchasing cycle price as a proxy measure for auction success. Despite some of the possible shortcomings (Millet, Parente, Fizel, & Venkataraman, 2004) associated with this measure, we use the price-deflation metrics to represent auction success primarily because the ultimate objective of the managers administering these procurement auctions in our client firm is price reduction, and consequently, they prefer using the price-deflation metrics as a measure for auction success. We compute the price deflation percentage by comparing the minimum bid for the relevant line item in previous purchasing cycles (or the actual cost if the line item is being auctioned for the first time) to its minimum bid in the current auction. Our hypothesis is portrayed in the general econometric model below:

$$P = f (Collusion, Z)$$

where P stands for price deflation and Z is a vector of control variables (other than the collusion metrics) that affect the auction success. According to the standard economic theory on collusion, $\partial P / \partial Collusion < 0$, which means that more collusion in an auction market inflates the bid price or lowers the auction success.

Auction success depends on many different factors. We focus on whether the phenomenon of a same set of bidders bidding together in a repeated fashion has any adverse effect on online auction success. Following Evans and Kessides (1994), Feinstien, Block, and Nold (1985) and Gupta (2001, 2002), we construct three different metrics, Metric 1 and Metric 2 and Metric 3, that capture the degree of multiple contact or repeated interaction among the suppliers across all auctions. It is important to note that unlike

these previous studies, we consider all logged-in bidders in each auction to compute Metric 1 and Metric 2. We do not require an actual bid by a bidder to be recognized for the purpose of our analysis because it is entirely possible that bidder coordination follows a strategy of no-bid behavior by certain bidders.

The first measure, Metric 1, is a simple average of the indices X(i), where i is the (pseudo)identity of the each logged-in supplier. Index X(i) is the ratio of two numbers: The numerator is the number of distinct other suppliers logged in along with supplier i in the auctions supplier i has participated in (excluding joint bids), and the denominator is the total number of suppliers (other than supplier i) in all auctions where supplier i took part. By construction X(i) would be higher when the number of different suppliers competing with bidder i is higher and therefore the scope of repeated interaction for supplier i is lower. If supplier i competes with a brand new set of bidders every time he/she participates in an auction, the index X(i) will take the value of one. It is straightforward to see that in this case, the number of distinct firms suppliers i competes with is the same as the total number of suppliers on all projects other than supplier i. Conversely, if supplier i logs in with the exact same set of bidders over all the auctions he/she participates in, X(i) will be 1/n, where n is the number of auctions i has logged in. The construction of Metric 1 is illustrated with the help of the following simple example:

Example: Suppose firms G, H, W, V, U, T, S, R, and Q are participating in four auctions in the following manner.

Supplier G has logged into three different auctions. A total of 12 other suppliers, in addition to supplier G and seven distinct firms besides firm G, participate in these three auctions. Therefore, X(G)=7/12. The equivalent indices for the other suppliers are reported in Table 2.

Table 1. Bidding example 1

Auctions	I	II	III	IV
Supplier	G	G	G	V
	H	H	H	T
	W	W	W	S
	V	T	S	R
	U	S	R	Q

Table 2. Value of index X

$$X(G) = X(H) = X(W) = 7/12.$$
$$X(V) = 8/8, X(U) = 4/4, X(T) = 7/8,$$
$$X(S) = 7/12, X(R) = 7/8, X(Q) = 4/4.$$

From Table 1 and Table 2 it is clear that index $X(i)$ is inversely related to the i'th supplier's propensity to compete with the same firms. Let us consider the indices $X(G)$, and $X(V)$. The low value of index $X(G)$ illustrates that supplier G has logged in with the same firms (H,W, and S) over several auctions. On the other hand, the high index value (1) for firm V captures the fact that it has not competed with any of the same suppliers on the auctions it participated in. The project metric, Metric 1(j), j = I, ...IV is an average of $X(i)$s for the suppliers who have logged into that particular auction, and the corresponding values are given below.

Metric 1(I) = (7/12 + 7/12 + 7/12 + 8/8 + 4/4) / 5 = .75

Metric 1 (II) =(7/12 +7/12 + 7/12 + 7/8 + 7/12) / 5 = .642

Metric 1 (III) = (7/12 + 7/12 + 7/12 + 7/12 + 7/8) / 5 = .642

Metric 1(IV) = (8/8 + 7/8 + 7/12 + 7/8 + 4/4) / 5 = .932

Note that the value of Metric 1 is inversely related to the occurrence of repeated interaction among the firms. We demonstrate this with the help of two extreme cases below. Consider the case in which the same five suppliers are logging into all four auctions.

As described above, $X(G) = 4/16 = 1/4 = X(H)$ = $X(W) = X(V) = X(U)$ and Metric 1 = (5/4)/5 = 1/4 = 1/n, where n is the number of projects. Therefore, if suppliers participate in many auctions, the value of Metric 1 is low and reflects a high collusion potential. Next, consider the scenario in which two suppliers never participate in more than one auction together. In other words, there is no repeated interaction among the suppliers.

In this case, $X(G) = X(H) = ... = X(W) = 4/4$ = 1, and the auction specific measure of repeated interaction, Metric 1 = 5/5 = 1. These examples suggest that the value of Metric 1 [$\Sigma X(i)/n$] varies between zero and one. Furthermore, it is evident

Table 3. Bidding example 2

Auctions	I	II	III	IV
Supplier	G	G	G	G
	H	H	H	H
	V	V	V	V
	U	U	U	U
	W	W	W	W

Table 4. Bidding example 3

Auctions	I	II	III	IV
Supplier	A	F	K	S
	B	G	L	T
	C	H	N	U
	D	I	Q	V
	E	J	R	W

that the greater the incidence of recurrent contact among the bidders, the lower the value of this index.

As the interaction amongst firms increases, so do the chances that they have formed a collusive bidding ring; that is, if the same three firms keep bidding together on auction after auction, it may increase the possibility of a collusive deal amongst them. With possible collusion in a reverse auction, we should expect the bids tendered by the suppliers to be higher than if there were no collusion. In other words, the price deflation will be lower. Since the value of Metric 1 varies *inversely* with the occurrence of repeated interaction, we expect the coefficient estimate of the variable Metric 1 in the regressions to be positive.

The second independent variable Metric 2 measures the pair-wise bonding strength of the suppliers. For each auction, Metric 2 averages the number of times each pair of firms logged in together weighted by the number of auctions each pair participated in. Suppose there are five auctions on which three suppliers G, H, and W log in along with other firms, with firm G logging into on all five auctions, H participating in four auctions, and W participating in three auctions. Now assume that G and H log in together in four auctions, H and W log in together in two auctions, W and G log in together on three auctions, and all three of them participate in auction number one. Then the specific measure of repeated interaction, Metric 2, for auction one would be [1/3] [(4 * 5

* 4) + (2 * 4 * 3) + (3 * 3 * 5)] = 49.7. Note that the value of this index is *directly* related to the degree of multiple contacts among the suppliers. In other words, more repeated contact between a *pair* of suppliers would produce a higher value of this metric, indicating a higher likelihood of collusion and poorer auction success. Accordingly, we would expect the coefficient estimate of the variable Metric 2 in the regressions to be negative.

Metric 1 and Metric 2 would be sensitive to the number of auctions the suppliers participated in on average. To capture this effect, we include a third independent variable Metric 3 that measures the average total number of auctions the suppliers in the auction participated in (logged in) over the total period. The variable Metric 3 can have two counteracting effects on auction success. If the average number of auctions attended by each supplier is higher, it may indicate more multiple contacts among suppliers. In our sample, we find that Metric 3 is negatively correlated with Metric 1, and positively correlated with Metric 2. This implies that the more each supplier participates, the higher the incidence of multiple contacts among them. On the other hand, if each supplier logs in on more auctions on average, it may also lead to more competitors per auction. Economic principle states that the more competitors there are, the more difficult it is to maintain a cartel, and thus the auction would be more successful. We denote the first effect *Metric 3 multiple contact effect* and the second one *Metric 3 competition effect*. We would expect the coefficient estimate of this variable in the regression to be negative if the first effect dominates and positive if the second effect dominates. The fourth independent variable or control variable Z is the number of distinct bidders logged in on each auction. As more competition should lead to higher auction success, the coefficient estimate of this variable in our regression should be positive.

AUCTION CHARACTERISTICS AND DATA

The data set used in our analysis consists of online reverse auctions conducted by a large multinational firm between the years 2000 and 2002 to procure a variety of products ranging from nuts and bolts to IT services. The data set comprises of first-price auctions where the lowest bidder wins the contract at its bid price. For each item auctioned, the purchasing agent of the firm specified the auction formats, identified the potential suppliers, and invited them to place bids in the auctions. The firm employed different auction designs that offered different degrees of information to the suppliers. The participating suppliers at all points in time were aware of the bidding terms, time remaining in the auction, and their own bidding history, but had only partial or no information about the bidding history of their competitors. At one end of this spectrum were auctions where the bidders only knew whether their own bid was accepted. These auctions are equivalent to traditional sealed bid or blind auctions. The rest of the auction formats provided the bidders with varied levels of transparency about the bids tendered. The degree of information available to the competitors ranged from knowing only their ranks in the auction to knowing all three of the following: their own current rank, the lowest bid submitted in that auction, and whether the reserve was met. For the purpose of our analysis, we group them into two different categories: blind auctions and not-blind auctions.

We have a total of 10,573 observations, with 1,004 blind and 9,569 not-blind auctions. We exclude the auctions with values less than $10,000 since they are not likely to have significant economic impact on our client firm. The auction values are calculated as sum of quantity times past purchase price across all line items of a particular auction. As described in the earlier section, the metric for auction success is based on last actual purchase price (or the actual cost for first-time line item auctions) and the lowest bid on current auction. To protect the confidentiality of the data, the dependent variable P depicting the auction success is computed by multiplying the percentage deflation in bid price by a secret positive constant. In an attempt to avoid outliers, our data set includes only auctions where the value of P lies between the range of positive 80% and negative 50%. Descriptive statistics for the variables used in this study are reported in Table 5 below.

The dependent variable P has a mean of 22.16% and a standard deviation of 16.47. We omit the minimum and maximum values of the adjusted price deflation variable P from our discussion to maintain the confidentiality of our data. Because we are interested in the effect of repeated interaction among bidders on auction success, our data set includes only auctions with more than two bidders. The average number of logged-in bidders per auction is approximately 4.3 with a standard deviation of 2.3, a minimum of 3 and maximum of 30. In blind auctions, however, the maximum number of logged-in bidders per auction is 12. The relatively small average number of logged-in bidders per auction indicates a higher probability of successful bidder collusion. Over the entire period, on average, the suppliers participated in 46 auctions with a standard deviation of 74.2, a minimum of 1 and maximum of 370 auctions. It is important to note that both metrics portraying the repeated interactions among the bidders are based on the (pseudo) identities of *all* logged-in

suppliers. The mean of the first metrics capturing multiple contact, Metric 1, is 0.45 with a standard deviation of 0.29, and the average of the second metric for multiple contact, Metric 2, is 581,926 with a standard deviation of 1,903,057, indicating that a substantial amount of repeat bidding has taken place in these online reverse auctions.

RESULTS

While there are many factors that determine the winning bid price, our analysis primarily focuses on whether frequent market interaction among the bidders has any detrimental impact on auction success. We test our hypothesis with three multiple regressions, and in each case auction success measured by adjusted price deflation is the dependent variable. As independent variables, in addition to the three metrics described earlier, we include the number of logged-in bidders. The first regression includes the complete data set while the remaining two are on a subset of the data. The first subset contains all non-blind auctions and the second one consists of blind auctions. The regression results are reported in Tables 6, 7, and 8, respectively. In general, the results are significant, with most of the coefficient estimates exhibiting the expected signs. The first regression conducted on the entire data set indicates a statistically significant and strong relationship between the dependent variable P, measured by adjusted price deflation and Metric

Table 5. Descriptive statistics of data

Variables	Mean	Standard Deviation	Minimum	Maximum
Metric 1	0.4567	0.2922	0.0432	1
Metric 2	581926.8	1903057	1	17866080
Metric 3	46.0967	74.2682	1	370.3333
Number of bidders	4.3386	2.3051	3	30
P	22.16078	16.4696	–	–

Number of Observations: 10573

Table 6. All auctions

Variables	Coefficient	Standard Error	t-statistic	p-value
Intercept	9.629	0.591	16.28	6.43E-59
Metric 1	6.014	0.706	8.51	1.96E-17
Metric 2	-1.8E-06	1.72E-07	-10.32	7.01E-25
Metric 3	0.111	0.005	21.60	2.7E-101
Number of bidders	1.31	0.06	19.65	1.58E-84

Number of Observations: 10573

Adjusted R^2: 0.103

F-Statistics: 303.87

F Significance: 0.000

1. More specifically, a 1% reduction in the value of this metric (indicating more repeated contact) results in a 6% reduction in the adjusted price deflation supporting our central premise that multiple contact among firms enhances bidder coordination and inflates bid price. The coefficient estimate of the variable Metric 2, albeit very small, is statistically significant and has the expected negative sign, again confirming our hypothesis. The variable Metric 3 has a positive and statistically significant coefficient estimate of 0.11, which indicates that in this market, the *Metric 3 competition effect* is more powerful. The fourth variable, number of logged-in bidders, has a significantly positive coefficient of 1.31, as we would expect if the Winners Curse effect were not dominating the competition effect.

Next, we test our hypothesis on two different subsets of our data, disseminating different levels of information to the suppliers on auction dynamics. The first subset includes not-blind auctions in which the bidders have a certain amount of knowledge about the status of their bids relative to those of the other bidders. The regression results again reject the null hypothesis of no effect of recurrent market contact among bidders on auction success in favor of the alternative hypothesis. In other words, it reveals the same trend as in the earlier instance where we included all observations: All coefficient estimates have the expected signs, that

is, the coefficient estimate of Metric 1 is positive, Metric 2 is negative, Metric 3 is positive (*Metric 3 competition effect* is dominant), and the number of bidders is positive. Furthermore, all coefficient estimates are statistically significant and all except for Metric 2 are numerically significant.

Finally, the third regression is estimated using blind auctions where the bidders have no information about how their bids stack up against the other bidders; they receive notification only if the buyer accepts their respective bid. As before, we observe qualitatively similar effects of the explanatory variables Metric 2, Metric 3, and the number of bidders on the dependent variable P. However, the effect of Metric 1 on the winning bid, though it has the expected sign, is statistically insignificant. This is not surprising because collusion in the context of multiple contacts among the competing firms over time is sustainable only in the presence of a credible threat of punishment for the deviating firms, which requires adequate knowledge of the underlying auction dynamics. Without such information on the bidding patterns or the member firms' standing in the market, successful coordination and thus price fixing become complicated and unattainable.

Overall, the results bear out our primary hypothesis that as the interaction between groups and pairs of bidders increase, the chances of collusion are strengthened and thus the price savings for

Table 7. Not-blind auctions

Variables	Coefficient	Standard Error	t-statistic	p-value
Intercept	10.94	0.63	17.19	2.69E-65
Metric 1	5.06	0.74	6.83	8.74E-12
Metric 2	-1.28E-06	2.02E-07	-6.34	2.32E-10
Metric 3	0.09	0.006	14.39	1.68E-46
Number of bidders	1.21	0.07	17.56	5.23E-68

Number of Observations: 9569
Adjusted R^2: 0.067
F-Statistics: 170.94
F Significance: 0.000

Table 8. Blind auctions

Variables	Coefficient	Standard Error	t-statistic	p-value
Intercept	7.03	2.13	3.29	0.001
Metric 1	2.51	3.72	0.67	0.49
Metric 2	-2.18E-06	3.8E-07	-5.72	-2.92E-06
Metric 3	0.13	0.01	11.57	3.5E-29
Number of bidders	1.94	0.28	6.95	6.35E-12

Number of Observations: 1004
Adjusted R^2: 0.296
F-Statistics: 106.94
F Significance: 0.000

the buyer firm conducting the auctions decrease. When the firms use the power of the Internet to conduct auctions primarily to help themselves realize added cost savings from procurement activities, it is vitally important for these firms to be aware that such collusion can be taking place in their auctions.

AN INTERPRETATION OF THE RESULTS FOR PRACTITIONERS

Possibility of collusion among suppliers in Internet auctions can be of enormous significance for the firms. It can cost the buyer firm large sums of money that could otherwise have been prevented with a little vigilance. In our analysis, we demonstrate that when the same set of suppliers bid together frequently on multiple auctions, it leads to lower auction success due to likely coordination among the bidders. The suppliers can coordinate their actions either through direct but secret communication with their rivals or through indirect exchange of information by meticulously monitoring the bidding process. The first form of coordination is possible when the firms get acquainted with their prospective competitors at technical conferences, trade events held by buyer firms, or via employee turnover. Therefore, companies using online reverse auctions for procurement purposes should exercise caution when inviting the suppliers. The purchasing firm should attempt to minimize the probability of bidder collaboration by lowering the possibility of recurring contact among the bidders. This can be achieved by inviting new suppliers to participate, by trying to increase bidder participation, and by carefully administering the invitations to prospective suppliers so that the same set of suppliers are less likely to bid together. When none of these is feasible, if suitable the purchasing firm can try to limit the possibility of collusion by calibrating auction designs that disseminate little information to the bidders, as lack of information in specific cases can make punishment strategies ineffective and successful coordination among bidders tricky.

In our analysis, we have provided a comprehensive account of how to construct the collusion metrics. One possible action by the practitioners is to monitor the suggested collusion metrics and auction success in their own purchasing operations. Over time, this should yield insights into which auctions are at high collusion risk and should be mitigated by inviting more or fresh suppliers and/or using a blind auction format.

Finally, our data set reveals that sometimes bidders logged into the system but did not place any bids. Research in traditional auction theory has established that this kind of bidder behavior, non-participation, could be indicative of a price conspiracy scheme. We have taken this into consideration while constructing our metrics for repeat bidding and we believe that the purchasing firm should be observant of this type of bidder conduct.

CONCLUSION

In this study, we have looked at a simple way to model the recurring interaction between firms participating in a B2B reverse auction and investigate the consequence of these frequent interactions on the cost savings of the buyer firms. We conclude that contacts among the firms over many auctions can encourage collusive activities, which eventually has a negative impact on the firms' bottom line. Thus, the purchasing firms in a reverse auction need to be aware of the market conditions that aid formation of a bidders' cartel, and need to examine the bidding patterns carefully to detect non-participation and repeated interactions among firms that discourage the ring members to diverge from collusive agreement. Unfortunately, due to data unavailability, we were unable to incorporate some of the explanatory variables that can affect the winning bid price and the likelihood of collusion. A more complete and detailed empirical analysis describing the price effect of collusion in a procurement auction market should include other independent variables, such as cost estimates of auctioned items, experience levels of suppliers, location of firms, distance of firms from the buyer, and so forth. It is possible that due to external circumstances, there is an increase in the transportation costs or the production costs of all participating firms, both of which can result in higher than normal bids. Though such information on cost estimates, distance, and experience of suppliers were not available in the data set provided to us by our client firm, it should be easily available to any firm using procurement auctions for sourcing. Nevertheless, our finding that price deflation, the measure of auction success in online reverse auctions, is significantly lower when repeated interaction among firms is prevalent provides a valuable insight to the purchasing firms; they can improve the auction success by undertaking appropriate measures to reduce the chances of recurring market contact among rivals that induces bid rigging.

FUTURE RESEARCH DIRECTIONS

In this chapter, we have proposed research methods that can be useful in analyzing the impact of bidder conduct on auction success. In particular, we study how repeated contact among the suppliers can depress the auction success, which is measured by the percentage price reduction. We first develop metrics that capture the frequency of supplier participation as well as the recurring market contacts among them. We then use these metrics to demonstrate that repetitive encounters among participating suppliers significantly lower the cost savings of the buyer firm by providing the bidders with a better opportunity to collude on bid price.

Even though we find ample evidence to support our central hypothesis, the study has room for improvement. A useful future extension would be a more rigorous analysis that implements additional pertinent factors. Verification of the applicability of our results through empirical testing will be useful as well.

First, our analysis is somewhat broad in the sense that it addresses only two types of auction formats: blind and not-blind. Businesses use many different auction designs that differ in closing rules (hard or soft close), ending time (early morning, evening, etc.), amount of information available to the participating suppliers, and so on. As bidder participation rate can vary across auction types, it would be interesting and useful to observe how, if at all, our key finding is affected by the structure of the auction. Second, our collusion metrics and price-reduction metrics are relatively easy to compute, and are therefore appealing to practitioners. However, there may be better alternative proxy measures. Future researchers should develop substitute collusion metrics that signal possible collusive activities and metrics for auction success. Third, as we have already mentioned, a more comprehensive study addressing the price effect of collusion should include other independent variables, such as cost estimates of auctioned items, types of products, location of firms, distance of supplier firms from the buyer firm, and experience levels of suppliers, to name a few. Finally, since our goal in this chapter is

to provide a research method that can be readily used by the practitioners, we have kept our statistical analysis techniques relatively simple and straightforward. A more sophisticated estimation technique, which may provide a better predictive power, is warranted.

REFERENCES

Bajari, P., & Ye, L. (2003). Deciding between competition and collusion. *Review of Economics and Statistics, 85,* 971-989.

Bajari, S., & Summers, G. (2002). Detecting collusion in procurement auctions: A selective survey of recent research. *Antitrust Law Journal, 70,* 143-170.

Bapna, R., Goes, P., & Gupta, A. (2003). Analysis and design of business to consumer online auctions. *Management Science, 49,* 42-50.

Beall, S., Carter, C., Carter, P., Germer, T., Hendrick, T., Jap, S., et al. (2003). *The role of reverse auctions in strategic sourcing.* Tempe, AZ: CAPS Research. Available at http://www.capsresearch. org/publications/pdfs-public/beall2003es.pdf

Evans, W. N., & Kessides, I. N. (1994). Living by the "Golden Rule": Multimarket contact in the U.S. airline industry. *Quarterly Journal of Economics, 109,* 341-366.

Feinstein, J. S., Block, M. K., & Nold, F. C. (1985). Asymmetric information and collusive behavior in auction markets. *American Economic Review, 75,* 441-460.

Froeb, L. M., Koyak, R. A., & Werden, J. G. (1993). What is the effect of bid-rigging on price? *Economic Letters, 42,* 419-423.

Gupta, S. (2001). The effect of bid rigging on price: A study of highway construction market. *Review of Industrial Organization, 19,* 453-457.

Gupta, S. (2002). Competition and collusion in a government procurement auction market. *Atlantic Economic Journal, 30,* 13-25.

McMillan, J. (1991). Dango: Japan's price-fixing conspiracies. *Economics and Politics, 3,* 201-218.

Millet, I., Parente, D. H., Fizel, J. L., & Venkataraman, R. R. (2004). Metrics for managing online procurement auctions. *Interfaces, 34*(3), 1-10.

Porter, H. R., & Zona, J. D. (1993). Detection of bid-rigging in procurement auctions. *Journal of Political Economy, 101,* 518-538.

Porter, H. R., & Zona, J. D. (1999). Ohio school milk markets: An analysis of bidding. *Rand Journal of Economics, 30,* 263-288.

Roth, A. E., & Ockenfels, A. (2002). Last minute bidding and the rules for ending second-price auctions: Evidence from eBay and Amazon auctions on the Internet. *The American Economic Review, 92,* 1093-1103.

ADDITONAL READINGS

Aoyagi, M. (2003). Bid rotation and collusion in repeated auctions. *Journal of Economic Theory, 112*(1), 79-105.

Banerji, A., & Meenakshi, J. (2004). Buyer collusion and efficiency of government intervention in wheat markets in northern India. *American Journal of Agricultural Economics, 86*(1), 236-253.

Bernard, J., Schulze, W., & Mount, T. (2005). Bidding behaviour in the multi-unit Vickrey and uniform price auctions. *Applied Economics Letters, 12*(10), 589-595.

Blume, A., & Heidhues, P. (2006). Private monitoring in auctions. *Journal of Economic Theory, 131*(1), 179-211.

Bolton, P., & Dewatripont, M. (2005). *Contract theory.* Cambridge, MA: MIT Press.

Brusco, S., & Lopomo, G. (2002). Collusion via signalling in simultaneous ascending bid auctions with heterogeneous objects. *Review of Economic Studies, 69*(2), 407-436.

Chen, C., & Tauman, Y. (2006). Collusion in one-shot second-price auctions. *Economic Theory, 28*(1), 145-172.

Chung, K., & Atila, A. (2002). *Optimal repeated auction with tacit collusion.* Theory workshop papers, University of California, Los Angeles.

Davis, D., & Wilson, B. (2002). Collusion in procurement auctions: An experimental examination. *Economic Inquiry, 40*(2), 213-230.

Eso, P., & Schummer, J. (2004). Bribing and signaling in second price auctions. *Games and Economic Behavior, 47*(2), 299-324.

Fabra, N. (2003). Tacit collusion in repeated auctions: Uniform versus discriminatory. *Journal of Industrial Economics, 51*(3), 271-293.

Hendricks, K., & Porter, R. (2000). *Collusion in auctions: The economic theory of auctions, Vol. 1,* (pp. 661-73). Elgar Reference Collection.

Ingraham, A. (2005). A test for collusion between a bidder and an auctioneer in sealed-bid auctions. *B.E. Journals in Economic Analysis and Policy: Contributions to Economic Analysis and Policy, 4*(1), 1-32.

Klemperer, P. (2002). How (not) to run auctions: The European 3G telecom auctions. *European Economic Review, 46*(4-5), 829-845.

Lambert-Mogiliansky, A., & Sonin, K. (2006). Collusive market sharing and corruption in procurement. *Journal of Economics and Management Strategy, 15*(4), 883-908.

Lee, I., & Hahn, K. (2002). Bid-rigging in auctions for Korean public-works contracts and potential damage. *Review of Industrial Organization, 21*(1), 73-88.

Lopomo, G., Marshall, R., & Marx, L. (2005). Inefficiency of collusion at English auctions. *B.E. Journals in Theoretical Economics: Contributions to Theoretical Economics, 5*(1), 1-26.

Lunander, A., & Nilsson, J. (2006). Combinatorial procurement auctions: A collusion remedy? *Rivista di Politica Economica, 96*(1-2), 65-90.

Macatangay, R. (2002). Tacit collusion in the frequently repeated multi-unit uniform price auction for wholesale electricity in England. *European Journal of Law and Economics, 13*(3), 257-273.

McCarty, C. (2002). Currency auctions: Minimizing collusive behavior. *Journal of East-West Business, 8*(1), 63-76.

Meenakshi, J., & Banerji, A. (2005). The unsupportable support price: An analysis of collusion and government intervention in paddy auction markets. *Journal of Development Economics, 76*(2), 377-403.

Menicucci, D. (2006). Full surplus extraction by a risk adverse seller in correlated environments. *Mathematical Social Sciences, 51*(3), 280-300.

Offerman, T., & Potters, J. (2006). Does auctioning of entry licences induce collusion? An experimental study. *Review of Economic Studies, 73*(3), 769-791.

Robinson, M. (2000). Collusion and the choice of auction: The economic theory of auctions. Volume 1 pp. 635-39, Elgar Reference Collection.

Sade, O., Schnitzlein, C., & Zender, J. (2006). Competition and cooperation in divisible good auctions: An experimental examination. *Review of Financial Studies, 19*(1), 195-235.

Saphores, J., Vincent, J., Marochko, V., Abrudan, I., Bouriaud, L., & Zinnes, C. (2006). *Detecting collusion in timber auctions: An application to Romania.* The World Bank, Policy Research Working Paper Series: 4105.

Schulenberg, S. (2003). Essays in auctions and collusion. Thesis (Ph. D.)--Pennsylvania State University, 2003. http://etda.libraries.psu.edu/theses/approved/WorldWideIndex/ETD-388/index.html.

Sherstyuk, K. (2002). Collusion in private value ascending price auctions. *Journal of Economic Behavior and Organization, 48*(2), 177-195.

Skrzypacz, A., & Hopenhayn, H. (2004). Tacit collusion in repeated auctions. *Journal of Economic Theory, 114*(1), 153-169.

Tu, Z. (2006). Three essays in auctions. (Doctoral dissertation, University of Pittsburgh).

IMPLICATIONS FOR PRACTITIONERS

Title: An Empirical Study of Collusion Potential Metrics and Their Impact on Online Reverse Auction Success

Short Description

This chapter studies the effect of bidder conduct on auction success by examining a business to business (B2B) online procurement auction market. We explore whether collaborative bidding is more likely when suppliers compete with each other on multiple auctions and/or over a longer time period. The data set used in our analysis consists of online reverse auctions conducted by a large multinational firm between the years 2000 and 2002 to procure a variety of products. It consists of only first-price auctions in which the supplier with the lowest bid wins the contract at the bid price. For each item auctioned, the manager in charge of administering the auction in our client firm stipulated the auction designs, identified the potential suppliers, and invited them to place bids for the items. The auction formats employed by the firm provided a varied amount of information to the suppliers. In each auction, the participating suppliers had complete information about the bidding terms, time remaining in the auction, and their own bidding history, but had only partial or no information about the bidding history of their competitors.

Our main objective in this chapter is to test the well-known notion that a price conspiracy scheme among competitors is easier to sustain in a long-term business relationship than in a one-time encounter. We apply different metrics representing recurring contacts among firms to investigate whether repeated interaction among suppliers indeed has an effect on online reverse auction success. The repeated interaction metrics in our analysis are computed to include *all* logged-in bidders, instead of the ones that tendered bids. This allows us to encompass the possibility of no-bid behavior by certain participants as a strategy to fix the price. We use multiple regression models to regress the collusion metrics against auction success, which confirms that winning bids are higher in online reverse auctions or auction success is lower when the same set of suppliers bid against each other regularly.

Findings

- The cost savings for the buyer firm is higher when more suppliers participate in a particular auction.
- Auction success is lower when the same set of suppliers bid against each other regularly and therefore can coordinate their actions.
- Auction success is higher when suppliers have less information on the process.

RECOMMENDATIONS

- The purchasing firm should try to minimize the probability of bidder cooperation by lowering the possibility of recurring contact among the bidders.
- The above can be accomplished by inviting new suppliers to join, by trying to increase bidder participation, and by cautiously managing the invitations to prospective suppliers so that the same set of suppliers are less likely to bid together.

- The buying firm should further try to limit the likelihood of bidder collusion by designing auction formats that disperse little information to the bidders.
- Practitioners should monitor the suggested collusion metrics and auction success in their own purchasing operations in order to acquire insights into high collusion risk auctions and should try to avoid those particular auction formats.
- Practitioners should also be observant of bidders who are logged into the system but do not tender any bids as that could be indicative of a price fixing scheme.

Chapter XVI
Do Reverse Auctions Violate Professional Standards and Codes of Conduct?

Joseph R. Muscatello
Kent State University, USA

Susan Emens
Kent State University, USA

ABSTRACT

During the e-business boom of the 1990s, reverse auctions became a new business tool for purchasing and procurement that promised increased reductions in supplier costs. The benefits of reverse auctions have been substantiated, but not without debate. One of the debates is the ethical considerations inherent with these new business processes. Our study investigates whether reverse auctions violate corporate or professional standards of conduct. This chapter examines some of the professional standards/codes of ethics available, including the Institute of Supply Chain Management (ISM) and a selected number of organizations, including Dell and GE. Further, the chapter presents a framework that can help an organization determine whether reverse auctions, and the way they are run, are ethical.

INTRODUCTION

The introduction of reverse auctions in the 1990s was believed to be a revolutionary new paradigm in the supplier bidding process. The term "reverse" emphasizes that competitive bidding between suppliers drives prices down, rather than competition among buyers driving prices up as in a forward auction (e.g., eBay auction) (Hur, Mabert, & Hartley, 2005). Because of the dramatic price reductions reported, reverse auctions have become a major, if not revolutionary, tool for many organizations (Hannon, 2003). Why has the reverse auction not become the revolutionary tool initially projected? There are a variety of reasons, including cost, ease of use, managerial acceptance, learning curves, and so forth. However, some researchers suggest that concerns with ethics and supplier relationships are barriers to reverse auction adoption (Hur et al., 2005; Jap, 2003; Handfield, Straight, & Stirling, 2002). This chapter builds on the ethical research by examining reverse auction ethics via professional standards and corporate codes of conduct, and seeks to build a framework for which reverse auction ethical codes can be developed.

Previous research has been published regarding negotiation problems such as honesty, mutual trust, deception, fairness, and other ethical issues in business (Campton & Dees, 1993, 1995). These papers focus on general negotiation problems that may or may not be applicable to reverse auctions since they are created from more traditional means of purchasing. Another avenue of research has focused on the release of information and the appropriateness or fairness to all suppliers in the negotiation if all suppliers do not receive the same data in a timely and accurate manner. Again, this may or may not be appropriate for reverse auctions and is not the focus of this research effort.

There have been several ethical studies on the reverse auction industry. However, most have focused on the ethical considerations of the practice of "sniping," which is the entry of a bid seconds before the close of the bidding process (Hur et al., 2005). Practitioners of sniping observe that it is both an effective strategy for winning auctions and a tactic well within the rules of limited-time auctions (Marcoux, 2003). This debate is ongoing because the tactics or rules of each individual auction can be vastly different. One of the few ethical studies not involving "sniping" asks an organization to review its internal ethics policies—look at its corporate ethics policy regarding supplier relationships, and ask itself and the market maker: "Do online reverse auctions violate

our ethics policy?" If the ethics policy contains specific references to fairness or fair competition, building long-term relationships, trust, respect, or conducting business free of deception or coercion, then using online reverse auctions likely violates and organization's code of ethics (Emiliani & Stec, 2004). This is one of the few references we have found regarding reverse auctions and code of ethics violations. This avenue of research seems ripe for new investigations.

This chapter does not focus on traditional buyer/supplier ethics, purchasing ethics, or the pros and cons of the usefulness of reverse auctions. In this chapter, we argue that ethics should be considered from the more philosophical side of the argument: That is, does the use of reverse auctions violate corporate or professional standards of conduct?

LITERATURE REVIEW

In order to discuss whether reverse auctions violate corporate or professional codes of conduct, we must review what has been published in the field of reverse auctions, especially ethical research, to help frame the actions that may be in violation.

Auctions have been widely studied in the fields of purchasing, operations, economics, supplier/buyer actions, and others. Most auction research has focused on identifying optimal auction designs in various settings (Rothkopf et al., 1998). In the 1990s, auctions moved into the Internet arena creating a new business process and unleashing a new set of studies based upon these new reverse auction processes. There were several modeling studies (Elmagraphy, 2002; Bapna, Goes, Gupta, & Karuga, 2002; Bapna, Goes, & Gupta, 2003), as well as case study and survey research that examined reverse auctions by examining critical factors leading to the overall success or failure (Smeltzer & Carr, 2002; Carter et al., 2004; Jap, 2003; Handfield et al., 2002; Emiliani, 2004). Researchers have also explored the overall perception of lower prices driven by reverse auctions and the financial impact (ROI, ROA, etc.) on the buyer/supplier enterprises (Hur et al., 2005; Mabert & Skeels, 2002; Jap, 2002; Smeltzer & Carr, 2002; Hartley, Lane, & Hong, 2004). These are certainly worthwhile efforts, and eventually researchers hope to build solid quantitative and qualitative models that can be used for selection, adoption, and adaptation of reverse auctions for the good of the adopting organization. However, the ethical considerations of adopting reverse auctions, beyond the work on sniping (Hur et al., 2005; Marcoux, 2003) deserves strong research review since ethics will certainly be a factor in a firm's adoption decision.

A construction industry survey on ethics published in *Contractor* magazine (2005) showed that 69% of respondents agreed or strongly agreed that reverse auctions are unethical. As research on reverse auctions is performed on other specific industries we may see the same kind of negative feedback from suppliers if organizations do not get a handle on the ethics issue.

Emiliani (2005) issued a set of guidelines that form an underpinning for potential reverse auction abuse. They are:

- Ambiguous or shifting auction rule
- Threatening incumbent suppliers to bid or risk losing the work
- Changing contract terms and conditions between RFQ and award
- Phantom bidding (buyer or market maker pretends to be a supplier)
- Drive down unit prices with no intention of switching sources
- Allowing unqualified suppliers to bid
- Showing the identities of the bidders and their bids
- Post-auction renegotiation
- Awarding only portions of the items in a bid package
- Forcing supplier to honor unreasonably low prices

- Providing incomplete or inaccurate specifications
- Allowing specification relief to winning bidders
- Including internal departments as bidders
- Repetitive rebidding to drive down prices
- Not informing bidders of outcomes

This is a good listing and subsequent starting point for the reverse auction ethics debate. However, since ethics is ever evolving in corporations, these areas of abuse may or may not be recognized as violations of codes of conduct. We seek to close this gap in the findings section after considering professional standards and corporate codes of conduct.

Another area of ethical consideration is the ethics of the supplier. Antitrust laws may be violated if unethical practices are used with reverse auctions. Collusion, selling below market price to eliminate competitors, and so forth is a concern to government agencies and businesses (Horlen, Eldin, & Ajinkya, 2005). There have been some major investigations by the U.S. Department of Justice regarding reverse auction antitrust violations. Mark (2006) summed up some of these violations and charges in his article in Business:

Two former Samsung officials and a former Hynix executive are the latest to be charged in the Department of Justice's (DoJ) ongoing investigation into a DRAM chip price-fixing conspiracy. The probe has already resulted in Korean-based Samsung and Hynix, Japan's Elpida and Infineon of Germany pleading guilty and paying $729 million in criminal fines. In addition, 13 former executives from the four companies and a former executive from U.S.-based Micron have pleaded guilty to conspiracy charges. All have been fined and sentenced to prison terms. 'The Antitrust Division will vigorously pursue individuals who engage in criminal cartel conspiracies,' Assistant Attorney General Thomas O. Barnett said in a statement. 'Criminal cartel enforcement is the Division's top *priority and both companies and individuals must comply with the antitrust laws.'*

The DoJ originally launched its investigation into price fixing by the world's DRAM makers in 2004. The DoJ claims the accused participated in the conspiracy through a series of telephone calls and meetings. As a result of the telephone calls and meetings, all three agreed to help rig an online auction of DRAM chips by either not submitting a bid or submitting intentionally high bids.

With these and other types of antitrust violations being discovered with the use of reverse auctions, the building of sound ethical principles becomes a must for all organizations who wish to participate in reverse auctions. The DoJ is taking a proactive stance against the use of reverse auctions and antitrust violations, and an organization must take the steps necessary to get their employees to comply.

In summary, the literature revealed that initial models, case studies, and surveys focused on the processes, designs, practices, and returns of reverse auctions and very little on the ethical considerations of adopting this technique or codes of conduct/professional standards violations, even though unethical behavior has been observed and documented. The review of the literature certainly presents a compelling case that some uses of Internet auctions are unethical and illegal. However, whose ethical standards do we apply and are they appropriate for reverse auctions?

PROFESSIONAL ETHICS AND CODES OF CONDUCT

Many businesses require any employee, regardless of rank, to sign and abide by a code of ethics or conduct when dealing with suppliers. Furthermore, professional societies such as the Institute for Supply Chain Management (ISM) require their members to abide by a code of conduct when dealing with suppliers. The temptation to take

"unethical gifts" from a supplier as an enticement for placing an order has been around for centuries. This chapter examines this important topic differently. We seek the answer to the ethical use of a reverse auction.

Ethics can be defined in a variety of ways. The Institute for Supply Chain Management (ISM) clearly states on their Web site, in the "Principles and Standards of Ethical Supply Management Conduct" section, that many parts of a suppliers bid can be considered confidential or proprietary. Therefore, if the buyer requests this type of information, they may be violating the ISM code of conduct. The confidential or proprietary examples as listed by the ISM are as follows:

Examples of information that may be considered confidential or proprietary include:

- Pricing
- Bid or quotation information
- Cost sheets
- Formulas and/or process information
- Design information
- Organizational plans, goals, and strategies
- Financial information
- Information that may influence stock prices
- Profit information
- Asset information
- Wage and salary scales
- Personal information about employees, officers, and directors
- Supply sources or supplier information
- Computer software programs

Many reverse auctions are open-bid, meaning all bidders have access to competitor's information. Because of the overall design of a reverse auction, auctioning the price of the product downward, the sharing of pricing information is paramount to the use of a reverse auction. Therefore, the mere use of a reverse auction comes with an ethical consideration clearly denoted by the ISM: the sharing of pricing information. But it does not stop there. Many auctions require designs, formula's costs sheets, financial information on a firm, the supplier's sources, and other information (Hur et al., 2005; Jap, 2003; Handfield, 2002; Emiliani, 2004). This could lead to unfair advantages and a new paradigm, "legalized espionage," where an organization bids just to find out the formally confidential and proprietary information about a competitor.

Many companies have language regarding the ethical behavior of its employees toward their suppliers. As Giampetro and Emiliani (2007) point out, "reverse auctions contradict the language many major companies use in their corporate codes of conduct. The following are excerpts from the codes of several large U.S.-based multinationals:

- *As Dell employees, we are committed to acting responsibly, honestly, and with integrity in all dealings with our suppliers... Vendor selection and purchasing decisions must be made objectively and in Dell's best interest, based upon evaluation of suitability, price, delivery, and quality.*
- *[General Electric's] relationships with suppliers are based on lawful, efficient, and fair practices...Following GE guidelines helps ensure our relationships will not damage GE's reputation.*
- *HP [Hewlett-Packard] suppliers are of great strategic importance... you have a duty to deal with suppliers fairly..."*

It is evident from these examples (and there are many more) that the use of reverse auctions may violate the code of conduct/ethics of a corporation simply because of the unique way that information is shared in most types of auctions (prices, delivery schedules, additions, etc.). Furthermore, the U.S. Federal Procurement Standards require corporations that do business with Federal agencies to establish and meet the Federal guidelines on ethics.

FINDINGS

The ethical use of reverse auctions is going to be debated for years to come. Each organization must carefully scrutinize what the effects of a reverse auction may have on its suppliers beyond the reduction of price and margin, and whether the use of reverse auctions violates its or a professional society's code of conduct. The rule "first, do no harm" should be applied to all reverse auction methodologies. CAPS Research (2003) stated that suppliers felt that reverse auctions were generally ethical if the playing field was even. Giampetro and Emiliani (2007) disagreed, concluding that reverse auctions are coercive with regards to incumbent suppliers, and are inconsistent with U.S. federal procurement standards and the Institute of Supply Management's "Principles and Standards of Ethical Supply Management Conduct."

This research effort finds that the use of reverse auctions may be unethical and in violation of professional standards or codes of conduct if any of the following conditions are met:

- The use of the reverse auction methodology is exclusionary to suppliers
- The reverse auction destroys the buyer-supplier relationship and trust
- The information asked for by the reverse auction process reveals confidential or proprietary information that may harm a supplier in the future
- The reverse auction does not indirectly or directly violate the integrity of either the buyer or vendor organizations
- The rules of engagement differ from supplier to supplier
- The reverse auction methodology does not violate a firms code of conduct/ethics

- The reverse auction methodology does not violate a professional organizations or governmental agencies code of conduct/ethics.

These conditions should be used as a framework to help determine whether using reverse auctions violates corporate or professional codes of conduct. Also, we find that those people or organizations that violate the rules of reverse auctions as suppliers are knowingly or unknowingly violating antitrust laws. It is difficult to see a situation in which supplier collusion, price fixing, or selling under the break-even price would not be in violation of an antitrust law.

CONCLUSION

This effort contributes to the debate of reverse auction ethics, which is relatively light compared to other areas of reverse auction research, by examining the effects of the reverse auction process against the ethical concerns of procurement established by businesses, governments, and professional societies. As with all studies on ethical behavior, hard rules are difficult to define and each organization will have to establish what criteria they will use. This study has limitations concerning the rules and only further research efforts will narrow down what is and is not ethical. Certainly, the widely held belief in distributed justice, that an advantage made available to some should not be denied to others without merit, will come into play.

The unethical conditions concluded from this research effort are meant as a framework for organizations pursuing reverse auction techniques and are certainly not an exhaustive list. Furthermore, each organization must decide if they do violate those codes, should reverse auctions be eliminated or have the rules changed? Ethical considerations are often determined by generally accepted practices that are not in violation of any laws. Reverse auctions may have rewritten the

ethical rules regarding buyer/supplier relationships. This research effort serves as a starting point for ethical inquiry into the use of reverse auctions and should provide a foundation for future research efforts.

FUTURE RESEARCH DIRECTIONS

There are still many areas related to the concept of ethics and ethical behavior in the use of the reverse auctions that should continue to be explored more in the future. Three areas that we believe have come to the forefront in our investigation of the current literature on reverse auction are the issue of possible mandated compliance to specific codes of conduct: the long-run quality of the supplier/buyer relationship and technology's role in helping prevent or facilitate the unethical behavior of buyers.

While some attention has been given to establishing the perception of the unethical nature of reverse auctions from the suppliers point of view (Giampetro & Emiliani, 2007) there are still many areas in ethics yet to explore. The long run effect on the buyer/supplier relationship is still largely unknown. What implications will this hold for the future of supply chain management in terms of collaboration and stability? Currently, most of the language specifically addressing ethical codes of behavior in relation to the reverse auction process remains at the industry association level as part of their professional standards for members. Yet at the corporate level, the language addressing codes of conduct with suppliers is very general, encouraging buyers to provide fair competition opportunities, promote transparency, and support management's philosophy of best practices. Thus for the reverse auction process, the supplier's fate is left to the mercy of the buyer's voluntary compliance with its industry association's specific code of ethics. If some buyers continue to abuse reverse auctions, choosing to drive margins down at the expense of their suppliers' survival, will this process fall under heightened scrutiny by regulators and result in a mandated compliance?

The attractiveness of using the reverse auctions from the buyer's standpoint is well documented in its ability to drive costs down. It is also known that such practices reduce procurement of any product to a commodity level, with price as the primary driver. Unfortunately, the process itself appears to be counter intuitive to the quality initiatives that most of these companies have implemented. The level of quality that has been sacrificed and its resultant impact on profitability is another area that needs further exploration. Additionally, future research could be directed toward answering the question of whether or not this violates a corporate code of ethics of responsibility to other stakeholders or contradicts the goals of maximizing shareholder wealth.

Finally, we see trends in the technology itself emerging that will address the concerns and perhaps the damages created by the reverse auction process. In order to maintain the positive elements perceived by both suppliers and buyers, that reverse auctions are a fairer process of awarding business through increased transparency, more technological safeguard mechanisms are needed. These safeguards would provide the assurance necessary that unethical behavior on the part of the buyer such as phantom bidding in the presence of multiple buyers is blocked.

REFERENCES

Bapna, R., Goes, P., & Gupta, A. (2003). An analysis of business to consumer online auctions. *Management Science, 49*(1), 85-101.

Bapna, R., Goes, P., Gupta, A., & Karuga, G. (2002). Optimal design of the online auction channel: Analytic, empirical and computational insights. *Decision Sciences, 33*(4), 557-577.

CAPS Research (2003). *Cross industry summary report*. CAPS Research, November.

Carter, C. R., Kaufman, L., Beall, S., Carter, P. L., Hendrick, T. E., & Petersen, K. J. (2004) Reverse auctions grounded theory from the buyer-supplier perspective. *Transportation Research, 40,* 229-254.

Contractor Magazine (2004). 84% find ethical violations.[Electronic version] *51*(6), 1.

Cramton, P. C., & Dees, J. G. (1993) Promoting honesty in negotiation: An excercise in practical ethics. *Business Ethics Quarterly, 3*(4), 359-394.

Dees, J.G., & Cramton, P. C. (1995) Deception and mutual trust: A reply to Strudler. *Business Ethics Quarterly, 5,* 823-832.

Elmaghraby, W. J. (2002). The importance of ordering in sequential auctions. *Management Science, 49*(5), 673-682.

Emiliani, M. L. (2004). Sourcing in the global aerospace supply chain using online reverse auctions. *Industrial Marketing Management, 33*(1), 65-73.

Emiliani, M. L., (2005). Regulating B2B online reverse auctions through voluntary codes of conduct. *Industrial Marketing Management, 34,*526-534.

Emiliani, M. L., & Stec, D. J. (2004). Aerospace parts supplier's reaction to online reverse auction. *Supply Chain Management, 9*(2), 139-153.

Giampetro, P., & Emiliani, M. L. (2007). Coercion and reverse auctions. *Supply Chain Management, 12*(2), 75-84.

Hartley, J. L., Lane, M. D., & Hong, Y. (2004). An exploration of the adoption of e-auctions in supply management. *IEEE Transactions, 51*(2), 153-161.

Handfield, R. B., Straight, S. L., & Stirling, W. A. (2002). Reverse auctions: How do supply managers really feel about them? *Inside Supply Management, 13*(11), 56-61.

Hannon, D. (2003). Purchasing shows e-sourcing adoption stalls. *Purchasing,* 12, August.

Horlen, J., Eldin, N., & Ajinkya, Y. (2005). Reverse auctions: Controversial bidding practice. *Journal of Professional Issues in Engineering, Education and Practice, 131*(1), 76-81.

Hur, D., Mabert, V. A., & Hartley, J. L. (2005). Getting the most out of e-auction investment. *Omega, 35,* 403-416.

Jap, S. D. (2003). An exploratory study of the introduction of on-line reverse auctions. *Journal of Marketing, 67,* 96-107.

Mabert, V. A., & Skeels, J. A. (2002). Internet reverse auctions: A valuable tool in experienced hands. *Business Horizons, 45*(4), 70-76.

Marcoux, A. M. (2003). Snipers, stalkers, and nibblers: Online auction business ethics. *Journal of Business Ethics, 46,* 163-173.

Mark, R. (2006). More indictments in DRAM price fixing probe. *Business, Internetnews.com,* October 19.

Rothkopf, M. H., Pekec, A., & Harstad, R. M. (1998). *Management Science, 44,* 1131-1147.

Smeltzer, L., & Carr, A. (2002). Reverse auctions in industrial marketing and buying. *Business Horizon, 45*(2), 47-52.

ADDITIONAL READING

(2006). Reverse auctions are found to be unethical; companies use coercion to force participation. *Manufacturing News, 13*(13), 1.

Bandyopadhyay, S., Rees, J., & Barron, J. M. (2006). Simulating sellers in online exchanges. *Decision Support Systems, 41*(2), 500-513.

Carbone, J. (2005, December 8). Reverse auctions become more strategic for buyers [Electronic version]. *Purchasing Magazine Online.*

Daly, S., & Nath, P. (2005). Reverse auctions for relationship marketers. *Industrial Marketing Management, 34*(2), 157-166.

Dani, S., Burns, N. D., & Backhouse, C. J. (2005). Buyer-supplier behaviour in electronic reverse auctions: A relationship perspective. *International Journal of Services and Operations Management, 1*(1), 22-34.

Emiliani, M. (2000). Business-to-business online auctions: Key issues for purchasing process improvement. *Supply Chain Management: An International Journal, 5*(4), 176-186.

Emiliani, M., & Stec, D. J. (2002). Realizing savings from online reverse auctions. *Supply Chain Management: An International Journal, 7*(1), 12-23.

Emiliani, M., & Stec, D. J. (2002). Squaring online reverse auctions with the Caux Round Table Principles for Business. *Supply Chain Management: An International Journal, 7*(2), 92-100.

Emiliani, M., & Stec, D. J. (2005). Wood pallet suppliers' reaction to online reverse auctions. *Supply Chain Management: An International Journal, 10*(4), 278-288.

Emiliani, M., Stec, D. J., & Grasso, L. P. (2005). Unintended responses to a traditional purchasing performance metric. *Supply Chain Management: An International Journal, 10*(3), 150-156.

Handfield, R. (2004). *Supply market intelligence: A managerial handbook for building sourcing strategies.* Canada: CRC Publications.

Hatipkarasulu, Y., & Gill, J., Jr. (2004). Identification of shareholder ethics and responsibilities in online reverse auctions for construction projects. *Science Engineering Ethics, 10*(2), 283-288.

Hawkins, T. (2005). Online auction rules get guarded assent. *Printing World, 9.*

Jap, S. D. (2002). Online reverse auctions: Issues, themes, and prospects for the future. *Academy of Marketing Science Review, 30*(4), 506-525.

Kenczyk, M. (2000). Reverse auctions are risky models for buying custom parts. *Machine Design, 73*(6), 148.

Leskelä, R., Teich, J., Wallenius, H., & Wallenius, J. (2007). Decision support for multi-unit combinatorial bundle auctions. *Decision Support Systems, 43*(2), 420-434.

Millet, I., Parente, D. H., Fizel, J., & Venkataraman, R. R. (2001, October). *Electronic reverse auctions - Success metrics & dynamics.* Paper presented at the IFIP Conference on Towards The E-Society: E-Commerce, E-Business, E-Government.

Online reverse auctions: Be careful! (2004). Retrieved September 25, 2004, from http://www.theclbm.com/research.html and http://www.theclbm.com/ora/ora_slides.pdf

Peace, A. G., Weber, J., Hartzel, K. S., & Nightingale, J. (2002). Ethical issues in ebusiness: A proposal for creating the ebusiness principles. *Business and Society Review, 107*(1), 41-60.

Reed, L. (2005). Online reverse auctions can be deceiving. *Air Conditioning Heating & Refrigeration News, 224*(8), 10.

Sawhney, M. (2003). Forward thinking about reverse auctions [Electronic Version]. *CIO Magazine.* Retrieved September 28, 2004 from http://www.cio.com/archive/060103/gains.html

Schooner, S. L., & Yukins, C. R. (2005). *Emerging policy and practice issues.* Paper presented at the West Government Contracts Year in Review Conference from http://ssrn.com/abstract=887355

Smart, A., & Harrison, A. (2003). Online reverse auctions and their role in buyer-supplier relationships. *Journal of Purchasing and Supply Management, 9*(5-6), 257-268.

Smeltzer, L. R., & Carr, A. S. (2003). Electronic reverse auctions: Promises, risks, and conditions for success. *Industrial Marketing Management, 32*(6), 481-488.

Smith, A. D. (2006). Supply chain management using electronic reverse auctions: A multi-firm case study. *International Journal of Services and Standards, 2*(2), 176-189.

Stein, A., & Hawking, P. (2002, July). *Reverse auction e-procurement: A supplier's viewpoint.* Paper presented at the Australian World Wide Web Conference, Twin Waters Resort, Sunshine Coast Queensland.

Tassabehji, R., Taylor, W. A., Beach, R., & Wood, A. (2006). Reverse e-auctions and supplier-buyer relationships: An exploratory study. *International Journal of Operations & Production Management, 26*(2), 166-184.

Tulder, R., & Mol, M. (2002). Reverse auctions or auctions reversed: First experiments by Philips. *European Management Journal, 20*(5), 447-456.

Tully, S. (2000). Going, going, gone! The B2B tool that really is changing the world. *Fortune, 141,* 132-145.

ADDITIONAL WEBSITES

American Society of Quality (http://www.asq.org)

Institute for Supply Chain Management (http://www.apics.org)

Baldridge Self Assessment (http://www.quality.nist.gov)

National Association of Purchasing Manager (http://www.napm.org/)

Center for Advanced Purchasing Studies (http://www.capsresearch.org/publications/index.htm)

Institute of Supply Management (www.ism.ws)

IMPLICATIONS FOR PRACTITIONERS

Title: Do reverse auctions violate professional standards and codes of conduct?

Short description

Because of the dramatic price reductions reported, reverse auctions have become a major, if not revolutionary, tool for many organizations (Hannon, 2003). Why has the reverse auction not become the revolutionary tool initially projected? There are a variety of reasons including cost, ease of use, managerial acceptance, learning curves, and so forth. However, some researchers suggest that concerns with ethics and supplier relationships are barriers to reverse auction adoption (Hur et al., 2005; Jap, 2003; Handfield et al., 2002). This chapter examines some of the professional standards/codes of ethics available including the Institute of Supply Chain Management (ISM) and a selected number of organizations including Dell and GE. Further, the chapter presents a framework that can help an organization determine if reverse auctions, and they way they are run, are ethical.

Findings

This research effort finds that the use of reverse auctions may be unethical and in violation of professional standards or codes of conduct if any of the following conditions are met:

- The use of the reverse auction methodology is exclusionary to suppliers.
- The reverse auction destroys the buyer-supplier relationship and trust.
- The information asked for by the reverse auction process reveals confidential or proprietary information that may harm a supplier in the future.
- The reverse auction does not indirectly or directly violate the integrity of either the buyer or vendor organizations.
- The rules of engagement differ from supplier to supplier.
- The reverse auction methodology does not violate a firms code of conduct/ethics.
- The reverse auction methodology does not violate a professional organizations or governmental agencies code of conduct/ethics.

RECOMMENDATIONS

Practitioners should examine:

- Their employers standards or codes of ethics in relation to reverse auctions
- Their professional standards or codes of ethics whether formal or informal
- Any governmental agencies standards or codes of ethics including international governments
- The effect on supplier relationships and the potential for disengaging key suppliers
- The rights of suppliers to retain confidential information
- The potential for abuse by the buyer or supplier
- The potential for collusion amongst supplying firms

- The limitations of reverse auctions and whether the effort will add value. Specifically, will it lower cost, increase quality or service, etc?
- The limitations of this study such as the limited number of firms and professional organizations studied. Often, a process that is unethical to one group may be perfectly acceptable to another.

Chapter XVII
Reverse Auction Impact on Mining Company

Radoslav Delina
Technical University of Kosice, Slovak Republic

Anton Lavrin
Technical University of Kosice, Slovak Republic

ABSTRACT

The case describes the initial implementation and evaluation of an e-procurement system, using reverse auctions, for a large manufacturer of brown coal in the Slovak Republic. One of the biggest problems when making decisions on e-business investments is unclear return on investment (ROI) and uncertainty about what method should be used for measuring the results. An outline of the reverse auction process is provided, followed by the presentation of a number of metrics that evaluate the current performance of the system versus intended future performance matrix. Specifically, it focuses on the ROI and other performance indicators that have been adjusted according to e-commerce specifics, particularly to procurement with dynamic pricing transactions. The case results proved that the investment into the e-commerce solution is highly effective in reducing input costs.

ORGANIZATION BACKGROUND

Hornonitrianske bane Prievidza (Upper Nitra Coal Mines, Prievidza, UNCMP) (http://www.hbp.sk/index.shtml.en) is the Slovakia's most important producer of brown coal which represents national primary source of energy. It is situated in the Upper Nitra Basin, the richest and largest brown coal deposit in the country. In 2002, the company produced 79% of the national coal output. As for the production portfolio, the coal dust for the energy industry was a core item and represented

85.6% of the company's total output. Sorted coal with the proportion of 14.4% was the second most important product. In terms of coal sales, Slovenske Elektrarne—Novaky Power Plant—was the most important business partner.

The company was founded by the government decree in 1993, when the Slovak Coal Mines, Corp. was split into seven independent companies (in order to privatise them later). The state owned enterprise UNCMP was one of them. It consisted of the following subsidiaries:

- Baňa Cigeľ (Cigeľ Mine),
- Baňa Handlová (Handlová Mine),
- Baňa Nováky (Nováky Mine),
- Banská mechanizácia a elektrifikácia Nováky (Mine Mechanization and Electrification, Nováky),
- Hlavná banská záchranná stanica Prievidza (Main Mine Rescue Station, Prievidza).

The Mining Mechanization and Electrification subsidiary was producing and repairing machinery of mining and driving processes.

The Main Mine Rescue Station, Prievidza provided services for all mining organizations in Slovakia. It also developed and marketed commercial activities of its own mainly in the field of professional counselling and training services, specific climbing equipment maintenance and distribution, distribution of gas pollutant analytical equipment, fire extinguishers, fire equipment, breathing and resuscitation equipment as well as inertisation equipment.

In 1996, the UNCMP was transformed into a state owned corporation that had to be closed down by June 30. However, on July 1 it was re-established by the National Property fund under the same name and 97% of its shares were sold to employess.

By January 1, 2003 in order to reduce costs and increase the mining process efficiecy Cigel Mine and Novaky Mine subsidiaries merged into a joint venture. The board of directors, after evaluation of production capacities and economic performance of the Handlova Mine, decided to close it down by October 1, 2003. All of its operations were overtaken by the UNCMP.

At present, the company headquarters is situated in Prievidza. Its main responsibilities include creating and applying mine development concepts, forecasting and long-term planning, performing global assessment and co-ordination of core activities.

The UNCMP belongs to the region's largest companies—in 2002, it had on average 6,183 employees. However, it turned out to be inefficient and the management had to apply measures improving the labor productvity (mainly layoffs). As a result, the 2002 average monthly salary rose to SKK 15,306, which represented an annual increase of about 6.9%.

The company's core activity is brown coal mining. Its mission is to use effectively existing brown coal resources of open deposits. The UNCMP also operates in the sector of engineering production and offers recreational and tourist services. Furthermore, considering the time limitations of current operations, it has been looking for and has desired to implement new manufacturing and entrepreneurial activities.

From the long term perspective, the management focuses on cost reduction and improving the efficiency of business processes. Considering current huge purchasing volumes, good industrial references, implementation simplicity and proclaimed fast return on investment [Pastore, 2001], the company decided to develop the reverse auction-based e-procurement model of its own. The reverse auction was selected mainly because of its dynamic pricing characteristics. Since real benefits are obtainable within the Web environment, the management chose a Web based solution. The main purpose was to create an effective procurement system that would use new information technologies and the Internet.

SETTING THE STAGE

Until 2002, all of the company's business operations were performed in a traditional "paper-based" way. In other words, once the request had been defined, the purchasing department made paper based orders using current prices from suppliers' catalogues. All of the purchases were performed individually for each subsidiary.

However, in 2002, the company management, in addition to achieving other corporate objectives, planned to prepare and launch several changes in auxiliary operations. The main purpose was to increase the purchasing economic efficiency by using modern ICT (Devaraj & Kohli, 2003). And so it was necessary to design a project that would help to create the centralized system of supply management, physical and electronic procurement and that would improve the existing procurement system as a whole.

Considering assumptions on large synergy effects obtained from the e-procurement (Subramaniam & Shaw, 2004; Harden & Heyman, 2002), the company decided to make significant changes in the supply system. The management decided to develop own Internet controlling system (ICS). It was based on reverse auction principle – online commodity auction. In general, commodity auctions represent virtual supermarket at which registered suppliers submit their product offers according to predefined clients' requirements. It is perceived as the most simple and most transparent way of trading in which all trades must be performed by providing and accepting a public offer.

The security of the system was maintained by the https security protocol using the SSL. Certificates with the mdSRSA algorithms (512 bits) protect the data exchange against unauthorized misuse. Furthermore, the security was enhanced by various login parameters and double login prevention.

The ICS included the following modules:

- **Registration:** Login and identification of buyers, suppliers, intermediaries, supervisor's and administrator's statistics.
- **Buyer for organization:** Submitting and recording commodity buying orders
- **Supplier:** Submitting commodity offers with maintaining records of already ordered items.
- **Goods delivery:** Delivering new items, maintaining records of already received and partially received commodities.
- **Statistics:** Data archiving, searching and restoring, processing printed reports on realized, deleted or postponed orders.
- **Supervisor:** Organizing work within internal and external auction board, lists of internal and external orders, approving order creation for external auction, verifying sending orders for selected suppliers.
- **Administrator:** Diversifying and modifying commodity kinds and groups, assigning users' IDs, passwords, editing e-mail notifications.
- **Automation:** Automated e-mail correspondence, automated auction prolongation, automated removal of required commodities without reaction

All purchases were performed by the centralized procurement system which meant that all purchasing orders obtained from each subsidiary were processed by the Department of centralized procurement (DCP). To secure normal operation of all subsidiaries it was necessary to provide the stable inflow of materials, spare parts, and other consumables or investment components. Orders were accumulated and assessed by the DCP. They were then consulted with the responsible manager. Next, the approved and specified orders with defined priority degree were selected and submitted by the DCP into the new information system (ICS). Its procurement process was based on dynamic pricing and was developed by external company according to the requirements of the UNCMP. Strategic and exceptional purchases were not performed by the new system.

The initial proposal did not include the automated processing of orders and other documents. Further development depended on success and efficiency of the e-procurement. Therefore, the company management decided to undergo a testing phase during which only a small fraction of the company procurement was affected and employee/supplier acceptance along with user friendliness were examined.

Newly established e-procurement office supervised the following activities:

- Accumulating and processing orders for material procurement submitted by the subsidiaries.
- Classifying orders according to the commodity sort and performing evaluation with the logistics center and inventory management.
- Performing procurement reevaluation and determining the procurement characteristics with the specification of the provisional financial cover.
- Preparing cumulative and approved orders for material procurement via the ICS in accordance with the instructions of the office for internal relations coordination (OIRC) and the office for purchase marketing (OPM).
- Performing contract finalization in accordance with signed general agreements and with the OPM and OIRC instructions (price instructions, delivery conditions, invoice maturity etc.).
- Following the trade development on the "exchange board" and approving the most advantageous offer.

- Providing complex delivery information for the department of the supply management and department of central inventory management (delivery dates, the list of consumption locations, quantities and dates, delivery conditions, customs declaration etc.).
- Supervising inventories.
- Checking and verifying accounting operations related to a particular delivery, verifying invoices on basis of enclosed and confirmed delivery notes and submitting into the ICS/MTZ system (checks on delivered quantity, prices, etc.).
- Dealing with delivery complaint notes, to propose solutions and submit the final decision to the OPM.
- Aggregating information on quality obtained from the branch OPMs and departments of the supply management and central inventory management with regards to particular commodities and suppliers, to provide information on quality and complaint notes processing at the OPMs.
- On basis of the predefined evaluation system to regularly evaluating suppliers and handing over results to the OPM.

The above-mentioned solution was based on the principles of dynamic pricing. The management wanted to evaluate all possible contracts on basis of two characteristics—the price and maturity date. Attributes such as the minimum requirements for suppliers invited to the e-reverse auction were not considered. The prices generated by the e-solutions were the prices for materials including all transportation costs. The winning offer was selected and sent to responsible managers for re-evaluation. Once the managers' consent was obtained orders for the winning offer were made.

From now on, the solution will be referred to as the e-auction because it fits best its basic characteristics. The auction start up process includes:

- Determination of the procurement conditions and date, which is approved of by the manager of the procurement office,
- Conditions are e-mailed to potential suppliers; none of them verifies their participation on the e-auction,
- E-auction is opened on a specified date and offers are expected,
- Each participant who submitted an offer would then see the anonymous results (offers without participant ID); this process continues until the end of the e-auction,
- Provided that the last offer contained a 3% lower price than the previous offer, the e-auction would be prolonged for another two hours,
- In case that the similar situation occurs afterwards, the auction will be prolonged for another half an hour, which might be additionally prolonged for another half an hour,
- The e-auction is closed and evaluated,
- Three hours after the auction closure the evaluation process starts (the OPM defines the most advantageous offer, however it might not be necessarily the winning offer),
- The form with e-auction results will enable to click on the e-auction winner for whom the purchase order is automatically generated and sent to,
- Once the purchase order is out, more detailed information are sent – business conditions, transport and storing conditions, etc.

At the beginning of the year the company applied the e-procurement solution to only 1% of the total volume of required commodities. Throughout the year the proportion of electronically procured commodities gradually increased to 2,5%. Later on, considering the results the management would

decide about the extent of further implementation in the future.

The e-procurement solution was also used in case of dominant suppliers whose prices were determined by bilateral agreements. The only advantage of this case was the automation of order processing. Material supply requirements and their parameters such as delivery dates were settled online by the e-auction as it had been requested. Throughout the examination period the company management was able to attract only 60% of all of its business partners.

Critical purchases (i.e. the ones necessary to realize in critically short time period) were excluded from the system. From the perspective of the company cash position it was irrelevant anyway.

The hardware and software equipment required for the new system cost SKK 600,000 and SKK 1,5 million respectively (exchange rate in the year of implementation was 1EUR=42SKK and 1USD=46SKK). The maintenance for the first year of operation was according to the contract free of charge (system guarantee). At that point, conditions of the system service and maintenance were frequently discussed in order to adapt the service agreeement. Licenses were in abeyance—the basic payment included only 5 user licenses. Business partners were not the system users.

Since during the period in question, there was neither financial metrics nor performance measurement, the management decided to implement the e-procurement solution on basis of best practice benchmarking and previously published case studies of the field (Neely, 2002; Barua, 1995; e-business w@tch, 2003; beep, 2003). In other words, the management made a research among companies in the field, which already implemented the solution and examined obtained results. This research indicated possible price savings 5-10%. However, later on during the testing period, the need for performance measurement reappeared. Unfortunately, the management knew only basic advantages presented in books (Turban, 2002) and needed IT financial metrics, which would be understandable and clear for all relevant parties (Barua, 2001; Best Practices LLC., 2001; eBusiness W@tch, 2003). Such metrics would be afterwards used for solution datamining and real time measuring. At that point, however, the priority was laid upon the reverse auction performance measurement since it was a new business model used within the company (Emiliani & Stec, 2002).

CASE DESCRIPTION

Reverse auctions and their popularity have had a tremendous impact on both manufacturers and on suppliers. Manufacturers have been able to streamline the vendor selection process and have made it easier on themselves to select the right supplier for each project. Reverse auctions have also forced suppliers to find new ways of staying competitive. Since price is not the only factor, vendors have been forced to bring more added value to their goods and services, such as extra warranties, maturity dates or other options.

Reverse auctions do offer a number of advantages. First, they do open up competition. Many manufacturers are today doing business with vendors they never knew existed a year ago simply because they were located on the other side of the globe. By allowing businesses to expand their horizons, reverse auctions have given them the tools to truly find the best and most affordable suppliers, depending on several attributes. Moreover, the reverse auctions speed up the entire procurement process. While before, the buyer has to create a complex RFP (Request for Proposal), distribute it to potential vendors, wait for their responses, then shift through each of their proposals individually in order to make a decision, today the entire process can be completed in 3-7 days instead of weeks or months (Neef, 2001; Emiliani & Stec, 2002).

Regardless of these benefits, reverse auctions still fall short in some areas. Because reverse auctions seem to emphasize cost over other qualifications, many buyers may choose the lowest bid only to find out that the shoddy workmanship, low quality products, and slow delivery times cost them more in the long run. Reverse auctions can also be detrimental to the supplier-buyer relationship that is essential for some goods. For example, if only a handful of vendors can provide the raw materials a company needs, and that company places the project up for auction instead of simply using its long-term vendor, chances are that they will lose the goodwill of that vendor and will find it difficult to work with them again. Furthermore, when only a small number of vendors can provide a specific good or service, reverse auctions do not always deliver cost savings and can sometimes cost the buyer more. However, the mentioned problems are being addressed by introducing additional evaluation criteria, e.g. rating of suppliers, product certifications, delivery times, etc.

Since most businesses feel that the strengths of reverse auctions outweigh their weaknesses, the company management decided to implement reverse auction solution into their procurement processes. Recent best practices benchmarks in the field enhanced their decision even more.

First of all, they had to analyze the suppliers' willingness to participate on the Internet based business model. In general, suppliers are not very fond of reverse auctions since they are forced to decrease the profit margins in order to obtain the contract (Kanaan & Praveen, 2001). However, in this case, suppliers agreed on participation because of a relatively dominant market position of the UNCMP and high volumes of its industry purchases. The number of participating suppliers had been low at the beginning but gradually increased because other suppliers quickly understood that accepting the model would be the only way of remain competitive.

The solution had the character of private auction—the company management did not consider the open number of suppliers. Therefore, it was necessary to create a network of prospective partners to whom the e–auction invitations would be sent. By doing this, another parameter of the offer evaluation was fulfilled—the suppliers' rating (suppliers did not need to be rated since they were selected by the UNCMP).

From the managers' perspective, the most important issue was to measure the effciency and performance of the e-commerce solution at its initial stage implementation. In order to obtain understandable results it was necessary to use traditional evaluation methods such as ROI, Cash flow or payback period (Neely, 2002; Grant 2002). According to The Dictionary of Modern Economics (Pearce, 1992):

- **Return on investment** (ROI) is defined as "A general concept referring to Earnings from the Investment of Capital, where the earnings are expressed as a proportion of the outlay. ROI = (Profits/Invested Capital)*100%".
- **Cash flow** is the amount of cash derived over a certain period of time from an income-producing property.
- **IRR** (Internal rate of return) is "the DIS-COUNT RATE which makes the NET PRESENT VALUE of a project equal to zero".
- **Net present value** (NPV) presents "The sum that results when the DISCOUNTED value of the expected costs of an investment are deducted from the discounted value of the expected returns".

Measurement Approach

The investigation on possibilities of procurement cost reduction is the first step for determining the e-solution impact. It is because the costs represent most important indicator for all savings to be obtained not only from hard (e.g., purchasing costs, maturity dates, personal costs, etc.) but also soft attributes (e.g., customer satisfaction—reduced cost on customers services, user friendliness—reduced cost on mistakes correction, training, etc.) (Delina, 2003; Subramaniam & Shaw, 2002). Procurement attributes affecting financial indicators are provided in Appendix 7. Potential reduction can be examined in two ways (Delina & Lavrin, 2004; VEGA, 2004). The first is the approximate calculation in which the first auction price is considered to be the catalogue price that we would have paid provided that we had used catalogue

Figure 1. Example of the price development

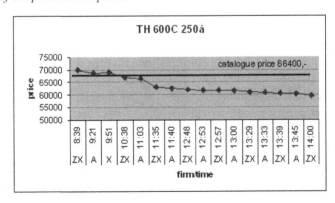

procurement. The second way is based on more precise research on the real catalogue price at the time of the auction performance (because the first price offered could be overestimated).

From the psychological perspective, it is assumed that the first price offered is higher than a real catalogue price. Participant does not lose anything if he submits a higher price. In case of a breakdown by another offer he would still remain competitive by reducing his own offer. Though, in case of a low attendance, he might end up with higher price than the one presented in a catalogue.

The next step is the calculation of savings resulting from better business conditions (e.g. better maturity dates). It is unambiguous and very easy to calculate from the auction data. Maturity dates as evaluation attributes are convenient because of their close relation to the liquidity management. Longer maturity dates obtained from e-auction allow company to use its available cash resources more efficiently (companies have liquid funds for longer time periods). As a result, the available cash can be invested and earn interest for the time corresponding to the prolonged maturity. The extent of benefits to be obtained from prolonged maturities depends on current situation of a given company (e.g., companies unable to obtain short term loans can perform planned activities, regardless of external capital; or if they are, they can borrow lesser amounts or nothing at all). For more information on cash flow and liquidity management, see Schaeffer, 2002.

Figure 1 shows the price development within the e-auction (see also Appendix 1). Maturity date savings varied from initial 30 to final 50 days. These savings were main benefits resulting from the e-solution. The only problem seemed to be with the identification of catalogue prices. Though, if the measurement process had been performed in time the procurement managers would have been able to estimate catalogue prices. On the other hand, the first price average in reverse auction is similar or equal to real catalogue price.

In case of B2B reverse auction, which is used very often for industrial procurement (Emiliani & Stec, 2002), it was necessary to identify savings for each auction. On their basis, one can calculate interests as secondary financial yields added to the price reduction.

The second aspect of dynamic transaction model is characterized by the opportunity to negotiate more convenient maturity dates. Better maturity dates can be also perceived as a kind of financial yield. It is because they provide additional time interest (Delina & Lavrin, 2003). For better illustration, it was assumed, that the interest rate is constant throughout the year.

It follows that if the maturity date is not the same as the date of the auction, financial indicators for reverse auction were derived as:

$$I_v = I_s + I_{md} =$$

$$= i \left[\sum_{j=1}^{n} (P_{0kj} - P_{dkj}) \frac{365 - k_j - d_{dkj}}{365} + \sum_{j=1}^{n} (P_{dkj} \frac{d_{dkj} - d_{0kj}}{365}) \right]$$

$$V = V_u + I_{md} = \sum_{j=1}^{n} (P_{0kj} - P_{dkj}) \cdot (1 + i \frac{365 - k_j - d_{dkj}}{365}) +$$

$$+ \frac{i}{365} \sum_{j=1}^{n} [P_{dkj}(d_{dkj} - d_{0kj})]$$

Explanatory Notes

Auction j is performed on day k, auction price is P_0, negotiated price is P_d and interest rate is I.

When maturity date is d, P_{dkj} is achieved price on day k by auction j, and interest from maturity date savings is I_{md}.

V_u: Financial yield from purchasing prices savings

I_v: Total amount of interests from savings

I_s: Amount of interests from better (reduced) price (from preserved cash)

V: Total financial yield (performance) from reverse auction

Apart from this, the management also needed to calculate traditional performance indicators such as the ROI.

For each e-commerce application, it is possible to determine savings that will occur as a result of the e-commerce technology application and the costs needed for its implementation. When the ROI is considered as a proportion of revenues on total assets, it is necessary to adjust the numerator and denominator by adding particular values. These changes cannot be simply added to the net profit, because we consider the pre-tax profit. The value of the numerator is extended by the value of the implemented solution and obtained savings (Delina 2003). As a result, the modified ROI formula respecting e-commerce characteristic (ROI_c) is expressed as follows:

$$ROI_c = \frac{P + C_r + I_v - D_e - C_c}{A + I + C_r - S - D_e + (TP_e + IP_e - S_i)}$$

where:

P   Is the pre tax profit from traditional operations (without the implementation of the e-solution).

C_r Is the value of identified cost reduction, (more about attributes see Delina & Lavrin, 2003); in terms of assets, the cost reduction increases money in bank accounts.

C_c Is the solution-carrying costs.

D_e Is the value of solution depreciation, (all hardware and software is assumed to be depreciated by a straight-line method, for more details on financial accounting principles see Eisen, 2003).

A   Is the value of assets without solution implementation.

S   Is the value of stock reduction (prices of material in warehouse).

TP_e Is the salvage value of tangible solution property as computers, accessories etc.

IP_e Is the salvage value of intangible property purchased or developed software solution.

S_i Is the installment on credit in year I.

The value of assets in case of not investing into the solution is obtained by adding the solution depreciation (*De*) and its financial yield (*V*) to the total value of assets.

On the other hand, when considering taxes and depreciation, it is more suitable to use Cash ROI (CROI):

$$CashROI = \frac{(P + Cr + I_v - D_e - C_c)(1-d) + D_c}{A + I_v - S + Cr - D_e + (TP_e + IP_e - S_i)}$$

where:

d   Is tax rate.

D_c Is value of complex depreciation.

In the case of added CashROI (ΔCROI), the expression is modified:

$$ROI_e = \frac{I_v + Cr - C_c - D_e}{A_e}$$

In order to get a clearer idea, it was also necessary to calculate the separate performance of the e-procurement solution (ROI_e), which is expressed as follows:

$$ROI_e = \frac{I_v + Cr - C_c - D_e}{A_e}$$

where:

A_e Is the value of solution assets:

$$A_e = TP_e + IP_e + I_v + Cr - S - D_e$$

RESULTS

Obtained results are presented in the table below in two ways. The column of the 2.5% procurement intensity shows real intensity status applied in the company. The next column presents the status that the company wants to achieve in the

Table 1. Results of Rox

Indicators	2.5% intensity	80% intensity
ROI_e / $CROI_e$	26.74% / 33.64%	95.08% / 68.49%
ROI_c / $CROI_c$	1.14% / 7.54%	2.13% / 8.8%
ROI_t / $CROI_t$	1.12% / 7.52%	1.12% / 7.52%
ΔROI / ΔCROI	0.02% / 0.022%	1.017% / 0.66%
ROC / CROC	45.63% / 57.4%	2414.5% / 1739%
In the case model		
ROI_e/$CROI_e$	-15.12% / -	92.3% / 66.5%
ROC/CROC	-25.8% / -	2343% / 1688.6%

Table 2. Result of other indicators

	2.5% intensity	80% intensity
Level of e-assets M_{vA}	0.06%	1.07%
Level of virtuality M_o	0.046%	0.67%

future once the solution efficiency is confirmed. The ROI_t indicator was the ROI without the e-procurement solution. The ROC represents the return on relevant cost (cost related only to the implementation and maintenance of the e-procurement solution). The CROI is the ROI respecting the cash flow (regarding taxes). The ΔROI represents an increase in the ROI. Financial yield from the solution is presented in Appendix 2 and basic values for investment calculation in Appendix 3. In general, the ROI should be higher as the average market interest rate (which was in this case 7%). From the table below we see, that the ROI from solution (ROI_e) was considerably higher and, therefore, the solution is very effective.

Moreover, the case model presented in the table above brought up the issue of solution related personal costs (48 man-days per month). By contrast, in practice personal costs were not included; because the personnel remained the same (they were still working also in traditional way) and no additional costs were charged (training was realized after identification of problems with acceptability of purchasing managers as mentioned below). Other calculations are presented in Appendix 4 and 5.

After the reexamination of the previous results it was found out that it was necessary to calculate other indicators (the significance of Δ(C)ROI, the profit or the CF growth and others), but especially the proportion of e-assets and the level of virtuality.

The indicator of the level of e-assets showed the proportion of assets generating online processes (A_e) on total assets (A_c). In other words, it is the part of the total capital (in %) invested into the e-solution. This is useful only for companies having their own e-solutions (see Table 2). The indicator needed to be calculated, because of very low ΔROI values. It is the specific case of mining companies, because they have huge assets in real estates.

$$M_{vA} = \frac{A_e}{A_c}$$

According to other specifics such as the value of the telework, the value of digital products and all financial flows, it was found out that the indicator of the level of virtuality was needed. This indicator expresses a proportion of financial flows related to the e-solution (O_e) on total financial inflows as well as outflows (O_c). In this particular case one can also consider the fixed asset depreciation generated by online processes. The indicator is also suitable for companies participating on outsourced electronic marketplaces whereby its value is extended by values of e-services.

$$M_O = \frac{O_e}{O_c}$$

The closer examination revealed that if one of these indicators is low, it could cause low added ROI, despite the fact that the performance of the e-solution was very high.

In order to evaluate the investment over a certain time period, it was assumed, that during the first year the company would procure electronically 2.5% of total procurement volume (this is the value that was actually achieved in practice), and during the remaining 3 years with the intensity of 80% (this was the plan for the future).

Internal rate of return (IRR) was calculated by back solver function using the MS Excel sheets. This and other indicators, shown in the table below, were very efficient in terms of presenting how the dynamic transaction solution of electronic commerce could be effective for companies.

As managers examined obtained results, the $ROI_e/CROI_e$ was perceived as very high along with very low ROI increase. This was caused by very high value of total assets and low value of intensity indicator (being just 2,5%). When they compared values of both indicators according to the intensity figures (2,5% and 80%), the ROI increase considerably augmented. However, the percentage on the total ROI was still low. This is because of the specifics of the mining industry, where the large majority of total assets is not related to the procurement processes. This is also the reason why the suitable measuring was needed for examination of the eF–assets level and the overall virtuality. It eventually helped to better understand obtained results.

Another very important fact was revealed. When the ROI was calculated with total assets we had to face the benefit paradox (low ROA paradox). Increasing e-solution related savings increased the value of total assets (used within the ROA calculation) by the cash position improvement. In that case, each additional saving meant that the rate of ROI (ROA) increases more slowly. Therefore, a better option was selected - instead of using total assets, only fixed assets were considered, which expressed return on really invested funds without unwanted cash increases. Or else, it is possible to use another option—use only the total cost (or TCO—total cost of ownership) per year (ROC). In both cases it was possible to calculate the real increase in the ROI.

Comparing ROI_e and ROC_e at the intensity of 2.5% and 80% of the case model respectively, it became apparent that the solution was not efficient at the 2.5% level. But the more the intensity grew, the more grew the solution efficiency.

Based on this, it would be useful to be able to determine the minimum amount of the procure-

Table 3. E-solution investment efficiency

Investment effectiveness for 4 years (stated by depreciation plan)				
IRR	401.16%			
N_e	1.02			
	1st year	**2nd year**	**3rd year**	**4th year**
Cf_e (in SKK)	1320180.4	36341944	40882120	40882120
NPV10% (in SKK)	87773208			

ment that would guarantee sufficient efficiency. In order to monitor the solution performance it would be better to measure individual performance of each process rather than overall company performance once the e-solution is fully imlemented (Subramaniam & Shaw, 2002;2004).

Developed metric for determination of the financial yield "*V*" was hardly quantifiable and therefore objective. Obtained results revealed that the total financial yield (performance) from a reverse auction *V* is also very useful and usable for the e-procurement intelligent agent automatically selecting the best offer. Furthermore, its implementation into a datamining system would help to continuously evaluate savings induced by the new business model (to other aspect of using measured attributes see Neely, et al, 2002).

After completing the measurement and reexamining the whole process an unexpected problem emerged. The responsible procurement managers reported that the e-solution was not suitable, not user friendly, etc. It was suggested that the real problem was in the transparency of the process. Since each participant (supplier) saw each offer, no fraud was possible. By contrast, under the previous circumstances the responsible employees were able to provide an inside information on prices of other competitors in order to obtain bribes. Once all the procedures became transparent the source of significant amounts of illegal money dried out. Such a problem should be solved continuously to assure effective human capital performance (Fitz-Enz, 2000). On the other hand, training and presentation of e-solution benefits for the whole company can be also helpful.

The following conclusions were reached once the managers evaluated all process and measurement results:

- A reverse auction is very useful and effective for "dominant" companies with high procurement volumes,
- It is a driving force for suppliers' utilization, though it is not very attractive for them

since they must decrease their margins significantly.

- Huge economies can be obtained while using a reverse auction, especially in cases where attributes other than price are examined.
- Maturity date examination within a reverse auction is very efficient.
- For the performance measurement and savings analysis it is also necessary, in some specific situations (e.g. high assets or low added ROI), to examine a level of e-assets and virtuality in order to recognize respective causalities.
- Provided that the financial metrics is developed, it is then easy to implement some of its elements for intelligent agents or datamining purposes.
- The return on assets is not very reliable in terms of measuring the total performance of the e-solution. In fact, it is quite a misleading indicator because of increasing the assets' value by the time interest (leading to the enforced financial position on bank accounts). It implies to higher assets value, and slow ROA increase because of increase in savings. This is the reason why the ROx was proposed to be modified (using only fixed assets or total costs).
- Measuring hard quantifiable attributes/savings is often a sufficient method for making a decision on the e-commerce solution implementation (soft benefits are auxiliary only).
- Personnel training is inevitable in order to obtain a fast and efficient e-commerce solution adoption.
- Transparency within the Internet procurement process will lead to significant fraud reduction.

Overview of Effects on Business

Implementation of online reverse auction brought the following results:

- Decreasing purchase prices by 7.5%
- Payback period of the investment was up to one year
- Improvement of the liquidity management (better maturity dates—at the end of the auction original maturity date was extended by 20 days)
- Improvement of the company performance. E-procurement results are slightly distorted because of high asset values (specific phenomenon of the mining industry)
- High value of reverse auction ROI (see Table 1)
- Elimination of corruption practices—this value was impossible to calculate
- Significant simplification of ordering procedures—single click on the auction winner will generate and send the order

CURRENT CHALLENGES/ PROBLEMS FACING THE ORGANIZATION

The problem of efficiency of smaller module solutions (reverse auction), the ones bringing the highest benefit, appeared during the evaluation process. It is expected to achieve lower performance results once the implementation of other e–commerce solutions (e.g. electronic order processing) is finished. One might also consider other research objectives such as the determination of a marginally efficient e-solution portfolio bringing the highest benefits with regards to additional investments. Though, this problem will be a subject to other analyses in the future. In the end, the company management believes that smaller e-solutions are more efficient than complex products of large IT companies.

During the e-solution implementation some individuals seemed to have problems with its acceptance mainly because of the significant fraud reduction. As a result, this phenomenon might negatively affect the overall efficiency and further solution implementation. The company management had to face the existing situation and organized several company training events followed by personal interviews explaining the necessity and efficiency of the solution. The trainings had to be organized in broader perspective since the general knowledge of e-commerce was very low. Despite a relatively high awareness among company top managers, the implementation process was slowed down by employees' fear from unknown technologies. So the real question that still remains unanswered is how to change employees' aversion towards e-commerce (especially of those who lost bribe money).

Another problem refers to the suitability of using the closed private auction; the ways of making other applicants (prospective suppliers) join the auction and the efficient rating control.

During the metrics verification process the need for real time efficiency monitoring along with its benefits appeared.

Once the performance metrics verification was approved of, the management agreed on the development of the metrics for quantifying labor savings and other benefits. Apparently, some economies will be achieved by the reduction of working positions or by a change in the workload. On the other hand, there will be much higher qualification requirements laid upon employees who would be assigned to the electronic commerce department. Naturally, it would go hand in hand with a higher salary. It means that the labor cost savings would be equal to the difference between the lay off costs and e-commerce department salary raise. Provided that these employees were transferred to other job position, the secondary benefit would be measured by increased productivity. This issue, however, is a question for future research.

The company management considers using electronic signature within the online procurement. All of of the remaining activities (obtaining goods, accepting them to a warehouse, invoice liquidation, performing payment orders, etc.) are planned to be performed electronically. This system is planned to be extended for all purchasing departments. Other challenge, for the future, is to enhance evaluation attributes also by the delivery time in order to promote more efficient stock management.

On basis of the approved project for a centralized procurement system, delivering, delivery management, and electronic procurement, focusing on greater economic effectiveness, further implementation started. The Procurement department was formed in order to provide procurement services within the whole company. New elements, such as purchase marketing, supply and storage logistics, assessment, contractor selection, and management of the purchase of strategic commodities have been included as a part of the procurement management. The solution is based on the utilization of new information technology and the Internet. Electronic procurement is an important element of the system.

REFERENCES

Barua, A., Konana, P., Whinston, A., & Yin, F. (2001). Measures for E-Business Value Assessment. *IT Pro, January-February*, 35-39.

Barua, A., Kriebel, C.H., & Mukhopadhyay, T.(1995). Information Technologies and business value: Ananalytic and empirical investigation. *Information Systems Research, 6*(1), 3-23.

BEEP (2003). *Best eEurope practices knowledge system.* Retrieved August 20, 2004, from http://www.beepknowledgesystem.org/default.asp

Best Practices LLC. (2001). *Developing a balanced scorecard of performance measures.* Chapel Hill, NC: Best Practices.

Delina, R., & Lavrin, A. (2003). Approach to the performance measuring of e-commerce solution in manufacturing firm. In Barros, L., Helo, P. & Kekäle (Eds.) *ICIL 2003, Proceedings International Conference on Industrial Logistics* (pp. 130-139). ICIL 2003; Vaasa, Finland, June 16-18, 2003. University of Southampton, UK.

Delina, R., & Lavrin, A. (2004, June 21-23). Performance measurement of e-procurement solution with dynamic pricing aspect. In R. Dienstbier (Ed.) *17th Bled eCommerce conference: eGlobal.* Bled, Slovenia.

Delina, R. (2003). Performance measuring of e-business solution in manufacturing firm. In Ghodous, P. (Ed.) *10th ISPE International Conference on Concurrent Engineering: Research and Applications* (pp. 455-462). Portugal; July 26-30, 2003. The Netherlands: A.A. Balkema.

Devaraj, S., & Kohli, R. (2003). Performance impacts of Information Technology: is actual usage the missing link? *Management Science, 49*(3), 273-289.

E-Business W@tch (2003) *The European e-Business Report.* (European Communities Publication No. NB-51-03-277-EN-C). Luxembourg: Office for Official Publications of the European Communities.

Eisen, P.J. (2003). *Accounting the Easy Way (Accounting the Easy Way).* Barron's Educational Series.

Emiliani, M. L., & Stec, D. J. (2002). Realizing savings from online reverse auctions. *Supply Chain Management, 7*(1), 12-23.

Fitz-Enz, J. (2000). *The ROI of human capital: Measuring the economic value of employee performance.* New York: American Management Association.

Grant, J.L. (2002). *Foundations of economic value added*, 2nd Edition. New York: John Wiley & Sons.

Harden, L., & Heyman, B. (2002). *The auction app: How companies tap the power of online auctions to maximize revenue growth.* New York: McGraw-Hill.

Kannan, P. K., & Praveen, K. K. (2001). Dynamic pricing on the Internet: Importance and implications for consumer behavior. *International Journal of Electronic Commerce, 5*(3), 63-84.

Neef, D. (2001). *E-procurement: From strategy to implementation.* NJ: Prentice Hall.

Neely, A. (2002). *Business performance measurement.* Cambridge: Cambridge University Press

Neely, A. (Ed.). (2002). *Measuring eBusiness performance in performance measurement: Theory and practice.* Cambridge: Cambridge University Press.

Pastore, M. (2001). *Businesses find ROI in e-procurement apps.* Retrieved August 20, 2004, from http://www.clickz.com/stats/sectors/b2b/article.php/727051.

Pearce, D. W. (1992). *The MIT dictionary of modern economics.* Cambridge, MA: The MIT Press.

Schaeffer, H. A. (2002). *Essentials of cash flow.* New York: Wiley.

Subramaniam, C., & Shaw, M. J. (2002). A Study on the value and impact of B2B e-commerce: The case of Web-based procurement. *International Journal of Electronic Commerce, 6*(4), 19-40.

Subramaniam, Ch., & Shaw, M.J. (2004) The effects of process characteristics on the value of B2B e-procurement,. *Information Technology and Management, 5*(1-2), 161-180.

Turban, E. (2002). Electronic commerce 2002: A managerial perspective (2nd edition). NJ: Prentice Hall

VEGA (2004) national project No1/1222/04—Effectiveness and Performance Measurement of Dynamic Transaction Methods in e-Business Solutions, financed by Ministry of Education of Slovak Republic

APPENDIX

Appendix 1

Price and maturity date development by specific product

TH 600C 250 units			
Company	time	Price	MD 30
ZX	8:39	70000	30
A	9:21	68750	30
X	9:51	69000	30
ZX	10:38	67000	30
A	11:03	66500	30
ZX	11:35	63000	30
A	11:40	62500	30
ZX	12:48	62000	30
A	12:53	61750	30
ZX	12:57	61700	30
A	13:00	61500	30
ZX	13:29	61000	30
A	13:33	60750	50
ZX	13:39	60500	50
A	13:45	60250	50
ZX	14:00	59500	50

Appendix 2

Savings and revenue from e-procurement solution

Evaluated attribute	Value SKK
(1) Savings from purchasing prices (for production)	1510722
(2) Savings from purchasing prices (for administration)	46416
Interest from (1)	22890.80
Interest from (2)	534.14
Interest earned from maturity date savings (for production)	61409.43
Total financial yield from e-procurement solution (V)	**1641972.40**

Appendix 3

Account assets of e-procurement solution

Account assets of e-procurement solution	Values in SKK
Tangible property	600000.-
Intangible property	1500000.-
Depreciation	525000.-
Carrying costs	0.-
Model's carrying costs	1500000.-

Appendix 4

Calculated indicators

	2.5% procurement intensity	80% procurement intensity
EVA (Economic Value Added)	573248	33863630
$EVA_{performance}$	36.4%	2150%
M'$_r$ – revenue growth	**1.75%**	**92.5%**
M'$_{ref}$ – CashFlow growth	**0.33%**	**9.92%**
Level of e-assets M_{vA}	**0.06%**	**1.07%**
Level of virtuality M_o	0.046%	0.67%
Economic value added (EVA) is a financial performance method to calculate the true economic profit of a corporation. EVA can be calculated as net operating after taxes profit minus a charge for the opportunity cost of the capital invested. (For more details see Grant, 2002) *Growth indicators are described as (Actual Indicator / Last Indicator) – 1 and present growth of indicator because of e-solution implementation.*		

Appendix 5

Indicators for comparison outsourced and internal solution

Comparison outsourced and internal solution (OUT / IN) (assumption: 1.5% transactions fees):				
	2.5% intensity		80% intensity	
ROC	**469.3%** / -25.8%		435.3% / **2343%**	
CROC	**333.2%** / -		309% / **1688.6%**	
IRR	152973128500 (!!!) / 401.16			
NPV10%	73351547 / **87773208**			
	1st year	2nd year	3rd year	4th year
CFe OUT	962777	29671894	33433120	33433120

Appendix 6a

Economic results from annual report '02

Income Statement	in thousand of Sk
	31.12.2002
Revenues from merchandise sold	546 549
Cost of sales	504 553
Gross profit	41 996
Production	3 127 609
Revenues from own products and services	2 884 210
Change in inventory	17 903
Capitalization	225 496
Production consumption	1 158 247
Value added	2 011 358
Staff costs	1 614 545
Taxes and fees	11 400
Depreciation and amortization expense	313 104
Usage and canceling of reserves and accounting for provisions to operating revenues	18 354
Additions to reserves and provisions to operating expenses	23 763
Other operating income	1 906 360
Other operating expenses	1 868 398
Operating loss	104 175
Finance income	82 724
Finance costs	173 487
Usage and canceling of reserves and accounting for provisions to finance income	4 335
Additions to reserves and provisions to finance costs	16 864
Finance loss	-103 292
Tax expense from operating activities - due	18 709
Tax expense from operating activities - deferred	384
Loss from operating activities	-17 523
Extraordinary revenues	6 322
Extraordinary expenses	80 197
Tax expense from extraordinary activities - due	-15 785
Loss from extraordinary activities	-58 090
Net loss	-75 613

continued on next page

Appendix 6b

Economic results from annual report '02 continued

Balance Sheet		in thousand of Sk
		31.12.2002
	TOTAL ASSETS	**4 730 745**
A.	Equity subscription receivable	0
B.	Non-current assets	3 581 641
B.I.	Long-term intangible assets	15 199
B.II.	Long-term tangible assets	3 375 933
B.III.	Long-term financial assets	190 509
C.	Current assets	1 047 172
C.I.	Inventory	174 865
C.II.	Long-term receivables	693
C.III.	Short-term receivables	769 085
C.IV.	Financial assets	102 530
D.	Prepayments and accrued income	101 932
	TOTAL EQUITY AND LIABILITIES	**4 730 745**
A.	Equity	3 572 100
A.I.	Registered capital	3 002 467
A.II.	Capital funds	645 246
A.III.	Funds created from net profits	0
A.IV.	Retained earnings	0
A.V.	Net loss	-75 613
B.	Liabilities	1 092 076
B.I.	Provisions	103 734
B.II.	Long-term payables	96 740
B.III.	Short-term payables	598 279
B.IV.	Bank loans	293 323
C.	Accruals and deferred income	66 569

continued on next page

Appendix 6c

Economic results from annual report '02 continued

Indicators Characterizing Company's Activities		
		2002
Total coal production	tonnes	2 786 033
Sorted coal	tonnes	402 512
Energetic coal	tonnes	2 383 521
Coal sales total	tonnes	2 787 581
Sorted coal	tonnes	401 728
of which: internal market	tonnes	306 303
other supply	tonnes	95 425
Energetic coal	tonnes	2 385 853
of which: Nováky Power Plant	tonnes	2 005 497
other supply	tonnes	380 356
Advance workings	metres	16 965
Revenues total	thousand SKK	5 692 253
Expenses total	thousand SKK	5 392 150
Profit and loss before tax	thousand SKK	-72 305
Income taxes	thousand SKK	3 308
Net profit	thousand SKK	-75 613
Number of employees	empl.	6 183
Average wages	empl./month	15 306
Labour productivity from mining	SKK/empl./month	37,55
Labour productivity from value added	SKK/empl./month	27 109

Appendix 7

Impact of Web based procurement (Delina 2003)

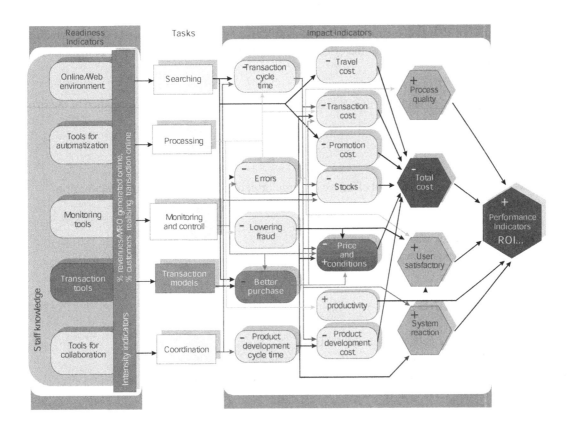

IMPLICATIONS FOR PRACTITIONERS[1]

Title: Reverse Auction Impact on Mining Company

Description

This chapter is a case study on the implementation of reverse auctions in a mining company. A major problem is the use of ROI as a metric for performance on the auction as it is not a good performance metric. The authors review, not only the effects on the business, but also reach some conclusions on the use of auctions.

A useful diagram of the impacts of various factors in a reverse auction on the performance of the firm is included.

Findings

- Reverse auctions are useful and effective on large or dominant firms with large purchasing volumes.
- Purchase prices were decreased by 7.5%.
- Investment payback was up to one year.
- Company performance was improved.

RECOMMENDATIONS

- Be sure to measure performance and savings.
- If financial metrics are use, the use of intelligent agents is possible.
- Be sure to train personnel on the use of the auction and its implementation.

LIMITATIONS

- This is a single case and the findings may not be generalized.

ENDNOTE

[1] Note that this section was written by D. H. Parente, Editor of Best Practices for Online Procurement Auctions, in order to be consistent with other chapters and provide value to practitioners reading the volume.

Chapter XVIII
A Reverse Auction Case Study:
The Final Chapter

Andrew Stein
Victoria University, Australia

Paul Hawking
Victoria University, Australia

David C. Wyld
Southeastern Louisiana University, USA

ABSTRACT

The reverse auction tool has evolved to take advantage of Internet technology and has been identified by many large organisations as a tool to achieve substantial procurement savings. As companies adopt this technology it is important for them to understand the implications of this type of procurement. This chapter re-visits a reverse auction event and discusses the impacts the reverse auction format had upon all participants involved in the auction. In late 2001 a small Australian supplier of transport and logistics services was asked to participate in a reverse auction for services they had provided for 5 years to a multi-national organisation. They were not successful in retaining their contract position and this chapter looks at the reverse auction and its business impacts 2 years after the initial auction. The case study is viewed through the eyes of the winning supplier, losing supplier, auction vendor, and buyer. The main outcomes show that the reverse auction struggles to adapt to fluid business conditions and is limited if it is used as only a price fixing mechanism. It did not engender co-operative supply chains or win-win situations between the auction players.

INTRODUCTION

Today, organisations spend over US$20 trillion globally on external goods and services, and thus, the supply chain is now the focus in cost reduction and efficiency increase (Minahan, 2001). As more and more innovative applications are developed, electronic commerce has increasingly adopted an ever-widening definition. One recent application that has sought the "e" treatment is procurement. Minahan (2001) defined e-procurement as:

The process of utilising Web-based technologies to support the identification, evaluation, negotiation, and configuration of optimal groupings of trading partners into a supply chain network, which can then respond to changing market demands with greater efficiency. (Minahan, 2001)

Activities that could be applied to the e-procurement process include:

- Advertisement of tenders
- Electronic submission of tenders
- Electronic ordering
- Internet sourcing via third parties
  Electronic mail between buyers and sellers
- Electronic mail in contract management
- Research into supplier markets
- Integration of procurement within the financial and inventory systems

Accordingly, there are a plethora of tools that have been developed to support these business activities. As organisations extend the reach of their information systems into the supply chain, e-procurement has become a driving force for achieving substantial cost savings. One mechanism that facilitates e-procurement is the reverse online auction. Reverse online auctions are delivered by intermediaries, many of whom promise to deliver savings of up to 20% for the buying organisations. The rhetoric of B2B collaboration

has "win-win" scenarios for all who participate in online auctions. But is this true? This chapter will re-visit a case study of an Australian reverse online auction asking the basic questions: what long-term impacts resulted from the original reverse auction? It will analyse the online auction from all viewpoints, questioning the value proposition of the reverse online auction as a tool in B2B e-commerce.

The Growth Of E-Procurement

Many research organisations predict massive growth in the B2B market. Bowles (2000) saw the global B2B market growing to US$968 million in 2002 and then US$1.551 billion in 2004. Yet, these figures pale into insignificance when considering other market analysts, predictions:

- **Gartner:** $US2.9 trillion by 2003
- **AMR:** $US5.7 trillion by 2004
- **Forrester:** $US7.29 trillion by 2004 (Diba, 2001; Hersch, 2000; Regan, 2001)

These predictions should be accepted with caution, however. In a recent article in *Management Research News,* Wyld (2002) cautions that we are entering the end of the "trough of disillusionment" phase of e-business, where exponential gains in efficiencies and cost reductions will be replaced with incremental progress. Yet, there does seem to be a sea change in how procurement is conducted in organisations. B2B has promised - and delivered in many instances - to drive costs down and streamline procurement operations (McGarvey, 2000). In fact, Metcalfe et al. (2001) predicted that European companies could achieve a 50% gain in productivity through adopting Internet-enabled B2B processes by 2010. Wyld (2000) developed an e-procurement model, presented in Figure 1, looking at the totality of the e-procurement process, from drivers through impact to imperatives. The model demonstrates some of the changes that are affecting the e-procurement value chain.

Organisations on the buying and selling side will need to address these challenges to capture both the tactical cost control and the more strategic market developments. One of the critical aspects will be decisions regarding buyers' employment of and sellers' participation in online auctions.

The Auction Economy

Batsone (1999) asked the question whether in the future, what if the price of everything would be negotiable? We have grown accustomed – both in the business and consumer marketplace – to the concept of market prices. Yet, at the heart of the auction economy is the concept of pricing, and more importantly, dynamic pricing. Dynamic pricing simply means that a good or service is priced according to what the market determines. The Web introduces the element of real-time pricing and further elevates the importance of personal price elasticities. Customers will determine the

price, depending upon the price/value trade-off. No longer is the supply/demand model determining price. Rather, a more complicated, customer-centric price/value trade-off determines pricing (Batsone, 1999). Many service-based companies use this principle when they have multiple – and sometimes hundreds – of price points for the one product, most notably airlines and hotels.

O'Malley (1998) saw the Web being "a giant bidding war," and Queree (2000) commented that online auctions were fast becoming a mainstream business model. The auction model has settled into the B2B marketplace and has been developed for various e-government applications (NSW, 2001). Wyld (2000) saw the auction model being adaptable for use in:

* Procurement
* Disposition of used assets
* Internal corporate management

Figure 1. The Wyld (2000) e-procurement model.

Drivers	Impacts	Imperatives
Fast pace of tech innovation	Shift of power from suppliers to buyers	Internal linkage between supply chain & portal
Economic Globalisation		Develop online supplier qualification
Rapid growth of e-business portal sector	Market makers increasing competition	Leverage suppliers into e-portal marketplaces
Large organisations become market makers		Develop vertical markets to force B2B and lower costs
Vertical trading communities	New product & services requirements	Build strategic alliances between e-commerce players
Demand for B2B solutions		

Source: Wyld (2000, p. 4).

There are several differing auction formats used in online auctions, including:

- English
- Yankee
- Dutch
- Sealed bid
- Vickrey
- Forward and Reverse Auctions (Wyld, 2000)

Kafka et al (2000) predicted that by 2004, $US 746 billion of business will be conducted through online auction models, based on dynamic pricing.

Reverse Auctions For E-Procurement

While many first think of eBay and *forward auctions* (where prices rise) when the subject of online auctions is discussed, *reverse auctions* play an important role in e-procurement strategies. In fact, growing numbers of firms worldwide, led by the global Fortune 1000 companies, have successfully used online auctions as a tool to reduce prices for goods and services (Emiliani, 2000). One of the pioneers of online B2B auctions for e-procurement is Freemarkets, which was established in 1995 and launched their online auction site in 1999. To date, they have conducted auctions involving more than 19,000 suppliers from more than 70 countries worth $US 30 billion (Freemarkets, 2002).

In the first quarter of 2000, they conducted auctions involving 47 Fortune 500 buyers and 4,000 suppliers (Freemarkets, 2002). Mayne Group, one of Australia's leading companies with major interests in health care and logistics, signed a 3-year deal in 2000 with Freemarkets to manage their procurement and operate online auctions. Other major B2B auction facilitators include:

Table 1. The reverse auction process

Step	Activities
1) Market Made (Client focus)	Make market (specifications)
	Identify Suppliers

2) Pre-Qualification (Supplier Focus)	Pre-Award Review
	    Contract/schedule, Specifications
	    Ability to deliver, Quality assurance
	    Past performance, Responsibilities
	    Set-up technicals

	Approved suppliers listing
	Identify specific terms & conditions
	Invite suppliers

3) Pre Auction Planning (Client/Supplier)	Set up Auction
	    Create auction content, Set-up security
	    Register bidders, Ensure readiness
	    Contingency planning

	Supplier Auction Strategy

4) Auction Activity (Supplier)	Conduct Auction
	    Suppliers bid real-time, Buyers monitors auction
	    Winners selected, Contingencies ready

5) Post Auction (Client)	Contract write-up

Source: Adapted from Buyers.gov, 2000.

- Ariba
- CommerceOne
- Andale
- Elcom.com
- Procuree
- Verticalnet

The B2B auction facilitators usually work with buyers to select bidders to participate in each auction, develop specifications in detail, and tailor the bidding process to the situation. This service is billed to buyers accordingly. There could be additional costs, based on a percentage of the anticipated savings (Messmer, 2000). Freemarkets (2002) promotes the ability of their auction format to decrease service prices by 16-18% and goods by 2-3%. The reverse auction process involves intensive work on behalf of the buyer and market maker to structure the bidding process and prepare suppliers for qualification. This process is represented in Table 1.

Reverse Auctions: State of Play

A recent comprehensive report by the CAPS Research Group (Beall et al., 2003) detailed the landscape for the operation and success for reverse auctions. The report recognises that reverse auctions are controversial and are implemented for many reasons:

- Get buyers and sellers to interact in a real-time Internet enabled world
- Recognise that service quality and product quality are "givens"
- Massive cost savings are possible

- ROI is rapid with reverse auction tools
- Cycle-time savings in the procurement process are significant
- Buyers can reach more suppliers and thereby increase competitive advantage

Whilst the literature shows rapid acceptance of the reverse auction format there are several impediments to the successful operation of reverse auctions:

- Unfamiliarity of the new procurement process and methodology.
- False premise that price is the only determinant of the reverse auction.
- Potential that the reverse auction will diminish buyer/supplier value trust network.

Reverse auctions are still in their formative years. Organisations are only now implementing their second and third iterations of reverse auctions. Issues to do with ethical use of reverse auctions and business viability of the reverse auction format are being developed. There is no doubt that the reverse auction tool is becoming part of mainstream procurement operations as shown in Table 2 (ISM, 2002).

Beall (2003, p. 60) concludes by mentioning the acceptance and potential impact that reverse auctions can have and makes the following points:

- Definite acceptance for highly standardized products and services
- Reported payback after a few uses of reverse auctions

Table 2. Use of online reverse auctions for procurement.

	Q1-2001	Q2-2001	Q3-2001	Q4-2001	Q1-2002	Q2-2002	Q3-2002	Q4-2002
All Companies	15.8%	15.0%	20.4%	17.4%	23.1%	20.2%	22.4%	18.8%

Source Data: ISM/Forrester. (2002). Reports on e-Business.

- Little evidence of reverse auctions harming buyer/supplier value trust network
- Late adopters rushing to catch first adopters
- Ethical concerns are less than existing negotiations practices
- Predicted growth of reverse auctions into the future

REVERSE AUCTION CASE STUDY

Methodology

The primary objective of this chapter was to return after 2 years to a study of an Australian example (Stein et al., 2003) of reverse auction procurement and analyse the auction process and outcomes. Whilst the growth of the reverse auction has been marked in recent years few studies have looked at long-term impacts of the process. The viewpoints of the winning and losing suppliers, auction vendor and buyer will be presented, as there is a dearth of literature of long-term case studies of participants in an online auction. This analysis will be presented as a case study. More specifically, the research question to be addressed in this study is: What are the long-term business impacts of the online auction?

Case study research methodology was used in this research, as this project represented an exploratory look at implications of reverse online auctions. Yin (1994, p. 35) emphasises the importance of asking "what" when analysing information systems. Yin goes further and emphasises the need to study contemporary phenomena within real-life contexts. Walsham (2000, p. 204) supports case study methodology and sees a need for a move away from traditional information systems research methods, such as surveys, toward more interpretative case studies, ethnographies and action research projects. Several works (Benbasat et al., 1987; Chan & Roseman, 2001; Lee, 1989)

have used case studies in presenting information systems case-study research. Cavaye (1996) used case study research to analyse inter-organisational systems and the complexity of information systems. The data collection process for the present research included:

- Examination of existing documentation
- Content analysis of e-mail
- Interview of actors
- Direct observations

The initial auction event was analysed (Stein et al., 2003) from the supplier organisation's viewpoint but this analysis will have emphasis on all participants and outcomes of the event.

The Initial Reverse Auction

In April 2001, AusBuyer[1] commissioned Auction.com to make a market for the logistics component of their manufacturing activities. The market was broken down into 19 channels, both state and nationally based. AusSupplier received notification that a contract that it had partially carried out for 5 years was to be auctioned on the Internet. AusSupplier started a 6-month exploration into online auctions and B2B procurement. Considerable time and financial resources were expended to first learn about and then to participate in a reverse online auction.

The Participants

AusSupplier is a micro-business, having two full-time and five part-time consultants. It is an "infomediary," or - in older parlance - a "middleman". AusSupplier turns over $AUD10 million and has a small client base. The role of the "infomediary" is to win a contract for packing and exporting commodities into the Asian marketplace. AusSupplier wins a contract from a large manufacturer (AusBuyer) and then negotiates transport and rates from shipping organisations. The commodity that was to be auctioned was worth about $AUD1.6 million per year. Currently, AusSupplier was responsible for about 20% of the contract, with a major transport company being responsible for the other 80%.

Auction.Com is a multi-national, market leading e-commerce company, specialising in e-procurement and auctions. It has about 1,000 employees worldwide and operates for about 140 large multi-national clients. It has conducted about $US 21 billion in auctions, resulting in savings of about $US 6 billion. It is obvious when looking at Auction.Com and AusSupplier, the difference in size, technology and more importantly, the chasm in understanding e-business.

AusBuyer is an Australian manufacturer that is part of a global organization, based in the United States. The global organisation was undergoing financial strain, due to the poor commodities market worldwide. In order to reduce costs AusBuyer turned to Auction.Com to conduct a number of auction events. This case study outlines the first of over 300 auction events conducted over the last two by Auction.com for Ausbuyer.

The Auction Process

The auction event was an Australia-wide procurement exercise, focusing on logistics and transport services. The entire procurement operation of AusBuyer was placed in 19 lots, with each lot undergoing a 1.5-hour auction. For AusSupplier the auction event went through five stages:

1. Market-made (client)
2. Pre-qualification (supplier)
3. Pre-auction planning & strategy (client/supplier)
4. Conduct auction (supplier)
5. Post-auction (client)

Stage 1

In stage 1 (Market-made), AusSupplier undertook research into the reverse auction process, and then received a CD containing Web-based bidding software and documentation from the manufacturer. This documentation consisted of over 50 files: tender documents, quote spreadsheets, specifications and information sheets. It was updated four times before the final auction. Initially, the deluge of information was overwhelming.

I have spent hours retrieving, printing, reading and just trying to make sense of the process. (Managing Director, AusSupplier, May 2001)

At this stage, considerable effort was expended to determine if AusSupplier could participate in more than one channel (auction). It was felt that other channels, including some interstate, could be bid for. However, a more conservative approach was adopted, due to uncertainty about the online auction process.

Stage 2

Stage 2, (pre-qualification), involves Auction.Com and AusBuyer weeding out non-performing suppliers. Yet, at the same time, they are trying to ensure an adequate number of bidders to be able to create the auction dynamic. AusSupplier had no idea how many other companies had pre-qualified; it only learned of the exact number at the auction event. Pre-qualification also introduces some financial parameters for the event. Auction.Com set the switching price at $AUD1.3million; that is, the price when AusBuyer would consider awarding the contract away from the existing supplier. Market research by AusSupplier showed the existing contract was worth $AUD 1.6million. The difference between the price of switching to a new supplier and the existing contract price was about 18%. This figure is similar to the figure quoted in the advertising material by Auction. Com, which quotes savings of 18%.

AusSupplier again had expended considerable resources at this stage:

- 2 site visits
- 4 sub-contractor meetings
- 200 phone calls
- 45 e-mails out
- 15 e-mails in
- 30 hours of managing director time
- 20 hours of consultants' time

Thus, the bill for participating in the reverse auction was climbing. Summarising the financial details thus far:

- AusSuppliers market entry price $AUD 2 million
- Existing contract price $AUD 1.6 million
- Reserve (switching) price $AUD 1.3 million

The AusSupplier's high market entry price ($AUD 2 million) was formulated on the basis of entry into an unknown scenario. It was formulated on the rate of moving the commodity by the tonnages quoted by AusBuyer, with a margin built in. At this stage, it became apparent that the auction format was introducing an element of incredulity to the quoting process.

We are flying in the dark, some cowboy could underbid us and have no real idea of what is involved in the job.... (Managing Director, AusSupplier, June 2001)

AusSupplier had no idea of how many others bidders there were, no idea of their market entry point and only one Auction.Com tutorial on a simulated auction. Being pre-qualified and

waiting for the auction became quite stressful for the AusSupplier. Questions were raised in regards to:

- What strategy should be adopted?
- What would happen if the power failed, or if the ISP went down?
- What would be the "bottom-line" position?
- Would AusSupplier be swept up in the auction dynamic?
- Who would press the buttons, and would they be able to keep their nerve?

Auction.Com conducted a training session from their Asian headquarters, and AusSupplier personnel had soon mastered the auction interface.

Stage 3

In Stage 3, (Auction Strategy), AusSupplier developed three strategies for the auction:

- Entry strategy
- Middle strategy
- End strategy

The *entry* strategy was to come in at the high pre-qualification bid after about 3 minutes and then watch the market develop. The *middle* strategy was to maintain control on the screen and drive the bids down in a controlled manner. During the auction event, AusSupplier would not know who were responsible for the other bids. The only strategy for the end was to be in the "*end game*," and if they did not have the lowest bid, then, at least, they would be under the switching cost at the end. It was believed that this would show AusBuyer that AusSupplier was a serious bidder. It was stated that AusBuyer was not under any obligation to accept the lowest bid. AusSupplier had seen sample auction events, and they knew the "*end game*" was frantic.

Stage 4

Stage 4, (auction), was delayed a week with a late flurry of updates and clarifications. Finally, the day of the auction arrived and at 10:33 a.m. AusSupplier pressed the bid accept button to indicate they were part of the event. Within 5 seconds, AusSupplier's early and middle strategies were destroyed. The screen showed there were three other bidders, with one bidder right on the switching price ($AUD 1.3 million). This was felt to be a ploy to scare off other bidders and AusSupplier was confident that this was the existing contractor, who had 80% of the existing contract. After about half an hour, another bidder entered and soon started to drive the bidding price down further. AusSupplier's strategy was to drive down the bids to the reserve price. As the scheduled auction time was nearing completion the bidding intensified and AusSupplier's phones were put on hold. A bid in the last minute extends the auction minute-by-minute. There were three bidders left. There was tension in AusSupplier personnel as the low price previously agreed upon was passed. This resulted in the staff member in front of the computer handing over control to the managing director.

The auction entered the phase that Auction. Com refers to as the *"auction dynamic,"* the dynamic that drives the price down even further. In fact, the reserve was driven down $90,000 in 7 minutes. The number of bids in the last 7 minutes tripled all bids in the previous 1.5 hours. The managing director became caught up in the auction dynamic, as he did not want to lose to the other bidders. AusSupplier's lowest bid was based on an agreed upon margin of 12%, but this was reduced to 5% towards the end of the auction.

AusSupplier did not win the auction, but that did not mean that they had not won the contract. They were in the game at the end, and they were determined to drive the market down to inflict some pain on the other bidders.

Stage 5

In Stage 5, (post-auction), AusSupplier was told that they would have to wait 5 weeks for the result. However, the answer came much earlier. AusSupplier was unsuccessful; they had lost the 20% of the contract that they had owned previously. The managing director took about 2 weeks to get over losing to the competition. There are several issues that need to be discussed concerning the winners and losers of reverse auction e-procurement.

DISCUSSION

What Are the Long-Term Business Impacts of the Online Auction

A full case study analysis of the auction event is described in Stein et al. (2003). The following analysis will focus on the long-term business impacts as experienced by all participants of the initial auction.

The Auction Vendor: Auction.com

So, who benefited initially from the auction event and was this benefit maintained over the course of the contract? Auction.com was the big winner by gaining their initial consulting fees for setting up the auction event and also a percentage of the savings from AusBuyer. They also used this auction event to demonstrate their auction technology to other large Australian companies. They were very successful in demonstrating their ability to achieve savings and this resulted in them conducting 300 reverse auctions for Ausbuyer in the following year. Many organisations have moved to reduce the cost of the reverse auction by moving from using auction vendors in an ASP format to conducting their own auctions (Beall et al., 2003, p. 8) on site.

One year after the auction, Auction.com (Rawlings, 2002) commented on the processes, transparency and fairness of reverse auctions. It is hard to argue with the auction vendor, as the growth in reverse auction has been significant (Beall et al., 2003:31). Auction.com did acknowledge the challenging nature of the reverse auction process but still felt that both suppliers and buyers were in a win-win situation. Auction.com commented on the acceptance of the reverse auction process by suppliers who appreciated the transparent nature of the process and the widening of markets for suppliers. It is interesting to note the impact of the reverse auction on middleman suppliers. In the case described above (Stein et al., 2003), the auction vendor was able to prune 20% from the contract price whilst charging something up to 20% for their fees. The sum effect is a transfer of profit margin from the supplier to the auction vendor and it is hard to imagine a more effective Internet enabled business strategy.

Beall et al. (2003, p. 11) point to the effect that changing external economic conditions can have on the effectiveness of the reverse auction format. The buyer is using the reverse auction tool to magnify their competitive advantage over their suppliers. The more suppliers the better, but what happens if the supply market tightens and suppliers have competitive advantage over buyers? Beall suggests that suppliers might then conduct forward auctions to sell their capacity to buyers. Again the auction vendor may be able to intercede and transfer buyer margin into auction vendor fees.

The original auction event as described above specified a contract length of 2 years; would a reverse auction be sustainable a second or third time? Would the auction vendor get a substantial fee for a claimed saving of another 20% on repeated buys? As described below the contract in this case lasted only 6 months before the commercial conditions were substantially changed. The auction vendor

was not penalised even though they play a major role in setting the market in the first stage of the reverse auction process. Indeed the more unsettled external market conditions render potential for auction.com to conduct more auctions.

The Winning Supplier

The auction produced one clear-cut winner, or did it? The winning supplier, prior to the auction, had 80% of the contract at a price of $AUD 1.28 million. They won the full contract at approximately the same price. Thus, they garnered 20% more work for a nominal extra margin. They did dispel the competing supplier and became the preferred supplier. As the winning supplier was a large national transport company and the losing supplier was an SME it is felt that the winning supplier took a loss-leader position to win the contract.

In the initial contract the predicted product tonnage was specified. Six months after the auction event additional logistics facilities became available to Ausbuyer, and they began to move products without using the winning supplier. The initial product specification in the RFQ was changed substantially. Would the winning or losing supplier be able to have redress in terms of changing contracts? Perhaps, but in the commercial environment where powerful multi-national buyers are using smaller suppliers the buyer dictates changes in contract conditions.

Two years after the initial auction, business circumstances have returned to those existing before the auction. The winning supplier has about 90% of the contract while the losing supplier has regained about 10%. Rates are as set in the reverse auction and essentially this example of a reverse auction had only two winners, Ausbuyer and Auction.com. Beall et al. (2003, p. 10) point to the use of reverse auctions for indirect and direct procurement for commodity-like products. Services or products that are irregular or subject to frequent change do not lend themselves for reverse auction formats; these could include:

- Design services
- Repair services
- Emergency deliveries
- Sudden surges in product demand

The dramatic change in product tonnages and changed transport options meant that the reverse auction was originally deciding a 2-year contract when in reality it was only a 6-month contract period. So would it be viable to conduct an auction every time the contract conditions changed markedly, or would Ausbuyer go back to the original suppliers and negotiate new terms and conditions? If negotiations are used, and Beall et al. (2003, p. 11) suggest they are, then the reverse auction again reverts to a price fixing role with more complex negotiations necessary to complete the contract. Does this then affect the claim by Auction.com that the new reverse auction process is all-encompassing and transparent?

The Losing Supplier

There were four losing bidders. AusSupplier had 20% of the contract prior to the auction but lost all entitlements to the contract. This was devastating to AusSupplier. At the time of the auction the AusSupplier management team pondered whether there would be a price to pay when the contract lapses and a premium paid to bring in another supplier to complete the contract. Indeed this is precisely what happened 18 months into the contract. The winning supplier could not service the contract with respect to margin and product tonnages. Ausbuyer contacted AusSupplier and asked that they again fulfil the role that they had prior to the reverse auction.

Another issue that AusSupplier had to contend with was the low availability of new markets that Auction.com had said would eventuate for suppliers. In 2 years only one potential new business

opportunity was sourced for AusSupplier through Auction.com. This opportunity was non-viable as it was in a product area that AusSupplier had no expertise in. The greatest impact for AusSupplier is in the area of supplier-buyer relations. Over a period of 2 years the trust that had been developed over a period of 15 years had been eroded; all together, the auction inspired a drop of 12% in margin. Was it worth the potential savings? Beall (2003, p. 11) indicates many suppliers drop previously "free" services because they are not value adding for them, or not affordable. Goodwill and trust are negated in favour of the letter of the contract and the last 30-minute drop in price as observed in the reverse auction. The price focus of the auction again seems to dominate accepted long-term business practices.

The Buyer

In the initial auction AusBuyer appeared to be the big winner, with a tangible savings of a 20% reduction in the cost of the contract. There were minimal switching costs, as they awarded the contract to the company who held the majority (80%) of the contract previously. However, from this Auction.com's costs need to be subtracted. An intangible benefit was the pre-qualifying process that identified future suitable suppliers. It appears the pre-qualifying process was flawed in one of the other auction events conducted on the same day when only one supplier was identified and this was the existing contractor. The auction event still went ahead and resulted in a 5% increase in the contract cost. In this case, the auction dynamic was missing, and therefore, no savings were made. AusBuyer used the reverse auction process over 300 times in the next year. There can be no doubt that reverse auctions can provide a value adding business process in the procurement area. Beall (2003, p. 11) supports this analysis when he comments on the benefit of reverse auctions to buyers:

For a growing number of buying firms, e-Reverse auctions have found an appropriate niche in their strategic sourcing toolkit, allowing them to efficiently source goods and services that are highly standardized, have sufficient spend volume, can be replicated by a reasonable number of qualified competitors, and have insignificant switching costs. (Beall et al., 2003, p. 13)

CONCLUSION

Many analysts (e.g., Deise et al., 2000; Wyld, 2000) believe that the use of the Internet - as a medium for business - provides the opportunity for companies to restructure their supply chains in collaboration with the other supply chain partners. One of the imperatives in the e-procurement model proposed by Wyld (2000) was to build strategic alliances between business partners. This involves both buyers and vendors, working collaboratively to provide cost efficiencies and add value to products and services. Many believe that this strategic collaboration is *essential* to survive in the e-world. This is the premise of the Value Trust Network (VTN). Raisch (2001) sees the supply chain being enhanced by the established relationships between buyers and suppliers, not just by the adoption of Internet technology. If reverse auction e-procurement is to enhance enterprise competitiveness, then value must be delivered to ease industry pain points, with trust being enhanced between suppliers and buyer (Emiliani & Stec, 2002; Jap, 2000; Raisch, 2001).

The question that needs to be asked is to what extent does a reverse online auction contribute to this value and trust? The whole issue of driving costs down to the lowest possible level would seem to present a serious impediment to the creation of any value *or* trust (Bartholomew, 2001). The attributes and skills that buyers would like to foster in their suppliers are placed at a lower priority to price. Mozer (2002) questions the elevation of cost savings over service offerings, suggesting

that buyers should be looking for the fairest price for the supplier of choice, rather than the lowest offer. Do companies really want their business to run on the lowest price?

Emiliani and Stec (2002) proposed several unresolved questions in their recent study of reverse auctions:

- Where do the cost savings come from?
- Are reverse auctions one-time events?
- Will online auction vendors replace the in-house buying function?
- Is there a conflict between supply chain management and online auctions?
- Do online auctions actually increase productivity?

The reverse auctioning method may indeed only be a short-term solution in a business world that is increasingly based on long-term alliances and partnerships. Whilst Rapport (1998) believes that a reverse online auction is only a "quick fix" to satisfy management objectives for increased shareholder value, Beall (2003) points to the reverse auction being one tool applicable for specific circumstances. Driving forces include the speedy ROI of reverse auction and the overall shortening of the whole procurement cycle.

In the case study presented in this chapter, the reverse auction:

- Did render massive cost savings
- Did replace existing in-house procurement
- Did increase supplier distrust
- Did have massive impacts on the suppliers, buyers and auction vendor
- Showed that price alone will not replace trust and negotiation in complex business interactions

REFERENCES

Bartholomew, D. (2001, September). Co$t vs. quality. *Industry Week, 34.*

Batsone, D. (1999). Going once, going twice. *Business 2, 4*(5), 141.

Beall, S., Carter, C., Carter, P., Germer, T., Hendrick, T., Jap, S. et al. (2003). *The role of reverse auctions in strategic sourcing.* CAPS Focus Study, Institute of Supply Management and W.P. Carey School of Business.

Benbasat, I., Goldstein, D., & Mead, M. (1987). The case research strategy in studies of information systems. *MIS Quarterly, 11*(3), 215-218.

Bowles, J. (2000). eMarketplaces: How digital marketplaces are shaping the future of B2B commerce. *Forbes, 166*(3), s20-s56.

Cavaye, A. (1996). Case study research: A multi-faceted approach for IS. *Information Systems Journal, 6*(3), 227-242.

Chan, R., & Roseman, M. (2001). Integrating knowledge into process models—A case study. *Proceedings of the Twelfth Australasian Conference on Information Systems,* Southern Cross University, Australia.

Deise, M., Nowikow, C., King, P., & Wright, A. (2000). *Executive's guide to e-business from tactics to strategy.* New York: PriceWaterhouseCoopers, John Wiley & Sons.

Diba, A. (2000). The B2B boom: What's what. *Fortune, 141*(10), 142.

Emiliani, M. (2000). Business-to-business online auctions: Key issues for purchasing process improvement. *Supply Chain Management, 5*(4), 176-186.

Emiliani, M., & Stec, D. (2001). Squaring online reverse auctions with the CAUX round table: Principles for business. *Supply Chain Management, 5*(4), 32-34.

Emiliani, M., & Stec, D. (2002). Realising savings from online reverse auctions. *Supply Chain Management, 7*(1), 12-23.

Freemarkets. (2002). *Why Freemarkets?* Retrieved February 20, 2002, from www.freemarkets.com/benefits/default.asp

Hersch, W. (2000). *Ebusiness: More friend than foe.* Retrieved February 20, 2002, from www.cco-nvergence.com/article/TCM20000728S0002

ISM (Institute for Supply Management)/Forrester. (2002). *Reports on e-business.* Retrieved November 20, 2002, from http://napm.org/isreport/forrester

Jap, S. (2000, November-December). Going-going-gone. *Harvard Business Review, 30.*

Kafka, S., Temkin, B., & Wegner, L. (2000). *B2B auctions go beyond price.* Retrieved February 20, 2002, from http://www.Forrester.com

Lee, A. (1989). Case studies as natural experiments. *Human Relations, 42*(2), 117-137.

McGarvey, R. (2000). From business: To business. *Entrepreneur, 28*(6), 96-100.

Messmer, E. (2000). Defense Dept.'s online auctions spark controversy. Retrieved February 20, 2002, from http://www.mwfusion.com/news/2000/0807reverse.html

Metcalf, D., Meringer, J., & Rehkopf, F. (2001). *Achieving B2B productivity.* Retrieved February 20, 2002, from www.Forrester.com

Minahan, T. (2001). *Strategic e-Sourcing: A framework for negotiating competitive advantage.* Aberdeen Group, Retrieved December 20, 2001, from www.aberdeen.com/ab_company/hottopics/esourcing

Mozer, E. (2002). E-procurement-Successfully using and managing reverse auctions. *Pharmaceutical Technology,* Retrieved October 20, 2002, from http://www.pharmtech.com

NSW. (2001). *E-procurement framework. NSW Government,* Retrieved December 20, 2001, from http://www.cpsc.nsw.gov.au/e-procurement/framework.htm

O'Malley, C. (1998, November). Internet: Do I hear a bid. *Popular Science, 253,* 52.

Queree, A. (2000, March 7). Rosky budness. *Rolling Stone,* 91-92.

Raisch, W. (2001). *The eMarketplace: Strategies for success in B2B eCommerce.* McGraw Hill, New York.

Rapport, A. (1998). *Creating shareholder value.* New York: The Free Press.

Rawlings, C. (2002, August 9). E-mail interview.

Regan, K. (2001). Is big talk a big pain for e-commerce. e*commercetimes,* Retrieved February 20, 2001, from http://www.ecommercetimes.com/perl/story/?id=7160

Stein, A., Hawking, P., & Wyld, D. (2003). The 20% solution: A case study on the efficacy of reverse auctions. *Management Research News, 26*(5), 35-45.

Walsham, G. (2000). Globalisation and IT: Agenda for research. *Organisational and social perspectives on information technology* (pp. 195-210). Boston: Kluwer Academic Publishers.

Wyld, D. (2000). *The auction model. The Price-WaterhouseCoopers Endowment for the Business of Government.* The Business of Government, University of Southern Louisiana.

Wyld, D. (2002). The electric company: How the supply chain is being reinvented through the rapid application of e-procurement processes in the business-to-business arena. *Management Research News,* (in press).

Yin, R. (1994). *Case study research, design and methods* (2nd ed.). Newbury Park: Sage Publications.

ENDNOTE

[1]   All company names are fictionalized.

This work was previously published in E-Commerce and M-Commerce Technologies, edited by P. C. Deans, pp. 230-252, copyright 2005 by IRM Press (an imprint of IGI Global).

IMPLICATIONS FOR PRACTITIONERS[1]

Title: A reverse auction case study: The final chapter

Description

This chapter is a primer for those who want to understand the online reverse auction. The authors return to a case after two. The viewpoints of the winning and losing suppliers, auction vendor and buyer are discussed.

The long-term business impacts of the online auction are discussed.

Findings

- The auction vendor benefited initially from the auction event.
- The winning supplier was able to actually take over more of the business—perhaps acting like a loss leader on the price.
- Two years after the initial event, the business situation with supply has returned to pre-auction conditions.
- With respect to the losing supplier(s), there was only one new business opportunity unlike the claims made by the original supplier.
- With respect to the buyer, there appeared to be a 20% reduction in costs and minimal switching costs. However, switching costs needed to be deducted.

RECOMMENDATIONS

- Firms should be aware of all costs and potential outcomes of the auction process.

CAVEATS

- This is a single study.

ENDNOTE

[1]   Note that this section was written by D. H. Parente, editor of *Best Practices for Online Procurement Auctions*, in order to be consistent with other chapters and provide value to practitioners reading the volume.

Section V
A Review of the Literature

Chapter XIX
Reverse Auctions:
A Topology and Synopsis of Current Research Efforts

Barbara Sherman
Computer Information Systems – Buffalo State College, USA

Joseph R. Muscatello
Kent State University, USA

ABSTRACT

Online reverse auctions are a relatively new phenomenon in business, although the practice of traditional auctions is centuries old. The online aspect of auctions is an example of a disruptive technology and its impact on the business world. The use of the Internet has changed the face of competition in supply and also changed the way buyers and suppliers interact. This chapter is a topological classification of the current literature on e-procurement auctions with the intent of organizing current and future research in online procurement auctions. Over 200 articles have been abstracted and reviewed. The authors develop three classification frames: content, theory, and methodology. Nineteen content areas are populated, including significant reference to the impact of auctions on the supply chain. In summary, this chapter seeks to increase the topic clarity of current research. The quality of each individual reverse auction paper is not evaluated. However, the classification should stimulate academics to pursue current and new avenues of reverse auction research.

INTRODUCTION

Reverse auctions tout the potential advantages buyers and suppliers can gain by utilizing the efficiencies created via the rapid, expansive growth of B2B transactions and subsequently, a potential for a larger, more open marketplace. However, the adoption of reverse auctions has raised concerns amongst both buyers and suppliers. Reverse auction adopters have been criticized for damaging supplier relationships, excluding ethical considerations, and changing the framework of accepted supply chain management and other tactical and strategic practices.

The reverse auction phenomenon has been both rapid and expansive, in all types and sizes of organizations; however, the theory and practicum development is still in its infancy. Thus, the research on reverse auctions has been furiously trying to "catch up" with the changes in the implementation, teaching, and practice of this technique.

The purpose of this paper is to provide a topological classification of research papers that can be used to further the academic and practitioner understanding of reverse auctions and to stimulate and assist further research efforts. The research to date suggests that many research auction avenues have been explored, and much progress has been made, but it is fragmented and unclassified. This paper seeks to increase the topic clarity of current research. It is not the intent of this effort to determine the usefulness or quality of each individual reverse auction paper. However, it is the intent of this research to stimulate and engage academics and practitioners to pursue current and new avenues of reverse auction research.

CURRENT REVERSE AUCTION RESEARCH AND TEACHING

The use of reverse auctions has gone from theory to reality with the wide spread use of B2B transactions via the Internet. The unprecedented expansion of useful management data has allowed even the smallest organizations to participate in reverse auctions. Because of the rapid expansion in business, most of the knowledge of reverse auctions has come from trial and error reports from actual business transactions. This has left a large void in theory development that researchers are only now beginning to fill.

Current business courses have also suffered due to the lack of research efforts in online reverse auctions. Few business books in operations management, procurement, purchasing, and so on include information about reverse auctions.

Many that do mention reverse auctions do so in elementary terms that are hardly useful to business students. In fairness, some schools and authors have done a significant amount of work to include reverse auctions in their coursework, but in general it is has not been adopted in most curricula to a reasonable level of significance, given its expansion of use in the business world.

This research effort seeks to spur the development of new ideas, tools, and techniques that can be included in future education and training curriculum and course development.

REVERSE AUCTION CATEGORIZATION—TOPICS

We have developed a comprehensive list of 212 articles using two of the most popular bibliographic databases for this topic, Proquest Direct and Elsevier Science Direct. After extensive review, we have categorized them into 19 topical areas. Each paper has been placed into one or more of the research areas based on its core research foci. Key words and phrases have been developed and mapped below to facilitate the organization of this paper and to increase the topological understanding. We have also provided a list of keywords common to the articles in the categories.

Strategies in Reverse Auctions:

- Sourcing strategies
- Synergy to existing strategies
- Equilibrium strategies
- Simulations
- Integration to organizational strategies and mission
- Innovation

Competitive Advantage:

- Strategic and Tactical Advantages
- Monetary, service, or other business outcomes

- Advantages guidelines and principles
- Disadvantages

Competitive Environment:

- New suppliers
- Competitive pressures
- Anti-competitive practices
- Required technology and processes

The Economics of Auctions:

- Goal identification
- Global economic changes
- Economic equilibriums
- Pricing strategies
- Economic models
- Financial models and returns
- Gaming

Negotiation in Online Procurement Auction:

- Savings vs. supplier relationships
- Allocations
- Split rewards
- Trust and security
- Communication complexities
- Non-human interactions
- Contracts

Efficiency in the Auction Process:

- Risk vs. reward
- Multi-attribute bids
- Cost reductions/savings
- Non-price related considerations
- Optimization

Risk or Uncertainty in the Reverse Auction:

- Jeopardizing current practices
- Liabilities
- Legalities
- Error rates

E-Auction Portals and Marketplace:

- New marketplaces
- Changing the dynamics of marketplaces
- E-marketplaces
- New business models
- Global marketplaces
- Exchanges
- Technology

The Product in the Online Reverse Auction:

- Product research and activities in online Reverse auctions

Buyers in the Reverse Auction:

- Buyer only attributes and issues

Buyer-Supplier Relationships (Dyad):

- Buyer-supplier interfaces
- Supplier only attributes and issues
- Buyer-supplier conduct
- Technology and other organizational integrations

Supply Chain Management and the Reverse Auction:

- Supply chain utilization
- Global sourcing and logistics
- Realizing the benefits
- Supply chain integration

Suppliers in the Reverse Auction:

- Supplier only attributes and issues

Ethics in Online Procurement Auctions:

- Perceptions
- Collusiveness and corruption
- Confidentiality

Quality:

- RFQ quality
- Multi-attribute issues
- Scoring models
- Information flows
- Types of auctions

Productivity or Performance Issues:

- Process alignments
- Utilization
- Payback
- Optimization
- Traditional vs. reverse auction comparisons
- Metrics

Auction Outcomes and Implementation:

- Barriers to implementation
- Barriers to participation
- Case study observations
- Decision making issues

Financial Issues in Reverse Auctions:

- Price reductions
- Total acquisition cost reductions
- Competitive pricing
- Percentage savings
- Trends

General or Uncategorized Auction Research:

- Online business communities
- Applications of frameworks

Table 1. Category of research in online reverse auctions

	Number of Citations
Strategies in reverse auctions	47
Competitive advantage:	20
Competitive environment	38
The economics of auctions	61
Negotiation in online procurement auctions	23
Efficiency in the auction process	36
Risk or uncertainty in the reverse auction	16
E-auction portals and marketplace	19
The product in the online reverse auction	28
Buyers in the reverse auction	36
Buyer-supplier relationships (Dyad)	53
Supply chain management and the reverse auction	36
Suppliers in the reverse auction	31
Ethics in online procurement auctions	13
Quality	22
Productivity or performance issues	17
Auction outcomes and implementation	19
Financial issues in reverse auctions	147
General or uncategorized auction research	14

- Case studies on outcomes
- Literature reviews

Table 1 identifies the categories of online procurement auction research as discovered in this research and is a concise presentation of the data above. It also includes the number of citations in each category. As mentioned previously, articles may appear in more than one category due to the foci of specific papers.

Referring to Table 1, financial issues, which include cost, price, and savings, are a large topic of the current research in online procurement auctions. The economics of auctions is also a well-researched topic, which is understandable as economists have long been interested in the topic.

Supply chain researchers have looked at the buyer, the supplier, and the dyad. The perspec-

tive of the product in the auction process is also studied in our set of papers.

Issues such as ethic, e-auction portals, and risk show promise for research. Additionally, productivity and auction implementation should provide a fertile area for publication.

The over 200 papers are categorized into these 19 areas in Appendix A. The classification provides the researcher with data that can be used to set a research agenda.

It is interesting to note that the categories map well to the conceptual research framework as constructed by Parente, Venkataraman, Fizel, & Millet (2004). In that paper, the systems theory approach places the research in an input-process-output framework. Note that in the categorization above, the product, buyer, supplier, and dyad are all included, as they are in the Parente et al. work (2004). This is shown in Figure 1 below.

Figure 1. The restructuring of these topics further identifies areas for future research

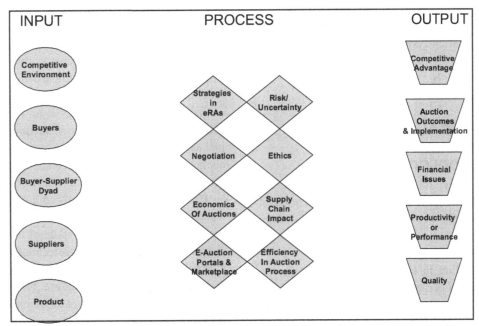

Table 2. Theoretical categorization

	Number of Citations
Economic theory	10
Auction theory	6
Game theory	4
Other theories	13

Table 3. Categorization by methodology

Experiment	14
Simulation	11
Empirical study	10
Field/case study	11
Survey	11

REVERSE AUCTION CATEGORIZATION— THEORETICAL FRAMEWORK

The second categorization of the research maps the papers to a number of theoretical frameworks. The papers are primarily categorized by economic theory, auction theory, and game theory. The other classification includes systems theory, utility theory, decision theory, computation theory, queuing theory, constraint theory, equivalence theory, and the information richness theory.

One look at a research agenda would certainly be to expand the game theory research as well as the "other" category. Use of the information richness theory, for example, would provide an interesting extension of auction research by using an information systems theoretical base.

The papers are shown in this categorization in Appendix B.

REVERSE AUCTION CATEGORIZATION— METHODOLOGY

The third categorization in this paper uses research methodology. In Appendix C, nearly 60 of the papers in our set are categorized by methodology. The array is fairly evenly spread.

According to Reisman and Xu (1992), the even spread of methodology may imply either a growth stage or a more mature stage of knowledge growth. Given the newness of the online environment, we would choose the growth stage. This means that there is room for research in any of the categories.

The papers are categorized by methodology in Appendix C.

FUTURE RESEARCH DIRECTIONS

There are several authors who present a variety of options for future research. Jap (2002) identifies four key aspects for the use of online reverse auctions: (1) the differences from physical auctions and those of the theoretical literature, (2) the conditions for using online reverse auctions, (3) the methods for structuring the auctions, and (4) the evaluations of auction performance. She further offers empirical evidence on these issues and concludes with discussions on three larger issues: cultural differences, ethical behavior, and long-term cost savings.

Jap identifies several issues as an agenda for future research in online reverse auctions. These include the conditions for using online reverse auctions, structuring online reverse auctions, and the evaluation of online reverse auctions.

Parente et al. (2004) identified a conceptual research framework using systems theory. She and her colleagues highlight the issue of increasing data availability given changes in technology. Such availability will allow researchers to adequately test hypotheses in the electronic era. They suggest that hypotheses are developed based on the conceptual research framework. These can be tested for both forward and reverse online auctions.

Carter and his associates (2004) report the results of a large-scale field study of a diverse group of buyers and their suppliers who have participated in reverse auctions. The purpose of their research was to explore implementation and use of electronic reverse auctions with a goal of generating reliable and valid grounded theory through the introduction of hypotheses to help guide future research. Since their study was qualitative, they suggest that additional research is needed to complement and expand on their findings.

Carter et al. (2004) focused on the perspective of the supply management function in the buying organization and the marketing and sales function for the supplier organizations. This area of research holds much promise for investigation.

Future research might tap the perspectives of other functional areas, such as engineering and manufacturing, particularly in the buying organization. Additionally, future research might also tap the perspectives of logistics service providers, as logistics services are frequently subject to electronic reverse auctions. Such research could examine how aspects of the supply chain relationship such as commitment and satisfaction are impacted by the use of electronic reverse auctions to source logistics services.

As the use of electronic reverse auctions becomes more prevalent and as time passes, the opportunity to examine the effect of repeat auctions will become increasingly viable. This could be accomplished through the analysis of archival data from electronic reverse auction providers, as well as by means of an experimental design or survey approach.

Much of the current growth in the electronic reverse auction has occurred during a period of worldwide economic recession, which has offered buyers relatively more power over suppliers. Research also needs to be conducted in a period of relative economic expansion, to see the impact when the roles are more likely to be reversed.

Germer, Carter, and Kaufmann (2004) suggest that additional research is needed to gain evidence on the proposed long-term benefits and concerns of auctions in purchasing (e.g., cycle time reductions, savings, or sourcing performance).

Another research question is raised when we review various work as to how to integrate auctions appropriately in the purchasing toolkit and in an auction-integrated sourcing process. This arena should be of vital interest for both academia and practice.

Cross-national studies are needed to examine similarities and differences that might be of interest in an international and decentralized purchasing organization.

REFERENCES

Carter, C. R., Kaufmann, L., Beall, S., Carter, P. L., Hendrick, T. E., & Petersen, K. J. (2004). Reverse auctions: Grounded theory from the buyer and supplier perspective. *Transportation Research Part E: Logistics and Transportation Review, 40*(3), 229-254.

Germer, T., Carter, P. L., & Kaufmann, L. (2004). *Purchasing auctions: A synthesis of current research.* Paper presented at the 15th Annual North American Research Symposium on Purchasing and Supply Management.

Jap, S. D. (2002). Online reverse auctions: Issues, themes, and prospects for the future. *Academy of Marketing Science Journal, 30*(4), 506-525.

Parente, D. H., Venkataraman, R. R., Fizel, J. F., & Millet, I. (2004). A conceptual research framework for analyzing online auctions in a B2B environment. *Supply Chain Management, An International Journal, 9*(4), 287-294.

Reisman, A., & Xu, X. (1992). On stages of knowledge growth in the management sciences. *IEEE Transactions on Engineering Management, 39*(2), 119-128.

APPENDIX A: REVERSE AUCTION REFERENCES BY CATEGORY

Strategies in Reverse Auctions

Number of Citations: 47

Anon. (2000). G-P selling mills, launches wood e-trade. *International Woodfiber Report, 6*(9), 1.

Anon. (2003). Reverse auction strategies offered. *Official Board Markets, 79*(24), 14.

Anton, J. J., & Yao, D. A. (1989). Split awards, procurement, and innovation. *The Rand Journal of Economics, 20*(4), 538-552.

Anton, J. J., & Yao, D. A. (1992). Coordination in split award auctions. *The Quarterly Journal of Economics, 107*(2), 681-707.

Arnold, U., Karner, H., & Schnabel, M. (2005). Target-oriented use of strategic sourcing tools: A critical analysis creating process awareness for electronic reverse auctions. *Journal of Purchasing and Supply Management, 11*(2-3), 116-128.

Bandyopadhyay, S., Rees, J., & Barron, J. M. (2006). Simulating sellers in online exchanges. *Decision Support Systems, 41*(2), 500-513.

Budde, J., & Gox, R. F. (1999). The impact of capacity costs on bidding strategies in procurement auctions. *Review of Accounting Studies, 4*(1), 5-13.

Carbone, J. (2005). Not just a cost-reduction tool [electronic industry]. *Purchasing, 134*(3), 43-44.

Carter, C. R., Kaufmann, L., Beall, S., Carter, P. L., Hendrick, T. E., & Petersen, K. J. (2004). Reverse auctions: Grounded theory from the buyer and supplier perspective. *Transportation Research Part E: Logistics and Transportation Review, 40*(3), 229-254.

Cox, A., Chicksand, D., Ireland, P., & Davies, T. (2005). Sourcing indirect spend: A survey of current internal and external strategies for non-revenue-generating goods and services. *Journal of Supply Chain Management, 41*(2), 39-51.

Dai, R., Narasimhan, S., & Wu, D. J. (2005). Buyer's efficient e-sourcing structure: Centralize or decentralize? *Journal of Management Information Systems, 22*(2), 141-164.

David, E., Azoulay-Schwartz, R., & Kraus, S. (In press). Bidding in sealed-bid and English multi-attribute auctions. *Decision Support Systems.*

Davis, B. (2006). Digital business: A more consolidated approach [oil industry]. *Petroleum Review, 60*(709), 32-34.

Emiliani, M. L. (2006). Executive decision-making traps and B2B online reverse auctions. *Supply Chain Management, 11*(1), 6-9.

Emiliani, M. L., & Stec, D. J. (2001). Online reverse auction purchasing contracts. *Supply Chain Management, 6*(3/4), 101-105.

Engelbrecht-Wiggans, R., & Katok, E. (2006). E-sourcing in procurement: Theory and behavior in reverse auctions with noncompetitive contracts. *Management Science, 52*(4), 581-596.

Gabert, S. (2003). Are reverse auctions friend or foe? *Printing News, 150*(14), 1-5.

Guilloux, V. (2002). Electronic auctions: An example in the advertising sector. *Décisions Marketing, 27,* 51-71.

Hannon, D. (2003). E-sourcing: CAPS research study defines staying power of e-auctions. *Purchasing, 132*(12), 48-49.

Hartley, J. L., Duplaga, E. A., & Lane, M. D. (2005). Reverse e-auctions: Exploring reasons for use and buyer's satisfaction. *International Journal of Integrated Supply Management, 1*(4), 410-420.

Hatton, J., & Young, B. (2004). Are e-auctions a good way to buy services? *Supply Management*, 28-29.

Hohner, G., Rich, J., Ng, E., Reid, G., Davenport, A. J., Kalagnanam, J. R., et al. (2003). Combinatorial and quantity-discount procurement auctions benefit Mars, Incorporated and its suppliers. *Interfaces, 33*(1), 23-35.

Ivang, R., & Soerensen, O. J. (2005). E-markets in the battle zone between relationship and transaction marketing! *Electronic Markets, 15*(4), 393-404.

Jap, S. D. (2002). Online reverse auctions: Issues, themes, and prospects for the future. *Academy of Marketing Science. Journal, 30*(4), 506-525.

Jofre-Bonet, M., & Pesendorfer, M. (2003). Estimation of a dynamic auction game. *Econometrica, 71*(5), 1443-1489.

Johnson, P. F., & Klassen, R. D. (2005). E-procurement. *MIT Sloan Management Review, 46*(2), 7-10.

Kehagias, D. D., Symeonidis, A. L., & Mitkas, P. A. (2005). Designing pricing mechanisms for autonomous agents based on bid-forecasting. *Electronic Markets, 15*(1), 53-62.

Kung, M., Monroe, K. B., & Cox, J. L. (2002). Pricing on the Internet. *The Journal of Product and Brand Management, 11*(4/5), 274-287.

Lancioni, R. (2005). Pricing issues in industrial marketing. *Industrial Marketing Management, 34*(2), 111-114.

Liebmann, L. (2001). Eyes wide shut: A look at B2B marketplaces. *Network Magazine, 16*(2), 112-114.

Mishra, D., & Veermani, D. (2006). An ascending price procurement auction for multiple items with unit supply. *IIE Transactions (Institute of Industrial Engineers), 38*(2), 127-140.

Mueller, B., (2001) UTC saves 30% using reverse auctions to purchase services. *Purchasing, 130*(18), 51, 54.

Myers, B. (2005). Fully loaded printing. *Printing News, 155*(10), 10.

Oliva, R. A. (2003). Business Web: Sold on reverse auctions. *Marketing Management, 12*(2), 44-47.

Raghavan, N. R. S., & Prabhu, M. (2004). Object-oriented design of a distributed agent-based framework for e-Procurement. *Production Planning and Control, 15*(7), 731-741.

Sandholm, T., Levine, D., Concordia, M., Martyn, P., Hughes, R., Jacobs, J., et al. (2006). Changing the game in strategic sourcing at procter & gamble: Expressive competition enabled by optimization. *Interfaces, 36*(1), 55-68, 95-97.

Schrader, R. W., Schrader, J. T., & Eller, E. P. (2004). Strategic implications of reverse auctions. *Journal of Business to Business Marketing, 11*(1,2), 61-82.

Settoon, R. P., & Wyld, D. C. (2003). The ski slope to prosperity: An analysis of the potential impact of reverse auctions in government procurement in five southeast asian nations. *Asia Pacific Journal of Marketing and Logistics, 15*(3), 3-19.

Smart, A., & Harrison, A. (2003). Online reverse auctions and their role in buyer-supplier relationships. *Journal of Purchasing and Supply Management, 9*(5-6), 257-268.

Stoddard, J. (2003). Going, going, gone reverse auctions. *Canadian Printer, 111*(3), 29.

Stoddard, J. (2003). Going, going, gone: Reverse auctions. *Gravure, August,* 46-48.

Suyama, T., & Yokoo, M. (2005). Strategy/false-name proof protocols for combinatorial multi-attribute procurement auction. *Autonomous Agents and Multi-Agent Systems, 11*(1), 7-21.

Swider, D. J., & Weber, C. (In press). Bidding under price uncertainty in multi-unit pay-as-bid procurement auctions for power systems reserve. *European Journal of Operational Research.*

Teich, J. E., Wallenius, H., Wallenius, J., & Zaitsev, A. (2006). A multi-attribute e-auction mechanism for procurement: Theoretical foundations. *European Journal of Operational Research, 175*(1), 90-100.

Van Tulder, R., & Mol, M. (2002). Reverse auctions or auctions reversed: First experiments by Philips. *European Management Journal, 20*(5), 447-456.

Wolfram, C. D. (1998). Strategic bidding in a multiunit auction: An empirical analysis of bids to supply electricity in England and Wales. *The Rand Journal of Economics, 29*(4), 703-725.

Yildirim, H. (2004). Piecewise procurement of a large-scale project. *International Journal of Industrial Organization, 22*(8-9), 1349-1375.

Competitive Advantage

Number of citations: 20

Barling, B. (2002). Expert advice: How can my organisation take advantage of reverse auctions without jeopardising existing supplier relationships? *Information Age*, 41.

Barrett, R. T., & Pugh, R. E. (2003). Procurement auctions in e-commerce. *Southern Business Review, 29*(1), 1-14.

Cox, A., Chicksand, D., Ireland, P., & Davies, T. (2005). Sourcing indirect spend: A survey of current internal and external strategies for non-revenue-generating goods and services. *Journal of Supply Chain Management, 41*(2), 39-51.

Daly, S. P., & Nath, P. (2005). Reverse auctions for relationship marketers. *Industrial Marketing Management, 34*(2), 157-166.

De Silva, D. G. (2005). Synergies in recurring procurement auctions: An empirical investigation. *Economic Inquiry, 43*(1), 55-66.

Goodwin, C. (2005). Electronic procurement. *Glass, 82*(5), 153.

Her, Y.-S., Imamoto, K., & Sakurai, K. (2005). Analysis and comparison of cryptographic techniques in e-voting and e-auction. *Research Reports on Information Science and Electrical Engineering of Kyushu University, 10*(2), 91-96.

Horlen, J., Eldin, N., & Ajinkya, Y. (2005). Reverse auctions: Controversial bidding practice. *Journal of Professional Issues in Engineering Education and Practice, 131*(1), 76-81.

Joia, L. A., & Zamot, F. (2002). Internet-based reverse auctions by the Brazilian government. *Electronic Journal on Information Systems in Developing Countries, 9.*

Kehagias, D. D., Symeonidis, A. L., & Mitkas, P. A. (2005). Designing pricing mechanisms for autonomous agents based on bid-forecasting. *Electronic Markets, 15*(1), 53-62.

Meij, S., & Pau, L. F. (2006). Auctioning bulk mobile messages. *Computational Economics, 27*(2-3), 395-430.

Mishra, D., & Veermani, D. (2006). An ascending price procurement auction for multiple items with unit supply. *IIE Transactions (Institute of Industrial Engineers), 38*(2), 127-140.

Rothkopf, M. H., Harstad, R. M., & Fu, Y. (2003). Is subsidizing inefficient bidders actually costly? *Management Science, 49*(1), 71-84.

Smart, A., & Harrison, A. (2003). Online reverse auctions and their role in buyer-supplier relationships. *Journal of Purchasing and Supply Management, 9*(5-6), 257-268.

Smeltzer, L. R., & Carr, A. (2002). Reverse auctions in industrial marketing and buying. *Business Horizons, 45*(2), 47-52.

Stein, A., Hawking, P., & Wyld, D. C. (2003). The 20% solution? A case study on the efficacy of reverse auctions. *Management Research News, 26*(5), 1-20.

Talluri, S., & Ragatz, G. L. (2004). Multi-attribute reverse auctions in B2B exchanges: A framework for design and implementation. *Journal of Supply Chain Management, 40*(1), 52-60.

Turner, B. (2003). Packs that think for themselves. *Packaging Magazine, 6*(14), 22.

van Heck, E., & Vervest, P. (1998). How should CIOs deal with Web-based auctions? *Communications of the ACM, 41*(7), 99-100.

Wang, J.-L., Yu, B.-X., & Wang, Y.-M. (2004). A general secure e-auction model based on bit commitment. *Chinese Journal of Computers, 27*(3), 347-351.

Competitive Environment

Number of Citations: 38

E-Anton, J. J., & Yao, D. A. (1992). Coordination in split award auctions. *The Quarterly Journal of Economics, 107*(2), 681-707.

Arozamena, L., & Cantillon, E. (2004). Investment incentives in procurement auctions. *The Review of Economic Studies, 71*(1), 1-18.

Bag, P. K. (1997). Optimal auction design and R&D. *European Economic Review, 41*(9), 1655-1674.

Bajari, P., & Ye, L. (2003). Deciding between competition and collusion. *The Review of Economics and Statistics, 85*(4), 971-989.

Brisset, K., & Thomas, L. (2004). Leniency program: A new tool in competition policy to deter cartel activity in procurement auctions. *European Journal of Law and Economics, 17*(1), 5.

Compte, O., & Jehiel, P. (2002). On the value of competition in procurement auctions. *Econometrica, 70*(1), 343-355.

Compte, O., Lambert-Mogiliansky, A., & Verdier, T. (2005). Corruption and competition in procurement auctions. *Rand Journal of Economics, 36*(1), 1-15.

Emiliani, M. L. (2004). Sourcing in the global aerospace supply chain using online reverse auctions. *Industrial Marketing Management, 33*(1), 65-72.

Engelbrecht-Wiggans, R., & Katok, E. (2006). E-sourcing in procurement: Theory and behavior in reverse auctions with noncompetitive contracts. *Management Science, 52*(4), 581-596.

Ewerhart, C., & Fieseler, K. (2003). Procurement auctions and unit-price contracts. *The Rand Journal of Economics, 34*(3), 569-581.

Gabert, S. (2003). Are reverse auctions friend or foe? *Printing News, 150*(14), 1-5.

Goodwin, C. (2005). Electronic procurement. *Glass, 82*(5), 153.

Gupta, S. (2002). Competition and collusion in a government procurement auction market. *Atlantic Economic Journal, 30*(1), 13-25.

Güth, W., Ivanova-Stenzel, R., & Kröger, S. (2006). Procurement experiments with unknown costs of quality. *Pacific Economic Review, 11*(2), 133-148.

Hirsch, S. (2005). Reverse auctions sharpen competition. *International Trade Forum,* (3), 14-15.

Hong, H., & Shum, M. (2002). Increasing competition and the winner's curse: Evidence from procurement. *The Review of Economic Studies, 69*(241), 871-898.

Horlen, J., Eldin, N., & Ajinkya, Y. (2005). Reverse auctions: Controversial bidding practice. *Journal of Professional Issues in Engineering Education and Practice, 131*(1), 76-81.

Hur, D., Hartley, J. L., & Mabert, V. A. (2006). Implementing reverse e-auctions: A learning process. *Business Horizons, 49*(1), 21-29.

Hur, D., Mabert, V. A., & Hartley, J. L. (In press). Getting the most out of reverse e-auction investment. *Omega.*

Iimi, A. (2004). (A

nti-)Competitive effect of joint bidding: Evidence from ODA procurement auctions. *Journal of the Japanese and International Economies, 18*(3), 416-439.

Iimi, A. (2006). Auction reforms for effective official development assistance. *Review of Industrial Organization, 28*(2), 109.

Ivang, R., & Soerensen, O. J. (2005). E-markets in the battle zone between relationship and transaction marketing! *Electronic Markets, 15*(4), 393-404.

Jap, S. D. (2003). An exploratory study of the introduction of online reverse auctions. *Journal of Marketing, 67*(3), 96-107.

Jin, M., & Wu, S. D. (2006). Supplier coalitions in online reverse auctions: Validity requirements and profit distribution scheme. *International Journal of Production Economics, 100*(2), 183-194.

Johnson, L. (1990). Gains from a unified European community public procurement market: An analysis using auction theory. *Brigham Young University Law Review, 1990*(4), 1727-1742.

Kehagias, D. D., Symeonidis, A. L., & Mitkas, P. A. (2005). Designing pricing mechanisms for autonomous agents based on bid-forecasting. *Electronic Markets, 15*(1), 53-62.

Kinney, S. (2000). RIP fixed pricing: The Internet is on its way to "marketizing" everything. *Business Economics, 35*(2), 39-44.

Kung, M., Monroe, K. B., & Cox, J. L. (2002). Pricing on the Internet. *The Journal of Product and Brand Management, 11*(4/5), 274-287.

MacDonald, J. M., Handy, C. R., & Plato, G. E. (2002). Competition and prices in USDA commodity procurement. *Southern Economic Journal, 69*(1), 128-143.

Reding, C. (2002). Assessing online reverse auctions. *Industrial Paint and Powder, 78*(9), 45-47.

Rothkopf, M. H., Harstad, R. M., & Fu, Y. (2003). Is subsidizing inefficient bidders actually costly? *Management Science, 49*(1), 71-84.

Sandholm, T., Levine, D., Concordia, M., Martyn, P., Hughes, R., Jacobs, J., et al. (2006). Changing the game in strategic sourcing at Procter & Gamble: Expressive competition enabled by optimization. *Interfaces, 36*(1), 55-68, 95-97.

Schrader, R. W., Schrader, J. T., & Eller, E. P. (2004). Strategic implications of reverse auctions. *Journal of Business to Business Marketing, 11*(1,2), 61-82.

Soudry, O. (2004). Promoting economy: Electronic reverse auctions under the EC directives on public procurement. *Journal of Public Procurement, 4*(3), 340-374.

Tunca, T. I., & Zenios, S. A. (2006). Supply auctions and relational contracts for procurement. *Manufacturing and Service Operations Management, 8*(1), 43-67.

Turner, B. (2003). Packs that think for themselves. *Packaging Magazine, 6*(14), 22.

Wagner, S. M., & Schwab, A. P. (2004). Setting the stage for successful electronic reverse auctions. *Journal of Purchasing and Supply Management, 10*(1), 11-26.

Yildirim, H. (2004). Piecewise procurement of a large-scale project. *International Journal of Industrial Organization, 22*(8-9), 1349-1375.

The Economics of Auctions

Number of citations: 61

Anon. (2003). Reverse auction strategies offered. *Official Board Markets, 79*(24), 14.

Anton, J. J., & Yao, D. A. (1989). Split awards, procurement, and innovation. *The Rand Journal of Economics, 20*(4), 538-552.

Anton, J. J., & Yao, D. A. (1992). Coordination in split award auctions. *The Quarterly Journal of Economics, 107*(2), 681-707.

Arminas, D. (2003). Beyond the quick wins [e-procurement]. *Supply Management*, 34-35.

Arozamena, L., & Cantillon, E. (2004). Investment incentives in procurement auctions. *The Review of Economic Studies, 71*(1), 1-18.

Bag, P. K. (1997). Optimal auction design and R&D. *European Economic Review, 41*(9), 1655-1674.

Bajari, P., & Ye, L. (2003). Deciding between competition and collusion. *The Review of Economics and Statistics, 85*(4), 971-989.

Bandyopadhyay, S., Rees, J., & Barron, J. M. (2006). Simulating sellers in online exchanges. *Decision Support Systems, 41*(2), 500-513.

Bartholomew, D. (2004). The juice flows again. *Industry Week, 253*(3), 31-34.

Belleflamme, P., & Bloch, F. (2004). Market sharing agreements and collusive networks. *International Economic Review, 45*(2), 387-411.

Bertsekas, D. P., & Castanon, D. A. (1992). Forward/reverse auction algorithm for asymmetric assignment problems. *Computational Optimization and Applications, 1*(3), 277-297.

Branco, F. (1997). The design of multidimensional auctions. *The Rand Journal of Economics, 28*(1), 63-81.

Brisset, K., & Thomas, L. (2004). Leniency program: A new tool in competition policy to deter cartel activity in procurement auctions. *European Journal of Law and Economics, 17*(1), 5.

Brosig, J., & Rei, J. P. (In press). Entry decisions and bidding behavior in sequential first-price procurement auctions: An experimental study. *Games and Economic Behavior.*

Budde, J., & Gox, R. F. (1999). The impact of capacity costs on bidding strategies in procurement auctions. *Review of Accounting Studies, 4*(1), 5-13.

Calveras, A., Ganuza, J.-J., & Hauk, E. (2004). Wild bids: Gambling for resurrection in procurement contracts. *Journal of Regulatory Economics, 26*(1), 41-68.

Chao, H.-P., & Wilson, R. (2002). Multi-dimensional procurement auctions for power reserves: Robust incentive-compatible scoring and settlement rules. *Journal of Regulatory Economics, 22*(2), 161.

Chen-Ritzo, C.-H., Harrison, T. P., Kwasnica, A. M., & Thomas, D. J. (2005). Better, faster, cheaper: An experimental analysis of a multiattribute reverse auction mechanism with restricted information feedback. *Management Science, 51*(12), 1753-1762.

Compte, O., & Jehiel, P. (2002). On the value of competition in procurement auctions. *Econometrica, 70*(1), 343-355.

Compte, O., Lambert-Mogiliansky, A., & Verdier, T. (2005). Corruption and competition in procurement auctions. *Rand Journal of Economics, 36*(1), 1-15.

Dai, R., Narasimhan, S., & Wu, D. J. (2005). Buyer's efficient e-sourcing structure: Centralize or decentralize? *Journal of Management Information Systems, 22*(2), 141-164.

Daly, S. P., & Nath, P. (2005). Reverse auctions for relationship marketers. *Industrial Marketing Management, 34*(2), 157-166.

Dasgupta, S., & Spulber, D. F. (1989). Managing procurement auctions. *Information Economics and Policy, 4*(1), 5-29.

Davis, D. D., & Wilson, B. J. (2002). Collusion in procurement auctions: An experimental examination. *Economic Inquiry, 40*(2), 213-230.

De Silva, D. G. (2005). Synergies in recurring procurement auctions: An empirical investigation. *Economic Inquiry, 43*(1), 55-66.

Ding, M., Eliashberg, J., Huber, J., & Saini, R. (2005). Emotional bidders: An analytical and experimental examination of consumers' behavior in a Priceline-like reverse auction. *Management Science, 51*(3), 352-364.

E-procurement adoptions progress slowly and steadily. (2002). *Purchasing, 131*(11), S8, S10.

Emiliani, M. L. (2004). Sourcing in the global aerospace supply chain using online reverse auctions. *Industrial Marketing Management, 33*(1), 65-72.

Engelbrecht-Wiggans, R., & Katok, E. (2006). E-sourcing in procurement: Theory and behavior in reverse auctions with noncompetitive contracts. *Management Science, 52*(4), 581-596.

Ewerhart, C., & Fieseler, K. (2003). Procurement auctions and unit-price contracts. *The Rand Journal of Economics, 34*(3), 569-581.

Gallien, J., & Wein, L. M. (2005). A smart market for industrial procurement with capacity constraints. *Management Science, 51*(1), 76-91.

Gupta, S. (2001). The effect of bid rigging on prices: A study of the highway construction industry. *Review of Industrial Organization, 19*(4), 451-465.

Gupta, S. (2002). Competition and collusion in a government procurement auction market. *Atlantic Economic Journal, 30*(1), 13-25.

Güth, W., Ivanova-Stenzel, R., & Kröger, S. (2006). Procurement experiments with unknown costs of quality. *Pacific Economic Review, 11*(2), 133-148.

Hong, H., & Shum, M. (2002). Increasing competition and the Winner's Curse: Evidence from procurement. *The Review of Economic Studies, 69*(241), 871-898.

Hur, D., Mabert, V. A., & Hartley, J. L. (In press). Getting the most out of reverse e-auction investment. *Omega.*

Iimi, A. (2006). Auction reforms for effective official development assistance. *Review of Industrial Organization, 28*(2), 109.

Jin, M., & Wu, S. D. (2006). Supplier coalitions in online reverse auctions: Validity requirements and profit distribution scheme. *International Journal of Production Economics, 100*(2), 183-194.

Jofre-Bonet, M., & Pesendorfer, M. (2000). Bidding behavior in a repeated procurement auction: A summary. *European Economic Review, 44*(4-6), 1006-1020.

Kim, I.-G. (1994). Price-preference vs. tariff policies in government procurement auctions. *Economics Letters, 45*(2), 217-222.

Kinney, S. (2000). RIP fixed pricing: The Internet is on its way to "marketizing" everything. *Business Economics, 35*(2), 39-44.

Luton, R., & McAfee, R. P. (1986). Sequential procurement auctions. *Journal of Public Economics, 31*(2), 181-195.

MacDonald, J. M., Handy, C. R., & Plato, G. E. (2002). Competition and prices in USDA commodity procurement. *Southern Economic Journal, 69*(1), 128-143.

Manelli, A. M., & Vincent, D. R. (2004). Duality in procurement design. *Journal of Mathematical Economics, 40*(3-4), 411-428.

Meij, S., & Pau, L. F. (2006). Auctioning bulk mobile messages. *Computational Economics, 27*(2-3), 395-430.

Mishra, D., & Veermani, D. (2006). An ascending price procurement auction for multiple items with unit supply. *IIE Transactions (Institute of Industrial Engineers), 38*(2), 127-140.

Naegelen, F. (2002). Implementing optimal procurement auctions with exogenous quality. *Review of Economic Design, 7*(2), 135-153.

Porter, R. H., & Zona, J. D. (1993). Detection of bid rigging in procurement auctions. *The Journal of Political Economy, 101*(3), 518-538.

Roelofs, M. R. (2002). Common value auctions with default: An experimental approach. *Experimental Economics, 5*(3), 233-252.

Rothkopf, M. H., Harstad, R. M., & Fu, Y. (2003). Is subsidizing inefficient bidders actually costly? *Management Science, 49*(1), 71-84.

Sampath, K., Saygin, C., Grasman, S. E., & Leu, M. C. (2006). Impact of reputation information sharing in an auction-based job allocation model for small and medium-sized enterprises. *International Journal of Production Research, 44*(9), 1777-1798.

Settoon, R. P., & Wyld, D. C. (2003). The ski slope to prosperity: An analysis of the potential impact of reverse auctions in government procurement in five southeast Asian nations. *Asia Pacific Journal of Marketing and Logistics, 15*(3), 3-19.

Snyder, C. M. (1996). A dynamic theory of countervailing power. *Rand Journal of Economics, 27*(4), 747-769.

Soudry, O. (2004). Promoting economy: Electronic reverse auctions under the EC directives on public procurement. *Journal of Public Procurement, 4*(3), 340-374.

Stoddard, J. (2003). Going, going, gone: Reverse auctions. *Gravure, August*, 46-48.

Tinham, B. (2004). Under the e-hammer. *Manufacturing Computer Solutions, 10*(3), 53.

Tunca, T. I., & Zenios, S. A. (2006). Supply auctions and relational contracts for procurement. *Manufacturing and Service Operations Management, 8*(1), 43-67.

Twentyman, J. (2005). Under pressure [business/industrial economics]. *Information Age*, 34-35.

Wang, R. (2000). Bidding and renegotiation in procurement auctions. *European Economic Review, 44*(8), 1577-1597.

Wang, S., Zheng, W., & Archer, N. (2005). The impact of Internet-based electronic marketplaces on buyer-supplier relationships. *Journal of Internet Commerce, 4*(3), 41-67.

Wolfram, C. D. (1998). Strategic bidding in a multiunit auction: An empirical analysis of bids to supply electricity in England and Wales. *The Rand Journal of Economics, 29*(4), 703-725.

Negotiation in Online Procurement Auctions

Number of Citations: 23

Barling, B. (2002). Expert advice: How can my organisation take advantage of reverse auctions without jeopardising existing supplier relationships? *Information Age*, 41.

Barrett, R. T., & Pugh, R. E. (2003). Procurement auctions in e-commerce. *Southern Business Review, 29*(1), 1-14.

Bichler, M., & Kalagnanam, J. (2005). Configurable offers and winner determination in multi-attribute auctions. *European Journal of Operational Research, 160*(2), 380-394.

Borkar, V. S., Dave, M. S., & Shyamasundar, R. K. (2005). Design and implementation of SeTiA: Secure multi auction system - I. Auction mechanisms. *Journal of Intelligent Systems, 14*(1), 45-68.

Borkar, V. S., Dave, M. S., & Shyamasundar, R. K. (2005). Design and implementation of SeTiA: Secure multi auction system – II. Architecture and implementation issues. *Journal of Intelligent Systems, 14*(1), 69-93.

Carbone, J. (2005). Not just a cost-reduction tool [electronic industry]. *Purchasing, 134*(3), 43-44.

Carter, C. R., Kaufmann, L., Beall, S., Carter, P. L., Hendrick, T. E., & Petersen, K. J. (2004). Reverse auctions: Grounded theory from the buyer and supplier perspective. *Transportation Research Part E: Logistics and Transportation Review, 40*(3), 229-254.

Dai, R., Narasimhan, S., & Wu, D. J. (2005). Buyer's efficient e-sourcing structure: Centralize or decentralize? *Journal of Management Information Systems, 22*(2), 141-164.

David, E., Azoulay-Schwartz, R., & Kraus, S. (In press). Bidding in sealed-bid and English multi-attribute auctions. *Decision Support Systems*.

Gattiker, T. F., Huang, X., & Schwarz, J. L. (2007). Negotiation e-mail, and Internet reverse auctions: How sourcing mechanisms deployed by buyers affect suppliers' trust. *Journal of Operations Management, 25*(1), 184-202.

Hatton, J., & Young, B. (2004). Are e-auctions a good way to buy services? *Supply Management*, 28-29.

Ivang, R., & Soerensen, O. J. (2005). E-markets in the battle zone between relationship and transaction marketing! *Electronic Markets, 15*(4), 393-404.

Jap, S. D. (2003). An exploratory study of the introduction of online reverse auctions. *Journal of Marketing, 67*(3), 96-107.

Naegelen, F. (2002). Implementing optimal procurement auctions with exogenous quality. *Review of Economic Design, 7*(2), 135-153.

Oliva, R. A. (2001). Discovering price discovery. *Marketing Management, 10*(4), 46-48.

Parkes, D. C., & Kalagnanam, J. (2005). Models for iterative multiattribute procurement auctions. *Management Science, 51*(3), 435-451.

Porter, A. M. (2000). E-auction model morphs to meet buyers' needs. *Purchasing, 128*(10), 31-32.

Raghavan, N. R. S., & Prabhu, M. (2004). Object-oriented design of a distributed agent-based framework for e-procurement. *Production Planning and Control, 15*(7), 731-741.

Shih, D.-H., Huang, S.-Y., & Yen, D. C. (2005). A new reverse auction agent system for m-commerce using mobile agents. *Computer Standards & Interfaces, 27*(4), 383-395.

Teich, J. E., Wallenius, H., Wallenius, J., & Koppius, O. R. (2004). Emerging multiple issue e-auctions. *European Journal of Operational Research, 159*(1), 1-16.

Teich, J. E., Wallenius, H., Wallenius, J., & Zaitsev, A. (2006). A multi-attribute e-auction mechanism for procurement: Theoretical foundations. *European Journal of Operational Research, 175*(1), 90-100.

Vail, S. (2005). The tender connection [electronic sourcing]. *Supply Management, 10*(15), 21-23.

Wang, R. (2000). Bidding and renegotiation in procurement auctions. *European Economic Review, 44*(8), 1577-1597.

Efficiency in the Auction Process

Number of Citations: 36

Anonymous. (2004). Buy better. *International Journal of Productivity and Performance Management, 53*(5/6), 560-561.

Arozamena, L., & Cantillon, E. (2004). Investment incentives in procurement auctions. *The Review of Economic Studies, 71*(1), 1-18.

Barrett, R. T., & Pugh, R. E. (2003). Procurement auctions in e-commerce. *Southern Business Review, 29*(1), 1-14.

Bichler, M., & Kalagnanam, J. (2005). Configurable offers and winner determination in multi-attribute auctions. *European Journal of Operational Research, 160*(2), 380-394.

Budde, J., & Gox, R. F. (1999). The impact of capacity costs on bidding strategies in procurement auctions. *Review of Accounting Studies, 4*(1), 5-13.

Dai, R., Narasimhan, S., & Wu, D. J. (2005). Buyer's efficient e-sourcing structure: Centralize or decentralize? *Journal of Management Information Systems, 22*(2), 141-164.

De Silva, D. G. (2005). Synergies in recurring procurement auctions: An empirical investigation. *Economic Inquiry, 43*(1), 55-66.

Elgart, E. G. (2001). Army reverse auctions: An e-commerce acquisition tool. *Public Manager, 30*(1), 13-16.

Ewerhart, C., & Fieseler, K. (2003). Procurement auctions and unit-price contracts. *The Rand Journal of Economics, 34*(3), 569-581.

Goodwin, C. (2005). Electronic procurement. *Glass, 82*(5), 153.

Güth, W., Ivanova-Stenzel, R., & Kröger, S. (2006). Procurement experiments with unknown costs of quality. *Pacific Economic Review, 11*(2), 133-148.

Hannon, D. (2003). E-sourcing: CAPS research study defines staying power of e-auctions. *Purchasing, 132*(12), 48-49.

Hohner, G., Rich, J., Ng, E., Reid, G., Davenport, A. J., Kalagnanam, J. R., et al. (2003). Combinatorial and quantity-discount procurement auctions benefit Mars, Incorporated and its suppliers. *Interfaces, 33*(1), 23-35.

Hu, C., & Lu, Y.-B. (2005). Procurement auction model with piecewise linear price curves and its genetic algorithm. *Industrial Engineering and Management, 10*(2), 76-80.

Iimi, A. (2006). Auction reforms for effective official development assistance. *Review of Industrial Organization, 28*(2), 109.

Jeong, W. S., Han, S. G., & Jo, G. S. (2003). Intelligent cyber logistics using reverse auction in electronic commerce. *Journal of Organizational Computing and Electronic Commerce, 13*(3-4), 191-209.

Jin, M., & Wu, S. D. (2006). Supplier coalitions in on-line reverse auctions: Validity requirements and profit distribution scheme. *International Journal of Production Economics, 100*(2), 183-194.

Jofre-Bonet, M., & Pesendorfer, M. (2003). Estimation of a dynamic auction game. *Econometrica, 71*(5), 1443-1489.

Joia, L. A., & Zamot, F. (2002). Internet-based reverse auctions by the Brazilian government. *Electronic Journal on Information Systems in Developing Countries, 9.*

Kehagias, D. D., Symeonidis, A. L., & Mitkas, P. A. (2005). Designing pricing mechanisms for autonomous agents based on bid-forecasting. *Electronic Markets, 15*(1), 53-62.

Kjerstad, E., & Vagstad, S. (2000). Procurement auctions with entry of bidders. *International Journal of Industrial Organization, 18*(8), 1243-1257.

Klafft, M., & Spiekermann, S. (2006). Reverse procurement and auctions for consumers - a new trend on the horizon of e-commerce? *Wirtschaftsinformatik, 48*(1), 36-45.

Luton, R., & McAfee, R. P. (1986). Sequential procurement auctions. *Journal of Public Economics, 31*(2), 181-195.

Meij, S., & Pau, L. F. (2006). Auctioning bulk mobile messages. *Computational Economics, 27*(2-3), 395-430.

Mishra, D., & Veermani, D. (2006). An ascending price procurement auction for multiple items with unit supply. *IIE Transactions (Institute of Industrial Engineers), 38*(2), 127-140.

Mullane, J. V., Peters, M. H., & Bullington, K. E. (2001). Entrepreneurial firms as suppliers in business-to-business e-commerce. *Management Decision, 39*(5/6), 388-393.

Parkes, D. C., & Kalagnanam, J. (2005). Models for iterative multiattribute procurement auctions. *Management Science, 51*(3), 435-451.

Peng, K., Boyd, C., & Dawson, E. (2006). Batch verification of validity of bids in homomorphic e-auction. *Computer Communications, 29*(15), 2798-2805.

Rothkopf, M. H., Harstad, R. M., & Fu, Y. (2003). Is subsidizing inefficient bidders actually costly? *Management Science, 49*(1), 71-84.

Sampath, K., Saygin, C., Grasman, S. E., & Leu, M. C. (2006). Impact of reputation information sharing in an auction-based job allocation model for small and medium-sized enterprises. *International Journal of Production Research, 44*(9), 1777-1798.

Sandholm, T., Levine, D., Concordia, M., Martyn, P., Hughes, R., Jacobs, J., et al. (2006). Changing the game in strategic sourcing at Procter & Gamble: Expressive competition enabled by optimization. *Interfaces, 36*(1), 55-68,95-97.

Settoon, R. P., & Wyld, D. C. (2003). The ski slope to prosperity: An analysis of the potential impact of reverse auctions in government procurement in five southeast Asian nations. *Asia Pacific Journal of Marketing and Logistics, 15*(3), 3-19.

Standifer, R. L., & Wall, J. A., Jr. (2003). Managing conflict in B2B e-commerce. *Business Horizons, 46*(2), 65-70.

Tunca, T. I., & Zenios, S. A. (2006). Supply auctions and relational contracts for procurement. *Manufacturing and Service Operations Management, 8*(1), 43-67.

Turner, B. (2003). Packs that think for themselves. *Packaging Magazine, 6*(14), 22.

Vail, S. (2005). The tender connection [electronic sourcing]. *Supply Management, 10*(15), 21-23.

Risk or Uncertainty in the Reverse Auction

Number of Citations: 16

Barling, B. (2002). Expert advice: How can my organisation take advantage of reverse auctions without jeopardising existing supplier relationships? *Information Age*, 41.

Bichler, M., & Kalagnanam, J. R. (2006). A non-parametric estimator for setting reservation prices in procurement auctions. *Information Technology and Management, 7*(3), 157-169.

Brandt, S. (2003). Business models, the Internet and printing industry associate. E-business in the printing field: Query whether it is the beginning of the end. *Deutscher Drucker Stuttgart, 39*(7), 24-26.

Calveras, A., Ganuza, J.-J., & Hauk, E. (2004). Wild bids: Gambling for resurrection in procurement contracts. *Journal of Regulatory Economics, 26*(1), 41-68.

Ding, M., Eliashberg, J., Huber, J., & Saini, R. (2005). Emotional bidders: An analytical and experimental examination of consumers' behavior in a Priceline-like reverse auction. *Management Science, 51*(3), 352-364.

Fraser, H., & Lanza, S. (2006). It matters which way you slice it: Risk management for the 2005 procurement auction of Italy's Acquirente Unico. *The Electricity Journal, 19*(1), 66-76.

Güth, W., Ivanova-Stenzel, R., & Kröger, S. (2006). Procurement experiments with unknown costs of quality. *Pacific Economic Review, 11*(2), 133-148.

Johnson, L. (1990). Gains from a unified European community public procurement market: An analysis using auction theory. *Brigham Young University Law Review, 1990*(4), 1727-1742.

Liebmann, L. (2001). Eyes wide shut: A look at B2B marketplaces. *Network Magazine, 16*(2), 112-114.

Lindorff, D. (2006). In this case, Talk isn't so cheap. *Treasury and Risk Management, 16*(4), 15.

Parente, D. H., Venkataraman, R. R., Fizel, J. L., & Millet, I. (2004). A conceptual research framework for analyzing online auctions in a B2B environment. *Supply Chain Management, 9*(4), 287-294.

Sandholm, T., Levine, D., Concordia, M., Martyn, P., Hughes, R., Jacobs, J., et al. (2006). Changing the game in strategic sourcing at Procter & Gamble: Expressive competition enabled by optimization. *Interfaces, 36*(1), 55-68, 95-97.

Smeltzer, L. R., & Carr, A. S. (2002). Reverse auctions in industrial marketing and buying. *Business Horizons, 45*(2), 47-52.

Smeltzer, L. R., & Carr, A. S. (2003). Electronic reverse auctions: Promises, risks and conditions for success. *Industrial Marketing Management, 32*(6), 481-488.

Swider, D. J., & Weber, C. (In Press) Bidding under price uncertainty in multi-unit pay-as-bid procurement auctions for power systems reserve. *European Journal of Operational Research.*

Tassabehji, R., Taylor, W. A., Beach, R., & Wood, A. (2006). Reverse e-auctions and supplier-buyer relationships: An exploratory study. *International Journal of Operations and Production Management, 26*(2), 166-184.

E-Auction Portals and Marketplace

Number of citations: 19

Anon. (2000). eCardboard launches new Web site. *Official Board Markets, 76*(39), 1.

Anon. (2000). G-P selling mills, launches wood e-trade. *International Woodfiber Report, 6*(9), 1.

Atkinson, W. (2000). Materials maker streamlines and saves with online buying. *Purchasing, 129*(11), 86-88.

Brandt, S. (2003). Business models, the Internet and printing industry associate. E-business in the printing field: Query whether it is the beginning of the end. *Deutscher Drucker Stuttgart, 39*(7), 24-26.

Davis, B. (2004). Trading places [e-trading exchanges]. *Professional Engineering, 17*(8), 34-35.

Ding, M., Eliashberg, J., Huber, J., & Saini, R. (2005). Emotional bidders: An analytical and experimental examination of consumers' behavior in a Priceline-like reverse auction. *Management Science, 51*(3), 352-364.

E-market traders. (2000). *Mind Your Own Business, 23*(10), 32.

Evans, B., & Bacheldor, B. (2003). Beyond e-procurement. *InformationWEEK,* (923), 44-45.

Goldsborough, R. (2000). Using the Net to travel the real world. *Tech Directions, 60*(5), 14.

Kung, M., Monroe, K. B., & Cox, J. L. (2002). Pricing on the Internet. *The Journal of Product and Brand Management, 11*(4/5), 274-287.

Li, Y., Shen, W., & Ghenniwa, H. (2004). Agent-based Web services framework and development environment. *Computational Intelligence, 20*(4), 678-692.

Liebmann, L. (2001). Eyes wide shut: A look at B2B marketplaces. *Network Magazine, 16*(2), 112-114.

McKendrick, J. (2000). Priceline.com: An inside look at the reverse auction master. *Electronic Commerce World, 10*(1), 30-34.

Mueller, B., (2001) UTC saves 30% using reverse auctions to purchase services. *Purchasing, 130*(18), 51, 54.

Oliva, R. A. (2001). Discovering price discovery. *Marketing Management, 10*(4), 46-48.

Rao, B. V., & Smith, B. C. (2006). Decision support in online travel retailing. *Journal of Revenue and Pricing Management, 5*(1), 72-80.

Stoddard, J. (2003). Going, going...gone. *Paper, Film and Foil Converter, 77*(5), 42.

Ulmer, D. B., & Tao, L. (2006). Architectural solutions to agent-enabling e-commerce portals with pull/push abilities. *WSEAS Transactions on Computers, 5*(5), 1026-1033.

Wang, S., Zheng, W., & Archer, N. (2005). The impact of Internet-based electronic marketplaces on buyer-supplier relationships. *Journal of Internet Commerce, 4*(3), 41-67.

Product

Number of Citations: 28

Boyle, E. J. (2003). Let's talk trends. *Paper, Film and Foil Converter, 77*(9), T30.

Brunelli, M. (2000). Web is changing basics of the print buy. *Purchasing, 128*(4), S96.

Castiglione, D. (2006). Court your customers. *Paperboard Packaging, 91*(1), 10.

Davis, B. (2004). Trading places [e-trading exchanges]. *Professional Engineering, 17*(8), 34-35.

Douglas, A. (2003). Damage limited [e-auctions]. *Supply Management*, 32-33.

Eso, M., Ghosh, S., Kalagnanam, J., & Ladanyi, L. (2005). Bid evaluation in procurement auctions with piecewise linear supply curves. *Journal of Heuristics, 11*(2), 147-173.

Goossens, D. R., Maas, A. J. T., Spieksma, F. C. R., & van de Klundert, J. J. (In press). Exact algorithms for procurement problems under a total quantity discount structure. *European Journal of Operational Research*.

Güth, W., Ivanova-Stenzel, R., & Kröger, S. (2006). Procurement experiments with unknown costs of quality. *Pacific Economic Review, 11*(2), 133-148.

Hatton, J., & Young, B. (2004). Are e-auctions a good way to buy services? *Supply Management*, 28-29.

Hu, C., & Lu, Y.-B. (2005). Procurement auction model with piecewise linear price curves and its genetic algorithm. *Industrial Engineering and Management, 10*(2), 76-80.

Jeong, W. S., Han, S. G., & Jo, G. S. (2003). Intelligent cyber logistics using reverse auction in electronic commerce. *Journal of Organizational Computing and Electronic Commerce, 13*(3-4), 191-209.

Joia, L. A., & Zamot, F. (2002). Internet-based reverse auctions by the Brazilian government. *Electronic Journal on Information Systems in Developing Countries, 9*.

Kauffman, R. G., & Leszczyc, P. T. L. P. (2005). An optimization approach to business buyer choice sets: How many suppliers should be included? *Industrial Marketing Management, 34*(1), 3-12.

Kim, Y. (2005). The effects of buyer and product traits with seller reputation on price premiums in e-auction. *The Journal of Computer Information Systems, 46*(1), 79-91.

Kung, M., Monroe, K. B., & Cox, J. L. (2002). Pricing on the Internet. *The Journal of Product and Brand Management, 11*(4/5), 274-287.

Lancioni, R. (2005). Pricing issues in industrial marketing. *Industrial Marketing Management, 34*(2), 111-114.

MacDonald, J. M., Handy, C. R., & Plato, G. E. (2002). Competition and prices in USDA commodity procurement. *Southern Economic Journal, 69*(1), 128-143.

Mueller, B., (2001) UTC saves 30% using reverse auctions to purchase services. *Purchasing, 130*(18), 51, 54.

Oliva, R. A. (2001). Discovering price discovery. *Marketing Management, 10*(4), 46-48.

Rao, B. V., & Smith, B. C. (2006). Decision support in online travel retailing. *Journal of Revenue and Pricing Management, 5*(1), 72-80.

Reding, C. (2002). Assessing online reverse auctions. *Industrial Paint and Powder, 78*(9), 45-47.

Smeltzer, L. R., & Carr, A. S. (2002). Reverse auctions in industrial marketing and buying. *Business Horizons, 45*(2), 47-52.

Smeltzer, L. R., & Carr, A. S. (2003). Electronic reverse auctions: Promises, risks and conditions for success. *Industrial Marketing Management, 32*(6), 481-488.

Stoddard, J. (2003). Going, going, gone: Reverse auctions. *Canadian Printer, 111*(3), 29.

Stoddard, J. (2003). Going, going, gone: Reverse auctions. *Gravure, August,* 46-48.

Twentyman, J. (2005). Under pressure [business/industrial economics]. *Information Age,* 34-35.

Vagstad, S. (2000). Centralized vs. decentralized procurement: Does dispersed information call for decentralized decision-making? *International Journal of Industrial Organization, 18*(6), 949-963.

Wagner, S. M., & Schwab, A. P. (2004). Setting the stage for successful electronic reverse auctions. *Journal of Purchasing and Supply Management, 10*(1), 11-26.

Buyers in the Reverse Auction

Number of Citations: 36

Anon. (2003). Reverse auction strategies offered. *Official Board Markets, 79*(24), 14.

Bandyopadhyay, S., Rees, J., & Barron, J. M. (2006). Simulating sellers in online exchanges. *Decision Support Systems, 41*(2), 500-513.

Bichler, M., & Kalagnanam, J. R. (2006). A non-parametric estimator for setting reservation prices in procurement auctions. *Information Technology and Management, 7*(3), 157-169.

Borkar, V. S., Dave, M. S., & Shyamasundar, R. K. (2005). Design and implementation of SeTiA: Secure multi auction system - I. Auction mechanisms. *Journal of Intelligent Systems, 14*(1), 45-68.

Borkar, V. S., Dave, M. S., & Shyamasundar, R. K. (2005). Design and implementation of SeTiA: Secure multi auction system - II. Architecture and implementation issues. *Journal of Intelligent Systems, 14*(1), 69-93.

Brunelli, M. (2000). Web is changing basics of the print buy. *Purchasing, 128*(4), S96.

Daly, S. P., & Nath, P. (2005). Reverse auctions and buyer-seller relationships: A rejoinder to Emiliani and Stec's commentary. *Industrial Marketing Management, 34*(2), 173-176.

David, E., Azoulay-Schwartz, R., & Kraus, S. (In press). Bidding in sealed-bid and

E-procurement adoptions progress slowly and steadily. (2002). *Purchasing, 131*(11), S8,S10.

English multi-attribute auctions. *Decision Support Systems.*

Emiliani, M. L. (2006). Executive decision-making traps and B2B online reverse auctions. *Supply Chain Management, 11*(1), 6-9.

Ewerhart, C., & Fieseler, K. (2003). Procurement auctions and unit-price contracts. *The Rand Journal of Economics, 34*(3), 569-581.

Fraser, H., & Lanza, S. (2006). It matters which way you slice it: Risk management for the 2005 procurement auction of Italy's Acquirente Unico. *The Electricity Journal, 19*(1), 66-76.

Güth, W., Ivanova-Stenzel, R., & Kröger, S. (2006). Procurement experiments with unknown costs of quality. *Pacific Economic Review, 11*(2), 133-148.

Hur, D., Mabert, V. A., & Hartley, J. L. (In press). Getting the most out of reverse e-auction investment. *Omega.*

Jeong, W. S., Han, S. G., & Jo, G. S. (2003). Intelligent cyber logistics using reverse auction in electronic commerce. *Journal of Organizational Computing and Electronic Commerce, 13*(3-4), 191-209.

Kehagias, D. D., Symeonidis, A. L., & Mitkas, P. A. (2005). Designing pricing mechanisms for autonomous agents based on bid forecasting. *Electronic Markets, 15*(1), 53-62.

Kim, Y. (2005). The effects of buyer and product traits with seller reputation on price premiums in e-auction. *The Journal of Computer Information Systems, 46*(1), 79-91.

Kinney, S. (2000). RIP fixed pricing: The Internet is on its way to "marketizing" everything. *Business Economics, 35*(2), 39-44.

Klafft, M., & Spiekermann, S. (2006). Reverse procurement and auctions for consumers: A new trend on the horizon of e-commerce? *Wirtschaftsinformatik, 48*(1), 36-45.

Luton, R., & McAfee, R. P. (1986). Sequential procurement auctions. *Journal of Public Economics, 31*(2), 181-195.

McKendrick, J. (2000). Priceline.com: An inside look at the reverse auction master. *Electronic Commerce World, 10*(1), 30-34.

Meij, S., & Pau, L. F. (2006). Auctioning bulk mobile messages. *Computational Economics, 27*(2-3), 395-430.

Myers, B. (2005). Fully loaded printing. *Printing News, 155*(10), 10.

Naegelen, F. (2002). Implementing optimal procurement auctions with exogenous quality. *Review of Economic Design, 7*(2), 135-153.

Oliva, R. A. (2003). Business Web: Sold on reverse auctions. *Marketing Management, 12*(2), 44-47.

Porter, A. M. (2000). E-auction model morphs to meet buyers' needs. *Purchasing, 128*(10), 31-32.

Purchasing survey. Buyers turn wary eyes on electronic auctions. (2000). *Purchasing, 129*(3), 109-110.

Reding, C. (2002). Assessing online reverse auctions. *Industrial Paint and Powder, 78*(9), 45-47.

Schrader, R. W., Schrader, J. T., & Eller, E. P. (2004). Strategic implications of reverse auctions. *Journal of Business to Business Marketing, 11*(1,2), 61-82.

Shih, D.-H., Huang, S.-Y., & Yen, D. C. (2005). A new reverse auction agent system for m-commerce using mobile agents. *Computer Standards & Interfaces, 27*(4), 383-395.

Snyder, C. M. (1996). A dynamic theory of countervailing power. *Rand Journal of Economics, 27*(4), 747-769.

Stoddard, J. (2003). Going, going, gone: Reverse auctions. *Canadian Printer, 111*(3), 29.

Stoddard, J. (2003). Going, going, gone: Reverse auctions. *Gravure, August,* 46-48.

Suyama, T., & Yokoo, M. (2005). Strategy/false-name proof protocols for combinatorial multi-attribute procurement auction. *Autonomous Agents and Multi-Agent Systems, 11*(1), 7-21.

Teich, J. E., Wallenius, H., Wallenius, J., & Koppius, O. R. (2004). Emerging multiple issue e-auctions. *European Journal of Operational Research, 159*(1), 1-16.

Teich, J. E., Wallenius, H., Wallenius, J., & Zaitsev, A. (2006). A multi-attribute e-auction mechanism for procurement: Theoretical foundations. *European Journal of Operational Research, 175*(1), 90-100.

Buyer-Supplier Relationship (Dyad)

Number of Citations: 53

Anonymous. (2004). Buy better. *International Journal of Productivity and Performance Management, 53*(5/6), 560-561.

Anton, J. J., & Yao, D. A. (1989). Split awards, procurement, and innovation. *The Rand Journal of Economics, 20*(4), 538-552.

Anton, J. J., & Yao, D. A. (1992). Coordination in split award auctions. *The Quarterly Journal of Economics, 107*(2), 681-707.

Bag, P. K. (1997). Optimal auction design and R&D. *European Economic Review, 41*(9), 1655-1674.

Barrett, R. T., & Pugh, R. E. (2003). Procurement auctions in e-commerce. *Southern Business Review, 29*(1), 1-14.

Bichler, M., & Kalagnanam, J. (2005). Configurable offers and winner determination in multi-attribute auctions. *European Journal of Operational Research, 160*(2), 380-394.

Carbone, J. (2005). Not just a cost-reduction tool [electronic industry]. *Purchasing, 134*(3), 43-44.

Carter, C. R., Kaufmann, L., Beall, S., Carter, P. L., Hendrick, T. E., & Petersen, K. J. (2004). Reverse auctions: Grounded theory from the buyer and supplier perspective. *Transportation Research Part E: Logistics and Transportation Review, 40*(3), 229-254.

Chen-Ritzo, C.-H., Harrison, T. P., Kwasnica, A. M., & Thomas, D. J. (2005). Better, faster, cheaper: An experimental analysis of a multiattribute reverse auction mechanism with restricted information feedback. *Management Science, 51*(12), 1753-1762.

Dai, R., Narasimhan, S., & Wu, D. J. (2005). Buyer's efficient e-sourcing structure: Centralize or decentralize? *Journal of Management Information Systems, 22*(2), 141-164.

Dasgupta, S., & Spulber, D. F. (1989). Managing procurement auctions. *Information Economics and Policy, 4*(1), 5-29.

Douglas, A. (2003). Damage limited [e-auctions]. *Supply Management,* 32-33.

Emiliani, M. L. (2005). Regulating B2B online reverse auctions through voluntary codes of conduct. *Industrial Marketing Management, 34*(5), 526-534.

Emiliani, M. L., & Stec, D. J. (2001). Online reverse auction purchasing contracts. *Supply Chain Management, 6*(3/4), 101-105.

Emiliani, M. L., & Stec, D. J. (2002). Realizing savings from online reverse auctions. *Supply Chain Management, 7*(1), 12-23.

Emiliani, M. L., & Stec, D. J. (2002). Squaring online reverse auctions with the Caux Round Table Principles for Business. *Supply Chain Management, 7*(2), 92-100.

Emiliani, M. L., & Stec, D. J. (2004). Aerospace parts suppliers' reaction to online reverse auctions. *Supply Chain Management, 9*(2), 139-153.

Engelbrecht-Wiggans, R., & Katok, E. (2006). E-sourcing in procurement: Theory and behavior in reverse auctions with noncompetitive contracts. *Management Science, 52*(4), 581-596.

Eso, M., Ghosh, S., Kalagnanam, J., & Ladanyi, L. (2005). Bid evaluation in procurement auctions with piecewise linear supply curves. *Journal of Heuristics, 11*(2), 147-173.

Gallien, J., & Wein, L. M. (2005). A smart market for industrial procurement with capacity constraints. *Management Science, 51*(1), 76-91.

Gattiker, T. F., Huang, X., & Schwarz, J. L. (2007). Negotiation e-mail, and Internet reverse auctions: How sourcing mechanisms deployed by buyers affect suppliers' trust. *Journal of Operations Management, 25*(1), 184-202.

Goossens, D. R., Maas, A. J. T., Spieksma, F. C. R., & van de Klundert, J. J. (In press). Exact algorithms for procurement problems under a total quantity discount structure. *European Journal of Operational Research.*

Hannon, D. (2003). E-sourcing survey: Purchasing survey shows e-sourcing adoption stalls. *Purchasing, 132*(12), 49-51.

Hartley, J. L., Duplaga, E. A., & Lane, M. D. (2005). Reverse e-auctions: Exploring reasons for use and buyer's satisfaction. *International Journal of Integrated Supply Management, 1*(4), 410-420.

Hartley, J. L., Lane, M. D., & Duplaga, E. A. (2006). Exploring the barriers to the adoption of e-auctions for sourcing. *International Journal of Operations & Production Management, 26*(2), 202-221.

Hartley, J. L., Lane, M. D., & Hong, Y. (2004). An exploration of the adoption of e-auctions in supply management. *IEEE Transactions on Engineering Management, 51*(2), 153-161.

Hatton, J., & Young, B. (2004). Are e-auctions a good way to buy services? *Supply Management,* 28-29.

Hazra, J., & Mahadevan, B. (2006). Impact of supply base heterogeneity in electronic markets. *European Journal of Operational Research, 174*(3), 1580-1594.

Hohner, G., Rich, J., Ng, E., Reid, G., Davenport, A. J., Kalagnanam, J. R., et al. (2003). Combinatorial and quantity-discount procurement auctions benefit Mars, Incorporated and its suppliers. *Interfaces, 33*(1), 23-35.

Hu, C., & Lu, Y.-B. (2005). Procurement auction model with piecewise linear price curves and its genetic algorithm. *Industrial Engineering and Management, 10*(2), 76-80.

Ivang, R., & Soerensen, O. J. (2005). E-markets in the battle zone between relationship and transaction marketing! *Electronic Markets, 15*(4), 393-404.

Jap, S. (2000). Going, going, gone. *Harvard Business Review, 78*(6), 30.

Jap, S. D. (2003). An exploratory study of the introduction of online reverse auctions. *Journal of Marketing, 67*(3), 96-107.

Kauffman, R. G., & Leszczyc, P. T. L. P. (2005). An optimization approach to business buyer choice sets: How many suppliers should be included? *Industrial Marketing Management, 34*(1), 3-12.

Kwak, M. (2002). Potential pitfalls of e-auctions. *MIT Sloan Management Review, 43*(2), 18.

Meere, A. (2001). Converters enter new bidding war. *Official Board Markets, 77*(32), 1.

Mullane, J. V., Peters, M. H., & Bullington, K. E. (2001). Entrepreneurial firms as suppliers in business-to-business e-commerce. *Management Decision, 39*(5/6), 388-393.

O'Brien, L. (2001). Relationships under the hammer [online auctions]. *Supply Management*, 30-31.

Oliva, R. A. (2001). Discovering price discovery. *Marketing Management, 10*(4), 46-48.

Parente, D. H., Venkataraman, R. R., Fizel, J. L., & Millet, I. (2004). A conceptual research framework for analyzing online auctions in a B2B environment. *Supply Chain Management, 9*(4), 287-294.

Parkes, D. C., & Kalagnanam, J. (2005). Models for iterative multiattribute procurement auctions. *Management Science, 51*(3), 435-451.

Pearcy, D. H., & Giunipero, L. C. (2006). The impact of electronic reverse auctions on purchase price reduction and governance structure: An empirical investigation. *International Journal of Services Technology and Management, 7*(3), 215-236.

Sandholm, T., Levine, D., Concordia, M., Martyn, P., Hughes, R., Jacobs, J., et al. (2006). Changing the game in strategic sourcing at Procter & Gamble: Expressive competition enabled by optimization. *Interfaces, 36*(1), 55-68, 95-97.

Smart, A., & Harrison, A. (2003). Online reverse auctions and their role in buyer-supplier relationships. *Journal of Purchasing and Supply Management, 9*(5-6), 257-268.

Smeltzer, L. R., & Carr, A. (2002). Reverse auctions in industrial marketing and buying. *Business Horizons, 45*(2), 47-52.

Standifer, R. L., & Wall, J. A., Jr. (2003). Managing conflict in B2B e-commerce. *Business Horizons, 46*(2), 65-70.

Stein, A., Hawking, P., & Wyld, D. C. (2003). The 20% solution? A case study on the efficacy of reverse auctions. *Management Research News, 26*(5), 1-20.

Talluri, S., & Ragatz, G. L. (2004). Multi-attribute reverse auctions in B2B exchanges: A framework for design and implementation. *Journal of Supply Chain Management, 40*(1), 52-60.

Tassabehji, R., Taylor, W. A., Beach, R., & Wood, A. (2006). Reverse e-auctions and supplier-buyer relationships: An exploratory study. *International Journal of Operations & Production Management, 26*(2), 166-184.

Tinham, B. (2004). Under the e-hammer. *Manufacturing Computer Solutions, 10*(3), 53.

Vail, S. (2005). The tender connection [electronic sourcing]. *Supply Management, 10*(15), 21-23.

Van Tulder, R., & Mol, M. (2002). Reverse auctions or auctions reversed: First experiments by Philips. *European Management Journal, 20*(5), 447-456.

Wang, S., Zheng, W., & Archer, N. (2005). The impact of Internet-based electronic marketplaces on buyer-supplier relationships. *Journal of Internet Commerce, 4*(3), 41-67.

Supply Chain Management and the Reverse Auction

Number of Citations: 36

Arminas, D. (2003). Beyond the quick wins [e-procurement]. *Supply Management*, 34-35.

Barrett, R. T., & Pugh, R. E. (2003). Procurement auctions in e-commerce. *Southern Business Review, 29*(1), 1-14.

Brandt, S. (2003). Business models, the Internet and printing industry associate. E-business in the printing field: Query whether it is the beginning of the end. *Deutscher Drucker Stuttgart, 39*(7), 24-26.

Carter, C. R., Kaufmann, L., Beall, S., Carter, P. L., Hendrick, T. E., & Petersen, K. J. (2004). Reverse auctions: Grounded theory from the buyer and supplier perspective. *Transportation Research Part E: Logistics and Transportation Review, 40*(3), 229-254.

Chen-Ritzo, C.-H., Harrison, T. P., Kwasnica, A. M., & Thomas, D. J. (2005). Better, faster, cheaper: An experimental analysis of a multiattribute reverse auction mechanism with restricted information feedback. *Management Science, 51*(12), 1753-1762.

Cox, A., Chicksand, D., Ireland, P., & Davies, T. (2005). Sourcing indirect spend: A survey of current internal and external strategies for non-revenue-generating goods and services. *Journal of Supply Chain Management, 41*(2), 39-51.

Daly, S. P., & Nath, P. (2005). Reverse auctions for relationship marketers. *Industrial Marketing Management, 34*(2), 157-166.

Davis, B. (2004). Trading places [e-trading exchanges]. *Professional Engineering, 17*(8), 34-35.

Davis, B. (2006). Digital business: A more consolidated approach [oil industry]. *Petroleum Review, 60*(709), 32-34.

Douglas, A. (2003). Damage limited [e-auctions]. *Supply Management*, 32-33.

Emiliani, M. L. (2004). Sourcing in the global aerospace supply chain using online reverse auctions. *Industrial Marketing Management, 33*(1), 65-72.

Emiliani, M. L. (2005). Regulating B2B online reverse auctions through voluntary codes of conduct. *Industrial Marketing Management, 34*(5), 526-534.

Emiliani, M. L. (2006). Executive decision-making traps and B2B online reverse auctions. *Supply Chain Management, 11*(1), 6-9.

Emiliani, M. L., & Stec, D. J. (2001). Online reverse auction purchasing contracts. *Supply Chain Management, 6*(3/4), 101-105.

Emiliani, M. L., & Stec, D. J. (2002). Realizing savings from online reverse auctions. *Supply Chain Management, 7*(1), 12-23.

Emiliani, M. L., & Stec, D. J. (2002). Squaring online reverse auctions with the Caux Round Table Principles for Business. *Supply Chain Management, 7*(2), 92-100.

Emiliani, M. L., & Stec, D. J. (2004). Aerospace parts suppliers' reaction to online reverse auctions. *Supply Chain Management, 9*(2), 139-153.

Evans, B., & Bacheldor, B. (2003). Beyond e-procurement. *InformationWEEK,* (923), 44-45.

Gattiker, T. F., Huang, X., & Schwarz, J. L. (2007). Negotiation e-mail, and Internet reverse auctions: How sourcing mechanisms deployed by buyers affect suppliers' trust. *Journal of Operations Management, 25*(1), 184-202.

Hannon, D. (2003). E-sourcing: CAPS research study defines staying power of e-auctions. *Purchasing, 132*(12), 48-49.

Hartley, J. L., Duplaga, E. A., & Lane, M. D. (2005). Reverse e-auctions: Exploring reasons for use and buyer's satisfaction. *International Journal of Integrated Supply Management, 1*(4), 410-420.

Hatton, J., & Young, B. (2004). Are e-auctions a good way to buy services? *Supply Management,* 28-29.

Hazra, J., & Mahadevan, B. (2006). Impact of supply base heterogeneity in electronic markets. *European Journal of Operational Research, 174*(3), 1580-1594.

Jeong, W. S., Han, S. G., & Jo, G. S. (2003). Intelligent cyber logistics using reverse auction in electronic commerce. *Journal of Organizational Computing and Electronic Commerce, 13*(3-4), 191-209.

Johnson, P. F., & Klassen, R. D. (2005). E-procurement. *MIT Sloan Management Review, 46*(2), 7-10.

Lancioni, R. (2005). Pricing issues in industrial marketing. *Industrial Marketing Management, 34*(2), 111-114.

Li, Y.-F. (2003). Reverse auction purchase: A new purchase model. *Industrial Engineering and Management, 8*(1), 71-73.

Mishra, D., & Veermani, D. (2006). An ascending price procurement auction for multiple items with unit supply. *IIE Transactions (Institute of Industrial Engineers), 38*(2), 127-140.

Parente, D. H., Venkataraman, R. R., Fizel, J. L., & Millet, I. (2004). A conceptual research framework for analyzing online auctions in a B2B environment. *Supply Chain Management, 9*(4), 287-294.

Settoon, R. P., & Wyld, D. C. (2003). The ski slope to prosperity: An analysis of the potential impact of reverse auctions in government procurement in five southeast Asian nations. *Asia Pacific Journal of Marketing and Logistics, 15*(3), 3-19.

Supporting the [ship repair industry]. (2005). *European Supply Chain Management,* 81-82.

Talluri, S., & Ragatz, G. L. (2004). Multi-attribute reverse auctions in B2B exchanges: A framework for design and implementation. *Journal of Supply Chain Management, 40*(1), 52-60.

Tassabehji, R., Taylor, W. A., Beach, R., & Wood, A. (2006). Reverse e-auctions and supplier-buyer relationships: An exploratory study. *International Journal of Operations & Production Management, 26*(2), 166-184.

Tunca, T. I., & Zenios, S. A. (2006). Supply auctions and relational contracts for procurement. *Manufacturing and Service Operations Management, 8*(1), 43-67.

Turner, B. (2003). Packs that think for themselves. *Packaging Magazine, 6*(14), 22.

Twentyman, J. (2005). Under pressure [business/industrial economics]. *Information Age*, 34-35.

Suppliers in the Reverse Auction

Number of Citations: 31

Anon. (2000). G-P selling mills, launches wood e-trade. *International Woodfiber Report, 6*(9), 1.

Atkinson, W. (2000). IT firm uses reverse auction for big contract labor buy. *Purchasing, 129*(11), 97-99.

Barling, B. (2002). Expert advice: How can my organisation take advantage of reverse auctions without jeopardising existing supplier relationships? *Information Age*, 41.

Beil, D. R., & Wein, L. M. (2003). An inverse-optimization-based auction mechanism to support a multiattribute RFQ process. *Management Science, 49*(11), 1529-1545.

Cohen, A. (2004). An auction to DIY for business travel [e-auction]. *Supply Management*, 28-29.

Cox, A., Chicksand, D., Ireland, P., & Davies, T. (2005). Sourcing indirect spend: A survey of current internal and external strategies for non-revenue-generating goods and services. *Journal of Supply Chain Management, 41*(2), 39-51.

Daly, S. P., & Nath, P. (2005). Reverse auctions for relationship marketers. *Industrial Marketing Management, 34*(2), 157-166.

Davis, B. (2004). Trading places [e-trading exchanges]. *Professional Engineering, 17*(8), 34-35.

Dochstader, J. (2003). Label industry matures. *Flexo, 28*(6), 13-16.

Emiliani, M. L. (2004). Sourcing in the global aerospace supply chain using online reverse auctions. *Industrial Marketing Management, 33*(1), 65-72.

Goodwin, C. (2005). Electronic procurement. *Glass, 82*(5), 153.

Hannon, D. (2003). E-sourcing: CAPS research study defines staying power of e-auctions. *Purchasing, 132*(12), 48-49.

Hannon, D. (2003). Pharmaceutical firm uses unique funding model. *Purchasing, 132*(12), 51.

Hirsch, S. (2005). Reverse auctions sharpen competition. *International Trade Forum*(3), 14-15.

Hur, D., Hartley, J. L., & Mabert, V. A. (2006). Implementing reverse e-auctions: A learning process. *Business Horizons, 49*(1), 21-29.

Jin, M., & Wu, S. D. (2006). Supplier coalitions in online reverse auctions: Validity requirements and profit distribution scheme. *International Journal of Production Economics, 100*(2), 183-194.

Kjerstad, E., & Vagstad, S. (2000). Procurement auctions with entry of bidders. *International Journal of Industrial Organization, 18*(8), 1243-1257.

Lancioni, R. (2005). Pricing issues in industrial marketing. *Industrial Marketing Management, 34*(2), 111-114.

Millet, I., Parente, D. H., Fizel, J. L., & Venkataraman, R. R. (2004). Metrics for managing online procurement auctions. *Interfaces, 34*(3), 171-179.

Mishra, D., & Veeramani, D. (In press). Vickrey-Dutch procurement auction for multiple items. *European Journal of Operational Research.*

Mishra, D., & Veermani, D. (2006). An ascending price procurement auction for multiple items with unit supply. *IIE Transactions (Institute of Industrial Engineers), 38*(2), 127-140.

Rao, B. V., & Smith, B. C. (2006). Decision support in online travel retailing. *Journal of Revenue and Pricing Management, 5*(1), 72-80.

Smeltzer, L. R., & Carr, A. S. (2003). Electronic reverse auctions: Promises, risks and conditions for success. *Industrial Marketing Management, 32*(6), 481-488.

Stoddard, J. (2003). Going, going...gone. *Paper, Film and Foil Converter, 77*(5), 42.

Supporting the [ship repair industry]. (2005). *European Supply Chain Management*, 81-82.

Tunca, T. I., & Zenios, S. A. (2006). Supply auctions and relational contracts for procurement. *Manufacturing and Service Operations Management, 8*(1), 43-67.

Twentyman, J. (2005). Under pressure [business/industrial economics]. *Information Age*, 34-35.

Vagstad, S. (2000). Centralized vs. decentralized procurement: Does dispersed information call for decentralized decision-making? *International Journal of Industrial Organization, 18*(6), 949-963.

Wagner, S. M., & Schwab, A. P. (2004). Setting the stage for successful electronic reverse auctions. *Journal of Purchasing and Supply Management, 10*(1), 11-26.

Wolfram, C. D. (1998). Strategic bidding in a multiunit auction: An empirical analysis of bids to supply electricity in England and Wales. *The Rand Journal of Economics, 29*(4), 703-725.

Yildirim, H. (2004). Piecewise procurement of a large-scale project. *International Journal of Industrial Organization, 22*(8-9), 1349-1375.

Ethics in Online Procurement Auctions

Number of Citations: 13

Anton, J. J., & Yao, D. A. (1989). Split awards, procurement, and innovation. *The Rand Journal of Economics, 20*(4), 538-552.

Bajari, P., & Ye, L. (2003). Deciding between competition and collusion. *The Review of Economics and Statistics, 85*(4), 971-989.

Carter, C. R., Kaufmann, L., Beall, S., Carter, P. L., Hendrick, T. E., & Petersen, K. J. (2004). Reverse auctions: Grounded theory from the buyer and supplier perspective. *Transportation Research Part E: Logistics and Transportation Review, 40*(3), 229-254.

Compte, O., Lambert-Mogiliansky, A., & Verdier, T. (2005). Corruption and competition in procurement auctions. *Rand Journal of Economics, 36*(1), 1-15.

Davis, D. D., & Wilson, B. J. (2002). Collusion in procurement auctions: An experimental examination. *Economic Inquiry, 40*(2), 213-230.

E-auction playbook II. (2002). *Purchasing, 131*(20), 35-37.

Gupta, S. (2001). The effect of bid rigging on prices: a study of the highway construction industry. *Review of Industrial Organization, 19*(4), 451-465.

Gupta, S. (2002). Competition and collusion in a government procurement auction market. *Atlantic Economic Journal, 30*(1), 13-25.

Iimi, A. (2004). (Anti-)Competitive effect of joint bidding: Evidence from ODA procurement auctions. *Journal of the Japanese and International Economies, 18*(3), 416-439.

Johnson, L. (1990). Gains from a unified European community public procurement market: An analysis using auction theory. *Brigham Young University Law Review, 1990*(4), 1727-1742.

Marshall, R. C., & Meurer, M. J. (2004). Bidder collusion and antitrust law: Refining the analysis of price fixing to account for the special features of auction markets. *Antitrust Law Journal, 72*(1), 83-118.

Porter, R. H., & Zona, J. D. (1993). Detection of bid rigging in procurement auctions. *The Journal of Political Economy, 101*(3), 518-538.

Snyder, C. M. (1996). A dynamic theory of countervailing power. *Rand Journal of Economics, 27*(4), 747-769.

Quality

Number of Citations: 22

Beil, D. R., & Wein, L. M. (2003). An inverse-optimization-based auction mechanism to support a multiattribute RFQ process. *Management Science, 49*(11), 1529-1545.

Bichler, M., & Kalagnanam, J. (2005). Configurable offers and winner determination in multi-attribute auctions. *European Journal of Operational Research, 160*(2), 380-394.

Branco, F. (1997). The design of multidimensional auctions. *The Rand Journal of Economics, 28*(1), 63-81.

Carbone, J. (2005). Not just a cost-reduction tool [electronic industry]. *Purchasing, 134*(3), 43-44.

Castiglione, D. (2006). Court your customers. *Paperboard Packaging, 91*(1), 10.

Chen-Ritzo, C.-H., Harrison, T. P., Kwasnica, A. M., & Thomas, D. J. (2005). Better, faster, cheaper: An experimental analysis of a multiattribute reverse auction mechanism with restricted information feedback. *Management Science, 51*(12), 1753-1762.

Douglas, A. (2003). Damage limited [e-auctions]. *Supply Management*, 32-33.

Elgart, E. G. (2001). Army reverse auctions: An e-commerce acquisition tool. *Public Manager, 30*(1), 13-16.

Gabert, S. (2003). Are reverse auctions friend or foe? *Printing News, 150*(14), 1-5.

Güth, W., Ivanova-Stenzel, R., & Kröger, S. (2006). Procurement experiments with unknown costs of quality. *Pacific Economic Review, 11*(2), 133-148.

Hohner, G., Rich, J., Ng, E., Reid, G., Davenport, A. J., Kalagnanam, J. R., et al. (2003). Combinatorial and quantity-discount procurement auctions benefit Mars, Incorporated and its suppliers. *Interfaces, 33*(1), 23-35.

Kim, Y. (2005). The effects of buyer and product traits with seller reputation on price premiums in e-auction. *The Journal of Computer Information Systems, 46*(1), 79-91.

Kinney, S. (2000). RIP fixed pricing: The Internet is on its way to "marketizing" everything. *Business Economics, 35*(2), 39-44.

Naegelen, F. (2002). Implementing optimal procurement auctions with exogenous quality. *Review of Economic Design, 7*(2), 135-153.

Snir, E. M., & Hitt, L. M. (2003). Costly bidding in online markets for IT services. *Management Science, 49*(11), 1504-1520.

Suyama, T., & Yokoo, M. (2005). Strategy/false-name proof protocols for combinatorial multi-attribute procurement auction. *Autonomous Agents and Multi-Agent Systems, 11*(1), 7-21.

Teich, J. E., Wallenius, H., Wallenius, J., & Koppius, O. R. (2004). Emerging multiple issue e-auctions. *European Journal of Operational Research, 159*(1), 1-16.

Tunca, T. I., & Zenios, S. A. (2006). Supply auctions and relational contracts for procurement. *Manufacturing and Service Operations Management, 8*(1), 43-67.

Turner, B. (2003). Packs that think for themselves. *Packaging Magazine, 6*(14), 22.

Twentyman, J. (2005). Under pressure [business/industrial economics]. *Information Age*, 34-35.

Vagstad, S. (2000). Centralized vs. decentralized procurement: Does dispersed information call for decentralized decision-making? *International Journal of Industrial Organization, 18*(6), 949-963.

Wang, J.-L., Yu, B.-X., & Wang, Y.-M. (2004). A general secure e-auction model based on bit commitment. *Chinese Journal of Computers, 27*(3), 347-351.

Productivity or Performance

Number of Citations: 17

Anonymous. (2004). Buy better. *International Journal of Productivity and Performance Management, 53*(5/6), 560-561.

Anton, J. J., & Yao, D. A. (1992). Coordination in split award auctions. *The Quarterly Journal of Economics, 107*(2), 681-707.

Bartholomew, D. (2004). The juice flows again. *Industry Week, 253*(3), 31-34.

Carter, C. R., Kaufmann, L., Beall, S., Carter, P. L., Hendrick, T. E., & Petersen, K. J. (2004). Reverse auctions: Grounded theory from the buyer and supplier perspective. *Transportation Research Part E: Logistics and Transportation Review, 40*(3), 229-254.

Chen-Ritzo, C.-H., Harrison, T. P., Kwasnica, A. M., & Thomas, D. J. (2005). Better, faster, cheaper: An experimental analysis of a multiattribute reverse auction mechanism with restricted information feedback. *Management Science, 51*(12), 1753-1762.

Douglas, A. (2003). Damage limited [e-auctions]. *Supply Management*, 32-33.

Goossens, D. R., Maas, A. J. T., Spieksma, F. C. R., & van de Klundert, J. J. (In press). Exact algorithms for procurement problems under a total quantity discount structure. *European Journal of Operational Research*.

Gupta, S. (2002). Competition and collusion in a government procurement auction market. *Atlantic Economic Journal, 30*(1), 13-25.

Hartley, J. L., Lane, M. D., & Hong, Y. (2004). An exploration of the adoption of e-auctions in supply management. *IEEE Transactions on Engineering Management, 51*(2), 153-161.

Jap, S. D. (2002). Online reverse auctions: Issues, themes, and prospects for the future. *Academy of Marketing Science. Journal, 30*(4), 506-525.

Johnson, P. F., & Klassen, R. D. (2005). E-procurement. *MIT Sloan Management Review, 46*(2), 7-10.

Kwak, M. (2002). Potential pitfalls of e-auctions. *MIT Sloan Management Review, 43*(2), 18.

Parente, D. H., Venkataraman, R. R., Fizel, J. L., & Millet, I. (2004). A conceptual research framework for analyzing online auctions in a B2B environment. *Supply Chain Management, 9*(4), 287-294.

Raghavan, N. R. S., & Prabhu, M. (2004). Object-oriented design of a distributed agent-based framework for e-procurement. *Production Planning and Control, 15*(7), 731-741.

Sampath, K., Saygin, C., Grasman, S. E., & Leu, M. C. (2006). Impact of reputation information sharing in an auction-based job allocation model for small and medium-sized enterprises. *International Journal of Production Research, 44*(9), 1777-1798.

Supporting the [ship repair industry]. (2005). *European Supply Chain Management*, 81-82.

Teich, J. E., Wallenius, H., Wallenius, J., & Koppius, O. R. (2004). Emerging multiple issue e-auctions. *European Journal of Operational Research, 159*(1), 1-16.

Auction Outcomes and Implementation

Number of Citations: 19

Anonymous. (2004). Buy better. *International Journal of Productivity and Performance Management, 53*(5/6), 560-561.

Arminas, D. (2003). Beyond the quick wins [e-procurement]. *Supply Management*, 34-35.

Arnold, U., Karner, H., & Schnabel, M. (2005). Target-oriented use of strategic sourcing tools: A critical analysis creating process awareness for electronic reverse auctions. *Journal of Purchasing and Supply Management, 11*(2-3), 116-128.

Atkinson, W. (2000). Materials maker streamlines and saves with online buying. *Purchasing, 129*(11), 86-88.

Barling, B. (2002). Expert advice: How can my organisation take advantage of reverse auctions without jeopardising existing supplier relationships? *Information Age*, 41.

Emiliani, M. L. (2004). Sourcing in the global aerospace supply chain using online reverse auctions. *Industrial Marketing Management, 33*(1), 65-72.

Emiliani, M. L. (2006). Executive decision-making traps and B2B online reverse auctions. *Supply Chain Management, 11*(1), 6-9.

Guilloux, V. (2002). Electronic auctions: An example in the advertising sector. *Décisions Marketing, 27*, 51-71.

Hur, D., Hartley, J. L., & Mabert, V. A. (2006). Implementing reverse e-auctions: A learning process. *Business Horizons, 49*(1), 21-29.

Klafft, M., & Spiekermann, S. (2006). Reverse procurement and auctions for consumers: A new trend on the horizon of e-commerce? *Wirtschaftsinformatik, 48*(1), 36-45.

Lancioni, R. (2005). Pricing issues in industrial marketing. *Industrial Marketing Management, 34*(2), 111-114.

Lauw, H. W., Hui, S. C., & Lai, E. (2004). Shared-storage auction ensures data availability. *IEEE Internet Computing, 8*(5), 22-28.

Millet, I., Parente, D. H., Fizel, J. L., & Venkataraman, R. R. (2004). Metrics for managing online procurement auctions. *Interfaces, 34*(3), 171-179.

Rao, B. V., & Smith, B. C. (2006). Decision support in online travel retailing. *Journal of Revenue and Pricing Management, 5*(1), 72-80.

Reding, C. (2002). Assessing online reverse auctions. *Industrial Paint and Powder, 78*(9), 45-47.

Smeltzer, L. R., & Carr, A. S. (2002). Reverse auctions in industrial marketing and buying. *Business Horizons, 45*(2), 47-52.

Smeltzer, L. R., & Carr, A. S. (2003). Electronic reverse auctions: Promises, risks and conditions for success. *Industrial Marketing Management, 32*(6), 481-488.

Tinham, B. (2004). Under the e-hammer. *Manufacturing Computer Solutions, 10*(3), 53.

Wagner, S. M., & Schwab, A. P. (2004). Setting the stage for successful electronic reverse auctions. *Journal of Purchasing and Supply Management, 10*(1), 11-26.

Financial Issues in Reverse Auctions

Number of Citations: 147

Anon. (2000). G-P selling mills, launches wood e-trade. *International Woodfiber Report, 6*(9), 1.

Anonymous. (2004). Buy better. *International Journal of Productivity and Performance Management, 53*(5/6), 560-561.

Anton, J. J., & Yao, D. A. (1989). Split awards, procurement, and innovation. *The Rand Journal of Economics, 20*(4), 538-552.

Anton, J. J., & Yao, D. A. (1992). Coordination in split award auctions. *The Quarterly Journal of Economics, 107*(2), 681-707.

Arminas, D. (2003). Beyond the quick wins [e-procurement]. *Supply Management,* 34-35.

Arnold, U., Karner, H., & Schnabel, M. (2005). Target-oriented use of strategic sourcing tools: A critical analysis creating process awareness for electronic reverse auctions. *Journal of Purchasing and Supply Management, 11*(2-3), 116-128.

Arozamena, L., & Cantillon, E. (2004). Investment incentives in procurement auctions. *The Review of Economic Studies, 71*(1), 1-18.

Atkinson, W. (2000). Materials maker streamlines and saves with online buying. *Purchasing, 129*(11), 86-88.

Bag, P. K. (1997). Optimal auction design and R&D. *European Economic Review, 41*(9), 1655-1674.

Bajari, P., & Ye, L. (2003). Deciding between competition and collusion. *The Review of Economics and Statistics, 85*(4), 971-989.

Bandyopadhyay, S., Rees, J., & Barron, J. M. (2006). Simulating sellers in online exchanges. *Decision Support Systems, 41*(2), 500-513.

Barling, B. (2002). Expert advice: How can my organisation take advantage of reverse auctions without jeopardising existing supplier relationships? *Information Age,* 41.

Barrett, R. T., & Pugh, R. E. (2003). Procurement auctions in e-commerce. *Southern Business Review, 29*(1), 1-14.

Bartholomew, D. (2004). The juice flows again. *Industry Week, 253*(3), 31-34.

Beil, D. R., & Wein, L. M. (2003). An inverse-optimization-based auction mechanism to support a multiattribute RFQ process. *Management Science, 49*(11), 1529-1545.

Bertsekas, D. P., & Castanon, D. A. (1992). Forward/reverse auction algorithm for asymmetric assignment problems. *Computational Optimization and Applications, 1*(3), 277-297.

Beyond the e-auction hype. (2000). *Purchasing, 128*(4), 60-63.

Bichler, M., & Kalagnanam, J. R. (2005). Configurable offers and winner determination in multi-attribute auctions. *European Journal of Operational Research, 160*(2), 380-394.

Bichler, M., & Kalagnanam, J. R. (2006). A non-parametric estimator for setting reservation prices in procurement auctions. *Information Technology and Management, 7*(3), 157-169.

Borkar, V. S., Dave, M. S., & Shyamasundar, R. K. (2005). Design and implementation of SeTiA: Secure multi auction system - I. Auction mechanisms. *Journal of Intelligent Systems, 14*(1), 45-68.

Boyle, E. J. (2003). Let's talk trends. *Paper, Film and Foil Converter, 77*(9), T30.

Branco, F. (1997). The design of multidimensional auctions. *The Rand Journal of Economics, 28*(1), 63-81.

Brandt, S. (2003). Business models, the Internet and printing industry associate. E-business in the printing field: Query whether it is the beginning of the end. *Deutscher Drucker Stuttgart, 39*(7), 24-26.

Brisset, K., & Thomas, L. (2004). Leniency program: A new tool in competition policy to deter cartel activity in procurement auctions. *European Journal of Law and Economics, 17*(1), 5.

Brosig, J., & Rei, J. P. (In press). Entry decisions and bidding behavior in sequential first-price procurement auctions: An experimental study. *Games and Economic Behavior.*

Brunelli, M. (2000). Web is changing basics of the print buy. *Purchasing, 128*(4), S96.

Budde, J., & Gox, R. F. (1999). The impact of capacity costs on bidding strategies in procurement auctions. *Review of Accounting Studies, 4*(1), 5-13.

Calveras, A., Ganuza, J.-J., & Hauk, E. (2004). Wild bids:Gambling for resurrection in procurement contracts*. *Journal of Regulatory Economics, 26*(1), 41-68.

Carbone, J. (2005). Not just a cost-reduction tool [electronic industry]. *Purchasing, 134*(3), 43-44.

Carr, S. M. (2003). Note on online auctions with costly bid evaluation. *Management Science, 49*(11), 1521-1528.

Carter, C. R., Kaufmann, L., Beall, S., Carter, P. L., Hendrick, T. E., & Petersen, K. J. (2004). Reverse auctions-: Grounded theory from the buyer and supplier perspective. *Transportation Research Part E: Logistics and Transportation Review, 40*(3), 229-254.

Castiglione, D. (2006). Court your customers. *Paperboard Packaging, 91*(1), 10.

Chen-Ritzo, C.-H., Harrison, T. P., Kwasnica, A. M., & Thomas, D. J. (2005). Better, faster, cheaper: An experimental analysis of a multiattribute reverse auction mechanism with restricted information feedback. *Management Science, 51*(12), 1753-1762.

Compte, O., & Jehiel, P. (2002). On the value of competition in procurement auctions. *Econometrica, 70*(1), 343-355.

Compte, O., Lambert-Mogiliansky, A., & Verdier, T. (2005). Corruption and competition in procurement auctions. *Rand Journal of Economics, 36*(1), 1-15.

Dai, R., Narasimhan, S., & Wu, D. J. (2005). Buyer's efficient e-sourcing structure: Centralize or decentralize? *Journal of Management Information Systems, 22*(2), 141-164.

Daly, S. P., & Nath, P. (2005). Reverse auctions for relationship marketers. *Industrial Marketing Management, 34*(2), 157-166.

Dasgupta, S., & Spulber, D. F. (1989). Managing procurement auctions. *Information Economics and Policy, 4*(1), 5-29.

David, E., Azoulay-Schwartz, R., & Kraus, S. (In press). Bidding in sealed-bid and English multi-attribute auctions. *Decision Support Systems.*

Davis, B. (2004). Trading places [e-trading exchanges]. *Professional Engineering, 17*(8), 34-35.

Davis, D. D., & Wilson, B. J. (2002). Collusion in procurement auctions: An experimental examination. *Economic Inquiry, 40*(2), 213-230.

Ding, M., Eliashberg, J., Huber, J., & Saini, R. (2005). Emotional bidders: An analytical and experimental examination of consumers' behavior in a priceline-like reverse auction. *Management Science, 51*(3), 352-364.

Dochstader, J. (2003). Label industry matures. *Flexo, 28*(6), 13-16.

Elgart, E. G. (2001). Army reverse auctions: An E-commerce acquisition tool. *Public Manager, 30*(1), 13-16.

Emiliani, M. L. (2004). Sourcing in the global aerospace supply chain using online reverse auctions. *Industrial Marketing Management, 33*(1), 65-72.

Emiliani, M. L. (2006). Executive decision-making traps and B2B online reverse auctions. *Supply Chain Management, 11*(1), 6-9.

Emiliani, M. L., & Stec, D. J. (2002). Realizing savings from online reverse auctions. *Supply Chain Management, 7*(1), 12-23.

Emiliani, M. L., & Stec, D. J. (2002). Squaring online reverse auctions with the Caux Round Table Principles for Business. *Supply Chain Management, 7*(2), 92-100.

Emiliani, M. L., & Stec, D. J. (2004). Aerospace parts suppliers' reaction to online reverse auctions. *Supply Chain Management, 9*(2), 139-153.

Engelbrecht-Wiggans, R., & Katok, E. (2006). E-sourcing in procurement: Theory and behavior in reverse auctions with noncompetitive contracts. *Management Science, 52*(4), 581-596.

Eso, M., Ghosh, S., Kalagnanam, J., & Ladanyi, L. (2005). Bid evaluation in procurement auctions with piecewise linear supply curves. *Journal of Heuristics, 11*(2), 147-173.

Ewerhart, C., & Fieseler, K. (2003). Procurement auctions and unit-price contracts. *The Rand Journal of Economics, 34*(3), 569-581.

Gabert, S. (2003). Are reverse auctions friend or foe? *Printing News, 150*(14), 1-5.

Gallien, J., & Wein, L. M. (2005). A smart market for industrial procurement with capacity constraints. *Management Science, 51*(1), 76-91.

Goldsborough, R. (2000). Using the Net to travel the real world. *Tech Directions, 60*(5), 14.

Goodwin, C. (2005). Electronic procurement. *Glass, 82*(5), 153.

Goossens, D. R., Maas, A. J. T., Spieksma, F. C. R., & van de Klundert, J. J. (In press). Exact algorithms for procurement problems under a total quantity discount structure. *European Journal of Operational Research.*

Guilloux*, V. (2002). Electronic auctions: An example in advertising sector. *Décisions Marketing, 27,* 51-71.

Günlük, O., Ladányi, L., & Vries, S. D. (2005). A branch-and-price algorithm and new test problems for spectrum auctions. *Management Science, 51*(3), 391-406.

Gupta, S. (2001). The effect of bid rigging on prices: A study of the highway construction industry. *Review of Industrial Organization, 19*(4), 451-465.

Gupta, S. (2002). Competition and collusion in a government procurement auction market. *Atlantic Economic Journal, 30*(1), 13-25.

Güth, W., Ivanova-Stenzel, R., & Kröger, S. (2006). Procurement experiments with unknown costs of quality. *Pacific Economic Review, 11*(2), 133-148.

Hannon, D. (2003). E-sourcing: CAPS research study defines staying power of e-auctions. *Purchasing, 132*(12), 48-49.

Hannon, D. (2003). Pharmaceutical firm uses unique funding model. *Purchasing, 132*(12), 51.

Hartley, J. L., Duplaga, E. A., & Lane, M. D. (2005). Reverse e-auctions: Exploring reasons for use and buyer's satisfaction. *International Journal of Integrated Supply Management, 1*(4), 410-420.

Hartley, J. L., Lane, M. D., & Hong, Y. (2004). An exploration of the adoption of e-auctions in supply management. *IEEE Transactions on Engineering Management, 51*(2), 153-161.

Hatton, J., & Young, B. (2004). Are e-auctions a good way to buy services? *Supply Management*, 28-29.

Hazra, J., & Mahadevan, B. (2006). Impact of supply base heterogeneity in electronic markets. *European Journal of Operational Research, 174*(3), 1580-1594.

Her, Y.-S., Imamoto, K., & Sakurai, K. (2005). Analysis and comparison of cryptographic techniques in e-voting and e-auction. *Research Reports on Information Science and Electrical Engineering of Kyushu University, 10*(2), 91-96.

Hirsch, S. (2005). Reverse auctions sharpen competition. *International Trade Forum*, (3), 14-15.

Hohner, G., Rich, J., Ng, E., Reid, G., Davenport, A. J., Kalagnanam, J. R., et al. (2003). Combinatorial and quantity-discount procurement auctions benefit Mars, Incorporated and its suppliers. *Interfaces, 33*(1), 23-35.

Hong, H., & Shum, M. (2002). Increasing competition and the Winner's Curse: Evidence from procurement. *The Review of Economic Studies, 69*(241), 871-898.

Hu, C., & Lu, Y.-B. (2005). Procurement auction model with piecewise linear price curves and its genetic algorithm. *Industrial Engineering and Management, 10*(2), 76-80.

Hur, D., Hartley, J. L., & Mabert, V. A. (2006). Implementing reverse e-auctions: A learning process. *Business Horizons, 49*(1), 21-29.

Hur, D., Mabert, V. A., & Hartley, J. L. (In press). Getting the most out of reverse e-auction investment. *Omega.*

Iimi, A. (2006). Auction reforms for effective official development assistance. *Review of Industrial Organization, 28*(2), 109.

Ivang, R., & Soerensen, O. J. (2005). E-markets in the battle zone between relationship and transaction marketing! *Electronic Markets, 15*(4), 393-404.

Jap, S. (2000). Going, going, gone. *Harvard Business Review, 78*(6), 30.

Jap, S. D. (2003). An exploratory study of the introduction of online reverse auctions. *Journal of Marketing, 67*(3), 96-107.

Jeong, W. S., Han, S. G., & Jo, G. S. (2003). Intelligent cyber logistics using reverse auction in electronic commerce. *Journal of Organizational Computing and Electronic Commerce, 13*(3-4), 191-209.

Jofre-Bonet, M., & Pesendorfer, M. (2003). Estimation of a dynamic auction game. *Econometrica, 71*(5), 1443-1489.

Johnson, L. (1990). Gains from a unified European community public procurement market: An analysis using auction theory. *Brigham Young University Law Review, 1990*(4), 1727-1742.

Kauffman, R. G., & Leszczyc, P. T. L. P. (2005). An optimization approach to business buyer choice sets: How many suppliers should be included? *Industrial Marketing Management, 34*(1), 3-12.

Kehagias, D. D., Symeonidis, A. L., & Mitkas, P. A. (2005). Designing pricing mechanisms for autonomous agents based on bid-forecasting. *Electronic Markets, 15*(1), 53-62.

Kim, I.-G. (1994). Price-preference vs. tariff policies in government procurement auctions. *Economics Letters, 45*(2), 217-222.

Kim, Y. (2005). The effects of buyer and product traits with seller reputation on price premiums in e-auction. *The Journal of Computer Information Systems, 46*(1), 79-91.

Kinney, S. (2000). RIP fixed pricing: The Internet is on its way to "marketizing" everything. *Business Economics, 35*(2), 39-44.

Kjerstad, E., & Vagstad, S. (2000). Procurement auctions with entry of bidders. *International Journal of Industrial Organization, 18*(8), 1243-1257.

Klafft, M., & Spiekermann, S. (2006). Reverse procurement and auctions for consumers: A new trend on the horizon of e-commerce? *Wirtschaftsinformatik, 48*(1), 36-45.

Kung, M., Monroe, K. B., & Cox, J. L. (2002). Pricing on the Internet. *The Journal of Product and Brand Management, 11*(4/5), 274-287.

Lancioni, R. (2005). Pricing issues in industrial marketing. *Industrial Marketing Management, 34*(2), 111-114.

Li, Y.-F. (2003). Reverse auction purchase: A new purchase model. *Industrial Engineering and Management, 8*(1), 71-73.

Liebmann, L. (2001). Eyes wide shut: A look at B2B marketplaces. *Network Magazine, 16*(2), 112-114.

Lindorff, D. (2006). In this case, talk isn't so cheap. *Treasury and Risk Management, 16*(4), 15.

Luton, R., & McAfee, R. P. (1986). Sequential procurement auctions. *Journal of Public Economics, 31*(2), 181-195.

MacDonald, J. M., Handy, C. R., & Plato, G. E. (2002). Competition and prices in USDA commodity procurement. *Southern Economic Journal, 69*(1), 128-143.

Marshall, R. C., & Meurer, M. J. (2004). Bidder collusion and antitrust law: Refining the analysis of price fixing to account for the special features of auction markets. *Antitrust Law Journal, 72*(1), 83-118.

McKendrick, J. (2000). Priceline.com: An inside look at the reverse auction master. *Electronic Commerce World, 10*(1), 30-34.

Meere, A. (2001). Converters enter new bidding war. *Official Board Markets, 77*(32), 1.

Meij, S., & Pau, L. F. (2006). Auctioning bulk mobile messages. *Computational Economics, 27*(2-3), 395-430.

Microprocessors: MPUs will see 13% growth in 2003. (2002). *Purchasing, 131*(19), 19-28.

Mishra, D., & Veeramani, D. (In press). Vickrey-Dutch procurement auction for multiple items. *European Journal of Operational Research.*

Mishra, D., & Veermani, D. (2006). An ascending price procurement auction for multiple items with unit supply. *IIE Transactions (Institute of Industrial Engineers), 38*(2), 127-140.

Mullane, J. V., Peters, M. H., & Bullington, K. E. (2001). Entrepreneurial firms as suppliers in business-to-business e-commerce. *Management Decision, 39*(5/6), 388-393.

Myers, B. (2005). Fully loaded printing. *Printing News, 155*(10), 10.

Naegelen, F. (2002). Implementing optimal procurement auctions with exogenous quality. *Review of Economic Design, 7*(2), 135-153.

Neal, D. (2004). NHS costs take a hammering [NHS electronic auction system]. *IT Week, 7*(16), 18.

O'Brien, L. (2001). Relationships under the hammer [online auctions]. *Supply Management*, 30-31.

Oliva, R. A. (2001). Discovering price discovery. *Marketing Management, 10*(4), 46-48.

Oliva, R. A. (2003). Business Web: Sold on reverse auctions. *Marketing Management, 12*(2), 44-47.

Parente, D. H., Venkataraman, R. R., Fizel, J. L., & Millet, I. (2004). A conceptual research framework for analyzing online auctions in a B2B environment. *Supply Chain Management, 9*(4), 287-294.

Parkes, D. C., & Kalagnanam, J. (2005). Models for iterative multiattribute procurement auctions. *Management Science, 51*(3), 435-451.

Pearcy, D. H., & Giunipero, L. C. (2006). The impact of electronic reverse auctions on purchase price reduction and governance structure: An empirical investigation. *International Journal of Services Technology and Management, 7*(3), 215-236.

Porter, A. M. (2000). E-auction model morphs to meet buyers' needs. *Purchasing, 128*(10), 31-32.

Porter, R. H., & Zona, J. D. (1993). Detection of bid rigging in procurement auctions. *The Journal of Political Economy, 101*(3), 518-538.

Raghavan, N. R. S., & Prabhu, M. (2004). Object-oriented design of a distributed agent-based framework for e-procurement. *Production Planning and Control, 15*(7), 731-741.

Reding, C. (2002). Assessing online reverse auctions. *Industrial Paint and Powder, 78*(9), 45-47.

Rothkopf, M. H., Harstad, R. M., & Fu, Y. (2003). Is subsidizing inefficient bidders actually costly? *Management Science, 49*(1), 71-84.

Sandholm, T., Levine, D., Concordia, M., Martyn, P., & et al. (2006). Changing the game in strategic sourcing at Procter & Gamble: Expressive competition enabled by optimization. *Interfaces, 36*(1), 55-68, 95-97.

Schrader, R. W., Schrader, J. T., & Eller, E. P. (2004). Strategic implications of reverse auctions. *Journal of Business to Business Marketing, 11*(1, 2), 61-82.

Settoon, R. P., & Wyld, D. C. (2003). The ski slope to prosperity: An analysis of the potential impact of reverse auctions in government procurement in five southeast Asian nations. *Asia Pacific Journal of Marketing and Logistics, 15*(3), 3-19.

Shih, D.-H., Huang, S.-Y., & Yen, D. C. (2005). A new reverse auction agent system for m-commerce using mobile agents. *Computer Standards & Interfaces, 27*(4), 383-395.

Smart, A., & Harrison, A. (2003). Online reverse auctions and their role in buyer-supplier relationships. *Journal of Purchasing and Supply Management, 9*(5-6), 257-268.

Smeltzer, L. R., & Carr, A. (2002). Reverse auctions in industrial marketing and buying. *Business Horizons, 45*(2), 47-52.

Snir, E. M., & Hitt, L. M. (2003). Costly bidding in online markets for IT services. *Management Science, 49*(11), 1504-1520.

Snyder, C. M. (1996). A dynamic theory of countervailing power. *Rand Journal of Economics, 27*(4), 747-769.

Soudry, O. (2004). Promoting economy: Electronic reverse auctions under the EC directives on public procurement. *Journal of Public Procurement, 4*(3), 340-374.

Standifer, R. L., & Wall, J. A., Jr. (2003). Managing conflict in B2B e-commerce. *Business Horizons, 46*(2), 65-70.

Stein, A., Hawking, P., & Wyld, D. C. (2003). The 20% solution? A case study on the efficacy of reverse auctions. *Management Research News, 26*(5), 1-20.

Stoddard, J. (2003). Going, going, gone: Reverse auctions. *Gravure, August*, 46-48.

Suyama, T., & Yokoo, M. (2005). Strategy/false-name proof protocols for combinatorial multi-attribute procurement auction. *Autonomous Agents and Multi-Agent Systems, 11*(1), 7-21.

Swider, D. J., & Weber, C. (In press). Bidding under price uncertainty in multi-unit pay-as-bid procurement auctions for power systems reserve. *European Journal of Operational Research*.

Talluri, S., & Ragatz, G. L. (2004). Multi-attribute reverse auctions in B2B exchanges: A framework for design and implementation. *Journal of Supply Chain Management, 40*(1), 52-60.

Tassabehji, R., Taylor, W. A., Beach, R., & Wood, A. (2006). Reverse e-auctions and supplier-buyer relationships: An exploratory study. *International Journal of Operations & Production Management, 26*(2), 166-184.

Teich, J. E., Wallenius, H., Wallenius, J., & Koppius, O. R. (2004). Emerging multiple issue e-auctions. *European Journal of Operational Research, 159*(1), 1-16.

Teich, J. E., Wallenius, H., Wallenius, J., & Zaitsev, A. (2006). A multi-attribute e-auction mechanism for procurement: Theoretical foundations. *European Journal of Operational Research, 175*(1), 90-100.

Tunca, T. I., & Zenios, S. A. (2006). Supply auctions and relational contracts for procurement. *Manufacturing and Service Operations Management, 8*(1), 43-67.

Turner, B. (2003). Packs that think for themselves. *Packaging Magazine, 6*(14), 22.

Twentyman, J. (2005). Under pressure [business/industrial economics]. *Information Age*, 34-35.

UTC saves 30% using reverse auctions to purchase services. (2001). *Purchasing, 130*(18), 51, 54.

Vagstad, S. (2000). Centralized vs. decentralized procurement: Does dispersed information call for decentralized decision-making? *International Journal of Industrial Organization, 18*(6), 949-963.

van Heck, E., & Vervest, P. (1998). How should CIOs deal with Web-based auctions? *Communications of the ACM, 41*(7), 99-100.

Wagner, S. M., & Schwab, A. P. (2004). Setting the stage for successful electronic reverse auctions. *Journal of Purchasing and Supply Management, 10*(1), 11-26.

Wang, R. (2000). Bidding and renegotiation in procurement auctions. *European Economic Review, 44*(8), 1577-1597.

Wolfram, C. D. (1998). Strategic bidding in a multi-unit auction: An empirical analysis of bids to supply electricity in England and Wales. *The Rand Journal of Economics, 29*(4), 703-725.

Yildirim, H. (2004). Piecewise procurement of a large-scale project. *International Journal of Industrial Organization, 22*(8-9), 1349-1375.

General or Uncategorized Auction Research

Number of Citations: 14

Abrache, J., Bourbeau, B., Gabriel Crainic, T., & Gendreau, M. (2004). A new bidding framework for combinatorial e-auctions. *Computers & Operations Research, 31*(8), 1177-1203.

Anon. (2002). Knight Ridder adopts e-sourcing and reverse auction solutions. *Newspaper Techniques,* (JUL), 60.

Anon. (2002). Reverse auction debate rages. *Official Board Markets, 78*(38), 12.

Anon. (2005). HMS Richmond to undergo refit as FSL secures major contract. *Jane's International Defense Review,* (FEB), 1.

De Silva, D. G., Jeitschko, T. D., & Kosmopoulou, G. (2005). Stochastic synergies in sequential auctions. *International Journal of Industrial Organization, 23*(3-4), 183-201.

Emiliani, M. L., & Stec, D. J. (2005). Commentary on "Reverse auctions for relationship marketers" by Daly and Nath. *Industrial Marketing Management, 34*(2), 167-171.

Fanning, B. (2002). Online reverse auctions create two procurement camps. *Purchasing, 131*(5), 36.

Germer, T., Carter, C. R., & Kauffman, L. (2004). *Purchasing auctions: A synthesis of current research.* Paper presented at the 15th Annual North American Research Symposium on Purchasing and Supply Management, Tempe, AZ.

Mabert, V. A., & Skeels, J. A. (2002). Internet reverse auctions: Valuable tool in experienced hands. *Business Horizons, 45*(4), 70-76.

Merrick, J. J., Jr. (2005). Tracking the U.S. Treasury: Footprints from the Treasury's debt buy-back program. *The Journal of Fixed Income, 15*(2), 37-39, 41-50, 54.

Raffa, L., & Esposito, G. (2006). The implementation of an e-reverse auction system in an Italian health care organization. *Journal of Public Procurement, 6*(1/2), 46-69.

Shih, D. H., Huang, S.-Y., & Lin, B. (2006). Linking secure reverse auction with Web service. *International Journal of Services and Standards, 2*(1), 15-31.

Townend, J. (1992). Recent developments in the gilt-edged market. *Bank of England. Quarterly Bulletin, 32*(1), 76-81.

APPENDIX B

THEORY

Economic Theory

Anton, J. J., & Yao, D. A. (1989). Split awards, procurement, and innovation. *The Rand Journal of Economics, 20*(4), 538-552.

Anton, J. J., & Yao, D. A. (1992). Coordination in split award auctions. *The Quarterly Journal of Economics, 107*(2), 681-707.

Arozamena, L., & Cantillon, E. (2004). Investment incentives in procurement auctions. *The Review of Economic Studies, 71*(1), 1-18.

Bajari, P., & Ye, L. (2003). Deciding between competition and collusion. *The Review of Economics and Statistics, 85*(4), 971-989.

Belleflamme, P., & Bloch, F. (2004). Market sharing agreements and collusive networks. *International Economic Review, 45*(2), 387-411.

Branco, F. (1997). The design of multidimensional auctions. *The Rand Journal of Economics, 28*(1), 63-81.

Gupta, S. (2001). The effect of bid rigging on prices: A study of the highway construction industry. *Review of Industrial Organization, 19*(4), 451-465.

Gupta, S. (2002). Competition and collusion in a government procurement auction market. *Atlantic Economic Journal, 30*(1), 13-25.

Güth, W., Ivanova-Stenzel, R., & Kröger, S. (2006). Procurement experiments with unknown costs of quality. *Pacific Economic Review, 11*(2), 133-148.

Luton, R., & McAfee, R. P. (1986). Sequential procurement auctions. *Journal of Public Economics, 31*(2), 181-195.

Auction Theory

Bichler, M., & Kalagnanam, J. R. (2006). A non-parametric estimator for setting reservation prices in procurement auctions. *Information Technology and Management, 7*(3), 157-169.

Gallien, J., & Wein, L. M. (2005). A smart market for industrial procurement with capacity constraints. *Management Science, 51*(1), 76-91.

Iimi, A. (2004). (Anti-)Competitive effect of joint bidding: Evidence from ODA procurement auctions. *Journal of the Japanese and International Economies, 18*(3), 416-439.

Johnson, L. (1990). Gains from a unified European community public procurement market: An analysis using auction theory. *Brigham Young University Law Review, 1990*(4), 1727-1742.

Snir, E. M., & Hitt, L. M. (2003). Costly bidding in online markets for IT services. *Management Science, 49*(11), 1504-1520.

Soudry, O. (2004). Promoting economy: Electronic reverse auctions under the EC directives on public procurement. *Journal of Public Procurement, 4*(3), 340-374.

Game Theory

Bandyopadhyay, S., Rees, J., & Barron, J. M. (2006). Simulating sellers in online exchanges. *Decision Support Systems, 41*(2), 500-513.

Jofre-Bonet, M., & Pesendorfer, M. (2003). Estimation of a dynamic auction game. *Econometrica, 71*(5), 1443-1489.

Roelofs, M. R. (2002). Common value auctions with default: An experimental approach. *Experimental Economics, 5*(3), 233-252.

Snyder, C. M. (1996). A dynamic theory of countervailing power. *Rand Journal of Economics, 27*(4), 747-769.

Other Theories

Theories that were used include: Systems theory, utility theory, decision theory, computation theory, queuing theory, constraint theory, equivalence theory, and information richness theory.

Bichler, M., & Kalagnanam, J. (2005). Configurable offers and winner determination in multi-attribute auctions. *European Journal of Operational Research, 160*(2), 380-394.

Carter, C. R., Kaufmann, L., Beall, S., Carter, P. L., Hendrick, T. E., & Petersen, K. J. (2004). Reverse auctions: Grounded theory from the buyer and supplier perspective. *Transportation Research Part E: Logistics and Transportation Review, 40*(3), 229-254.

Chen-Ritzo, C.-H., Harrison, T. P., Kwasnica, A. M., & Thomas, D. J. (2005). Better, faster, cheaper: An experimental analysis of a multiattribute reverse auction mechanism with restricted information feedback. *Management Science, 51*(12), 1753-1762.

Dai, R., Narasimhan, S., & Wu, D. J. (2005). Buyer's efficient e-sourcing structure: Centralize or decentralize? *Journal of Management Information Systems, 22*(2), 141-164.

David, E., Azoulay-Schwartz, R., & Kraus, S. (In press). Bidding in sealed-bid and English multi-attribute auctions. *Decision Support Systems.*

Engelbrecht-Wiggans, R., & Katok, E. (2006). E-sourcing in procurement: Theory and behavior in reverse auctions with noncompetitive contracts. *Management Science, 52*(4), 581-596.

Gattiker, T. F., Huang, X., & Schwarz, J. L. (2007). Negotiation e-mail, and Internet reverse auctions: How sourcing mechanisms deployed by buyers affect suppliers' trust. *Journal of Operations Management, 25*(1), 184-202.

Jeong, W. S., Han, S. G., & Jo, G. S. (2003). Intelligent cyber logistics using reverse auction in electronic commerce. *Journal of Organizational Computing and Electronic Commerce, 13*(3-4), 191-209.

Kauffman, R. G., & Leszczyc, P. T. L. P. (2005). An optimization approach to business buyer choice sets: How many suppliers should be included? *Industrial Marketing Management, 34*(1), 3-12.

Millet, I., Parente, D. H., Fizel, J. L., & Venkataraman, R. R. (2004). Metrics for managing online procurement auctions. *Interfaces, 34*(3), 171-179.

Parente, D. H., Venkataraman, R. R., Fizel, J. L., & Millet, I. (2004). A conceptual research framework for analyzing online auctions in a B2B environment. *Supply Chain Management, 9*(4), 287-294.

Sampath, K., Saygin, C., Grasman, S. E., & Leu, M. C. (2006). Impact of reputation information sharing in an auction-based job allocation model for small and medium-sized enterprises. *International Journal of Production Research, 44*(9), 1777-1798.

Teich, J. E., Wallenius, H., Wallenius, J., & Zaitsev, A. (2006). A multi-attribute e-auction mechanism for procurement: Theoretical foundations. *European Journal of Operational Research, 175*(1), 90-100.

APPENDIX C CATEGORIZATION BY METHODOLOGY

Experiment

Bandyopadhyay, S., Rees, J., & Barron, J. M. (2006). Simulating sellers in online exchanges. *Decision Support Systems, 41*(2), 500-513.

Brosig, J., & Rei, J. P. (In press). Entry decisions and bidding behavior in sequential first-price procurement auctions: An experimental study. *Games and Economic Behavior.*

Chen-Ritzo, C.-H., Harrison, T. P., Kwasnica, A. M., & Thomas, D. J. (2005). Better, faster, cheaper: An experimental analysis of a multiattribute reverse auction mechanism with restricted information feedback. *Management Science, 51*(12), 1753-1762.

Davis, D. D., & Wilson, B. J. (2002). Collusion in procurement auctions: An experimental examination. *Economic Inquiry, 40*(2), 213-230.

Ding, M., Eliashberg, J., Huber, J., & Saini, R. (2005). Emotional bidders: An analytical and experimental examination of consumers' behavior in a priceline-like reverse auction. *Management Science, 51*(3), 352-364.

Engelbrecht-Wiggans, R., & Katok, E. (2006). E-sourcing in procurement: Theory and behavior in reverse auctions with noncompetitive contracts. *Management Science, 52*(4), 581-596.

Gattiker, T. F., Huang, X., & Schwarz, J. L. (2007). Negotiation e-mail, and Internet reverse auctions: How sourcing mechanisms deployed by buyers affect suppliers' trust. *Journal of Operations Management, 25*(1), 184-202.

Güth, W., Ivanova-Stenzel, R., & Kröger, S. (2006). Procurement experiments with unknown costs of quality. *Pacific Economic Review, 11*(2), 133-148.

Hur, D., Mabert, V. A., & Hartley, J. L. (In press). Getting the most out of reverse e-auction investment. *Omega.*

Jap, S. D. (2003). An exploratory study of the introduction of online reverse auctions. *Journal of Marketing, 67*(3), 96-107.

Jeong, W. S., Han, S. G., & Jo, G. S. (2003). Intelligent cyber logistics using reverse auction in electronic commerce. *Journal of Organizational Computing and Electronic Commerce, 13*(3-4), 191-209.

Parkes, D. C., & Kalagnanam, J. (2005). Models for iterative multiattribute procurement auctions. *Management Science, 51*(3), 435-451.

Roelofs, M. R. (2002). Common value auctions with default: An experimental approach. *Experimental Economics, 5*(3), 233-252.

Van Tulder, R., & Mol, M. (2002). Reverse auctions or auctions reversed: First experiments by Philips. *European Management Journal, 20*(5), 447-456.

Simulation

Bandyopadhyay, S., Rees, J., & Barron, J. M. (2006). Simulating sellers in online exchanges. *Decision Support Systems, 41*(2), 500-513.

Gallien, J., & Wein, L. M. (2005). A smart market for industrial procurement with capacity constraints. *Management Science, 51*(1), 76-91.

Gattiker, T. F., Huang, X., & Schwarz, J. L. (2007). Negotiation e-mail, and Internet reverse auctions: How sourcing mechanisms deployed by buyers affect suppliers' trust. *Journal of Operations Management, 25*(1), 184-202.

Her, Y.-S., Imamoto, K., & Sakurai, K. (2005). Analysis and comparison of cryptographic techniques in e-voting and e-auction. *Research Reports on Information Science and Electrical Engineering of Kyushu University, 10*(2), 91-96.

Hur, D., Mabert, V. A., & Hartley, J. L. (In press). Getting the most out of reverse e-auction investment. *Omega.*

Jeong, W. S., Han, S. G., & Jo, G. S. (2003). Intelligent cyber logistics using reverse auction in electronic commerce. *Journal of Organizational Computing and Electronic Commerce, 13*(3-4), 191-209.

Kehagias, D. D., Symeonidis, A. L., & Mitkas, P. A. (2005). Designing pricing mechanisms for autonomous agents based on bid-forecasting. *Electronic Markets, 15*(1), 53-62.

Meij, S., & Pau, L. F. (2006). Auctioning bulk mobile messages. *Computational Economics, 27*(2-3), 395-430.

Mishra, D., & Veeramani, D. (In press). Vickrey-Dutch procurement auction for multiple items. *European Journal of Operational Research.*

Mishra, D., & Veermani, D. (2006). An ascending price procurement auction for multiple items with unit supply. *IIE Transactions (Institute of Industrial Engineers), 38*(2), 127-140.

Sampath, K., Saygin, C., Grasman, S. E., & Leu, M. C. (2006). Impact of reputation information sharing in an auction-based job allocation model for small and medium-sized enterprises. *International Journal of Production Research, 44*(9), 1777-1798.

Empirical Study

De Silva, D. G. (2005). Synergies in recurring procurement auctions: An empirical investigation. *Economic Inquiry, 43*(1), 55-66.

Ding, M., Eliashberg, J., Huber, J., & Saini, R. (2005). Emotional bidders: An analytical and experimental examination of consumers' behavior in a Priceline-like reverse auction. *Management Science, 51*(3), 352-364.

Hong, H., & Shum, M. (2002). Increasing competition and the Winner's Curse: Evidence from procurement. *The Review of Economic Studies, 69*(241), 871-898.

Iimi, A. (2004). (Anti-)Competitive effect of joint bidding: Evidence from ODA procurement auctions. *Journal of the Japanese and International Economies, 18*(3), 416-439.

Kauffman, R. G., & Leszczyc, P. T. L. P. (2005). An optimization approach to business buyer choice sets: How many suppliers should be included? *Industrial Marketing Management, 34*(1), 3-12.

Klafft, M., & Spiekermann, S. (2006). Reverse procurement and auctions for consumers: A new trend on the horizon of e-commerce? *Wirtschaftsinformatik, 48*(1), 36-45.

Parente, D. H., Venkataraman, R. R., Fizel, J. L., & Millet, I. (2004). A conceptual research framework for analyzing online auctions in a B2B environment. *Supply Chain Management, 9*(4), 287-294.

Pearcy, D. H., & Giunipero, L. C. (2006). The impact of electronic reverse auctions on purchase price reduction and governance structure: An empirical investigation. *International Journal of Services Technology and Management, 7*(3), 215-236.

Tassabehji, R., Taylor, W. A., Beach, R., & Wood, A. (2006). Reverse e-auctions and supplier-buyer relationships: An exploratory study. *International Journal of Operations & Production Management, 26*(2), 166-184.

Wolfram, C. D. (1998). Strategic bidding in a multiunit auction: An empirical analysis of bids to supply electricity in England and Wales. *The Rand Journal of Economics, 29*(4), 703-725.

Field/Case Study

Carbone, J. (2005). Not just a cost-reduction tool [electronic industry]. *Purchasing, 134*(3), 43-44.

Carter, C. R., Kaufmann, L., Beall, S., Carter, P. L., Hendrick, T. E., & Petersen, K. J. (2004). Reverse auctions: Grounded theory from the buyer and supplier perspective. *Transportation Research Part E: Logistics and Transportation Review, 40*(3), 229-254.

Hartley, J. L., Lane, M. D., & Duplaga, E. A. (2006). Exploring the barriers to the adoption of e-auctions for sourcing. *International Journal of Operations & Production Management, 26*(2), 202-221.

Hur, D., Hartley, J. L., & Mabert, V. A. (2006). Implementing reverse e-auctions: A learning process. *Business Horizons, 49*(1), 21-29.

Hur, D., Mabert, V. A., & Hartley, J. L. (In press). Getting the most out of reverse e-auction investment. *Omega*.

Joia, L. A., & Zamot, F. (2002). Internet-based reverse auctions by the Brazilian government. *Electronic Journal on Information Systems in Developing Countries, 9*.

Li, Y., Shen, W., & Ghenniwa, H. (2004). Agent-based Web services framework and development environment. *Computational Intelligence, 20*(4), 678-692.

Smart, A., & Harrison, A. (2003). Online reverse auctions and their role in buyer-supplier relationships. *Journal of Purchasing and Supply Management, 9*(5-6), 257-268.

Stein, A., Hawking, P., & Wyld, D. C. (2003). The 20% solution? A case study on the efficacy of reverse auctions. *Management Research News, 26*(5), 1-20.

Tassabehji, R., Taylor, W. A., Beach, R., & Wood, A. (2006). Reverse e-auctions and supplier-buyer relationships: An exploratory study. *International Journal of Operations & Production Management, 26*(2), 166-184.

Wang, S., Zheng, W., & Archer, N. (2005). The impact of Internet-based electronic marketplaces on buyer-supplier relationships. *Journal of Internet Commerce, 4*(3), 41-67.

Survey

Barling, B. (2002). Expert advice: How can my organisation take advantage of reverse auctions without jeopardising existing supplier relationships? *Information Age*, 41.

Boyle, E. J. (2003). Let's talk trends. *Paper, Film and Foil Converter, 77*(9), T30.

Cox, A., Chicksand, D., Ireland, P., & Davies, T. (2005). Sourcing indirect spend: A survey of current internal and external strategies for non-revenue-generating goods and services. *Journal of Supply Chain Management, 41*(2), 39-51.

E-procurement adoptions progress slowly and steadily. (2002). *Purchasing, 131*(11), S8, S10.

Emiliani, M. L., & Stec, D. J. (2004). Aerospace parts suppliers' reaction to online reverse auctions. *Supply Chain Management, 9*(2), 139-153.

Hannon, D. (2003). E-sourcing survey: Purchasing survey shows e-sourcing adoption stalls. *Purchasing, 132*(12), 49-51.

Hartley, J. L., Lane, M. D., & Duplaga, E. A. (2006). Exploring the barriers to the adoption of e-auctions for sourcing. *International Journal of Operations & Production Management, 26*(2), 202-221.

Hartley, J. L., Lane, M. D., & Hong, Y. (2004). An exploration of the adoption of E-auctions in supply management. *IEEE Transactions on Engineering Management, 51*(2), 153-161.

Pearcy, D. H., & Giunipero, L. C. (2006). The impact of electronic reverse auctions on purchase price reduction and governance structure: An empirical investigation. *International Journal of Services Technology and Management, 7*(3), 215-236.

Purchasing survey. Buyers turn wary eyes on electronic auctions. (2000). *Purchasing, 129*(3), 109-110.

Wagner, S. M., & Schwab, A. P. (2004). Setting the stage for successful electronic reverse auctions. *Journal of Purchasing and Supply Management, 10*(1), 11-26.

346

Compilation of References

Abrams, Z. (2006). *Revenue maximization when bidders have budgets*. Paper presented at the seventeenth annual ACM-SIAM Symposium on Discrete Algorithms, Miami, FL.

Adams, W. J., & Yellen, J. L. (1976). Commodity bundling and the burden of monopoly. *The Quarterly Journal of Economics, 90*(3), 475-498.

Akacum, A., & Dale, B. G. (1995). Supplier partnering: Case study experiences. *International Journal of Purchasing and Materials Management, 31*(1), 37-44.

Anderson, P., & Anderson, E. (2002). The new e-commerce intermediaries. *MIT Sloan Management Review, 43*(4), 53-62.

Anderson, J. C., & Narus, J. A. (1990). A model of distributor-firm and manufacture-firm working partnership. *Journal of Marketing, 54*(January), 42-58.

Armstrong, J. S., & Overton, T. S. (1977). Estimating nonresponse bias in mail surveys. *Journal of Marketing Research, 14*(3), 396-402.

Arnold, U. & Essig, M. (2001). Electronic procurement in supply chain management: An information economics-based analysis of electronic markets, their facilities and their limits. *Journal of Supply Chain Management, 37*(4), 43-49.

Arnold, U. & Kärner, H. (2003). eReadiness deutscher lieferanten - Empirische erhebung zum aktuellen stand und den zukünftigen entwicklungen. *quiBiq.de, DeSK Deutscher eSupplier Katalog*. Stuttgart. pp. 7-35.

Arnold, U., Kärner, H. & Schnabel, M. (2005). Target oriented use of strategic sourcing tools: A critical analysis creating process awareness for electronic reverse auctions. *Journal of Purchasing and Supply Management, 11*(2-3), 116-128.

Ashenfelter, O., & Genesore, D. (1992). Testing for price anomalies in real estate auctions. *American Economic Review: Papers and Proceedings, 82,* 501-505.

AT Kearney (2001). *Creating differentiated value networks: How companies can get real value out of e-markets*. Chicago: AT Kearney.

Athey, S., & Levin, J. (2001). Information and competition in U.S. forest service timber auctions. *Journal of Political Economy, 109*(2), 375-417.

Ausubel, L. M., & Milgrom, P. (2005). The lovely but lonely Vickrey auction. In P. Crampton, R. Steinberg, & Y. Shoham (Eds.), *Combinatorial auctions* (pp. 17-40). Cambridge, MA: MIT Press.

Avery, C., & Hendershott, T. (2000). Bundling and optimal auctions of multiple products. *Review of Economic Studies, 67*(3), 483-497.

Backhaus, K., Aufderheide, D. & Späth, G. M. (1994). *Marketing für systemtechnologien: Entwicklung eines theoretisch-ökonomisch begründeten geschäftstypenansatzes*. Stuttgart.

Bajari, P., & Ye, L. (2003). Deciding between competition and collusion. *Review of Economics and Statistics, 85,* 971-989.

Bajari, S., & Summers, G. (2002). Detecting collusion in procurement auctions: A selective survey of recent research. *Antitrust Law Journal, 70,* 143-170.

Bakos, J.Y. (1991). A strategic analysis of electronic marketplaces. *MIS Quarterly, 15*(1), 295-310.

Bakos, J.Y. (1998). The emerging role of electronic marketplaces on the Internet. *Communications of the ACM, 41*(8), 35-42.

Bakos, Y., & Brynjolfsson, E. (2000). Bundling and competition on the Internet. *Marketing Science, 19*(1), 63-82.

Balcan, M.-F., Chen, J., Devanur, N., & Kumar, A. (2006). Transcript of Panel discussion: Models for Sponsored Search: What are the right questions? [Electronic Version]. *Second Workshop on Sponsored Search Auctions* Retrieved April 5, 2007. from http://research.microsoft.com/~hartline/papers/panel-SSA-06.pdf

Banks Jeffrey, Mark Olson, David Porter, Stephen Rassenti, & Vernon Smith (2005) Theory, experiment and the Federal Communications Commission spectrum auctions. *Journal of Economic Behavior and Organization* (forthcoming).

Bapna, R., Goes, P., & Gupta, A. (2003). Analysis and design of business to consumer online auctions. *Management Science, 49,* 42-50.

Bapna, R., Goes, P., & Gupta, A. (2003). An analysis of business to consumer online auctions. *Management Science, 49*(1), 85-101.

Bapna, R., Goes, P., Gupta, A., & Karuga, G. (2002). Optimal design of the online auction channel: Analytic, empirical and computational insights. *Decision Sciences, 33*(4), 557-577.

Barney, J. B., & Hansen, M. H. (1994). Trustworthiness as a source of competitive advantage. *Strategic Management Journal, 15,* 175.

Barratt, M.A., & Rosdahl, K. (2002). Exploring business-to-business marketsites. *European Journal of Purchasing and Supply Management, 8*(2), 111-122.

Barratt, M., & Oliveira, A. (2001). Exploring the experiences of collaborative planning initiatives. *International Journal of Physical Distribution & Logistics Management, 31*(4), 266.

Bartholomew, D. (2001, September). Co$t vs. quality. *Industry Week,* 34.

Barua, A., Konana, P., Whinston, A., & Yin, F. (2001). Measures for E-Business Value Assessment. *IT Pro, January-February,* 35-39.

Barua, A., Kriebel, C.H. & Mukhopadhyay, T.(1995). Information Technologies and business value: Ananalytic and empirical investigation. *Information Systems Research, 6*(1), 3-23.

Batsone, D. (1999). Going once, going twice. *Business 2, 4*(5), 141.

Beall, S., Carter, C., Carter, P., Germer, T., Hendrick, T., Jap, S., et al. (2003). *The role of reverse auctions in strategic sourcing* (CAPS Research Report). Tempe, Arizona: Institute of Supply Management.

Beam, C., Segev, A., Bichler, M., & Krishnan, R. (1999). On negotiations and deal making in electronic markets. *Information Systems Frontiers, 1*(3), 241-258.

Beam, C. & Segev, A. (1998). Auctions on the Internet: A Field Study. *Working Paper 98-WP-1032, The Fisher Center for Management and Information Technology,* University of California, Berkeley.

BEEP (2003). *Best eEurope practices knowledge system.* Retrieved August 20, 2004, from http://www.beepknowledgesystem.org/default.asp

Beil, D. R., & Wein, L. M. (2003). An inverse-optimization-based auction mechanism to support a multiattribute RFQ process, *Management Science, 49*(11), 1529-1545.

Benbasat, I., Goldstein, D., & Mead, M. (1987). The case research strategy in studies of information systems. *MIS Quarterly, 11*(3), 215-218.

Berg, J. E., Forsythe, R., Nelson, F. D., & Rietz, T. A. (2001). Results from a dozen years of election futures markets research. Forthcoming in C. A. Plott & V. Smith (Eds.), *Handbook of Experimental Economic Results.*

Berg, J. E., & Rietz, T. A. (2003). Prediction markets as decision support systems. *Information Systems Frontiers, 5*(1), 79-93.

Berger, A.J., & Gattorna, J.L. (2001). *Supply chain cybermastery.* Aldershot: Gower.

Best Practices LLC. (2001). *Developing a balanced scorecard of performance measures.* Chapel Hill, NC: Best Practices.

Bichler, M. (2000). An experimental analysis of multi-attribute auctions. *Decision Support Systems, 29*(3), 249-268.

Bichler, M. (2001). *The future of e-Markets: Multi-dimensional market mechanisms.* Cambridge: Cambridge University Press.

Bichler, M., & Kalagnanam, J. (2005). Configurable offers and winner determination in multi-attribute auctions. *European Journal of Operational Research, 160*(2), 380-394.

Bichler, M., & Klimesch, R. (2000). Simulation multivariater auktionen—eine analyse des otc-handels mit finanzderivaten. *Wirtschaftsinformatik, 42*(3), 244-252.

Bichler, M., & Segev, A. (2001). Methodologies for the design of negotiation protocols on e-markets. *Computer Networks, 37*(2), 137-152.

Bikhchandani, S., de Vries, S., Schummer, S. & Vohra, R.V. (2001). *Linear Programming and Vickrey Auctions: Mathematics of the Internet: E-auction and Markets.* Springer-Verlag.

Billington, C., Callioni, G., Crane, B., Ruark, J., D. , & et al. (2004). Accelerating the profitability of Hewlett-Packard's supply chains. *Interfaces, 34*(1), 59.

Blecherman, B., & Camerer, C. (1998). *Is there a winner's curse in the market for baseball players?* mimeograph, Brooklyn Polytechnic University, Brooklyn.

Bloch, N., & Catfolis, T. (2001). B2B e-marketplaces: How to succeed. *Business Strategy Review, 12*(3), 20-28.

Boehmer, J. (2005). GE curtails hotel auctions. *Business Travel News, 22*(8), 6.

Borgs, C., Chayes, J., Etesami, O., Immorlica, N., Jain, K., & Mahdian, M. (2007, May). *Dynamics of bid optimization in online advertisement auctions.* Paper presented at the 16th International World Wide Web Conference (WWW2007), Banff, Alberta, Canada.

Bounds, G. (1996). Toyota supplier development. In G. Bounds (Ed.), *Cases in quality* (pp. 3-25). Chicago: R. D. Irwin.

Bowersox, D. J., & Closs, D. J. (1996). *Logistical management.* New York: McGraw-Hill.

Bowersox, D. J. (1990). The strategic benefits of logistics alliances. *Harvard Business Review, 68*(4), 36.

Bowles, J. (2000). eMarketplaces: How digital marketplaces are shaping the future of B2B commerce. *Forbes, 166*(3), s20-s56.

Branco, F. (1996). Common value auctions with independent types. *Economic Design, 2*(3), 283-309.

Branco, F. (1997). The design of multidimensional auctions. *RAND Journal of Economics, 28*(1), 63-81.

Brandt, F., & Weiss, G. (2001). Antisocial agents and Vickrey auctions. In J. J. C. Meyer & M. Tambe (Eds.), *Intelligent Agents 8*(2333), 335-347.Springer-Verlag.

Brunelli, M. (2000). Online auctions save millions for Quaker Oats and SmithKline Beecham. *Purchasing, 128*(4), S22.

Bucklin, L. (1973). A theory of channel control. *Journal of Marketing, 37*, 39-47.

Bulow, J., & Klemperer, P. (1996). Auctions versus negotiations. *The American Economic Review, 86*(1), 180-194.

Buono, A. F. (1997). Enhancing strategic partnerships: Intervening in network organizations. *Journal of Organizational Change, 10*(3), 251-266.

Burnes, B., & New, S. (1996). *Strategic advantage and supply chain collaboration.* London: AT Kearney.

Burt, D. N., Dobler, D. W., & Starling, S. L. (2003). *World class supply management - the key to supply chain management* (7th ed.). New York: McGraw-Hill Higher Education.

Burt, R., Norquist, W., & Anklesaria, J. (1990). *Zero base pricing: Achieving world class competitiveness through reduced all-in-cost.* Chicago: Probus Publishing.

Bush, D. (2006). *E-sourcing benchmark survey: Analysis of e-sourcing marketplace and adoption levels.* Carmel, Indiana: Iasta.com.

Büyüközkan, G. (2004). A success index to evaluate e-marketplaces. *Production Planning and Control, 15*(7), 761-774.

Buyya, R., Stockinger, H., Giddy, J. & Abramson, D. (2001). Economic Models for Management of Resources in Peer-to-Peer and Grid Computing. *Proceedings of the international symposium on the convergence of information technologies and communications, ITCom '01*, Denver, USA.

Campbell, C. M., & Levin, D. (2000). Can the seller benefit from an insider in common-value auctions? *Journal of Economic Theory, 91*(1), 106-120.

Capen, E., Clapp R., & Campbell, W. (1971). Competitive bidding in high-risk situations. *Journal of Petroleum Technology, 23*(6), 641-653.

CAPS (2006). *CAPS research: Report of cross-industry standard benchmarks.* Retrieved May 22, 2006, from http://www.capsresearch.org/publications/pdfs-protected/CrossInd052006.pdf.

CAPS Research (2003). *Cross industry summary report.* CAPS Research, November.

Carter, C., Beal, S., Carter, P., Hendrick, T., Kaufman, L., & Petersen, K. (2004). Reverse auctions-grounded theory from the buyer and supplier perspective. *Transportation Research Part E, 40*(3), 229-254.

Carter, C., & Stevens, C. (Forthcoming). Electronic reverse auction configuration and its impact on buyer price and supplier perceptions of opportunism: A laboratory experiment. *Journal of Operations Management.*

Carter, P. & Petersen, H.J. (2005). Impact of technology on purchasing and supply. In: Essig, M. (Ed.), *Perspektiven des Supply Management*, (pp. 251-290), Berlin.

Casper, C. (2000). B2B exchanges: All buzz, not bite? *Food* Logistics, *34*, (September 15), 14.

Cassing, J., & Douglas, R. (1980). Implication of the auctions mechanism in baseball's free agency draft. *Southern Economic Journal, 46,* 110-120.

Cavaye, A. (1996). Case study research: A multi-faceted approach for IS. *Information Systems Journal, 6*(3), 227-242.

Cavinato, J. L., & Kauffman, R. G. (Eds.). (1999). *The purchasing handbook* (6th ed.). New York: McGraw-Hill.

Chan, R., & Roseman, M. (2001). Integrating knowledge into process models—A case study. *Proceedings of the Twelfth Australasian Conference on Information Systems,* Southern Cross University, Australia.

Che, Y. K. (1993). Design competition through multidimensional auctions. *RAND Journal of Economics, 24*(4), 668-680.

Chen, I. J., Paulraj, A., & Lado, A. A. (2004). Strategic purchasing, supply management, and firm performance. *Journal of Operations Management, 22*(5), 505-523.

Chen, K. Y., Fine, L., & Humberman, B. A. (2004). Eliminating public knowledge biases in information-aggregation mechanisms. *Management Science, 50*(7), 983-994.

Chen, K. Y., & Plott, C. (2002). *Information aggregation mechanisms: concept, design, and implementation for a sales forecasting problem.* Unpublished manuscript, California Institute of Technology.

Chen, Y., Mullen, T., & Chu, C. H. (2004, June). *Theoretical investigation of prediction markets with aggregate uncertainty.* Paper presented at the 7th International Conference on Electronic Commerce Research (ICECR-7), Dallas, TX.

Chen, Y., Mullen, T., & Chu, C. H. (2006). An in-depth analysis of information markets with aggregate uncertainty. *Electronic Commerce Research, 6,* 201-220.

Chen, Y., Chu, C. H., Mullen, T., & Pennock, D. M. (2005, June). *Information Markets vs. Opinion Pools: An Empirical Comparison*. Paper presented at the ACM Conference on Electronic Commerce (EC-05), Vancouver, British Columbia, Canada.

Chen-Ritzo, C.; Harrison, T. P., Kwasnica, A. M., & Thomas, D. J. (2005). Better, faster, cheaper: An experimental analysis of a multi-attribute reverse auction mechanism with restricted information feedback. *Management Science*,

Choi, T. Y., & Hartley, J. L. (1996). An exploration of supplier selection practices across the supply chain. *Journal of Operations Management, 14*(4), 333-343.

Chopra, S., & Meindl, P. (2007). *Supply chain management: Strategy, planning, operation* (3rd ed.). Upper Saddle River, NJ: Prentice Hall.

Chung, L.K., Nixon, B.A., Yu, E. & Mylopoulos J. (2000). *Non-Functional Requirements in Software Engineering*. Kluwer Publishing.

Claro, D. P., Claro, P. B. d. O., & Hagelaar, G. (2006). Coordinating collaborative joint efforts with suppliers: The effects of trust, transaction specific investment and information network in the Dutch flower industry. *Supply Chain Management, 11*(3), 216-224.

Click Fraud (2005). [Electronic Version]. *Marketing Experiments Journal*. Retrieved April 5, 2007, from www.marketingexperiments.com/internet-online-advertising/click-fraud.html

Coase, R. H. (1937). The Nature of the firm. *Economica, 4*, 386-405.

Compte, O. (2002). *The winner's curse with independent private values*, Mimeograph CERAS-ENPC.

Contractor Magazine (2004). 84% find ethical violations.[Electronic version] *51*(6), 1.

Cooper, M. C., Ellram, L., Gardner, J. T., & Hanks, A. M. (1997). Meshing multiple alliances. *Journal of Business Logistics, 18*(1), 67-89.

Cowgill, B. (2005). *Putting crowd wisdom to work*. Retrieved April 5, 2007, from http://googleblog.blogspot.com/2005/09/putting-crowd-wisdom-to-work.html

Cramton, P. C., & Dees, J. G. (1993) Promoting honesty in negotiation: An excercise in practical ethics. *Business Ethics Quarterly, 3*(4), 359-394.

Crawford, V., & Irriberi, N. (2005). *Level-k auctions: Can a non-equilibrium model of strategic thinking explain the winner's curse and overbidding in private value auctions?* Working Paper.

Darby, M. R., Karni, E. (1973). Free Competition and the Optimal Amount of Fraud. *Journal of Law and Economics, 16*(4), 67-88.

Dasgupta, S., & Maskin, E. (2000). Efficient auctions. *The Quarterly Journal of Economics, 65*(2), 341-388.

Davies, G. (2002). Entering the second generation of online reverse auctions. *Inside Supply Management, 5*(6), 54.

Davila, A., Gupta, M., & Palmer, R. (2003). Moving procurement systems to the Internet: The adoption and use of e-procurement technology models. *European Management Journal, 21*(1), 11-23.

Davis, F., Bagozzi, R. P., & Warshaw, P. R. (1989). User acceptance of computer technology: A comparison of two theoretical models. *Management Science, 35*(8), 982-1003.

Davis, F. D. (1989). Perceived usefulness, perceived ease of use, and user acceptance of information technology. *MIS Quarterly, 13*(3), 319-340.

Day, G.S., Fein, A.J., & Ruppersberger, G. (2003). Shake-outs in digital markets: Lessons from B2B exchanges. *California Management Review, 45*(2), 131-250.

Day R., & S Raghavan (2003). *CAMBO: Combinatorial Auctions using Matrix Bids with Order*. Working Paper, University of Maryland.

De Boer, L., Harink, J., Heijboer, G. (2002). A conceptual model for assessing the impact of electronic procurement.

European Journal of Purchasing & Supply Management, 8(1), 25-33.

Dees, J.G., & Cramton, P. C. (1995) Deception and mutual trust: A reply to Strudler. *Business Ethics Quarterly, 5,* 823-832.

Degraeve, Z., & Roodhooft, F. (1999). Effectively selecting suppliers using total cost of ownership. *Journal of Supply Chain Management, 35*(1), 5-10.

Deise, M., Nowikow, C., King, P., & Wright, A. (2000). *Executive's guide to e-business from tactics to strategy.* New York: PriceWaterhouseCoopers, John Wiley & Sons.

Delina, R. & Lavrin, A. (2003). Approach to the performance measuring of e-commerce solution in manufacturing firm. In Barros, L., Helo, P. & Kekäle (Eds.) *ICIL 2003, Proceedings International Conference on Industrial Logistics* (pp. 130-139). ICIL 2003; Vaasa, Finland, June 16-18, 2003. University of Southampton, UK.

Delina, R. & Lavrin, A. (2004, June 21-23). Performance measurement of e-procurement solution with dynamic pricing aspect. In R. Dienstbier (Ed.) *17th Bled eCommerce conference: eGlobal.* Bled, Slovenia.

Delina, R. (2003). Performance measuring of e-business solution in manufacturing firm. In Ghodous, P. (Ed.) *10th ISPE International Conference on Concurrent Engineering: Research and Applications* (pp. 455-462). Portugal; July 26-30, 2003. The Netherlands: A.A. Balkema.

DeMaio, H.B. (2001). *B2B and beyond: New business models built on trust.* New York: Wiley.

Dessauer, J. (1981). *Book Publishing.* New York: Bowker.

Devaraj, S. & Kohli, R. (2003). Performance impacts of Information Technology: is actual usage the missing link? *Management Science, 49*(3), 273-289.

Diba, A. (2000). The B2B boom: What's what. *Fortune, 141*(10), 142.

Dickson, P. (1994). *Marketing management* (2nd ed.). Fort Worth: Dryden Press/Harcourt-Brace.

Dillman, D. A. (2000). *Mail and Internet surveys: The tailored design method* (2nd ed.). New York: Wiley & Sons.

Do, T.T., Faulkner, S. & Kolp, M. (2002). The Structure-in-5 as a Multi-Agent Architectural Pattern. *IAG Working Paper 38/02, IAG School of Management,* Université catholique de Louvain.

Do, T.T., Kolp, M. & Pirotte, A. (2003). Social Patterns for Designing Multiagent Systems. *Proceedings of the 15th*

Doney, P. M., & Cannon, J. P. (1997). An examination of the nature of trust in buyer-seller relationships. *Journal of Marketing, 61*(2), 35-52.

Drew, S. (2003). Strategic uses of e-commerce by SMEs in the east of England. *European Management Journal, 21*(1), 79.

Dyer, J., & Nobeoka, K. (2000). Creating and managing a high-performance knowledge sharing network: The Toyota case. *Strategic Management Journal, 21,* 345-367.

Dyer, J. H., & Hatch, N. W. (2004). Using supplier networks to learn faster. *MIT Sloan Management Review, 45*(3), 57-63.

E-Business W@tch (2003) *The European e-Business Report.* (European Communities Publication No. NB-51-03-277-EN-C). Luxembourg: Office for Official Publications of the European Communities.

Edelman, B., & Ostrovsky, M. (2007). Strategic bidder behavior in sponsored search auctions. *Decision Support Systems, 43*(1), 192-198.

Edelman, B., Ostrovsky, M., & Schwarz, M. (2007). Internet advertising and the generalized second price auction: Selling billions of dollars worth of keywords. *American Economic Review, 97*(1), 242-259.

Eisen, P.J.(2003). *Accounting the Easy Way (Accounting the Easy Way).* Barron's Educational Series.

Ellram, L. (1990). The supplier selection decision in strategic partnerships. *Journal of Purchasing & Materials Management, 26*(4), 8-14.

Elmaghraby, W. J. (2002). The importance of ordering in sequential auctions. *Management Science, 49*(5), 673-682.

Emiliani, M. (2006). Executive decision-making traps and B2B online reverse auctions. *Supply Chain Management: An International Journal, 11*(1), 6-9.

Emiliani, M., & Stec, D. (2001). Online reverse auction purchasing contracts. *Supply Chain Management: An International Journal, 6*(3), 101-105.

Emiliani, M., & Stec, D. (2002). Realizing savings from on-line reverse auctions. *Supply Chain Management: An International Journal, 7*(1), 12-23.

Emiliani, M., & Stec, D. (2004). Aerospace parts suppliers' reaction to online reverse auctions. *Supply Chain Management: An International Journal, 9*(2), 139-153.

Emiliani, M., & Stec, D. (2005). Wood pallet suppliers' reaction to online reverse auctions. *Supply Chain Management: An International Journal, 10*(4), 278-287.

Emiliani, M., Stec, D., & Grasso, L. (2005). Unintended responses to a traditional purchasing performance metric. *Supply Chain Management: An International Journal, 10*(3), 150-156.

Emiliani, M. L., & Stec, D. J. (2001). Online reverse auction purchasing contracts. *Supply Chain Management, 6*(3/4), 101-105.

Emiliani, M. L., & Stec, D. J. (2002). Squaring online reverse auctions with the Caux Round Table principles for business. *Supply Chain Management, 7*(2), 92-100.

Emiliani, M. L., & Stec, D. J. (2001). Online reverse auction purchasing contracts. *Supply Chain Management, 6*(3/4), 101-105.

Emiliani, M., & Stec, D. (2000). Business to business online auctions: Key issues for purchasing process improvement. *Supply Chain Management, 5*(4), 176-186.

Emiliani, M.L. (2004). Sourcing in the global aerospace supply chain using online reverse auctions. *Industrial Marketing Management, 33*(1), 65-72.

Emiliani, M.L. (2005). Regulating b2b online reverse auctions through voluntary codes of conduct. *Industrial Marketing Management, 34*(5), 526-534.

Evans, W. N., & Kessides, I. N. (1994). Living by the "Golden Rule": Multimarket contact in the U.S. airline industry. *Quarterly Journal of Economics, 109,* 341-366.

Faulkner, S., Kolp, M. & Do, T.T. (2004). The SKwyRL Perspective on Agent-Oriented Design Patterns. *Proceedings of the 6th International Conference on Enterprise Information Systems, ICEIS '04*, Porto, Portugal.

Faulkner, S. (2004). *An Architectural Framework for Describing BDI-Multi-Agent Information Systems.* Unpublished doctoral thesis, University of Louvain, Belgium.

Feigenbaum, J., Fortnow, L., Pennock, D. M., & Sami, R. (2003, June). *Computation in a distributed information market.* Paper presented at the 4th Annual ACM Conference on Electronic Commerce (EC'03), San Diego, CA.

Feinstein, J. S., Block, M. K., & Nold, F. C. (1985). Asymmetric information and collusive behavior in auction markets. *American Economic Review, 75,* 441-460.

Feng, J., Bhargava, H. K., & Pennock, D. M. (2007). Implementing sponsored search in Web search engines: Computational evaluation of alternative mechanisms. *Informs Journal on Computing, 19*(1), 137-148.

Fisher, L. (1976). *Industrial marketing: An analytical approach to planning and execution.* London: Business Books Limited.

Fisher, M. L. (1997). What is the right supply chain for your product? *Harvard Business Review, 75*(2), 105.

Fitz-Enz, J. (2000). *The ROI of human capital: Measuring the economic value of employee performance.* New York: American Management Association.

Forsythe, R., & Lundholm, F. (1990). Information aggregation in an experimental market. *Econometrica, 58,* 309-347.

Freemarkets. (2002). *Why Freemarkets?* Retrieved February 20, 2002, from www.freemarkets.com/benefits/default.asp

French, S. (1985). Group consensus probability distributions: A critical survey. *Bayesian Statistics, 2,* 183-202.

Friedman, M., & Blanshay, M. (2001). *Understanding B2B.* Chicago: Dearborn Trade.

Froeb, L. M., Koyak, R. A., & Werden, J. G. (1993). What is the effect of bid-rigging on price? *Economic Letters, 42,* 419-423.

Gamma Erich, Richard Helm, Ralph Johnson, & John Vlissides (1995). *Design Patterns.* Addison-Wesley.

Gampfer, R. (2003). *Auktionen und auktionsplattformen zwischen unternehmen im internet,* Aachen.

Garcia-Dastugue, S. J., & Lambert, D. M. (2003). Internet-enabled coordination in the supply chain. *Industrial Marketing Management, 32*(3), 251.

Gates, B. (1995). *The road ahead.* London: Viking.

Gattiker, T. (2005). Individual user adoption and diffusion of internet reverse auctions at Shell Chemical. *Practix: Best Practices in Purchasing and Supply Chain Management, 8*(4), 1-6.

Gattiker, T. F., Huang, X., & Schwarz, J. L. (2007). Negotiation, email, and Internet reverse auctions: How sourcing mechanisms deployed by buyers affect suppliers' trust. *Journal of Operations Management, 25*(1), 184-202.

Gefen, D., Karahanna, E., & Straub, D. W. (2003). Trust and TAM in online shopping: An integrated model. *MIS Quarterly, 27*(1), 51-90.

Genest, C., & Zidek, J. V. (1986). Combining probability distributions: A critique and an annotated bibliography. *Statistical Science, 1*(1), 114-148.

Germer, T., Carter, P. L., & Kaufmann, L. (2004). *Purchasing auctions: A synthesis of current research.* Paper presented at the 15th Annual North American Research Symposium on Purchasing and Supply Management.

Giampetro, P., & Emiliani, M. L. (2007). Coercion and reverse auctions. *Supply Chain Management, 12*(2), 75-84.

Goldsby, T. J., & Eckert, J. A. (2003). Electronic transportation marketplaces: A transaction cost perspective. *Industrial Marketing Management, 32*(3), 187-198.

Goodhue, D., & Thompson, R. (1995). Task-technology fit and individual performance. *MIS Quarterly, 19*(2), 213-236.

Goodhue, D. L. (1995). Understanding user evaluations of information systems. *Management Science, 41*(12), 1827-1844.

Goodman, J. (2005). *Pay-per-percentage of impressions: An advertising method that is highly robust to fraud.* Paper presented at the Workshop on Sponsored Search Auctions.

Google. Adwords Help Center. Retrieved April 5, 2007, from https://adwords.google.com/support/

Google. Keyword Tool. Retrieved April 5, 2007, from https://adwords.google.com/select/KeywordToolExternal

Google. Tips for success. Retrieved April 5, 2007, from https://adwords.google.com/select/tips.html

Google. Traffic Estimator. Retrieved April 5, 2007, from https://adwords.google.com/select/TrafficEstimatorSandbox

Grant, J.L. (2002). *Foundations of economic value added,* 2nd Edition. New York: John Wiley & Sons.

Green, S. B., & Salkind, N. J. (2003). *Using SPSS for Windows and Macintosh.* Upper Saddle River, NJ: Prentice Hall.

Grieger, M. (2003). Electronic marketplaces: A literature review and a call for supply chain management research. *European Journal of Operational Research, 144*(2), 280-294.

Griffiths, A. (2003). Trusting an auction. *Supply Chain Management, 8*(3/4), 190-194.

Grossman, S. J. (1981). An introduction to the theory of rational expectations under asymmetric information. *Review of Economic Studies, 48*(4), 541-559.

Grubb, A. (2000). *B2B Darwinism: How e-marketplaces survive (and succeed)*. New York: Deloitte Research.

Gupta, S., Ghosh, I., & Millet, I. (2008). An empirical study of collusion potential metrics and their impact on online reverse auction success In D. Parente (Ed.), *Best Practices in Online Procurement Auctions*. Hershey, PA: IGI Global Publishing.

Gupta, S. (2001). The effect of bid rigging on price: A study of highway construction market. *Review of Industrial Organization, 19,* 453-457.

Gupta, S. (2002). Competition and collusion in a government procurement auction market. *Atlantic Economic Journal, 30,* 13-25.

Guttman, R.H., Moukas, A.G. & Maes, P. (1998). Agent-mediated electronic commerce: A survey. *Knowledge Engineering Review, 13*(3), 45-69.

Hahn, R. W., & Tetlock, P. C. (2005). Making development work. *Policy Review, 132,* [Electronic version]. Stanford, CA: Hoover Institution.

Hakansson, N. H. (1982). Changes in the financial market: Welfare and price effects and the basic theorems of value conservation. *The Journal of Finance, 37*(4), 977-1005.

Handfield, R. B., Straight, S. L., & Stirling, W. A. (2002). Reverse auctions: How do supply managers really feel about them? *Inside Supply Management, 13*(11), 56-61.

Hannon, D. (2003). Purchasing shows e-sourcing adoption stalls. *Purchasing,* 12, August.

Hanson, R. D. (1999). Decision markets. *IEEE Intelligent Systems, 14*(3), 16-19.

Harden, L., & Heyman, B. (2002). *The auction app: How companies tap the power of online auctions to maximize revenue growth*. New York: McGraw-Hill.

Hartley, J. L., Duplaga, E. A., & Lane, M. D. (2005). Reverse e-auctions: Exploring reasons for use and buyer's satisfaction. *International Journal of Integrated Supply Management, 1*(4), 410-420.

Hartley, J. L., Lane, M. D., & Hong, Y. (2004). An exploration of the adoption of e-auctions in supply management. *IEEE Transactions on Engineering Management, 51*(2), 153-161.

Heide, J. B., & John, G. (1990). Alliances in industrial purchasing: The determinants of joint action in buyer-supplier relationships. *Journal of Marketing Research, 37*(1), 24-36.

Heide, J. B., & John, G. (1998). The role of dependence balancing in safeguarding transaction-specific assets in conventional channels. *Journal of Marketing, 52*(1), 20-35.

Hersch, W. (2000). *Ebusiness: More friend than foe*. Retrieved February 20, 2002, from www.cconvergence.com/article/TCM20000728S0002

Hines, P., & Rich, N. (1997). Supply-chain management and time-based competition: The role of the suppler association. *International Journal of Physical Distribution & Logistics Management, 27*(3/4), 210-221.

Hines, P., & Rich, N. (1998). Outsourcing competitive advantage: The use of supplier associations. *International Journal of Physical Distribution & Logistics Management, 28*(7), 524-536.

Hines, P., Rich, N., & Easin, A. (1999). Value stream mapping: a distribution strategy application. *Benchmarking, 6*(1), 60-71.

Hohner, G., Rich, J., Ng, E., Reid, G., Davenport, A. J., Kalagnanam, J. R., et al. (2003). Combinatorial and quantity-discount procurement auctions benefit Mars, Incorporated and its suppliers. *Interfaces, 33*(1), 23-35.

Hong, H., & Shum, M. (2002). Increasing competition and the winner's curse: Evidence from procurement. *Review of Economic Studies, 69*(4), 871-898.

Horlen, J., Eldin, N., & Ajinkya, Y. (2005). Reverse auctions: Controversial bidding practice. *Journal of Professional Issues in Engineering, Education and Practice, 131*(1), 76-81.

Hoyt, J., & Huq, F. (2000). From arms-length to collaborative relationships in the supply chain: An evolutionary process. *International Journal of Physical Distribution & Logistics Management, 30*(9), 750-764.

Hsiao, R. L. (2003). Technology fears: Distrust and cultural persistence in electronic marketplace adoption. *Journal of Strategic Information Systems, 12*(3), 169-199.

Hsieh, L.-F. (2004). The buyer-supplier long-term partnership effects upon the buyer's operational performance in the Taiwan center-satellite factory system. *International Journal of Technology Management, 28*(2), 243.

Huber, B., Sweeney, E., & Smyth, A. (2004). Purchasing consortia and electronic markets: A procurement direction in integrated supply chain management. *Electronic Markets, 14*(4), 284-294.

Hur, D., Mabert, V. A., & Hartley, J. L. (2007). Getting the most out of reverse e-auction investment. *Omega, 35*(4), 403.

Hur, D., Mabert, V. A., & Hartley, J. L. (2005). Getting the most out of e-auction investment. *Omega, 35*, 403-416.

Immorlica, N., Jain, K., Mahdian, M., & Talwar, K. (2005). *Click fraud resistant methods for Learning click-through rates.* Paper presented at the Workshop on Internet and Network Economics (WINE), (pp. 34-45).

ISM (Institute for Supply Management)/Forrester. (2002). *Reports on e-business.* Retrieved November 20, 2002, from http://napm.org/isreport/forrester

Izushi, H. (1999). Can a development agency foster co-operation among local firms? The case of the welsh development agency's supplier association programme. *Regional Studies, 33*(8), 739-750.

Jackwerth, J. C., & Rubinstein, M. (1996). Recovering probability distribution from options prices. *Journal of Finance, 51*(5), 1611-1631.

Jansen, B. (2006). Paid search. *IEEE Computer, 39*(7), 88-90.

Jap, S. D. (2000). Going, going, gone. *Harvard Business Review, 78*(6), 30-38.

Jap, S. D. (2007). The Impact of online reverse auction design on buyer-supplier relationships. *Journal of Marketing, 71*(1), 146-159.

Jap, S. (2002). Online reverse auctions: Issues, themes and prospects for the future. *Marketing Science Institute—Journal of the Academy of Marketing Science—Special Issue on Marketing to and Serving Customers through the Internet, 30*(4), 506-525.

Jap, S. D. (2003). An exploratory study of the introduction of online reverse auctions. *Journal of Marketing, 67*(3), 96-107.

Jayaram, J., Kannan, V. R., & Tan, K. C. (2004). Influence of initiators on supply chain value creation. *International Journal of Production Research, 42*(20), 4377-4399.

Johnson, P. F., & Klassen, R. D. (2005). E-procurement. *MIT Sloan Management Review, 46*(2), 7.

Johnston, D. A., McCutcheon, D. M., Stuart, F. I., & Kerwood, H. (2004). Effects of supplier trust on performance of cooperative supplier relationships. *Journal of Operations Management, 22*(1), 23-38.

Jonsson, P., & Zineldin, M. (2003). Achieving high satisfaction in supplier-dealer working relationships. *Supply Chain Management, 8*(3-4), 224-241.

Jost, G., Dawson, M., & Shaw, D. (2005). Private sector consortia working for a public sector client - factors that build successful relationships: Lessons from the UK. *European Management Journal, 23*(3), 336-350.

Kafka, S., Temkin, B., & Wegner, L. (2000). *B2B auctions go beyond price.* Retrieved February 20, 2002, from http://www.Forrester.com

Kagel, J., & Levin, D. (1986). The winner's curse and public information in common value auctions. *American Economic Review, 76*, 894-920.

Kannan, V. R., & Tan, K. C. (2002). Supplier selection and assessment: Their impact on business performance. *Journal of Supply Chain Management, 38*(4), 11-21.

Kannan, P. K., & Praveen, K. K. (2001). Dynamic pricing on the Internet: Importance and implications for consumer behavior. *International Journal of Electronic Commerce, 5*(3), 63-84.

Kauffman, R.J. &Walden, E.A. (2001). Economics and Electronic Commerce: Survey and Research Directions. *International Journal of Electronic Commerce, 5*(4), 5-117.

Kaufmann, L., & Carter, C. (2004). Deciding on the mode of negotiation: To auction or not to auction electronically. *Journal of Supply Chain Management, 40*(2), 15-26.

Kaufmann, L. (2003). Elektronische verhandlungen - Erste empirische befunde zu auktionen im einkauf. In: Weber J. & Deepen, J. (Eds.), *Erfolg durch Logistik - Erkenntnisse aktueller Forschung,* (pp. 197-216), Bern.

Kern, T., Willcocks, L. P., & Heck, E. V. (2002). The winner's curse in IT outsourcing: Strategies for avoiding relational trauma. *California Management Review, 44*(2), 47-69.

King, R. (2006). Workers, place your bets [Electronic Version]. *Business Week online.* Retrieved April 5, 2007 from www.businessweek.com/technology/content/aug2006/tc20060803_012437.htm

Kisiel, R. (2002). Supplier group seeks conduct code for auctions. *Automotive News, 67,* 16F.

Kiviat, B. (2004). The end of management? *Time, July 6.*

Klemperer, P., (1999). Auction theory: A guide to the literature. *Journal of Economic Surveys, 13*(3), 227-286.

Kolp, M., Giorgini, P. & Mylopoulos, J. (2003). Organizational Patterns for Early Requirements Analysis. *Proceedings of the 15th International Conference on Advanced Information Systems Engineering, CAiSE '03,* Velden, Austria.

Koppius, O. R. (2002). *Information architecture and electronic market performance.* Unpublished Doctoral Dissertation, Erasmus University, Rotterdam, The Netherlands.

Koppius, O. R., & Van Heck, E. (2002). The role of product quality information, market state information

and transaction costs in electronic auctions. *Academy of Management Proceedings, TIM,* I1-16.

Kräkel, M. (1992). *Auktionstheorie und interne organisation,* Berlin.

Krishna, V. (2002). *Auction theory*: Academic Press.

Krüger, W. & Homp, C. (1997). *Kernkompetenz-management: Steigerung von flexibilität und schlagkraft im wettbewerb.* Wiesbaden: Gabler.

Kumar, S., Bragg, R., & Creinin, D. (2003). Managing supplier relationships. *Quality Progress, 36*(9), 24-30.

Kumar, M. & Feldman, S.I. (1998). Internet Auctions. *Proceedings of the 3rd USENIX Workshop on Electronic Commerce,* Boston, USA.

Kurbel, K. & Loutchko, I. (2001). A Framework for Multiagent Electronic Marketplaces: Analysis and Classification of Existing Systems. *Proceedings of International Congress on Information Science Innovations, ISI '01,* American University in Dubai

Kwak, M. (2001). Searching for search costs. *MIT Sloan Management Review, 42*(3), 8-9.

Kwak, M. (2002). Potential pitfalls of e-auctions. *MIT Sloan Management Review, 43*(2), 18.

Kwon, I., & Suh, T. (2004). Trust, commitment and relationships in supply-chain management: A path analysis. *Supply Chain Management, 10*(1), 26-34.

Laffont, J., & Tirole, J. (1991). Auction design and favoritism. *International Journal of Industrial Organization, 9*(1), 9-42.

Lahaie, S. (2006). *An analysis of alternative slot auction designs for sponsored search.* Paper presented at the Seventh ACM Conference on Electronic Commerce, Ann Arbor, MI.

Le, T. T., Rao, S. S., & Truong, D. (2004). Industry-sponsored marketplaces: A platform for supply chain integration or a vehicle for market aggregation? *Electronic Markets, 14*(4), 295-307.

Lee, H. L., Padmanabhan, V., & Whang, S. (1997). The bullwhip effect in supply chains. *Sloan Management Review, 38*(3), 93.

Lee, A. (1989). Case studies as natural experiments. *Human Relations, 42*(2), 117-137.

Leenders, M. R., & Fearon, H. E. (1997). *Purchasing and Supply Management* (11th ed.). Chicago: Richard D. Irwin.

Leenders, M., Fearon, H., AE, F., & Johnson, P. (2002). *Purchasing and supply management* (12 ed.). Boston: McGraw-Hill Irwin.

Levaux, J. (2001). B2B exchanges: Will they survive? *World Trade, 14*(3), 32-35.

Liker, J., & Choi, T. (2004). Building deep supplier relationships. *Harvard Business Review, 82*(12), 104-113.

Lilien, G., & Wong, M. A. (1984). An exploratory investigation of the structure of the buying center in the metalworking industry. *Journal of Marketing Research, 21*(1), 1-11.

Liu, D., Chen, J., & Whinston, A. B. (2006). *Weighted unit-price auctions.* Paper presented at the Second Workshop on Sponsored Search Auctions, Ann Arbor, MI.

Liu, L. & Yu, E. (2004). Designing information systems in social context: a goal and scenario modelling approach. *Information Systems, 29*, 187-203.

Lorenz, J., & Dougherty, E. (1983). *Bonus bidding and bottom lines: Federal off-shore oil and gas.* SPE 12024, 58th Annual Fall Technical Conference.

Lucking-Reiley, D. (2000). Auctions on the Internet: What's being auctioned, and how? *Journal of Industrial Economics, 48*(3), 227-252.

Lucking-Reiley, David (1999) Using field experiments to test equivalence between auction formats: Magic on the Internet. *American Economic Review, 89*(5), 1063-1080.

Lundholm, R. (1991). What affects the efficiency of the market? Some answers from the laboratory. *The Accounting Review, 66*, 486-515.

Mabert, V. A., & Schoenherr, T. (2001). Evolution of on-line auctions in b2b procurement. *Praxtix, 5*(1), 15-19.

Mabert, V. A., & Schoenherr, T. (2001). An online RFQ system: A case study. *PRACTIX – Best Practices in Purchasing/Supply Chain, 4*(2), 1-6.

Mabert, V. A., & Skeels, J. A. (2002). Internet reverse auctions: Valuable tool in experienced hands. *Business Horizons, 45*(4), 70-76.

Mabert, V. A., Soni, A. K., & Venkataramanan, M. A. (2003). The impact of organization size on enterprise resource planning (ERP) implementations in the US manufacturing sector. *Omega, 31*(3), 235-246.

Mabert, V. A., & Venkataramanan, M. A. (1998). Special research focus on supply chain linkages: Challenges for design and management in the 21st century. *Decision Sciences, 29*(3), 537.

Malone, T.W., Yates, J. & Benjamin, R.I. (1987). Electronic markets and electronic hierarchies. *Communication of the Association for Computing Machinery, 30*(6), 1987, 484-497.

Mao Weiliang, Sheng H., & Ding Peng (2001). An XML-based language for coordination protocol description in multi-agent system. In *Proceedings of 14th International Conference on Industrial and Engineering Applications of Artificial Intelligence and Expert Systems (IEA/AIE2001)* (pp.708-717).

Marcoux, A. M. (2003). Snipers, stalkers, and nibblers: Online auction business ethics. *Journal of Business Ethics, 46*, 163-173.

Mares, V., & Harstad, R. M. (2003). Private information revelation in common-value auctions. *Journal of Economic Theory, 109*(2), 264-282.

Mark, R. (2006). More indictments in DRAM price fixing probe. *Business, Internetnews.com*, October 19.

Mayer, R. C., Davis, J. H., & Schooman, F. D. (1995). An integration model of organizational trust. *Academy of Management, The Academy of Management Review, 20*(3), 709-735.

McAfee, R.P. & McMillan, J. (1987). Auction and bidding. *Journal of Economic Literature, 25*(2), 669-738.

McAfee, R. P., McMillan, J., & Whinston, M. D. (1989). Multiproduct monopoly, commodity bundling, and correlation of values. *The Quarterly Journal of Economics, 104*(2), 371-383.

McCabe, K., Rassenti, S., & Smith, V. (1991). Testing Vickrey's and other simultaneous multiple unit versions of the English auction. Isaac, R.M. (Ed.), *Research in Experimental Economics, Vol. 4* (pp. 45-79). JAI Press.

McGarvey, R. (2000). From business: To business. *Entrepreneur, 28*(6), 96-100.

McMillan, J. (1991). Dango: Japan's price-fixing conspiracies. *Economics and Politics, 3,* 201-218.

Meakin, A. (2002). *Options and opportunities in business-to-business e-commerce.* Unpublished MEng dissertation, University of Oxford.

Meier, R.L., Williams, M.R. & Singley, R.B. (2002). The strategic role of reverse auctions in the quotation and selection process. *PRACTIX, Best Practices in Purchasing & Supply Chain Management, 5*(3), 13-17.

Messmer, E. (2000). Defense Dept.'s online auctions spark controversy. Retrieved February 20, 2002, from http://www.mwfusion.com/news/2000/0807reverse.html

Metcalf, D., Meringer, J., & Rehkopf, F. (2001). *Achieving B2B productivity.* Retrieved February 20, 2002, from www.Forrester.com

Mikoucheva, A., & Sonin, K. (2004). Information revelation and efficiency in auctions. *Economics Letters, 83*(3), 277-284.

Milgrom, P., & Weber, R. (1982). A theory of auctions and competitive bidding. *Econometrica, 50*(5), 1089-1122.

Millet, I., Parente, D. H., Fizel, J. L., & Venkataraman, R. R. (2004). Metrics for managing online procurement auctions. *Interfaces, 34*(3), 171-179.

Min, H., & Galle, W. P. (2003). E-purchasing: Profiles of adopters and nonadopters. *Industrial Marketing Management, 32,* 227-233.

Min, H. (1994). International supplier selection: A multi-attribute utility approach *International Journal of Physical Distribution & Logistics Management, 24*(5), 24-33.

Minahan, T. (2001). *Strategic e-Sourcing: A framework for negotiating competitive advantage.* Aberdeen Group, Retrieved December 20, 2001, from www.aberdeen.com/ab_company/hottopics/esourcing

Mizrachi, J. (2002). Focusing on "bundling" and "IRS" (no, not that IRS) in real estate transactions. *The Real Estate Finance Journal, 17*(3), 13-17.

Monczka, R., Trent, R., & Handfield, R. (2005). *Purchasing and supply chain management* (3rd ed.). Cincinnati: Southwestern.

Morgan, R. M., & Hunt, S. D. (1994). The commitment-trust theory of relationship marketing. *Journal of Marketing, 58*(3), 20-38.

Mozer, E. (2002). E-procurement-Successfully using and managing reverse auctions. *Pharmaceutical Technology,* Retrieved October 20, 2002, from http://www.pharmtech.com

Mylopoulos J., Kolp M. & Castro J. (2001). UML for Agent-Oriented Software Development: The Tropos Proposal. *Proceedings of the 4th International Conference on the Unified Modeling Language, UML '01,* Toronto, Canada.

Nair, A. (2005). Emerging Internet-enabled auction mechanisms in supply chain. *Supply Chain Management, 10*(3/4), 162.

Neef, D. (2001). *E-procurement: From strategy to implementation.* NJ: Prentice Hall.

Neely, A. (Ed.)(2002) *Measuring eBusiness performance in performance measurement: Theory and practice.* Cambridge: Cambridge University Press.

Nelson, P. (1970). Information and consumer behavior. *Journal of Political Economy, 78*(2), 311-329.

New, S.J. (1998). The implications and reality of partnership. In B. Burnes & B. Dale (Eds.), *Working in partner-*

ship: Best practice in customer-supplier relationships (pp. 9-20). Aldershot: Gower.

New, S.J. (2002). *Understanding the e-marketspace: Making sense of B2B.* Saïd Business School, Oxford.

Nisan Noam. (2000). Bidding and allocation in combinatorial auctions. In *Proceedings of the 2ⁿᵈ ACM Conference on Electronic Commerce* (pp. 1-12).

NSW. (2001). *E-procurement framework. NSW Government,* Retrieved December 20, 2001, from http://www.cpsc.nsw.gov.au/e-procurement/framework.htm

O'Brien, J., & Srivastava, S. (1991). Dynamic stock markets with multiple assets: An experimental analysis. *Journal of Finance, 46,* 1811-1838.

O'Malley, C. (1998, November). Internet: Do I hear a bid. *Popular Science, 253,* 52.

Papazoglou M.P. (2001). Agent-Oriented Technology in Support of E-Business. *Communications of the ACM, 44*(4), 71-77.

Parente, D. H., Venkataraman, R., Fizel, J., & Millet, I. (2004). A conceptual research framework for analyzing online auctions in a B2B environment. *Supply Chain Management, 9*(3/4), 287-294.

Pastore, M. (2001). *Businesses find ROI in e-procurement apps.* Retrieved August 20, 2004, from http://www.clickz.com/stats/sectors/b2b/article.php/727051.

Paulraj, A., & Chen, I. J. (2005). Strategic supply management and dyadic quality performance: A path analytical model. *Journal of Supply Chain Management, 41*(3), 4-18.

Pavlou, P. A. (2002). Institution-based trust in interorganizational exchange relationships: The role of online B2B marketplaces on trust formation. *Journal of Strategic Information Systems, 11*(3/4), 215-243.

Pavlou, P. A. (2002). Trustworthiness as a source of competitive advantage in online auction markets. *Best Paper Proceedings, Academy of Management, Denver, CO,* 9-14.

Pavlou, P. A., & Gefen, D. (2004). Building effective online marketplaces with institution-based trust. *Information Systems Research, 15*(1), 37.

Pearce, D. W. (1992). *The MIT dictionary of modern economics.* Cambridge, MA: The MIT Press.

Pekec, A., & Rothkopf, M. H. (2003). Combinatorial auction design. *Management Science, 49*(11), 1485-1503.

Pennock, D. M., Lawrence, S., Nielsen, F. A., & Giles, C. L. (2001). *Extracting collective probabilistic forecasts from Web games.* Paper presented at the 7th ACM SIG-KDD International Conference on Knowledge Discovery and Data Mining, San Francisco, CA.

Picot, A. (1991). Ein neuer ansatz zur gestaltung der leistungstiefe. *Zeitschrift für betriebswirtschaftliche Forschung, 43*(4), 336-357.

Picot, A., Bortenländer, C., & Röhrl, H. (1997). Organization of electronic markets: Contributions from the new institutional economics. *Information Society, 13*(1), 107-123.

Pinker, E. J., Seidmann, A., & Vakrat, Y. (2003). Managing online auctions: Current business and research issues. *Management Science, 49*(11), 1457-1484.

Pinker, E.J., Seidmann, A. & Vakrat, Y. (2001). The Design of Online Auctions: Business Issues and Current Research. *Working Paper CIS-01-05, W. E. Simon Graduate School of Business Administration,* University of Rochester, Canada.

Plott, C., & Sunder, S. (1988). Rational expectations and the aggregation of diverse information in laboratory security markets. *Econometrica, 56,* 1085-1118.

Plouffe, C. R., Vandenbosch, M., & Hulland, J. (2001). Intermediating technologies and multi-group adoption: A comparison of consumer and merchant adoption intentions toward a new electronic payment system. *The Journal of Product Innovation Management, 18*(2), 65.

Polgreen, P. M., Nelson, F. D., & Neumann, G. R. (2006). Using prediction markets to forecast trends in infectious diseases. *Microbe, 1*(10), 459-465.

Porter, M. E. (1980). *Competitive strategy: Techniques for analysing industries and competitors.* New York: Macmillan, Free Press.

Porter, A. M. (2000). Buyers turn wary eyes on electronic auctions. *Purchasing, 129*(3), 109.

Porter, H. R., & Zona, J. D. (1993). Detection of bid-rigging in procurement auctions. *Journal of Political Economy, 101,* 518-538.

Porter, H. R., & Zona, J. D. (1999). Ohio school milk markets: An analysis of bidding. *Rand Journal of Economics, 30,* 263-288.

Prahinski, C., & Benton, W. C. (2004). Supplier evaluations: communication strategies to improve supplier performance. *Journal of Operations Management, 22*(1), 39-62.

Pressey, A., & Tzokas, N. (2004). Lighting up the "dark side" of international export/import relationships: Evidence from UK reporters. *Management Decision, 42*(5/6), 694-708.

Presutti, W. D. (2003). Supply management and e-procurement: Creating value added in the supply chain. *Industrial Marketing Management, 32*(3), 219-226.

Presutti, W. D., & Zuffoletti, J. (2002). The buyer-seller relationship and the impact of reverse auctions. In G. Antionette, L. C. Giunipero, and C. Sawchuk (Eds.), *E-purchasing Plus* Goshen, NY: JGC Enterprises.

Prigg, M. (2000, December 3). How sharing can change the way business works. *Sunday Times Special Supplement, B2B: Collaborating with Partners in the Digital Economy,* pp. 2-3.

Queree, A. (2000, March 7). Rosky budness. *Rolling Stone,* 91-92.

Rachlevsky-Reich B., Ben-Shaul, I., Tung Chau, N., Lo, A. & Poggio, T. (1999). GEM: A Global Electronic Market System. *Special issue on information systems for electronic commerce, Information Systems, 24*(6), 495-518.

Raisch, W.R. (2001). *The eMarketplace: Strategies for success in B2B eCommerce.* New York: McGraw-Hill.

Ramchurn, S.D., Huynh, D. & Jennings N.R. (2004). Trust in Multi-Agent Systems. *The Knowledge Engineering Review, 19*(1), 1-25.

Ramsdell, G. (2000). The real business of B2B. *McKinsey Quarterly, 3,* 174-185.

Rapport, A. (1998). *Creating shareholder value.* New York: The Free Press.

Rawlings, C. (2002, August 9). E-mail interview.

Raymond L. (1990). Organization context and information systems success: A contingency approach. *Journal of Management Information Systems, 6*(4), 5-20.

Re R., Braga R.T.V. & Masiero P.C. (2001). A Pattern Language for Online Auctions Management. *Proceedings of the 8th Conference on Pattern Languages of Programs,* PLoP '01, Illinois, USA.

Regan, K. (2001). Is big talk a big pain for e-commerce. *ecommercetimes,* Retrieved February 20, 2001, from http://www.ecommercetimes.com/perl/story/?id=7160

Reicheld, F. F., & Schefter, P. (2000). E-loyalty: Your secret weapon on the Web. *Harvard Business Review, 78*(4), 105-113.

Reisman, A., & Xu, X. (1992). On stages of knowledge growth in the management sciences. *IEEE Transactions on Engineering Management, 39*(2), 119-128.

Resnick P. & Zeckhauser R. (2002). Trust Among Strangers in Internet Transactions: Empirical Analysis of eBayís Reputation System. *Advances in Applied Microeconomics, 11,* 77-106.

Rhode, P. W., & Strumpf, K. S. (2007). *Manipulating political stock markets: A field experiment and a century of observational data.* University of Arizona.

Ribeiro, R. A. (1996). Fuzzy multiple attribute decision making: A review and new preference elicitation techniques. *Fuzzy Sets and Systems, 78*(2), 155-181.

Richins, M. L., & Dawson, S. (1992). A consumer values orientation for materialism and its measurement: scale development and validation. *Journal of Consumer Research, 19,* 303-316.

Rodriguez-Aguilar J. A., P. Noriega, C. Sierra, & J. Padget (1997). FM96.5: A Java-based electronic auction house. *Proceedings of the Second International Conference on the Practical Application of Intelligent Agents and Multi-Agent Technology (PAAM'97).* 207-224.

Rogers, D. L. (2001). The future of software bundling after United States v. Microsoft. *Intellectual Property and Technology Law Journal, 13*(12), 1-11.

Roll, R. (1986). The hubris hypothesis of corporate takeovers. *Journal of Business, 59,* 197-216.

Roll, R. (1984). Orange juice and weather. *American Economic Review, 74,* 861-880.

Roth, A. E., & Ockenfels, A. (2002). Last minute bidding and the rules for ending second-price auctions: Evidence from eBay and Amazon auctions on the Internet. *The American Economic Review, 92,* 1093-1103.

Rothkopf, M. H., Pekec, A., & Harstad, R. M. (1998). *Management Science, 44,* 1131-1147.

Sairamesh, J., Stanbridge, P., Ausio, J., Keser, C., & Karabulut, Y. (2005). *Business models for virtual organization management and interoperability*: Deliverable document 01945 prepared for TrustCom. and the European Commission, 1-20.

Sandholm, T., Levine, D., Concordia, M., Martyn, P., Hughes, R., Jacobs, J., et al. (2006). Changing the game in strategic sourcing at Procter & Gamble: Expressive competition enabled by optimization. *Interfaces, 36*(1), 55-68.

Sandholm T. (2002). eMediator: A next generation electronic commerce server. *Computational Intelligence. 18*(4), 656-676.

Sashi, C. M., & O'Leary, B. (2002). The role of Internet auctions in the expansion of B2B markets. *Industrial Marketing Management, 31*(2), 103-110.

Schaeffer, H. A. (2002). *Essentials of cash flow.* New York: Wiley.

Schafer, J. B. (2002). *MetaLens: A Framework for Multisource Recommendations.* Unpublished doctoral

thesis, Department of Computer Science, University of Northern Iowa, USA.

Schoenherr, T. (2005). *An exploratory study of bundling in B2B online procurement auctions.* Doctoral dissertation, Indiana University, Indiana.

Schoenherr, T., & Mabert, V. A. (2006). Bundling for B2B procurement: Current state and best practices. *International Journal of Integrated Supply Management, 2*(3), 189-213.

Schwab, A.P. (2003). *Elektronische verhandlungen in der beschaffung.* St. Gallen.

Scott, C., & Westbrook, R. (1991). New Strategic Tools for Supply Chain Management. *International Journal of Physical Distribution and Logistics Management, 21*(1), 23-33.

Sculley, A.B., & Woods, W.W.A. (1999). *B2B exchanges: The killer application in the business-to-business Internet revolution.* Hamilton, Bermuda: ISI Books.

Servan-Schreiber, E., Wolfers, J., Pennock, D. M., & Galebach, B. (2004). Prediction markets: Does money matter? *Electronic Markets, 14*(3), 243-251.

Simatupang, T. M., & Sridharan, R. (2005). The collaboration index: A measure for supply chain collaboration. *International Journal of Physical Distribution & Logistics Management, 35*(1), 44.

Simchi-Levi, D., Kaminsky, P., & Simchi-Levi, E. (2000). *Designing and managing the supply chain: Concepts, strategies, and case studies* (1ˢᵗ ed.). Boston: Irwin McGraw-Hill.

Simon, H. (1955). A behavioral model of rational choice. *Quarterly Journal of Economics, 69*(1), 99-118.

Skjott-Larsen, T., Kotzab, H., & Grieger, M. (2003). Electronic marketplaces and supply chain relationships. *Industrial Marketing Management, 32*(3), 199-210.

Smart, A., & Harrison, A. (2003). Online reverse auctions and their role in buyer-supplier relationships. *Journal of Purchasing & Supply Management, 9*(5-6), 257-268.

Smeltzer, L. R., & Carr, A. S. (2003). Electronic reverse auctions: Promises, risks and conditions for success. *Industrial Marketing Management, 32*(6), 481-488.

Smeltzer, L. & Ruzicka, M. (2000). Electronic reverse auctions: Integrating the tool with the strategic-sourcing process. *PRACTIX, Best Practices in Purchasing & Supply Chain Management, 3*(4), 1-6.

Smeltzer, L. R., & Carr, A. (2002). Reverse auctions in industrial marketing and buying. *Business Horizons, 45*(2), 47-52.

Smith, N. (2002). Dynamic pricing effects on strategic sourcing and supplier relations. *Leaders for Manufacturing Thesis.* Massachusetts Institute of Technology.

Southard, P. B., & Parente, D. H. (2007). Supplier consortia: A classification framework. *In process*, 1-16.

Sparks, L., & Wagner, B. (2003). Retail exchanges: A research agenda. *Supply Chain Management, 8*(1), 17-25.

Spekman, R. F. (1988). Strategic supplier selection: Understanding long-term buyers' relationship. *Business Horizon, July-August,* 75-81.

Spremann, K. (1990). Asymmetrische information. *Zeitschrift für Betriebswirtschaft, 60*(5/6), 561-586.

Standing, C., Love, P. E. D., Stockdale, R., & Gengatharen, D. (2006). Examining the relationship between electronic marketplace strategy and structure. *IEEE Transactions on Engineering Management, 53*(2), 297-311.

Stein, A., Hawking, P., & Wyld, D. C. (2003). The 20% solution?: A case study on the efficacy of reverse auctions. *Management Research News, 26*(5), 1-20.

Story, L. (2006, October 30). Marketers demanding better count of the clicks. *New York Times.*

Strecker, S., & Seifert, S. (2003). *Preference revelation in multi-attribute bidding procedures: An experimental analysis.* Paper presented at the 14th International Workshop on Database and Expert Systems Applications (DEXA'03).

Stremersch, S., & Tellis, G. J. (2002). Strategic bundling of products and prices: A new synthesis for marketing. *Journal of Marketing, 66*(1), 55-72.

Stuart, I., Deckert, P., McCutcheon, D., & Kunst, R. (1998). Case study: A leveraged learning network. *Sloan Management Review, 39*(4), 81-93.

Subramaniam, C., & Shaw, M. J. (2002). A Study on the value and impact of B2B e-commerce: The case of Web-based procurement. *International Journal of Electronic Commerce, 6*(4), 19-40.

Subramaniam, Ch., & Shaw, M.J. (2004) The effects of process characteristics on the value of B2B e-procurement,. *Information Technology and Management, 5*(1-2), 161-180.

Sunder, S. (1995). Experimental asset markets. In J. H. K. a. A. E. Roth (Ed.), *The handbook of experimental economics* (pp. 445-500). Princeton, NJ: Princeton University Press.

Szymanski, B. K., & Lee, J. S. (2006, June). *Impact of ROI on bidding and revenue in sponsored search advertisement auctions.* Paper presented at the Second Workshop on Sponsored Search Auctions, Ann Arbor, MI.

Talluri, S., & Ragatz, G. L. (2004). Multi-attribute reverse auctions in B2Bexchanges: A framework for design and implementation. *Journal of Supply Chain Management, 40*(1), 52-61.

Tassabehji, R., Taylor, W., Beach, R., & Wood, A. (2006). Reverse e-auctions and supplier-buyer relationships: An exploratory study. *International Journal of Operations and Production Management, 26*(2), 166-184.

Teich, J., Wallenius, H., Wallenius, J., & Koppius, O. (2004). Emerging multiple issue e-auctions. *European Journal of Operational Research, 159*(1), 1-16.

Tella, E., & Virolainen, V.-M. (2005). Motives behind purchasing consortia. *International Journal of Production Economics, 93-94,* 161-168.

Terpend, R. and Krause, D. R. (under review). Thinking Outside the Box: A Typology of Commodity Sourcing Strategies. *Journal of Operations Management.*

The Oxford Modern English Dictionary. (1996). (2nd ed.) . New York: Oxford University Press.

Timmers, P. (2000). *Electronic commerce: Strategies and models for business-to-business trading.* Chichester, UK: Wiley.

Turban, E. (2002). Electronic commerce 2002: A managerial perspective. 2nd edition. NJ: Prentice Hall

Tuzhilin, A. (2006). *The Lane's Gifts v. Google Report.* Retrieved Oct 16, 2007 from http://googleblog.blogspot.com/pdf/Tuzhilin_Report.pdf

van Tulder, R. J. M., & Mol, M. (2002). Reverse auctions or auctions reversed: First experiments by Philips. *European Management Journal, 20*(5), 447-56.

Varian, H. R. (2006). *Position auctions.* (Technical Working Paper). Berkeley, CA: Univeristy of California. Forthcoming in *International Journal of Industrial Organization.*

VEGA (2004) national project No1/1222/04 - Effectiveness and Performance Measurement of Dynamic Transaction Methods in e-Business Solutions, financed by Ministry of Education of Slovak Republic

Venkatesh, V., & Davis, F. (2000). A theoretical extension of the technology acceptance model: Four longitudinal field studies. *Management Science, 46*(2), 186-204.

Venkatesh, V., Morris, M. G., Davis, G. B., & Davis, F. D. (2003). User acceptance of information technology: Toward a unified view. *MIS Quarterly, 27*(3), 425-478.

Vickrey, W. (1961). Counterspeculation, auctions, and competitive sealed tenders. *Journal of Finance, 16,* 8-27.

Wagner, S. M., & Schwab, A. P. (2004). Setting the stage for successful electronic reverse auctions. *Journal of Purchasing and Supply Management, 10*(1), 11-26.

Walsham, G. (2000). Globalisation and IT: Agenda for research. *Organisational and social perspectives on information technology* (pp. 195-210). Boston: Kluwer Academic Publishers.

Wathne, K. H., & Heide, J. B. (2000). Relationship governance in supply chain network. *Journal of Marketing, 68*(1), 73-89.

Weiber, R. & Adler, J. (1995). Informationsökonomisch begründete typologisierung von kaufprozessen. *Zeitschrift für betriebswirtschaftliche Forschung, 47*(1), 43-65.

Weiss M. (2003). Pattern-Driven Design of Agent Systems: Approach and Case Study. *Proceedings of the 15th International Conference on Advanced Information Systems Engineering, CAISE '03*, Velden, Austria.

Williamson, O. E. (1979). Transaction-cost economics: The governance of contractual relations. *Journal of Law and Economics, 22,* 3-61.

Williamson, O. E. (1989). Transaction cost economics. In: Schmalensee, R. & Willig, R.D. (Eds.), *Handbook of Industrial Organization:Vol. 1,* (pp. 135-182). Amsterdam.

Williamson, O. E. (1990). *Die ökonomischen institutionen des kapitalismus: Unternehmen, märkte, kooperationen.* Tübingen, Germany.

Williamson, O. E. (1991). Comparative economic Oorganization: Vergleichende ökonomische organisationstheorie: Die analyse diskreter strukturalternativen. In: Ordelheide, D., Rudolph, B. & Büsselmann, E. (Eds.), *Betriebswirtschaftslehre und ökonomische Theorie* (pp. 13-49). Stuttgart, Germany: Schaeffer-Poeschel.

Williamson, O. E., (1985). *The economic institutions of capitalism.* New York: Free Press.

Wilson, D. T. (1995). An integrated model of buyer-seller relationships. *Journal of the Academy of Marketing Science, 23*(4), 335-345

Wolfers, J., & Zitzewitz, E. (2005). *Interpreting prediction market prices as probabilities.* Wharton School, University of Pennsylvania.

Wurman P. R., M. P. Wellman, & Walsh W. E. (1998). The Michigan Internet auctionbot: A configurable auction server for human and software agents. In *Proceedings of the Second International Conference on Autonomous Agents (AGENTS)* (pp. 301-308).

Wyld, D. (2000). *The auction model. The PriceWaterhouseCoopers Endowment for the Business of Government.* The Business of Government, University of Southern Louisiana.

Wyld, D. (2002). The electric company: How the supply chain is being reinvented through the rapid application of e-procurement processes in the business-to-business arena. *Management Research News,* (in press).

Yahoo! (2006, August 16, 2006). *Yahoo! and go2 Sign Mobile Search Advertising Distribution Agreement; Yahoo! Advertisers to Reach Consumers Through go2's Mobile Local Content Channels.* Retrieved April 5, 2007, from http://yhoo.client.shareholder.com/press/ReleaseDetail.cfm?ReleaseID=207538

Yahoo! (2007). *Search marketing overview: Quality index.* Retrieved April 5, 2007, from http://help.yahoo.com/l/us/yahoo/ysm/sps/start/overview_qualityindex.html

Yahoo! Search Marketing: Sponsored Search. Retrieved April 5, 2007, from http://searchmarketing.yahoo.com/srch/index.php

Yap C. S. (1990). Distinguishing characteristics of organizations using computers. *Information and Management, 18*(2), 97-107.

Yen, B. P.-C., & Ng, E. O. S. (2003). The impact of electronic commerce on procurement. *Journal of Organizational Computing and Electronic Commerce, 13*(3 & 4), 167-189.

Yin, R. (1994). *Case study research, design and methods* (2nd ed.). Newbury Park: Sage Publications.

Yu E. (1995). *Modelling Strategic Relationships for Process Reengineering.* Unpublished doctoral thesis, Dept. of Computer Science, University of Toronto, Canada.

Yu E. (1997). Why Agent-Oriented Requirements Engineering. *Proceedings of 3rd International Workshop on Requirements Engineering: Foundations for Software Quality*, Barcelona, Spain.

Yu E. (2001). Agent-Oriented Modelling: Software Versus the World. *Proceedings of the 2nd International Workshop on Agent-Oriented Software Engineering*, AOSE '01, Montreal, Canada.

Zajac, E. J. & Olsen, C. P. (1993). From transaction cost to transaction value analysis: Implications for the study of interorganizational strategies. *Journal of Management Studies, 30*(1), 131-145.

About the Contributors

Diane H. Parente is an associate professor of management at the Sam & Irene Black School of Business at Penn State, Erie. She received her PhD from the University at Buffalo. Her current research interests are interdisciplinary and include on-line procurement auctions, supply chain management from a multi-functional perspective, and the strategic impact of cross-functional processes. She has published in *Interfaces, International Journal of Operations and Production Management, Journal of Public Policy & Marketing, Health Care Management Review, Psychological Reports,* and *Information Resources Management Journal,* among others. Dr. Parente has previous industry experience in a variety of functional and cross-functional positions in the manufacturing, banking, and insurance industries.

* * * *

Prof. Dr. h.c. Ulli Arnold is professor (full chair) of business-to-business marketing and purchasing management at the University of Stuttgart in Germany. His main research interests are strategic supply management, industrial goods marketing, and nonprofit organization management. He realized some research projects on purchasing management in cooperation with CAPS, the Center for Advanced Purchasing Studies, at Arizona State University in Tempe. Professor Arnold is co-editor of several scientific journals and serves as member of the review board of the *Journal of Supply Chain Management* and the *Journal of Purchasing and Supply Management.* He has published several books and articles on supply chain management, industrial marketing, and nonprofit organizations. He has held lectures as guest professor at universities in Sweden, China, Poland, Hungary, India, Russia, USA, France, and Switzerland.

Janet M. Duck is on faculty at Penn State University's World Campus, as well as the Department of Management and Organization for the Great Valley School of Graduate Professional Studies, PSU. She earned a PhD in workforce education and development from Penn State University, University Park, and an MBA from Lebanon Valley College, Annville, PA. Dr. Duck teaches courses in organizational behavior, human resource management, organizational communication, organizational development, organizational change, and corporate culture in both the Penn State online MBA program as well as the resident MBA program. Dr. Duck's research interests include group dynamics in online teaching environments, collaborative teaching models for online learning, sources of group efficacy, team motivation, and organizational change. She is an active member and presenter for the Association of Business Simulation and Experiential Learning (ABSEL). Dr. Duck has over 15 years of industry experience as an organizational development and human resource specialist in domestic and international settings.

Susan Emens is an assistant professor in business management and related technologies at Kent State University's Trumbull Campus. Susan Emens received her MA in economics and MBA from Kent State University. She has over 15 years of experience working in the private sector for simulation software and technology-related firms. Her research interests are in the areas of quality assessment and business applications in nonprofit organizations. She is an active member of several professional societies and is a past board member of APICS Cleveland Chapter.

M. L. "Bob" Emiliani is a professor in the School of Technology at Connecticut State University in New Britain, CT, where he teaches courses in supply chain management. Prior to joining academia, Bob worked in the industry for 15 years and had management responsibility in engineering (R&D, new product development) and operations (manufacturing and supply chain). He also had responsibility for implementing Lean principles and practices in both manufacturing and supply networks at Pratt & Whitney.

Bob has authored or co-authored over 30 peer-reviewed management papers, many on the topic of supply chain management and e-business. He is the North American Regional Editor of *Supply Chain Management: An International Journal* and is a member of the editorial review board of *Industrial Marketing Management*. Bob is also the principal author of the Shingo Prize winning book *Better Thinking, Better Results: Case Study and Analysis of an Enterprise-Wide Lean Transformation* (second edition, 2007) and *REAL LEAN: Understanding the Lean Management System* (Volume 1, 2007).

John Fizel is the director of Pennsylvania State University's online MBA program (iMBA) and a professor of economics. He received his PhD from the University of Wisconsin. Dr. Fizel conducts research in applied microeconomics including areas such as nursing home efficiency, oil market pricing, executive compensation and tenure, mutual fund performance, labor arbitration, and online auctions. Recently, Dr. Fizel's primary focus has been on sports economics, in which he has co-edited a number of books including *Handbook of Sports Economics Research, International Sports Economics,* and *Economics of College Sports.*

Tom Gattiker, PhD CFPIM, is assistant professor of operations management at Boise State University, where he teaches operations management and supply chain management. His research interests include the use of information and Internet technology in operations and supply chain management, environmental purchasing, and negotiations. His research appears in *The Journal of Operations Management, The International Journal of Production Research, MIS Quarterly, Information and Management, Production and Inventory Management Journal, Quality Management Journal, Decision Sciences Journal of Innovative Education* and other journals and books. He is an associate editor at the *Journal of Supply Chain Management.* He is co-editor of the upcoming special issue on innovative data sources in the *Journal of Operations Management.* He was the 1999 APICS Education and Research Foundation George and Marion Plossl Fellow. Before obtaining his PhD from the University of Georgia, he held a variety of positions in operations and inventory management, most recently at Rockwell Automation/ Reliance Electric. He is certified in production and inventory management by the American Production and Inventory Control Society.

Indranil Ghosh is assistant professor of economics at Winston-Salem State University. Previously he served as a lecturer in economics at Pennsylvania State University at Erie. He earned his PhD from Southern Methodist University in Dallas. His current research interests are Mechanism Design, Game Theory and Analysis of Auctions. His teaching interests are microeconomics and managerial economics at both the undergraduate and the MBA level.

Srabana Gupta is an associate professor of economics at St. Thomas University. She received her PhD in economics from Warrington College of Business at the University of Florida. Her research interests include auctions, competition issues, agency theory, and international business.

Kholekile Gwebu is an assistant professor of decision sciences at the Whittemore School of Business and Economics, University of New Hampshire. He holds a PhD in management and information systems from Kent State. His research interests include agent-based simulation, multi-attribute auctions, and e-commerce.

Eric Jackson received his PhD from Michigan State University. His research interests include SCM, project management, and complex dynamic systems. He was the technical director for a multinational specialty chemical firm for ten years. He has served as managerial assistant for *Decision Science Journal* and as an engineering and business consultant for firms in Ohio and Michigan. He has published works in *Journal of Operations Management, Transportation Journal,* and *Journal of the Transportation Research Forum*

Peggy D. Lee received her PhD from George Washington University. She is assistant professor of management at Pennsylvania State University in Great Valley, where she teaches operations management and supply chain management. Dr. Lee has an MBA from the University of North Carolina at Chapel Hill and a BA from the University of Michigan at Ann Arbor. She also holds a graduate certificate in project management. Her industry experience includes executive and managerial positions in telecommunications and banking. Her research, which focuses on supply chain integration and the application of social network theories to the buyer-supplier relationship, has been published in *Supply Chain Forum*, the *International Journal of Information and Operations Management Education*, and the *Journal of Business and Industrial Management* (forthcoming).

Vincent A. Mabert is the John and Esther Reese Professor and professor of operations management in the operations and decision technologies department at the Kelley School of Business, Indiana University. He received his PhD from Ohio State University. He conducts research and consults in the areas of work force planning, order scheduling, enterprise resource planning systems, new product development, and manufacturing system design. His publications include articles in *Management Science, Decision Sciences, IIE Transactions, Journal of Operations Management, The Accounting Review,* and the *Academy of Management Journal*. Routinely he consults with the Rand Corporation concerning supply chain management issues for the United States military. He has been active and held officer positions in a number of professional societies including Industrial Engineering, INFORMS, APICS, and Decision Sciences. Professor Mabert is vice president of the Harvey Foundation and a Fellow of the Decision Sciences Institute.

Ido Millet is a professor of MIS at Penn State, Erie. He received his PhD in decision sciences from the Wharton School at the University of Pennsylvania. Research interests include the Analytic Hierarchy Process (AHP), business intelligence, and online reverse auctions. He is also a consultant and software developer (www.MilletSoftware.com). He has published in *Interfaces, the Journal of the Operations Research Society, Journal of Management Systems, Computers & Operations Research*, and the *European Journal of Operations Research,* among others.

Tracy Mullen is an assistant professor of information sciences and technology at the Pennsylvania State University, University Park. She received her PhD in electrical engineering and computer science from the University of Michigan. Her research interests include prediction markets, e-commerce, and intelligent agents. She is a member of *IEEE, ACM*, and *AAAI.*

Joseph R. Muscatello is an assistant professor of business management and related technology at Kent State University, Geauga. He received his DBA from Cleveland State University. His current research interests include enterprise resource planning systems, supply chain management, forecasting, project management, and the impact of technology on manufacturing organizations. He has published in *Omega, International Journal of Operations and Production Management, Information Resource Management Journal, Applied Computing and Informatics, Journal of Business Forecasting, Journal of Safety Research, Business Technology Educator,* and the *Business Process Management Journal.* Dr. Muscatello has previous executive-level industry experience in chemical and metal manufacturing and strategic consulting.

Dipl.-Kfm. techn. Martin Schnabel is assistant chair of business-to-business marketing and purchasing management at the University of Stuttgart in Germany. After 5 years of experience as an electronics technician he studied business administration at the University of Stuttgart with the main focus on finance, marketing, and supply management. His main research interests are supply chain management and electronic procurement with a focus on electronic reverse auctions. His main teaching fields are international marketing and electronic procurement. At the department of business administration he is responsible for international students exchange programs.

Tobias Schoenherr is an assistant professor of operations and supply chain management in the College of Business at Eastern Michigan University. He received his PhD in operations management and decision sciences from the Kelley School of Business at Indiana University, from which he also obtained his BSc and MB. In addition, he holds a Diplom-Betriebswirt (FH) from the European School of Business, Reutlingen University, Germany. Dr. Schoenherr's current research interests include supply chain management, electronic procurement and reverse auctions, e-commerce, industrial marketing, and ERP systems. His work has appeared or is forthcoming in the *International Journal of Operations and Production Management, The Journal of Supply Chain Management, Business Horizons, Omega, the Journal of International Technology and Information Management,* and *PRACTIX,* among others. He has been involved in several professional associations, including the Decision Sciences Institute, the Institute for Supply Management, the Global Manufacturing Research Group, POMS, APICS, ASQ, and INFORMS.

Barbara Ann Sherman, PhD (University at Buffalo, management systems), is teaching assistant professor in computer science at the University at Buffalo. Dr. Sherman has an MS in computer information and control engineering from the University of Michigan at Ann Arbor. She previously earned the CPIM certification (Certified in Production and Inventory Management). She has a strong combination of both industry and academic experience.

Peter B. Southard, PhD, is an assistant professor of management at the Sam & Irene Black School of Business, Pennsylvania State University, Erie. Peter has taught supply chain management, operations management, operations planning and control systems, information systems, business strategy, and statistics for over eight years on both the graduate and undergraduate level. His industry experience includes eight years in financial services as a senior vice president and branch manager of a private bank and six years with the United States Department of Agriculture (USDA) in their lending branch, known then as the Farmers Home Administration (FmHA). He has published in *Communications of the ACM, Journal of Management Decision, International Journal of Operations and Production Management, Journal of Information Technology and Information Management,* and *Benchmarking: An International Journal,* among others.

Jing Wang is an assistant professor of decision sciences at the Whittemore School of Business and Economics, University of New Hampshire. Her research focuses on the area of virtual organizations, open source software, and agent-based decision support systems.

Index

A